SSB Constable

Sashastra Seema Bal

Latest Edition
Practice Kit

10 Tests

10 Mock Test

Based On Real Exam Pattern

✓ Thoroughly Revised and Updated

✓ Detailed Analysis of all MCQs

Title	: SSB Constable Sashastra Seema Bal
Author Name	: Mr. Rohit Manglik
Published By	: EduGorilla Community Pvt. Ltd.
Publishers Address	: 12/651, First Floor Opp. Arvindo Park, Near Jama Masjid, Indira Nagar, Lucknow, Uttar Pradesh-226016, India

Copyright EduGorilla

Disclaimer EduGorilla

Compiled and created by EduGorilla Community Pvt. Ltd

Printed By EduGorilla Community Pvt. Ltd.

ROHIT MANGLIK
CEO, EduGorilla

Dear Applicants,

People say *"Success comes to those who work hard."* But I've seen people working hard for their exams day in and day out for marginal success. While others succeed in their examinations by putting in just half the work. So are they God Gifted? No! I believe that it's because they work *smart* and not just *hard*. Similarly, for your exams, you should strategize your preparation so as to increase the likelihood of success. Well with EduGorilla get ready to increase your *chances of selection* in your exam by *16x*.

EduGorilla helps you in not only working *hard* but also working in a *smart and strategic* manner. With EduGorilla's preparation package, you get a chance to make your exam preparation easy, and a fun learning path towards selection. Finding the right path to your preparations can be difficult if you don't know in which direction to head. Don't worry, we have you covered! EduGorilla will be your guide to success in your journey. With our Preparation Package, you can prepare strategically and beat the exam in just one attempt.

EduGorilla's Preparation Package includes-

• **Test Series**   • **Books**

Our preparation package is handcrafted as per the latest changes, expert opinions, and students' discretion. Thus, enabling you to get through each stage of the selection process for your exam.

Our Books are designed by the teachers and experts of the respective exam with a combined 150+ years of experience; to provide you with easy, efficient, and effective learning. Our books are smart, in the sense that not only do they give you the answers to the questions but also provide similar questions for practice.

EduGorilla's competent Test Series gives you real-time experience and confidence through which you can clear your offline or online exam in just one attempt. We currently host 94,000+ mock tests for 1,480+ competitive and academic exams.

Thus, EduGorilla misses no chance to assist you in your preparation and covers all stages of the exam, so that you don't have to look anywhere else.

We provide complete preparation packages for defense, banking, teaching, and other National & State-Level exams. Hence, it doesn't matter which exam you aspire to because you will reach your success.

ALL THE BEST !
Let EduGorilla be your Guide to Success.

Rohit Manglik,
Founder and CEO, EduGorilla

INTRODUCTION

EduGorilla focuses on guiding students to succeed in their examinations. With that in mind, our book, titled "SSB Constable : Sashastra Seema Bal", has been drafted through the collective efforts of our distinguished experts with 150+ years of combined experience. This book consists of questions that are created following the latest changes in the syllabus and exam pattern. We compiled the book on the basis of questions that are most likely to appear in the SSB Constable. Through EduGorilla's "SSB Constable : Sashastra Seema Bal" your chances of success will increase 16x.

EduGorilla does this through our Complete Preparation Package. This package consists of well-conceptualized and structured content in the form of questions that are tailor-made according to your needs and will help you practice for exams in a smart way by pinpointing all the necessary information. It also provides hints and solutions, along with a smart answer sheet for your self-evaluation. You can assess your shortcomings and work accordingly on areas that may require more of your attention.

EduGorilla promises to help you succeed in your examination and accomplish your dream goals. We believe in our aspirants and see them at the top of the merit list. And the first step towards the top is to start preparing with us. EduGorilla's "SSB Constable : Sashastra Seema Bal" includes the following attributes.

➤ Well-Researched Content

➤ Top-Notch Quality

➤ Detailed Answers and Analysis

➤ Smart Answer Sheet

➤ Exam Relevant Questions

Therefore, EduGorilla fortifies your preparation and makes it durable enough to help you stand tall and beat the examination.

SSB Constable
Scan QR code for Eligibility, Exam Pattern, Syllabus and more.

Book ID: 1344

TABLE OF CONTENTS

1. Which of the following books is not authored by Nirad C. Chaudhuri?
   (a) A Passage to India
   (b) Autobiography of an Unknown Indian
   (c) The Continent of Circe: An Essay on People of India
   (d) Scholar Extraordinary

2. The government of the Satavahana Kingdom was organized on the traditional lines where the kingdom was divided into:
   (a) Gupta Dynasty   (b) Janapadas
   (c) Amataya   (d) Gamika

3. During the 15-16th century, for commercial trade, Hundi was commonly used. What does Hundi refer to?
   (a) A form of currency used to purchase goods
   (b) A kind of bank used to keep money
   (c) A marketplace where goods can be bartered
   (d) Bills of exchange

4. Who among the following was popularly known as Napoleon of ancient India?
   (a) Samudragupta   (b) Chandragupta II
   (c) Kamishka   (d) Ashoka

5. The arrest of Mahatma Gandhi and his associates in 1942 led to riots in Bihar. Rail service came to a complete standstill in this. The maximum affected district was:
   (a) Munger   (b) Gone
   (c) Patna   (d) Shahabad

6. On July 6, 1942, at Wardha, Mahatma Gandhi discussed his 'Quit India' movement in the Working Committee of the Congress, then the chairman of that committee was:
   (a) Chakravarti Rajagopalachari
   (b) Abul Kalam Azad
   (c) Jawaharlal Nehru
   (d) Anne Besant

7. Through which states does the Kaveri river pass?
   (a) Gujarat, Madhya Pradesh, Tamil Nadu
   (b) Karnataka, Kerala, Tamil Nadu
   (c) Karnataka, Kerala, Andhra Pradesh
   (d) Madhya Pradesh, Maharashtra, Tamil Nadu

8. The states through which Konkan Rail passes are-
   (a) Maharashtra-Goa-Karnataka
   (b) Maharashtra-Karnataka-Kerala
   (c) Maharashtra-Goa-Kerala
   (d) Maharashtra-Goa-Karnataka-Kerala

9. Bhakra-Nangal Joint Project is-
   (a) Haryana-Punjab-Rajasthan
   (b) Haryana-Punjab-Delhi
   (c) Himachal Pradesh-Delhi
   (d) Punjab-Delhi-Rajasthan

10. Which of the following became the country's first carbon-neutral power exchange in December 2022?
    (a) Multi Commodity Exchange
    (b) Hindustan Power Exchange
    (c) Power Exchange of India Ltd.
    (d) Indian Energy Exchange

11. Renowned Singer-composer 'Krishnakumar Kunnath', who fondly known as KK, has passed away in when and which city?
    (a) 31st May 2022 (Kolkata)
    (b) 30th May 2022 (Chennai)
    (c) 29th May 2022 (Mumbai)
    (d) 28th May 2022 (Ahmedabad)

12. Consider the following statements.
    1. TOPS is a flagship program of the Ministry of Youth Affairs and Sports which is an attempt to provide assistance to India's top athletes.
    2. Mohammed Arif Khan became the first Indian Alpine Skier to qualify for the Winter Olympic Games 2022 to be held in Beijing.
    3. Aditi Ashok is related to the shooting sport.
    Which of the above statements are correct?
    (a) 1 and 2 only   (b) 2 and 3 only
    (c) 1 and 3 only   (d) 1, 2 and 3

13. Which of the following is a rescue operation initiated by the Government of India to aid Syria and Turkey, after an earthquake hit both countries on 6 February 2023?
    (a) Operation Mitree   (b) Operation Rescue
    (c) Operation Dost   (d) Operation Madad

14. Which one from among the following planets is largest in size ?
    (a) Earth   (b) Venus
    (c) Mars   (d) Mercury

15. Which one of the following statements about biodiversity is not correct?
    (a) The term 'biodiversity' was coined by Walter G. Rosen in 1986.
    (b) The term 'biodiversity hotspots' was coined by Norman Myers in 1988.
    (c) The regions having richest biodiversity are called 'biodiversity hotspots'.
    (d) More than 100 hotspots of biodiversity are identified in the world.

16. Which is not a biotic factor?
    (a) Plants   (b) Animals
    (c) Micro-organisms   (d) Rocks

17. Which of the following are correct about the Rajya Sabha?
    1. It is not subject to dissolution.
    2. It has a term of five years.
    3. One-third of its members retire after every two years.
    4. Its member shall not be less than 25 years of age.
    Select the correct answer using the code given below:
    Codes:
    (a) 1, 2 and 3   (b) 2, 3 and 4
    (c) 1 and 3   (d) 2 and 4

18. The Parliament in India consists of
    (i) President

(ii) Rajya Sabha
(iii) Lok Sabha
(iv) Vice President
Select the correct answer using the code given below:
Codes:

(a) (i), (ii) and (iii)   (b) (ii) and (iii)
(c) (ii), (iii) and (iv)   (d) (i), (ii), (iii) and (iv)

19. The Constitutional advisor to the Constituent Assembly was:

(a) Sachidanand Sinha   (b) K. M. Munshi
(c) B. N. Rao   (d) T.T. Krishnamachari

20. The National Education Policy (NEP), 2020 commits to raising the total expenditure by states and centre on education to _____ of GDP.

(a) 2%   (b) 4%
(c) 6%   (d) 8%

21. Indian Development Forum (IDF) was earlier known as-

(a) Bharat Sahayata Club
(b) Bharat Sahayata Bank
(c) World Bank
(d) None of the above

22. Revised Value-Added Tax relates to-

(a) Sales tax   (b) Income tax
(c) Wealth tax   (d) Excise duty

23. Who created a new national record in 100 meter race in the competition held in Rae Bareli?

(a) Ravi Kumar   (b) Amlan Borgohain
(c) Kamal Tiwari   (d) Raj Kishore

24. Which of the following statements about National Research Foundation (NRF), proposed in National Education Policy (2020) is correct?

(a) It does not fund research activities at state universities.
(b) It provides funding to research projects in science as well as non-science disciplines.
(c) It will be headed by the secretary of the Ministry of Education.
(d) It aims to increase the expenditure of the government on Research and Development (R&D) to 2.5 percent of GDP by 2025.

25. Which is/are a/the core technique(s) that enabled the birth of Modern Biotechnology?

(a) Genetic Engineering
(b) Sterile Ambience in Chemical Engineering
(c) Both (A) and (B)
(d) Neither (A) nor (B)

Mathematics

26. Direction : Simplify the given expression.
$$3\frac{1}{6} + 7\frac{2}{3} - 4\frac{1}{4} = ? + 2\frac{1}{6}$$

(a) $8\frac{7}{15}$ (b) $5\frac{4}{11}$
(c) $7\frac{3}{10}$ (d) None of these

27. A man sold two chairs for Rs. 800 each. On one he profit 20% and on another he loses 20%. How much does he profit% or loss% in the whole transaction?

(a) 5% loss   (b) 4% profit
(c) 4% loss   (d) 5% profit

28. A salesman sells an item at a price that is higher than the cost price by 30% and uses a weight which is 20% less. Find his total profit.

(a) 60%   (b) 62.5%
(c) 65%   (d) 50%

29. What is the difference between compound interest and simple interest on $Rs.\,6000$ for 2 years at 4% per annum?

(a) $Rs.\,14.\,40$ (b) $Rs.\,19.\,20$
(c) $Rs.\,9.\,60$ (d) $Rs.\,19.\,60$

30. A sum of money becomes $2\frac{1}{2}$ times in 6 years when invested at compound interest. How many times does the sum become when it is invested for 18 years?

(a) $\frac{5}{2}$ (b) $\frac{25}{4}$
(c) $\frac{125}{8}$ (d) $\frac{625}{16}$

31. Direction: Below given a question and three statements numbered I, II and III. You have to decide whether the data provided in the statements are sufficient to answer the question. Read all the statements and give answer:

A metal block of density $'D'$ and mass $'M'$, in the form of a cuboid, is beaten into a thin square sheet of thickness $'t'$, and rolled to form a cylinder of the same thickness. Find the inner radius of the cylinder.

Statement I: Cuboid has dimensions $10\,cm$ $x\ 5\,cm\ x\ 12\,cm$
Statement II: Thickness $'t' = 1.5\,cm$
Statement III: Mass of block, $M = 216$ kg

(a) Either statement III alone or statements I and II together are sufficient.
(b) Only statement III is sufficient.
(c) Statement I and Statement II together are sufficient.
(d) Only statement I, II, and III together are sufficient.

32. Direction: Each of the questions below consists of a question and three statements numbered I, II and III given below it. You have to decide whether the data provided in the statements are sufficient to answer the question. Read all the statements and give answer:

What is the ratio of the volume of the cube to the volume of the cuboid?

I. The Total Surface Area of the cuboid is 352 cm^2 and the ratio of the length, breadth and height of the cuboid is $3:2:1$.
II. The Total Surface Area of the cube is 726 cm^2.
III. The length of the cuboid is 1.5 times of the breadth of the cuboid and 3 times of the height of the cuboid. The difference between the height and the length of the cuboid is 8 cm.

(a) The data in statements I alone is sufficient to answer the question, while the data in statement II aand III is not sufficient to answer the question.
(b) The data in statements II aand III is sufficient to answer the question, while the data in statement I is not sufficient to answer the question.
(c) The data in statements I and II or in statement

II and III is sufficient to answer the question.

(d) The data in all the statements I, II and III is not sufficient to answer the question.

33. When a number a increases by 20% and then decrease by 20 we get 160 . If a number decreases by 20% and increases by 20 , what will we get?

(a) 144   (b) 140

(c) 152   (d) 148

34. The average age of husband, wife and their child 3 years ago was 27 years and that of wife and the child 5 years ago was 20 years. The present age of the husband is:

(a) 40 years   (b) 35 years

(c) 45 years   (d) 55 years

35. The average marks of 25 students is 45 . Later at the time of recalculation of marks it is found that the marks of one student is wrongly taken as 82 instead of 28 . Find the correct average marks of students.

(a) 42.84   (b) 48.84

(c) 42.20   (d) 47.84

36. In an election, there are two parties A and B involved. 18% of the total votes were invalid and the ratio of votes received by A and B is 5 : 3. If the number of votes polled in favor of B was 615, then find the total number of votes polled.

(a) 5000   (b) 4000

(c) 2000   (d) 3000

37. A can do a particular work in 6 days. B can do the same work in 8 days. A and B signed to do it for Rs. 3200. They completed the work in 3 days with the help of C. How much is to be paid to C?

(a) Rs. 500   (b) Rs. 600

(c) Rs. 450   (d) Rs. 400

38. 2 men and 3 women can do a work in 6 days, 3 men and 9 women can complete the work in 3 days. How many men will do the same amount of work as done by 12 women?

(a) 3 men   (b) 4 men

(c) 6 men   (d) 7 men

39. A can plough a square field of side 10 m in 10 hours and that can be done by B in 5 hours. In how much time a new field having a 50% larger side and square in shape is ploughed if A and B plough together?

(a) 6.5 hours   (b) 9.5 hours

(c) 7.5 hours   (d) 5.5 hours

40. The ratio of the speed of 2 cars is 5: 4. According to this, what would be the ratio of their time to go to the same distance?

(a) 5: 4   (b) 6: 4

(c) 6: 4   (d) 4: 5

41. A person can ride a boat in the opposite direction of the stream at a speed of 10 km/h. And its speed in the direction of current is 16 km/h. Show the speed of the boat in calm water:

(a) 17 km/h   (b) 13 km/h

(c) 30 km/h   (d) 29 km/h

42. HCF of $\frac{9}{10}, \frac{18}{35}, \frac{12}{25}$ is

(a) $\frac{18}{35}$ (b) $\frac{3}{35}$

(c) $\frac{120}{350}$ (d) $\frac{3}{350}$

43. When Jaynav was born, his father was 32 years older than his brother and his mother was 25 years older than his sister. If Jaynav's brother is 6 years older than him and his mother is 3 years younger than his father, then how old was Jaynav's sister when he was born?

(a) 10 years   (b) 12 years

(c) 14 years   (d) 15 years

Ques (44-45): Study the bar graph and answer the questions based on it.

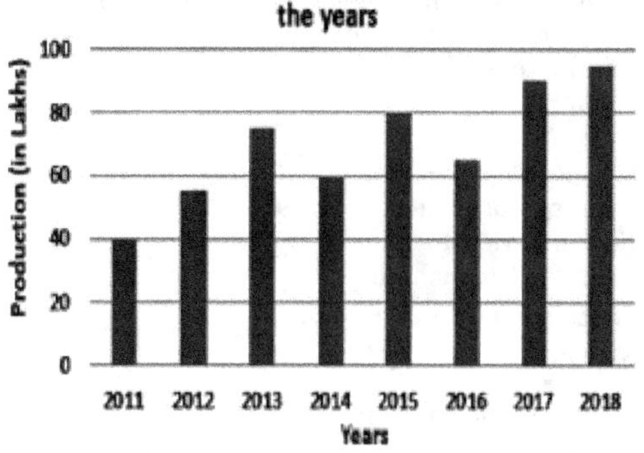

Production of Toys by company (in Lakhs) over the years

44. In which year the percentage increase in production was maximum as compared to the previous year?

(a) 2013   (b) 2012

(c) 2015   (d) 2017

45. In how many of the given years was the production of toys more than the average production of the given years?

(a) 2   (b) 1

(c) 3   (d) 4

46. If $a^4 + b^4 + a^2b^2 = 16$, and $a^2 + b^2 + ab = 8$, then find the value of $a^2 + b^2 - ab$.

(a) 1   (b) 2

(c) 3   (d) 8

47. In $\triangle ABC$, $AB = 20$ cm, $BC = 7$ cm and $CA = 15$ cm. Side BC is produced to D such that $\triangle DAB \sim \triangle DCA$. DC is equal to:

(a) 9 cm   (b) 8 cm

(c) 10 cm   (d) 7 cm

48. If $\sin(2\alpha + \beta) = 1$ and $\sin(\alpha - 2\beta) = \frac{1}{2}$, then find the value of $(\alpha + \beta)$.

(a) 76°   (b) 36°

(c) 48°   (d) 56°

49. If three dice are rolled under the condition that no two dice show the same face, then what is the probability that one of the faces is having the number 6?

(a) $\frac{5}{6}$ (b) $\frac{5}{9}$

(c) $\frac{1}{2}$ (d) $\frac{5}{12}$

50. Out of 6 teachers and 8 students a committee of 11 is to be formed. In how many ways can this be done such that the committee has exactly 4 teachers?

(a) 140   (b) 140

(c) 125   (d) 120

Reasoning

51. BRIGHT is related to JSCSGF in the same way as JOINED is related to....?
(a) HNIEFO   (b) JPKEFO
(c) JPKMDC   (d) JPKCDM

52. Find the missing number.
16 : 4 : : 9 : ?
(a) 1   (b) 2
(c) 25   (d) 4

53. Pointing to an old woman, Aryan said "Her son is my son's uncle and she has no daughter." How is Aryan related to old woman?
(a) Mother   (b) Sister
(c) Son   (d) Daughter

54. Suresh, the son of Mahesh is married to Sia, whose sister Jia is married to Amar, the brother of suresh. How is Jia related to Mahesh?
(a) Daughter-in-law   (b) Cousin
(c) Sister-in-law   (d) Sister

55. Select the odd image pair which is different from other image pairs.
(a)
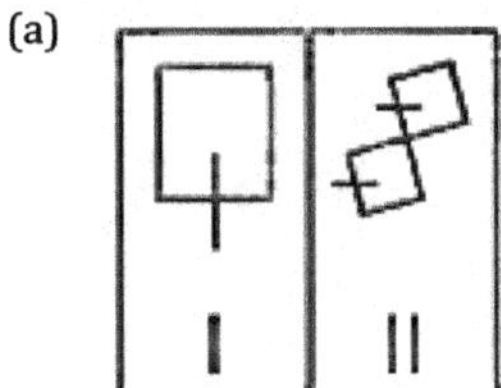

(b)
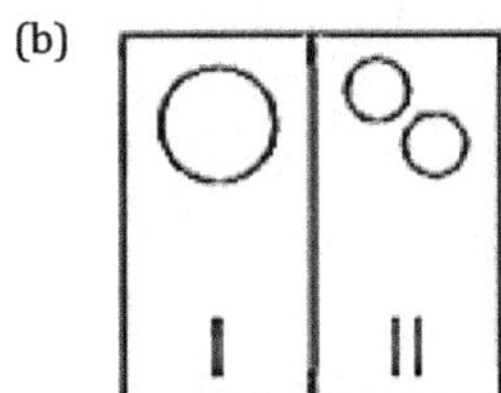

(c)
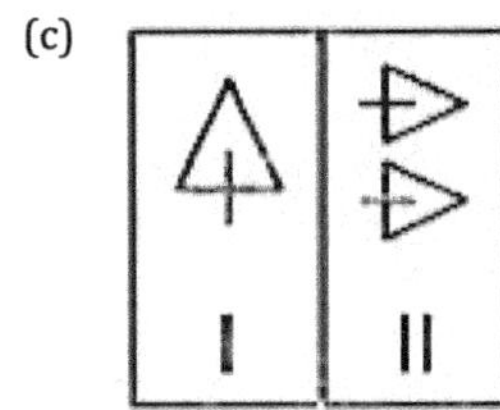

(d)
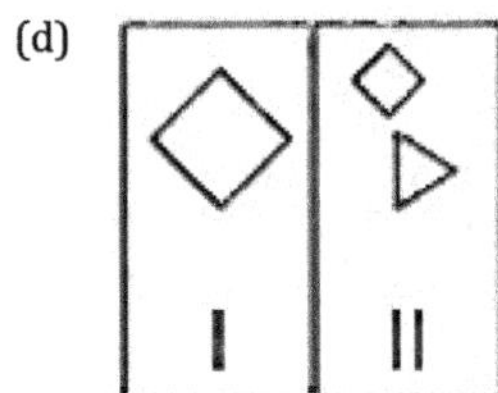

56. Identify the odd one from the given series.

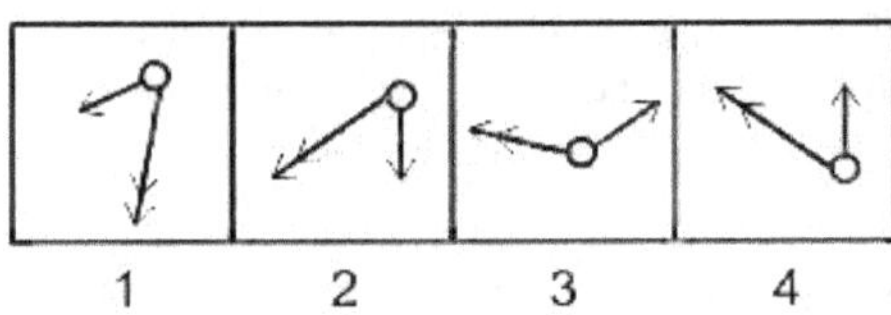

(a) 3   (b) 4
(c) 2   (d) 1

57. **Direction:** In the given question, in three out four figures, figure (i) is related to figure (ii) in same particular manner. Spell out the pair in which relationship does not exist between figure (i) and figure (ii).

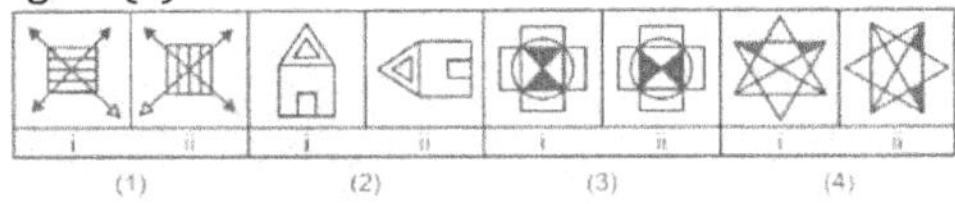

(a) (1)   (b) (2)
(c) (3)   (d) (4)

58. Jyoti travels 15 km towards south and then takes a left turn and travels 10 km further again she takes a left turn and travels 15 km further. How far is she from his original position?
(a) 17 km   (b) 10 km
(c) 13 km   (d) 15 km

59. A man is facing north. He turns 90° in the clockwise direction and then 135° in the anti-clockwise direction. Which direction is he facing now?
(a) East   (b) North-West
(c) North   (d) South

60. If in a coding system, FIXED is coded as 86 and COMPANY is coded as 101 , then how will INTERIM be coded in the same coding system ?
(a) 102   (b) 100
(c) 99   (d) 101

61. In a certain code language, 'CLOT' is written as ' 6243040' . How will ' MOSAIC' be written in that language?
(a) 2630382186   (b) 2630382206
(c) 2830382183   (d) 2632362186

62. Study the problem figures given below and identify one of the alternative figures from the answer figures which should continue the sequence of the problem :
Problem figures:

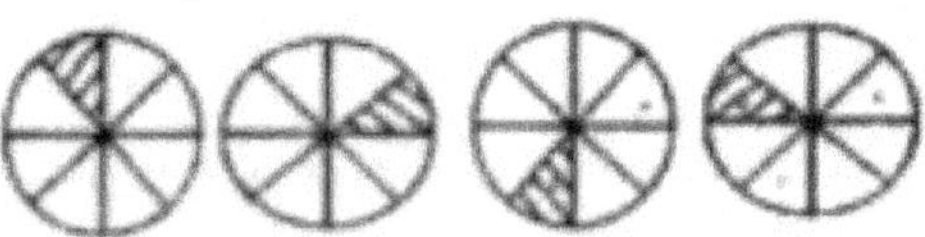

Answer figures:

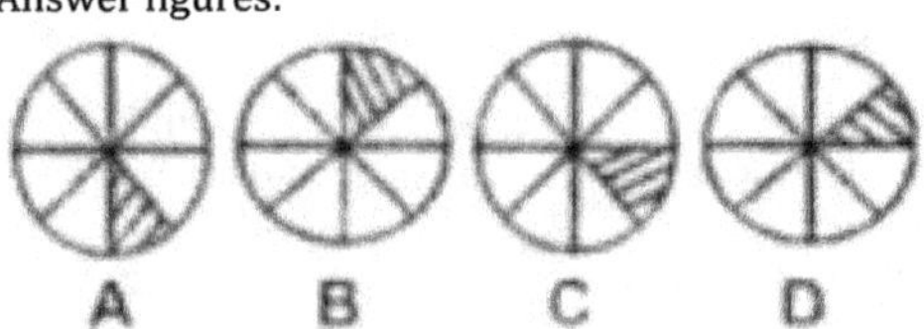

(a) A   (b) B
(c) C   (d) D

63. Study the problem figures and choose the option from the answer figures that will continue the sequence of

the problem figures.
Problem Figures:

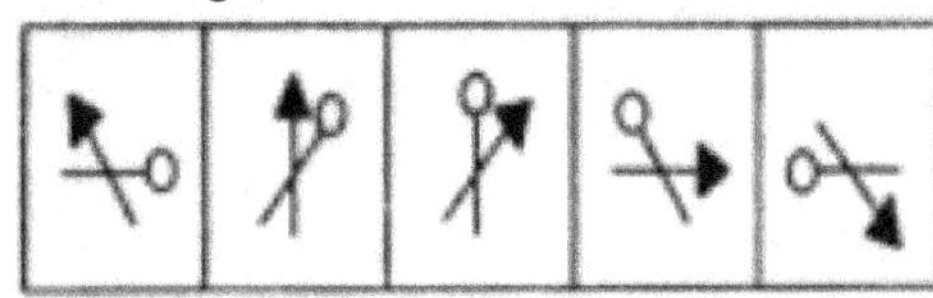

Answer figures:

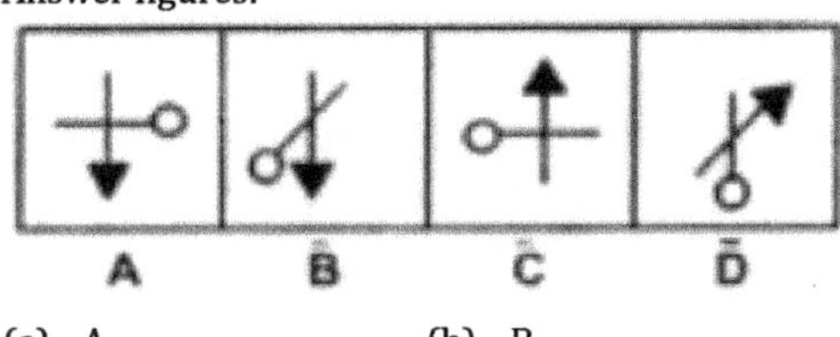

(a)   A
(b)   B
(c)   C
(d)   D

Ques (64-65): Direction: Identify the diagram that best represents the relationship among classes given below:

64. Tie, Shirt and Shoe

(a)

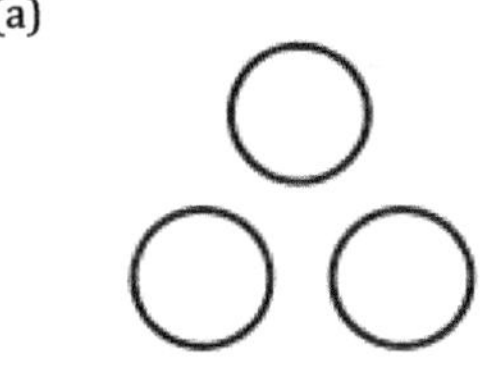

(b)

(c)

(d)

65. Ornaments, Gold, Silver.

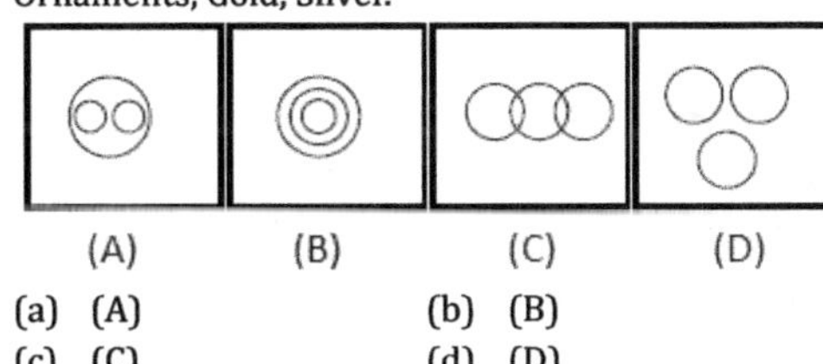

(a)   (A)
(b)   (B)
(c)   (C)
(d)   (D)

66. What will come in place of the question mark (?) in the following number series?
8 72 288 (?) 1800 3528

(a)   850
(b)   800
(c)   1000
(d)   820

67. Which number will replace the question mark (?) in the following series.
11, 13, 10, 15, 8, 19, 6, 23, ?
(a)   2
(b)   4
(c)   3
(d)   1

68. In a row of boys. Srinath is 7 th from the left and Venkat is 12 th from the right. If they interchange their positions, Srinath becomes 22 nd from the left. How many boys are there in the row?
(a)   19
(b)   31
(c)   33
(d)   34

69. Kamal is 11th from the front in a row of girls. Leela is 3 places ahead of Sunita, who is 22nd from the lead. How many girls are there between Kamal and Leela in this row?
(a)   6
(b)   8
(c)   7
(d)   9

Ques (70-71): Direction: In the following question below some statements are given followed by some conclusions. Taking the given statements to be true even if they seem to be at variance from commonly known facts, read all the conclusions and then decide which of the given conclusions logically follows the given statements.

70. Statements:
I. All cars are machines.
II. No machine is a bike.
Conclusions:
I. No bike is a machine.
II. No car is a bike.
(a)   Only conclusion I follows.
(b)   Only conclusion II follows.
(c)   Both conclusions I and II follows.
(d)   Neither conclusion I nor conclusion II follows.

71. Statements:
I. Some Gs are Mg.
II. No Mg is Fr.
Conclusions:
I. Some Gs are Fr.
II. No Gs is Mg.
III. Some Mg are Fr.
IV. All Mg are Fr.
(a)   Only I follows
(b)   Only II follows
(c)   Only III follows
(d)   None follows

72. Direction: Read the instructions carefully and answer the question below.
A, B, C, D, E, F, G, and H are the eight male members sitting around a circular table. Four of them are facing the inward direction and four are facing the outward direction. These eight people are married to eight girls namely L, M, N, O, P, Q, R, and S but not necessarily in the same order. No three consecutive people are facing the same direction.
Only one person is sitting between B and the husband of L. Both the immediate neighbours of D are facing the same direction. Either R or P is the wife of D. The husband of Q is facing the outward direction and he is sitting to the immediate right of D. B is sitting third to the right of the person who is the husband of R and they are facing the same direction. The husband of P and the husband of Q are facing the same direction.

The wife of D is sitting third to the left of F. Neither O nor P is the wife of B. G is sitting third to the right of C. The husband of L is sitting third to the left of E. Only one person is sitting between F and the husband of M and they are facing the same direction. The husband of S is sitting third to the right of H. A is an immediate neighbour of the husband of M. C is sitting third to the right of the husband of M and they are facing different directions.

Who is sitting second to the left of the husband of Q?

(a) D
(b) G
(c) B
(d) C

73. **Direction:** Read the instructions carefully and answer the question below.

Ten persons Sagar, Anurag, Sanket, Vinit, Amit, Rajesh, Aditya, Himanshu, Akshay and Sujit are sitting in a circular park facing away from the centre but not necessarily in the same order. Sanket is sitting fourth to the right of Akshay. Three persons are sitting between Sujit and Sanket. Rajesh is an immediate neighbour of Sujit. Amit is sitting fourth to the right of Rajesh. Amit is an immediate neighbour of Sagar. Himanshu is sitting third to the right of Sagar. Three persons are sitting between Himanshu and Vinit. Aditya is sitting third to the left of Anurag.

How many persons are sitting between Sujit and Aditya?

(a) 3
(b) 2
(c) 4
(d) 5

74. Select the word which is different from the others.

(a) Clove
(b) Cardamom
(c) Saffron
(d) Cashewnut

75. Select the letter which is different from the others.

(a) CDF
(b) IJL
(c) MNQ
(d) STV

General Hindi

76. प्रश्न में सही वर्तनी चुनिये:

(a) भास्कर
(b) भाषकृ
(c) भाश्कर
(d) भाशकर

77. प्रश्न में सही वर्तनी चुनिये:

(a) उर्ध्व
(b) ऊर्ध्व
(c) उर्धव
(d) ऊर्धव

78. कुजगह फोड़ा और ससुर वैद्य - कहावत का अर्थ है:

(a) दोनों में दोष
(b) मरीज वैद्य में संपर्क
(c) दोनों का त्याग
(d) धर्म संकट की स्थिति

79. 'लश्कर में ऊंट बदनाम' का अर्थ है:

(a) गुणवान का बदनाम
(b) ऊंट का सदा एकरस
(c) मोल-ताल कर बदनाम होना
(d) दोष किसी का पर नाम किसी और का

80. 'सदा एक समान' रहने पर लोकोक्ति प्रयुक्त होती है:

(a) साँच को आँच नहीं
(b) सावन हरे न भादो सूखे
(c) भागते चोर की लंगोटी ही सही
(d) सहज पे सो मीठा होय।

81. स्त्रीलिंग शब्द अलग कीजिए:

(a) हुलास
(b) हरकत
(c) हमला
(d) हवाला

82. भील का स्त्रीलिंग है:

(a) भालू
(b) भीलनी
(c) भिलीनी
(d) भालना

83. 'बिना पलक झपकाए' के लिए एक शब्द है:

(a) निष्पलक
(b) निस्पृह
(c) निर्निमेष
(d) निर्विकार

84. प्राणदा के लिए अनेक शब्द है:

(a) प्राण रहने का मंत्र
(b) जीवन देने वाली दवा
(c) जीवन चाहने वाली राह
(d) प्राण रहने का अभ्यास

85. व्याकरण में 'वचन' का सही अर्थ क्या है?

(a) संख्या
(b) बोली
(c) भाषा
(d) प्रतिज्ञा

86. निम्नलिखित शब्दों में से किस शब्द में प्रत्यय है?

(a) निकाय
(b) ऊंचाई
(c) दुर्बोध
(d) आत्मकथा

87. 'सु' उपसर्ग से बना शब्द है?

(a) ससुराल
(b) ससुर
(c) सुबोध
(d) इनमें से सभी

88. 'जाति' शब्द का बहुवचन रूप क्या होगा?

(a) जातिऐं
(b) जातियाँ
(c) जातिओं
(d) जातियां

89. 'चाय' शब्द का प्रयोग किस वचन में होता है?

(a) एकवचन
(b) द्विवचन
(c) बहुवचन
(d) कोई नहीं

Ques (90-91): निर्देश: वाक्य के अशुद्ध भाग (त्रुटिपूर्ण भाग) का चयन कीजिए।

90. मैं पटना गया (a)/ तो उस समय (b)/मेरे पास (c)/केवल बीस रुपये मात्र थे। (d)

(a) (a)
(b) (b)
(c) (c)
(d) (d)

91. एक वर्ष से मैं जिस पुस्तक की रचना में संलग्न था (a)/ आज उसे छपे आकार में देखकर (b)/ मेरी प्रसन्नता का ठिकाना नहीं है। (c)/ कोई त्रुटि नहीं (d)

(a) (a)
(b) (b)
(c) (c)
(d) (d)

92. 'स्वर्ग' शब्द का विलोम है:

(a) बैकुंठ
(b) देवलोक
(c) नरक
(d) परमधाम

93. 'राग' शब्द का विलोम है:

(a) अनुराग
(b) विराग
(c) आसक्ति
(d) अनुरक्ति

94. 'स्वाधीन' शब्द का विलोम है:

(a) स्वतंत्र
(b) स्वच्छंद

95. निम्नलिखित में से कौन-सा शब्द ' पहाड़ ' का पर्यायवाची नहीं है?
    (a) अचल
    (b) अचला
    (c) गिरि
    (d) अद्रि

96. 'स्वाधीन' में प्रयुक्त संधि का नाम है:
    (a) गुण संधि
    (b) दीर्घ संधि
    (c) व्यंजन संधि
    (d) यण संधि

97. 'विधायक' में कौन सी संधि है?
    (a) गुण संधि
    (b) अयादि संधि
    (c) व्यंजन संधि
    (d) विसर्ग संधि

98. 'तथोक्तम्' में प्रयुक्त संधि का नाम है-
    (a) वृद्धि संधि
    (b) दीर्घ संधि
    (c) विसर्ग संधि
    (d) गुण संधि

99. निम्नलिखित में से जायसी की रचना कौनसी है?
    (a) कवितावली
    (b) चंदायन
    (c) पद्मावत
    (d) हंस जवाहिर

100. गोरख बानी किस साहित्य की रचना है?
    (a) सिद्ध साहित्य
    (b) नाथ साहित्य
    (c) रासो साहित्य
    (d) जैन साहित्य

// Smart Answer Sheet //

Correct — Percentage of students who answered correctly.

Skipped — Percentage of students who skipped.

Q.	Ans.	Correct / Skipped	Q.	Ans.	Correct / Skipped	Q.	Ans.	Correct / Skipped
1	A	26.42% / 4.58%	2	B	61.94% / 1.82%	3	D	50.05% / 1.14%
4	A	82.07% / 0.0%	5	C	47.19% / 1.97%	6	B	46.44% / 1.89%
7	B	27.47% / 3.5%	8	D	47.85% / 1.57%	9	A	55.88% / 1.19%
10	D	18.61% / 4.56%	11	A	84.32% / 0.0%	12	A	40.89% / 1.35%
13	C	77.93% / 0.0%	14	A	54.01% / 1.64%	15	D	54.51% / 1.16%
16	D	47.01% / 1.66%	17	C	43.98% / 1.03%	18	A	79.3% / 0.0%
19	C	83.3% / 0.0%	20	C	53.59% / 1.76%	21	A	59.43% / 1.22%
22	A	47.34% / 1.36%	23	B	12.8% / 3.14%	24	B	62.43% / 1.3%
25	C	40.35% / 1.19%	26	D	64.5% / 1.35%	27	C	40.28% / 1.61%
28	B	43.04% / 1.83%	29	C	45.68% / 1.44%	30	C	16.13% / 3.88%
31	C	47.89% / 1.6%	32	C	20.93% / 3.51%	33	B	68.48% / 1.73%
34	A	46.02% / 1.86%	35	A	41.69% / 1.88%	36	C	16.54% / 4.47%
37	D	21.11% / 3.53%	38	B	14.0% / 4.33%	39	C	47.67% / 1.96%
40	D	87.76% / 0.0%	41	B	85.47% / 0.0%	42	D	64.51% / 1.14%
43	A	43.42% / 1.69%	44	D	54.05% / 1.38%	45	D	41.63% / 1.92%
46	B	58.05% / 1.69%	47	A	51.52% / 1.21%	48	C	50.15% / 1.35%
49	C	46.55% / 1.45%	50	D	58.66% / 1.7%	51	D	43.46% / 1.11%
52	A	58.65% / 1.36%	53	C	50.87% / 1.43%	54	A	66.42% / 1.98%
55	D	62.98% / 1.35%	56	A	46.47% / 1.71%	57	B	64.81% / 1.17%
58	B	84.15% / 0.0%	59	B	45.05% / 1.35%	60	B	25.27% / 4.08%
61	A	52.26% / 1.3%	62	B	77.75% / 0.0%	63	B	63.45% / 1.05%
64	A	47.44% / 1.18%	65	A	55.29% / 1.78%	66	B	50.18% / 1.0%
67	B	50.36% / 1.93%	68	C	55.35% / 1.1%	69	B	45.47% / 1.15%
70	C	45.14% / 1.47%	71	C	43.3% / 1.55%	72	C	55.51% / 1.87%
73	C	61.53% / 1.62%	74	D	46.18% / 1.27%	75	C	65.55% / 1.97%
76	A	84.78% / 0.0%	77	B	81.27% / 0.0%	78	D	62.6% / 1.44%
79	D	67.53% / 1.72%	80	B	84.28% / 0.0%	81	B	54.46% / 1.75%
82	B	85.98% / 0.0%	83	C	80.03% / 0.0%	84	B	61.33% / 1.48%
85	A	48.1% / 1.06%	86	B	79.63% / 0.0%	87	C	78.14% / 0.0%
88	B	82.61% / 0.0%	89	A	60.19% / 1.35%	90	C	67.76% / 1.42%
91	B	48.46% / 1.47%	92	C	82.7% / 0.0%	93	B	89.95% / 0.0%
94	C	89.39% / 0.0%	95	B	85.74% / 0.0%	96	B	51.61% / 1.46%
97	B	82.63% / 0.0%	98	D	42.99% / 1.8%	99	C	43.86% / 1.43%
100	B	64.19% / 1.54%						

// Hints and Solutions //

1(A). A Passage to India is not authored by Nirad C. Chaudhuri.

Nirad C. Chaudhuri , born in Kishorganj, East Bengal, British India (now in Bangladesh), Bengali author and scholar who was opposed to the withdrawal of British colonial rule from the Indian subcontinent and the subsequent rejection of Western culture in independent India. He dedicated his first book, The Autobiography of an Unknown Indian (1951), to the memory of the British Empire.

2(B). The government of the Satavahana Kingdom was organized on the traditional lines where the kingdom was divided into Janapadas.

Satvahana Kingdom:
- Simuka was the founder of the Satavahana Dynasty.
- It majorly comprised the present states of Andhra Pradesh, Maharashtra and Telangana.
- Their kingdom also included parts of Gujarat, Karnataka as well as Madhya Pradesh.

3(D). The correct answer is Bill of exchange.

Hundi
- Hundi is a financial instrument that was developed in Medieval India for use in trade and credit transactions.
- A Hundi is an unconditional order in writing made by a person directing another to pay a certain sum of money to a person named in the order.
- Hundis, being a part of the informal system have no legal status and are not covered under the Negotiable Instruments Act, 1881.
- It is regarded as bills of exchange, they were more

often used as equivalents of cheques issued by indigenous bankers.

4(A). The correct answer is Samudragupta.
Samudragupta
- Samudragupta (335-375 AD) of the Gupta Dynasty is known as the Napoleon of India.
- He was the first significant ruler of the Gupta Dynasty.
- The caste status of Samudra Gupta and his successors remains uncertain.
- He was a great warrior.
- Samudragupta was a brilliant commander and a great conqueror is proved by Harisena's description of his conquests.

5(C). The maximum affected district was Patna. There was no law and order in Patna for two days after the Secretariat firing (August 11, 1942).

6(B). The chairman of the Working Committee of the Congress was Abul Kalam Azad. The meeting between Gandhi and Azad was likely focused on the strategic and tactical aspects of the freedom struggle.

7(B). Kaveri river rises on Brahmagiri Hill of the Western Ghats in southwestern Karnataka state, flows in a southeasterly direction for 475 miles (765 km) through the states of Karnataka, Kerala, and Tamil Nadu, and descends the Eastern Ghats in a series of great falls.

8(D). The Konkan Railway Project passes through four states - Goa, Maharashtra, Karnataka, and Kerala. The tunnel at Karbude near Ratnagiri on this rail route is 6.5 km long, which is the longest rail tunnel in the world.

9(A). Bhakra Nangal is a joint venture of the Punjab, Haryana, and Rajasthan states designed to harness the precious water of the Sutlej for the benefit of the concerned states.

10(D). Indian Energy Exchange (IEX) became the country's first carbon-neutral power exchange in December 2022.
IEX voluntarily cancelled CERs (certified emissions reductions) from clean projects. As per UNEP 2022 report, global greenhouse gas (GHG) emissions must be cut 45% by 2030 to limit global warming to 1.5 degrees. Ever since its incorporation, it has held an influential market share. IEX operates a day-ahead market based on closed auctions with double-sided bidding and uniform pricing.

11(A). Singer-composer KK, whose real name was "Krishnakumar Kunnath", died in Kolkata on 31st May 2022 at the age of 53. His debut album 'Pal' was released in 1999. He has recorded songs in Hindi, Tamil, Telugu, Kannada, Malayalam, Marathi and Bengali, among other languages.

12(A). Five golfers including Aditi Ashok among 10 more athletes added to TOPS.
- TOPS (Target Olympic Podium Scheme) is a flagship program of the Ministry of Youth Affairs and Sports which is an attempt to provide assistance to India's top athletes. So, statement 1 is correct.
- The Scheme looks to add a premium to the preparations of these athletes so that they can win medals in the Olympics.
Players included in TOPS scheme:

- Ace rider Fouaad Mirza, golfers Anirban Lahiri, Aditi Ashok and Diksha Dagar and Alpine Skier Mohammed Arif Khan are among the 10 athletes added by the Ministry of Youth Affairs and Sports' Mission Olympic Cell (MOC) to the list of athletes who would be provided support under the Target Olympic Podium Scheme. So, statement 3 is not correct.
- Mohammed Arif Khan became the first Indian Alpine Skier to qualify for the Winter Olympic Games 2022 to be held in Beijing. So, statement 2 is correct.
So, statement 1 and 2 only is correct.

13(C). Operation Dost is a rescue operation initiated by the Government of India to aid Syria and Turkey, after an earthquake hit both countries on 6 February 2023. Under the operation, India has deployed a field hospital, supplies, and rescue personnel to the earthquake-stricken countries of Turkey and Syria.

14(A). In the given options, Earth is is the largest planet.

15(D). Around the world, 36 areas qualify as hotspots. They represent just 4% of Earth's land surface, but they support more than half of the world's plant species as endemics — i.e., species found no place else — and nearly 43% of bird, mammal, reptile, and amphibian species as endemics.

16(D). Rocks is not a biotic factor. Biotic factors are living organisms in the ecosystem. Examples of biotic factors are animals, birds, plants, fungi, and other similar organisms.

17(C). Rajya Sabha is a permanent house. It never dissolves like Lok Sabha. Members have a term of six year. One-third of its members retire every two years. Its member shall not be less than 30 years of age.

18(A). The Parliament consists of two Houses Lok Sabha and Rajya Sabha and the President of India.

19(C). The Constitutional advisor to the Constituent Assembly was B. N. Rao.

20(C). The National Education Policy (NEP), 2020 commits to raising the total expenditure by states and centre on education to 6% of GDP.
- The National Education Policy 2020 has set the target to increase public investment in the education sector to reach 6 percent of Gross Domestic Product (GDP) at the earliest.
- After almost three decades, the government is ready to transform the country's education system by making some impactful suggestions.
- While the National Education Policy 2020 (NEP 2020) aims at making India a global knowledge superpower by providing high-quality education to all.
- The policy focuses on almost doubling the Gross Enrolment Ratio (GER) in higher education, including vocational education, from 26.3 percent to 50 percent by 2035.
- Currently, the expenditure on education by centre and states as a proportion of GDP is 3.1 percent in 2019/20 (budget estimates) and has inched up by a meagre 30 basis points in the past six years.

21(A). From the 1990s, Bharat Sahayata Club came to be known as Indian Development Forum (IDF).

22(A). Revised Value-Added Tax relates to Sales tax.

23(B). On National Sports Day (29 Aug), Indian sprinter Amlan Borgohain set a new national record with a timing of 10.25 seconds in the men's 100m race at the Inter-Railway Athletics Championships in Rae Bareli, Uttar Pradesh.

24(B). 'It provides funding to research projects in science as well as non-science disciplines' statement about National Research Foundation (NRF), proposed in National Education Policy (2020) is correct.
The primary activities of the NRF will be to:
- Fund competitive, peer-reviewed grant proposals of all types and across all disciplines. (It will fund research projects across four major disciplines –Sciences; Technology; Social Sciences; and Arts and Humanities).
- Seed, grow, and facilitate research at academic institutions, particularly at universities and colleges where research is currently in a nascent stage, through mentoring of such institutions;
- Act as a liaison between researchers and relevant branches of government as well as industry, so that research scholars are constantly made aware of the most urgent national research issues, and so that policymakers are constantly made aware of the latest research breakthroughs; so as to allow breakthroughs to be optimally brought into policy and/or implementation and recognize outstanding research and progress.
- In the budget 2021-22, NRF has been allocated 50,000 crores over the next 5 years.

25(C). Among many, the two core techniques that enabled birth of modern biotechnology are:
Genetic engineering : Techniques to alter the chemistry of genetic material (DNA and RNA), to introduce these into host organisms and thus change the phenotype of the host organism.
The techniques of genetic engineering which include creation of recombinant DNA, use of gene cloning and gene transfer

26(D). Given,
$$3\tfrac{1}{6} + 7\tfrac{2}{3} - 4\tfrac{1}{4} = ? + 2\tfrac{1}{6}$$
$$\Rightarrow 3\tfrac{1}{6} + 7\tfrac{2}{3} - 4\tfrac{1}{4} - 2\tfrac{1}{6} = ?$$
$$\Rightarrow ? = (3+7-4-2) + \left(\tfrac{1}{6} + \tfrac{2}{3} - \tfrac{1}{4} - \tfrac{1}{6}\right)$$
$$\Rightarrow ? = 4 + \frac{2+8-3-2}{12}$$
$$\Rightarrow ? = 4 + \frac{5}{12}$$
$$\Rightarrow ? = 4 + \frac{48+5}{12}$$
$$\Rightarrow ? = 4\tfrac{5}{12}$$

27(C). Given:
The selling price of each chair = Rs. 800, Profit = 20%, Loss = 20%
Formula:
$$\text{Profit \%} = \left(\frac{\text{S.P}-\text{C.P}}{\text{C.P}}\right) \times 100$$
$$\text{Loss \%} = \left(\frac{\text{C.P}-\text{S.P}}{\text{C.P}}\right) \times 100$$
Where, C.P = Cost Price and S.P = Selling Price
According to the question,
C.P of the first chair is:
$$\text{C.P} \times \frac{120}{100} = 800$$
$$\Rightarrow \text{C.P} = 666.66$$
and C.P of second chair is:

$$\text{C.P} \times \frac{80}{100} = 800$$
$$\Rightarrow \text{C.P} = 1000$$
The total C.P of two chairs are:
= 1000 + 666.66
= 1666.66
The total S.P of two chairs are:
= 800 + 800
= 1600
So that, the S.P is less than the C.P
$$\Rightarrow \text{Loss \%} = \left(\frac{1666.66-1600}{1666.66}\right) \times 100$$
$$= \frac{66.66 \times 100}{1666.66}$$
= 3.99% in approx 4%.
∴ The total loss percentage is 4%.

28(B). Let the customer bought 1 kg of item
Actual amount received by the customer
$$= 1 - \left(\frac{20}{100} \times 1\right) = 0.8 \text{ kg}$$
Let the cost price of 1 kg be Rs. 100
Actual price of 80gm $= 100 \times (0.80) = \text{Rs.80}$
New marked price $= 100 + \left(\frac{30}{100}\right) \times 100 = \text{Rs.130}$
Price paid by the customer $= \text{Rs. }130$
Profit earned by the shopkeeper
$= 130 - 80 = \text{Rs.50}$
Profit percentage $= \left(\frac{50}{80}\right) \times 100 = 62.5\%$

29(C). Given-
Principal $P = Rs.\,6000$
Time $T = 2$ years
Rate $R = 4\%$ per annum
According to the formula-
$$d = \frac{P \times R^2}{10000}$$
where d is the difference between compound interest and simple interest
$$\Rightarrow d = \frac{6000 \times 4^2}{10000}$$
$$\Rightarrow d = Rs.\,9.60$$

30(C). Given-
A sum of money becomes $2\tfrac{1}{2}$ times in 6 years when invested at compound interest.
Let the sum $= Rs.\,P$
Amount $A = 2\tfrac{1}{2} \times P$
$$\Rightarrow A = Rs.\,\frac{5P}{2}$$
Time $T = 6$ years
According to the formula-
$$A = P\left(1 + \frac{R}{100}\right)^T \text{ where } R \text{ is rate}$$
$$\Rightarrow \frac{5P}{2} = P\left(1 + \frac{R}{100}\right)^6$$
$$\Rightarrow \frac{5}{2} = \left(1 + \frac{R}{100}\right)^6 \text{ -------- EQUATION (1)}$$
When the sum of money is invested for 18 years,
New amount $A' = P\left(1 + \frac{R}{100}\right)^{18}$
$$\Rightarrow A' = P\left[\left(1 + \frac{R}{100}\right)^6\right]^3$$
From EQUATION (1),
$$\Rightarrow A' = P\left[\left(\frac{5}{2}\right)^3\right]$$
$$\Rightarrow A' = \frac{125P}{8}$$
The sum of money becomes $\frac{125}{8}$ times when it is invested for 18 years.

31(C). If we have the dimensions, from Statement a,
Volume of cuboid $= 10 \times 5 \times 12 = 600 \text{ cm}^3$
If thickness is 't' and let side of square sheet be S, then,

$600 = (S^2) \times (t)$

If $t = 1.5$ cm is taken from Statement II,

$\frac{600}{1.5} = (S^2) = 400$

$S = 20$ cm

Height of cylinder $= S = 20\ cm$ [As square sheet is rolled so the side of the cylinder will be equal to side of square]

Outer circumference $= S = 20$ cm $= 2\pi r$ Or,

$r = \frac{10}{\pi} \approx 3.185$

Thickness taken, $t = 1.5$ cm

So inner radius $= 3.185 - 1.5 = 1.685$ cm

Whereas Statement III has no significance anywhere.

But none of the statement alone can answer the question individually.

So, answer is using statement I and II together is sufficient.

32(C). Statement I:

Total Surface Area of cuboid $= 2(lb + bh + hl)$

Let length $= 3x$, breadth $= 2x$, height $= x$

$352 = 2(3x \times 2x + 2x \times x + x \times 3x)$

$176 = (6x^2 + 2x^2 + 3x^2)$

$176 = 11x^2$

$x^2 = 16$

$x = 4$

Length $= 12$ cm, Breadth $= 8$ cm, Height $= 4$ cm

Volume $= lbh$

$= 12 \times 8 \times 4 = 384$ cm^3

Statement II:

Total Surface Area of cube $= 6\,s^2$

$384 = 6\,s^2$

$s^2 = 64$

$s = 8$ cm

Volume of the cube $= s^3$

$= 8^3 = 512$ cm^3

Statement III:

Height of the cuboid $= x$ cm, length $= 3x$, breadth $= 2x$

Difference $= 3x - x$

$8 = 2x$

$x = 4$

Length $= 12$ cm, breadth $= 8$ cm, height $= 4$ cm

Volume $= lbh$

$= 12 \times 8 \times 4 = 384$ cm^3

We can solve this question with the help of either statement I and II or statement II and III.

33(B). Given,

If a number is increased by 20% and decreased by 20, then the resultant number is 160.

Let the number be x

According to the question, we have.

$x + (20\% \times x) - 20 = 160$

$\Rightarrow x + \frac{20}{100} \times x = 160 + 20$

$\Rightarrow x + \frac{x}{5} = 180$

$\Rightarrow \frac{6x}{5} = 180$

$\Rightarrow x = \frac{(180 \times 5)}{6}$

$\Rightarrow 150$

Now, the number is decreased by 20% and then increased by 20\)

So, $150 - (20\%$ of $150\,) + 20$

$\Rightarrow 150 - \frac{20}{100} \times 150 + 20$

$\Rightarrow 150 - 30 + 20 = 140$

$\therefore$ The required number is 140.

34(A). Given,

The average age of husband, wife and their child 3 years ago was 27 years and that of wife and the child 5 years ago was 20 years.

Sum of the present ages of husband, wife and child

$= (27 \times 3 + 3 \times 3)$ years

$= 90$ years

Sum of the present ages of wife and child

$= (20 \times 2 + 5 \times 2)$ years

$= 50$ years

Husband's present age

$= (90 - 50)$ years

$= 40$ years

35(A). Given,

The average marks of 25 students $= 45$

Correct value $= 28$

Incorrect value $= 82$

We know that,

Average $= \dfrac{\text{Sum of all the terms}}{\text{Total number of terms}}$

The average marks of 25 students $= 45$

$\therefore$ Sum of marks of all students $= 45 \times 25 = 1125$

To find the correct average we have to subtract the incorrect value and add the correct value.

Sum of marks after correction

$= (1125 - 82 + 28) = 1071$

$\therefore$ Correct average $= \dfrac{1071}{25} = 42.84$

The correct average marks of students is 42.84.

36(C). Given:

The ratio of votes received by A and B = 5 : 3

Invalid vote = 18% of total votes

Votes received by B = 18%

Let the total number of votes polled be x

18% of votes were invalid, so remaining votes = 0.82x

The ratio of votes received by A and B = 5 : 3

Let the number of votes received by A and B be 5y and 3y respectively

According to the question,

$\Rightarrow$ 3y = 615

$\Rightarrow$ y = 205

$\Rightarrow$ 5y = 5 × 205 = 1025

$\Rightarrow$ Votes received by A = 1025

Now total votes received by A and B = 1025 + 615 = 1640

Now,

$\Rightarrow$ 0.82x = 1640

$\Rightarrow$ x = 2000

$\therefore$ Total number of votes polled = 2000

Hence, the correct option is (D).

37(D). Given:

Amount of work A can do in 1 day $= 1/6$

Amount of work B can do in 1 day $= 1/8$

Calculation:

Amount of work $A + B$ can do in 1 day $= 1/6 + 1/8 = 7/24$

Amount of work $A + B + C$ can do in 1 day $= 1/3$

Amount of work C can do in 1 day $= 1/3 - 7/24 = 1/24$

Work done by A in 1 day : work done by B in 1 day : work done by C in 1 day

$\Rightarrow 1/6 : 1/8 : 1/24 = 4 : 3 : 1$

Amount to be paid to $C = 3200 \times (1/8) = $ Rs. 400

$\therefore$ The amount to be paid to C is Rs. 400.

38(B). Given:

2 men and 3 women can do a work in 6 days

3 men and 9 women can complete the work in 3 days

Calculation:

Let the efficiency of man be M and woman be W

According to question,

$(2M + 3W) \times 6 = (3M + 9W) \times 3$

$\Rightarrow 12M + 18W = 9M + 27W$

$\Rightarrow 12M - 9M = 27W - 18W$

$\Rightarrow 3M = 9W$

$\Rightarrow 1M = 3W$

$\Rightarrow 1W = \left(\frac{1}{3}\right)M$

$\Rightarrow 12W = \left\{\left(\frac{1}{3}\right) \times 12\right\}M$

$\Rightarrow 12W = 4M$

$\therefore$ The amount of work done by 12 women is equal to the work of 4 men.

39(C). Given:

Length of the side of square-shaped field = 10 m

Time taken by A to plough the field = 10 hours

Time taken by B to plough the field = 5 hours

Percentage increase in the side of the new square-shaped field = 50%

Formula:

Area of Square = $(\text{side})^2$

Work efficiency = $\dfrac{(\text{Total Work})}{(\text{Total time})}$

Calculation:

Area of the field to be ploughed = $(\text{side})^2 = 100 \text{ m}^2$

The efficiency of A to plough the field = $\dfrac{(\text{Area of field})}{(\text{Total Time})}$

$= \dfrac{100}{10} = 10 \text{ m}^2/\text{hour}$ ---(1)

The efficiency of B to plough the field = $\dfrac{(\text{Area of field})}{(\text{Total Time})}$

$= \dfrac{100}{5} = 20 \text{ m}^2/\text{hour}$ ---(2)

Length of side of new field = $10 + \left[10 \times \left(\frac{50}{100}\right)\right]$

$= 10 + 5 = 15 \text{ m}$

Area of new field = $(\text{side})^2$

$= 15^2$

$= 225 \text{ m}^2$

Colletive efficiency of A and B = $(10 + 20) \text{ m}^2/\text{hour}$ ---(By adding (1) and (2))

$= 30 \text{ m}^2/\text{hour}$

Total time taken by A and B to plough together = $\dfrac{(\text{Area of field})}{(\text{Collective efficiency of A and B})}$

$= \dfrac{225}{30}$

$= 7.5$ hours

$\therefore$ A and B will take 7.5 hours to plough the new field.

40(D). Time and speed are inversely proportional.

So, expected ratio = 4: 5

41(B). The boat moves 10 km/h in the opposite direction of the stream to the person. And its speed in the direction of the stream is 16 km/h

According to the given formula,

Speed of boat in calm water

$$= \dfrac{(Speed\,in\,the\,current\,of\,the\,stream + Speed\,in\,the\,op posite\,direction\,of\,the\,stream)}{2}$$

Speed of boat in calm water $= \dfrac{10+16}{2} = 13 \text{ km/h}$

42(D). Given:

$\dfrac{9}{10}, \dfrac{18}{35}, \dfrac{12}{25}$

Formula Used:

HCF of fraction $= \dfrac{(\text{HCF of numerator})}{(\text{LCM of denominator})}$

Considering the given fractions

HCF of (9, 18 and 12) = 3

LCM of (10, 35 and 25) = 350

$\therefore$ HCF of $\dfrac{9}{10}, \dfrac{18}{35}, \dfrac{12}{25} = \dfrac{3}{350}$

43(A). When Jaynav was born, his brother's age = 6 years

His father's age = (6 + 32) years = 38 years

His mother's age = (38 - 3) years = 35 years

His sister's age = (35 - 25) years = 10 years

44(D). Production in 2017 = 90, Production in 2016 = 65

In 2017, Percentage increase in production

$= \left\{\dfrac{(90-65)}{65}\right\} \times 100 = 38.46\%$

So, we can clearly see that the percentage increase in production was the maximum in the Year 2017.

45(D). Average production of toys

$= \dfrac{(40+55+75+60+80+65+90+95)}{8} \Rightarrow \dfrac{560}{8} = 70$

Now we can see in the graph that in the years 2013, 2015, 2017 & 2018 the production of toys is more than the average production of toys.

46(B). Given:

$a^4 + b^4 + a^2b^2 = 16$ and $a^2 + b^2 + ab = 8$

we know that,

$a^4 + b^4 + a^2b^2 = \left(a^2 + b^2 + ab\right)\left(a^2 + b^2 - ab\right)$

$\Rightarrow 16 = 8\left(a^2 + b^2 - ab\right)$

$\Rightarrow \left(a^2 + b^2 - ab\right) = 2$

$\therefore$ The value of $\left(a^2 + b^2 - ab\right)$ is 2.

47(A). Given:

In $\triangle ABC$

$AB = 20$ cm, $BC = 7$ cm and $CA = 15$ cm and $\triangle DAB \sim \triangle DCA$

Let $CD = x$ and $AD = y$

From given,

$\triangle DAB \sim \triangle DCA$

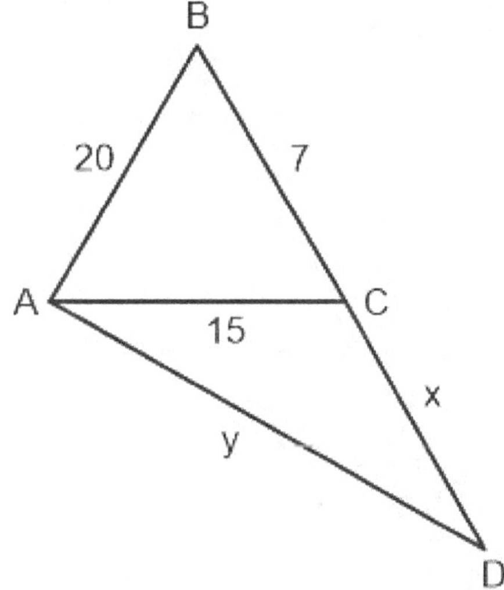

So, $\dfrac{\text{AB}}{\text{AC}} = \dfrac{\text{DB}}{\text{AD}} = \dfrac{\text{AD}}{\text{DC}}$

If we take the first $\dfrac{\text{AB}}{\text{AC}} = \dfrac{\text{DB}}{\text{AD}}$ two part of the

equation, we get
$$\frac{20}{15} = \frac{7+x}{y}$$
$$\Rightarrow \frac{4}{3} = \frac{7+x}{y}$$
$$\Rightarrow y = \frac{3}{4} \times (7+x) = \frac{21+3x}{4} \quad ....(1)$$
If we take the $\frac{AB}{AC} = \frac{AD}{DC}$ first and third part of the equation, we get
$$\frac{y}{x} = \frac{4}{3}$$
$$\Rightarrow y = \frac{4x}{3} \quad ....(2)$$
From (1) and (2), we get
$$\frac{21+3x}{4} = \frac{4x}{3}$$
$$\Rightarrow 16x = 63 + 9x$$
$$\Rightarrow 7x = 63$$
$$\Rightarrow x = 9$$
$\therefore$ The length of CD is 9 cm.

48(C). Given:
$$\Rightarrow \sin(2\alpha + \beta) = 1$$
$$\Rightarrow \sin(2\alpha + \beta) = \sin 90°$$
$$\Rightarrow (2\alpha + \beta) = 90° \quad .....(1)$$
$$\Rightarrow \sin(\alpha - 2\beta) = \frac{1}{2}$$
$$\Rightarrow \sin(\alpha - 2\beta) = \sin 30° \quad .....(2)$$
Multiply by 2 in equation (1)
$$\Rightarrow (4\alpha + 2\beta) = 180° \quad .....(3)$$
Add equation (1) and equation (2)
$$\Rightarrow 5a = 210°$$
$$\Rightarrow \alpha = 42°$$
Put $a = 42°$ in equation (1)
$$\Rightarrow 84° + \beta = 90°$$
$$\Rightarrow \beta = 6°$$
$$\therefore (\alpha + \beta) = 42° + 6° = 48°$$

49(C). A die is thrown: Sample space $S = \{1, 2, 3, 4, 5, 6\}$
Now, possible outcomes of three dice the condition that no two dice show the same face = $6 \times 5 \times 4 = 120$
Now, the number of one of the faces is having the number $6 = 1 \times 5 \times 4 \times 3! = 60$
$\therefore$ The probability that one of the faces is having the number $6 = \frac{60}{120} = \frac{1}{2}$

50(D). Given: There are 6 teachers and 8 students out of which we need to form a committee of 11 members such that the committee has exactly 4 teachers in it. If out 11 members of committee 4 are teachers then 7 members are students.
So, the committee compromises of 4 teachers and 7 students.
No. of ways in which 4 teachers can be selected from 6 teachers = $^6C_4$
No. of ways in which 7 students can be selected from 8 students = $^8C_7$
So, the number of ways in which the committee can be formed = $^6C_4 \times {}^8C_7$
As we know that, $^nC_r = \frac{n!}{r! \times (n-r)!}$
$$\Rightarrow {}^6C_4 \times {}^8C_7$$
$$= \left(\frac{6!}{(6-4)!4!} \times \frac{8!}{(8-7)!7!}\right)$$
$$= \left(\frac{6!}{(2)!4!} \times \frac{8!}{(1)!7!}\right)$$
$$= 120$$
So, the committee can be formed in 120 ways.

51(D).

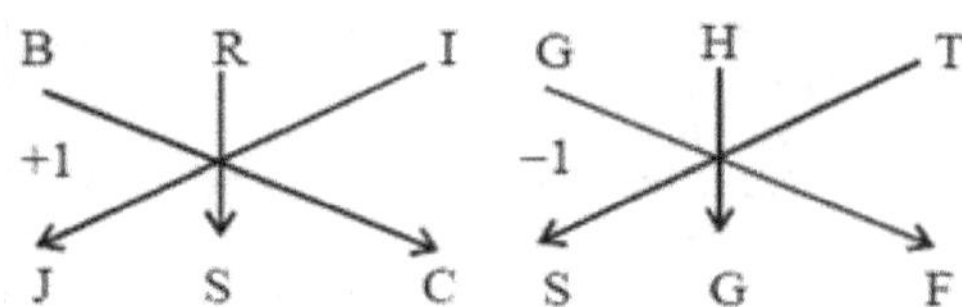

Similarly,

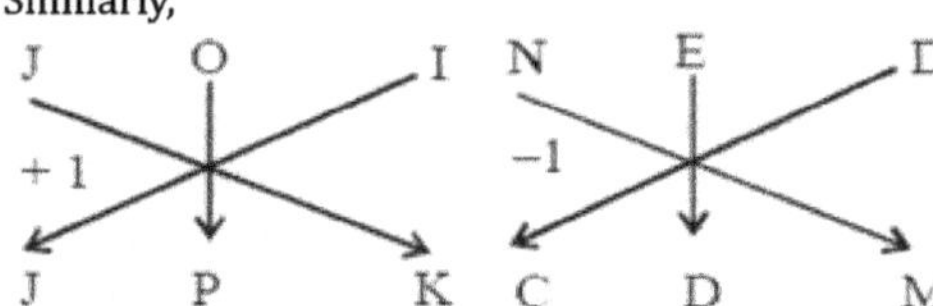

52(A). $16 = (4)^2$, and $4 - 2 = 2 \Rightarrow (2)^2 = 4$
So, it become
$\Rightarrow 16 : 4$
Similarly,
$9 = (3)^2$, and $3 - 2 = 1 \Rightarrow (1)^2 = 1$
So, it become
$\Rightarrow 9 : 1$

53(C). Preparing the family tree using the following symbols:

Symbol in Diagram	Meaning
◯	Female
▢	Male
══	Married Couple
───	Siblings
│	Difference of a generation

Possible tree diagram will be:

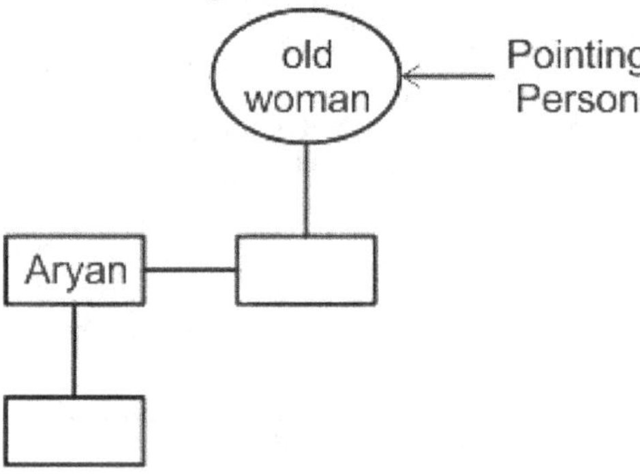

So, Aryan is the son of an old woman because she has no daughter.
So, the correct answer is "Son".

54(A). Symbols used to draw family tree:

Symbol in Diagram	Meaning
◯	Female
☐	Male
═══	Married Couple
───	Siblings
│	Difference of a generation

Drawing the family tree as per the given information

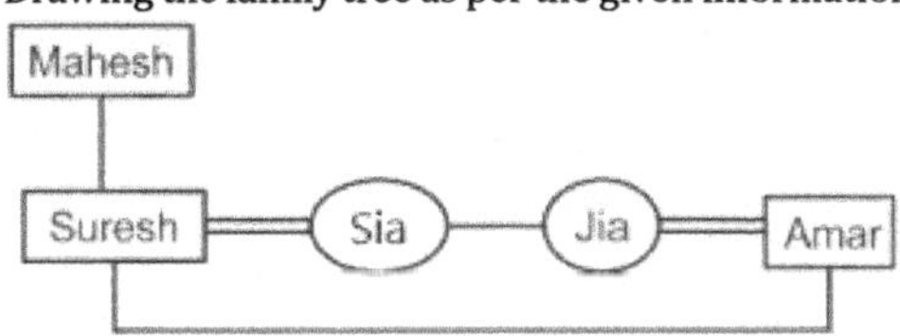

As Amar is brother of Suresh, Amar is also a son of Mahesh.
So, Jia is daughter-in-law of Mahesh.
So, the correct answer is "Daughter-in-law".

55(D). The logic follows here is:
All the given figure in option (A), (B), and (C) follows the pattern of: Right side image is the double of the left side except the option (D) in which right side image is different from the left side.

56(A). The logic follows here is:
The figure 1, 2 and 4 are acute angles, while figure 3 is an obtuse angle.
Thus, figure 3 is not similar to the other figures.

57(B). In each pair of figures (i) and (ii), the relationship is such that figure (i) is rotated 90° clockwise to form figure (ii). In option (B) when figure (i) is rotated 90° clockwise, it does not form figure (ii).
So, option figure (2) is the odd one.

58(B). We can draw the following diagram:

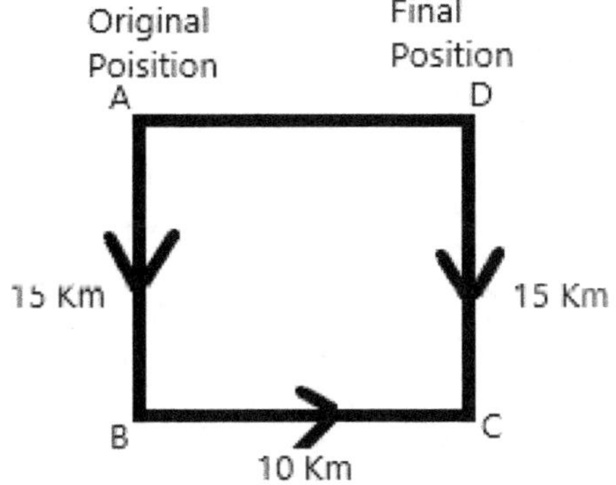

∵ AD = BC = 10 km
So, the required distance = 10 km

59(B). Given data:
1) A man is facing north. He turns 90° in the clockwise direction.
2) Then turns 135° in the anti-clockwise direction.
The direction and angle diagram is shown below:

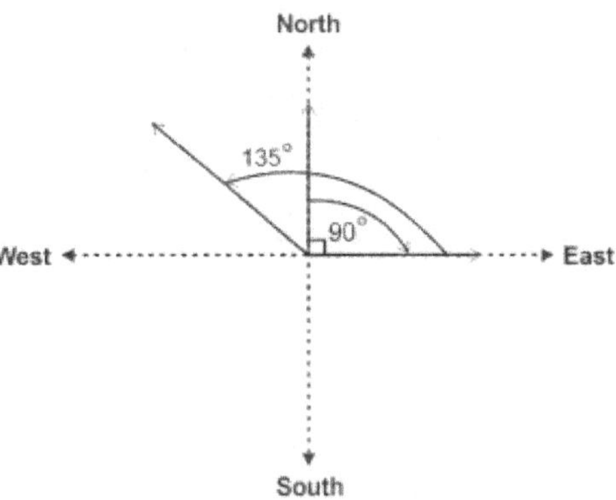

So, 'North-West' is the correct answer.

60(B). The pattern here followed is:
$FIXED$
Write the opposite of this,
$URCVW$
Now, take the sum of the positional value and subtract 1 from it.
$(21 + 18 + 3 + 22 + 23) - 1$
$87 - 1 = 86$
$COMPANY$
Write the opposite of this,
$XLNKZMB$
$(24 + 12 + 14 + 11 + 26 + 13 + 2) - 1$
$102 - 1 = 101$
Similarly,
$INTERIM$
Write the opposite of this,
$RMGVIRN$
$(18 + 13 + 7 + 22 + 9 + 18 + 14) - 1$
$101 - 1 = 100$

61(A). The logic followed here is:
'CLOT' is written as '6243040'.

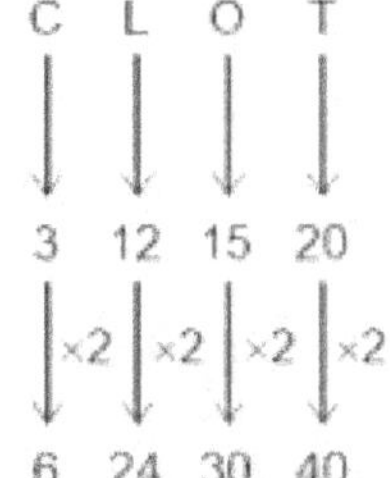

Similarly,
'MOSAIC' will be written as:

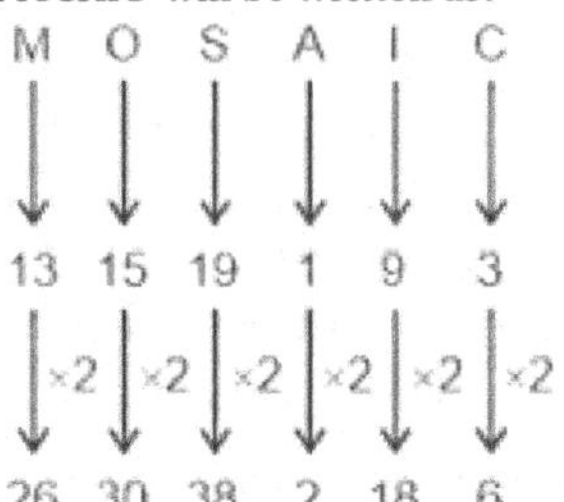

62(B). The figure in the answer figure that will complete the figural series given in the problem figures is shown below:

The next figure in the series will be figure B.

63(B). In the given figure, the oblique symbol is deflected 45° in the clockwise direction while the circular symbol is deflected 45° in the anti-clockwise direction.

Thus, the next figure in the series will be figure B.

64(A). Tie, Shirt and Shoe are all separate items, entirely different from each other.

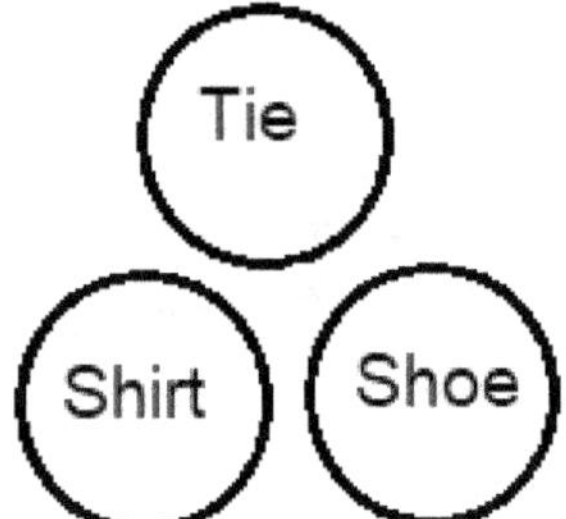

65(A).

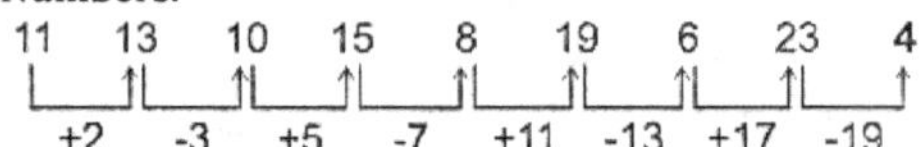

66(B). The pattern of given series is:
$$\to 8 = 2^3$$
$$\to 72 = 2^3 + 4^3$$
$$\to 288 = 2^3 + 4^3 + 6^3$$
$$\to ? = 2^3 + 4^3 + 6^3 + 8^3$$
$$\to ? = 800$$
$$\to 1800 = 2^3 + 4^3 + 6^3 + 8^3 + 10^3$$
$$\to 3528 = 2^3 + 4^3 + 6^3 + 8^3 + 10^3 + 12^3$$
Thus, the missing number is 800.

67(B). The pattern follows here is;
Addition and Subtraction of consecutive Prime Numbers.

11	13	10	15	8	19	6	23	4
+2	-3	+5	-7	+11	-13	+17	-19	

Thus, "(B)" is the correct answer.

68(C). Srinath is 7th from the left and Venkat is 12th from the right.
Now, If they interchange their positions, Srinath becomes 22nd from the left.
So, Srinath is 22 from the left and 12 from the right.
So, he has 21 boys before him and 11 boys after him.
Thus, the total number of boys = number of boys before him + Number of boys after him + Srinath
=21+11+1=33
Thus, there are 33 boys.

69(B). Kamal is 11th from the front in a row of girls. Leela is 3 places ahead of Sunita, who is 22nd from the lead.
According to the given information,

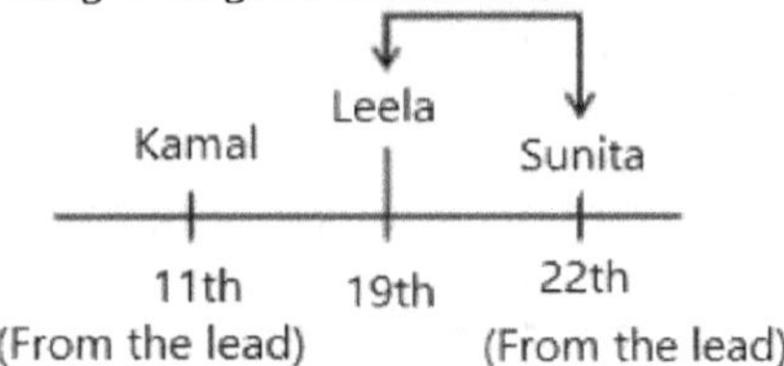

Girls in row between Kamal and Leela = 19 - 11 = 8

70(C). The least possible Venn Diagram is as follows:

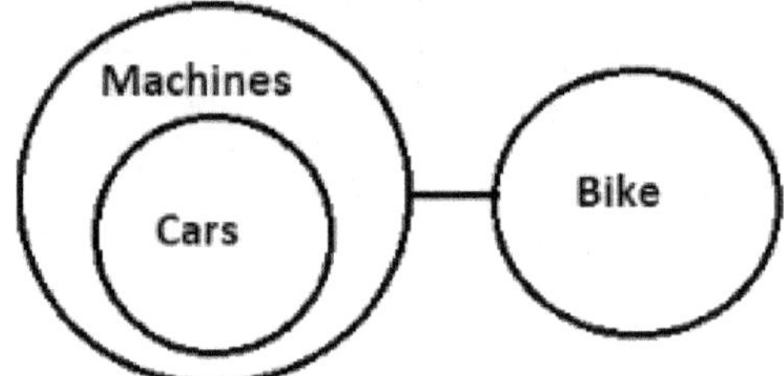

Conclusions :
I. No bike is a machine – True (It is true as no machine is a bike).
II. No car is a bike – True (It is true as all cars are machines and no machine is a bike).

71(C). The least possible Venn diagram for the given statements is as follows:

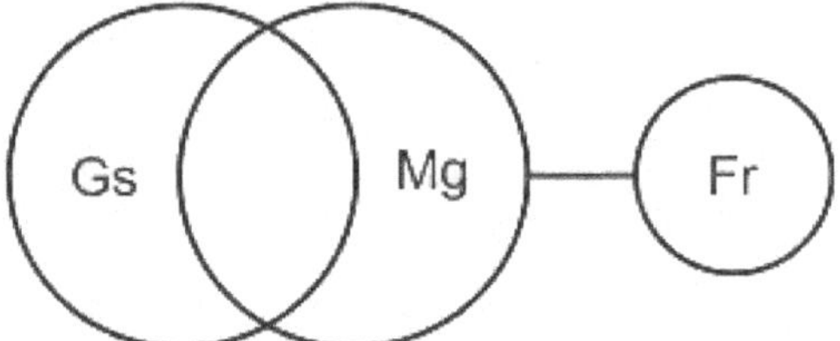

Conclusions:
I. Some Gs are Fr. → False (it is possible but not definite)
II. No Gs is Mg. → False (as some Gs are Mg)
III. Some Mg are Fr. → False (as no Mg is Fr)
IV. All Mg are Fr. → False (as no Mg is Fr)
So, none of the conclusion follows.

Q.72 1) B is sitting third to the right of the person who is the husband of R and they are facing the same direction.
(As it is a circular arrangement, we can randomly place the husband of R on any seat and then we can place B according to the direction the husband of R is facing.)

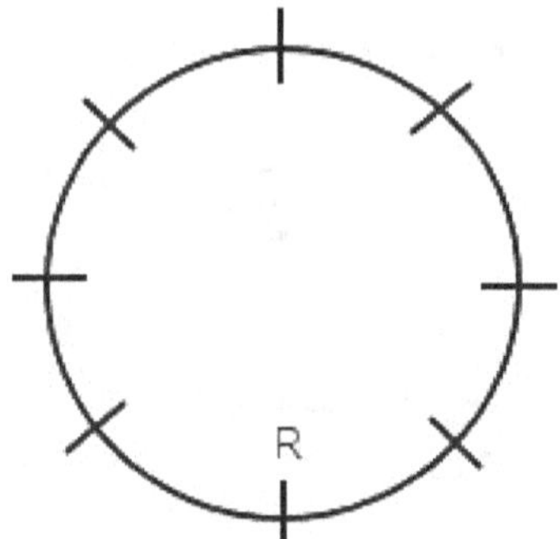

2) Both the immediate neighbours of D are facing the same

direction.
(Implies, the immediate neighbours of D are facing a different direction than D.)
3) The husband of Q is facing the outward direction and he is sitting to the immediate right of D.
(Implies, D must be facing the inward direction. It also means that the other immediate neighbour of D must also be facing the outward direction and B is facing the inward direction.)
4) Either R or P is the wife of D.
5) The husband of P and the husband of Q are facing the same direction.
(Implies, the husband of P is also facing the outward direction. It means that R is the wife of D.)

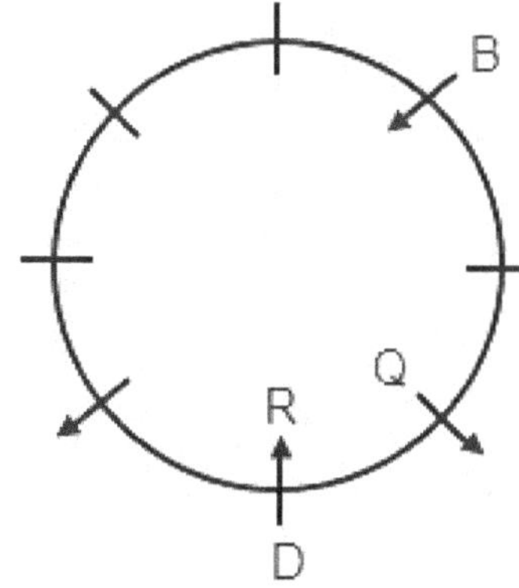

6) Only one person is sitting between B and the husband of L.
(Implies, the husband of L is sitting second to the right of B because the husband of Q is sitting second to the left of B.)

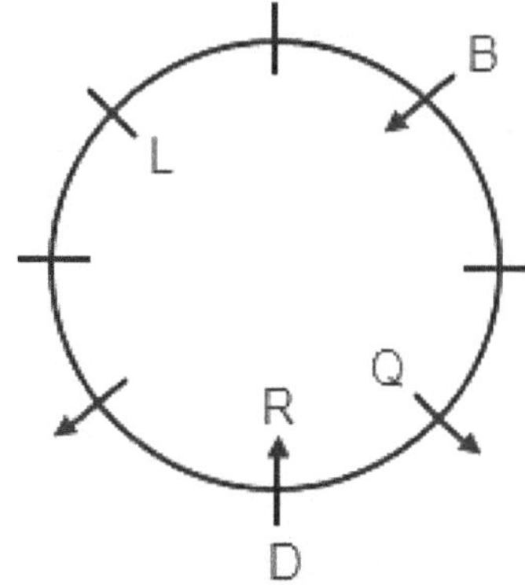

7) The wife of D is sitting third to the left of F.
(It is only possible if F is the husband of L and F is facing the outward direction.)
8) Only one person is sitting between F and the husband of M and they are facing the same direction.
(Implies, the husband of M is sitting second to the left of F because B is facing the inward direction.)

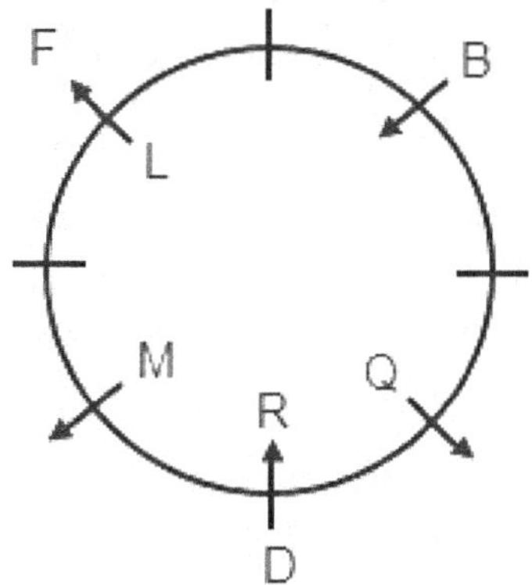

9) C is sitting third to the right of the husband of M and they are facing different directions.
(Implies, C is sitting between F and B. Also, C is facing the inward direction because the husband of M is facing the outward direction.)
10) The husband of L is sitting third to the left of E.
(Implies, E is sitting to the immediate left of B and E is facing the outward direction as it is the only possibility. Also, now that we have identified the four people who are facing the outward direction, we can say that all the other people are facing the inward direction.)

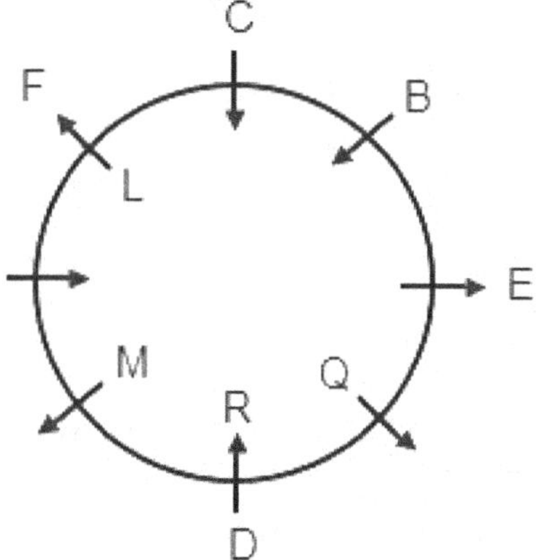

11) A is an immediate neighbour of the husband of M.
(Implies, A is sitting to the immediate left of F.)

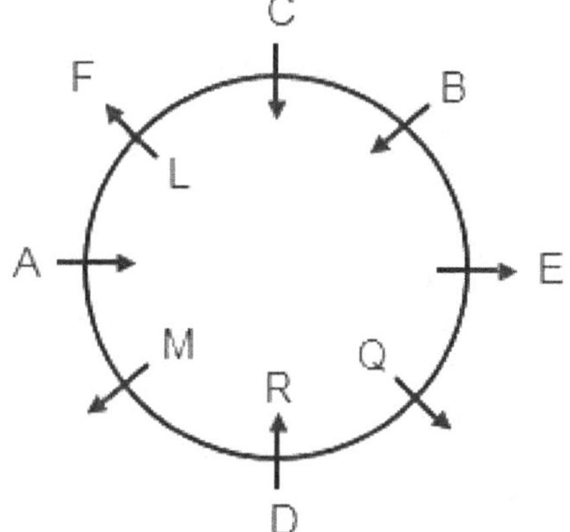

12) G is sitting third to the right of C.
(Implies, G is the husband of M. Now, that only H is left to be placed, we can safely say that H is sitting to the immediate right of D.)
13) The husband of S is sitting third to the right of H.
(Implies, A is the husband of S.)

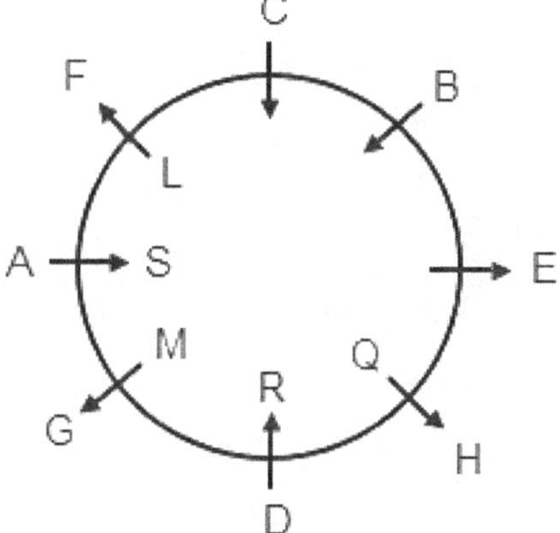

14) Neither O nor P is the wife of B.

(Implies, N is the wife of B as it is the only option left. Also, O and P are the wives of C and E but not necessarily in the same order.)

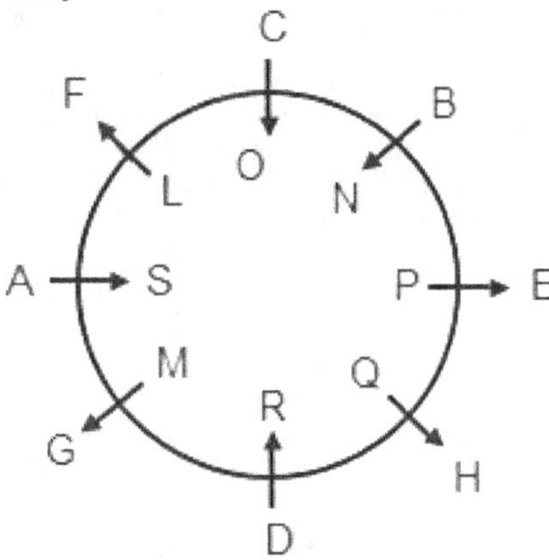

72(C). Clearly, B is sitting second to the left of H who is the husband of Q.

Q.73 Ten persons: Sagar, Anurag, Sanket, Vinit, Amit, Rajesh, Aditya, Himanshu, Akshay, and Sujit
Face Direction: Away from the center.
1) Sanket is sitting fourth to the right of Akshay.

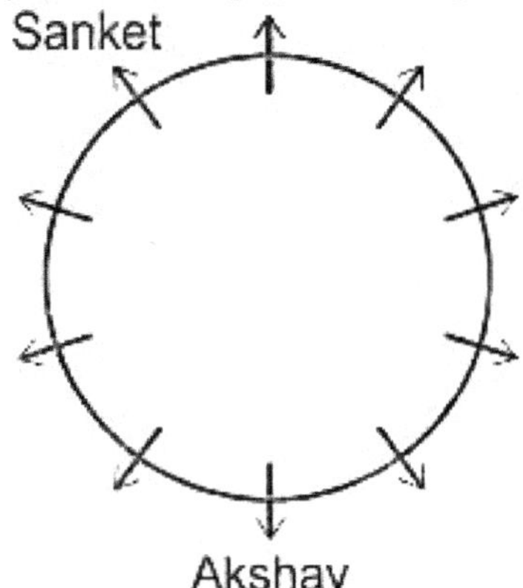

2) Three persons are sitting between Sujit and Sanket

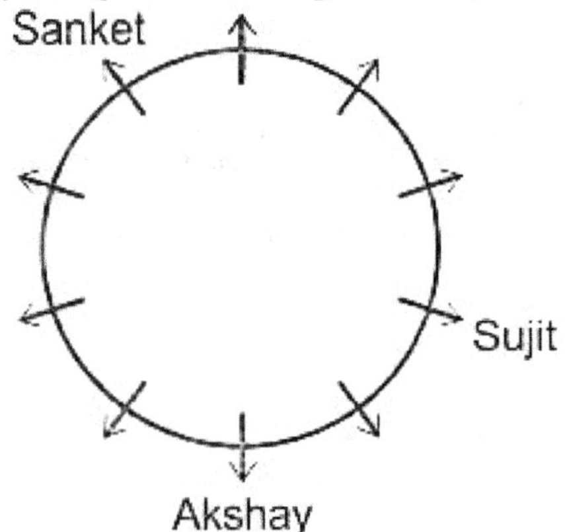

3) Rajesh is an immediate neighbor of Sujit.
4) Amit is sitting fourth to the right of Rajesh.

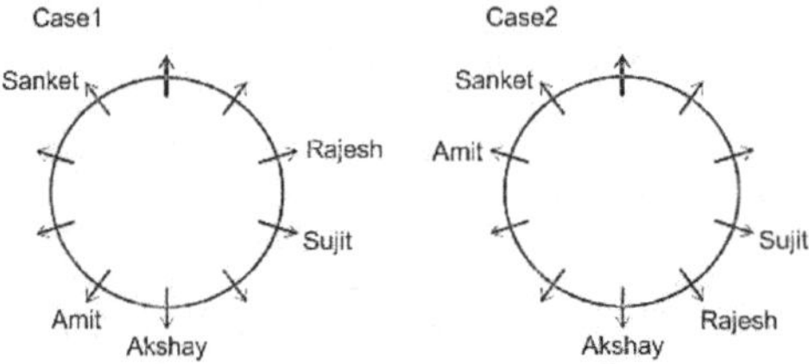

5) Amit is an immediate neighbor of Sagar.

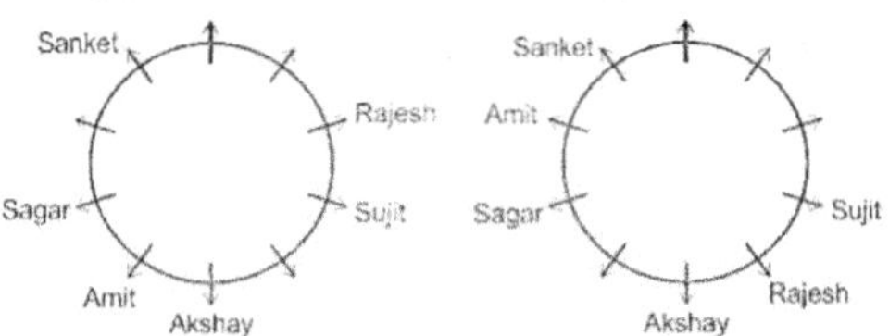

6) Himanshu is sitting third to the right of Sagar.
7) Three people are sitting between Himanshu and Vinit.

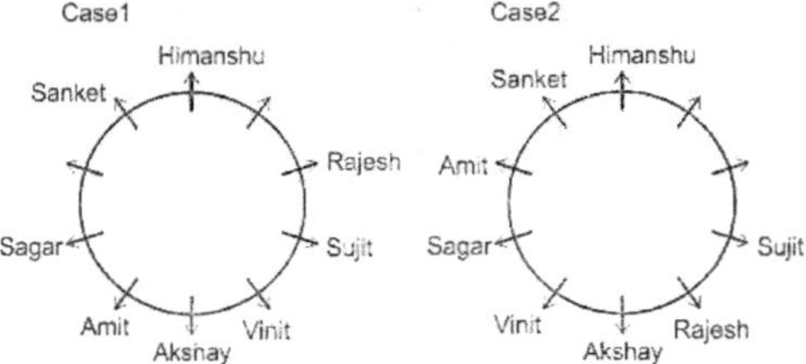

8) Aditya is sitting third to the left of Anurag.
(In case 2, Aditya can not sit third to the left of Anurag so we can eliminate case 2)
The final arrangement will be as follows:

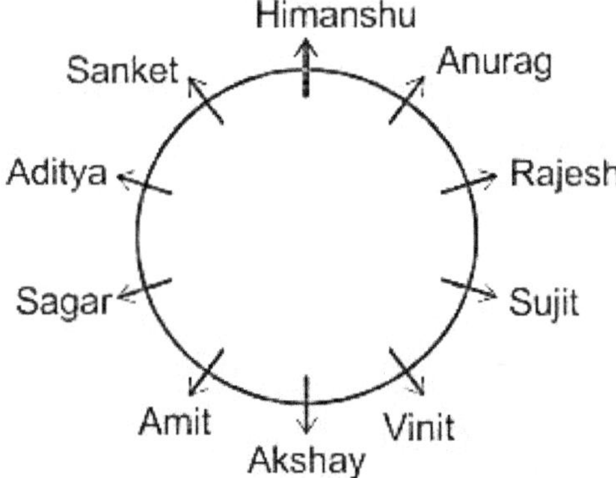

73(C). Thus, 4 persons are sitting between Sujit and Aditya.

74(D). Except for cashew nut, all are spices.
Cashew is commonly eaten as food. People also use cashew to make medicine. It is used for stomach and intestinal (gastrointestinal) ailments.

75(C). Here, it follows a pattern of +1 between 1st and 2nd characters and of +2 between 2nd and 3rd characters as shown below:

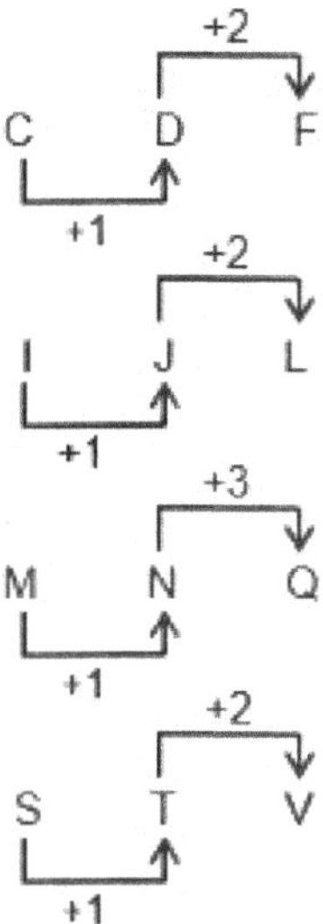

Thus, MNQ is odd letter group.

76(A). प्रश्न में सही वर्तनी भास्कर है।
भास्कर का अर्थ "सूर्य" होता है।
उदाहरण: श्याम ने भास्कर की ऊर्जा की तरह प्रभावशाली कार्य किया था ।

77(B). प्रश्न में राही वर्तनी ऊर्ध्व है।
ऊर्ध्व का अर्थ "ऊपर की ओर गया हुआ" होता है ।
उदाहरण : विमान की अधिरचना अंतर्भित्ति ऊर्ध्व विस्तार है।

78(D). कुजगह फोड़ा और ससुर वैद्य - कहावत का अर्थ है: धर्म संकट की स्थिति।
• वाक्य प्रयोग - एक ओर मेरा सारा काम पड़ा है, दूसरी ओर मुझे जल्दी निकलना है, कुजगह फोड़ा और ससुर वैद्य ।
• अन्य विकल्प सार्थक नहीं हैं।

79(D). 'लश्कर में ऊंट बदनाम' का अर्थ 'दोष किसी का पर नाम किसी और का' है।
• वाक्य प्रयोग - चोरी तुमने की और पकड़ी मैं गई, लश्कर में ऊँट बदनाम ।
• अन्य विकल्प सार्थक नहीं हैं।

80(B). 'सदा एक समान' रहने पर 'सावन हरे न भादो सूखे' लोकोक्ति प्रयुक्त होती है ।
• सावन हरे न भादो सूखे - लोकोक्ति का अर्थ है: सदा समान रहना ।
• वाक्य प्रयोग - तुम्हारे कहने पर राम को कोई असर नहीं पड़ेगा वह सावन हरे न भादो सूखे का प्यादा है ।

81(B). दिए गए विकल्पों में से हरकत स्त्रीलिंग शब्द है ।
• हरकत का अर्थ है - शरारत, गति, चेष्टा, आदि ।
• अन्य सभी विकल्प पुल्लिंग शब्द है।

82(B). दिए गए विकल्पों में से भील का स्त्रीलिंग शब्द भीलनी है ।
• भीलनी का अर्थ है - भील की स्त्री।
• भील पुल्लिंग है और भीलनी स्त्रीलिंग
• जिन शब्दों से स्त्री जाति का बोध होता है उन्हें स्त्रीलिंग शब्द कहते हैं।

83(C). 'बिना पलक झपकाए' के लिए एक शब्द 'निर्निमेष' होगा।
अन्य विकल्प :
• निष्पलक: जो पलकों से रहित हो ।
• निस्पृह: जिसे किसी प्रकार का लोभ या लालसा न हो ।
• निर्विकार: जिसमें कोई विकार न हो ।

84(B). 'जीवन देने वाली दवा' के लिए एक शब्द 'प्राणदा' होगा।

• प्राणदा के पर्यायवाची - समृद्धि, ऋद्धि, हरीतकी, आदि ।
• अन्य विकल्प सही उत्तर नहीं हैं।

85(A). संज्ञा, सर्वनाम, विशेषण और क्रिया के जिस रूप से संख्या का बोध हो, उसे 'वचन' कहते हैं। दूसरे शब्दों में, शब्दों के संख्याबोधक विकारी रूप का नाम 'वचन' है। वचन के दो प्रकार हैं: एकवचन और बहुवचन।

86(B). दिए गए विकल्पों में 'ऊंचाई' शब्द में प्रत्यय है।
'ऊंचाई' शब्द 'आई' प्रत्यय के योग से बना है,
'ऊंचा + 'आई' = 'ऊंचाई'
प्रत्यय वे शब्द हैं जो दूसरे शब्दों के अन्त में जुड़कर, अपनी प्रकृति के अनुसार, शब्द के अर्थ में परिवर्तन कर देते हैं।

87(C). दिए गए विकल्पों में 'सुबोध' शब्द में 'सु' उपसर्ग है।
सु + बोध = सुबोध, यह विशेषण शब्द है।
इसका अर्थ है सरल और बोधगम्य।
जो शब्दांश शब्दों के प्रारम्भ में जुड़ कर उनके अर्थ में कुछ विशेषता लाते हैं, वे उपसर्ग कहलाते हैं।

88(B). 'जाति' शब्द का बहुवचन रूप 'जातियाँ' होगा। बहुवचन शब्द 'जातियाँ' से एक से अधिक वंश, कुल, जन्म, उत्पत्ति का बोध होता है।

89(A). 'चाय' शब्द का प्रयोग एकवचन में होता है।

90(C). वाक्य के (c) भाग में त्रुटि है, क्योंकि केवल और मात्र का अर्थ एक ही होता है।
शुद्ध वाक्य:
"मैं पटना गया तो उस समय मेरे पास केवल बीस रुपये थे।" हे।

91(B). वाक्य के (b) भाग में त्रुटि है, "आज उसे छपे आकार में देखकर" के स्थान पर "आज उसे छपे रूप में देखकर" होगा।
शुद्ध वाक्य:
एक वर्ष से मैं जिस पुस्तक की रचना में संलग्न था आज उसे छपे रूप में देखकर मेरी प्रसन्नता का ठिकाना नहीं है।

92(C). 'स्वर्ग' का विलोम शब्द 'नरक' है। स्वर्ग का अर्थ – देवलोक । नरक का अर्थ – पापियों के रहने का स्थान, गंदी एवं घृणित जगह।

93(B). 'राग' का विलोम शब्द 'विराग' है। राग का अर्थ – प्रेम। विराग का अर्थ – राग का अभाव।

94(C). 'स्वाधीन' का सही विलोम शब्द 'पराधीन' है। स्वाधीन का अर्थ – स्वयं के अधीन । पराधीन का अर्थ – किसी अन्य के अधीन ।

95(B). 'पहाड़' का पर्यायवाची 'अचला' नहीं है। 'पहाड़' के पर्यायवाची शब्द: नग, भूधर, महीधर, शैल, नगपति, शिखर, तुंग, धरणीधर, पर्वत अचल, गिरि, अद्रि, आदि है।

96(B). 'स्वाधीन' में प्रयुक्त संधि का नाम दीर्घ संधि है। दीर्घ संधि स्वर संधि का एक भेद अथवा प्रकार है। जब दो शब्दों की संधि करते समय (अ, आ) के साथ (अ, आ) हो तो 'आ' बनता है, जब (इ, ई) के साथ (इ, ई) हो तो 'ई' बनता है, जब (उ, ऊ) के साथ (उ, ऊ) हो तो 'ऊ' बनता है। इस संधि को हम ह्रस्व संधि भी कह सकते हैं।
दीर्घ संधि के उदाहरण :
स्व + आधीन = स्वाधीन
सर्व + अधिक = सर्वाधिक
अंड + आकार = अंडाकार

97(B). 'विधायक' में अयादि संधि है। जब संधि करते समग्र ए , ऐ , ओ , औ के साथ कोई अन्य स्वर हो तो (ए का अय), (ऐ का आय), (ओ का अव), (औ – आव) बन जाता है। यही अयादि संधि कहलाती है।
अयादि संधि के उदाहरण :
विधायक = विधे + अक
श्रवण = श्री + अन
पावक = पौ + अक
पावन = पौ + अन

98(D). 'तथोक्तम्' में प्रयुक्त संधि का नाम गुण संधि है। जब दो भिन्न - भिन्न ध्वनि वाले स्वरों का मेल होता है तथा उनकी संधि से उत्पन्न नया स्वर उन दोनों से भिन्न गुण वाला होता है , तो ऐसी संधि गुण संधि कहलाती है।

उदाहरण -

तथा + उक्तम् = तथोक्तम्

स्व + इच्छा = स्वेच्छा

वीर + उचित = वीरोचित

99(C). '**पद्मावत**' जायसी की रचना है।

मलिक मुहम्मद जायसी (1467-1542) हिन्दी साहित्य के भक्ति काल की निर्गुण प्रेमाश्रयी धारा के कवि थे।

उनकी 21 रचनाओं के उल्लेख मिलते हैं।

जायसी की प्रमुख रचनाएं निम्नलिखित हैं:

- पद्मावत
- अखरावट
- आखिरी कलाम
- कहरनाम
- चित्ररेखा
- कान्हावत

100(B). गोरख बानी **नाथ साहित्य** की रचना है।

- इसके रचनाकार का नाम: गोरख नाथ है।
- गोरखबानी के सम्पादक: पीताम्बर दत्त बड़थ्वाल है।
- इसका रचनाकाल: 12 वीं शती से 14 वीं शती माना है।
- सिद्ध साहित्य: सरहपा प्रथम कवि. 729ई समय।
- रासो साहित्य : परमल रासो, पृथ्वीराज रासो मुख्य रचनाएँ।
- जैन साहित्य: पुष्यदन्त, स्वयम्भू प्रमुख।

General Knowledge

1. Who is the author of the book 'Republic'?
   (a) Leo Tolstoy   (b) Leo Tolstoy
   (c) Plato   (d) TS Eliot

2. With respect to Indus valley civilization, consider the following statements:
   1) In the entire Indus valley sites, Mohenjodaro was the only place having evidences of coffin burial.
   2) Both male and female were allowed to take part in the Political organization.
   Which of the statements given above is/are correct?
   (a) 1 only   (b) 2 only
   (c) Both 1 and 2   (d) Neither 1 nor 2

3. Examine the following statements:
   A. The non-cooperation movement brought all sections of Indians into the freedom struggle.
   B. Violent incident took place at Chauri-Chaura
   Choose the correct answer:
   (a) Only A is correct
   (b) Only B is correct
   (c) Both A and B are correct
   (d) Both A and B are incorrect

4. Examine the following statements:
   A. 'Indian Association' was established in Benaras.
   B. The 'Dhaka Anushilan Samiti' was started in the year 2009.
   C. 'The East India Association' was founded by Dadabhai Naoroji.
   D. The 'Treaty of Salbai' was signed in 1782.
   Choose the correct answer:
   (a) A and B only   (b) B and C only
   (c) C and D only   (d) A, C and D only

5. Which Indian leader participated in the first Round Table Conference in London?
   (a) Maulana Muhammad Ali
   (b) Maulana Abul Kalam Azad
   (c) Mahatma Gandhi
   (d) Pt. Jawaharlal Nehru

6. Who started Individual civil disobedience?
   (a) Vinoba Bhave   (b) Jawaharlal Nehru
   (c) Sardar Patel   (d) Shaukat Ali

7. 'Transhumance' refers to:
   (a) migration of animals in ranches
   (b) human migration in search of job
   (c) seasonal movement of people and their herds from valley to mountain and vice versa
   (d) migration of nomads

8. Match List - I with List - II and select the correct answer using the codes given below the Lists:

List - I (Rivers)	List - II (Their Tributaries)
a. Krishna	1. Chambal
b. Brahmaputra	2. Indravati
c. Godavari	3. Tista
d. Yamuna	4. Bhima

   (a) a - 4, b - 3, c - 2, d - 1 (b) a - 3, b - 4, c - 1, d - 2
   (c) a - 4, b - 3, c - 1, d - 2 (d) a - 3, b - 4, c - 2, d - 1

9. The power plant of Manikaran based on geothermal energy is in the State of:
   (a) Arunachal Pradesh   (b) Himachal Pradesh
   (c) Jammu and Kashmir (d) Uttarakhand

10. HLFT-42 was in news recently. What is it related to?
    (a) Hypersonic Jet
    (b) Oral Vaccine of COVID-19
    (c) Supersonic jet trainer
    (d) Newly discovered Asteroid

11. In which country the meeting of National Security Advisors of Shanghai Cooperation Organisation, 2023 was held?
    (a) China   (b) Uzbekistan
    (c) India   (d) Russia

12. According to the Economic Survey 2022-23, what is the estimated GDP growth rate of India?
    (a) 6.5 %   (b) 7.0 %
    (c) 7.2 %   (d) 7.6 %

13. Consider the following statements in respect of the ICC U-19 World Cup 2022.
    1. It was an international limited-overs cricket tournament, held in January-February 2022 in West Indies.
    2. 16 teams took part in the game, and It was the fourteenth edition of the Under-19 Cricket World Cup.
    3. It was the first tournament, held in West Indies.
    Which of the above statement is/are correct?
    (a) 1 and 2 only   (b) 1 and 3 only
    (c) 2 and 3 only   (d) 1, 2, and 3

14. The pH value of Milk of Magnesia is approximately:
    (a) Zero   (b) 7
    (c) 10   (d) 14

15. Which one of the following compounds is used in 'black and white' photography?
    (a) AgF (b) $AgBr$
    (c) $AgCO_2$ (d) Ag_2SO_4

16. Most plants are present in:
    (a) lithosphere   (b) hydrosphere
    (c) atmosphere   (d) photosphere

17. In which year was the Royal Commission of Agriculture set up to examine and report the status of India's agricultural and rural economy and in which year did it submit the report?
    (a) 1926, 1928   (b) 1938, 1940
    (c) 1942, 1944   (d) 1946, 1947

18. In which year was the national commission on Farmers set up?
    (a) 2001   (b) 2004
    (c) 2006   (d) 2007

19. India has successively passed through all the phases of demographic transition and is now widely believed to have entered the final phase which is normally characterized by rapidly declining ______.

(a) migration   (b) crop rate
(c) fertility   (d) interest rate

20. Which of the following is/are social security scheme(s)?
1. Atal Pension Yojana
2. Pradhan Mantri Jeevan Jyoti Bima Yojana
3. Pradhan Mantri Suraksha Bima Yojana
Select the correct answer using the code given below:
(a) 1 only   (b) 2 and 3 only
(c) 1, 2 and 3   (d) 1 and 3 only

21. At present the country has adopted?
(a) Partial convertibility of Indian currency
(b) Full convertibility of Indian currency
(c) Full current account convertibility
(d) Full convertibility of capital account

22. Modvat which will be implemented from April 2001 replaces:
(a) Sales tax   (b) Custom duty
(c) State excise duty   (d) Central excise duty

23. Who has won the women's singles championship title at the Australian Open 2022?
(a) Ashleigh Barty   (b) Jessica Pegula
(c) Barbora Krejcikova   (d) None of above

24. Which of the following seaweed species are commercially exploited in India?
1. Kappaphycus alvarezii
2. Gracilaria edulis
3. Gelidiella acerosa
4. Sargassum spp
Select correct code:
(a) 1 and 2 only   (b) 2, 3 and 4
(c) 1, 3 and 4   (d) 1, 2, 3 and 4

25. Consider the following statements about Low Earth Orbit (LEO)
1. It is an Earth-centered orbit with an altitude of 2,000 km or less.
2. The International Space Station conducts operations in LEO.
3. Major disadvantage of Low Earth orbit is that it requires a high amount of energy for satellite placement.
4. Spy satellites cannot use LEO.
Which of the above statements is/are NOT correct?
(a) 1 and 2 only   (b) 1, 2 and 3
(c) 3 and 4 only   (d) 2, 3 and 4

Mathematics

26. Evaluate :
(-2) x (-3) x (-4) x (-5) x (-6)
(a) - 360   (b) 360
(c) - 720   (d) 720

27. In what ratio should sugar costing ₹ 40 per kg be mixed with sugar costing ₹ 48 per kg, so as to earn a profit of 20% by selling the mixture at ₹ 54 per kg?
(a) 2 : 3   (b) 4 : 7
(c) 3 : 5   (d) 5 : 8

28. Reshma buys two articles A and B for ₹ 1,734 . She sells A at a loss of 16% and sells B at a gain of 20% . The selling price of both the articles is the same. If A is sold for ₹ 1,147.50 , then the gain percent on A is:
(a) 12   (b) 10
(c) 12.5   (d) 10.5

29. Find the rate of interest if compound interest for 2 years is Rs. 84 and simple interest for two years is Rs. 80 .
(a) 12%   (b) 8%
(c) 10%   (d) 9%

30. A sum amounts to Rs. 6,050 in 2 years and to Rs. 6,655 in 3 years at a certain rate percentage per annum when the interest is compounded yearly. What is the simple interest on a sum of Rs. 6,000 at the same rate for $5 \frac{3}{4}$ years?
(a) Rs. 3,450   (b) Rs. 3,150
(c) Rs. 3,300   (d) Rs. 3,200

31. **Direction:** Each of the questions below consists of a question and two statements numbered I and II given below it. You have to decide whether the data provided in the statements are sufficient to answer the question. Read both the statements and give answer:
Find the height of the cylinder.
I. The Curved surface area of the cylinder is 396 cm^2 and the total surface area of the cylinder is 1628 cm^2 .
II. The radius of the cylinder is 0.5 cm more than the 3 times of the height of the cylinder.
(a) The data in statements I alone is sufficient to answer the question, while the data in statement II alone is not sufficient to answer the question.
(b) The data in statements II alone is sufficient to answer the question, while the data in statement I alone is not sufficient to answer the question.
(c) The data in statements I alone or in statement II alone is sufficient to answer the question.
(d) The data in both the statements I and II is not sufficient to answer the question.

32. The sides of a right triangle $ABC, AB = 30 \text{ cm}, AC = 40 \text{ cm}$ and $BC = 50 \text{ cm}$. Draw $AY \perp BC$ and BX as the angle bisector of $\angle CBA$ meeting AC at $X. AY$ and BX both cut at point O . Then, find the area of the $\triangle ABY$ (in sq. cm)?
(a) 225   (b) 216
(c) 324   (d) 135

33. The sum of two positive numbers is 20% of the sum of their square and 25% of the difference of their squares. If the numbers are x & y then $\frac{x+y}{x^2}$ is equal to:
(a) $\frac{1}{4}$ (b) $\frac{3}{8}$
(c) $\frac{1}{3}$ (d) $\frac{2}{9}$

34. The average of 12 numbers is 18.5 The average of first six numbers Is 16.8 and that of the last seven numbers is 17.4 If the 6th number is excluded, then what is the average (correct to one decimal place) of remaining 11 numbers?
(a) 20.1   (b) 17.9
(c) 18.4   (d) 18.9

35. The average monthly salary of 30 employees and 5 managers is Rs. 80000 . One manager with salary Rs. 180000 is replaced by a new manager. If the average

monthly salary now becomes Rs. 78500 , then what is the monthly salary of the new manager?
(a) Rs. 142500
(b) Rs. 132000
(c) Rs. 127500
(d) Rs. 154500

36. Club A has won 30% of the first 60 matches it had played in a particular season. Then the minimum possible number of additional matches Club A should play to achieve a success rate of 44% in that season is:
(a) 15
(b) 20
(c) 30
(d) 25

37. A can do a piece of work in 60 days. He works at it for 15 days, and then B alone finishes the remaining work in 30 days. In how many days can A and B working together finish the same work?
(a) 22 days
(b) 25 days
(c) 20 days
(d) 24 days

38. To do a certain work, A and B work on alternate days with B beginning the work on the first day. A alone can complete the same work in 24 days. If the work gets completed in $11\frac{1}{3}$ days, then B alone can complete $\frac{7}{9}^{th}$ part of the original work in:
(a) 4 days
(b) 6 days
(c) $5\frac{1}{2}$ days
(d) $4\frac{1}{2}$ days

39. A and B can do a piece of work together in 15 days while A alone can do it in 25 days. They start working together but B leaves 5 days before the completion of the work. For how many days did A and B work together?
(a) 10
(b) 13
(c) 9
(d) 12

40. A car travels a distance of 840 km at a uniform speed. If the speed of the car is 10 kmph more, it takes two hours less to cover the same distance. The original speed of the car is:
(a) 80 kmph
(b) 50 kmph
(c) 75 kmph
(d) 60 kmph

41. A person crosses a 455-meter long distance in 35 minutes. What is his speed in km/hr ?
(a) 0.52
(b) 0.95
(c) 0.62
(d) 0.78

42. The HCF and LCM of two numbers are 6 and 864 respectively. If one number is 96 , find the other number.
(a) 84
(b) 45
(c) 54
(d) 24

43. A man is 24 years older than his son. In two years, his age will be twice the age of his son. The present age of his son is:
(a) 14 years
(b) 18 years
(c) 20 years
(d) 22 years

44. When $x^2 + y^2 = 30$ and $x + y = 20$ then find the value of xy .
(a) 180
(b) 182
(c) 185
(d) 187

45. If lines $\frac{x-1}{-3} = \frac{y-2}{2k} = \frac{z-3}{2}$ and

$\frac{x-1}{3k} = \frac{y-5}{1} = \frac{z-6}{-5}$ are mutually perpendicular, then k is equal to-
(a) $\frac{-10}{7}$
(b) $-\frac{7}{10}$
(c) -10
(d) -7

46. Let ABC be a triangle right angled at C , then what is $\tan A + \tan B$ equal to?
(a) $\frac{a}{bc}$
(b) $\frac{a^2}{bc}$
(c) $\frac{b^2}{ca}$
(d) $\frac{c^2}{ab}$

47. If $P(A \cup B) = \frac{5}{6}, P(A \cap B) = \frac{1}{3}$ and $P(\text{not A}) = \frac{1}{2}$, then which one of the following is not correct?
(a) $P(B) = \frac{2}{3}$
(b) $P(A \cap B) = P(A)P(B)$
(c) $P(A \cup B) > P(A) + P(B)$
(d) P(not A and not B) = P(not A) P(not B)

48. Out of 7 consonants and 4 vowels, how many words can be formed such that it contains 3 consonants and 2 vowels?
(a) 36000
(b) 55000
(c) 25200
(d) 75000

49. **Direction:** The line graph shows the Sales per employee of a certain company. Study the diagram and answer the following question.

In which year were the Sales per employee greater than that of the previous year?
(a) 2014
(b) 2015
(c) 2017
(d) 2016

50. **Directions:** Study the given line graph carefully and answer the following questions accordingly.
The given line graph shows the number of Hindi Newspapers and English Newspapers sold in five different districts of Mumbai on a particular day.

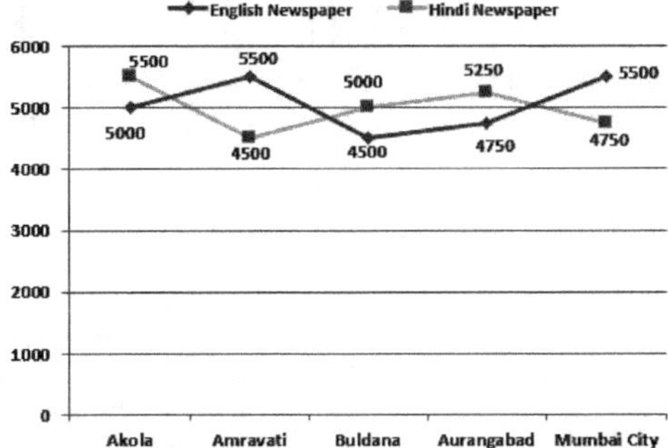

What is the respective ratio of the total number of Hindi Newspaper sold in Aurangabad and Mumbai City together to the total number of English Newspaper sold in Akola and Amravati together?

(a) 23 : 18   (b) 45 : 43

(c) 39 : 40   (d) 20 : 21

Reasoning

51. Select from the following a pair of birds having excellent sight and can distinctly see things from a distance four times as far as we can.

(a) Crow and Owl

(b) Kite and Vulture

(c) Indian Robin and Eagle

(d) Barbet and Crow

52. Select from the following, a pair of diseases caused/ spread by mosquitoes :

(a) Malaria and Dengue

(b) Cholera and Chikungunya

(c) Cholera and Malaria

(d) Chikungunya and Typhoid

53. If Rani is the wife of Ram and Rahul is the father of Sunil and Ram. What is Rahul to Rani?

(a) Brother   (b) Husband

(c) Father in law   (d) Father

54. Pointing at a boy, Naveen says, "His grandmother's only daughter is my grandmother's daughter." What relationship can that boy have with Naveen?

(a) Maternal Uncle   (b) Nephew

(c) Brother-in-Law   (d) Brother

55. In the given question has four Terms. Three terms are alike in some way. One term is different from three others. Find out the correct term which is different from three others:

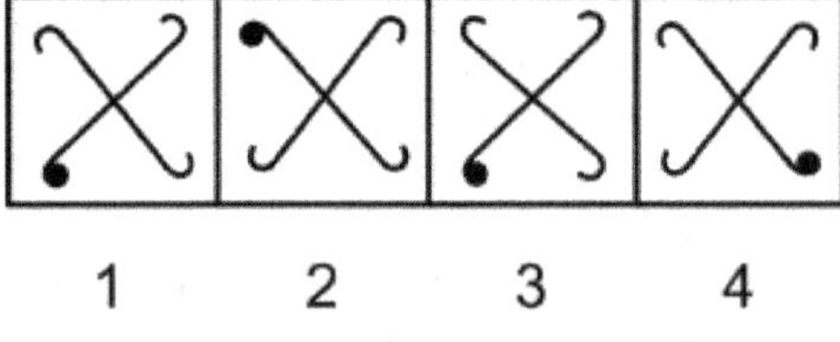

    1   2   3   4

(a) 1   (b) 2

(c) 3   (d) 4

56. In the given question has four Terms. Three terms are alike in some way. One term is different from three others. Find out the correct term which is different from three others:

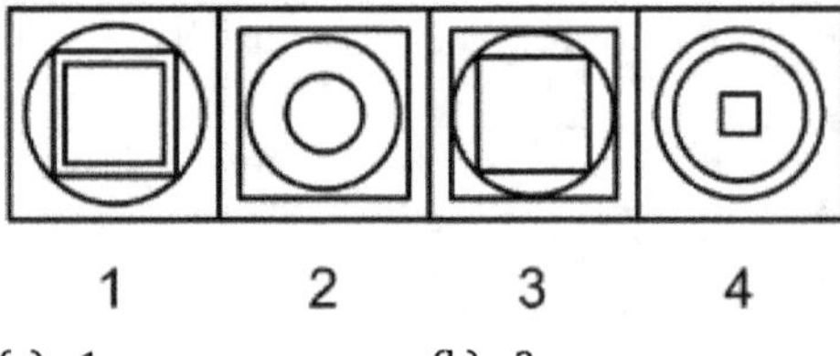

    1   2   3   4

(a) 1   (b) 2

(c) 3   (d) 4

57. In the given question has four Terms. Three terms are alike in some way. One term is different from three others. Find out the correct term which is different from three others:

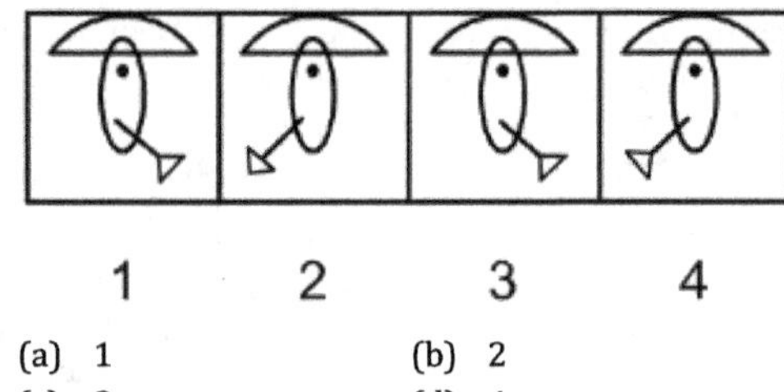

    1   2   3   4

(a) 1   (b) 2

(c) 3   (d) 4

58. House Q is to the South-East of house P. House R is to the East of house Q. House T is to the North of house R and house S is to the South of house R. In which direction is house Q with respect to house T?

(a) North-West   (b) South

(c) West   (d) South-West

59. A fishing boat sails 10 km North in still water, then turns West and sails 12 km, then turns North and sails 15 km, then turns to its left and sails 12 km. Where is the boat now with reference to its starting position?

(a) North-West   (b) South-East

(c) South-West   (d) North-East

60. In a code language, LEAVE is written as RKGBK. How will FLOAT be written in that language?

(a) MSUGZ   (b) LRVGY

(c) LRUFA   (d) LRUGZ

61. In a certain code language, 'WRITE' is written as 'RWIET', and 'MONTHLY' is written as 'NOMTYLH'. How will 'AMSTERDAM' be written in that language?

(a) TSMAEMADR   (b) STNAEMAER

(c) TSNAEFADR   (d) STMAEAMER

Ques (62-63): Direction: Select the Answer figure that will complete the series of question figures.

62. Problem Figures: Answer Figures:

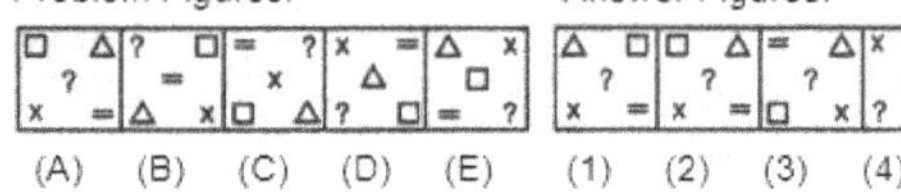

(A)   (B)   (C)   (D)   (E)   (1)   (2)   (3)   (4)

(a) (1)   (b) (2)

(c) (3)   (d) (4)

63. Question figure:

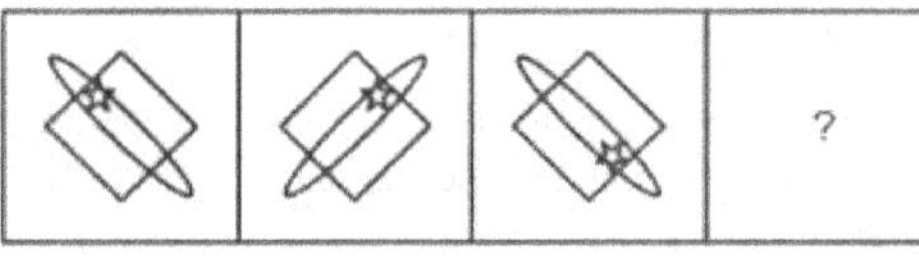

Option figure:

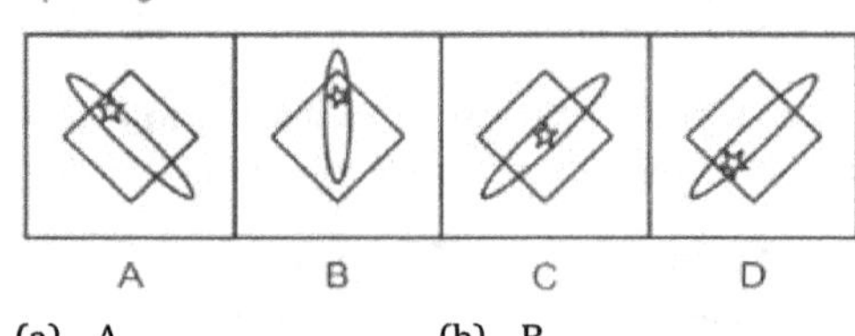

    A   B   C   D

(a) A   (b) B

(c) C   (d) D

Ques (64-65): Direction: Identify the diagram that best represents the relationship among classes given below:

64. India, Maharashtra and Kerala

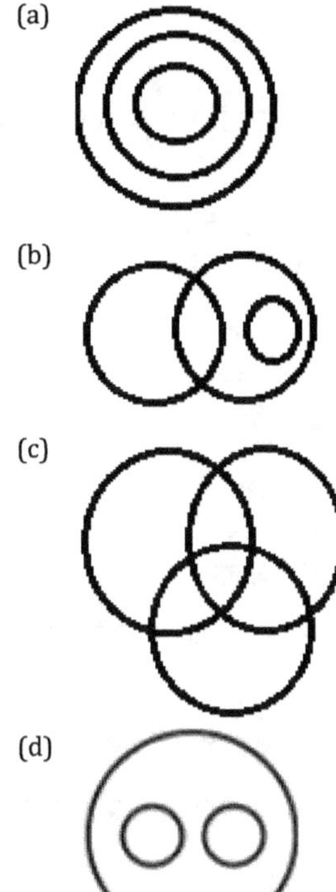

65. Wheat, Tea, Plant and Coffee

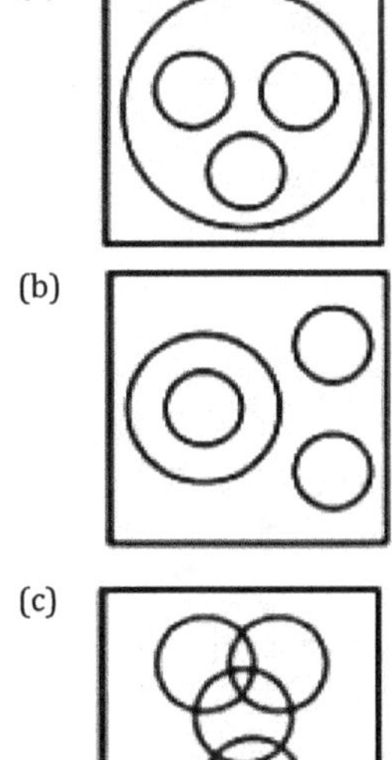

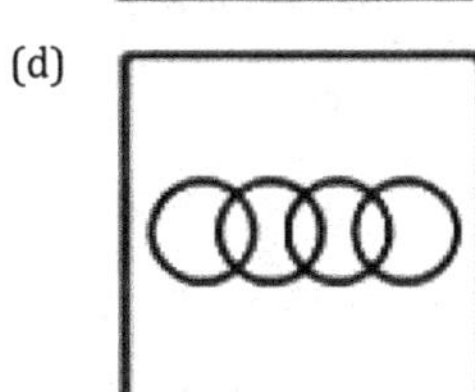

66. **Direction:** In the given series, a number/letter/word/term is missing. Choose the correct alternative from the given ones that will complete the series.

24, 37, 50, 63, ?

(a) 86   (b) 57

(c) 76   (d) 87

67. **Direction:** What should come in place of the question mark '?' in the following number series?

2, 11, 54, 215, 644, ?

(a) 1280   (b) 1278

(c) 1287   (d) 1295

68. Among five rods, P, Q, R, S and T, the weight of T is 20 kg. The weight of S is half the weight of P. The weight of Q is one-fourth the weight of P. R's weight is twice the weight of Q. The weight of P is twice the weight of T. Which rod is the lightest among all?

(a) P   (b) S

(c) Q   (d) R

69. In a school, there are five students A, B, C, D and E. 'A' scored less marks than 'B'. 'C' scored less marks than 'D'. 'B' scored less marks than 'C' and 'A' scored more marks than 'E'. Who scored the highest marks out of these 5 students?

(a) A   (b) B

(c) C   (d) D

Ques (70-71): Direction: In the following question below some statements are given followed by some conclusions. Taking the given statements to be true even if they seem to be at variance from commonly known facts, read all the conclusions and then decide which of the given conclusions logically follows the given statements.

70. **Statements:**
I. Some green are big.
II. All big are blue.
Conclusions:
I. Some blue are green.
II. Some big are green.

(a) Only conclusion I follows

(b) Only conclusion II follows

(c) Both conclusion follows

(d) Neither conclusion I nor conclusion II follows

71. **Statements:**
I. Some monkeys are milk.
II. No milk is a fruit.
Conclusions:
I. All fruit are milk.
II. All monkeys are fruit.

(a) Only conclusion I follows.

(b) Only conclusion II follows.

(c) Both conclusions I and II follow.

(d) Neither conclusion I nor conclusion II follows.

72. **Direction:** Study the following information and answer the given questions.

Eight friends Ravi, Rakesh, Rajesh, Ram, Rahul, Raj, Ritesh, and Rishi are sitting around a circular park. Some of them facing away from the center and some are facing inside the center. One person sits between Rakesh and Rishi. Rakesh sits second to the right of Ram who is facing towards the center. Raj who is facing the center is not an immediate neighbor of Ram and Rishi. Ritesh who is not an immediate neighbor of Rakesh sitting to the immediate right of Rishi. Rajesh is not an immediate neighbor of Ram. More than 2 person is sitting between Rajesh and Ravi from both sides and Ritesh is facing away from the centre. Rajesh and Rahul face the same direction as Raj but opposite to Rakesh. Ravi is not sitting second to the right of Ritesh but facing the direction same as Ritesh.

Who is sitting immediate right of Rakesh?

(a) Raj   (b) Ritesh

(c) Rahul   (d) Rakesh

73. **Direction:** Read the following information carefully and answer the following questions.

Eight persons A, B, C, D, P, Q, R and S are sitting around two concentric circular table such as one circular table is inscribed in another one. All of them facing towards the center. Persons A, B, C and D are sitting around the inner circle and remaining four persons P, Q, R and S are sitting around the outer circle. They like different colors Red, Green, Blue, Pink, Yellow, Silver, Cyan and Magenta. The persons of outer circle are sitting exactly behind the person sitting around the inner circle and the person sits in inner circle exactly in front of outer circle. All the sitting arrangements and color's choice is not necessarily in the same order.

B is second to the right of the person who likes Yellow color. S is an immediate neighbor of the one who sits behind B. Person likes Pink color sits in front of S. There is only one person sits between A and B. Person sits behind C likes Silver color and sits immediate left of Q. S is an immediate neighbor of both Q and R. C does not like Pink color. Person sits immediate left of R likes Cyan color. B likes Red color. Person sits in front of P likes Blue color. Person sits behind B does not like Magenta color and R likes Magenta color.

Who sits behind D?

(a) Person likes Yellow color.

(b) Person likes Red color.

(c) P

(d) Person likes Cyan color.

74. Select the letter which is different from the others.

(a) CEIO   (b) WYCI

(c) VXBF   (d) UWAG

75. Select the number which is different from the others.

(a) 170   (b) 290

(c) 360   (d) 530

General Hindi

76. 'वांगमय' शब्द की शुद्ध वर्तनी कौन सी होगी?

(a) वांगमय्   (b) वाङ्मय

(c) वागमय   (d) कोई भी नहीं

77. "विरहणी" शब्द की शुद्ध वर्तनी कौन सी होगी?

(a) विरहिणी   (b) वीरहिणी

(c) विरहीणी   (d) विरहनी

78. निम्नलिखित प्रश्न में, चार विकल्पों में से, उस विकल्प का चयन करे जो दिए गए मुहावरे का सही अर्थ वाला विकल्प है।
मूंग की दाल खाने वाला।

(a) सोच समझकर काम करना

(b) सीधा-साधा व्यक्ति

(c) कमजोर

(d) सुंदर होना

79. निम्नलिखित प्रश्न में, चार विकल्पों में से; उस विकल्प का चयन करें जो दिए गए मुहावरे का सही अर्थ वाला विकल्प है।
शहद लगाकर चाटना।

(a) किसी चीज़ को व्यर्थ लेकर बैठे रहना

(b) कीमती होना

(c) पसंदीदा होना

(d) बढ़ा-चढ़ा कर कहना

80. निम्नलिखित प्रश्न में, चार विकल्पों में से, उस विकल्प का चयन करें जो दिए गए मुहावरे का सही अर्थ वाला विकल्प है।
हिसाब बैठना।

(a) सही लगना   (b) ध्यान देना

(c) पूछताछ करना   (d) सुभीता होना

81. स्त्रीलिंग शब्द है:

(a) सलाद   (b) सनक

(c) सारस   (d) राष्ट्र

82. निम्नलिखित में से पुल्लिंग शब्द छाँटिए:

(a) चाहत   (b) रंगत

(c) मेहनत   (d) आहार

83. 'जानने की इच्छा रखने वाला'- इस शब्द समूह के लिए एक शब्द बताइए।

(a) पिपासु   (b) उत्साही

(c) जिज्ञासु   (d) इनमें से कोई नहीं

84. 'उपकार को मानने वाला'- इस शब्द समूह के लिए एक शब्द बताइए।

(a) कृपालु   (b) कृतज्ञ

(c) कृतघ्न   (d) आज्ञाकारी

85. 'डिब्बा' शब्द का स्त्रीलिंग शब्द क्या होगा?

(a) डिब्बे   (b) डिब्बों

(c) डिबिए   (d) डिबिया

86. निम्नलिखित शब्दों में किसका लिंग परिवर्तन हिन्दी भाषा में प्रचलित नहीं है?

(a) कोयल   (b) भैंसा

(c) बहन   (d) चाचा

87. कौन-सा शब्द स्त्रीलिंग है?

(a) परिषद   (b) सियार

(c) सहारा   (d) इनमे से कोई नहीं

88. निम्नलिखित में से किस शब्द का बहुवचन नहीं होगा?

(a) दूध   (b) रायता

(c) दही   (d) उपरोक्त सभी

89. दिये गए विकल्पों में से बहुवचन शब्द पहचानिए।

(a) थाली   (b) रीति

(c) सखियाँ   (d) लड़की

90. निम्नलिखित प्रत्येक प्रश्न में तीन गद्यांश दिये गये हैं। त्रुटि वाले वाक्यांश को चुनें और उसके अनुरूप (A), (B), (C) पर चिन्ह लगाएँ। यदि वाक्य त्रुटिहीन हो, तो (D) पर चिन्ह लगाएँ:

(a) हमारी दुग्धशाला में शुद्ध गाय का घी बिकता है

(b) मिलावट सिद्ध करने पर

(c) पाँच हजार रुपये का पुरस्कार प्राप्त करें।

(d) कोई त्रुटि नहीं

91. निम्नलिखित प्रत्येक प्रश्न में तीन गद्यांश दिये गये हैं। त्रुटि वाले वाक्यांश को चुनें और उसके अनुरूप (A), (B), (C) पर चिन्ह लगाएँ। यदि वाक्य त्रुटिहीन हो, तो (D) पर चिन्ह लगाएँ।

(a) महापुरुष किसी भी देश, जाति अथवा धर्म में जन्म लेकर

(b) उसी देश, जाति अथवा धर्म तक सीमित नहीं रहते

(c) वे तो सम्पूर्ण मानवता के पथ प्रदर्शक होते हैं।

(d) कोई त्रुटि नहीं

92. "योगी" का विपरीतार्थक शब्द है:

    (a) रोगी   (b) निरोगी

    (c) जोगी   (d) भोगी

93. 'कपडा' का पर्याय बताइए।

    (a) चलन   (b) वसन

    (c) गगन   (d) जंगल

94. प्रश्न के नीचे दिए गए विकल्पों में से उचित विकल्प का चयन कीजिए: निम्नलिखित में से कौन-सा शब्द अद्वितीय का पर्यायवाची शब्द है?

    (a) आश्चर्यजनक   (b) अनोखा

    (c) अनुपम   (d) अपूर्व

95. 'कवयित्री' का निम्न में से कौन सा सही विलोम शब्द है?

    (a) कवि   (b) कबि

    (c) कवी   (d) कबी

96. किस शब्द में "मधु + आचार्य" की संधि है?

    (a) मध्वाचार्य   (b) मधचार्य

    (c) मधूचार्य   (d) माधोचार्य

97. 'भव्याकृतिः' का संधि विच्छेद है-

    (a) भव्या + आकृतिः   (b) भव्य + आकृतिः

    (c) भव् + आकृतिः   (d) भव्य + आकतिः

98. 'आ + अ = आ' किस संधि का नियम है?

    (a) दीर्घ संधि   (b) गुण संधि

    (c) वृद्धि संधि   (d) यण संधि

99. 'राजा भोज का सपना' कहानी के कहानीकार है:

    (a) प्रेमचंद   (b) मोहन राकेश

    (c) शिवप्रसाद सितारेहिंद   (d) भारतेंदु हरिश्चंद्र

100. सूर्यकांत त्रिपाठी 'निराला' ने निम्न में से किस पत्रिका का सम्पादन किया?

    (a) मतवाला   (b) सरस्वती

    (c) कल्पना   (d) प्रतीक

// Smart Answer Sheet //

Correct — Percentage of students who answered correctly.

Skipped — Percentage of students who skipped.

Q.	Ans.	Correct / Skipped	Q.	Ans.	Correct / Skipped	Q.	Ans.	Correct / Skipped
1	C	12.21% / 3.61%	2	D	41.3% / 1.36%	3	C	49.44% / 1.38%
4	C	53.76% / 1.52%	5	A	45.07% / 1.54%	6	A	56.11% / 1.23%
7	C	47.88% / 1.74%	8	A	66.58% / 1.41%	9	B	65.18% / 1.01%
10	C	18.7% / 3.09%	11	C	53.34% / 1.1%	12	A	77.01% / 0.0%
13	D	81.97% / 0.0%	14	C	61.41% / 1.42%	15	B	43.31% / 1.3%
16	A	83.33% / 0.0%	17	A	21.27% / 3.24%	18	B	50.96% / 1.52%
19	C	81.23% / 0.0%	20	C	59.76% / 1.01%	21	C	85.61% / 0.0%
22	D	63.6% / 1.91%	23	A	55.8% / 1.28%	24	D	60.96% / 1.17%
25	C	42.87% / 1.99%	26	C	77.97% / 0.0%	27	C	42.84% / 1.4%
28	C	43.6% / 1.23%	29	C	43.02% / 1.53%	30	A	24.1% / 4.62%
31	A	47.61% / 1.06%	32	B	53.1% / 1.64%	33	D	64.35% / 1.85%

Q.	Ans.	Correct / Skipped	Q.	Ans.	Correct / Skipped	Q.	Ans.	Correct / Skipped
34	A	77.47% / 0.0%	35	C	17.14% / 4.56%	36	A	56.94% / 1.65%
37	D	57.54% / 1.61%	38	B	47.14% / 1.37%	39	D	65.0% / 1.95%
40	D	50.1% / 1.06%	41	D	58.73% / 1.08%	42	C	61.34% / 1.94%
43	D	45.35% / 1.06%	44	C	43.41% / 1.18%	45	A	26.77% / 4.46%
46	D	76.58% / 0.0%	47	C	14.3% / 3.94%	48	C	88.07% / 0.0%
49	D	67.93% / 1.08%	50	D	83.09% / 0.0%	51	B	54.78% / 1.49%
52	A	60.14% / 1.9%	53	C	83.92% / 0.0%	54	D	68.53% / 1.57%
55	A	40.94% / 1.04%	56	C	81.34% / 0.0%	57	B	52.55% / 1.67%
58	D	44.18% / 1.49%	59	A	47.22% / 1.51%	60	D	83.93% / 0.0%
61	A	46.02% / 1.16%	62	B	53.02% / 1.67%	63	D	48.24% / 1.17%
64	D	54.83% / 1.07%	65	A	69.06% / 1.26%	66	C	89.82% / 0.0%
67	C	78.74% / 0.0%	68	C	15.31% / 3.14%	69	D	85.71% / 0.0%
70	C	49.89% / 1.66%	71	D	64.48% / 1.23%	72	C	44.1% / 1.46%
73	D	61.89% / 1.78%	74	C	60.39% / 1.92%	75	C	44.52% / 1.69%
76	B	58.41% / 1.59%	77	A	52.0% / 1.73%	78	B	64.31% / 1.47%
79	A	55.29% / 1.78%	80	D	65.7% / 1.12%	81	B	49.8% / 1.45%
82	D	46.05% / 1.56%	83	C	76.16% / 0.0%	84	B	30.47% / 3.4%
85	D	53.03% / 1.95%	86	A	53.06% / 1.73%	87	A	15.08% / 4.33%
88	D	52.11% / 1.5%	89	C	80.75% / 0.0%	90	A	40.3% / 1.12%
91	D	78.46% / 0.0%	92	D	69.11% / 1.05%	93	B	80.16% / 0.0%
94	C	59.4% / 1.79%	95	A	86.42% / 0.0%	96	A	59.53% / 1.47%
97	A	48.64% / 1.92%	98	A	88.2% / 0.0%	99	C	59.58% / 1.4%
100	A	66.32% / 1.72%						

// Hints and Solutions //

1(C). Plato is the author of the book 'Republic'.
- Plato was an ancient Greek philosopher.
- He was born in 428-7 B.C.E and died in 348-7 B.C.E.
- He was the student of Socrates and the teacher of Aristotle.
- Plato is known for his work " the Republic"

2(D). Not Mohenjodaro, it was Harappa which was the only place having evidences of coffin burial. Harappa was excavated in the year 1921 by Daya Ram Sahni. It is situated at Montgomery district of Punjab (Now in Pakistan) on the left bank of Ravi. Other notable features include:
1. City followed grid planning.
2. Row of six granaries.
3. Only place having evidences of coffin burial.
4. Evidence of fractional burial and coffin burial.
5. Cemetery-H of alien people.
There is no idea about the political organization of the Harappans. Perhaps, the Harappan rulers were more concerned with commerce than conquests,

and Harappa was possibly ruled by the class of merchants.

3(C). The Non-Cooperation Movement launched by Mahatma Gandhi on August 1, 1920.
It was the first mass movement organized nationwide during India's struggle for freedom.
The movement could cement Hindu-Muslim unity and bring Muslim masses into the national movement.
It was a platform from which mass united non-cooperation could be declared against the government.
The Movement was supposed to be firmly based on non-violence, but people failed to learn or fully understand the method of non-violence. Gandhi premised his idea of movement on the idea that a violent movement could be easily suppressed by the colonial regime who could use the incidents of violence as an excuse to use their armed might against people. But Violent incident took place at Chauri-Chaura in 1922 February which forced Gandhi to withdraw the movement.

4(C). Indian Association, a nationalist political group in India that favoured local self-government and served as a preparatory agent for the more truly national Indian National Congress.
The association was founded in Bengal in 1876 by Surendranath Banerjee and Ananda Mohan Bose. Therefore statement A is incorrect.
The Anushilan Samiti was established by Pramathanath Mitra, a barrister from Calcutta on 24 March 1902. Therefore statement B is incorrect.
It was headed by Barindra Kumar Ghosh, younger brother of Sri Aurobindo Ghosh.
It soon displaced the Indian League.
The East India Association was an organization established by some Indian students in London on 1 October 1866 on the initiative of Dadabhai Naoroji. Therefore statement C is correct.
The Treaty of Salbai was signed on 17 May 1782 between the British East India Company and the Marathas.

5(A). The Congress did not participate in the First Round Table Conference (1930). Many leaders of other parties had participated, such as Maulana Muhammad Ali, Aga Khan, Jinnah, Mu. Shafi, Srinivas Shastri, etc.

6(A). Vinobha Bhave was the first Individual Satyagrahi. Bhoodan Movement was started in 1951 by Acharya Vinoba Bhave at Pochampally village (Telangana), India.

7(C). 'Transhumance' refers to seasonal movement of people and their herds from valley to mountain and vice versa.
It is the seasonal movement of livestock (such as sheep) between mountain and lowland pastures either under the care of herders or in company with the owners. They move between higher pastures in summer and lower valleys in winter. The movements are mostly predictable, each year, herders follow the rhythm of the seasons and pass over the same trails and pasturelands that they already know.

8(A). The rivers with their source and opening place and tributaries are described in the table given below:

River	Source	Mouth	Tributaries
Krishna	Mahabaleshwar, Maharashtra	Hamsaladeevi, Bay of Bengal	Ghataprabha River, Malaprabha River, Bhima River, Tungabhadra River, and Musi River.
Brahmaputra	Himalayas	The Ganges, Bay of Bengal	Teesta River, Lohit, Danba Qu, Subansiri River
Godavari	Triambakeshwar, Maharashtra	Bay of Bengal	Purna, Kadam, Pranahita, Indravati, Pravara, Sindphana, Manjira, Manair, Kinnerasani
Yamuna	Yamunotri, Champasar Glacier	Ganges, Triveni Sangam	Tons River, Hindon River, Ken River, Betwa River, Chambal river

9(B). The power plant of Manikaran based on geothermal energy is in the State of Himachal Pradesh.
Geothermal energy is energy from the shallow ground hot water and hot rock found some miles or deeper to the extremely high temperatures of molten rock called magma. An experimental geothermal power plant of 5 MW capacity has been set up at Manikaran in Himachal Pradesh. Manikaran is located in the Parvati Valley on the river Parvati, in the Kullu District of Himachal Pradesh.

10(C). HAL unveiled next gen supersonic trainer HLFT-42 at Aero India 2023. Hindustan Aeronautics Limited (HAL) has unveiled the design of a new supersonic jet trainer HLFT-42 for combat aircraft training of the Indian Air Force (IAF) at Aero India 2023.

11(C). The meeting of the National Security Advisors of the Shanghai Cooperation Organisation, 2023 was held in the country of India.

12(A). Finance Minister Nirmala Sitharaman presented the Economic Survey on 31 January 2023 during the budget session. The survey has estimated the GDP growth rate to be 6.5 % for the financial year 2023-24, while the growth for the ongoing year has been projected at 7 per cent.

13(D). 2022 ICC Under-19 Cricket World Cup:
- It was an international limited-overs cricket tournament, held in January-February 2022 in West Indies. So, Statement 1 is correct.
- 16 teams took part in the game. It was the fourteenth edition of the Under-19 Cricket World Cup. So, Statement 2 is correct.
- It was the first tournament, held in West Indies. Bangladesh were the defending champions. So, Statement 3 is correct.
- Matches were played in Antigua, Saint Kitts, Guyana, and Trinidad.
- The final match was played at Sir Vivian Richards Stadium in Antigua.
- New Zealand withdrew from the tournament because of extensive mandatory quarantine restrictions for minors on their return home.
- Scotland was named as their replacement.
- ICC U-19 World Cup final 2022, India cruised to a four-wicket victory against England, at Sir Vivian Richards Stadium in Antigua, on

February 5, 2022.
So, statement 1, 2, and 3 is correct.

14(C). Milk of Magnesia is basic in nature. The pH value of the Milk of Magnesia is 10.5.

15(B). Silver Bromide (AgBr) is used in black and white photography.
$$2\,AgBr + hv\,(light) \to 2Ag\,(s) + Br_2$$

16(A). Most plants are present in lithosphere. This is the place where we find the soil which enables the growth of most of the plants and also the cimatic conditions are suitable.

17(A). The Royal Commission of Agriculture was set up in 1926 to examine and report the status of India's agricultural and rural economy and it submitted the report in 1928.
- The Royal Commission of Agriculture was set up under the chairmanship of Lord Linlithgow.
- The aim was to examine India's agricultural and rural economy as early as 1926 that had submitted its report in 1928 .
- Later on, various other committees were set up they were Gregory Committee in 1943 (mainly to focus on food availability, supplies, distribution, and control price), the Maitra committee (1950) , Mehta Committee (1957) , Venkatappaiah committee (1966) .
- The government set up the ' National Commission on Agriculture ' in 1970 to review the progress of agriculture and suggests for its improvement and modernization that submitted its report in 1976 .
- In 2004, the ' National Commission for Farmers ' was constituted that submitted its fifth and final report in October 2006.
- The report was popularly known as the M.S Swaminathan Committee Report .

18(B). The national commission on Farmers was set up in 2004.
National Commission on Farmers:
- It was constituted on November 18, 2004, under the chairmanship of Professor M.S. Swaminathan.
- The aim of the commission was to address the nationwide calamity of farmers suicides in India.
- The commission also contained:
- Full-time Members – Ram Badan Singh, Y.C. Nanda
- Part-time Members – R. L. Pitale, Jagadish Pradhan, Chanda Nimbkar (yet to join), Atul Kumar Anjan
- Member Secretary – Atul Sinha
- Based on the studies the NCF submitted four reports in December 2004, August 2005, December 2005 and April 2006.
- The fifth report was submitted in October 2006 it suggested achieving the goal of "faster and more inclusive growth" as envisaged in the Approach to 11th Five Year Plan.

19(C). India has successively passed through all the phases of demographic transition and is now widely believed to have entered the final phase. which is normally characterized by rapidly declining fertility .
Fertility is the ability to produce a child .

20(C). The correct answer is 1, 2 and 3.

Atal P ension Yojana	• The scheme was launched on 9th Ma y 2015, with the objective of creating a universal social security system for all Indians, especially the poor, the un derprivileged, and the workers in the unorganized sector. • Any citizen of India can join the APY s cheme. The age of the subscriber sho uld be between 18-40 years. • It provides a minimum guaranteed pe nsion ranging from Rs 1000 to Rs 500 0 on attaining 60 years of age.
Pradh an Ma ntri Je evan J yoti Bi ma Yoj ana	• It is a life insurance scheme launched in 2015 for people between 18 and 5 0 years of age with bank accounts. • It provides a cover of Rs. 2 Lakh on n atural death or death by accidents (te rm plan insurance). • The annual premium for the scheme i s Rs. 330.
Pradh an Ma ntri Su raksh a Bim a Yoja na	• It is a life Insurance Scheme to provid e insurance cover at a minimal annua l premium for death or disability by a ccidents. • The risk coverage of the scheme for a ccidental death or full disability is Rs. 2 lakhs and for partial disability is Rs. 1 lakh. • Anyone who falls in the age bracket o f 18-70 years can avail the benefit of t his scheme. • The annual premium is a meager am ount of Rs. 12.

21(C). At present the country has adopted full current account convertibility under which the Government of India declared the rupee as convertible on current account from August 9, 1994.

22(D). In the budget for the year 2000-2001, the three rates of excise duty (8, 16, 24 percent) were replaced by a single Modvatable rate of 16%, called Modvat.

23(A). Australian tennis player Ashleigh Barty has won the title by defeating Daniel Collins of America in the women's singles final of the Australian Open. Ashleigh Barty was the first Australian woman since Wendy Turnbull in 1980 to reach the Australian Open singles final and has now become the first Australian champion since Chris O'Neill in 1978.

24(D). Seaweed Farming:
In Budget 2021, the Finance Minister has proposed to set up a multi-purpose seaweed park in Tamil Nadu. It will be a part of the Seaweed Farming promotion in India.
Seaweed: It is the name given to the many species of marine algae and plants. These species grow in water bodies such as rivers, seas and oceans. The practice of cultivating and harvesting seaweed is known as Seaweed Farming.
Seaweed Species in India: The commercially exploited seaweed species in India mainly include Kappaphycus alvarezii, Gracilaria edulis, Gelidiella acerosa, Sargassum spp. and Turbinaria spp. So, statements 1, 2, 3 and 4 are correct.

25(C). Low earth orbit refers to an altitude up to 2,000 km or less.

A satellite in the LEO can monitor activities on the ground and water surfaces.

A Low Earth orbit requires the lowest amount of energy for satellite placement. Hence, statement 3 is NOT correct.

It provides high bandwidth and low communication latency. Satellites and space stations in LEO are more accessible for crew and servicing.

Earth observation satellites and spy satellites use LEO as they are able to see the surface of the Earth clearly by being close to it. Hence, statement 4 is NOT correct.

The International Space Station is in a LEO about 330 km to 420 km above Earth's surface.

26(C). (-2) x (-3) x (-4) x (-5) x (-6), can be written as = 2 x 3 x 4 x 5 x (-6) = - 720

27(C). Given,

Sugar costing ₹ 40 per kg be mixed with sugar costing ₹ 48 per kg.

As we know,

$$\text{Selling price} = (100 + \text{profit}) \times \frac{\text{cost price}}{100}$$

Let the cost price of whole mixture be ₹ x.

$$x = 54 \times \frac{100}{120}$$

$$\Rightarrow x = ₹\,45$$

Ratio = (48 − 45) : (45 − 40)

= 3 : 5

∴ The ratio is 3 : 5.

28(C). Given,

Let, CP of article A and B be A and B respectively.

$A + B = ₹\,1734 \ldots \ldots (1)$

Loss % of A = 16%

Gain % of B = 20%

SP_1 of $A = SP_1$ of B

SP_2 of A = ₹ 1, 147.50

SP = Selling price, CP = cost price

As we know,

$$SP = CP \times \frac{(100 + \text{Gain }\%)}{100}$$

$$SP = CP \times \frac{(100 - \text{Loss }\%)}{100}$$

$$\text{Gain} = SP - CP$$

$$\text{Gain }\% = \left(\frac{\text{Gain}}{CP}\right) \times 100$$

$$SP = CP \times \frac{(100 - \text{Loss }\%)}{100}$$

$$SP_1 \text{ of } A = A \times \frac{(100 - 16)}{100}$$

$$\Rightarrow SP_1 \text{ of } A = 0.84A \quad \cdots (2)$$

$$SP = CP \times \frac{(100 + \text{Gain }\%)}{100}$$

$$SP_1 \text{ of } B = B \times \frac{(100 + 20)}{100}$$

$$\Rightarrow SP_1 \text{ of } B = 1.2B \quad \cdots (3)$$

Equating equations (2) and (3)

$$\Rightarrow 0.84A = 1.2B$$

$$\Rightarrow A = \frac{10B}{7}$$

Putting value of A in equation (1),

$$\Rightarrow \frac{10B}{7} + B = 1734$$

$$\Rightarrow \frac{17B}{7} = 1734$$

$$\Rightarrow CP \text{ of } B = ₹\,714$$

$$\Rightarrow A = 1734 - 714$$

$$\Rightarrow CP \text{ of } A = ₹\,1020$$

SP_2 of A = ₹ 1147.50

Gain $_2 = SP_2 - CP$

$= 1147.50 - 1020$

$= ₹\,127.5$

$$\text{Gain }\% = \left(\frac{\text{Gain}_2}{CP}\right) \times 100$$

$$= \left(\frac{127.5}{1020}\right) \times 100$$

$$= 12.5\%$$

29(C). Given:

Compound interest = Rs. 84 .

Simple interest = Rs. 80

Time = 2 years

Simple interest remains the same for every year.

So, simple interest for the 1 st year = simple interest for the 2 nd year = Rs. $\frac{80}{2}$

$\Rightarrow$ Rs. 40

Again, compound interest for the 1 st year = Rs. 40

Now, the compound interest for the 2 nd year = Rs. $(84 - 40)$

$\Rightarrow$ Simple interest for the 2 nd $+ R\% \times$ Simple interest for the 1 st year = Rs. 44

$$\Rightarrow 40 + \left(\frac{R}{100}\right) \times 40 = \text{Rs. } 44$$

$$\Rightarrow \left(\frac{R}{100}\right) \times 40 = \text{Rs. } 4$$

$$\Rightarrow R = \frac{400}{40}$$

$$\Rightarrow R = 10\%$$

∴ The rate percent per annum is 10% .

30(A). Given:

A sum amounts to Rs. 6,050 in 2 years and to Rs. 6,655 in 3 years at a certain rate percentage per annum when the interest is compounded yearly.

As we know, that

$$\text{Simple interest} = \frac{PNR}{100}$$

$$\text{Compound interest} = P\left(1 + \frac{R}{100}\right)^N - P$$

Where,

P = Principal

R = rate of interest and

N = time period

Accordingly,

$$6050 = P\left(1 + \frac{R}{100}\right)^2$$

$$\text{And, } 6655 = P\left(1 + \frac{R}{100}\right)^3$$

Dividing,

$$\left(1 + \frac{R}{100}\right) = \frac{6655}{6050}$$

$$\Rightarrow \frac{R}{100} = \frac{6655}{6050} - 1$$

$$\Rightarrow \frac{R}{100} = \frac{605}{6050}$$

$$\Rightarrow R = 10\%$$

Simple interest on a sum of Rs. 6,000 at the same rate for $5\frac{3}{4}$ years $= 6000 \times \frac{10}{100} \times \frac{23}{4}$

= Rs. 3450

∴ The required simple interest is Rs. 3450.

31(A). From Statement I:

Let radius = r, height = h

Curved surface area = $2\pi rh$

$$396 = 2 \times \frac{22}{7} \times r \times h$$

$$r \times h = 63$$

Total Surface area = $2\pi rh + 2\pi r^2$

$$1628 = \frac{22}{7}\left(rh + r^2\right)$$

$$rh + r^2 = 259$$

$$63 + r^2 = 259$$

$$r^2 = 259 - 63 = 196$$

$$r = 14$$

$$r \times h = 63$$

$$14 \times h = 63$$

$h = 4.5 \text{ cm}$
Statement I is alone sufficient to answer the question.
From Statement II:
$r = 3h + 0.5$
Statement II is not alone sufficient to answer the question.

32(B). Given:
$AB = 30\ cm$, $BC = 50\ cm$, $AC = 40\ cm$
Formula used:
Area of triangle $= \frac{1}{2} \times \text{Base} \times \text{Height}$
$AY = \frac{(AC \times AB)}{BC}$ where,
$AY \perp CB$

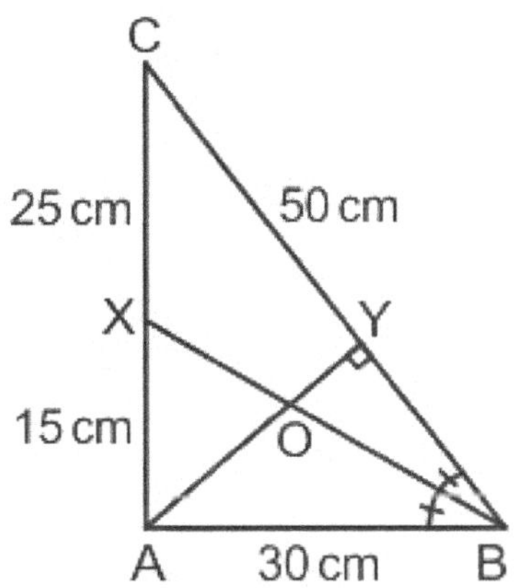

BX is the angle bisector of $\angle B$.
$\therefore \frac{CX}{XA} = \frac{BC}{AB}$
$\Rightarrow \frac{CX}{XA} = \frac{50}{30}$
$\Rightarrow \frac{CX}{XA} = \frac{5}{3}$
$\therefore 8 \text{ units} = 40$
$\Rightarrow 5 \text{ units} = 25 \text{ cm}, 3 \text{ units} = 15 \text{ cm}$
So, $CX = 25 \text{ cm}$ and $AX = 15 \text{ cm}$
$AY = \frac{(AC \times AB)}{BC}$
$\Rightarrow AY = \frac{(40 \times 30)}{50}$
$\Rightarrow AY = 24 \text{ cm}$
$BY = \frac{AB^2}{BC}$
$\Rightarrow BY = \frac{(30 \times 30)}{50}$
$\Rightarrow BY = 18 \text{ cm}$
$\therefore$ Area of $\triangle ABY = \frac{1}{2} \times BY \times AY$
$\Rightarrow \frac{1}{2} \times 18 \times 24$
$\Rightarrow 216 \text{ sq. cm}$

33(D). According to the question,
$x + y = \left(x^2 + y^2\right) \times \frac{1}{5}$
Again, $x + y = \left(x^2 - y^2\right) \times \frac{1}{4}$
$\therefore \frac{x^2 + y^2}{5} = \frac{x^2 - y^2}{4}$
$\Rightarrow 5x^2 - 5y^2 = 4x^2 + 4y^2$
$\Rightarrow 5x^2 - 4x^2 = 5y^2 + 4y^2$
$\Rightarrow x^2 = 9y^2$
$\Rightarrow x = 3y$
$\therefore \frac{x + y}{x^2} = \frac{x^2 + y^2}{5x^2}$
$= \frac{9y^2 + y^2}{5 \times 9y^2}$
$= \frac{10y^2}{45y^2}$

$= \frac{2}{9}$

34(A). Given:
Average of 12 numbers $= 18.5$
Sum of 12 numbers $= 18.5 \times 12 = 222$
Average of first 6 numbers $= 16.8$
Sum of first 6 numbers $= 16.8 \times 6 = 100.8$
Average of last 7 numbers $= 17.4$
Sum of last 7 numbers $= 17.4 \times 7 = 121.8$
6th number $= 100.8 + 121.8 - 222$
$= 222.6 - 222 = 0.6$
Sum of 11 number $= 222 - 0.6 = 221.4$
Average of 11 number $= \frac{221.4}{11} = 20.1$

35(C). Given:
Average monthly salary of 30 employees and 5 managers $=$ Rs 80000
Total salary of 30 employees and 5 managers $= 35 \times 80000 = 2800000$
Let the salary of new manager be $= x$
$\Rightarrow \frac{(2800000 - 180000 + x)}{35} = 78500$
$\Rightarrow x = 2747500 - 2620000 = \text{Rs. } 127500$
$\therefore$ Salary of new manager $= \text{Rs. } 127500$

36(A). Given,
Winning percentage of the first 60 matches $= 30\%$
Won matches by Club A $= 60 \times \frac{30}{100} = 18$
Let Club A played minimum Y more matches and wins them all.
Then, total matches played $= 60 + Y$
Total matches won $= 18 + Y$
So, $44\% (60 + Y) = 18 + Y$
$\Rightarrow \frac{44}{100} \times (60 + Y) = 18 + Y$
$\Rightarrow \frac{11}{25} \times (60 + Y) = 18 + Y$
$\Rightarrow 660 + 11Y = 25 \times 18 + 25Y$
$\Rightarrow 14Y = 660 - 450$
$\Rightarrow Y = \frac{210}{14} = 15$
$\therefore$ The minimum no of matches to be played is 15.

37(D). Given,
A can do a piece of work $= 60$ days
Number of days A works $= 15$ days
B alone finish the remaining work $= 30$ days
As we know,
Work $=$ Efficiency $\times$ Time
Time taken by A to complete the work $= \left(\frac{60}{15}\right) = 4$ days
Number of days B works $= \left(1 - \frac{1}{4}\right) = \frac{3}{4}$ days
Time taken by B to complete the work $= \left(\frac{4}{3} \times 30\right) = 40$ days
Now,
LCM of 60 and 40 is 120.
Efficiency of $A = \left(\frac{120}{60}\right) = 2$ units/day
Efficiency of $B = \left(\frac{120}{40}\right) = 3$ units/day
Time taken by A and B together to complete a work $= \lceil \frac{120}{(2+3)} \rceil$
$= \frac{120}{5}$ days
$= 24$ days

38(B). Given:
Time taken by A to finish a task alone $= 24$ days
Calculation:
Let the total work be $= 1$
A alone can finish the task in 24 days

$\Rightarrow A'$ s one-day work $= 1/24$

A and B complete the whole task in $= 11\frac{1}{3}$ days

A and B work on alternate days, with B beginning so, we can say B will work only 6 days

$\Rightarrow$ A will work only $11\frac{1}{3} - 6 = 5\frac{1}{3}$ days

If A' s one day work $= 1/24$ of work A completes in 1 day

$\Rightarrow$ A's $5\frac{1}{3}$ days work $= 1/24 \times 5\frac{1}{3} = 1/24 \times 16/3$

$\Rightarrow 2/9$

Remaining work $= 1 - 2/9 = 7/9$

$\therefore$ B does the 7/9th part of the work in 6 days.

39(D). As we know,

Efficiency ratio is inversely proportional to time

Efficiency ratio of $(A + B)$ and $A = 25 : 15 = 5 : 3$

Efficiency of $B = 5 - 3 = 2$

Efficiency ratio of A to $B = 3 : 2$

$\Rightarrow$ Total work $= 5 \times 15 = 75$ units

$\Rightarrow$ Work done by A in 5 days $= 5 \times 3 = 15$ units

$\therefore$ Remaining work $= 75 - 15 = 60$ units

$\therefore$ Time taken by A and B to complete 60 units

$= \frac{60}{5} = 12$ days

40(D). Let the original speed of the car is x km/hr.

Then, time taken in moving 840 km $= \frac{840}{x}$ hr

If speed is going 10 km/hr more $= x + 10$

Then, time taken in moving 840 km $= \frac{840}{x+10}$ hr

$\therefore \frac{840}{x} - \frac{840}{x+10} = 2$

$\Rightarrow 840(x + 10) - 840x = 2x(x + 10)$

$\Rightarrow 2x^2 + 20x - 8400 = 0$

$\Rightarrow x^2 + 70x - 60x - 4200 = 0$

$\Rightarrow (x + 70)(x - 60) = 0$

$\Rightarrow x = 60$ or $x = -70$

If $x = -70$ is not true because the speed is not negetive.

So, speed is 60 km/hr.

41(D). Given:

Covers 455 meters in 35 minutes

Speed $= \frac{\text{Distance}}{\text{Time}}$

Speed $= 455$ meters / 35 minutes

But we need speed in km/hr

We know that,

1 km = 1000 meters

1 hour = 60 minutes

$\Rightarrow$ Speed $= \frac{\left(\frac{455}{1000}\right)}{\left(\frac{35}{60}\right)}$

$\Rightarrow$ Speed $= \frac{(455 \times 60)}{(1000 \times 35)}$

$\Rightarrow$ Speed $= 0.78$ km/hr

$\therefore$ Speed of a person is 0.78 km/hr.

42(C). Given:

HCF $= 6$

LCM $= 864$

One number $= 96$

Second number $= ?$

Let, the second number is x .

LCM $\times$ HCF = First number $\times$ Second number

$\Rightarrow 864 \times 6 = 96 \times x$

$\Rightarrow x = \frac{864 \times 6}{96}$

$\Rightarrow x = 54$

43(D). Let the son's present age be x years.

Then, man's present age $= (x + 24)$ years

So, according to the question,

$\Rightarrow (x + 24) + 2 = 2(x + 2)$

$\Rightarrow x + 26 = 2x + 4$

$\Rightarrow x = 22$

44(C). Given:

$x + y = 20$

$x^2 + y^2 = 30$

Formula Used:

$(x + y)^2 = x^2 + y^2 + 2xy$

$\Rightarrow (20)^2 = x^2 + y^2 + 2xy$

$\Rightarrow 400 = 30 + 2xy$

$\Rightarrow 400 - 30 = 2xy$

$\Rightarrow 370 = 2xy$

$\Rightarrow xy = 185$

45(A). Given:

The lines $\frac{x-1}{-3} = \frac{y-2}{2k} = \frac{z-3}{2}$ and $\frac{x-1}{3k} = \frac{y-5}{1} = \frac{z-6}{-5}$ are mutually perpendicular.

As we know that, if a, b, c are the direction ration ratios of a line passing through the point (x_1, y_1, z_1), then the equation of line is given by:

$\frac{x-x_1}{a} = \frac{y-y_1}{b} = \frac{z-z_1}{c}$

Let $L_1 : \frac{x-1}{-3} = \frac{y-2}{2k} = \frac{z-3}{2}$ and

$L_2 = \frac{x-1}{3k} = \frac{y-5}{1} = \frac{z-6}{-5}$

Now by comparing L_1 and L_2 with $\frac{x-x_1}{a} = \frac{y-y_1}{b} = \frac{z-z_1}{c}$ we get

$\Rightarrow a_1 = -3, \ b_1 = 2k, c_1 = 2, a_2 = 3k, b_2 = 1$ and $c_2 = -5$

As we know that if two lines are perpendicular then

$a_1 \cdot a_2 + b_1 \cdot b_2 + c_1 \cdot c_2 = 0$

$\Rightarrow a_1 \cdot a_2 + b_1 \cdot b_2 + c_1 \cdot c_2 = -9k + 2k - 10 = 0$

$\Rightarrow -7k = 10$

$\Rightarrow k = \frac{-10}{7}$

46(D). According to question,

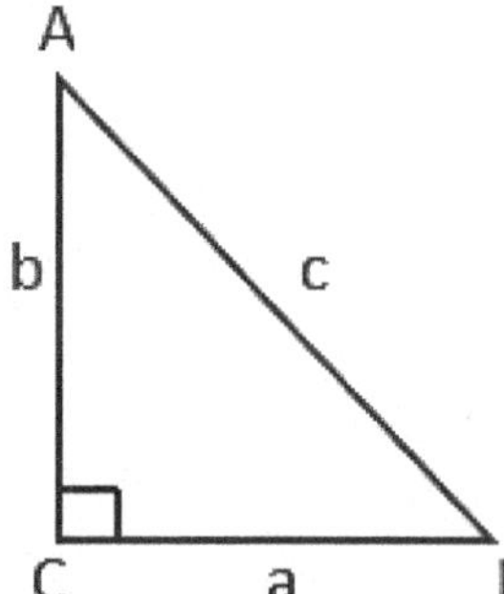

We know that

$\tan = \frac{\text{perpendicular}}{\text{base}}$

So,

$\tan A = \frac{a}{b}, \tan B = \frac{b}{a}$

$\tan A + \tan B = \frac{a}{b} + \frac{b}{a}$

$= \frac{a^2 + b^2}{ab}$

Using pythagoras theorem,

$a^2 + b^2 = c^2$

$\therefore \tan A + \tan B = \frac{c^2}{ab}$

47(C). Given:

$P(A \cup B) = \frac{5}{6}, P(A \cap B) = \frac{1}{3}, P(\overline{A}) = \frac{1}{2}$

So, $P(A) = 1 - P(\overline{A}) = 1 - \frac{1}{2} = \frac{1}{2}$

As we know,

$P(A \cup B) = P(A) + P(B) - P(A \cap B)$

$\Rightarrow P(A \cup B) = 1 - P(\bar{A}) + P(B) - P(A \cap B)$

$\Rightarrow \frac{5}{6} = 1 - \frac{1}{2} + P(B) - \frac{1}{3}$

$\Rightarrow \frac{5}{6} = \frac{1}{2} - \frac{1}{3} + P(B)$

$\Rightarrow \frac{5}{6} = \frac{1}{6} + P(B)$

$\Rightarrow \frac{5}{6} - \frac{1}{6} = P(B)$

$\Rightarrow P(B) = \frac{4}{6}$

$\therefore P(B) = \frac{2}{3}$

So, option (A) is true.

$P(A \cap B) = P(A)P(B) = \frac{1}{2} \times \frac{2}{3} = \frac{1}{3}$

So, option (B) is also true.

$P(A) + P(B) = \frac{1}{2} + \frac{2}{3} = \frac{7}{6} > P(A \cup B)$

So, option (C) is not true.

48(C). Given,

There are 7 consonants and 4 vowels

Here, we have to find how many words can be formed such that it has 3 consonants and 2 vowels.

No. of ways to select 2 vowels out of 4 vowels = $^4C_2$

No. of ways to select 3 consonants out of 7 consonants = $^7C_3$

$\therefore$ No. of words that can be formed which contains 3 consonants and 2 vowels = $^4C_2 \times ^7C_3$

As we know that,

$^nC_r = \dfrac{n!}{r! \times (n-r)!}$

$\Rightarrow ^4C_2 \times ^7C_3 = 6 \times 35 = 210$

The no. of ways to arrange words containing 3 consonants and 2 vowels = $210 \times 5! = 25200$.

49(D). The sales per employee increases in the year 2016 as compared to the previous year.

∴ Sales per employee in 2016 is greater than that of the previous year.

50(D). Total number of Hindi Newspaper sold in Aurangabad and Mumbai City together = 5250 + 4750 = 10,000

Total number of English Newspaper sold in Akola and Amravati together = 5000 + 5500 = 10,500

∴ Required Ratio = 10000 : 10500 = 20 : 21

51(B). Kite and Vulture is a pair of birds having excellent sight and can distinctly see things from a distance four times as far as we can.

52(A). Malaria and Dengue is a pair of diseases caused/spread by mosquitoes.

53(C).

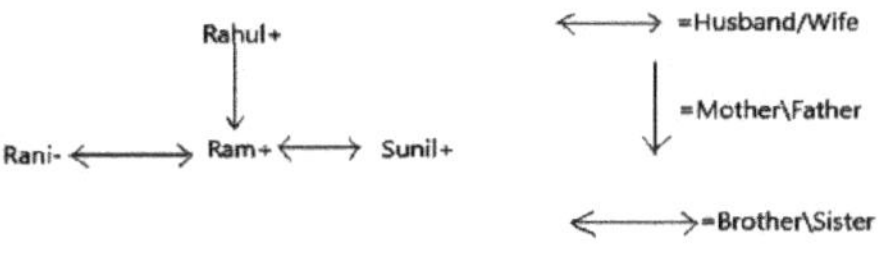

Rahul is the father in law of Rani.

54(D). According to the given information,

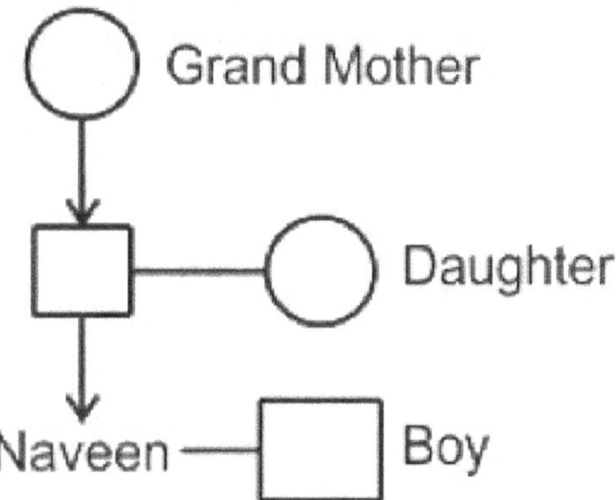

The family tree will be as follows,

So, 'Brother' is the correct answer.

55(A). Figure 1 is different from the other three.

Figures 2, 3 and 4 have two 'S' shaped lines facing their scoop sides, i.e. they are facing each other. Whereas, in figure 1 the scoop sides of the two rows are not facing each other.

56(C). Figure 3 is different from the other three figures.

At least one shape is one after the other in Figures 1, 2 and 4. Whereas in 3 the shapes are placed alternately.

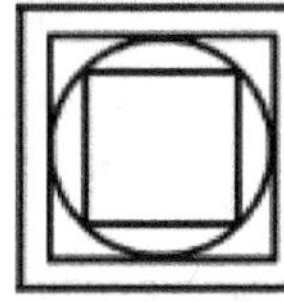

57(B). Figure 2 is different from the other three figures.

In option (B) only, the vertex of the triangle is on the outside and the vertex is not connected to the line segment, whereas in the other three figures, the vertex of the triangle is connected to the line segment.

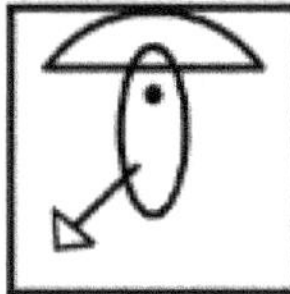

58(D). Drawing the diagram according to the given information:

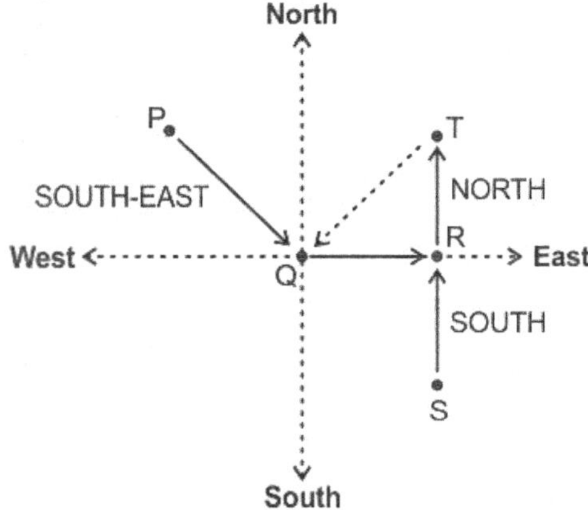

So, house Q is in South-West direction with respect to house T.

59(A). The direction path is shown in the figure below:

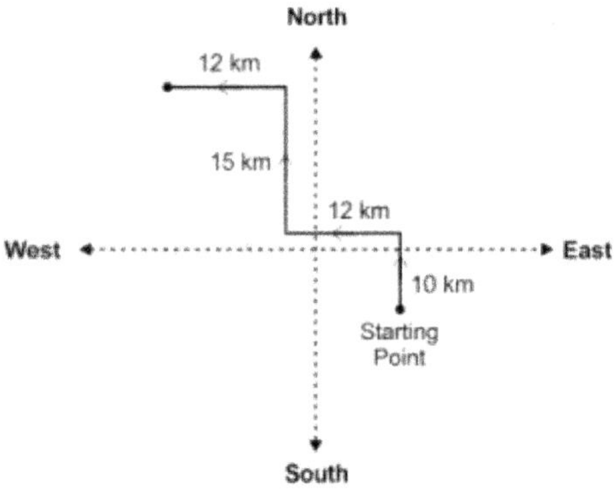

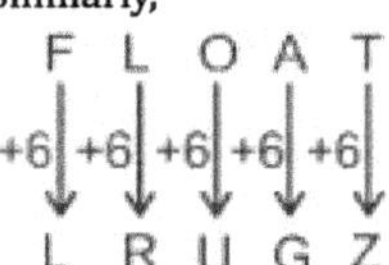

So, the boat is now in the North-West direction of starting position.

60(D). The logic is as:

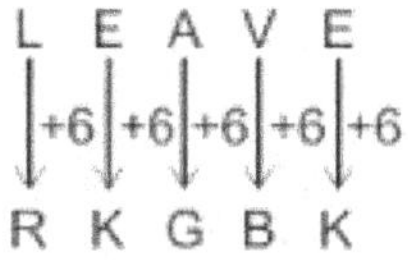

$$L \xrightarrow{+6} R$$
$$E \xrightarrow{+6} K$$
$$A \xrightarrow{+6} G$$
$$V \xrightarrow{+6} B$$
$$E \xrightarrow{+6} K$$

Similarly,

$$F \xrightarrow{+6} L$$
$$L \xrightarrow{+6} R$$
$$O \xrightarrow{+6} U$$
$$A \xrightarrow{+6} G$$
$$T \xrightarrow{+6} Z$$

Thus, FLOAT will be written as LRUGZ.

61(A). Given: 'WRITE' is written as 'RWIET', and 'MONTHLY' is written as 'NOMTYLH'.
The logic followed here is:

W R I T E
R W I E T

And,

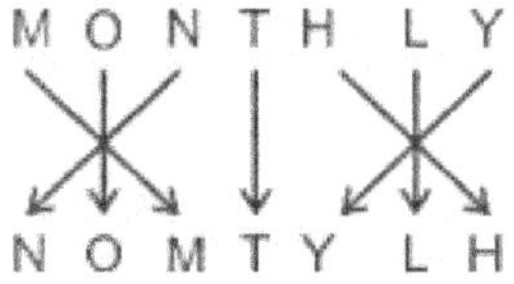

M O N T H L Y
N O M T Y L H

Similarly,

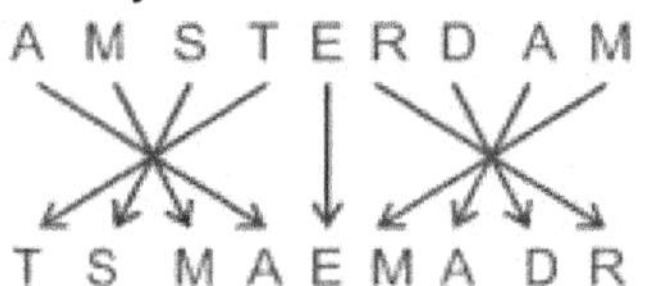

A M S T E R D A M
T S M A E M A D R

So, TSMAEMADR is the correct answer.

62(B). In each step, the elements move in the sequence. Figure (2) will continue the same series as established by the five Problem Figures.

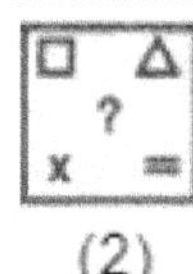

(2)

63(D). The logic followed here is:
In each figure the complete central image turns 90 degrees in clockwise direction.
Answer figure:

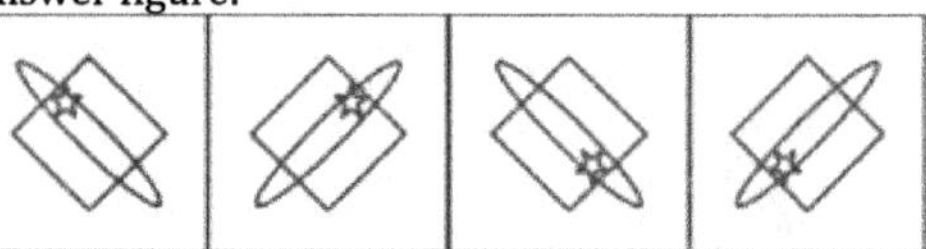

Therefore, the answer figure D will complete the series.

64(D). Maharashtra and Kerala both are states of India.

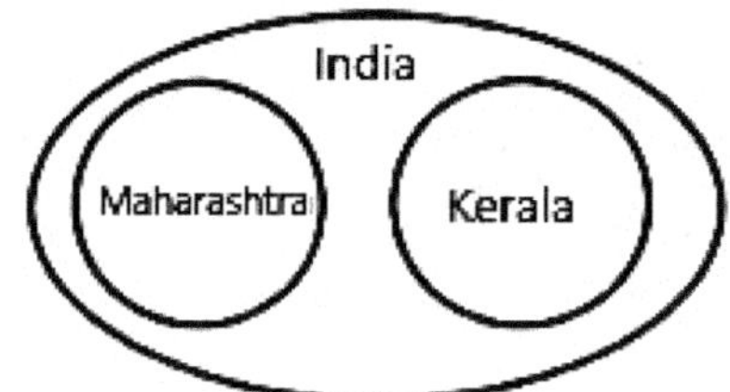

65(A). Given elements: Wheat, Tea, Plant and Coffee

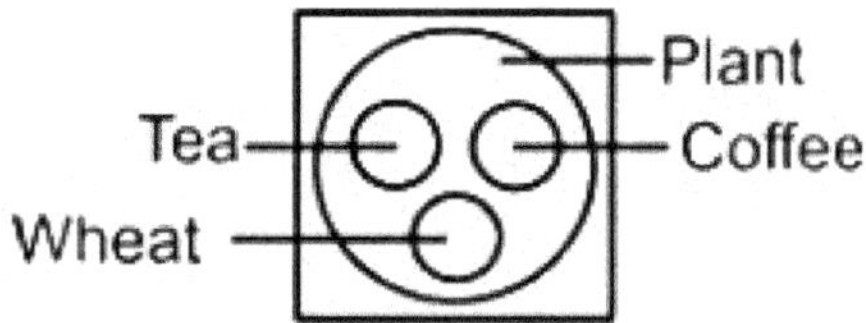

66(C). Here, the pattern in the series is,
24 + 13 = 37
37 + 13 = 50
50 + 13 = 63
63 + 13 = 76.
So, '76' completes the series.

67(C). The series follows following pattern:
$2 \times 6 - 1 = 11$
$11 \times 5 - 1 = 54$
$54 \times 4 - 1 = 215$
$215 \times 3 - 1 = 644$
$644 \times 2 - 1 = 1287$
∴ The value of ? is 1287

68(C). Given:
The weight of T = 20 kg
(A) The weight of P is twice the weight of T:
P = 2 × T
P = 2 × 20
P = 40 kg

(B) The weight of S is half the weight of P:
S = P ÷ 2
S = 40 ÷ 2
S = 20
(C) The weight of Q is one-fourth of the weight of P:
Q = P ÷ 4
Q = 40 ÷ 4
Q = 10 kg
(D) R's weight is twice the weight of Q:
R = 2 × Q
R = 2 × 10
R = 20 kg
So, Rod "Q" is the lightest among all.

69(D).   Given data :
Five students: A, B, C, D and E
1) 'A' scored less marks than 'B'.
A < B
2) 'C' scored less marks than 'D'.
C < D
3) 'B' scored less marks than 'C' and 'A' scored more marks than 'E'.
B < C
E < A
On combining all three statements we get,
E < A < B < C < D

70(C).   The least possible Veen diagram for the given statements is as follows,

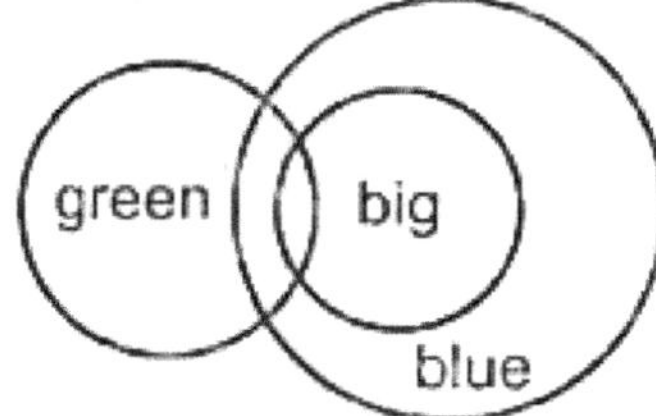

Conclusions:
I. Some blue are green → True
II. Some big are green → True (Some green are big)
Thus, both the conclusion follows.

71(D).   The least possible Venn Diagram is as follows:

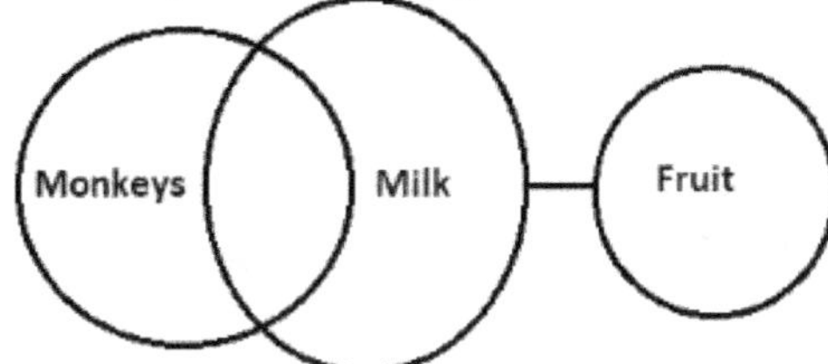

Conclusions :
I. All fruit are milk – False (It is false as no milk is a fruit).
II. All monkeys are fruit – False (As no milk is fruit therefore part of the milk which is monkey definitely not fruit. So, false).

Q.72 8 person: Ravi, Rakesh, Rajesh, Ram, Rahul, Raj, Ritesh, and Rishi.
1) Rakesh sits second to the right of Ram who is facing towards the center.
2) One person sits between Rakesh and Rishi.

Case 1

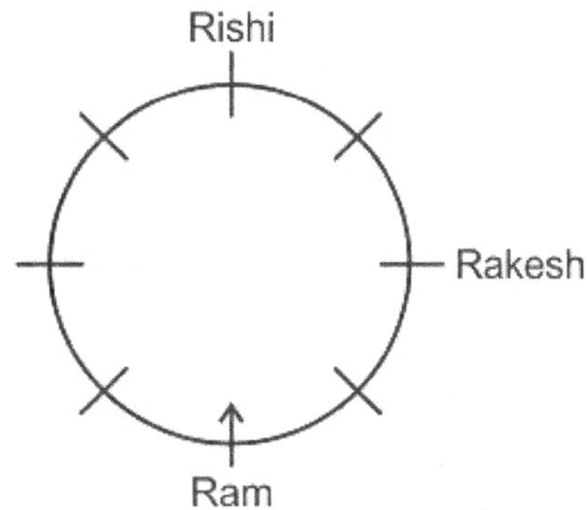

3) Raj who is facing the center is not an immediate neighbor of Ram and Rishi.

Case 1

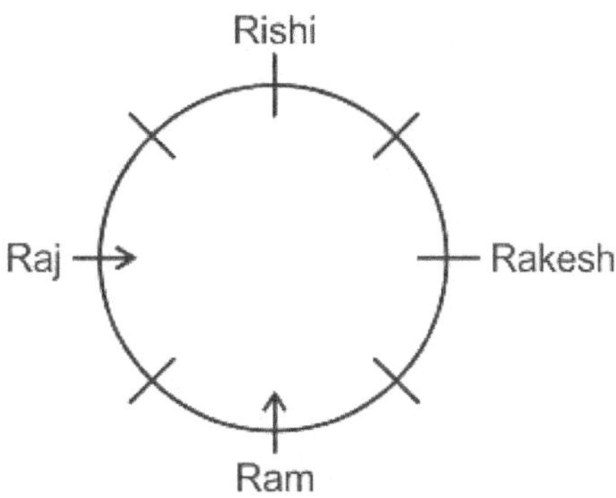

4) Ritesh who is not an immediate neighbor of Rakesh sitting to the immediate right of Rishi. (From here we say that Rishi is facing inside).

Case 1

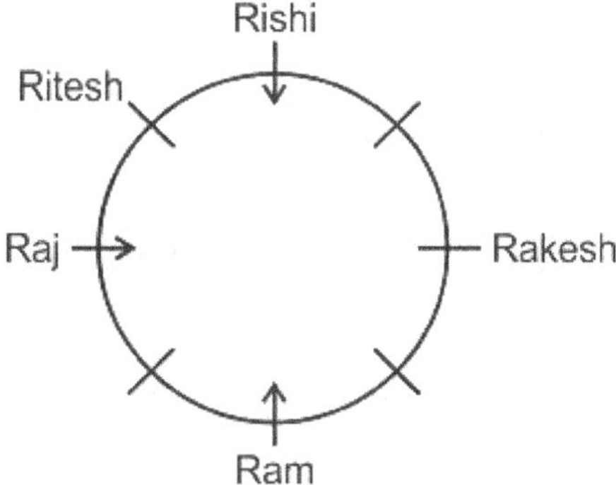

5) More than 2 person is sitting between Rajesh and Ravi.
6) Rajesh and Rahul face the same direction as Raj but opposite to Rakesh.

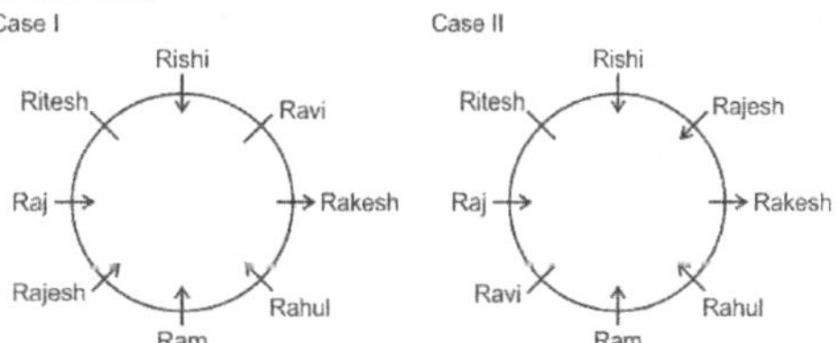

7) Ritesh is facing away from the center.
8) Ravi is not sitting second to the right of Ritesh but facing the direction same as Ritesh. So case 1 not follows.

Case 2

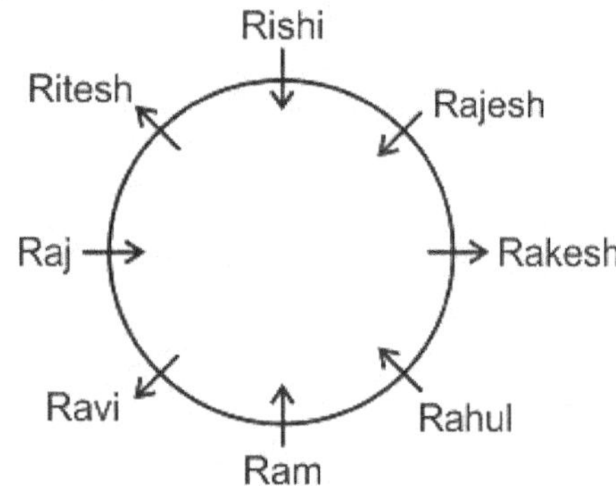

The final arrangement:
Case 2

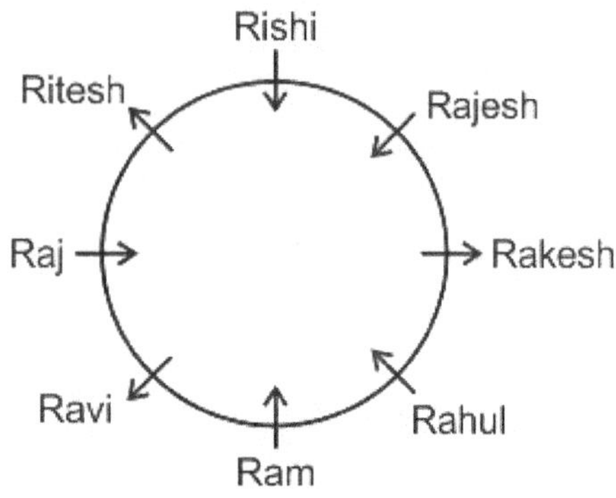

72(C). From the above figure, we say that Rajesh is sitting immediate right of Rakesh.
So, Rahul is sitting immediate right of Rakesh.

Q.73 Eight persons A, B, C, D, P, Q, R and S.
Eight colors: They like different colors Red, Green, Blue, Pink, Yellow, Silver, Cyan and Magenta.
Number of circles: Two.
Inner circle: A, B, C and D.
Outer circle: P, Q, R and S.
1) B is second to the right of the person who likes Yellow color.
2) B likes Red color.
3) There is only one person sits between A and B.
The possible sitting arrangement for the given statements is as follows,

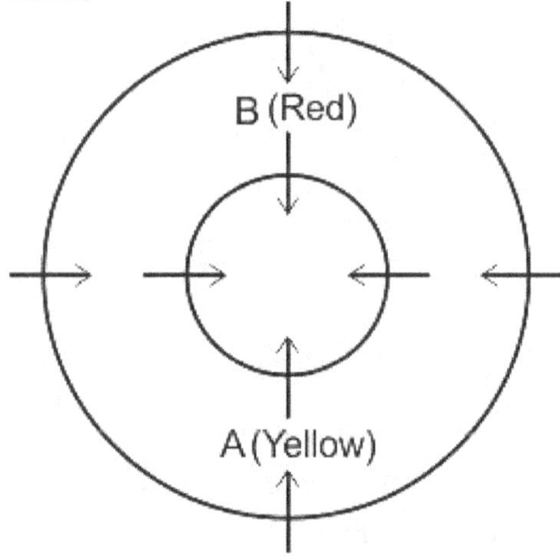

4) S is an immediate neighbor of the one who sits behind B.
5) Person likes Pink color sits in front of S.
There are two possible cases for the given statements,
Case1:

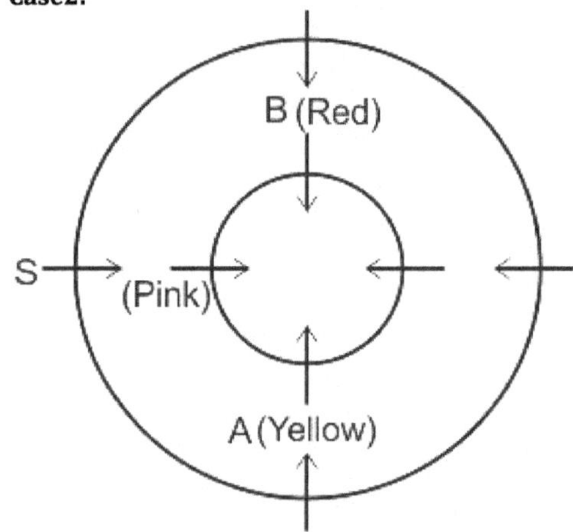

Case2:

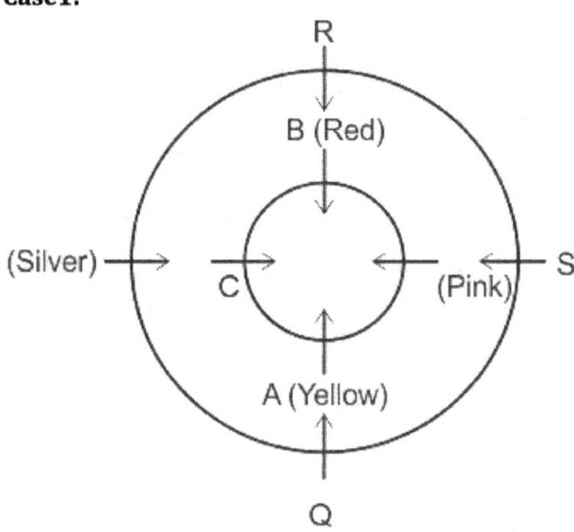

6) S is an immediate neighbor of both Q and R.
7) Person sits behind C likes Silver color and sits immediate left of Q.
8) C does not like Pink color.
Case1:

Case2:

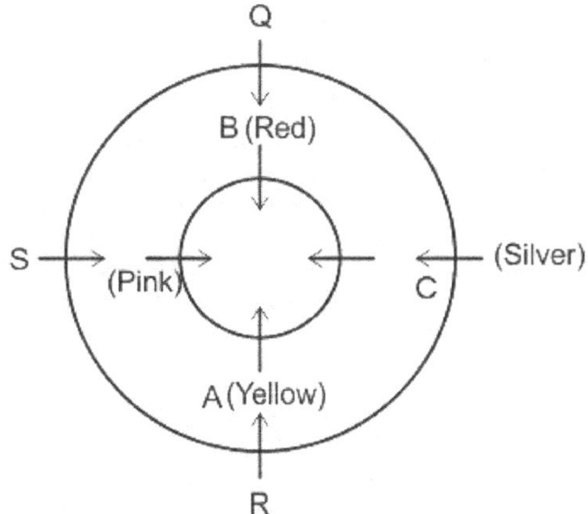

9) Person sits immediate left of R likes Cyan color.
10) Person sits behind B does not like Magenta color and R likes Magenta color. This statement eliminate case 1.
11) Person sits in front of P likes Blue color.
Therefore the final arrangement is as follows,

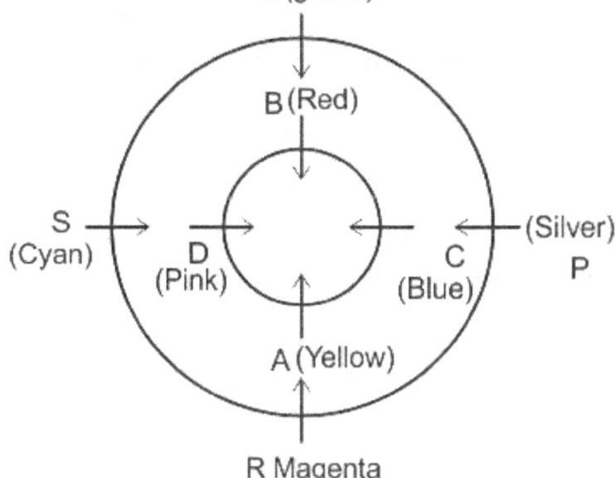

73(D). So, person likes Cyan color sits behind D.

74(C). The pattern is:
$$C \xrightarrow{+2} E \xrightarrow{+4} I \xrightarrow{+6} O$$
$$W \xrightarrow{+2} Y \xrightarrow{+4} C \xrightarrow{+6} I$$
$$V \xrightarrow{+2} X \xrightarrow{+4} B \xrightarrow{+4} F$$
$$U \xrightarrow{+2} W \xrightarrow{+4} A \xrightarrow{+6} G$$
VXBF is odd in the given option.

75(C). The pattern followed here is:
$13^2 = 169 + 1 = 170$
$17^2 = 289 + 1 = 290$
$19^2 = 361 - 1 = 360$
$23^2 = 529 + 1 = 530$
So, 360 is an odd number.

76(B). 'वांग्मय' शब्द की शुद्ध वर्तनी वाङ्मय होगी। 'वांग्मय' यह संस्कृत का शब्द है, जिसका हिंदी अर्थ होता है "साहित्य"।

77(A). "विरहणी" शब्द की शुद्ध वर्तनी विरहिणी होगी।
विरहिणी - प्रिय या पति से बिछुड़ी हुई दुःखिनी नायिका।

78(B). "मूंग की दाल खाने वाला" मुहावरे का सही अर्थ "सीधा-साधा" व्यक्ति है।

79(A). "शहद लगाकर चाटना" मुहावरे का सही अर्थ "किसी चीज़ को व्यर्थ लेकर बैठे रहना" है।

80(D). "हिसाब बैठना" मुहावरे का सही अर्थ "सुभीता होना (ऐसी स्थिति जो किसी व्यक्ति या बात के लिए अनुकूल हो)" है।

81(B). सनक स्त्रीलिंग शब्द है। सनक का अर्थ- पागलपन, खब्त, धुन, झोंक आदि है ।

82(D). आहार पुल्लिंग शब्द है। आहार का अर्थ है - भोजन। पुल्लिंग: जिन शब्दों से पुरुष जाति का बोध होता है उन्हें पुल्लिंग शब्द कहते हैं। जैसे:माता, बहन, पुस्तक, पार्वती, आदि।

83(C). 'जानने की इच्छा रखने वाला' समूह के लिए एक शब्द 'जिज्ञासु' होगा।

84(B). 'उपकार को मानने वाला' के लिए एक शब्द 'कृतज्ञ' है।

85(D). 'डिब्बा' शब्द का स्त्रीलिंग 'डिबिया' होगा।
'लिंग' का शाब्दिक अर्थ प्रतीक या चिह्न अथवा निशान होता है। संज्ञाओं के जिस रूप से उसकी पुरुष या स्त्री जाति का पता चलता है, उसे 'लिंग' कहा जाता है।
लिंग दो प्रकार के होते हैं: स्त्रीलिंग [जो स्त्री-जाति का बोध कराता है।] और पुल्लिंग [जो पुरुष-जाति का बोध कराता है।]

86(A). कोयल शब्द का लिंग परिवर्तन हिन्दी भाषा में प्रचलित नहीं है। अन्य शब्दों के लिंग बदले जा सकते हैं जैसे भैंसा का स्त्रीलिंग भैंस, बहन का पुल्लिंग भाई और चाचा का स्त्रीलिंग चाची होता है, परंतु कोयल शब्द का लिंग परिवर्तन नहीं होता।

87(A). परिषद शब्द स्त्रीलिंग है।
परिषद:
- परिषद एक तरह का -सभा,वैदिक युग में राजा द्वारा बुलाई जानेवाली विद्वानों की सभा।
- समानार्थी शब्द - परिषद

सियार:
- लिंग - पुल्लिंग
- सियार जातिवाचक संज्ञा है
- समानार्थी शब्द - श्रृगाल , श्रृगाल , गीदड़, श्रृंगाल

सहारा:
- लिंग - पुल्लिंग
- सहारा जातिवाचक संज्ञा है
- समानार्थी शब्द - अवलंब, आश्रय

88(D). उपर्युक्त शब्द "दूध, रायता, दही" केवल एकवचन होते हैं। द्रव्यसूचक संज्ञायें सदैव एकवचन में प्रयोग होती है। जैसे- पानी, तेल, घी, दूध आदि।
वचन- संज्ञा, सर्वनाम, विशेषण और क्रिया आदि की व्याकरण सम्बन्धी श्रेणी है जो इनकी संख्या की सूचना देती है (एक, दो, आदि)।

89(C). 'सखियाँ' शब्द बहुवचन है जिसका एकवचन रूप 'सखी' होगा।
अन्य विकल्प:
- थाली – थालियाँ
- लड़की – लड़कियां
- रीति – रीतियाँ

90(A). त्रुटि वाला वाक्यांश ' हमारी दुग्धशाला में शुद्ध गाय का घी बिकता है' है। इस वाक्यांश का सही अनुरूप - 'हमारी दुग्धशाला में गाय का शुद्ध घी बिकता है' होगा।

91(D). वाक्यांशों में कोई त्रुटि नहीं है।

92(D). "योगी" का विपरीतार्थक शब्द भोगी है।
- योगी का अर्थ : योग साधना करनेवाला व्यक्ति।
- भोगी का अर्थ : इंद्रिय सुखभोग की इच्छा करनेवाला, विषयासक्त।

93(B). 'कपड़ा' का पर्याय 'वसन' है।
'कपड़ा' के अन्य पर्यायवाची शब्द 'वस्त्र, अंबर, पट, चीर, अंशुष्क, आच्छादन, चैल' आदि हैं।
अन्य विकल्प:
- 'चलन' के पर्यायवाची- अनिल, समीर, वायु पवन, पवमान, प्रभंजन, मातरिश्वा, मारुत, वात।
- 'गगन' के पर्यायवाची- अंतरिक्ष, अंबर, अधर, अभ्र, अर्श, आसमान, उर्ध्वलोक, आकाश, गगनमंडल।
- 'जंगल' के पर्यायवाची- अरण्य, विपिन, कांतार, वन, बीहड़, गहन, कानन, विटप।

94(C). 'अद्वितीय' का पर्यायवाची शब्द 'अनुपम' होता है।

इसके अन्य पर्यायवाची शब्द-बेजोड़, विचित्र, विलक्षण, अद्भुत, प्रधान, मुख्य आदि है।
अन्य विकल्प असंगत है।

95(A). 'कवयित्री' का विलोम शब्द 'कवि' है।
'कवयित्री' का अर्थ 'कविताएँ लिखने वाली महिला' होता है।
'कवि' का अर्थ 'कविताएँ लिखने वाला पुरुष' होता है।
विपरीत (उल्टा) अर्थ बताने वाले शब्दों को विलोम शब्द कहते हैं। जैसे- रात - दिन, सुख - दुःख आदि।

96(A). "मधु + आचार्य" शब्द मिलकर "मध्वाचार्य" शब्द बनाते है तथा 'मधु + आचार्य = मध्वाचार्य' में उ + आ= वा का मेल हो रहा है अत: इसमें यण संधि होगी। यण संधि स्वर संधि का एक भेद अथवा प्रकार है। जब संधि करते समय इ, ई के साथ कोई अन्य स्वर हो तो ' य ' बन जाता है, जब उ, ऊ के साथ कोई अन्य स्वर हो तो ' व् ' बन जाता है , जब ऋ के साथ कोई अन्य स्वर हो तो ' र ' बन जाता है।
जैसे:
अनु + अय = अन्वय
सु + अस्ति = स्वस्ति
सु + आगत = स्वागत

97(A). 'भव्याकृतिः' का संधि विच्छेद 'भव्या + आकृतिः' होता है। इसमें स्वर संधि है। जब दो स्वर आपस में जुड़ते हैं या दो स्वरों के मिलने से उनमें जो परिवर्तन आता है, तो वह स्वर संधि कहलाती है। जैसे :

विद्यालय : विद्या + आलय
पर्यावरण : परी + आवरण
मुनींद्र : मुनि + इंद्र

98(A). 'आ + अ = आ' दीर्घ संधि का नियम है। संधि करते समय अगर (अ, आ) के साथ (अ, आ) हो तो 'आ' बनता है, जब (इ, ई) के साथ (इ , ई) हो तो 'ई' बनता है, जब (उ, ऊ) के साथ (उ ,ऊ) हो तो 'ऊ' बनता है। जब ऐसा होता है तो हम इसे दीर्घ संधि कहते हैं। इस संधि को हृस्व संधि भी कहा जाता है।
उदाहरण:

विद्या + अभ्यास : विद्याभ्यास (आ + अ = आ)
परम + अर्थ : परमार्थ (अ + अ = आ)
कवि + ईश्वर : कवीश्वर (इ + ई = ई)

99(C). 'राजा भोज का सपना' कहानी 1905 में प्रकाशित हुई थी। इस कहानी में राजा भोज के उस सपने की चर्चा हुई है, जिसके बाद उनकी ज़िन्दगी बदल गई और उन्होंने अच्छे कार्य किए। 'राजा भोज का सपना' कहानी के कहानीकार शिवप्रसाद सितारेहिंद है। अत: सही उत्तर विकल्प (C) शिवप्रसाद सितारेहिंद है।
राजा शिवप्रसाद 'सितारेहिन्द' हिन्दी के उन्नायक एवं साहित्यकार थे। वे शिक्षा-विभाग में कार्यरत थे। राजा साहब 'आम फहम और खास पसंद' भाषा के पक्षपाती और ब्रिटिश शासन के निष्ठावान् सेवक थे। भारतेंदु हरिश्चंद्र ने इन्हें गुरु मानते हुए भी इसलिए इनका विरोध भी किया था। फिर भी इन्हीं के उद्योग से उस समय परम प्रतिकूल परिस्थितियों में भी शिक्षा विभाग में हिंदी का प्रवेश हो सका। साहित्य, व्याकरण, इतिहास, भूगोल आदि विविध विषयों पर इन्होंने प्राय: 35 पुस्तकों की रचना की जिनमें इनकी 'सवानेह उमरी' (आत्मकथा), 'राजा भोज का सपना', 'आलसियों का कोड़ा', 'भूगोल हस्तामलक' और 'इतिहासतिमिरनाशक' उल्लेख्य हैं।

100(A). मतवाला पत्रिका के संपादक ' सूर्यकांत त्रिपाठी निराला ' जी थे 1 सूर्यकांत त्रिपाठी निराला मूलत: छायावादी कवि था निराला का साहित्य ही नहीं साहित्यिक पत्रकारिता में भी महत्वपूर्ण योगदान था। पत्रिका मतवाला से उनका विशेष लगाव रहा था। 23 अगस्त, 1923 को जब मतवाला निकला, तो उसपर छपा मोटो निराला ने ही तैयार किया था।
निराला आधुनिक मार्क्सवादी या प्रगतिवादी कवि हैं। इन्हें हिंदी मुक्त छन्द का प्रवर्तक माना जाता है। निराला जी की अन्य प्रमुख कृतियाँ हैं - अनामिका, परिमल, गीतगुंज, कुकुरमुत्ता, अणिमा आदि।
दिए गए विकल्पों में से 'मतवाला' पत्रिका सूर्यकांत त्रिपाठी 'निराला' जी की है। अन्य सभी पत्रिका इनकी नहीं हैं। अतः सही विकल्प (A) मतवाला है।

General Knowledge

1. What is the name of the Arabic book by Al-Biruni?
   - (a) Kitab-ul-Hind
   - (b) Hindustan-nama
   - (c) Tarikh-e-Hindustan
   - (d) Fatawa-e-Hindustani

2. **Direction:** Consider the following statements with reference to the Vijayanagara Kingdom.
   1. The Vijayanagar rulers produced a new style of architecture called the Dravida style.
   2. In Lepakshi, near Hindupur, in present Andhra Pradesh, there are glorious examples of Vijayanagara paintings on the walls of the Shiva temple.
   3. Their capital city, Vijayanagar, stood on the north bank of river Tungabhadra.

   Which of the statements given above is/are correct?
   - (a) 1 and 2 only
   - (b) 1 and 3 only
   - (c) 2 and 3 only
   - (d) 2 only

3. **Direction:** With reference to the cultural history of India consider the following pairs.
   1. Sun Temple- Konark
   2. Dashavtara Vishnu Temple- Deogarh
   3. Vishwanatha Temple-Madurai
   4. Meenakshi Temple- Mahabalipuram

   Which of the pairs given above is/are correctly matched?
   - (a) 1 and 2 only
   - (b) 1, 2 and 4 only
   - (c) 2, 3 and 4 only
   - (d) 3 and 4 only

4. **Direction:** Consider the following statements with reference to Temple Architecture in India.
   1. Two broad orders of temples in the country are known— Nagara in the north and Dravida in the south.
   2. The second major type of architectural form in the Dravida order is the phamsana.

   Which of the statements given above is/are correct?
   - (a) 1 only
   - (b) 2 only
   - (c) Both 1 and 2
   - (d) Neither 1 nor 2

5. Which leader presided over the Calcutta Congress session in 1906?
   - (a) Bal Gangadhar Tilak
   - (b) Gopal Krishna Gokhale
   - (c) Arvind Ghosh
   - (d) Dadabhai Naoroji

6. Quit India Movement was started in-
   - (a) In 1940 AD
   - (b) In 1941 AD
   - (c) In 1942 AD
   - (d) In 1945 AD

7. Fine-grained bed of ephemeral lake in a desert is also known as:
   - (a) Playa
   - (b) Oasis
   - (c) Drumlin
   - (d) Natural levee

8. The Constitution (35 Amendment) Act of 1974 is related to which one of the following States?
   - (a) Mizoram
   - (b) Sikkim
   - (c) Nagaland
   - (d) Arunachal Pradesh

9. Which one of the following best describes the electoral system of India ?
   - (a) First-Past-the-Post System
   - (b) Proportional Representation
   - (c) Mixed System
   - (d) General Ticket

10. 'Sonzal-2022' is an annual youth festival held in which state/UT?
    - (a) Andhra Pradesh
    - (b) Himachal Pradesh
    - (c) Jammu and Kashmir
    - (d) Uttarakhand

11. 'Omorgus Khandesh' is a newly found species of which insect?
    - (a) Bees
    - (b) Beetle
    - (c) Ladybugs
    - (d) Ants

12. Union Minister Anurag Thakur inaugurated India's first Drone Skill Training Conference in which city in December 2022?
    - (a) Patna
    - (b) Chennai
    - (c) Kolkata
    - (d) Bengaluru

13. Which portal has been launched by the Central Government for claim disbursement through National Crop Insurance Portal (NCIP)?
    - (a) Saras Portal
    - (b) USOF Portal
    - (c) MTCTE Portal
    - (d) Digiclaim Portal

14. What is the colour of the precipitate obtained by passing CO_2 gas through lime water?
    - (a) Green
    - (b) Blue
    - (c) White
    - (d) Brown

15. Which one of the following pairs of elements is liquid at room temperature and at normal pressure?
    - (a) Gallium and Bromine
    - (b) Mercury and Bromine
    - (c) Gallium and Mercury
    - (d) Gallium and Caesium

16. Animals that feed on other dead animals are called:
    - (a) parasites
    - (b) decomposers
    - (c) scavengers
    - (d) omnivores

17. Who among the following elects the Rajya Sabha Members?
    - (a) Voters in Assembly Constituencies
    - (b) Voters in Parliamentary Constituencies
    - (c) Lok Sabha Members
    - (d) Members of Legislative Assemblies (MLAs)

18. Which of the following systems of government was adopted by India?
    - (a) Parliamentary and Unitary
    - (b) Presidential and Federal
    - (c) Presidential and Unitary
    - (d) Parliamentary and Federal

19. Which one of the following Fundamental Rights is violated due to practice of untouchability in India?
    - (a) Right to Equality
    - (b) Right to Freedom
    - (c) Right against Exploitation
    - (d) Right to Constitutional Remedies

20. NIDHI is an umbrella scheme for the promotion of:

(a) young and aspiring innovators
(b) scientific research
(c) primary health care
(d) primary education in rural areas

21. The capital adequacy standard for commercial banks by the Government of India is:
(a) 5%
(b) 6%T
(c) 7%
(d) 8%

22. The control of interest of banks is based on the recommendation of _______.
(a) Chelliah Committee
(b) Dantawalla committee
(c) Narsimha Committee
(d) None of these

23. _______ country will host the 2026 Asian Games.
(a) Japan
(b) Malaysia
(c) Singapore
(d) Vietnam

24. Which of the following correctly describes the term 'homemade leverage'?
(a) It refers to overnight borrowing a substantial amount of cash for intraday stock trading.
(b) It refers to the practice of printing currency in order to insulate the economy from black swan events.
(c) It refers to the unfair trade advantage reaped by an economy by devaluating its own currency.
(d) It is the use of personal borrowing by investors to change the amount of financial leverage of the firm.

25. What is the importance of using Pneumococcal Conjugate Vaccines in India?
1. These vaccines are effective against pneumonia as well as meningitis and sepsis.
2. Dependence on antibiotics that are not effective against drug-resistant bacteria can be reduced.
3. These vaccines have no side effects and cause no allergic reactions.
Select the correct answer using the code given below:
(a) 1 only
(b) 1 and 2 only
(c) 3 only
(d) 1, 2 and 3

Mathematics

26. The value of $\left(\frac{-1}{729}\right)^{-\frac{1}{2}}$ is:
(a) $\frac{1}{81}$
(b) -81
(c) $-\frac{1}{81}$
(d) 81

27. A person has planned to sell his old laptop for Rs. 4500 , he would lose 10% . To gain 20% of profit, he should sell it for:
(a) Rs. 6000
(b) Rs. 7000
(c) Rs. 7200
(d) Rs. 8500

28. A man bought 50 cricket balls each at the price of Rs. 50 each. After some days he sold 40 of them at Rs. 55 each and remaining 10 at Rs. 40 each. Calculate his gain or loss percentage.
(a) Loss, 4%
(b) Gain, 5%

(c) Loss, 6%
(d) Gain, 4%

29. The simple interest on a certain sum of money invested at a certain rate for 2 years is Rs 1200 . The compound interest of the same sum of money invested at the same rate of interest for 2 years is Rs 1290 . What was the principal?
(a) Rs. 12000
(b) Rs. 16000
(c) Rs. 6000
(d) Rs. 4000

30. A certain sum of money fetched an interest of Rs. 1800 at 15% per annum simple interest for 2 years. Find the sum.
(a) Rs. 5000
(b) Rs. 4000
(c) Rs. 8000
(d) Rs. 6000

31. A hollow sphere of internal and external diameters 4 cm and 8 cm, respectively is melted into a solid cone of base diameter 8 cm. The height of the cone is:
(a) 11 cm
(b) 12 cm
(c) 14 cm
(d) 16 cm

32. How many bullets can be made out of a lead circular cylinder 28 cm high and 6 cm radius, each bullet being 1.5 cm in diameter?
(a) 1279
(b) 1792
(c) 2179
(d) 2772

33. If (the product of the common positive factors of 36 and 48) =999 + 9 × _______, then the number which will come in the blank space is:
(a) 90
(b) 9
(c) 27
(d) 81

34. The average weight of 8 gold coins is 20 g per coin. The average weight of 12 silver coins is 35 g per coin. What is the average weight per coin for 20 coins?
(a) 25 g
(b) 29 g
(c) 21 g
(d) 31 g

35. The average weight of 3 persons of group A is 60 kg, the average weight of 2 other persons of Group B is 70 kg, then find out the average weight of all persons.
(a) 40 kg
(b) 54 kg
(c) 64 kg
(d) 70 kg

36. The population of a particular city is 5,00,000. If the annual birth rate is 5% and the annual death rate is 1%, then what will be the population of the city after 3 years?
(a) 5,95,502
(b) 5,62,432
(c) 4,44,498
(d) 4,42,368

37. Two teachers A and B can complete an academic work in 10 days and 15 days respectively. They started the work together, but A left after 5 days and another teacher C joined, who alone can complete the work in 60 days. In how many days the work got completed?
(a) 7
(b) 5
(c) 6
(d) 2

38. A and B can do a job together in 7 days. A is $1\frac{3}{4}$ times as efficient as B . The same job can be done by A alone in :
(a) $9\frac{1}{3}$ days
(b) $\frac{1}{11}$ days
(c) $12\frac{1}{4}$ days
(d) $16\frac{1}{3}$ days

39. A is thrice as good a workman as B and is, therefore, able to finish a piece of work in 60 days less than B. The time (in days) in which they can do it working together is:

(a) 22   (b) $22\frac{1}{2}$

(c) 23   (d) $23\frac{1}{4}$

40. A person travelled 132 km by auto, 852 km by train and 248 km by bike. It took 21 hours in all. If the speed of train is 6 times the speed of auto and 1.5 times speed of bike, what is the speed of train?

(a) $78\,\text{kmh}^{-1}$ (b) $104\,\text{kmh}^{-1}$

(c) $96\,\text{kmh}^{-1}$ (d) $88\,\text{kmh}^{-1}$

41. The speed of a boat in still water is 9km/hr. It covers a distance of 42 km upstream in 6 hours. What is the speed (in km/hr) of the stream?

(a) 1.2   (b) 1.5

(c) 1.6   (d) 2

42. Given HCF of $(16, 100) = 4$, what is the LCM of $(16, 100)$?

(a) 400   (b) 398

(c) 440   (d) 300

43. Raj is currently 12 years older than Ravi after 8 years the ratio of their age will be 15: 12. How old is Raj's age at present?

(a) 42   (b) 49

(c) 56   (d) 52

44. The following Venn diagram represents which of the given options?

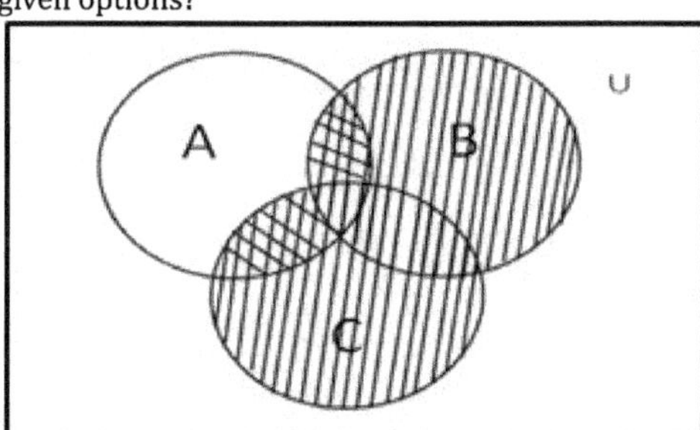

(a) $A \cup (B \cap C)$ (b) $A \cap (B \cup C)$

(c) $(A \cap B) \cup C$ (d) $(A \cup B) \cap C$

45. A triangle with vertices (4, 0), (-1, -1) and (3, 5) is:

(a) isosceles and right-angled

(b) isosceles but not right-angled

(c) right-angled but not isosceles

(d) neither right-angled nor isosceles

46. If $\sin\theta\cos\theta = k$, where $0 \leq \theta \leq \frac{\pi}{2}$, then which one of the following is correct?

(a) $0 \leq k \leq 1$ (b) $0 \leq k \leq 0.5$ only

(c) $0.5 \leq k \leq 1$ only   (d) $0 < k < 1$

47. The sum of deviations of n number of observations measured from 2.5 is 50. The sum of deviations of the same set of observations measured from 3.5 is -50. What is the value of n?

(a) 50   (b) 60

(c) 80   (d) 100

48. How many different 4 – letter words can be formed with the letter of the word 'MUNCH' when U & N are always to be included?

(a) 72   (b) 62

(c) 12   (d) 42

Ques (49-50): Direction: Study the following pie chart carefully and answer the question given beside.

The following pie chart gives the information about the percentage distribution of the JIO users in five different states out of 6 crores users in these states.

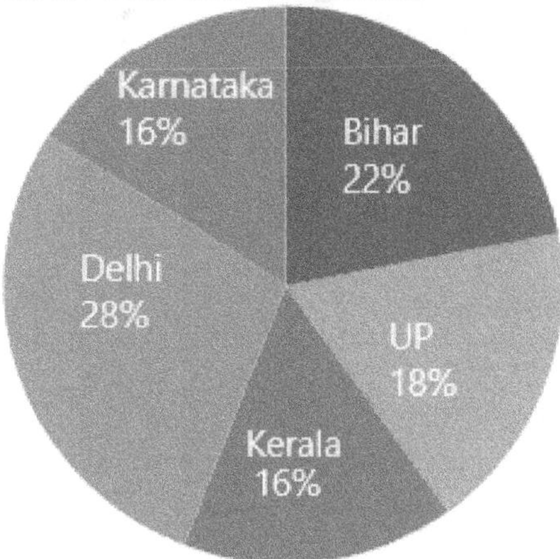

49. If the total number of Airtel users in Bihar is 2500000 less than the total number of JIO users in that state then what is the total number of Airtel users in Bihar?

(a) 10700000   (b) 13200000

(c) 11200000   (d) 11500000

50. If the total number of Idea users in Delhi is 15% of the sum of the total number of Idea users in these five states then the total number of JIO users in Delhi is what percent more than the total number of Idea users in Delhi? (It is given that the sum of the total number of Idea users in these five states is 2.5 crores)

(a) 358%   (b) 368%

(c) 348%   (d) 338%

Reasoning

51. Direction: In the following question find out the alternative which will replace the question mark (?).

MKJ : LHE :: TPL : ?

(a) QJF   (b) RNH

(c) SMG   (d) VKE

52. Direction : Select the option that is related to the third letter-cluster in the same way as the second letter-cluster is related to the first letter-cluster.

PRISM : NTJSQ :: CLAPS : ?

(a) TQBMD   (b) TOBKD

(c) TOBKD   (d) DNBRT

53. Pointing to a boy, a lady said, "He is the son of my grandmother's only child's husband's only daughter's brother." How is the boy related to the lady?

(a) Nephew   (b) Son

(c) Brother   (d) Grandson

54. Read the information carefully and answer the following question.

A + B means A is the father of B

A - B means A is the mother of B

A ★ B means A is the sister of B
A / B means A is the brother of B
In the given expression M/N*O+P , how is N related to P?

(a) Maternal Uncle   (b) Paternal Uncle
(c) Maternal Aunt   (d) Paternal Aunt

55. Direction: Select the odd figure out of the given series of figures.

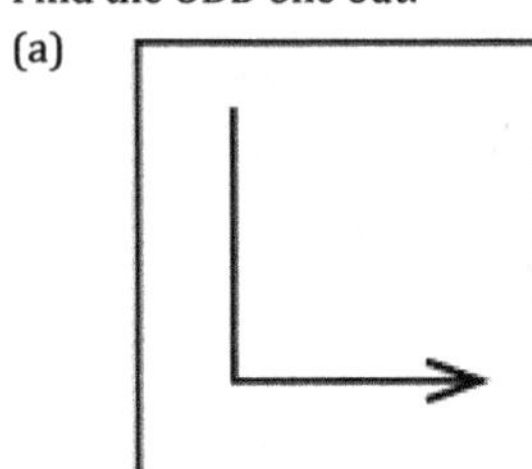

(A)   (B)   (C)   (D)

(a) (A)   (b) (B)
(c) (C)   (d) (D)

56. Find the ODD one out:

(a)
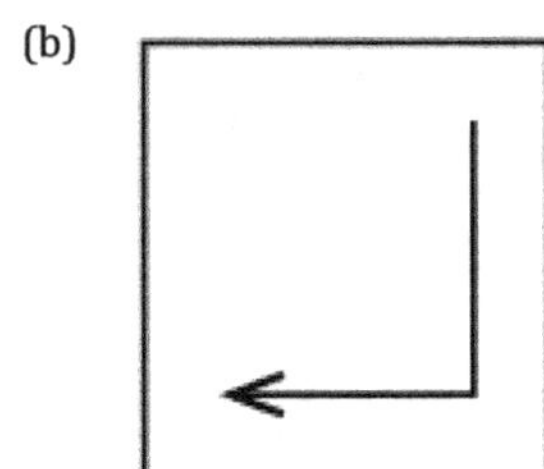

(b)
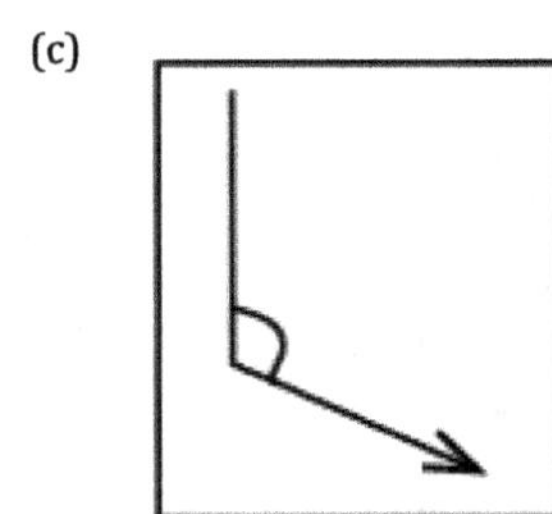

(c)
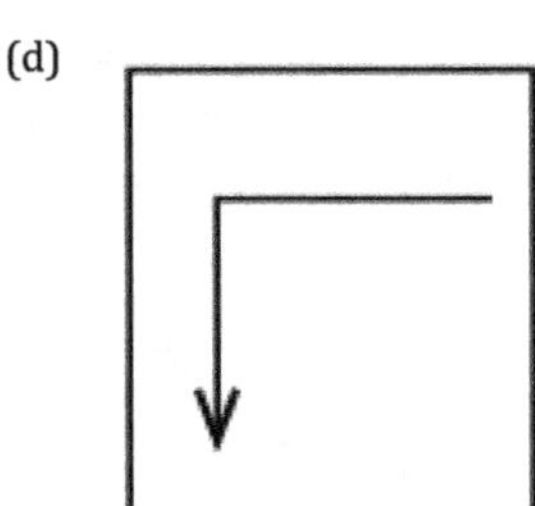

(d)

57. Find the odd one out.

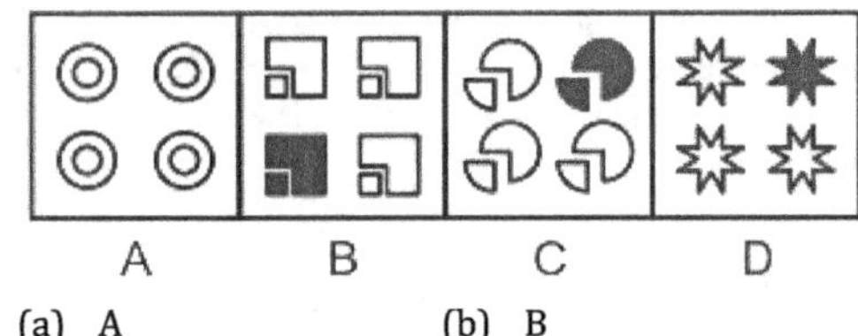

A   B   C   D

(a) A   (b) B
(c) C   (d) D

58. Sudha travels 8 km to the South. Then she turns to the right and walks 4 km. Then again she turns to her right and moves 8 km forward. How many km away is she from the starting point?

(a) 7   (b) 6
(c) 4   (d) 8

59. Y is to the East of X, which is to the North of Z, if P is to the South of Z, then P is in which direction with respect to Y?

(a) North   (b) South
(c) South-East   (d) None of these

60. In the following question, select the related letters from the given alternatives.

W × J : 5 x 1 : : M × V : ?

(a) 4 × 1   (b) 4 × 3
(c) 4 × 4   (d) 5 × 2

61. In a certain code language, ' *PLAN* ' is written as ' *KOZM* '. How will ' *FLICK* ' be written in that language?

(a) *UORXP*   (b) *UQRXR*
(c) *UOZXP*   (d) *WNRXP*

62. Which of the answer figure will complete the figural series given in the problem figures?

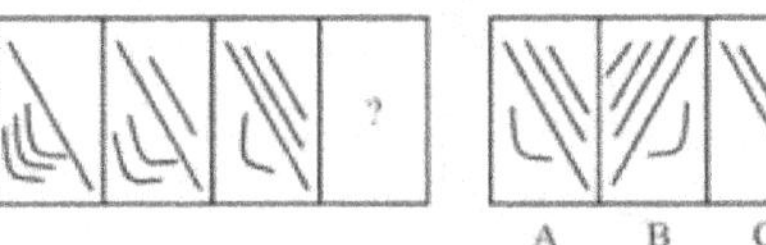

Problem Figure   Answer Figure

A   B   C   D

(a) A   (b) B
(c) C   (d) D

63. Which of the answer figures will complete the figural series given in the problem figures?

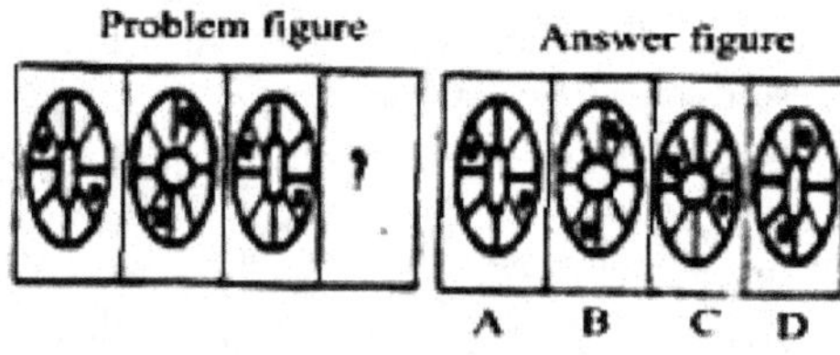

Problem figure   Answer figure

A   B   C   D

(a) A   (b) B
(c) C   (d) D

Ques (64-65): Direction: Identify the diagram that best represents the relationship among classes given below:

64. Doctors, Lawyers, and Professionals

(a)

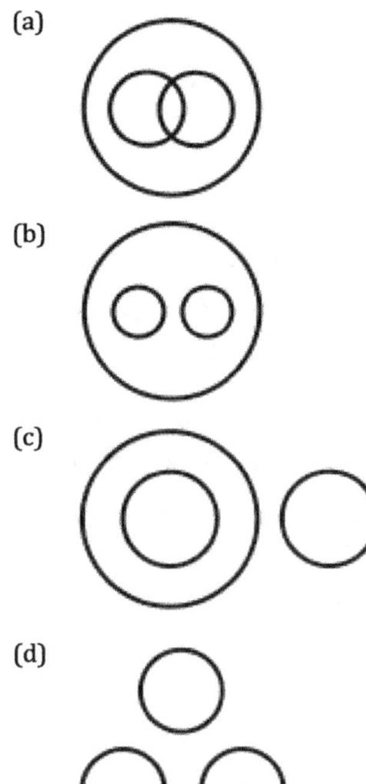

(b)

(c)

(d)

65. Words, Synonyms, Antonymous

(a)

(b)

(c)

(d)

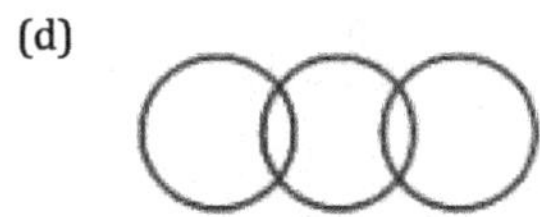

66. Direction: What will come in place of question mark in the following series.

4096, 1024, 256, ? 16, 4

(a) 64   (b) 48
(c) 40   (d) 60

67. Direction: What will come in place of the question mark (?) in the following number series ?

435, 354, 282, 219, 165, (?)

(a) 103   (b) 112
(c) 120   (d) 130

68. In a row of students, Ramesh is ninth from the left and Suman is sixth from the right. When Ramesh and Suman interchange their places, Ramesh becomes fifteenth from the left. Tell what will be the position of

Suman from the right after the interchange?

(a) 6th   (b) 13th
(c) 14th   (d) 15th

69. E is older than C. D is older than C but younger than E. A is younger than B and C. C is older than B. Who is the youngest?

(a) C   (b) D
(c) B   (d) A

Ques (70-71): Direction: In the following question below some statements are given followed by some conclusions. Taking the given statements to be true even if they seem to be at variance from commonly known facts, read all the conclusions and then decide which of the given conclusions logically follows the given statements.

70. Statements:
1. Some flowers are white.
2. Some white are round.
Conclusions:
I. Some flowers are round.
II. Every round is either white or a flower.

(a) Only conclusion II follows
(b) Both conclusions I and II follows
(c) Only conclusion I follows
(d) Neither conclusion I nor II follows

71. Statements:
Some Poets are poems.
No poem is the song.
Conclusions:
I. Some Poems are not songs.
II. Some songs are poems.

(a) Only Conclusion I follows
(b) Only Conclusion II follows
(c) Either Conclusion I or II follows
(d) Neither Conclusion I nor II follows

72. Select the option which is different from the others.

(a) 12 - 24 - 48   (b) 36 - 72 - 144
(c) 25 - 50 - 115   (d) 53 - 106 - 212

73. Select the word which is different from the others.

(a) Dining table   (b) Wardrobe
(c) Refrigerator   (d) Sofa

Ques (74-75): Direction: Study the given question carefully and answer the question.

Nine friends Ram, Rahul, Sagar, Rajesh, Anurag, Amit, Vinit, Sanket, and Shekhar are sitting in a row and all of them are facing North. Each of them likes different colour viz. Red, Orange, Green, Violet, Black, Blue, Purple, Yellow and Indigo but not necessarily in the same order.

Shekhar who likes the Blue colour is not sitting at any of the extreme ends. Ram and Sagar are sitting together. Sanket sits to the immediate left of Vinit who neither likes Yellow nor Indigo colour. The person who likes the Black colour sits second to the right of a person who likes Indigo colour. Only two persons are sitting between Rahul and Rajesh, who is sitting at the extreme end. The person who likes the Green colour sits at one of the places to the right of the person who likes the Indigo colour. Only one person is sitting between the person who likes Violet and the Green colour. The person who likes the Purple colour is sitting at one of the extreme ends, but he is not a neighbour of the person who likes the Blue colour. Rahul, who likes the Black colour sits second to the left of Shekhar. Amit who likes the Orange colour is a neighbour of both Ram and Rahul.

74. Who is sitting immediate left of Amit?

(a) Ram	(b) Rahul
(c) Sagar	(d) Shekhar

75. Who likes Red colour?
- (a) Ram
- (b) Anurag
- (c) Amit
- (d) Vinit

General Hindi

76. वर्तनी के अनुसार शुद्ध शब्द का चयन कीजिए।
- (a) निवृत्ति
- (b) निवृती
- (c) निर्बृत्ति
- (d) निर्वृत्ति

77. अशुद्ध वर्तनी वाले शब्द का चयन कीजिए।
- (a) अन्दर
- (b) उधृत
- (c) नैतिक
- (d) मार्गदर्शन

78. "खटाई में पड़ना" मुहावरे का आशय है।
- (a) बहुत कष्ट होना
- (b) नुकसान होना
- (c) पछतावा होना
- (d) निर्णय न होना

79. 'नौ दिन चले अढ़ाई कोस' लोकोक्ति का भावार्थ है:
- (a) काम करने की बहुत धीमी गति
- (b) पैदल चलने की आदत होनी चाहिए चाहे बहुत धीरे-धीरे ही चलें
- (c) व्यक्ति कौ नौ दिन तक प्रतिदिन अढ़ाई कोस पैदल चलना चाहिए
- (d) पैदल चलने में बहुत समय लगता है, इसलिए पैदल न चलें, समय की बचत करें

80. विकल्प में दी गई लोकोक्तियों में सही लोकोक्ति का चयन कीजिए।
- (a) अधजल लोटा छलकत जाए
- (b) अपनी अपनी ढपली सबका राग
- (c) अंधों में काना राजा
- (d) अपना हाथ हरि

81. निम्न में कौन सा शब्द पुल्लिंग है?
- (a) दया
- (b) माया
- (c) भाषा
- (d) आभार

82. निम्न में कौन सा शब्द पुल्लिंग है?
- (a) आशा
- (b) कष्ट
- (c) क्षमा
- (d) सेना

83. नीचे लिखे वाक्य के लिए एक शब्द बताइए:
जो युद्ध में स्थिर रहता है
- (a) यशस्वी
- (b) सत्याग्रही
- (c) युधिष्ठिर
- (d) अश्वारोह

84. शैव कहते है:
- (a) जो शक्ति की उपासना करता है
- (b) जो शिव की उपासना करता है
- (c) जो विष्णु की उपासना करता है
- (d) जो किसी की उपासना नहीं करता है।

85. नीचे दिए गये विकल्पों में से तत्सम - तद्भव शब्दो का कौन सा युग्म सही सुमेलित नहीं है?
- (a) आम्र - आम
- (b) अंगरखा - अंगरक्षक
- (c) अक्षोट - अखरोट
- (d) अर्द्ध - अंधा

86. नीचे दिए गये विकल्पों में निजवाचक सर्वनाम की पहचान करें:
- (a) आप
- (b) स्वयं
- (c) अपना
- (d) उपरोक्त सभी

87. नीचे दिए गये विकल्पों में से तत्सम - तद्भव शब्दो का कौन सा युग्म सही सुमेलित नहीं है?
- (a) धृष्ट - ढीठ
- (b) धूम्र - धुआँ
- (c) प्रहेलिका - फूल
- (d) प्रतिवेशिक - पड़ोसी

88. हिन्दी में कितने वचन होते हैं?
- (a) दो
- (b) तीन
- (c) चार
- (d) पाँच

89. एकारांत संज्ञा शब्द को बहुवचन बनाते समय क्या किया जाता है?
- (a) अंतिम स्वर के बाद 'याँ' लगा देते हैं ।
- (b) अंतिम स्वर को हटा कर 'याँ' लगा देते हैं ।
- (c) 'ई' को ह्रस्व करके अंतिम स्वर के बाद 'याँ' लगा देते हैं ।
- (d) 'ई' को ह्रस्व करके अंतिम स्वर के बाद 'ओं' लगा देते हैं ।

90. निम्नलिखित प्रत्येक प्रश्न में तीन गद्यांश दिये गये हैं। त्रुटि वाले वाक्यांश को चुनें और उसके अनुरूप (A), (B), (C) पर चिन्ह लगाएँ। यदि वाक्य त्रुटिहीन हो, तो (D) पर चिन्ह लगाएँ:
- (a) पल्स-पोलियो से बचाव के लिए
- (b) सबसे सरलतम उपाय
- (c) शिशुओं को निरोधक खुराक देना है
- (d) कोई त्रुटि नहीं

91. निम्नलिखित प्रत्येक प्रश्न में तीन गद्यांश दिये गये हैं। त्रुटि वाले वाक्यांश को चुनें और उसके अनुरूप (A), (B), (C) पर चिन्ह लगाएँ। यदि वाक्य त्रुटिहीन हो, तो (D) पर चिन्ह लगाएँ।
- (a) महामहिम राष्ट्रपति
- (b) हमारे संस्थान में स्वर्ण जयंती समारोह का
- (c) उद्घाटन करेगा
- (d) कोई त्रुटि नहीं

92. 'आविर्भाव' का विलोम शब्द है-
- (a) तिरोभाव
- (b) विरक्ति
- (c) अंत
- (d) अधोगति

93. किस विकल्प में सही विलोम-युग्म नहीं है?
- (a) अमावस्या-पूर्णिमा
- (b) आचार-अनाचार
- (c) गुप्त-मुक्त
- (d) कुटिल-सरल

94. 'कोप' का विलोम शब्द है-
- (a) कृपा
- (b) असंतुष्ट
- (c) खेद
- (d) इनमें से कोई नहीं

95. 'वनिता' शब्द का पर्यायवाची शब्द है-
- (a) महिला
- (b) शफरी
- (c) विधु
- (d) जानकी

96. 'देशांतर' का संधि विच्छेद बताइये।
- (a) दशा + अंतर
- (b) दिश + अंतर
- (c) दिशा + अंतर
- (d) दश + अंतर

97. 'स्वध् + आ' ____ संधि का उदाहरण है।
- (a) स्वर संधि
- (b) विसर्ग संधि
- (c) व्यंजन संधि
- (d) अयादि संधि

98. 'लाकृति' का संधि विच्छेद होगा:
- (a) लृ + आकृति
- (b) ला + आकृति
- (c) ल + आकृति
- (d) इनमे से कोई नहीं

99. 'रामचरितमानस' किसकी रचना है?
- (a) तुलसीदास
- (b) जायसी
- (c) कबीर
- (d) सूरदास

100. निम्नलिखित में से 'शैलेश मटियानी' की रचना नहीं है:

(a) आकाश कितना अनन्त है
(b) सर्पगन्धा
(c) बावन नदियों का संगम
(d) एक सड़क सत्तावन गलियाँ

// Smart Answer Sheet //

Correct — Percentage of students who answered correctly.

Skipped — Percentage of students who skipped.

Q.	Ans.	Correct / Skipped	Q.	Ans.	Correct / Skipped	Q.	Ans.	Correct / Skipped
1	A	82.64% / 0.0%	2	A	66.97% / 1.81%	3	A	20.26% / 4.6%
4	A	63.75% / 1.89%	5	D	78.29% / 0.0%	6	C	81.57% / 0.0%
7	A	47.43% / 1.33%	8	B	48.71% / 1.69%	9	A	42.68% / 1.31%
10	C	89.0% / 0.0%	11	B	57.32% / 1.68%	12	B	50.11% / 1.35%
13	D	86.96% / 0.0%	14	C	59.94% / 1.62%	15	B	14.42% / 4.84%
16	C	53.78% / 1.75%	17	D	54.62% / 1.72%	18	D	56.61% / 1.1%
19	A	79.75% / 0.0%	20	A	40.08% / 1.29%	21	D	58.24% / 1.75%
22	C	62.86% / 1.25%	23	A	88.61% / 0.0%	24	D	63.84% / 1.6%
25	B	63.5% / 1.83%	26	D	81.31% / 0.0%	27	A	40.35% / 1.15%
28	D	59.79% / 1.63%	29	D	56.17% / 1.31%	30	D	58.46% / 1.15%
31	C	46.74% / 1.53%	32	B	54.97% / 1.98%	33	D	47.3% / 1.54%
34	B	56.77% / 1.54%	35	C	86.39% / 0.0%	36	B	77.39% / 0.0%
37	A	14.17% / 4.67%	38	B	62.82% / 1.22%	39	B	47.42% / 1.21%
40	C	17.39% / 3.86%	41	D	29.94% / 4.63%	42	D	44.64% / 1.54%
43	D	49.92% / 1.61%	44	B	83.41% / 0.0%	45	A	51.23% / 1.72%
46	B	89.87% / 0.0%	47	D	56.19% / 1.14%	48	A	88.82% / 0.0%
49	A	47.88% / 1.12%	50	C	80.83% / 0.0%	51	C	68.31% / 1.09%
52	A	69.64% / 1.54%	53	A	62.11% / 1.73%	54	D	67.61% / 1.17%
55	D	65.42% / 1.37%	56	C	50.2% / 1.66%	57	A	50.98% / 1.38%
58	C	80.23% / 0.0%	59	D	56.61% / 1.78%	60	C	14.47% / 3.09%
61	A	23.74% / 3.24%	62	C	46.1% / 1.14%	63	B	49.44% / 1.24%
64	B	65.75% / 1.06%	65	B	62.85% / 1.59%	66	A	17.79% / 4.45%
67	C	17.51% / 4.09%	68	A	31.98% / 4.44%	69	D	48.53% / 1.4%
70	D	52.5% / 1.53%	71	B	81.86% / 0.0%	72	C	54.71% / 1.1%
73	C	44.04% / 1.46%	74	A	69.49% / 1.58%	75	D	61.42% / 1.38%
76	A	52.05% / 1.13%	77	B	66.9% / 1.9%	78	D	83.29% / 0.0%
79	A	55.03% / 1.36%	80	C	51.78% / 1.51%	81	D	67.24% / 1.22%
82	B	84.14% / 0.0%	83	C	80.16% / 0.0%	84	B	42.98% / 1.09%
85	D	54.31% / 1.77%	86	D	41.52% / 1.94%	87	C	48.06% / 1.13%
88	A	86.27% / 0.0%	89	C	84.65% / 0.0%	90	B	40.6% / 2.0%
91	C	42.71% / 1.22%	92	A	69.8% / 1.63%	93	C	78.23% / 0.0%
94	A	89.25% / 0.0%	95	A	52.02% / 1.35%	96	C	67.72% / 1.45%
97	B	54.92% / 1.32%	98	A	84.25% / 0.0%	99	A	84.34% / 0.0%
100	D	57.71% / 1.79%						

// Hints and Solutions //

1(A). The correct answer is Kitab-ul-Hind.
- Al-Biruni was an Iranian scholar.
  - He is considered the father of modern geodesy.
  - Al-Biruni is a traveler who called Kerala as Malabar.
  - Kitab-ul-Hind is the Arabic book authored by Al-Biruni.
  - Kitab al-Tafhim is the book authored by Al-Biruni in both Persian and Arabic languages.
  - He traveled to the Indian subcontinent in 1017.
  - Tārīkh al-Hind (History of India) is a book authored by Al-Biruni based on his study of Indian culture.
  - His birthday was celebrated as the day of the surveying engineer in Iran.
- Notable work of Al-Biruni are:
  - The Remaining Signs of Past Centuries.
  - Gems.
  - The Mas'udi Canon.
  - Understanding Astrology.
- Tarikh-e-Hindustan is the book authored by Molvi Mohammad Zaka Ulla.

2(A). The Vijayanagar rulers were great builders. During this period, palaces, temples, huge halls (mahamantapa), forts, towers, public buildings, dams, tanks and canals were constructed.
The Vijayanagar rulers produced a new style of architecture called a Dravida style.
Paintings at the Virabhadra temple and Lepakshi temple show the excellence of Vijayanagar painters.
In Lepakshi, near Hindupur, in present Andhra Pradesh, there are glorious examples of Vijayanagara paintings on the walls of the Shiva temple.

3(A). Konark Sun Temple is situated in Konark, a town in the district of Puri in Odisha.
The Dashavatara Temple is an early 6th century Vishnu Hindu temple located at Deogarh, Uttar Pradesh which is 125 kilometers from Jhansi, in the Betwa River valley in northern-central India.
Meenakshi Amman Temple, also known as Minakshi-Sundareshwara Temple, is one of the oldest and most important temples in India. Located in the city of Madurai, the temple has a great mythological and historical significance.
The Vishvanatha Temple is a Hindu temple in Madhya Pradesh, India. It is located among the western group of Khajuraho Monuments, a UNESCO World Heritage site.

4(A). By evolving the Nagara and the Dravida styles, the Gupta art ushers in a formative and creative age in the history of Indian architecture with considerable scope for future development.
Two broad orders of temples in the country are known— Nagara in the north and Dravida in the

south.

5(D). Dadabhai Naoroji presided over the Calcutta Congress session in 1906 .During the Calcutta session of 1906,there was a possibility of division in the Congress on the question of the president.

6(C). Quit India Movement was started in August, 1942. Gandhiji had given the slogan 'Do or Die' in this.

7(A). Fine-grained bed of ephemeral lake in a desert is also known as Playa. It occupies the flat central basins of desert plains.

8(B). The status of Sikkim as a protectorate state was terminated and Sikkim was given the status of 'Associate State' of India. The state of Sikkim was given an associate status in the Indian Constitution in the year 1974.

9(A). In India, all key representatives except the President, Vice President, Members of Rajya Sabha, and Members of the state legislative council are elected via the first-past-the-post (FPTP) system. It is the main electoral system of India.

10(C). Jammu and Kashmir Lieutenant Governor Manoj Sinha inaugurated the annual youth festival 'Sonzal-2022' on November 23, 2022 at the University of Kashmir.
The festival is an opportunity for young artists to showcase their talents and 'Sonzal' provides them with a platform to achieve the dream of 'Ek Bharat, Shreshta Bharat'.

11(B). A new beetle species 'Omorgus Khandesh' was found in western ghats in India, according to a paper published in the New Zealand-based journal Zootaxa in February 2023. The beetle is important for forensic science as it helps detect the time of death of an animal or human.

12(B). Union Minister Anurag Thakur inaugurated India's first Drone Skill Training Conference in Chennai on 06 December 2022. He also launched 1000 planned Drone Centre of Excellence at Garuda Aerospace's Manufacturing unit in Chennai, and also flagged off Garuda Aerospace's Drone Yatra, 'Operation 777'. Operation 777 is meant to demonstrate the efficacy of drones across 777 districts in India.

13(D). Union Minister of Agriculture & Farmers Welfare, Shri Narendra Singh Tomar launched National Crop Insurance Portal's digitized claim settlement module namely DigiClaim under the ambit of Pradhan Mantri Fasal Bima Yojana (PMFBY).

14(C). When carbon dioxide gas is passed through or over limewater, it turns milky due to the formation of calcium carbonate.

15(B). Bromine and mercury are the two elements that remain liquid at room temperature and standard pressure.

16(C). A scavenger is an organism that mostly consumes dead and decaying biomass, such as meat or rotting plant. Vultures are scavengers that feed on carrion (dead animals).

17(D). Election of Rajya Sabha Members:
- The Single Transferable Vote system (STV), the third variant of PR, is followed for Rajya Sabha elections.
- Under the system, every State has a specific quota of seats in the Rajya Sabha.
- The members of the Rajya Sabha are elected by the respective members of State legislative assemblies.
- This means the voters are the Members of Legislative Assemblies(MLAs) in that State.
- Every MLA is required to rank candidates according to his or her preference and a candidate must secure a minimum quota of votes to be declared the winner.

18(D). The parliamentary system of government is a form of government in which the power to make and execute laws is held by the Parliament. In India, the parliamentary form of government exists both at the Centre and in the States. The President of India is only a constitutional head. The real powers are enjoyed by the Prime Minister who is aided by the Council of Ministers.
The Constitution provides for a Parliamentary form of government which is federal in structure with certain unitary features. The constitutional head of the Executive of the Union is the President.

19(A). Right to equality (Articles 14-18):
1. Equality before the law and equal protection of laws (Article 14).
2. Prohibition of discrimination on grounds of religion, race, caste, sex or place of birth (Article 15).
3. Equality of opportunity in matters of public employment (Article 16).
4. Abolition of untouchability and prohibition of its practice (Article 17).
5. Abolition of titles except military and academic (Article 18).
Thus, Right to equality is violated due to practice of untouchability in India.

20(A). The correct answer is young and aspiring innovators.
Department of Science and Technology (DST) has announced National Initiative for Developing and Harnessing Innovations (NIDHI) is an umbrella program for nurturing ideas and innovations (knowledge-based and technology-driven) into successful startups.

21(D). In April 1992, Reserve Bank fixed 8% capital adequacy norm and directed all the banks to complete it in three years.

22(C). The control of interest of banks is based on the recommendation of Narsimha Committee, with the aim to examine all aspects of the financial system's structure, system, functions, etc.

23(A). Japan will host the 2026 Asian Games.
- The games will be held in Japan's Aichi prefecture and its capital city Nagoya. J
- apan has hosted the Asian Games twice before, at Tokyo in 1958 and Hiroshima in 1994.
- Asian Games 2018 have already been awarded to the Indonesian cities of Jakarta and Palemban, the 2022 edition will be held in the Chinese city of Hangzhou.
- The Asian Games also known as Asiad, are held every 4 years.

24(D). Homemade leverage is used by an individual investor to artificially adjust the leverage of a company. An individual investing in a company with no leverage can recreate the effect of leverage using homemade leverage, which includes taking out personal loans on the investment. However, differences in the tax rate between the corporation and the individual will likely disrupt the ability of the investor to construct the leveraging scenario accurately.

25(B). Pneumococcal disease
- It is caused by bacteria which can lead to infections in the lungs, blood, and brain.
- It causes health problems in children younger than 5 years of age.
- The greatest risk for infection is for children younger than 2, adults over 65, people with certain medical conditions, and cigarette smokers.
- These diseases also include pneumonia, meningitis, sepsis, blood infections, and ear infections.

26(D). Given:
$$\left(-\frac{1}{729}\right)^{-\frac{2}{3}}$$
$$= (-729)^{\frac{2}{3}}$$
$$= (-9)^{3 \times \frac{2}{3}}$$
$$= (-9)^2$$
$$= 81$$

27(A). Given:
A person has planned to sell his old laptop for Rs. 4500, he would lose 10%.
Formula Used:
Selling price = Cost price - loss% of cost price
Selling price of laptop $= 4500$
Loss percent $= 10\%$
$\Rightarrow 4500 =$ cost price -10% of cost price
$\Rightarrow 4500 = 90\%$ of cost price
Cost price $=$ Rs. 5000
Now according to question he need 20% profit
So new selling price $=$ cost price $+20\%$ of cost price
$= 5000 + 20\%$ of 5000
$= 5000 + 1000$
$=$ Rs. 6000
$\therefore$ He will sell at Rs. 6000 to gain 20% on cost price.

28(D). Given:
Cost Price (C.P.) of 50 balls $= 50 \times 50 =$ Rs. 2500
Selling Price (S.P.) of 50 balls $= 40 \times 55 + 10 \times 40 = 2200 + 400 =$ Rs. 2600
So, we are having gain and it is equal to $2600 - 2500 =$ Rs. 100
$\text{Gain}\% = \frac{gain}{C.P.} \times 100$
$\text{Gain }\% = \frac{100}{2500} \times 100 = 4\%$

29(D). Let, the principal $=$ Rs. $100x$ and rate of interest $= r\%$
Simple interest for 2 years $=$ Rs. 1200
$\therefore$ Simple interest for 1 year $=$ Rs. $\frac{1200}{2} =$ Rs. 600
$\therefore$ Compound interest for 1st year $=$ Rs. 600
$\therefore$ Compound interest for 2nd year $=$ Rs. $(1290 - 600) =$ Rs. 690
$\therefore$ Difference between compound and simple interest for 2nd year $=$ Rs. $(690 - 600) =$ Rs. 90
According to the question,
$\Rightarrow 600 \times 1 \times \frac{r}{100} = 90$
$\Rightarrow 6r = 90$
$\Rightarrow r = 15$
$\therefore$ Rate of interest $= 15\%$
According to the question,

$\Rightarrow 100x \times 2 \times \frac{15}{100} = 1200$
$\Rightarrow 30x = 1200$
$\Rightarrow x = 40$
$\therefore$ The principal $=$ Rs. (100×40)
$=$ Rs. 4000

30(D). Let the sum of money be Rs. $100x$.
Simple Interest at 15% per annum for 2 years $= 2 \times (15\%$ of $100x) =$ Rs. $30x$
So, according to the question,
$30x = 1800$
$\Rightarrow x = 60$
Therefore, Sum $=$ Rs. $100x =$ Rs. $(100 \times 60) =$ Rs. 6000

31(C). Given:
Internal diameter of hollow sphere $(d) = 4$ cm
Internal radius of hollow sphere $(r) = \frac{4}{2} = 2$ cm
External diameter of hollow sphere $(D) = 8$ cm
External radius of hollow sphere $(R) = \frac{8}{2} = 4$ cm
As we know,
Volume of the Hollow sphere $= \frac{4}{3}\pi \left(R^3 - r^3\right)$
$= \frac{4}{3}\pi \left(4^3 - 2^3\right)$
$= \frac{4}{3}\pi(64 - 8)$
$= \frac{4}{3}\pi(56)$ cm^3
Diameter of the cone $(d_1) = 8$ cm
Radius of the cone $(r_1) = \frac{8}{2} = 4$ cm
Let the height of the cone be h cm
Volume of the cone $= \frac{1}{3}\pi r_1^2 h$
$= \frac{1}{3}\pi \times 4^2 h$
$= \frac{16}{3}\pi h$
Volume of the cone $=$ Volume of the hollow sphere
$\Rightarrow \frac{16}{3}\pi h = \frac{4}{3}\pi \times 56$
$\Rightarrow 16h = 4 \times 56$
$\Rightarrow h = \frac{4 \times 56}{16}$
$\Rightarrow h = \frac{56}{4}$
$\Rightarrow h = 14$ cm
So, the height of the cone is 14 cm.

32(B). Given,
Height of cylinder $= 28$ cm
Radius of cylinder $= 6$ cm
Diameter of bullet $= 1.5$ cm
$\Rightarrow$ Radius of bullet $= \frac{1.5}{2}$ cm
As we know,
The volume of cylinder $= \pi r^2 h$
The volume of bullet $= \frac{4}{3}\pi r^3$
The volume of cylinder $=$ Number of bullet $\times$ The volume of a bullet
Let assume that n bullets can be made.
According to the question,
$\Rightarrow \pi r^2 h = n\left(\frac{4}{3}\pi r^3\right)$
$\Rightarrow \pi(6)^2(28) = n\left[\frac{4}{3}\pi\left(\frac{1.5}{2}\right)^3\right]$
$\Rightarrow n = 1792$
$\therefore$ 1792 bullets can be made.

33(D). Factors of $36 = 1, 2, 3, 4, 6, 9, 12, 18, 36$
Factors of $48 = 1, 2, 3, 4, 6, 8, 12, 16, 24, 48$
Common factor for 36 and $48 = 1, 2, 3, 4, 6, 12$
$1 \times 2 \times 3 \times 4 \times 6 \times 12 = 999 + 9 \times x$
$\Rightarrow 1728 = 999 + 9 \times x \Rightarrow x = \frac{729}{9} = 81$

34(B). As we know,

$$\text{Average weight} = \frac{\text{Sum of Observation}}{\text{Total number of obsrvation}}$$

The average weight of 8 gold coins = 20 g
Total weight of 8 coins = 160 g
The average weight of 12 silver coins = 35 g
Total weight of 12 silver coins = 420 g

The average weight for 20 coins = $\frac{160+420}{8+12}$

$= \frac{580}{20}$

$= 29$ g

∴ The average weight for 20 coins is 29 g.

35(C). Given,

The average weight of 3 persons of group A = 60 kg
The average weight of 2 persons of Group B = 70 kg
We know that,

$$\text{Average} = \frac{\text{Total sum of all quantities}}{\text{total number of quantities}}$$

Total weight of group A people = $60 \times 3 = 180$ kg
Total weight of group B people = $70 \times 2 = 140$ kg
Total weight = $140 + 180 = 320$ kg

∴ Average weight of all persons = $\frac{320}{5} = 64$ kg

36(B). Given:

The Population of a town = 5,00,000
The annual birth rate is 5%
The annual death rate is 1%
Calculation:
Net change = Birth rate - death rate
5 % - 1 % = 4%

Increasing after one year = 5,00,000 × 104 % = $5,00,000 \times \frac{104}{100}$ =5,20,000

Increasing after two year = 5,20,000 × 104 % = $5,20,000 \times \frac{104}{100} = 5,40,800$

Increasing after three year = 5,40,800 × 104 % = $5,40,800 \times \frac{104}{100} = 5,62,432$

Total population after three years 5,62,432.

37(A). Let total work be $60x$ units (LCM of 10, 15, 60)
Efficiency of $A = 6x$ units/day
Efficiency of $B = 4x$ units/day
Efficiency of $C = x$ units/day
Work done in 5 days by A and $B = (6x + 4x) \times 5 = 50x$ units
Remaining work = $60x - 50x = 10x$ units
This work is completed by B and C.
Time taken to complete the remaining work

$= \frac{10x}{(4x+x)}$

$= \frac{10x}{5x}$

$= 2$ days

∴ Total time taken to complete the work $= 5 + 2 = 7$ days

38(B). Given,

A and B can do a job together in 7 days. A is $1\frac{3}{4}$ times as efficient as B.

(A's 1 day's work) : (B's 1 day's work)

$= \frac{7}{4} : 1 = 7 : 4$.

Let A's and B's 1 day's work be $7x$ and $4x$ respectively.

Then, $7x + 4x = \frac{1}{7}$

$\Rightarrow 11x = \frac{1}{7}$

$\Rightarrow x = \frac{1}{77}$

∴ A's 1 day's work $= \left(\frac{1}{77} \times 7\right)$

$= \frac{1}{11}$

39(B). Let the number of days in which B can finish the work be 'd'.

∵ A is thrice as good a workman as B.

Thus A will take $\frac{1}{3}$ rd time as B.

∴ Number of days in which A can finish the work = $\frac{d}{3}$

Given, A can finish a piece of work in 60 days less than B

∴ d − 60 = $\frac{d}{3}$

$\Rightarrow \frac{2d}{3} = 60$

$\Rightarrow$ d = 90 days

Thus,
Number of days B take to finish the work = 90 days

In one day B can finish $\frac{1}{90}$ th of the work

Number of days A take to finish the work = $\frac{d}{3} = 30$ days

In one day A can finish $\frac{1}{30}$ th of the work.

Now, in one day A and B working together can finish part of the work = $\frac{1}{30} + \frac{1}{90}$

$\Rightarrow$ In one day A and B working together can finish part of the work = $\frac{4}{90} = \frac{2}{45}$

∴ Number of days it will take to finish the work when A and B are working together = $\frac{45}{2} = 22\frac{1}{2}$

40(C). Let the speed of auto be x kmh^{-1}.
So, the speed of the train will be 6x and that of bike will be

$= \frac{6x}{1.5} = 4x$

As per the given information,
Time taken by auto + Time taken by train + Time taken by bike = 21 hours

$\Rightarrow \frac{132}{x} + \frac{852}{6x} + \frac{248}{4x} = 21$

or, $\frac{132}{x} + \frac{142}{x} + \frac{62}{x} = 21$

or, $21x = 132 + 142 + 62 = 336$

∴ $x = \frac{336}{21} = 16$

∴ Speed of the train = $6x = 6 \times 16 = 96$ kmh^{-1}

41(D). Let, the speed of the stream = x km/hr
Speed of the boat = 9 km/hr
Upstream speed = (9 - x) km/hr
According to the problem,

$\Rightarrow$ 6(9 - x) = 42

$\Rightarrow$ 9 - x = 7

$\Rightarrow$ x = 2

∴ Speed of the stream = 2 km/hr

42(D).

2	6, 100
2	3, 50
3	3, 25
5	1, 25
5	1, 5
	1, 1

$6 = 2 \times 3$
$100 = 2 \times 2 \times 5 \times 5$
LCM of 6 and 100 = $2 \times 2 \times 3 \times 5 \times 5 = 300$

43(D). Given:

Raj currently 12 years older than Ravi.
After 8 years the ratio of their age = 15: 12

Raj is currently 12 years older than Ravi.
Difference between raj and Ravi = 12 years
After 8 years' age ratio of Raj and Ravi = 15 : 12
Ratio of age difference = 15 – 12 = 3
Then, 3 = 12
⇒ 1 = 4
Now, Raj age after 8 years = 15 × 4 = 60
Present age of Raj = 60 – 8 = 52 years
∴ Present age of Raj is 52 years.

44(B). The given Venn diagram represents $A \cap (B \cup C)$.

45(A). First, we will calculate the distance between all pairs of points from the given pairs.
First consider the points (4, 0) and (-1, -1).
The distance is given as follows:
$$d_1 = \sqrt{(4 - (-1))^2 + (0 - (-1))^2}$$
$$= \sqrt{25 + 1}$$
$$= \sqrt{26}$$
Now consider the pair (-1, -1) and (3, 5).
The distance is given as follows:
$$d_2 = \sqrt{(3 - (-1))^2 + (5 - (-1))^2}$$
$$= \sqrt{16 + 36}$$
$$= 2\sqrt{13}$$
Now consider the pair (4, 0) and (3, 5).
The distance is given as follows:
$$d_3 = \sqrt{(3 - (4))^2 + (5 - (0))^2}$$
$$= \sqrt{1 + 25}$$
$$= \sqrt{26}$$
Therefore, two distances are equal thus, the triangle is isosceles.
The greatest side is of length $2\sqrt{13}$.
As we can see that, $d_2{}^2 = d_1{}^2 + d_3{}^2$
Therefore, by using the inverse of the Pythagorean theorem, we conclude that the triangle is right-angled.

46(B). Given:
$$\sin\theta\cos\theta = k$$
$$\frac{2\sin\theta\cos\theta}{2} = k$$
$$\frac{\sin 2\theta}{2} = k$$
$$\Rightarrow \text{Max value} = 0.5, \text{ at } \theta = \frac{\pi}{4}$$
$$\Rightarrow \text{Min value} = 0, \text{ at } \theta = 0 \text{ and } \theta = \frac{\pi}{2}$$
$$\therefore 0 \le k \le 0.5$$

47(D). Let, data value be $a_1, a_2, a_3, \ldots, a_n$
$$(a_1 - 2.5) + (a_2 - 2.5) + (a_3 - 2.5) + \ldots + (a_n - 2.5) = 50$$
$$(a_1 + a_2 + a_3 + \ldots\ldots + a_n) - 2.5(n) = 50$$
$$(a_1 + a_2 + a_3 + \ldots\ldots + a_n) = 50 + 2.5n \text{ and}$$
$$(a_1 - 3.5) + (a_2 - 3.5) + - (a_n - 3.5) = -50$$
$$(a_1 + a_2 + a_3 + \ldots\ldots + a_n) - 3.5(n) = -50$$
$$(a_1 + a_2 + a_3 + \ldots + a_n) = -50 + 3.5n$$
Now, $-50 + 3.5n = 50 + 2.5n$
$$\Rightarrow n = 100$$

48(A). Given:
5 letter word MUNCH is given.
Since U and N are always included so first we select 2 letters from remaining 3 letters M, C and H, which can be done in ${}^3C_2 = 3$ ways.
Now these 4 letters can be arrange in $4! = 24$ ways.
So, the required number is 72 ways (3×24).

49(A). Given,
The percentage distribution of the JIO users in Bihar = 22%

The total number of JIO users in Bihar = 22% of 60000000
$$= 60000000 \times \frac{22}{100}$$
$$= 13200000$$
The total number of airtel users in Bihar = 13200000 – 2500000
$$= 10700000$$

50(C). Given,
The percentage distribution of the JIO users in Delhi = 28%
The percentage distribution of the Idea users in Delhi = 15%
The total number of JIO users in Delhi = 28% of 6 crores
$$= \frac{28 \times 6}{100} \text{ crores}$$
$$= 1.68 \text{ crores}$$
The total number of Idea users in Delhi = 15% of 2.5 crores
$$= \frac{15 \times 2.5}{100} \text{ crores}$$
$$= 0.375 \text{ crores}$$
The required percentage $= \dfrac{(1.68 - 0.375) \times 100}{0.375}$
$$= 348\%$$

51(C). Logic: We are subtracting the consecutive odd number from the (Staring from 1) from the Letters place value.

<pre>
M   K   J
│-1 │-3 │-5
↓   ↓   ↓
L   H   E
</pre>

Similarly,

<pre>
T   P   L
│-1 │-3 │-5
↓   ↓   ↓
S   M   G
</pre>

52(A). The logic follows here is:

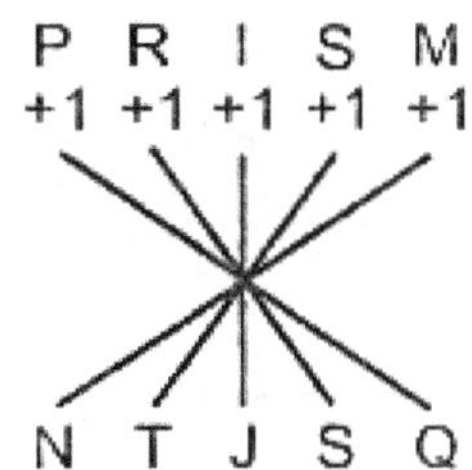

Similarly;

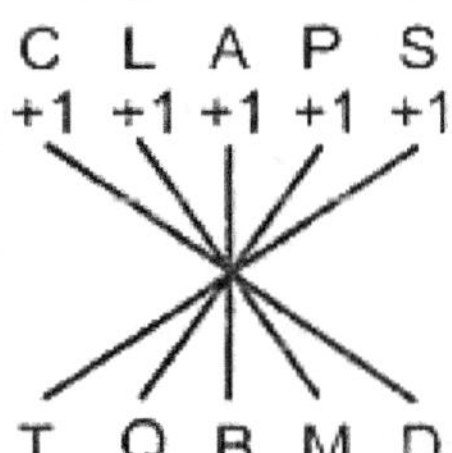

53(A). By using the following symbols in the table given below, we can draw the following family tree:

Symbol in Diagram	Meaning
◯	Female
▢	Male
═══	Married Couple
───	Siblings
│	Difference of A Generation

Given Statement: Pointing to a boy, a lady said, "He is the son of my grandmother's only child's husband's only daughter's brother."

Here, the boy is the son of the lady's grandmother's only child's husband's (Lady's father) only daughter's (i.e the lady's) brother (lady's brother).

Thus the following family tree can be drawn :

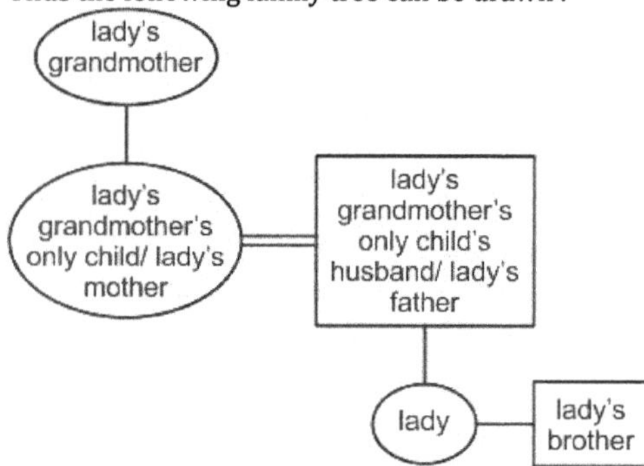

Thus, the boy is the 'Nephew' of the lady.
So, the correct answer is "Nephew".

54(D). As per the given information,

Symbol in Diagram	Meaning
◯	Female
▢	Male
═══	Married Couple
───	Siblings
│	Difference of A Generation

Given:

A + B means A is the father of B
A - B means A is the mother of B
A ⋆ B means A is the sister of B
A / B means A is the brother of B
Let us first decode the given symbols and then draw a family tree

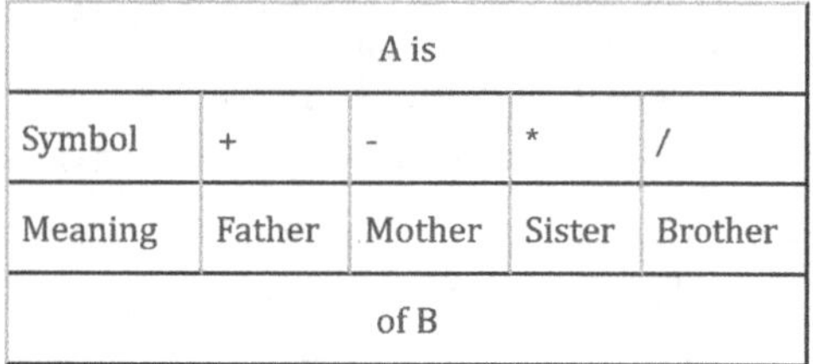

A is			
Symbol	+	-	⋆	/
Meaning	Father	Mother	Sister	Brother
of B			

On checking: M/N*O+P
1) M/N
Here, M is brother of N.
2) N*O
Here, N is sister of O.
3) O+P
Here, O is father of P.
• Thus, the following family tree can be drawn:

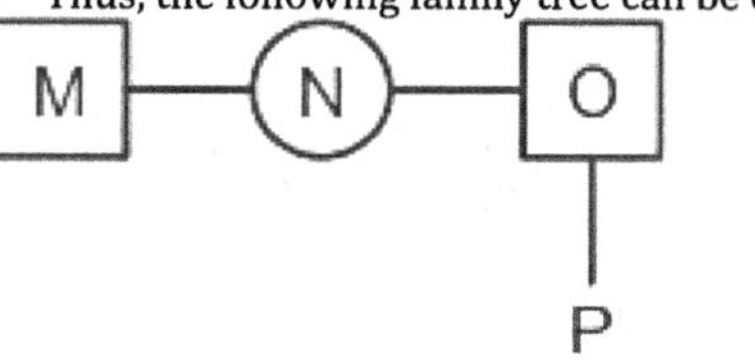

• Clearly N is 'Paternal Aunt' of P.
So, the correct answer is " Paternal Aunt ".

55(D). Penguin, Tortoise, and Crocodile can live on land as well as water but fish cannot survive on land. Thus figure (D) is the odd one out.

56(C).

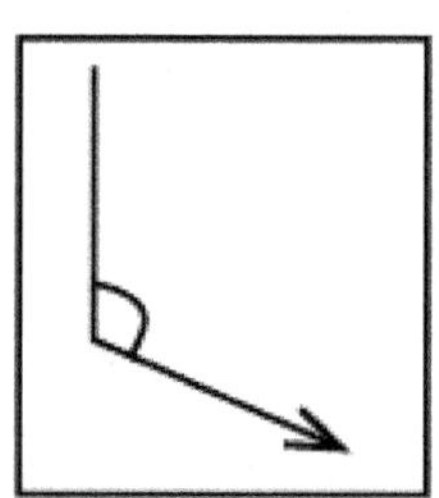

Except for C all others are at 90°.

57(A).

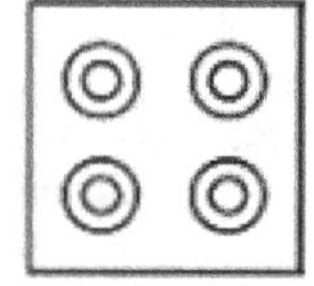

All option except '(A)' has one of the images shaded, while option (A) has no image shaded.

58(C). According to the question,

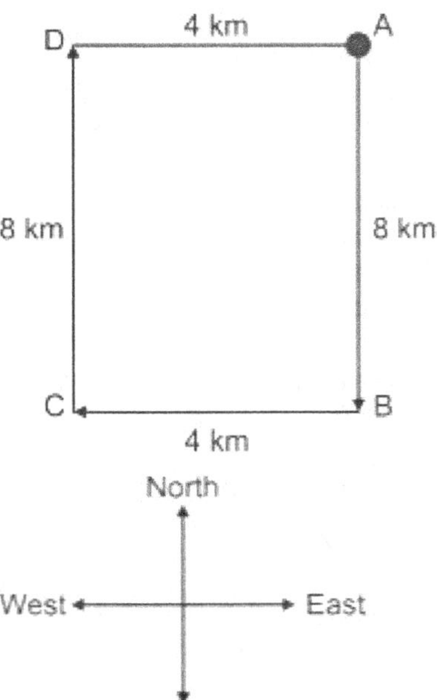

Required distance = AD
= 4 km

59(D).

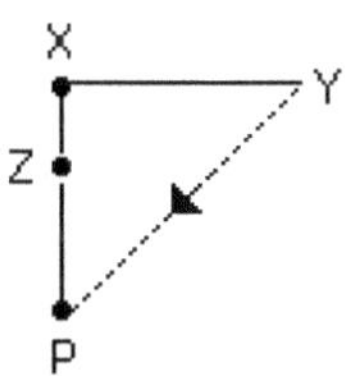

P is in South-West of Y.

60(C). The pattern followed here is,
W → 23th letter → 2 + 3 = 5
J → 10th letter → 1 + 0 = 1
Similarly,
M → 13th letter → 1 + 3 = 4
V → 22th letter → 2 + 2 = 4
→ M × V: 4 × 4
So, 4 × 4 is the correct answer.

61(A). The logic followed here is:
Alphabets given in the coded language are the opposite alphabet of the word *PLAN* '.

$$P \xrightarrow{16 + 11 = 27} K$$
$$16 \qquad\qquad 11$$

$$L \xrightarrow{12 + 15 = 27} O$$
$$12 \qquad\qquad 15$$

$$A \xrightarrow{1 + 26 = 27} Z$$
$$1 \qquad\qquad 26$$

$$N \xrightarrow{13 + 14 = 27} M$$
$$14 \qquad\qquad 13$$

Similarly,
Opposite alphabets of the word ' *FLICK* ' are:

$$F \xrightarrow{6 + 21 = 27} U$$
$$6 \qquad\qquad 21$$

$$L \xrightarrow{12 + 15 = 27} O$$
$$12 \qquad\qquad 15$$

$$I \xrightarrow{9 + 18 = 27} R$$
$$9 \qquad\qquad 18$$

$$C \xrightarrow{3 + 24 = 27} X$$
$$3 \qquad\qquad 24$$

$$K \xrightarrow{11 + 16 = 27} P$$
$$11 \qquad\qquad 16$$

62(C). The next figure in the problem figure will be the answer figure C because the curved line is decreasing by one and the straight line is increasing by one.

63(B). The next term of the given problem figure will be the answer figure with option (B).
In the given series, the shaded portion is moving in clockwise direction skipping adjacent position.

64(B). Doctors and lawyers are entirely different. But, both are Professionals.

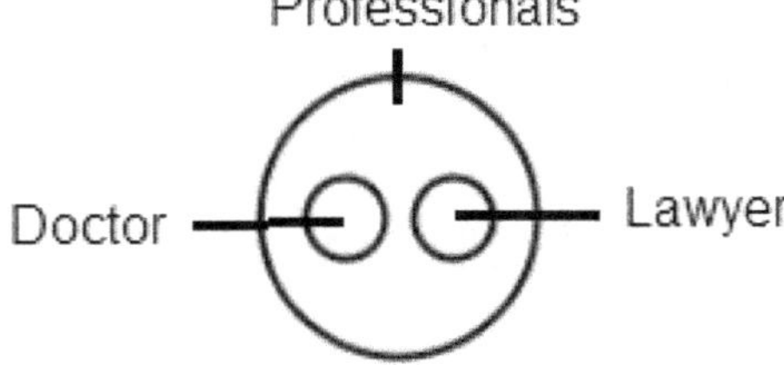

65(B). A word with nearly same meaning is called a synonym and a word with opposite meaning is an antonym.
So,
Synonyms and Antonyms are words.
The correct Venn diagram is,

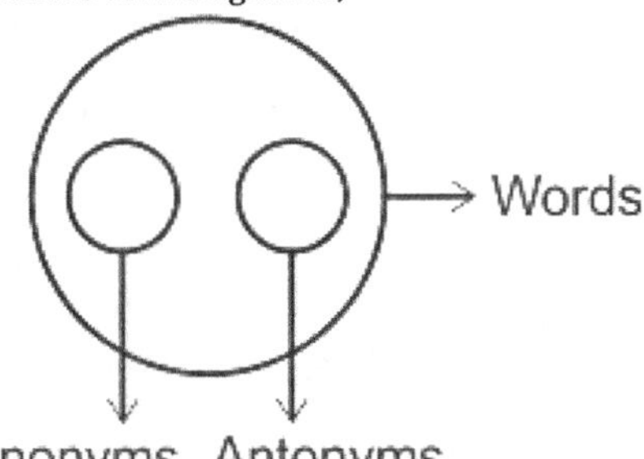

66(A). We can see in the above series next number is obtained by dividing each term by 4.
4096 ÷ 4 = 1024
1024 ÷ 4 = 256
256 ÷ 4 = 64
64 ÷ 4 = 16
16 ÷ 4 = 4
Thus, the number in place of ? should be 64.

67(C). The pattern of the number series is :
435 - 9 × 9 = 354
354 - 9 × 8 = 282

$282 - 9 \times 7 = 219$
$219 - 9 \times 6 = 165$
$165 - 9 \times 5 = 120$

68(A). Given,
In a row of students, Ramesh is ninth from the left and Suman is sixth from the right. When Ramesh and Suman interchange their places, Ramesh becomes fifteenth from the left.

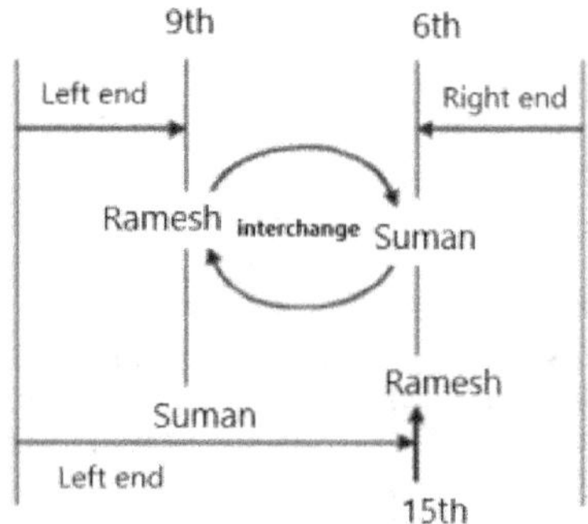

Thus the position of Suman changed from right to
$= 6 + 5 + \text{Suman}$
$= 6 + 5 + 1 = 12$
Thus Suman will be 12th from the right.

69(D). The logic followed here is:
1. E is older than C.
$E > C$
2. D is older than C but younger than E.
$E > D > C$
3. A is younger than B and C.
$B > A$ and $C > A$
4. C is older than B.
$C > B$
Combining all the statements together, we get:
$E > D > C > B > A$
Clearly, A is the youngest.

70(D). The least possible Venn diagram for the given statements is as follows,

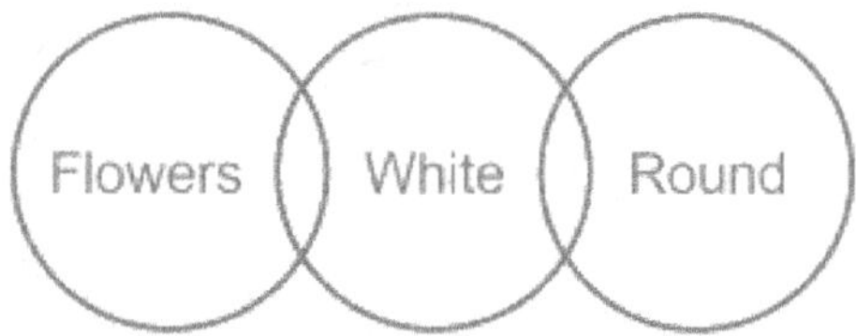

Conclusions:
I. Some flowers are round → False (It is possible but not definite)
II. Every round is either white or a flower → False (some rounds are white)
So, 'Neither conclusion I nor II follows' is the correct answer.

71(B). From the following Statement we have these diagram:

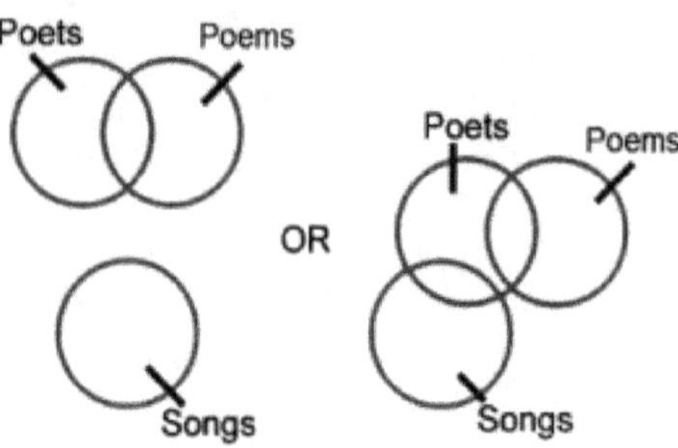

From the above diagram, we can have a conclusion that only I conclusion is true.

72(C). From options:
(A) 12 - 24 - 48 → 12 - 12 × 2 - 24 × 2
(B) 36 - 72 - 144 → 36 - 36 × 2 - 72 × 2
(C) 25 - 50 - 115 → 25 - 25 × 2 - 50 × 2 ≠ 115 (it should be 25 - 50 - 100)
(D) 53 - 106 - 212 → 53 - 53 × 2 - 106 × 2
So, the correct answer is 25 - 50 - 115.

73(C). All options except "Refrigerator" are examples of furniture, while "Refrigerator" is an electronic device.

Ques (74-75): Names of person: Ram, Rahul, Sagar, Rajesh, Anurag, Amit, Vinit, Sanket, and Shekhar.
Colors: Red, Orange, Green, Violet, Black, Blue, Purple, Yellow, and Indigo.
1) Only two person are sitting between Rahul and Rajesh, who is sitting at the extreme end.
2) Rahul, who likes the Black color sits second to the left of Shekhar.

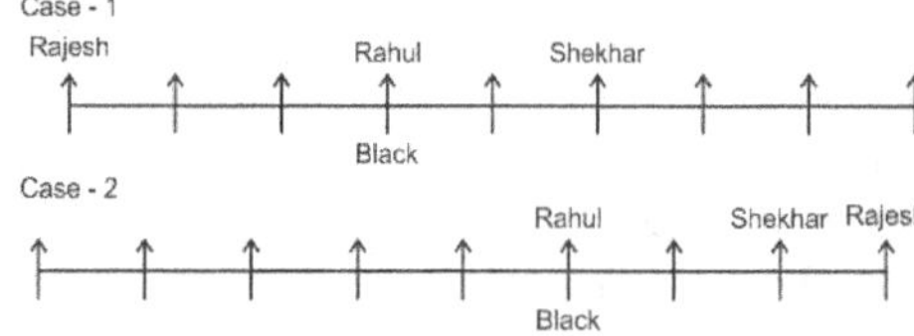

3) The person who likes the Black color sits second to the right of a person who likes Indigo color.
4) Shekhar who likes the Blue color is not sitting at any of the extreme ends.

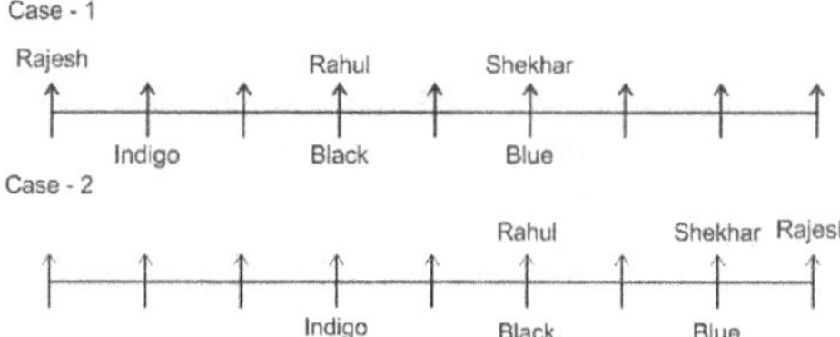

5) Amit who likes the Orange color is a neighbor of both Ram and Rahul.
6) Ram and Sagar are sitting together.

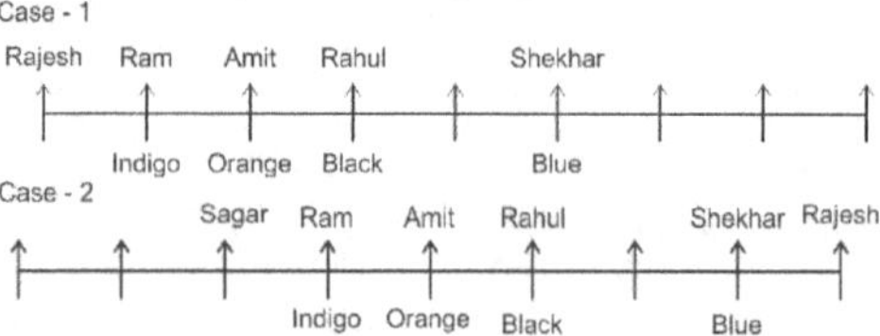

(In case 1 there is no place for Sagar as according to statement 6 Ram and Sagar are sitting together. So, here we can eliminate Case 1)
7) Sanket sits to the immediate left of Vinit who neither likes Yellow nor Indigo color.
8) The person who likes the Purple color is sitting at one of the

extreme ends, but he is not a neighbor of the person who likes the Blue color.

(As the person who likes purple color is not a neighbor of the person who likes blue color, the person who likes purple color will be at the left end only)

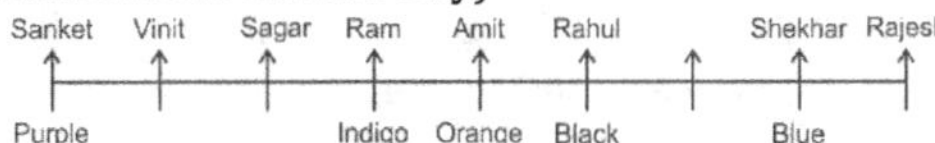

9) The person who likes the Green color sits at one of the places to the right of the person who likes Indigo color.

(The person who likes the Green color sits at the extreme right end or third from the right end).

10) Only one person is sitting between the person who likes Violet and the Green color.

(The person who likes the Violet color will also sit either at the extreme right end or third from the right end)

The only person remaining is Anurag, so the vacant position will be taken by Anurag.

According to statement 7, Vinit does not like the Yellow or Indigo color, so the only color remaining i.e., Red is liked by Vinit, and Sagar likes Yellow color

The final arrangement will be as follows:

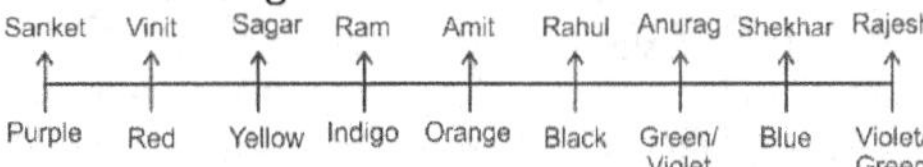

74(A). So, Ram is sitting immediate left of Amit.

75(D). So, Vinit likes red colour.

76(A). उपरोक्त शब्दों में 'निवृत्ति' वर्तनी के अनुसार शुद्ध रूप है, अन्य सभी शब्द वर्तनी के अनुसार गलत शब्द है।
वर्तनी का अर्थ: वर्तनी शब्द विशेष के लेखन में उस शब्द की एक-एक करके आने वाली ध्वनियों में लिपि चिह्न निर्धारित करती है। इस प्रकार उच्चारित शब्द के लेखन में प्रयोग होने वाले लिपि चिह्नों के व्यवस्थित रूप को वर्तनी कहते हैं।
निवृत्ति का अर्थ - मुक्त होना।

77(B). 'उधृत' की वर्तनी यहाँ अशुद्ध है।
शुद्ध शब्द: उद्धृत शब्द यहाँ वर्तनी और उच्चारण की दृष्टि से शुद्ध सार्थक शब्द है।
जिसका अर्थ है- जड़ से उखाड़ा हुआ, पृथक किया हुआ।

78(D). निर्णय न होना, यहाँ सही विकल्प है। अन्य विकल्प असंगत है।
खटाई में पड़ना एक प्रचलित हिंदी मुहावरा है जिसका अर्थ किसी काम का अनिश्चित होने से है।
जैसे- इस बार की परीक्षा का परिणाम खटाई में पड़ गया है।

79(A). लोकोक्ति – नौ दिन चले अढ़ाई कोस, लोकोक्ति का अर्थ – काम करने की बहुत धीमी गति।
वाक्य – राजू ने दस महीने में मात्र एक पाठ याद किया है। यह तो वही बात हुई – 'नौ दिन चले अढ़ाई कोस'।

80(C). उपरोक्त सभी विकल्पों में 'अंधों में काना राजा' उचित लोकोक्ति है।
लोकोक्ति: अंधों में काना राजा, अर्थ: गुणहीन व्यक्तियों में कम गुण वाला व्यक्ति माना जाता है।
वाक्य: गाँव में जब लोगों ने देखा के कोई भी अच्छा उम्मीदवार चुनाव में खड़ा नहीं है तो उन्होंने पांचवीं पास श्यामलाल को ही गांव का मुखिया बना दिया जैसे अंधों में काना राजा।

81(D). उपर्युक्त शब्दों में से 'आभार' पुल्लिंग शब्द है।
"उन्होंने सभी के प्रति आभार व्यक्त किया।" वाक्य से स्पष्ट कि 'आभार' शब्द का प्रयोग पुल्लिंग में किया जाता है। शेष विकल्प 'दया, माया, भाषा' स्त्रीलिंग शब्द हैं।

82(B). उपर्युक्त में से 'कष्ट' शब्द पुल्लिंग है। 'कष्ट' शब्द का प्रयोग पुल्लिंग में किया जाता है, जैसे - मुझे बहुत कष्ट हुआ। इस प्रकार सही विकल्प 'कष्ट' है। अन्य विकल्प 'आशा, क्षमा, सेना' स्त्रीलिंग शब्द हैं।

83(C). 'जो युद्ध में स्थिर रहता है' वाक्य के लिए एक शब्द 'युधिष्ठिर' होता है। युधिष्ठिर, हिंदू धर्म के अनुसार, या तो एक व्यक्ति का नाम हो सकता है या किसी शक्तिशाली व्यक्ति को संदर्भित करने के लिए इस्तेमाल किया जा सकता है।

84(B). भगवान शिव तथा उनके अवतारों को मानने वालों और भगवान शिव की उपासना करने वाले लोगों को शैव कहते हैं।

85(D). "अर्द्ध - अंधा" युग्म सही सुमेलित नहीं है।
"अर्द्ध" का सही तद्भव "आधा" होगा।

86(D). जो सर्वनाम तीनों पुरूषों (उत्तम, मध्यम और अन्य) में निजत्व का बोध कराता है, उसे निजवाचक सर्वनाम कहते हैं। जैसे-
1. मैं खुद लिख लूँगा।
2. तुम अपने आप चले जाना।
3. वह स्वयं गाडी चला सकती है।
उपर्युक्त वाक्यों में खुद, अपने आप और स्वयं शब्द निजवाचक सर्वनाम हैं।

87(C). दिए गए विकल्पो में "प्रहेलिका - फूल" युग्म सही सुमेलित नहीं है।
"प्रहेलिका" का सही तद्भव "पहेली" होगा तथा "फूल" "पुष्प" का तद्भव है।

88(A). हिन्दी में दो वचन होते हैं- एकवचन और बहुवचन ।
वचन: संज्ञा के जिस रुप से संख्या का बोध होता हो उसे वचन कहते हैं। वचन का प्रयोग संख्या का बोध करवाने के लिए किया जाता है।
जैसे - लड़का एकवचन और लड़के बहुवचन।

89(C). ईकारांत संज्ञा शब्द को बहुवचन बनाते समय 'ई' को ह्रस्व करके अंतिम स्वर के बाद 'याँ' लगा देते हैं।
जैसे - नारी - नारियाँ, थाली - थालियाँ।

90(B). त्रुटि वाला वाक्यांश ' सबसे सरलतम उपाय ' है। इस वाक्यांश का सही रूप 'सबसे सरल उपाय या सरलतम उपाय' है।

91(C). त्रुटि वाला वाक्यांश ' उद्घाटन करेगा ' है। इस वाक्यांश का सही रूप 'उद्घाटन करेंगे' होगा क्योंकि सम्माननीय व्यक्तियों के लिए सदैव बहुवचन का प्रयोग किया जाता है।

92(A). 'आविर्भाव' का सही विलोम शब्द 'तिरोभाव' है। आविर्भाव का अर्थ – प्रकट होना, उत्पत्ति। तिरोभाव का अर्थ – अदृश्य हो जाना, अदर्शन।

93(C). 'गुप्त-मुक्त' सही विलोम-युग्म नहीं है। गुप्त का अर्थ- 'छिपा हुआ' होता है। मुक्त का अर्थ- 'स्वतंत्र, छूटा हुआ' होता है।

94(A). 'कोप' का विलोम शब्द 'कृपा' है। कोप शब्द का अर्थ गुस्सा करना होता है, अतः इसका विपरीत अर्थ 'कृपा करना' होता है।

95(A). 'वनिता' शब्द का पर्यायवाची शब्द 'महिला' है। 'वनिता' के अन्य पर्यायवाची शब्द हैं- योषिता, स्त्री, औरत, नारी, योषा, आदि।

96(C). 'देशांतर' का संधि विच्छेद दिशा + अंतर होता है। इसमें दीर्घ संधि है। ह्रस्व स्वर या दीर्घ स्वर अ ,आ, इ , ई, उ , ऊ आपस में मिलते है तो स्वर दीर्घ हो जाता है। तो उसे दीर्घ संधि कहते है। जैसे –
धर्म + अर्थ – धर्मार्थ
स्वर + अर्थ - स्वार्थ
परम + अर्थ – परमार्थ

97(B). 'स्वध् + आ' विसर्ग संधि का उदाहरण है। 'स्वध् + आ' की संधि 'स्वाहा' होती है। विसर्ग का स्वर या व्यंजन के साथ मेल होने पर जो परिवर्तन होता है, उसे विसर्ग संधि कहते है।
उदाहरण -
निः + चय = निश्चय
दुः + चरित्र = दुश्चरित्र
ज्योति: + चक्र = ज्योतिश्चक्र
निः + छल = निश्छल

98(A). 'लाकृति' का संधि विच्छेद 'लृ + आकृति' होता है। इसमें यण संधि है। यण संधि स्वर संधि का एक भेद अथवा प्रकार है। जब संधि करते समय इ, ई के साथ कोई अन्य स्वर हो तो 'य' बन जाता है,

जब उ, ऊ के साथ कोई अन्य स्वर हो तो 'व्' बन जाता है, जब ऋ के साथ कोई अन्य स्वर हो तो 'र' बन जाता है।

जैसे:

अनु + अय = अन्वय

सु + अस्ति = स्वस्ति

सु + आगत = स्वागत

धातु + इक = धात्विक

अनु + ईक्षा = अन्वीक्षा

वधू + आगमन = वध्वागमन

99(A). रामचरितमानस तुलसीदास की सबसे प्रमुख कृति है। इसकी रचना संवत 1631 ई. की रामनवमी को अयोध्या में प्रारम्भ हुई थी किन्तु इसका कुछ अंश काशी (वाराणसी) में भी निर्मित हुआ था, यह इसके किष्किन्धा काण्ड के प्रारम्भ में आने वाले एक सोरठे से निकलती है, उसमें काशी सेवन का उल्लेख है।

'रामचरितमानस' एक चरित-काव्य है, जिसमें राम का सम्पूर्ण जीवन-चरित वर्णित हुआ है। इसमें 'चरित' और 'काव्य' दोनों के गुण समान रूप से मिलते हैं।

अन्य विकल्प:

रचनाकार	परिचय	प्रमुख रचनाएँ
जायसी	मलिक मुहम्मद जायसी हिन्दी साहित्य के भक्ति काल की निर्गुण प्रेमाश्रयी धारा के कवि थे। जायसी का जन्म सन 1467 ई के आसपास माना जाता है। वे उत्तर प्रदेश के जायस नामक स्थान के रहनेवाले थे। उनके नाम में जायसी शब्द का प्रयोग, उनके उपनाम की भाँ	पद्मावत, अखरावट, आख़िरी कलाम, कहर नामा, चित्ररेखा, कान्हावत आदि।
कबीर	ति, किया जाता है। भारत के महान संत और आध्यात्मिक कवि कबीर दास का जन्म वर्ष 1440 में हुआ था। इस्लाम के अनुसार 'कबीर' का अर्थ महान होता है। संत कबीर दास हिंदी साहित्य के भक्ति काल के इ कलौते ऐसे कवि हैं, जो आजीवन समाज और लोगों के बीच व्याप्त आडंबरों पर कुठाराघात करते रहे। वह कर्म प्रधान समाज के पैरोकार थे और इसकी झलक उनकी रचनाओं में साफ़ झलकती है। लोक कल्याण हेतु ही मानो उनका समस्त जीवन था। कबीर को वास्तव में एक सच्चे विश्व - प्रेमी का अनुभव था। कबीर की सबसे बड़ी विशेषता यह थी कि उनकी प्रतिभा में अबाध गति और अदम्य प्रखरता थी। समाज में कबीर को जागरण युग का अग्रदूत कहा जाता है।	बीजक
सूरदास	सूरदास हिन्दी के भक्तिकाल के महान कवि थे। हिन्दी साहित्य में भगवान श्री कृष्ण के अनन्य उपासक और ब्रजभाषा के श्रेष्ठ कवि महात्मा सूरदास हिंदी साहित्य के [सूर्य] माने जाते हैं।	सूरसागर, सूर सारावली, साहित्य-लहरी, नल-दमयन्ती, ब्याहलो आदि।

100(D). दिए गए विकल्पों में से 'एक सड़क सत्तावन गलियाँ रचना शैलेश मटियानी की नहीं है। यह उपन्यास कमलेश्वर द्वारा रचित है।

कमलेश्वर के अन्य उपन्यास हैं - डाक बंगला, समुद्र में खोया हुआ आदमी, काली आँधी, आगामी अतीत, सुबह...दोपहर...शाम, रेगिस्तान, लौटे हुए, मुसाफ़िर, वही बात, एक और चंद्रकांता, कितने पाकिस्तान, अंतिम सफर आदि।

General Knowledge

1. The timeless Indian novel 'Devdas' was written by:
   (a) Rabindranath Tagore
   (b) Bankim Chandra Chatterjee
   (c) Mirza Ghalib
   (d) Sarat Chandra Chattopadhyay

2. Montague-Chelmsford Reforms introduced ______ which was a kind of double government in the provinces.
   (a) Dual
   (b) Self-Government
   (c) Legislative Reform
   (d) Dyarchy

3. The fear of the Phallus worship was replaced in the ______ by its recognition as an official ritual.
   (a) Rig Veda
   (b) Sama Veda
   (c) Yajur Veda
   (d) Atharva Veda

4. After the death of King Ashoka the ______ declined rapidly.
   (a) Maurya Dynasty
   (b) Chola Dynasty
   (c) Chalukya Dynasty
   (d) Gupta Dynasty

5. Where was the All India Kisan Mahasabha organized for the first time?
   (a) Calcutta
   (b) Madras
   (c) Lucknow
   (d) Patna

6. Where did the Moplah rebellion of 1921 take place?
   (a) Kashmir
   (b) B. N. W. F. P
   (c) Kerala
   (d) Assam

7. Where does Bhagirathi and Alaknanda join the Ganges?
   (a) Karna Prayag
   (b) Dev Prayag
   (c) Rudra Prayag
   (d) Gangotri

8. Breaking of a rock in place is called:
   (a) erosion
   (b) weathering
   (c) mass destruction
   (d) degradation

9. The longest river in Europe is:
   (a) Rhine
   (b) Rhone
   (c) Danube
   (d) Volga

10. As per the World Bank report "Migration and Development Brief', India was set to receive how many billion dollars as remittances in 2022?
    (a) $75 billion
    (b) $100 billion
    (c) $125 billion
    (d) $150 billion

11. In December 2022, the CM of which state declared a seed farm, located in Aluva, as the first carbon-neutral farm in the country?
    (a) Kerala
    (b) Odisha
    (c) Gujarat
    (d) Punjab

12. ________ has been appointed as India's next Ambassador to Kuwait in October 2022.
    (a) Ravi Prakash
    (b) Satish Singh
    (c) Kumar Ranjan
    (d) Adarsh Swaika

13. To raise awareness about Yoga, Mobile app "Namaste Yoga" launched by whom in India?
    (a) Ministry of Health and Family Welfare
    (b) Ministry of Home Affairs
    (c) Ministry of Ayush
    (d) None of these

14. Which one of the following methods can be used to separate anthracene from a mixture of salt and anthracene?
    (a) Distillation
    (b) Sublimation
    (c) Evaporation
    (d) Chromatography

15. Shoots of plant show upward movement and it can be designated to be:
    (a) Negatively phototropic
    (b) Positively chemotropic
    (c) Positively hydrotropic
    (d) Negatively geotropic

16. Too much use of insecticides will cause:
    (a) air pollution
    (b) noise pollution
    (c) water pollution
    (d) all of these

17. Which of the following is/are function(s) of the Election Commission of India?
    1. Registration and recognition of political parties.
    2. Allot election symbols to political parties or candidates.
    3. Preparing electoral rolls.
    4. Advising the President or Governor in matters relating to the disqualification of sitting legislators except under Schedule 10.
    (a) 1, 2 and 3 only
    (b) 2, 3 and 4 only
    (c) 1, 3 and 4 only
    (d) 1, 2, 3 and 4

18. Which of the following is included in the members of Zilla Panchayat?
    (a) Member of Legislative Assembly
    (b) Member of Legislative Council
    (c) Member of Lok Sabha
    (d) All of the above

19. Constitutional government means:
    (a) a representative government of a nation with federal structure
    (b) a government whose Head enjoys nominal powers
    (c) a government whose Head enjoys real powers
    (d) a government limited by the terms of the Constitution

20. Chief Minister Raj Neer Scheme was launched on:
    (a) 13 March 2020
    (b) 2 October 2019
    (c) 1 December 2019
    (d) 1 January 2021

21. The objective of the Eleventh Five Year Plan is-
    (a) Eradication of poverty
    (b) Inclusive economic growth
    (c) Development with social justice
    (d) Development of minorities

22. Rainbow revolution is related to-
    (a) Green revolution
    (b) White revolution
    (c) Blue revolution
    (d) All of the above

23. Which country won the maximum number of medals

at 2020 Summer Olympic Games (played in 2021)?
(a) United States of America
(b) People's Republic of China
(c) Japan
(d) Great Britain

24. Consider the following statements with reference to the Limited Liability Partnership (LLP):
1. In an LLP, each partner is not responsible or liable for another partner's misconduct or negligence.
2. The internal governance structure of a company and LLP both are regulated by statute, Companies Act, 2013.
Which of the statements given above is/are correct?
(a) 1 only
(b) 2 only
(c) Both 1 and 2
(d) Neither 1 nor 2

25. Consider the following statements:
1. Maitri and Bharati are the two permanent research stations of India in Antarctica.
2. National Centre for Polar and Ocean Research (NCPOR) is the nodal agency for India's scientific expeditions in Antarctica and the Arctic.
Which of the statements given above is/are correct?
(a) 1 only
(b) 2 only
(c) Both 1 and 2
(d) Neither 1 nor 2

Mathematics

26. **Direction** : Simplify the given expression.
$$\frac{32}{100} \times 850 - ? = \frac{14}{100} \times 640$$
(a) 127.8
(b) 153.5
(c) 175.6
(d) 182.4

27. A person sells a watch at a profit of 26% . If he had bought it at 20% less and sold for ₹ 81.60 less, he would have gained 32% . What is the original cost price (in ₹) of the watch?
(a) 400
(b) 480
(c) 450
(d) 360

28. Ram buys 70 articles for Rs. 890 and sold 60 articles for Rs. 890 . What is his gain percent?
(a) $17\frac{1}{3}\%$
(b) 25%
(c) 20%
(d) $16\frac{2}{3}\%$

29. What is the total earning after 2 years from Rs. 18,750 on variable compound interest if the rate of interest for the first year is 4% and for the second, it is 8% ?
(a) Rs. 1,740
(b) Rs. 1,760
(c) Rs. 1,670
(d) Rs. 2,310

30. There is 100% increase to an amount in 8 years, at simple interest. Find the compound interest of Rs. 8000 after 2 years at the same rate of interest.
(a) Rs. 2500
(b) Rs. 2000
(c) Rs. 2250
(d) Rs. 2125

31. The perimeter of a rectangle having area equal to 144 cm^2 and sides in the ratio 4 : 9 is:
(a) 52 cm
(b) 56 cm
(c) 60 cm
(d) 64 cm

32. The radius of a circular wheel is $1\frac{3}{4}$ m. How many revolutions will it make in traveling 11 $\left(\pi = \frac{22}{7}\right)$.
(a) 1000
(b) 1100
(c) 900
(d) 1200

33. The number 40 is divided into two parts in such way that two times the square of the first number exceeds the second number by 5 . Find the two numbers.
(a) $\frac{7}{2}$ and $\frac{73}{2}$
(b) $\frac{5}{2}$ and $\frac{75}{2}$
(c) $\frac{9}{2}$ and $\frac{71}{2}$
(d) $\frac{11}{2}$ and $\frac{69}{2}$

34. There are 96 students in a class, out of which the number of girls is 40% more than that of the boys. The average score in mathematics of the boys is 40% more than the average score of girls. If the average score in mathematics of all the students is 63, then what is the average score of the girls in mathematics?
(a) 55
(b) 54
(c) 51
(d) 57

35. Ajay working in a Cellular company as a salesman. His monthly salary is Rs. 200 . But he gets a bonus as per given rule. If he sells sim cards of Rs. x then his bonus will be $\left[\left(\frac{x}{100}\right)^2 + 10\right]$. In the first quarter of the year, his average sale was Rs. 3000 per month. In the next 5 five-month his average sale was Rs. 5000 per month and for next four-/month his average sale was Rs. 8000 per month. What is the average earning per month for the whole year?
(a) Rs. 3350
(b) Rs. 3610
(c) Rs. 3560
(d) Rs. 3750

36. When the price of a machine was increased by 20% , the number of machines sold was decreased by 25% . What was the percentage decrease change in the total revenue?
(a) 5%
(b) 20%
(c) 15%
(d) 10%

37. Three taps A, B, and C can fill a tank in 180, 20 , and 90 minutes respectively. If all the taps are opened together, then in how many minutes will the tank be filled?
(a) 15
(b) 25
(c) 30
(d) 35

38. 14 workers can construct a wall in 20 days than in how many days 20 workers will construct 2 such walls?
(a) 20 days
(b) 35 days
(c) 28 days
(d) 21 days

39. Reenu can do a work in 15 days. Reenu and Meenu together can do the same work in 10 days. If they got Rs. 600 for that work, find the share of Reenu and Meenu respectively.
(a) Rs. 400, Rs. 200
(b) Rs. 300, Rs. 300
(c) Rs. 500, Rs. 100
(d) Rs. 350, Rs. 150

40. The speed of a boat in still water is 12 km/hr more than that of current. If the speed of the current is $1.25x$ km/hr and the time taken by the boat to cover 160 km in downstream is 5 hours then find the value of 'x'.
(a) 8
(b) 6
(c) 4
(d) 10

41. How many minutes Raman's will take to cover a distance of 400 meters. if he runs at a speed of 20 km/

hr?

(a) 2 minute   (b) 1.5 minute
(c) 1.2 minute   (d) 2.5 minute

42. HCF of 36 and 144 is:
(a) 36   (b) 144
(c) 4   (d) 2

43. The present ages of a father and his son are in the ratio $3 : 1$. 10 years ago, the father is 24 years older than his son. Find the present age of the son.
(a) 12 years   (b) 10 years
(c) 20 years   (d) 24 years

44. If $a + b + c = 45$ and $ab + bc + ca = 254$. Find the value of $a^2 + b^2 + c^2 = ?$
(a) 1517   (b) 1516
(c) 1515   (d) 1518

45. If the latus rectum of an ellipse is equal to half of its minor axis, then its eccentricity is:
(a) $\frac{1}{2}$ (b) $\frac{1}{\sqrt{2}}$
(c) $\frac{\sqrt{3}}{2}$ (d) $\frac{\sqrt{3}}{4}$

46. If $\sec^4 \theta - \sec^2 \theta = 3$ then the value of $\tan^4 \theta + \tan^2 \theta$ is:
(a) 8   (b) 4
(c) 6   (d) 3

47. A data set of n observations has mean 2M, while another data set of 2n observations has mean M. What is the mean of the combined data sets?
(a) M (b) $\frac{3M}{2}$
(c) $\frac{2M}{3}$ (d) $\frac{4M}{3}$

48. The number of rectangles that you can find on a chess board is:
(a) 1376   (b) 1236
(c) 1296   (d) 372

Ques (49-50): Direction: Study the following table carefully to answer the question given below.
The table given below represent the annual income of Arunoday and Annual expenditure of Geet (in thousand) from 2002 – 2006.

Year	Annual income of Aru noday	Annual expenditure o f Geet
2002	650	400
2003	700	300
2004	500	300
2005	700	150
2006	800	200

The table given below represent the respective ratio of the annual income of Geet and (Arunoday + Geet) and the respective ratio of the annual expenditure of Arunoday and (Arunoday + Geet)

Year	Annual income	Annual expenditure
2002	4 : 9	3 : 5
2003	4 : 11	2 : 5
2004	3 : 8	4 : 7
2005	2 : 9	5 : 8
2006	3 : 11	3 : 5

Note: Annual income = Annual expenditure + Annual saving

49. Find the difference (in thousand) in the average annual savings of Arunoday in 2002 and 2006 together and that of Geet in the same two years together?
(a) 160   (b) 165
(c) 155   (d) 175

50. Find the ratio of annual income of Geet in 2003 and 2005 together to annual expenditure of Arunoday in 2004 and 2006 together.
(a) 6 : 11   (b) 5 : 7
(c) 3 : 7   (d) 6 : 7

51. Select the related word from the give alternatives
Deer : Fawn :: Horse : ?
(a) Lamb   (b) Foal
(c) Calf   (d) Toad

52. In the following options consists of pair of words. Choose the best pair to match with the pair in the question.
Run : Walk
(a) Heavy Rain : Drizzle   (b) Jog : Run
(c) Dive : Swim   (d) Bounce : Gallop

53. Martha said to Linda, "Your mother's father's only son's only sister is my father's wife". How is Linda related to Martha?
(a) Aunt   (b) Sister
(c) Cousin   (d) Niece

54. Mahathir is Najma's husband. Najma's son, kamran's wife Reshma has a son named Ashraf. Ashraf's only sister is Urja. How is Mahathir related to Urja?
(a) Father   (b) Grandfather
(c) Cousin   (d) Uncle

55. Choose the figure which is different from the rest.

(1)   (2)   (3)   (4)   (5)

(a) (1)   (b) (2)
(c) (3)   (d) (4)

56. Select the odd figure:
(a)

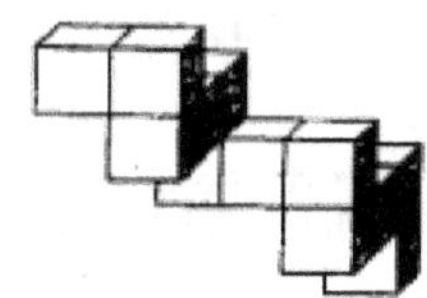

(b)

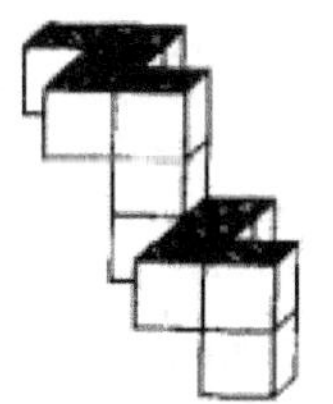

(c)

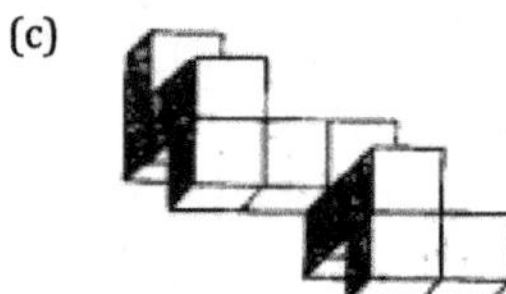

(d)

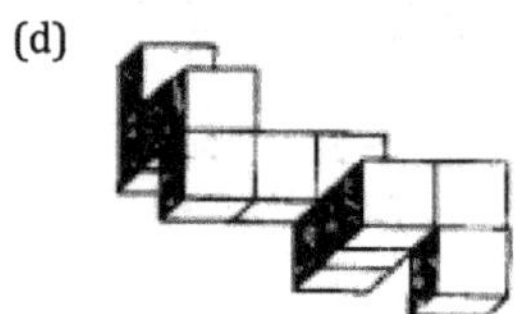

57. **Direction:** Select the odd image pair which is different from other image pairs.

(a)

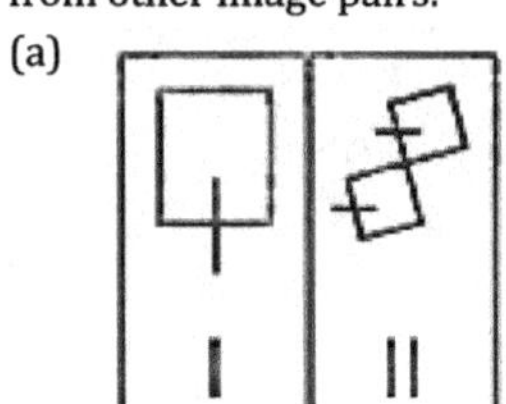

(b)

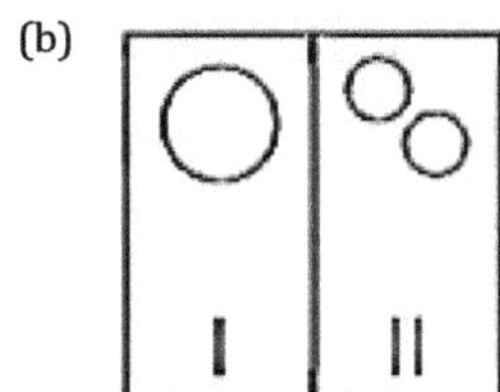

(c)

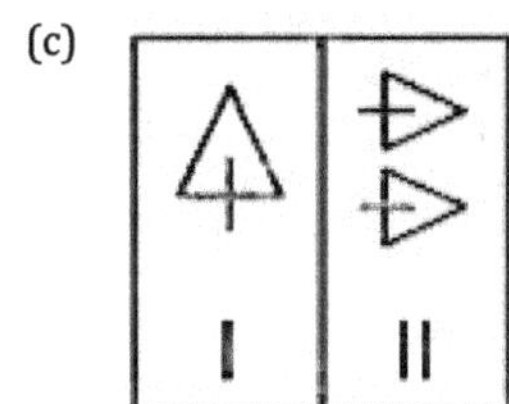

(d)

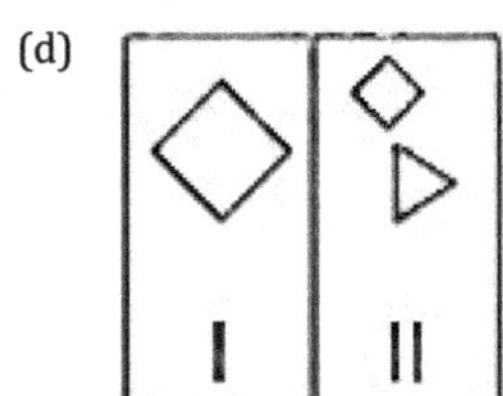

58. **Direction:** Study the following information carefully and answer the questions given below.

Taiyab from his home, he goes 3 km north to the railway station then he turns right and goes 6 km to reach a movie theatre. He then goes 8 km south to reach a lake and from there he takes a left turn and goes for 2 km to reach a hospital. At last, he takes one more left turn and goes for 5 km to reach his office.

What is the shortest distance between the railway station and the lake?

(a) 9 km   (b) 5 km

(c) 4 km   (d) 10 km

59. X walks 3 km away from his starting point. He turns right and travels a further 8 km. He turns left and walks ahead, but notices that he is in the opposite direction of what he is supposed to be in. He started by walking towards east. In which direction is he supposed to go?

(a) North   (b) East

(c) West   (d) South

60. In a certain code language, "SYSTEM" is written as "VATRCK" and "POLICE" is written as "SQMGAC". How will "FAMILY" be coded in that language?

(a) ICNGJW   (b) ICNJGW

(c) ICNGIW   (d) ICMGIW

61. In a certain code language, 'BRIGHT' is written as 'YCBDWW', and 'PAIN' is written as 'SDVU'. How will 'LATER' be written in that language?

(a) WZYVQ   (b) YZWQV

(c) QVYZW   (d) QWERT

62. Find the next figure for the given series:

Question figure:

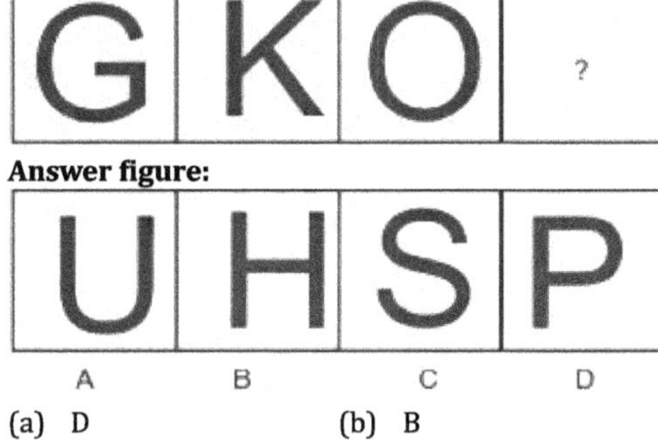

Answer figure:

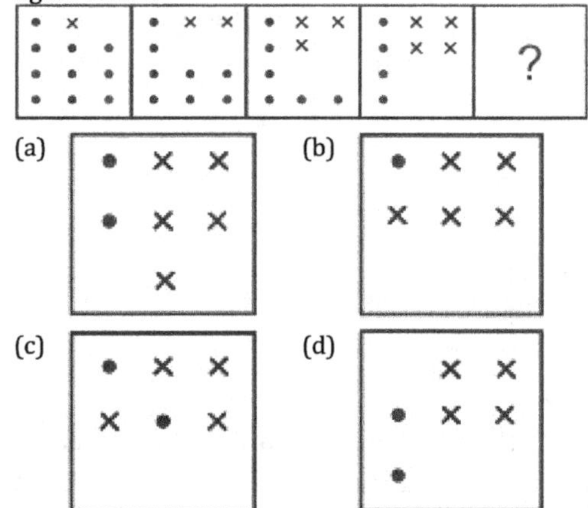

(a) D   (b) B

(c) A   (d) C

63. Select the figure that will come next in the following figure series.

(a)   (b)

(c)   (d)

Ques (64-65): Direction: Identify the diagram that best represents the relationship among classes given below:

64. Thief, Police and Criminal

(a)

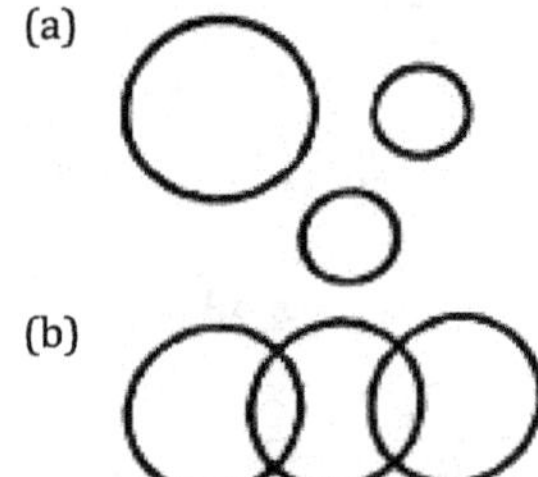

(b)

(c)

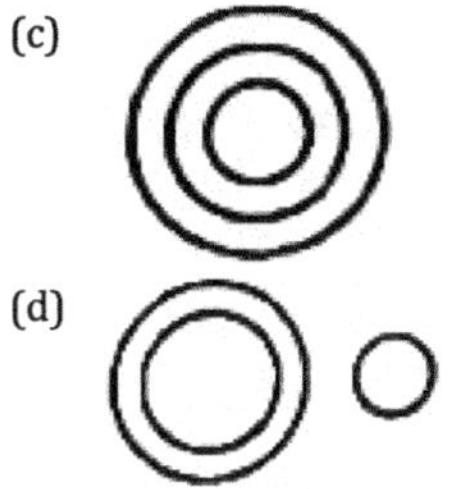

(d)

65. Squirrels, Parrots, Mammals

(a)   (b)

(c)   (d)

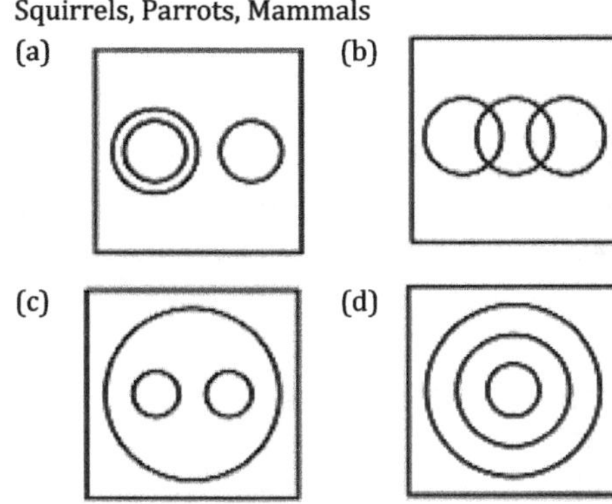

66. In the following number series, a wrong number is given. Find out the wrong number.
850, 843, 829, 808, 788, 745, 703

(a) 843   (b) 829
(c) 808   (d) 788

67. **Direction:** Select the number from among the given options that can replace the question mark (?) in the following series.
214, 197, 179, 160, ?

(a) 147   (b) 159
(c) 140   (d) 149

68. In a row of children, Deepa is 9th from the left and Vijay is 13th from the right. When these two interchange their positions, Deepa becomes 17th from the left. Tell where will Vijay be from the right?

(a) 9th   (b) 21st
(c) 20th   (d) 7th

69. O, P, Q, R, S, and T are standing on a bench according to their height. P is taller than O but shorter than S. Only S is taller than T. R is shorter than P but taller than Q. Who is the shortest?

(a) O
(b) Q
(c) P
(d) Cannot be determined

Ques (70-71): Direction: In the following question below some statements are given followed by some conclusions. Taking the given statements to be true even if they seem to be at variance from commonly known facts, read all the conclusions and then decide which of the given conclusions logically follows the given statements.

70. **Statements:**
All A's are B.
Some B's are D.
Some A's are C.
Some E's are B's as well as D's.
Conclusions:
i. Some C's are B.

ii. Some E's are A.
(a) If only conclusion I follows
(b) If only conclusion II follows
(c) If both conclusion I and II follows
(d) If none of the conclusion I and II follows

71. **Statements:**
Some sky is blue.
Some blue is not white.
Conclusions:
I. No white is blue.
II. Some white is blue.
(a) Only I follows   (b) Only II follows
(c) Either I or II follows   (d) None follows

Ques (72-73): Direction: Read the instructions carefully and answer the question below.

A, B, C, D, E, F, G, and H are the eight male members sitting around a circular table. Four of them are facing the inward direction and four are facing the outward direction. These eight people are married to eight girls namely L, M, N, O, P, Q, R, and S but not necessarily in the same order. No three consecutive people are facing the same direction.

Only one person is sitting between B and the husband of L. Both the immediate neighbours of D are facing the same direction. Either R or P is the wife of D. The husband of Q is facing the outward direction and he is sitting to the immediate right of D. B is sitting third to the right of the person who is the husband of R and they are facing the same direction. The husband of P and the husband of Q are facing the same direction. The wife of D is sitting third to the left of F. Neither O nor P is the wife of B. G is sitting third to the right of C. The husband of L is sitting third to the left of E. Only one person is sitting between F and the husband of M and they are facing the same direction. The husband of S is sitting third to the right of H. A is an immediate neighbour of the husband of M. C is sitting third to the right of the husband of M and they are facing different directions.

72. Who is the husband of S?
(a) B   (b) E
(c) F   (d) A

73. Who is sitting to the immediate right of the husband of N?
(a) D   (b) C
(c) E   (d) B

74. Select the option which is different from the others.
(a) Camels and Roar   (b) Dogs and Bark
(c) Birds and Chirp   (d) Horse and Neigh

75. Select the word which is different from the others.
(a) Vanilla   (b) Biscuits
(c) Bun   (d) Muffin

General Hindi

76. निम्नलिखित शब्दों में वर्तनी के अनुसार शुद्ध शब्द का चयन कीजिए:
(a) अन्ताक्षरी   (b) अन्त्याक्षरी
(c) अन्तअक्षरी   (d) अन्ताक्षरि

77. निम्नलिखित शब्दों में वर्तनी के अनुसार शुद्ध शब्द का चयन कीजिए:
(a) सुषमा   (b) सुशमा
(c) शुषमा   (d) सुसमा

Ques (78-80): निर्देश: निम्नलिखित प्रत्येक कहावत के लिए चार-चार समानार्थक वाक्यांश दिए गए हैं। उनमें से सही उत्तर के रूप में विकल्प का

चयन कीजिए और उत्तर-पत्र पर चिह्न लगाइए।

78. पत्थर को जोंक नहीं लगती
    (a) सबल का शोषण नहीं होता
    (b) मजबूत चीज़ आसानी से खराब नहीं होती
    (c) दो धूर्तों में प्रायः टकराव नहीं होता
    (d) हठी पर कोई प्रभाव नहीं होता

79. विहंगम दृष्टि
    (a) गहरी नज़र
    (b) तीखी नज़र
    (c) मंद नज़र
    (d) सरसरी नज़र

80. काटो तो खून नहीं
    (a) पीड़ा शांत हो जाना
    (b) बिल्कुल निर्जीव हो जाना
    (c) भय के कारण स्तब्ध हो जाना
    (d) गुस्सा शांत हो जाना

81. पुल्लिंग संज्ञा के स्थान पर स्त्रीलिंग कर देने से 'काला' विशेषण का क्या रूप होगा?
    (a) काले
    (b) काला
    (c) कालों
    (d) काली

82. 'कव्वाली' शब्द में कौन सा लिंग है?
    (a) पुल्लिंग
    (b) स्त्रीलिंग
    (c) नपुंसकलिंग
    (d) उभयलिंग

83. 'बुरे भाव से की गई संधि' को कहते हैं:
    (a) दुरभिसंधि
    (b) छद्मसंधि
    (c) कूट-संधि
    (d) दुष्ट-संधि

84. कौनसा वाक्यांश युग्म संगत नहीं है?
    (a) कोई काम करने की इच्छा - चरिष्णु
    (b) आकाश में असंख्य तारों का प्रकाश पुंज - नीहारिका
    (c) जो पहले कभी न हुआ हो - अभूतपूर्व
    (d) जो हृदय को पिघला दे - हृदयद्रावक

85. निम्नलिखित में से देशज शब्द का चयन कीजिए:
    (a) मुग़ल
    (b) बेगम
    (c) सुराग
    (d) डिबिया

86. 'स्त्रीत्व' शब्द में कौन-सी संज्ञा है?
    (a) भाववाचक संज्ञा
    (b) व्यक्तिवाचक संज्ञा
    (c) जातिवाचक संज्ञा
    (d) द्रव्यवाचक संज्ञा

87. निम्नलिखित में से कौन-सा शब्द विदेशज है?
    (a) मटरगश्ती
    (b) इडली
    (c) ताम्बूल
    (d) बाजरा

88. नीचे दिए गए शब्द का सही बहुवचन वाला विकल्प पहचानिए।
    मामा
    (a) मामें
    (b) मामियाँ
    (c) मामाओं
    (d) मामा

89. नई **दवाई** की खोज जारी है। में **दवाई** का बहुवचन रूप क्या होगा?
    (a) दवाईयाँ
    (b) दवाइयाँ
    (c) दवाएँ
    (d) दवइयाँ

Ques (90-91): निर्देश: वाक्य के अशुद्ध भाग (त्रुटिपूर्ण भाग) का चयन कीजिए।

90. राजा दशरथ को (a)/ चार पुत्र राम, लक्ष्मण, भरत और शत्रुघ्न (b)/ पैदा हुए थे। (c)/ कोई त्रुटि नहीं (d)
    (a) (a)
    (b) (b)
    (c) (c)
    (d) (d)

91. आज भ्रष्टाचार हर क्षेत्र में (a)/ शिष्टाचार के रूप में (b)/जाना जाता है। (c)/कोई त्रुटि नहीं (d)
    (a) (a)
    (b) (b)
    (c) (c)
    (d) (d)

92. "अभिसरण" का विलोम शब्द क्या है?
    (a) अनुसरण
    (b) प्रसारण
    (c) मिश्रण
    (d) अपसरण

93. निम्न में से कौन-सा एक युग्म विपरीतार्थक नहीं है?
    (a) कंजूस - उदार
    (b) ऊँच - नीच
    (c) उदय - उग्र
    (d) उत्थान - पतन

94. निम्नलिखित अनुलोम-विलोम युग्मों में से कोई एक युग्म सही नहीं है, चयन कीजिए:
    (a) पुरस्कार-दंड
    (b) पुरस्कार-पुरुस्कृत
    (c) पाप-पुण्य
    (d) पाप-पुन्य

95. दिवंगत शब्द का समानार्थक शब्द चुनिए -
    (a) बुजुर्ग
    (b) स्वर्गवासी
    (c) पूर्व
    (d) सुर

96. 'भागवद्भक्ति' का संधि विच्छेद बताइये।
    (a) भवत् + भक्ति
    (b) भागव + भक्ति
    (c) भागत् + भक्ति
    (d) भागवत् + भक्ति

97. अयादि संधि में "ऐ" के बदले क्या हो जाता है?
    (a) अय्
    (b) आय्
    (c) अव्
    (d) आव्

98. किस क्रम में संधि का सही प्रयोग नहीं हुआ है?
    (a) देवी + अर्पण = देव्यर्पण
    (b) वि + ऊह = व्यूह
    (c) दै + इनी = दायिनी
    (d) अभि + अर्थी = अभ्यर्थी

99. भक्तमाल के रचनाकार है:
    (a) अग्रदास
    (b) नन्ददास
    (c) रसखान
    (d) नाभादास

100. "सत्यवती कथा" के रचनाकार निम्न में से कौन है?
    (a) चिंतामणि
    (b) बिहारी
    (c) ईश्वर दास
    (d) केशवदास

// Smart Answer Sheet //

Correct — Percentage of students who answered correctly.

Skipped — Percentage of students who skipped.

Q.	Ans.	Correct / Skipped	Q.	Ans.	Correct / Skipped	Q.	Ans.	Correct / Skipped
1	D	16.63% / 4.84%	2	D	76.07% / 0.0%	3	C	19.22% / 3.13%
4	A	49.9% / 1.05%	5	C	78.12% / 0.0%	6	C	56.46% / 1.52%
7	B	88.4% / 0.0%	8	B	66.24% / 1.87%	9	D	80.68% / 0.0%
10	B	69.97% / 1.84%	11	A	64.09% / 1.08%	12	D	11.91% / 3.93%
13	C	26.44% / 3.5%	14	B	53.25% / 1.28%	15	D	80.06% / 0.0%
16	C	53.7% / 1.15%	17	D	22.1% / 3.32%	18	D	15.39% / 4.06%
19	D	16.79% / 4.56%	20	A	58.52% / 1.92%	21	B	49.05% / 1.6%
22	D	66.56%	23	A	62.37%	24	A	50.92%

		1.57%			1.69%			1.18%
25	C	68.96% / 1.9%	26	D	48.78% / 1.76%	27	A	57.2% / 1.9%
28	D	49.01% / 1.82%	29	D	81.21% / 0.0%	30	D	14.51% / 4.07%
31	A	83.57% / 0.0%	32	A	76.87% / 0.0%	33	C	45.58% / 1.25%
34	B	22.73% / 4.95%	35	B	30.09% / 4.35%	36	D	30.75% / 4.66%
37	A	31.28% / 4.25%	38	C	89.85% / 0.0%	39	A	42.68% / 1.4%
40	A	12.04% / 3.1%	41	C	22.44% / 4.23%	42	A	90.0% / 0.0%
43	A	56.87% / 1.3%	44	A	49.35% / 1.01%	45	C	68.8% / 1.5%
46	D	47.8% / 1.14%	47	D	42.72% / 1.81%	48	B	79.81% / 0.0%
49	B	10.5% / 4.26%	50	D	62.05% / 1.03%	51	B	87.89% / 0.0%
52	A	67.29% / 1.91%	53	B	44.24% / 1.29%	54	B	41.63% / 1.11%
55	D	82.48% / 0.0%	56	D	45.34% / 1.47%	57	D	40.28% / 1.2%
58	D	32.69% / 4.79%	59	C	55.5% / 1.77%	60	A	56.36% / 1.38%
61	A	58.82% / 1.4%	62	D	69.65% / 1.5%	63	A	78.44% / 0.0%
64	D	80.41% / 0.0%	65	A	64.31% / 1.33%	66	D	68.13% / 1.04%
67	C	59.72% / 1.08%	68	B	16.56% / 3.79%	69	D	64.66% / 1.56%
70	A	63.53% / 1.76%	71	C	44.99% / 1.13%	72	D	49.45% / 1.4%
73	B	40.86% / 1.78%	74	A	88.5% / 0.0%	75	A	85.67% / 0.0%
76	B	52.59% / 1.8%	77	A	41.19% / 1.8%	78	D	56.62% / 1.0%
79	D	51.52% / 1.88%	80	C	61.78% / 1.51%	81	D	88.65% / 0.0%
82	B	82.54% / 0.0%	83	A	63.48% / 1.84%	84	A	69.05% / 1.68%
85	D	59.02% / 1.45%	86	A	23.18% / 3.93%	87	A	66.3% / 1.48%
88	D	64.26% / 1.85%	89	B	68.41% / 1.09%	90	A	11.37% / 3.35%
91	C	78.18% / 0.0%	92	D	40.09% / 1.98%	93	C	64.75% / 1.22%
94	B	30.28% / 4.39%	95	B	52.45% / 1.49%	96	D	21.79% / 3.08%
97	B	52.4% / 1.1%	98	C	51.53% / 1.65%	99	D	77.4% / 0.0%
100	C	47.13% / 1.31%						

// Hints and Solutions //

1(D). The timeless Indian novel 'Devdas' was written by Saratchandra Chattopadhyay.
- Sarat Chandra Chattopadhyay (1876-1938) wrotes Devdas in 1901 at the age of 17.
- His other famous novels are Pather Dabi, Srikanta, Parineeta, Datta, etc.
- Ilis nickname is Nyailia.
- He is also known as Anila Devi.

2(D). Montague-Chelmsford Reforms introduced **Dyarchy** which was a kind of double government in the provinces.
- Montague-Chelmsford Reforms introduced Dyarchy which was a kind of double government in the provinces.
- The Montagu–Chelmsford Reforms were enacted by the colonial government to gradually install self-governing institutions in British India.
- The amendments are named after Edwin Montagu, Secretary of State for India from 1917 to 1922, and Lord Chelmsford, Viceroy of India from 1916 to 1921.
- The Central Legislative Assembly and the Council of State would now make up the Imperial Legislative Council.
- The Dual Government System, or dyarchy, was to be followed by the provinces.
- The review commission (Simon Commission) was led by Sir John Simon, who suggested further constitutional changes.

3(C). The fear of the Phallus worship was replaced in the **Yajur Veda** by its recognition as an official ritual.
Yajur Veda:
- The fear of the Phallus worship was replaced in the Yajur Veda by its recognition as an official ritual.
- Harappans worshipped Mother Goddess but the female deities played a minor part in the Vedic religion.
- Aryans were said to provide spouses to their gods by later Vedic times.
- But the fear of the Phallus worship was replaced in the Yajur Veda by its recognition as an official ritual.

RigVeda:
- The oldest religious text in the world.
- It is the collection of hymns, composed around 1700 BC, contains 1,028 hymns and is divided into 10 mandalas.
- The third mandala contains the Gayatri Mantra.

Samaveda:
- It is called the book of chants.
- Itis a collection of melodies.
- The hymns of the Samaveda were recited by Udgatri at the Soma sacrifice.
- It contains Dhrupad Raga.

Atharva Veda:
- It is a book of magical formulas.
- Mentioned in the Gotra is found in Atharvaveda.

4(A). After the death of King Ashoka, the **Maurya Dynasty** declined rapidly.
- The later Mauryas ruled from 232 BC-185 BC .
- Ashoka's death was followed by the division of the Mauryan Empire into two parts– Western and Eastern regions .
- The Western part came to be ruled by Kunala (son of Ashoka) and the Eastern part came to be ruled by Dasaratha .
- The last Mauryan ruler, Brihadratha , was assassinated in 185 BC by his commander-in-chief, Pushyamitra Sunga .

5(C). The All India Kisan Sabha was organized for the first time in Lucknow, Uttar Pradesh, India, in 1936.

6(C). The Moplah rebellion of 1921 take place in Kerala.

7(B). Dev Prayag is one of the Panch Prayag of Alaknanda River where Alaknanda and Bhagirathi rivers meet.
Dev Prayag is located in the hilly areas of Uttrakhand. Bhagirathi originates from Gangotri and Alaknanda originates from Badrinath, both of which are considered sacred destinations for Hindus across the world. Dev prayag is the last prayag of River Alaknanda. It is believed that Lord Rama and King

Dushratha did penance here.

8(B). Breaking of a rock in place is called weathering. Weathering is the method of disintegrating or breaking up rock minerals not removing them. Weathering refers to the breakdown or disintegration and decomposition of rocks in situ through mechanical and chemical changes in rock. The nature and magnitude of weathering differs from place to place and region to region. Weathering can be caused by wind, water, ice, plants, gravity, and changes in temperature.

9(D). The Volga is the longest river in Europe.
- It is the national river of Russia flowing at a distance of 2294 miles.
- It originates in the Valdai Hills northwest of Moscow and discharges into the Caspian Sea.
- It has two main tributaries named Kama and Oka.
- The Danube is Europe's second longest river, after the Volga and flows through 10 countries.

10(B). As per the World Bank report "Migration and Development Brief', India was set to receive $100 billion as remittances in 2022. In 2021 India received $89.4 billion in remittances. India is the 1st country in the world to receive $100 billion in remittances from migrant workers abroad. With a share of 23% of total remittances, the US surpassed the UAE as the top source country in 2020-21.

11(A). Kerala CM Pinarayi Vijayan on 10 December 2022 declared a seed farm, located in Aluva, as the first carbon-neutral farm in the country. The Kerala government has announced to start of Carbon-neutral farms in all its assembly constituencies. Women's associations will be formed to implement this in tribal areas. As many as 170 tons of more carbon have been procured at the farm.

12(D). Dr Adarsh Swaika, a joint secretary in the Ministry of External Affairs, has been appointed India's next Ambassador to Kuwait. Swaika has succeeded Sibi George as the Indian envoy in Kuwait. Also, Avtar Singh, Director in the Ministry of External Affairs, has been appointed as India's next Ambassador to the Republic of Guinea.

13(C). To raise awareness about Yoga, the Mobile app "Namaste Yoga" was launched by Ministry of Ayush in India.
- The event was organized by the Ministry of Ayush in association with the Morarji Desai National Institute of Yoga.
- The event brought together several Yoga Gurus and experienced Yoga exponents on the virtual platform, to appeal to the world community to adopt Yoga in their daily life for the betterment of both the individual self and mankind.
- The event underlined the importance of the central theme of IDY 2021 "Be With Yoga, Be At Home".
- As a part of the event, a mobile application devoted to Yoga named "Namaste Yoga", was also launched.
- The Namaste Yoga" app has been designed as an information platform for the public, with the aim to raise awareness about yoga and make it accessible to the larger community.

14(B). To separate anthracene from a mixture of salt and anthracene, sublimation can be used.

15(D). Shoots of plant show upward movement and it can be designated to be Negatively geotropic.

16(C). Too much use of insecticides will cause water pollution. Water pollution is at rise due to persistent organic chemicals present in pesticides.

17(D). The Election Commission of India is an autonomous constitutional authority responsible for administering Union and State election processes in India. Part XV of the Indian constitution deals with elections and establishes a commission for these matters.
Functions of ECI:
- It ensures that political parties and candidates adhere to the Model Code of Conduct.
- Regulates and registers political parties as per eligibility to contest in elections. So, statement 1 is correct.
- Put a limit on campaign expenditure per candidate to all parties.
- All political parties must submit annual reports to the ECI to be able to claim the tax benefit on the contributions.
- Guarantees that all political parties regularly submit audited financial reports.
- Supervise, control and conduct all elections to Parliament and State Legislatures.
- Prepares electoral rolls. So, statement 3 is correct.
- Managing the election process from notification of election dates to the declaration of results.
- It can cancel the polls in event of any irregularity like rigging, booth capture, violence, etc.
- Allot election symbols to political parties or candidates. So, statement 2 is correct.
- Advising to the President or Governor in matters relating to the disqualification of sitting legislators except under Schedule 10. So, statement 4 is correct.
- It acts as a court for settling disputes related to the granting of recognition and allotment of symbols to political parties.

18(D). Zila Parishad or District Council:
- It is the third tier in the Panchayati Raj system added to the Constitution by the 73rd Constitutional Amendment Act of 1992.
- It is an elected body and its members shall be elected directly by the people.
- The chairperson and vice-chairman are to be elected indirectly by and from amongst the elected members.
- The members of the Panchayat Samiti (link between gram panchayat and Zila Parishad) are ex officio members of the Zila Parishad.
- The Deputy Chief Executive Officer from the General Administration Department at the district level is ex-Officio Secretary of Zila Parishad.
- The Chief Executive Officer, who is an IAS Officer or Senior State Service Officer heads the administrative set-up of the Zila Parishad.
- In each district of the state, the members of the Zilla Panchayat are members of the Lok Sabha, members of the Legislative Assembly, members of the Legislative Councils and Rajya Sabha members.
- One-third of the total seats are reserved for women and reservation of seats for scheduled caste and scheduled tribe according to the

proportion of their population.

19(D). Constitutional government means a government limited by the terms of the Constitution.

Constitutional government:

- The core element of constitutional government is the existence of a Rule-of-Law or set of basic laws that bind both public office-holders and all members of a society within a given territory.
- Presently most states avail of a constitution, which directs the organization of the state, the relations between the public offices within the state, as well the human and civil rights of the individual.
- The Constitution seeks to regulate political power.
- Constitutional government means a limited government.
- A constitutional government is conducted according to rules and principles which are binding on all political actors and which therefore help to constrain the unfettered excise of power by separating it or dividing it.

20(A). Chief Minister Raj Neer Scheme was launched on 13 March 2020.

Under this scheme, will be waived if the monthly water consumption of domestic consumers in the urban area of the state is less than 15000 liters.

21(B). The development target of the 11th plan was kept at 9%, whereas in the last year it will be up to 10%. The objective of this plan was kept inclusive growth.

22(D). The different colors of the rainbow revolution indicate different agricultural practices, such as the Green Revolution (food grains), the White Revolution (milk), the Yellow Revolution (oilseeds), the Blue Revolution (fish farming).

23(A). The United States was represented by the United States Olympic & Paralympic Committee (USOPC) at the 2020 Summer Olympics in Tokyo. The country finished the Games with 113 medals, the most amongst all nations: 39 gold, 41 silver, and 33 bronze. US won the maximum number of medals at 2020 Summer Olympic Games (played in 2021). These individual totals were each the highest of the Games. This was the third consecutive Summer Olympics that the U.S. was the medal table leader. The medal total was slightly lower than five years prior in Rio de Janeiro, where the United States won 46 gold and 121 total medals.

24(A). Following are the important points associated with Limited Liability Partnership (LLP):

- Budget 2021 proposed Decriminalisation of the Limited Liability Partnership (LLP) Act, 2008.
- It is a partnership in which some or all partners (depending on the jurisdiction) have limited liabilities. In an LLP, each partner is not responsible or liable for another partner's misconduct or negligence. So, statement 1 is correct.
- The LLP can continue its existence irrespective of changes in partners. It is capable of entering into contracts and holding property in its own name.
- The LLP is a separate legal entity, is liable to the full extent of its assets but the liability of the partners is limited to their agreed contribution in the LLP.

- The internal governance structure of a company is regulated by statute (i.e. Companies Act, 2013) whereas for an LLP it would be by a contractual agreement between partners. So, statement 2 is incorrect.

25(C). Maitri and Bharati are the two permanent research stations of India in Antarctica. Thus, statement 1 is correct.

National Centre for Polar and Ocean Research (NCPOR) is the nodal agency for India's scientific expeditions in Antarctica and the Arctic. Thus, statement 2 is correct.

26(D). Given,
$$\frac{32}{100} \times 850 - ? = \frac{14}{100} \times 640$$
$$\Rightarrow 16 \times 17 - ? = 14 \times 6.4$$
$$\Rightarrow 272 - ? = 89.6$$
$$\Rightarrow ? = 272 - 89.6$$
$$\Rightarrow ? = 182.4$$
Hence, the correct option is (D)

27(A). Given:
Profit $= 26\%$
New selling Price $= ₹ 81.60$
New Profit $= 32\%$
Formula Used:
$$\text{Selling price} = \frac{\text{cost price}}{100} \times (100 + \text{profit} \%)$$
Let the Cost price be x.
Selling Price $= 1.26x$
New Cost Price $= 0.8x$
New Selling Price $= 1.26x - 81.60$
$$1.26x - 81.60 = \frac{(0.8x)}{100} \times (100 + 32)$$
$$\Rightarrow x = \frac{81.60}{0.204}$$
$$\Rightarrow x = 400$$
$\therefore$ The original cost price of the watch is $₹ 400$.

28(D). Given:
CP (Cost price) of 70 article $=$ Rs. 890
SP (Selling price) of 60 article $=$ Rs. 890
$$\text{Profit} \% = \frac{(\text{Selling price-Cost price})}{\text{Cost price}} \times 100$$
CP of 70 article is 890
$\Rightarrow$ CP of 420 article $=$ Rs. 5340
$\Rightarrow$ SP of 60 article $=$ 890
$\Rightarrow$ SP of 420 article $=$ Rs. 6230
Profit $= 6230 - 5340 =$ Rs. 890
$\therefore$ Profit $\% = \frac{890}{5340} \times 100$
$$= 16\frac{2}{3}\%$$

29(D). Given:
Principal $(P) = 18,750$, Rate $r_1 = 4\%$ and $r_2 = 8\%$
We know that,
$$\text{Amount} = P\left(1 + \frac{r_1}{100}\right)\left(1 + \frac{r_2}{100}\right)$$
$$\text{Amount} = 18750\left(1 + \frac{4}{100}\right)\left(1 + \frac{8}{100}\right)$$
$$\text{Amount} = 18,750 \times \frac{104}{100} \times \frac{108}{100}$$
$$\text{Amount} = 21,060$$
Compound Interest $=$ Amount $-$ Principal
$\Rightarrow 21,060 - 18,750 =$ Rs. 2310

30(D). We know that,
$$\text{Simple Interest (SI)} = \frac{P \times r \times t}{100}$$
For Compound Interest (CI):
$$A = P\left(1 + \frac{r}{100}\right)^t$$
A is the amount at the end of time t
P is the principal

t is time

r is rate

For Simple Interest (SI), there is 100% increase to amount, thus A = 2P

$\Rightarrow$ Simple Interest (SI) = p

Time is 8 years.

$\therefore p = \frac{p \times r \times t}{100}$

$\Rightarrow r = \frac{100}{8}$

$\Rightarrow r = 12.5\%$

Now, $P = $ Rs. 8000, $t = 2$ years and $r = 12.5\%$

$A = 8000\left(1 + \frac{12.5}{100}\right)^2$

$\Rightarrow A = 8000 \times \left(\frac{100+12.5}{100}\right)^2$

$\Rightarrow A = 8000 \times (1.125)^2$

$\Rightarrow A = $ Rs. 10125

$CI = A - P$

Where CI = Compound Interest

A = Amount

P = Principal

$\Rightarrow CI = 10125 - 8000 = $ Rs. 2125

31(A). Given:

The area of the rectangle is 144 cm ^{2} and the sides are in the ratio $4 : 9$.

Let the length be $4x$ and the breadth be $9x$.

Area of a rectangle = length $\times$ breadth

$\Rightarrow 144 = 4x \times 9x$

$\Rightarrow 144 = 36x^2$

$\Rightarrow x^2 = \frac{144}{36}$

$\Rightarrow x^2 = 4$

$\Rightarrow x = \sqrt{4}$

$\Rightarrow x = 2$ cm

Therefore, the length $= 4 \times 2 = 8$ cm and the breadth $= 18$ cm

Now, to find the perimeter.

Perimeter of a rectangle = 2 (Length + Breadth)

Perimeter $= 2(8 + 18)$

Perimeter $= 2 \times 26$

Perimeter $= 52$ cm

Therefore, the perimeter $= 52$ cm

32(A). Given:

Traveling $= 11$ km $= 11000$ m

The radius of the circular wheel

$r = 1\frac{3}{4} = \frac{7}{4} = 1.75$ m

Circumference of a circular wheel $= 2\pi r$

$= 2 \times \frac{22}{7} \times 1.75$ m

Number of revolutions

$= \frac{\text{Distance to be covered}}{\text{Circumference of circle}}$

$= \frac{11000}{2 \times \frac{22}{7} \times 1.75}$

$= \frac{11000}{11}$

$= 1000$

33(C). Given,

Number $= 40$

Let one part is a and other is $(40 - a)$

$\Rightarrow 2a^2 = (40 - a) + 5$

$\Rightarrow 2a^2 + a - 45 = 0$

$\Rightarrow 2a^2 + 10a - 9a - 45 = 0$

$\Rightarrow 2a(a + 5) - 9(a + 5) = 0$

$\Rightarrow (2a - 9)(a + 5) = 0$

$\Rightarrow a = \frac{9}{2}$ or $a = -5$

One number must be $\frac{9}{2}$.

Second number $= 40 - \frac{9}{2} = \frac{71}{2}$

$\therefore$ Two numbers are $= \frac{9}{2}$ and $\frac{71}{2}$.

34(B). Given:

Total student $= 96$

As we know,

Average $= \frac{\text{Sum of observation}}{\text{Number of observations}}$

Let the number of boys be x.

Sum of boys and girls $= 96$

Number of girls $= 96 - x$

The number of girls is 40% more than boys.

$\frac{140x}{100} = 96 - x$

$\Rightarrow 14x = 960 - 10x$

$\Rightarrow x = 40$

Number of girls $= 56$

Total sum of boys and girls marks $= 96 \times 63 = 6048$

Let the average of girls is M.

Sum of average of girls $= 56M$

The average of boys is 40% of girls $= \frac{140}{100} \times M$

Sum of boys $= 1.4 \text{ M} \times 40 = 56 \text{ M}$

According to the question,

$56M + 56M = 6048$

$\Rightarrow M = \frac{6048}{112}$

$\Rightarrow M = 54$

$\therefore$ The average score of the girls in mathematics is 54.

35(B). When Ajay sells sim cards of Rs. x then his bonus will be $\left[\left(\frac{x}{100}\right)^2 + 10\right]$

Bonus for the first three month

$= \left[\left(\frac{3000}{100}\right)^2 + 10\right] \times 3$

$= $ Rs. 2710

Bonus for the next five month

$= \left[\left(\frac{5000}{100}\right)^2 + 10\right] \times 5$

$= $ Rs. 12550

Bonus for the next four month

$= \left[\left(\frac{8000}{100}\right)^2 + 10\right] \times 4$

$= $ Rs. 25640

Total earning as bonus for whole year,

$= 2710 + 12550 + 25640$

$= $ Rs. 40900

His average bonus $= \frac{40900}{12}$

$= $ Rs. 3410

Thus his average earning for whole year,

$= 3410 + 200$

$= $ Rs. 3610

36(D). Let the price of a machine be Rs. 100 and let original sales be 100 pieces.

As the price of the machine is increased by 20%.

And the number sold is decreased by 25%.

New price $= 100 + \frac{20}{100} \times 100 = 120$

Number of sales after price rise $= 100 - \frac{25}{100} \times 100 = 75$

Initial revenue $= 100 \times 100 = 10000$

New revenue $= 120 \times 75 = 9000$

Decrease in revenue

$= \left(\frac{(10000 - 9000)}{10000}\right) \times 100$

$= 10\%$

$\therefore$ Decrease in revenue by 10%.

37(A). Tap A can fill the tank $= 180$ minutes

Tap A's one-minute work $= \frac{1}{180}$

Tap B can fill the tank $= 20$ minutes

Tap B's one-minute work $= \frac{1}{20}$

Tap C can fill the tank $= 90$ minutes

Tap C's one-minute work $= \frac{1}{90}$

When all the taps are opened together,

$A + B + C = \left(\frac{1}{180} + \frac{1}{20} + \frac{1}{90}\right) = \frac{(1+9+2)}{180} = \frac{12}{180} = \frac{1}{15}$

So, $(A + B + C)$ working together can fill the whole tank in 15 minutes.

38(C). Time is taken $= \dfrac{\text{Total work}}{\text{Efficiency}}$

As, 14 workers can construct a wall in 20 days

So, 1 worker construct a wall in $20 \times 14 = 280$ days

$\Rightarrow$ 20 works construct a wall in $\frac{280}{20} = 14$ days

$\Rightarrow$ 20 workers construct 2 such walls in $14 \times 2 = 28$ days

$\therefore$ 20 workers construct 2 walls in 28 days.

39(A). Given:

Reenu can do a work in 15 days

Reenu and Meenu can do a work in 10 days

Total wages = Rs. 600

Calculation:

Reenu finishes the work in 15 days

$\therefore$ Part of work done by Reenu in one day $= \frac{1}{15}$

Working together they complete the work in 10 days.

$\Rightarrow$ Part of Work done by both in 1 day $= \frac{1}{10}$

$\therefore$ Part of Work done by Meenu in 1 day $= \frac{1}{10} - \frac{1}{15} = \frac{1}{30}$

The wages will be in ratio of their efficiency i.e.

Ratio of wages of Reenu : Meenu $= \frac{1}{15} : \frac{1}{30} = 2 : 1$

Share of Reenu $= 600 \times \frac{2}{3} =$ Rs. 400

Share of Meenu $= 600 - 400 =$ Rs. 200

40(A). Given,

The speed of the current is $1.25x$ km/hr.

And the speed of a boat in still water is 12 km/hr more than that of current.

According to the question,

The speed of a boat + The speed of the current $= \dfrac{\text{Distance}}{\text{(Time taken by the boat)}}$

$1.25x + 1.25x + 12 = \frac{160}{5}$

Or, $2.5x = 20$

Or, $x = 8$

41(C). Speed of Raman $= 20\,\text{km} / \text{hr}$

After convert in km/hr to m/s,

$= \frac{5}{18} \times 20 = \frac{50}{9}\,\text{m/s}$

We know that, Time $= \dfrac{\text{distance}}{\text{speed}}$

$\Rightarrow$ Time $= \frac{400}{\frac{50}{9}}$

$\Rightarrow$ Time $= 400 \times \frac{9}{50}$

$\Rightarrow$ Time $= 8 \times 9$

$\Rightarrow$ Time $= 72$ sec

$\Rightarrow 72$ sec $= \frac{72}{60} = \frac{6}{5} = 1.2$ minute

42(A). Factor of $36 = 2 \times 2 \times 3 \times 3$

Factor of $144 = 2 \times 2 \times 2 \times 3 \times 3$

Taking common factor, we get

HCF $= 2 \times 2 \times 3 \times 3 = 36$

43(A). Let the present age of the son is x years and the present age of the father is $3x$ years.

We know that the difference between the ages of any two person at any time is equal.

It is given that, $3x - x = 24$

$\Rightarrow 2x = 24$

$\Rightarrow x = 12$

Therefore, the present age of the son $= 12$ years.

44(A). Given:

$a + b + c = 45$ and $ab + bc + ca = 254$

Formula Used:

$(a + b + c)^2 = a^2 + b^2 + c^2 + 2(ab + bc + ca)$

$\Rightarrow (45)^2 = a^2 + b^2 + c^2 + 2 \times (254)$

$\Rightarrow 2025 = a^2 + b^2 + c^2 + 508$

$\Rightarrow a^2 + b^2 + c^2 = 2025 - 508$

$\therefore a^2 + b^2 + c^2 = 1517$

45(C). In an ellipse $\frac{x^2}{a^2} + \frac{y^2}{b^2} = 1, a > b$:

The length of the latus rectum is equal to $\frac{2b^2}{a}$.

Minor axis of ellipse $= 2b$

Its eccentricity is given by: $e = \sqrt{1 - \frac{b^2}{a^2}}$

According to the question, the latus rectum of the ellipse is equal to half of its minor axis. Therefore,

$\Rightarrow \frac{2b^2}{a} = \frac{2b}{2}$

$\Rightarrow a = 2b$

Now, the eccentricity of the ellipse

$\left(e\right) = \sqrt{1 - \frac{b^2}{a^2}} = \sqrt{1 - \frac{b^2}{4b^2}} = \frac{\sqrt{3}}{2}$

46(D). We know that,

$\Rightarrow \sec^2\theta = 1 + \tan^2\theta$

We have,

$\Rightarrow \left(\sec^2\theta\right)^2 - \sec^2\theta = 3$

$\Rightarrow \left(1 + \tan^2\theta\right)^2 - \left(1 + \tan^2\theta\right) = 3$

$\Rightarrow \left(1 + \tan^4\theta + 2\tan^2\theta\right) - \left(1 + \tan^2\theta\right) = 3$

$\Rightarrow 1 + \tan^4\theta + 2\tan^2\theta - 1 - \tan^2\theta = 3$

$\Rightarrow \tan^4\theta + \tan^2\theta = 3$

47(D). Given:

$n_1 = n$ and $x_1 = 2M$

$n_2 = 2n$ and $x_2 = M$

The combined mean will be:

$= \frac{(n \times 2M) + (2n \times M)}{n + 2n}$

$= \frac{4nM}{3n}$

$= \frac{4M}{3}$

48(B). Number of horizontal lines in chess board $= 9$

Number of vertical lines in chess board $= 9$

2 horizontal lines and 2 vertical lines will for 1 rectangle box

Number of rectangle $= {}^9C_2 \times {}^9C_2$

$\Rightarrow 36 \times 36 = 1296$

49(B). For Arunoday:

In 2002:

Annual income = Rs. 650 thousand

Annual expenditure $= 400 \times \frac{3}{2} = 600$ thousand

$\therefore$ Saving (annual) $= 50$ thousand

Similarly, annual saving in $2006 = 800 - \left(200 \times \frac{3}{2}\right) = 500$ thousand

For Geet,

Annual saving in $2002 = \left(650 \times \frac{4}{5}\right) - 400 = 120$ thousand

Annual saving in $2006 = \left(800 \times \frac{3}{8}\right) - 200 = 100$ thousand

∴ Required difference of average $= \frac{1}{2}[(500 + 50) - (120 + 100)] = 165$ thousand

50(D). Income of Geet in 2003 and $2005 = 700 \times \frac{4}{7} + 700 \times \frac{2}{7} = $ Rs. 600 thousand

Expenditure of Arunoday in 2004 and $2006 = 300 \times \frac{4}{3} + 200 \times \frac{3}{2}$

$= $ Rs. 700 thousand

∴ Required ratio $= \frac{600}{700} = 6 : 7$

51(B). The logic is:

Deer : Fawn → The young one of a Deer is called fawn.

Similarly,

Horse : ? → The young one of a Horse is called foal.

52(A). The logic is:

Run : Walk → Run means to move at a speed faster than walk.

Similarly,

Heavy Rain : Drizzle → Heavy rain means to drizzle fast or drizzle means light rain falling in very fine drops.

53(B).

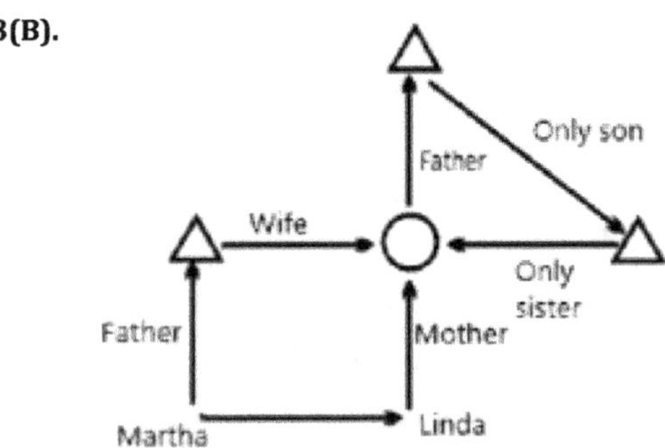

From the above figure, it is clear that Linda is the sister of Martha.

54(B).

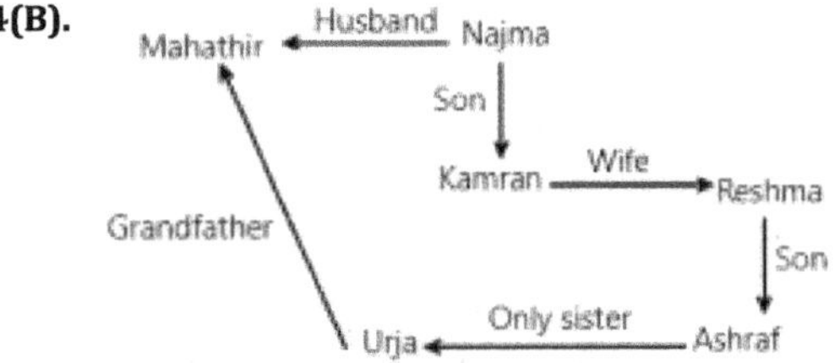

It is clear from the picture that Mahathir will have grandfather's relation with energy.

55(D). Except figure (4) in all other figures, the arrow and the sign lie towards the black end of the main figure.

56(D). All three options have two black parts but option (D) has three black parts.

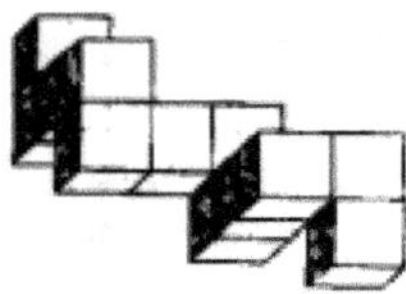

57(D). The logic follows here is:

All the given figure in option (A), (B), and (C) follows the pattern of: Right side image is the double of the left side except the option (D) in which right side image is different from the left side.

58(D). From the given information the displacements are as shown below:

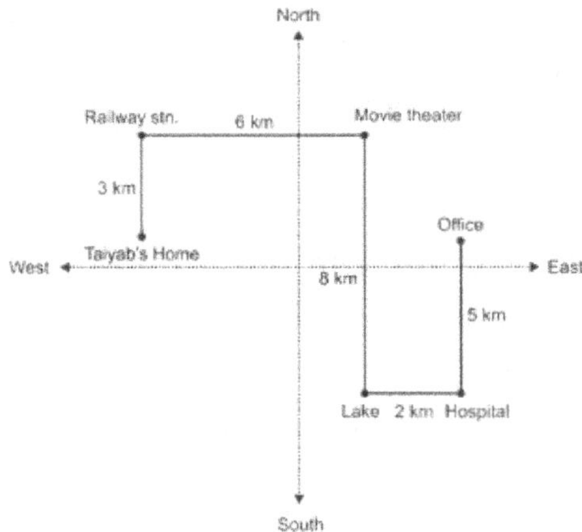

The distance between the railway station and the movie theatre = 6 km

The distance between the movie theatre and the lake = 8 km

Using the Pythagoras theorem, the shortest between the railway station and the lake is 10 km.

59(C). Drawing the diagram according to the given information,

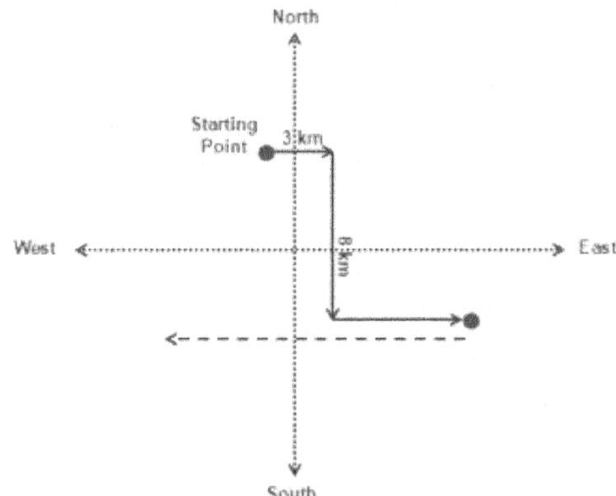

He notices that he is in the opposite direction of what he is supposed to be in. He started by walking towards the east, so at the current point, he is facing East.

Here, at the East, he is noticed that he is in the opposite direction.

Therefore, He needs to go West direction.

60(A). The pattern followed here is as follows:

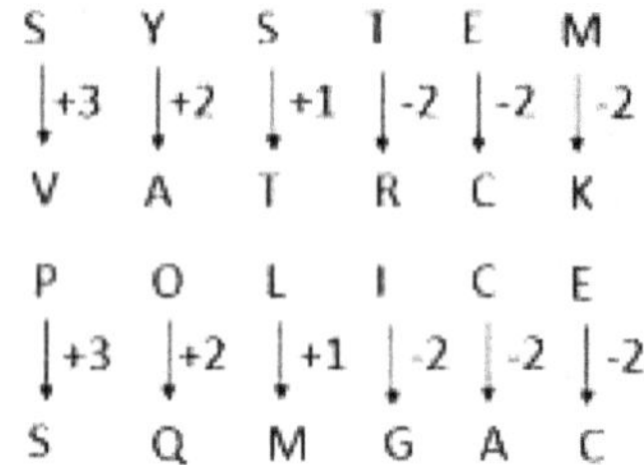

Similarly,

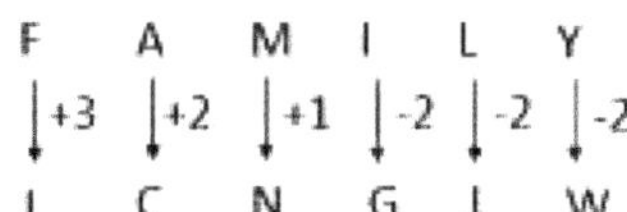

61(A). Logic:
Reverse the Word.
Single-digit place value - 5 and double-digit place value + 5
'BRIGHT' → 'YCBDWW'
Reverse order of 'BRIGHT' = 'THGIRB'

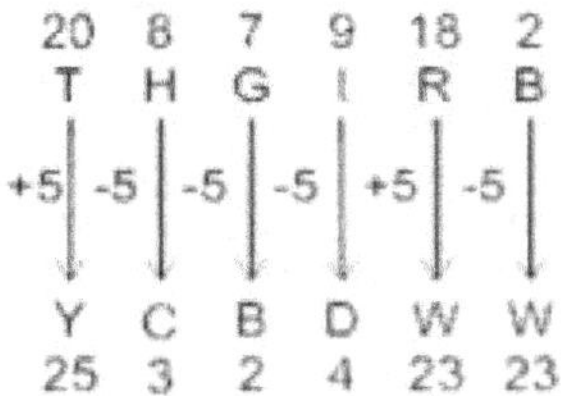

And,
'PAIN' → 'SDVU'
Reverse order of 'PAIN' = 'NIAP'

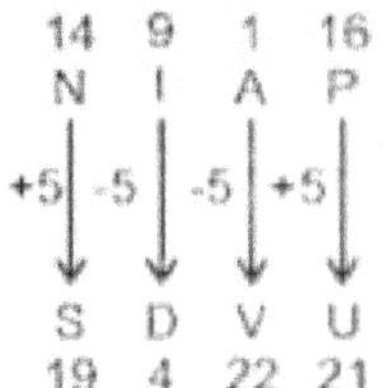

Similarly,
'LATER' → ?
Reverse order of 'LATER' = 'RETAL'

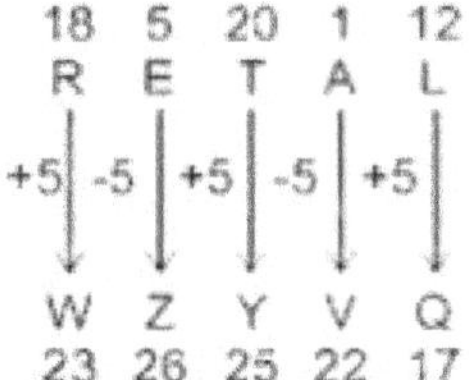

62(D). We know that:

Alphabets	A	B	C	D	E	F	G	H	I	J	K	L	M
Positional value	1	2	3	4	5	6	7	8	9	10	11	12	13
Positional value	26	25	24	23	22	21	20	19	18	17	16	15	14
Alphabets	Z	Y	X	W	V	U	T	S	R	Q	P	O	N

The logic followed here is:
G + 4 = K;
K + 4 = O;
O + 4 = S.
So, answer figure 'C' will be the next figure for the given series.

63(A). Given figure,

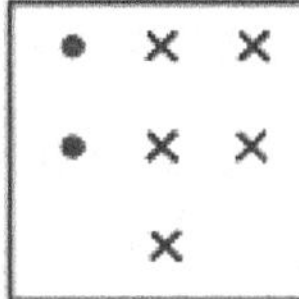

In the first figure, there is only one 'x', in the second figure, there are two 'x' and so on. Following the same pattern, there would be five 'x' in the final figure. (This eliminates two options with four 'x'.) Also, in each of the figures, the 'x' is either in the second column or the third column.

Thus, the above figure will come next in the given figure series.

64(D). Thief comes under the class criminal. But police is different from the both thief and criminal. From above it is clear that option (D) represents the best relationship between Police, Thief and Criminal. As shown in given venn - diagram.

65(A). The Venn diagram that best represents the relationship between Squirrels, Parrots, and Mammals is shown below:

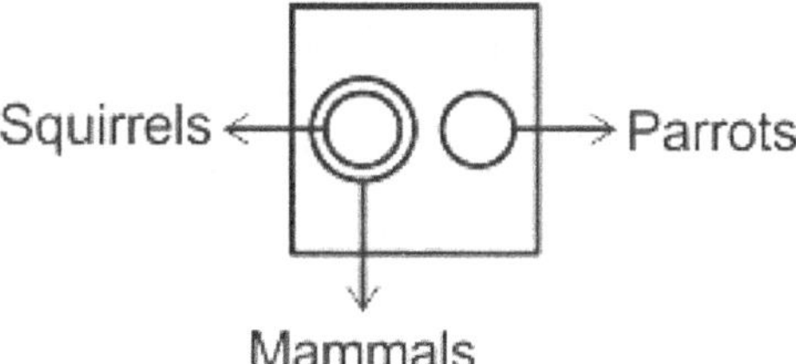

All squirrels are mammals. Parrot is a bird.

66(D). The pattern of given series is:
→ 850 – 843 = 7 [7 x 1]
→ 843 – 829 = 14 [7 x 2]
→ 829 – 808 = 21 [7 x 3]
→ 808 – 788 = 20* [28 = 7 x 4]
→ 788 – 745 = 43* [35 = 7 x 5]
→ 745 – 703 = 42 [7 x 6]
If we replace 788 by 780, then 808 – 780 = 28 & 780 – 745 = 35
So the wrong term is 788.

67(C). The logic follows here is:

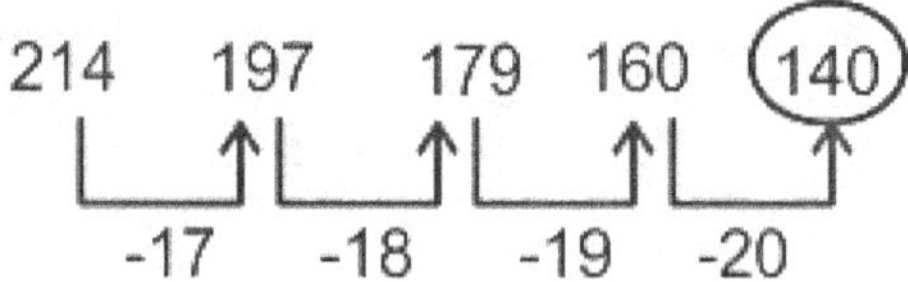

68(B). Given,

In a row of children, Deepa is 9th from the left and Vijay is 13th from the right. When these two interchange their positions, Deepa becomes 17th from the left.

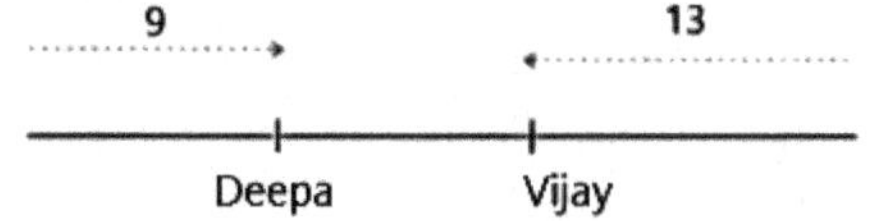

After interchanging,

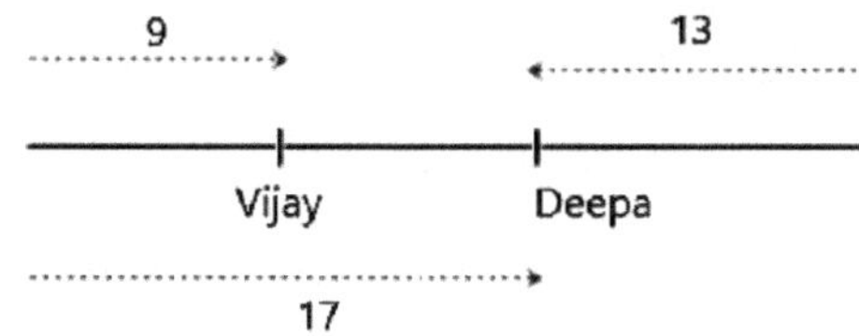

Then,

Present position of Deepa = 17

Former position of Deepa = 9

Difference of present and former position of Deepa
= 17 - 9 = 8

Former position of Vijay = 13

Present position of Vijay = difference of present and previous position of Deepa + former position of Vijay

$= (17 - 9) + 13 = 21$ st

69(D). Arranging the students according to their height:
P is taller than O but shorter than S.
S, P, O
Only S is taller than T.
S, T, P, O
R is shorter than P but taller than Q.
S, T, P, R,
The height of Q is not mentioned correctly.
Therefore, we c annot determined shortest.

70(A). The least possible Venn diagram is:

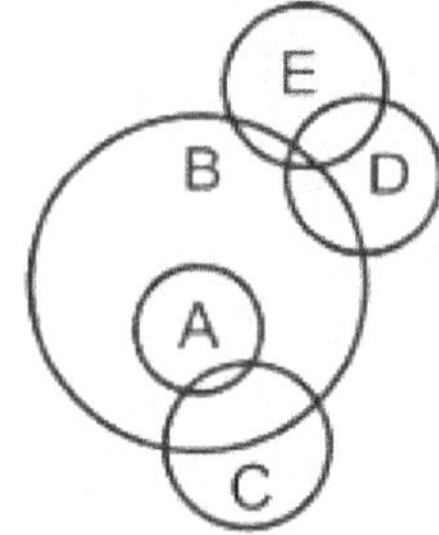

i. Some C's are B. → True (As, all A's are B and some A's are C → Some C's are B)
ii. Some E's are A. → False (As, there is no definite relation between E and A. Hence, false)
So, only conclusion I follows.

71(C). The least possible diagram for the given statements is as follows,

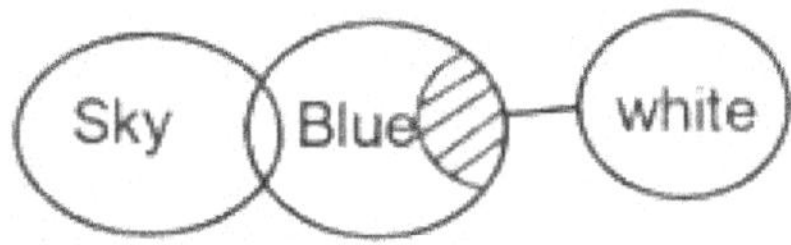

Conclusions:
I. No white is Blue. → False (It is possible but not definite)
II. Some white is blue. → False (It is possible but not definite)
Conclusions I and II are complementary pair.
So, either conclusion I or II follows.

Ques (72-73): 1) B is sitting third to the right of the person who is the husband of R and they are facing the same direction. (As it is a circular arrangement, we can randomly place the husband of R on any seat and then we can place B according to the direction the husband of R is facing.)

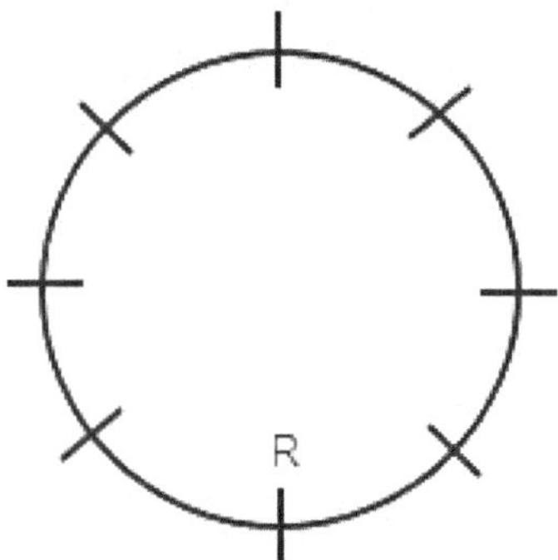

2) Both the immediate neighbours of D are facing the same direction.
(Implies, the immediate neighbours of D are facing a different direction than D.)
3) The husband of Q is facing the outward direction and he is sitting to the immediate right of D.
(Implies, D must be facing the inward direction. It also means that the other immediate neighbour of D must also be facing the outward direction and B is facing the inward direction.)
4) Either R or P is the wife of D.
5) The husband of P and the husband of Q are facing the same direction.
(Implies, the husband of P is also facing the outward direction. It means that R is the wife of D.)

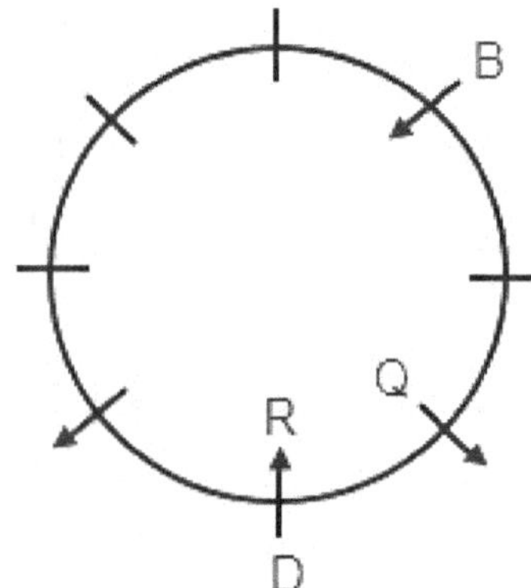

6) Only one person is sitting between B and the husband of L.
(Implies, the husband of L is sitting second to the right of B because the husband of Q is sitting second to the left of B.)

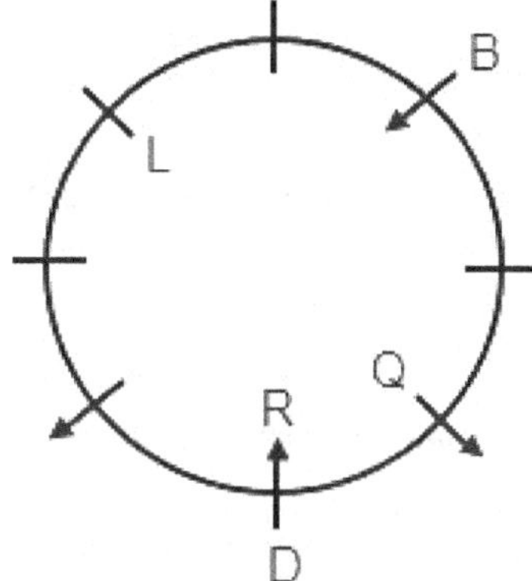

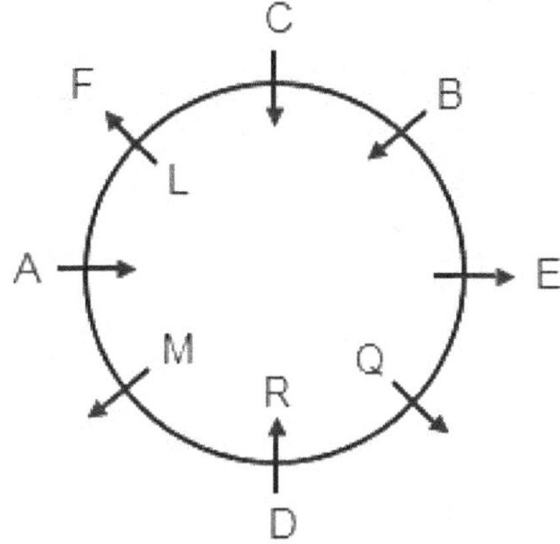

7) The wife of D is sitting third to the left of F.
(It is only possible if F is the husband of L and F is facing the outward direction.)

8) Only one person is sitting between F and the husband of M and they are facing the same direction.
(Implies, the husband of M is sitting second to the left of F because B is facing the inward direction.)

12) G is sitting third to the right of C.
(Implies, G is the husband of M. Now, that only H is left to be placed, we can safely say that H is sitting to the immediate right of D.)

13) The husband of S is sitting third to the right of H.
(Implies, A is the husband of S.)

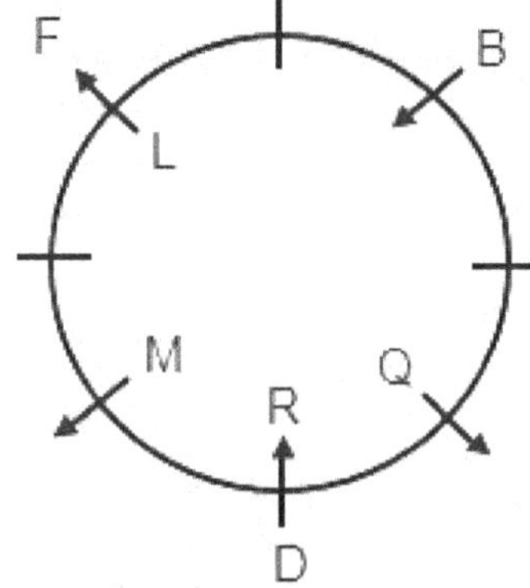

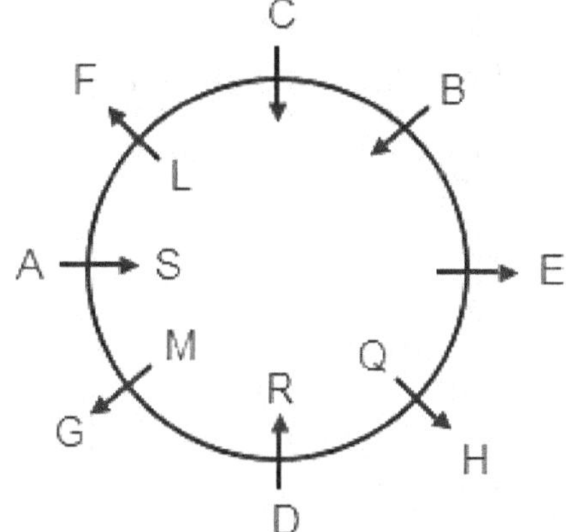

9) C is sitting third to the right of the husband of M and they are facing different directions.
(Implies, C is sitting between F and B. Also, C is facing the inward direction because the husband of M is facing the outward direction.)

10) The husband of L is sitting third to the left of E.
(Implies, E is sitting to the immediate left of B and E is facing the outward direction as it is the only possibility. Also, now that we have identified the four people who are facing the outward direction, we can say that all the other people are facing the inward direction.)

14) Neither O nor P is the wife of B.
(Implies, N is the wife of B as it is the only option left. Also, O and P are the wives of C and E but not necessarily in the same order.)

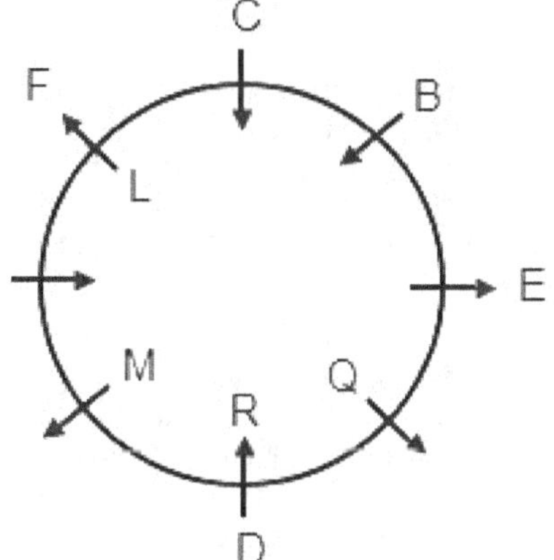

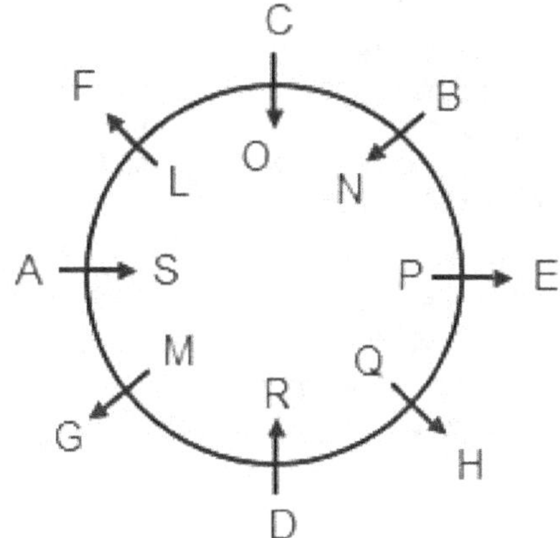

11) A is an immediate neighbour of the husband of M.
(Implies, A is sitting to the immediate left of F.)

72(D). Clearly, A is the husband of S.

73(B). Clearly, C is sitting to the immediate right of B who is the husband of N.

74(A). In 'Dogs and Bark', 'Birds and chirp' and 'Horse and Neigh', the second word is the cry of the first word. So, 'Camels and Roar' is a different word pair.

75(A). Biscuits, buns, and muffins are bakery products while vanilla is not.

So, vanilla is the odd word.

76(B). वर्तनी के अनुसार शुद्ध शब्द 'अन्त्याक्षरी' है। 'अन्त्याक्षरी' शब्द का अर्थ होता है- एक प्रकार का खेल या प्रतियोगिता जिसमें कोई एक कविता पढ़ता और दूसरा उस कविता के अंतिम अक्षर से आरम्भ होनेवाली दूसरी कविता पढ़ता है।

77(A). वर्तनी के अनुसार शुद्ध शब्द 'सुषमा' है। भाषा की वर्तनी का अर्थ उस भाषा में शब्दों को वर्णों से अभिव्यक्त करने की क्रिया को कहते हैं।

78(D). पत्थर को जोंक नहीं लगती कहावत का अर्थ 'हठी पर कोई प्रभाव नहीं पड़ता है।'

79(D). 'विहंगम दृष्टि' या विहंगावलोकन का अर्थ 'सरसरी नज़र' है।

80(C). 'काटो तो खून नहीं' कहावत का सही अर्थ 'भय के कारण स्तब्ध हो जाना है।

81(D). पुल्लिंग संज्ञा के स्थान पर स्त्रीलिंग कर देने से 'काला' विशेषण का सही रूप 'काली' होगा। जो शब्द संज्ञा की विशेषता बताते हैं वह विशेषण कहलाते हैं।

82(B). 'कव्वाली' शब्द में स्त्रीलिंग है। कव्वाली विदेशज शब्द है। वे शब्द जो किसी अन्य भाषा से हिन्दी में स्वीकार कर लिए गए हैं विदेशज शब्द कहलाते हैं।

83(A). 'बुरे भाव से की गई संधि' के लिए एक शब्द **'दुरभिसंधि'** होगा।
वाक्यांश - भाषा को सुंदर, आकर्षक और प्रभावशाली बनाने के लिए अनेक शब्दों के स्थान पर एक शब्द का प्रयोग किया जाता है तो वह वाक्यांश के लिए एक शब्द कहलाता है।

84(A). **कोई काम करने की इच्छा -** चरिष्णु वाक्यांश युग्म संगत नहीं है।
अन्य विकल्प संगत हैं।
सही युग्म है- कोई काम करने की इच्छा - चिक्कीर्षा
प्राप्ति की तीव्र इच्छा - चरिष्णु

85(D). उपर्युक्त विकल्पों में 'डिबिया' देशज शब्द है। अतिरिक्त विकल्प विदेशज शब्द के उदाहरण हैं।
देशज शब्द: वे शब्द जिनकी उत्पत्ति के मूल का पता न हो परन्तु वे प्रचलन में हों। ऐसे शब्द देशज शब्द कहलाते हैं। ये शब्द आम तौर पर क्षेत्रीय भाषा में प्रयोग किये जाते हैं।
विदेशज शब्द: विदेशी भाषाओं से हिंदी में आये शब्दों को विदेशी शब्द कहा जाता है। इन विदेशी भाषाओं में मुख्यतः अरबी, फारसी, तुर्की, अंग्रेजी व पुर्तगाली शामिल है।

86(A). 'स्त्रीत्व' शब्द में भाववाचक संज्ञा है।
भाववाचक संज्ञा: जिन शब्दों से किसी प्राणी या पदार्थ के गुण, भाव, स्वभाव या अवस्था का बोध होता है, उन्हें भाववाचक संज्ञा कहते हैं। भाववाचक संज्ञा बनाते समय शब्दों के अंत में प्रायः पन, त्व, ता आदि शब्दों का प्रयोग किया जाता है।

87(A). उपर्युक्त विकल्पों में से ' मटरगश्ती ' एक विदेशज शब्द हैं।
जो शब्द विदेशी भाषा के हैं, परंतु हिंदी में उन शब्दों का बहुत प्रचलन होता है। ऐसे शब्द विदेशी या विदेशज शब्द कहलाते हैं। मटरगश्ती (पश्तो शब्द) जिसका अर्थ होता है " मस्ती " करना ,अन्य विकल्पों के शब्द देशज हैं। इसलिए सही विकल्प ' मटरगश्ती ' है।

88(D). मामा का बहुवचन शब्द मामा होगा।
संबद्ध दर्शाने वाली कुछ संज्ञायें एकवचन और बहुवचन में एक समान रहती है। जैसे- ताई, मामा, दादा, नाना, चाचा आदि।
मामा माँ के भाई को कहते हैं जिसका तत्सम शब्द 'मातुल' होता है।

89(B). दवाई एकवचन शब्द है जबकि इसका बहुवचन दवाइयाँ होता है।
इस तरह के अन्य शब्दों के बहुवचन शब्दों को यहाँ देख सकते हैं- तिथि- तिथियाँ, रीति-रीतियाँ आदि।
इस प्रकार 'दवाई' का बहुवचन 'दवाइयाँ' रहेगा। इसलिए सही विकल्प 'दवाइयाँ है।

90(A). वाक्य के (a) भाग में त्रुटि है, "राजा दशरथ को" के स्थान पर "राजा दशरथ के" होगा।
शुद्ध वाक्य:
"राजा दशरथ के चार पुत्र राम, लक्ष्मण, भरत और शत्रुघ्न पैदा हुए थे।"

91(C). वाक्य के (c) भाग में त्रुटि है, "जाना जाता है।" के स्थान पर "माना जाता है।" होगा।
शुद्ध वाक्य:
"आज भ्रष्टाचार हर क्षेत्र में शिष्टाचार के रूप में माना जाता है।"

92(D). अभिसरण का विलोम शब्द अपसरण है।
अपसरण एक तरह का काम, कर्तव्य या उत्तरदायित्व छोड़कर भाग जाने की क्रिया
वाक्य में प्रयोग - अपसरण कायरता का सूचक है।

93(C). 'उदय-उग्र' सही विलोम युग्म नहीं है।
- 'उदय' का सही विलोम शब्द 'अस्त' है।
- 'उग्र' का सही विलोम शब्द 'सौम्य' है।
- अन्य सभी विकल्प सही विलोम युग्म हैं।

94(B). दिए गए विकल्पों में से 'पुरस्कार-पुरुस्कृत' यह विकल्प अनुचित विकल्प है।
पुरुस्कृत शब्द न तो पुरस्कार का उचित विलोम शब्द है और न ही वर्तनीगत शुद्ध है। इसका शुद्ध रूप है पुरस्कृत जिसका अर्थ है - जिसने पुरस्कार प्राप्त किया हो।

95(B). बुजुर्ग वृद्ध का, पूर्व पहले का और सुर देवता का समानार्थी शब्द है, जबकि दिवंगत का समानार्थी स्वर्गवासी है।

96(D). 'भागवद्भक्ति' का संधि विच्छेद 'भागवत् + भक्ति' होता है। इसमें व्यंजन संधि है। व्यंजन से स्वर अथवा व्यंजन के मेल से उत्पत्र विकार को व्यंजन संधि कहते हैं। एक व्यंजन के दूसरे व्यंजन या स्वर से मेल को व्यंजन-संधि कहते हैं। व्यंजन से स्वर अथवा व्यंजन के मेल से उत्पत्र संधि को व्यंजन संधि कहते हैं।
किसी वर्ग के पहले वर्ण – क् ,च् , ट् ,त् , का मेल किसी स्वर या किसी वर्ग के तीसरे , चौथे वर्ण या , य , र , ल , व , ह। से हो तो पहला वर्ण तीसरे वर्ण (ग् ,ज् ,ड् ,द् ,ब्) में बदलता है।
भागवत् + भक्ति – भागवद्भक्ति
जगत् + ईश – जगदीश

97(B). अयादि संधि में "ऐ" के बदले 'आय' हो जाता है।
जब संधि करते समय ए , ऐ , ओ , और के साथ कोई अन्य स्वर हो तो (ए का अय), (ऐ का आय), (ओ का अव), (औ – आव) बन जाता है। यही अयादि संधि कहलाती है।
अयादि संधि के उदाहरण:
श्री + अन : श्रवण
पौ + अक : पावक
पौ + अन : पावन

98(C). 'दै + इनी = दायिनी' संधि का सही प्रयोग नहीं हुआ है। 'दायिनी' का संधि विच्छेद 'दै + इनी' होता है। इसमें अयादि संधि है। इस संधि का नियम ऐ + इ = आयि है। जब संधि करते समय ए , ऐ , ओ , और के साथ कोई अन्य स्वर हो तो (ए का अय), (ऐ का आय), (ओ का अव), (औ – आव) बन जाता है। यही अयादि संधि कहलाती है।

99(D). "भक्तमाल" के रचनाकार "नाभादास" है। भक्तमाल का रचना वर्ष 1585 ईस्वी है। 'भक्तमाल' की रचना ब्रजभाषा में हुई है। इसकी भाषा शैली प्रौढ़ एवं परिमार्जित है। भक्तमाल' में नाभादास ने छप्पय छंद में अपने पूर्ववर्ती अथवा समसामयिक लगभग दो सौ भक्तों का चरित्रगान किया है।

100(C). "सत्यवती कथा" की रचना "ईश्वर दास" ने की है।
रचना वर्ष :- 1501 ईस्वी
उक्त पुस्तक दिल्ली के बादशाह सिकंदर शाह (सं. 1546-1574) के समय में लिखी गई।
आचार्य रामचंद्र शुक्ल ने सत्यवतीकथा को अवधी की सबसे पुरानी रचना माना है।

दोहे और चौपाइ छंद है। पाँच-पाँच चौपाइयों (अर्धालियों) पर एक दोहा है।

General Knowledge

1. Tughlaq Nama was written by_____.
   - (a) Amir Khusrau
   - (b) Al-Biruni
   - (c) Fani Badayuni
   - (d) Hiuen Tsang

2. With reference to Satavahana rulers, consider the following statements:
   1. Achievements of Gautamiputra Satkarni are mentioned in Nashik Prasasti.
   2. They started granting tax-free lands to Brahmins.
   3. The Romans first started with the southernmost part of India under Satavahana dominion.
   Which of the statements given above is/are correct?
   - (a) 1 and 2 only
   - (b) 1,2 and 3
   - (c) 2 and 3 only
   - (d) 1 and 3 only

3. With reference to the Vernacular Press Act, 1878 , consider the following statements:
   1. It was directed only against Indian language newspapers.
   2. It sought to suppress the criticism against Lord Lytton's administration.
   3. It was repealed by Lord Ripon
   - (a) 1 and 3 only
   - (b) 3 only
   - (c) 1,2 and 3
   - (d) 1 and 2 only

4. Consider the following statements with regard to Morley Minto Reforms of 1909.
   1. It increased the number of elected members in both the Imperial Legislative Council and provincial councils.
   2. It introduced a separate electorate for Muslims, Sikhs and Christians.
   Which of the statements given above is/are correct?
   - (a) 1 only
   - (b) 2 only
   - (c) Both 1 and 2
   - (d) Neither 1 nor 2

5. Which Urdu poet saw the Revolt of 1857?
   - (a) Mir Taki Mir
   - (b) Jok
   - (c) Galib
   - (d) Iqbal

6. The Mundas raised a rebellion:
   - (a) in 1885 AD
   - (b) in 1888 AD
   - (c) in 1890 AD
   - (d) in 1895 AD

7. Garo tribe is-
   - (a) In Assam
   - (b) In Manipur
   - (c) In Mizoram
   - (d) In Meghalaya

8. Kaveri water dispute is-
   - (a) of Andhra Pradesh and Tamil Nadu
   - (b) of Andhra Pradesh and Karnataka
   - (c) of Karnataka and Tamil Nadu
   - (d) of Tamil Nadu and Pondicherry

9. The Shivalik range was formed in-
   - (a) Eozoic
   - (b) Paleozoic
   - (c) Mesozoic
   - (d) Cenozoic

10. Who has been appointed as the chief of Air India's low-cost airline business with effect from January 1, 2023?
    - (a) Rajeeva Laxman Karandikar
    - (b) Aloke Singh
    - (c) Dinesh Kumar Shukla
    - (d) Arun Kumar Singh

11. Which of the following has been named India's most accessible app for persons with disabilities in a report titled "Making the Digital Ecosystem Disabled Friendly" released in February 2023 ?
    - (a) WhatsApp
    - (b) PhonePe
    - (c) Telegram
    - (d) Ajio

12. In January 2023, with which of the following has Indian Space Research Organization signed an MoU to help Indian Space tech start-ups?
    - (a) IBM
    - (b) Microsoft
    - (c) Google
    - (d) Adobe

13. The government has approved the implementation of the Inter-Operable Criminal Justice System (ICJS) project by the Ministry of Home Affairs, during the period from 2022 - 2023 to which year?
    - (a) 2024 - 25
    - (b) 2025 - 26
    - (c) 2026 - 27
    - (d) 2027 - 28

14. Rough endoplasmic reticulum (RER) looks rough under the microscope because of the attachment of which one of the following cell organelles to its surface?
    - (a) Centrioles
    - (b) Plastids
    - (c) Lysosomes
    - (d) Ribosomes

15. Which one of the following is known as Wood Spirit?
    - (a) Methanol
    - (b) Ethanol
    - (c) Formaldehyde
    - (d) Acetaldehyde

16. Which of the following leads to global warming?
    - (a) Water pollution
    - (b) Soil pollution
    - (c) Air pollution
    - (d) Noise pollution

17. Who is the head of the District Planning and Development Council?
    - (a) State Finance Minister
    - (b) District Development Officer
    - (c) District Planning Officer
    - (d) State Chief Minister

18. Which of the following states has a Legislative Council?
    1. Kerala, 2. Himachal Pradesh, 3. Delhi. 4. Bihar
    Code:
    - (a) 1 and 4
    - (b) 1 and 2
    - (c) 2 and 3
    - (d) Only 4

19. The Legislative Council in a State may be constituted or dissolved:
    - (a) by the Legislative Assembly of this State
    - (b) by central parliament
    - (c) on the recommendation of the Governor by the Central Parliament
    - (d) by the President, on the recommendation of the Governor

20. Which of the following statements about the Pradhan Mantri Gram Sadak Yojana are correct?
    1. It is part of Government of India's poverty reduction strategy.
    2. It is a centrally sponsored scheme for rural development.
    3. It provides connectivity in rural areas.

Select the correct answer using the code given below:
(a) 1,2 and 3
(b) 1 and 3 only
(c) 2 and 3 only
(d) 1 and 2 only

21. The most important item exported from India is-
(a) Leather goods
(b) Clothes
(c) Tea
(d) Rice

22. Which of the following is a state tax?
(a) Income tax
(b) Land revenue
(c) Customs
(d) Excise duty

23. Mumtaz Khan, who was named the Emerging Player of the Year 2022 by the International Hockey Federation (FIH), belongs to which district?
(a) Azamgarh
(b) Lucknow
(c) Banda
(d) Chitrakoot

24. The proposed Agricultural Infrastructure and Development cess will be applicable on which of the following products?
(a) Alcohol beverages
(b) Gold
(c) Petrol and Diesel
(d) All of the above

25. Consider the following statements regarding Digilocker.
1. It is an initiative under the Digital India program by the Ministry of Electronics & Information Technology.
2. Issuer, Requester, and Resident are the key stakeholders in the DigiLocker system.
Which among the above statements is/are correct?
(a) 1 only
(b) 2 only
(c) Both 1 and 2
(d) Neither 1 nor 2

Mathematics

26. **Direction:** Simplify the given expression.
$$\left(2^2 \times 2^3\right)^3 \div (512 \div 16)^5 \times (32 \times 64)^4 = (2 \times 2)^{?+3}$$
(a) 16
(b) 14
(c) 15
(d) 12

27. An article is sold at a profit of 15%. If both the cost price and the selling price of the article are reduced by Rs.140 each, then the profit percentage becomes 19.2%. The cost price of the article is:
(a) Rs. 560
(b) Rs. 720
(c) Rs. 680
(d) Rs. 640

28. A and B started a business with Rs. 1500 and Rs. 2500 and got a profit Rs. 800 Half of the profit is shared equally the remaining is shared according to their investment. Find their profits respectively.
(a) Rs. 400 & Rs. 400
(b) Rs. 500 & Rs. 300
(c) Rs. 300 & Rs. 500
(d) Rs. 350 & Rs. 450

29. Reet invested an amount of Rs A for 2 years at 12% compound interest and received some amount of interest. Sonali invested Rs (A + 1500) for 3 years at 8% simple interest and received same amount of interest as Reet received. Find the amount that is invested by Reet.
(a) Rs 20000
(b) Rs 25000
(c) Rs 30000
(d) Rs 27500

30. The simple interest on a sum of Rs. 4,800 for $4\frac{1}{2}$ years at a certain rate per annum is Rs. 1,684.80 , What will be the amount of the same sum at the same rate for $6\frac{2}{3}$ years at simple interest?
(a) Rs. 7,096
(b) Rs. 7,087
(c) Rs. 7,296
(d) Rs. 7,196

31. A figure is formed by revolving a rectangular sheet of dimensions 7 cm ×4 cm about its length. What is the volume of the figure thus formed?
(a) 352 cm^3
(b) 296 cm^3
(c) 176 cm^3
(d) 15.59 cm^3

32. A square of a side 12 cm is made from a single wire. The same wire is then bent to form a equilateral triangle. Find the area of equilateral triangle.
(a) $64cm^2$
(b) $24\sqrt{3}cm^2$
(c) $64\sqrt{3}cm^2$
(d) $16cm^2$

33. Consider all 3− digit numbers (without repetition of digits) obtained using three nonzero digits which are multiples of 3 . Let S be their sum.
Which of the following is/are correct?
1. S is always divisible by 74 .
2. S is always divisible by 9 .
select the correct answer using the code given below:
(a) 1 only
(b) 2 only
(c) Both 1 and 2
(d) Neither 1 nor 2

34. The average age of a class of 40 students is 12 years. if the teacher's age is also included, the average increases by one year. Find the age of the teacher.
(a) 54 years
(b) 55 years
(c) 53 years
(d) 52 years

35. The average of three numbers is 28 . The first number is half of the second and the third number is twice the second. The third number is:
(a) 18
(b) 12
(c) 36
(d) 48

36. When 20% of a number is added to 36 then the resultant number is 200% of the actual number. Then find 40% of actual number.
(a) 10
(b) 8
(c) 12
(d) 6

37. A, B and C together can complete a piece of work in 30 minutes. A and B together can complete the same work in 50 minutes. C alone can complete the work in:
(a) 150 minutes
(b) 80 minutes
(c) 60 minutes
(d) 75 minutes

38. A and B work alternately for a day to do a piece of work and B starts the work. A alone can complete the work in 48 days. If the work is completed in $11\frac{1}{3}$ days, then in how many days can B alone complete the work?
(a) $8\frac{1}{2}$ days
(b) $6\frac{1}{2}$ days
(c) $6\frac{3}{4}$ days
(d) $8\frac{1}{4}$ days

39. 'A' does 30% of a work in 30 days. He then call 'B' and they together finish the 'remaining work in 20 days. How long 'B' alone would take to do the whole work?
(a) 40
(b) 80
(c) 120
(d) 160

40. A train is moving at a speed of 72 km/h. If the length of the train is 220 meters, then how long will it take to

cross the 330 metre long platform?

(a) 48.5 seconds   (b) 11 seconds

(c) 16.5 seconds   (d) 27.5 seconds

41. Excluding stoppages, the speed of a bus is 54 kmph and including stoppages, it is 45 kmph. For how many minutes does the bus stop per hour?

(a) 9   (b) 10

(c) 12   (d) 20

42. The HCF and the LCM of two polynomials are $3x + 1$ and $30x^3 + 7x^2 - 10x - 3$ respectively. If one polynomial is $6x^2 + 5x + 1$, then what is the other polynomial?

(a) $15x^2 + 4x + 3$ (b) $15x^2 + 4x - 3$

(c) $15x^2 - 4x + 3$ (d) $15x^2 - 4x - 3$

43. A man was 32 years old when his first son was born. When his son was seven years old, his wife was 35 years old. The difference between the age of the man and his wife is _______.

(a) 7 years   (b) 3 years

(c) 4 years   (d) 5 years

44. What is the value of $1 - 2 + 3 - 4 + 5 \ldots 101$?

(a) 51   (b) 55

(c) 110   (d) 111

45. The equation of the ellipse whose vertices are at ($\pm$ 5, 0) and foci at ($\pm$ 4, 0) is-

(a) $\dfrac{x^2}{25} + \dfrac{y^2}{9} = 1$ (b) $\dfrac{x^2}{9} + \dfrac{y^2}{25} = 1$

(c) $\dfrac{x^2}{16} + \dfrac{y^2}{25} = 1$ (d) $\dfrac{x^2}{25} + \dfrac{y^2}{16} = 1$

46. If cot 35° = m, then sec 55° =?

(a) $\sqrt{(1 + m^2)}$ (b) $\sqrt{m}$

(c) $\sqrt{(1 - m^2)}$ (d) m^2

47. The term independent of x in the binomial expansion of $\left(\dfrac{2}{x^2} - \sqrt{x}\right)^{10}$ is equal to:

(a) 180   (b) 120

(c) 90   (d) 72

48. How many ways 6 rings can be worn in 4 fingers such that no fingers are without ring?

(a) 84   (b) 360

(c) 120   (d) 240

Ques (49-50): Direction: The bar graph given below shows the earning of a company (in million Rs.) from 1991 to 1999. Read it and answer the following questions correctly.

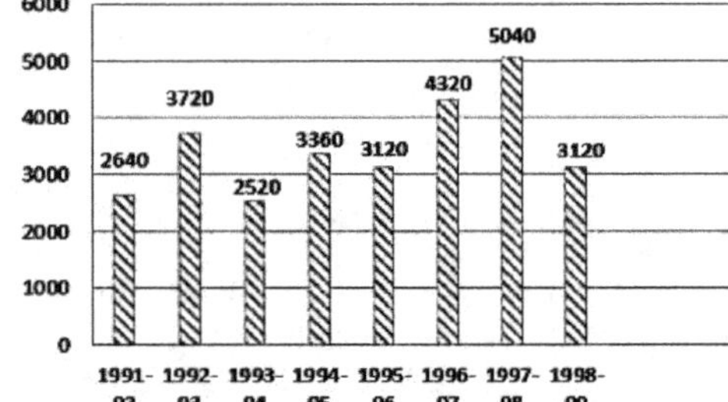

49. The earnings of the company in 1996-97 were approximately what percent of the average earning over the period under review?

(a) 90%   (b) 110%

(c) 115%   (d) 125%

50. The ratio of number of years, in which earnings of a company are below the average earning, to those in which the earnings are above the average is:

(a) 2 : 6   (b) 3 : 4

(c) 5 : 3   (d) None of these

51. Victory is to Joy as _______ is to Sorrow.

(a) Defeat   (b) Depression

(c) Loneliness   (d) Cry

52. A FISH is to GILLS then a MAN is to _____.

(a) Ear   (b) Eye

(c) Lungs   (d) Nose

53. Ratnakar says, "I am the brother of Rashmi, who is the grand-daughter of Sadanand and Surekha". Rashmi says, "I am the daughter of Rajani, who is the daugther-in-law of Surekha". What is the relation between Ratnakar and Sadanand?

(a) Father-Son

(b) Paternal Grandfather-Grandson

(c) Maternal Grandfather-Grandson

(d) Uncle-Nephew

54. If A&B means A is the husband of B, A#B means B is the son of A. A@B means B is the sister of A and A%B means B is the brother of A, then which of the following expressions definitely means that S is the brother of T?

(a) P&Q#R@S%T   (b) Q&S#T@R%P

(c) R@S%T#Q&P   (d) Q&P#T%S@R

55. Which of the options is the wrong figure in the series?

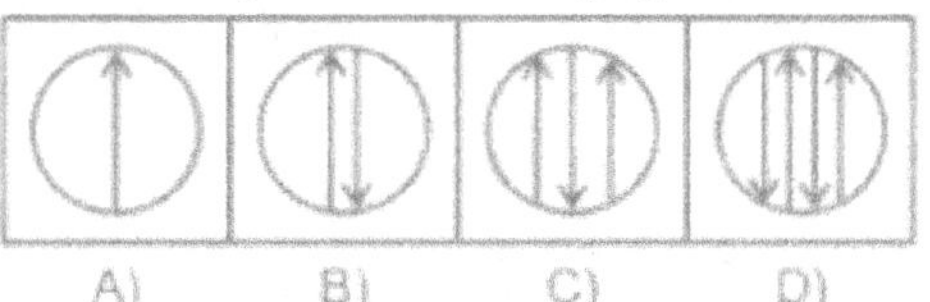

(a) A   (b) B

(c) C   (d) D

56. Direction: Out of the four option figures, three are similar in a certain manner. However, one figure is not like the other three select the figure which is different from the rest.

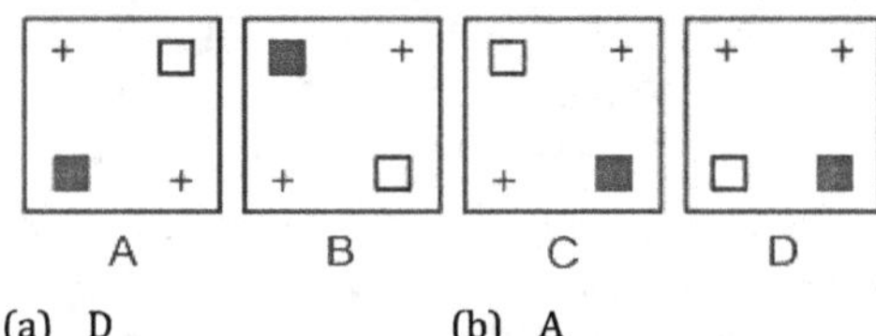

(a) D   (b) A

(c) B   (d) C

57. Direction: In the question, a group of four figures is given. Candidates must choose one odd figure.

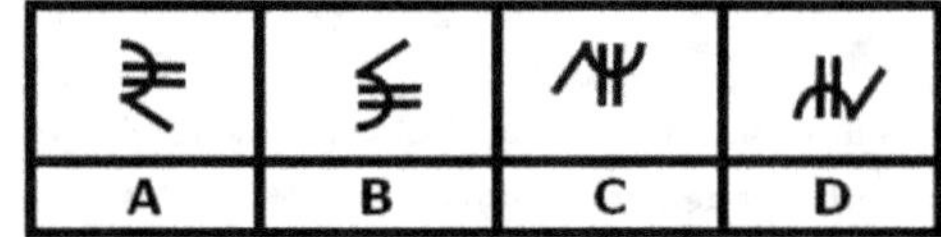

(a) (A)   (b) (B)
(c) (C)   (d) (D)

58. If North becomes North-East then what will North-East become?
(a) East   (b) West
(c) North   (d) South

59. Rasik walked 20 m towards the north. Then he turned right and walks 30 m. Then he turns right and walks 35 m. Then he turns left and walks 15 m. Finally, he turns left and walks 15 m. In which direction and how many meters is he from the starting position?
(a) 15 m West   (b) 30 m East
(c) 30 m West   (d) 45 m East

60. In a certain code language, A is coded as 2 , M is coded as 26 and Z is coded as 52 . How will BET be coded in the same code language?
(a) 44   (b) 46
(c) 50   (d) 54

61. If in a certain code language "APTITUDE" is written as "ZKGRGFWV", then how is "BEYOND" is coded in that language?
(a) YVBLMW   (b) WMLVBY
(c) YBVLMN   (d) YLMWEB

62. Which answer figure will complete the series of figures given in the problem figure?

Problem Figure

Answer Figure

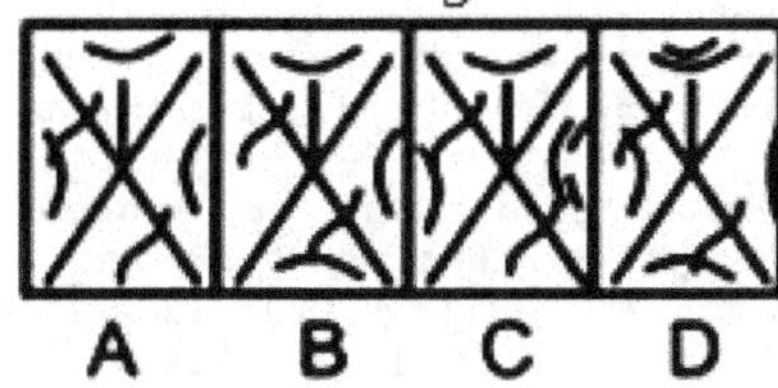

(a) A   (b) B
(c) C   (d) D

63. Which answer figure will complete the series of figures given in the problem figure?

Problem figure

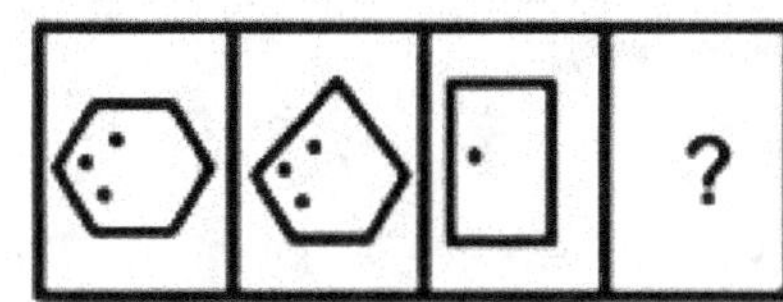

Answer figure

(a) A   (b) B
(c) C   (d) D

Ques (64-65): Direction: Identify the diagram that best represents the relationship among classes given below:

64. student, teacher, school
(a)
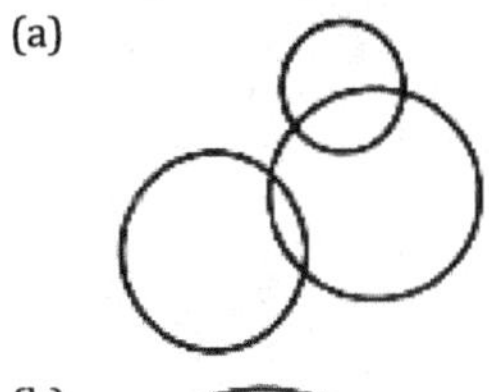

(b)

(c)

(d)
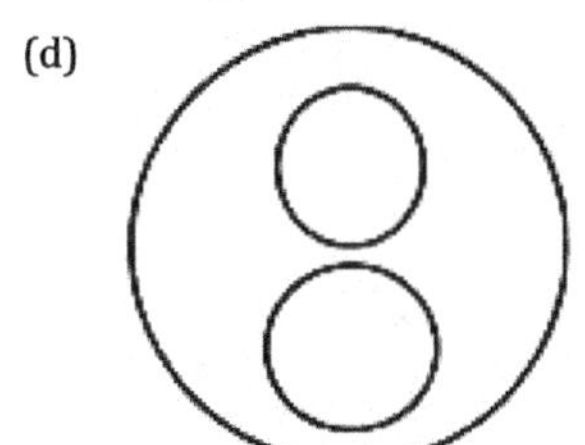

65. Male, Skaters, Brown-Haired People
(a) 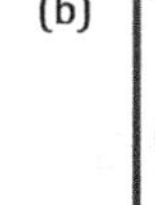   (b) 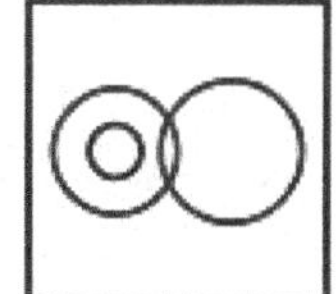

(c)    (d) 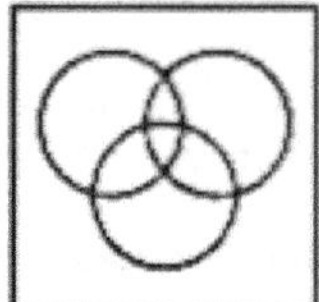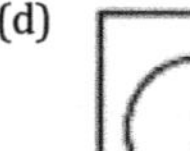

66. **Direction:** What will come in place of the question mark (?) in the following number series.
    227, 221, 211, 199, 187, ?
    (a) 181　　　　　　　(b) 175
    (c) 180　　　　　　　(d) 177

67. Which number will replace the question mark (?) in the following series?
    22, 46, 94, 190, ?
    (a) 412　　　　　　　(b) 370
    (c) 382　　　　　　　(d) 394

68. In a class Anil ranks 7th from the top, Rohit is 7 ranks ahead of Sumit and 3 ranks behind Anil. Vijay, who is 4th from the bottom is 32 ranks behind Sumit. How many students are there in the class?
    (a) 39　　　　　　　(b) 49
    (c) 52　　　　　　　(d) 62

69. Height of five students A, K, L, M and T are compared. Height of K is more than only two students. Height of M is greater than T and Height of T is greater than K. How many students are smaller than T ?
    (a) 3　　　　　　　(b) 4
    (c) 5　　　　　　　(d) 1

Ques (70-71): Direction: In the following question below some statements are given followed by some conclusions. Taking the given statements to be true even if they seem to be at variance from commonly known facts, read all the conclusions and then decide which of the given conclusions logically follows the given statements.

70. **Statements:**
    All donkeys are horses.
    No cow is a horse.
    Conclusions:
    I. Some cows are donkeys
    II. Some horses are donkeys.
    III. No donkeys is a cow.
    (a) Both conclusions II and III follows
    (b) Only conclusion II follows
    (c) Only conclusion III follows
    (d) Either conclusion II or III follows

71. **Statements:**
    1. All books are red.
    2. No copy is red.
    Conclusions:
    I. Some books are copies.
    II. No book Is a copy.
    III. All the copies are books.
    (a) Only II follows.　　　(b) I and II follows.
    (c) II and III follows.　　(d) Only I follows.

72. Select the letter which is different from the others.
    (a) PNST　　　　　　(b) LJON
    (c) RPUT　　　　　　(d) NLQP

73. Select the letter which is different from the others.
    (a) PV　　　　　　　(b) TW
    (c) LO　　　　　　　(d) EH

74. **Direction:** Read the given information and carefully answer the following questions.
    A certain number of people are sitting in a straight line, facing south. Some of them like different colors. The distance between two adjacent people is the same. P sits fourth to the right of Q, who sits sixth to the

right of Z. At least two people sit between W and Z. The person who likes red color sits exactly between the person who likes pink color and the person who likes blue color. The person who likes yellow color sits at one of the extreme ends. P does not like the yellow color and V likes blue color. No person sits to the right of P. W likes red color. S is an immediate neighbor of Z but does not like pink color. V, who is an immediate neighbor of Q, sits sixth to the right of the person who likes pink color. Not more than four persons sit between the one who likes yellow and the one who likes Red.

How many people are sitting in the row?
    (a) 9　　　　　　　(b) 12
    (c) 14　　　　　　(d) 15

75. **Direction:** Read the instructions carefully and answer the question below.
    Twelve people of a family, A, B, C, D, E, F, G, H, I, J, K, and L are sitting in three rows facing north. Each row has four seats at equal distance. The seats of these rows are arranged in such a way that the first seat of the first row is exactly in front of the first seat of the second row and the first seat of the second row is exactly in front of the first seat of the third row and so on. Also, these people are sitting in such a way that the people sitting in the first row are younger than 20 years, the people sitting in the row immediately behind it i.e. row 2 are older than 20 years but younger than 50 years and the people sitting in the row that is immediately behind row 2 are older than 50 years. Also, the age of each of these people is a natural number.
    J is 6 years younger than F but 30 years younger than G. The difference between the ages of A and L is 47 years. The age of B is one third the age of the person who is sitting immediately behind E but half the age of the person who is sitting to his immediate left. The difference between the ages of the two people who are sitting on the extreme ends in the third row is 8 years. The age of H is 45 years less than the person sitting immediately behind him. L is 15 years older than the person who is sitting second to his left. J is sitting immediately in front of F. B is sitting to the immediate left of the person who is sitting right in front of D. E is sitting two seats ahead of C whose age is numerically an even number. H is sitting second to the left of J and H is 21 years younger than J. The age of the person sitting right behind A is 1 year less than twice the age of A. The age of K is 1 year less than thrice the age of the person who is sitting immediately behind him. A is sitting second to the left of the person who is 39 years old. K is sitting third to the right of E and the sum of their ages is 25 years.

    What is the difference between the ages of the person who is sitting on the leftmost seat of the 1st row and the person who is sitting on the rightmost seat of the 3rd row?
    (a) 45 years　　　　(b) 71 years
    (c) 67 years　　　　(d) 55 years

76. इनमें से शुद्ध वर्तनी का रूप है:
    (a) निरझरणी　　　　(b) निरझरिणी
    (c) निर्झरिणी　　　　(d) निर्झरणी

77. निम्नलिखित में से शब्द का शुद्ध रूप कौन सा है?

(a) उर्वर   (b) ऊर्वर
(c) उरवर   (d) उउर्वर

78. 'छक्के छुड़ाना' इस मुहावरे का अर्थ क्या है?
(a) हराना   (b) हारना
(c) जीतना   (d) जिताना

79. 'पाटी पढ़ना' - मुहावरे का अर्थ क्या है?
(a) खुश होना   (b) ध्यान करना
(c) सबक सीखना   (d) नगाड़ा बजाना

80. 'सिर उठाना' इसका तात्पर्य क्या है?
(a) विरोध करना   (b) शुरू होना
(c) साहसी बनना   (d) लज्जा का त्याग करना

81. **निर्देश:** लिंग बदलिए:-
शेर (स्त्रीलिंग)
(a) शेरी   (b) शेरनी
(c) शेरणी   (d) सेरनी

82. **निर्देश:** लिंग बदलिए:
कुत्ता (स्त्रीलिंग)
(a) कुतिया   (b) कुतीया
(c) खुतिया   (d) खुतीया

83. दिए गए विकल्पों में 'संध्या और रात के बीच का समय' को एक शब्द गें क्या कहेंगे?
(a) गोधूली   (b) गोधूल
(c) गोधूलि   (d) गोदुली

84. वाक्यांश के लिए एक शब्द के अनुचित विकल्प की पहचान कीजिए।
(a) इंद्रियों से संबन्धित - ऐंद्रिक
(b) जहां कोई दूसरा न हो - एकाक्ष
(c) जो कल्पना से परे हो - कल्पनातीत
(d) जो बात छिपाई जाए - गोपनीय

85. निम्नलिखित में से कौन-सा शब्द विदेशज है?
(a) खिड़की   (b) बाल्टी
(c) पगड़ी   (d) कटोरा

86. निम्नलिखित में से देशज शब्द का चयन कीजिए:
(a) इनाम   (b) फुनगी
(c) पेट्रोल   (d) पार्सल

87. निम्न में से पुल्लिंग शब्द है:
(a) रात   (b) बात
(c) गीत   (d) मात

88. गुड़िया शब्द का बहुवचन _______ है।
(a) गुड़ियों   (b) गुड़ियाएं
(c) गुड़ियाँ   (d) गुड़ियाओं

89. **निर्देश:** नीचे दिए गए शब्द का सही बहुवचन वाला विकल्प पहचानिए।
मंत्री
(a) मंत्रियाँ   (b) मंत्रिमत
(c) गंत्रीगण   (d) मंत्रिगंण

90. निम्नलिखित प्रत्येक प्रश्न में तीन गद्यांश दिये गये हैं। त्रुटि वाले वाक्यांश को चुनें और उसके अनुरूप (A), (B), (C) पर चिन्ह लगाएँ। यदि वाक्य त्रुटिहीन हो, तो (D) पर चिन्ह लगाएँ।
(a) हमारी दुग्धशाला में शुद्ध गाय का घी बिकता है
(b) मिलावट सिद्ध करने पर
(c) पाँच हजार रुपये का पुरस्कार प्राप्त करें।
(d) कोई त्रुटि नहीं

91. निम्नलिखित प्रत्येक प्रश्न में तीन गद्यांश दिये गये हैं। त्रुटि वाले वाक्यांश को चुनें और उसके अनुरूप (A), (B), (C) पर चिन्ह लगाएँ। यदि वाक्य त्रुटिहीन हो, तो (D) पर चिन्ह लगाएँ।
(a) अपने परिवार एवं प्रियजनों के विषय में
(b) स्वास्थ्य संबंधी कुशल समाचार
(c) शीघ्र भेजने की अनुकम्पन करें
(d) कोई त्रुटि नहीं

92. 'मूर्त' शब्द का विलोम है-
(a) अमूर्त   (b) प्रतिमूर्त
(c) सम्मूर्त   (d) अदृष्ट

93. 'वक्ता' शब्द का विलोम है-
(a) आयोजक   (b) प्रयोजक
(c) श्रोता   (d) व्याख्याता

94. निम्नलिखित में से कौन-सा शब्द 'कुशल' का पर्यायवाची नहीं है?
(a) दक्ष   (b) अक्ष
(c) निपुण   (d) प्रवीण

95. निम्नलिखित में से कौन-सा शब्द 'पक्षी' का पर्यायवाची नहीं है?
(a) द्विज   (b) खग
(c) पंथी   (d) विहग

96. किस क्रम में संधि का सही प्रयोग नहीं हुआ है?
(a) शब्द + इतर = शब्देतर   (b) अनु + दित = अनुदित
(c) रजनी + ईश = रजनीश   (d) अहम् + कार = अहंकार

97. 'आ + औ = औ' किस संधि का नियम है?
(a) यण संधि   (b) वृद्धि संधि
(c) गुण संधि   (d) दीर्घ संधि

98. किस शब्द में 'धनुः + टंकार' की संधि है?
(a) धनुःटंकार   (b) धनुष्टंकार
(c) धनुस्तकार   (d) धनुस्तंकार

99. 'प्रभु जी तुम चंदन हम पानी' इस पंक्ति के रचनाकार है?
(a) चंदनदास   (b) मलूकदास
(c) नानक   (d) संत रैदास

100. "अनुराग बाँसुरी" किस कवि की रचना है?
(a) मंझन   (b) देव
(c) नूर मुहम्मद   (d) जायसी

// Smart Answer Sheet //

Correct   Percentage of students who answered correctly.

Skipped   Percentage of students who skipped.

Q.	Ans.	Correct / Skipped	Q.	Ans.	Correct / Skipped	Q.	Ans.	Correct / Skipped
1	A	31.98% / 4.01%	2	A	56.55% / 1.7%	3	C	25.22% / 3.81%
4	A	49.57% / 1.15%	5	C	24.99% / 3.4%	6	D	80.77% / 0.0%
7	D	52.19% / 1.05%	8	C	56.04% / 1.71%	9	D	47.62% / 1.07%
10	B	63.95% / 1.26%	11	A	41.29% / 1.32%	12	B	65.18% / 1.81%
13	B	61.47% / 1.21%	14	D	54.7% / 1.81%	15	A	53.66% / 1.62%
16	C	78.6% / 0.0%	17	B	55.99% / 1.04%	18	D	57.03% / 1.03%

Q	Ans	%	Q	Ans	%	Q	Ans	%
19	A	49.21% / 1.6%	20	A	61.81% / 1.38%	21	B	59.22% / 1.28%
22	B	31.57% / 3.35%	23	B	86.62% / 0.0%	24	D	67.08% / 1.68%
25	C	51.34% / 1.25%	26	B	45.39% / 1.37%	27	D	62.86% / 1.11%
28	D	61.8% / 1.37%	29	B	14.38% / 4.98%	30	C	67.65% / 1.52%
31	D	53.45% / 1.91%	32	C	51.17% / 1.57%	33	C	80.55% / 0.0%
34	C	80.92% / 0.0%	35	D	54.12% / 1.36%	36	B	47.33% / 1.58%
37	D	83.33% / 0.0%	38	C	48.35% / 1.45%	39	A	83.22% / 0.0%
40	D	78.74% / 0.0%	41	B	79.97% / 0.0%	42	D	31.93% / 4.77%
43	C	85.2% / 0.0%	44	A	42.66% / 1.74%	45	A	50.96% / 1.58%
46	A	67.8% / 1.28%	47	A	29.73% / 4.23%	48	B	81.55% / 0.0%
49	D	83.9% / 0.0%	50	C	76.83% / 0.0%	51	A	85.13% / 0.0%
52	C	78.95% / 0.0%	53	B	52.25% / 1.93%	54	D	29.41% / 4.33%
55	D	43.09% / 1.57%	56	A	65.51% / 1.9%	57	B	55.29% / 1.58%
58	A	82.2% / 0.0%	59	D	56.97% / 1.37%	60	D	66.61% / 1.45%
61	A	67.71% / 1.14%	62	B	64.84% / 1.69%	63	C	65.19% / 1.48%
64	D	42.19% / 1.4%	65	D	89.58% / 0.0%	66	D	32.96% / 3.21%
67	C	24.71% / 3.37%	68	C	29.22% / 4.83%	69	A	67.61% / 1.04%
70	A	32.9% / 3.26%	71	A	63.12% / 1.89%	72	A	49.67% / 1.3%
73	A	64.42% / 1.25%	74	B	77.88% / 0.0%	75	C	26.2% / 3.02%
76	C	47.66% / 1.04%	77	A	67.53% / 1.58%	78	A	46.9% / 1.91%
79	C	84.76% / 0.0%	80	A	89.89% / 0.0%	81	B	67.46% / 1.09%
82	A	46.78% / 1.54%	83	C	47.34% / 1.98%	84	B	48.08% / 1.49%
85	B	58.27% / 1.66%	86	B	48.61% / 1.0%	87	C	64.56% / 1.15%
88	C	69.98% / 1.12%	89	C	45.29% / 1.5%	90	A	51.91% / 1.92%
91	C	49.14% / 1.64%	92	A	81.12% / 0.0%	93	C	57.56% / 1.7%
94	B	88.39% / 0.0%	95	C	87.24% / 0.0%	96	B	31.0% / 4.84%
97	B	59.33% / 1.53%	98	B	21.09% / 4.78%	99	D	85.77% / 0.0%
100	C	50.65% / 1.02%						

// Hints and Solutions //

1(A).
- Tughlaq Nama was written by Amir Khusrau.
- Amir Khusrau was born in 1253 in Patiyali, Delhi Sultanate (now in Uttar Pradesh).
- Khusrau was referred to as the "voice of India" or "Parrot of India" (Tuti-e-Hind).

Hence the correct option is (A).

2(A). The Satavahanas appeared as the successors of the Mauryas in the Deccan region.

The Matsya Purana lists their origin and rule for over 450 years. The Satavahanas were also known as Andhras, Andhrajatiyah and Andhrabhrityas in Purana. It was founded by Simuka. They emerged at the banks of the Godavari river in Maharashtra and Andhra state.

Gautamiputra Satkarni (86-110 AD):

He was the greatest ruler of this dynasty.

His achievements are mentioned in Nashik inscription. So, statement 1 is correct.

They were the first rulers to give land grants to brahmans, sometimes to Buddhist monks. They granted tax-free villages to them. Also, the cultivated fields and villages granted to them were declared free from intrusion by the royal policemen, soldiers and other royal officers. So, statement 2 is correct.

The Romans first started trade with the southernmost part of India. Their earliest coins are found in the Tamil kingdoms which lay outside the Satavahana kingdom dominions. So, statement 3 is incorrect.

3(C). It was directed only against Indian language newspapers. It sought to suppress the criticism against Lord Lytton's administration. It was repealed by Lord Ripon.

In British India, the Vernacular Press Act (1878) was enacted to curtail the freedom of the Indian press and prevent the expression of criticism toward British policies notably, the opposition that had grown with the outset of the Second Anglo-Afghan War (1878–80)

4(A). This reform increased the number of elected members in both the Imperial Legislative Council and the provincial councils. But most of the elected members were elected indirectly. So, Statement 1 is correct.

Morley Minto Reform introduced a separate electorate for the Muslims, not for the Sikhs and Christians . So, Statement 2 is incorrect.

5(C). The Revolt of 1857 was witnessed by the Urdu poet Galib. The era of famous poet Asadullah Khan Galib is from 1806 to 1869.

6(D). Munda rebellion is also called 'Ulgulan'. This rebellion started in 1895 AD . In 1895, Birsa Munda declared himself the messenger of God. The headquarters of the Birsa movement was Khuti.

7(D). The Garo tribe is an indigenous ethnic group that is native to the Garo Hills in the northeastern Indian state of Meghalaya.

8(C). There is a dispute between Karnataka and Tamil Nadu over the sharing of Kaveri water. The major cities situated on the banks of this river are Srirangapatna and Thanjavur.

9(D). The Shivalik range was formed in the Pleistocene period. The Pleistocene comes under the Cenozoic period.

10(B). Aloke Singh has been appointed as the chief of Air India's low-cost airline business with effect from January 1, 2023.

Aloke Singh joined Air India Express in November 2020. Aviation veteran Aloke Singh will take charge as the chief executive officer (CEO) of Air India's low-cost airline business, comprising AirAsia India and Air India Express, from January 1, 2023. Singh is currently the CEO of Air India Express.

11(A). WhatsApp has been named India's most accessible app for persons with disabilities in a report titled "Making the Digital Ecosystem Disabled Friendly" released in February 2023. WhatsApp was the only app related as "highly accessible" based on the Web Content Accessibility Guidelines (WCAG), which serve as the global benchmark for determining the disabled-friendliness of a website.

12(B). Indian Space Research Organization and Microsoft signed an MoU to help Indian Space tech start-ups in January 2023.

13(B). The government has approved the implementation of the Inter-Operable Criminal Justice System (ICJS) project by the Ministry of Home Affairs, during the period from 2022 - 23 to 2025 - 26. The project will be implemented as a Central Sector Scheme. National Crime Records Bureau (NCRB) will be responsible for the implementation of the project in association with National Informatics Center (NIC).

14(D). The endoplasmic reticulum(ER) is a complex network of membrane-bound structure which runs through the cytoplasm.
Within the folds of the ER membranes, we can find spaces called Cisternae.
It is connected to both the outer nuclear membrane as well as a cell membrane.
The membrane has the same structure as the plasma membrane but ribosomes do not have membranes.

15(A). Methyl alcohol or Methanol (CH_3OH) is also called wood alcohol, or wood spirit, i.e. alcohol (an organic compound) consisting of a methyl group (CH_3) linked with a hydroxyl group (OH).
Destructive distillation of wood was the method used formerly to produce it.
The direct combination of carbon monoxide gas and hydrogen in the presence of a catalyst is the modern method of preparing methanol.
Syngas, a mixture of hydrogen and carbon monoxide derived from biomass, is increasingly used for methanol production in modern times.

16(C). Air pollution leads to global warming. Air pollution is the release of harmful substances into the atmosphere, including carbon dioxide, methane, nitrous oxide, and other greenhouse gases.

17(B). District Development Officer is the head of the District Planning and Development Council.

18(D). The constitution originally provided that the legislature would be bicameral in populous states. This provision was - Andhra Pradesh, Bihar, Madhya Pradesh, Tamil Nadu, Maharashtra, Karnataka, Punjab, Uttar Pradesh and P. Bengal.

19(A). It is left to the Legislative Assembly of the State to recommend to the Parliament that where there is a Legislative Council, it should be abolished (abolished) and where there is no Legislative Council, it should be established; As stated in Article 169.

20(A). The correct answer is 1, 2 and 3.
PMGSY - Phase I was launched in December 2000 as a 100 % centrally sponsored scheme with an objective to provide single all-weather road connectivity to eligible unconnected habitation of designated population size.

21(B). Textiles and clothing are an important part of India's export economy.

22(B). Land revenue is a tax of the state governments. Except for agriculture, all taxes such as income tax, customs duty, and excise duty are taxes collected by the central government.

23(B). Mumtaz Khan, who was named the Emerging Player of the Year by the International Hockey Federation (FIH), hails from the Lucknow district of Uttar Pradesh. India's young hockey player Mumtaz Khan has been awarded the 'FIH Rising Women's Star of the Year 2021-22' award.

24(D). The proposed Agricultural Infrastructure and Development cess will be applicable on Alcohol beverages, Gold and Petrol and Diesel.
Agricultural Infrastructure and Development cess: Union Budget 2021: The Minister proposed an Agriculture Infrastructure and Development Cess (AIDC) on a small number of items.
Items covered under Agricultural Infrastructure and Development cess are:
- Petrol, Diesel gold, silver, alcohol beverages, crude palm oil, crude soya bean and sunflower oil, apples, coal, lignite and peat specified fertilizers, peas, Kabuli chana, Bengal gram, lentil and cotton.

25(C). IRDAI (Insurance Regulatory Authority of India) in a Circular dated 9th February 2021, has advised all Insurance companies for issuance of Digital Insurance Policies via DigiLocker.
- Digilocker is an initiative under the Digital India program by the Ministry of Electronics & Information Technology where citizens can get authentic documents/certificates in digital format from original issuers of these certificates. Thus, statement 1 is correct .
- It aims at eliminating or minimising the use of physical documents and will enhance the effectiveness of service delivery, making these hassle-free and friendly for the citizens.
- The circular also mentions that the insurers should inform their retail policyholders about Digilocker and how to use it.
- In the insurance sector, Digilocker will drive a reduction in costs, elimination of customer complaints relating to non-delivery of policy copy, improved turn around time of insurance services, faster claims processing and settlement, reduction in disputes, reduction in fraud and improvement in customer contactability .
- The following are the key stakeholders in the DigiLocker system:
  - Issuer : Entity issuing e-documents to individuals in a standard format and making them electronically available e.g. CBSE, Registrar Office, Income Tax department, etc.
  - Requester : Entity requesting secure access to a particular e-document stored within a repository (e.g. University, Passport Office, Regional Transport Office, etc.)
  - Resident: An individual who uses the Digital Locker service based on the Aadhaar number. Thus, statement 2 is correct.

26(B). Given:
$$\left(2^2 \times 2^3\right)^3 \div (512 \div 16)^5 \times (32 \times 64)^4 = (2 \times 2)^{?+3}$$
On solving we get,
$$= \frac{\left(2^5\right)^3}{\left(\frac{512}{16}\right)^5} \times \left(2^5 \times 2^6\right)^4 = \left(2^2\right)^{?+3}$$

$= \dfrac{(2^{15})}{(2^5)^5} \times (2^{44}) = (2^2)^{?+3}$

$= \dfrac{(2^{15})}{(2^{25})} \times (2^{44}) = (2^2)^{?+3}$

$= (2)^{34} = (2)^{(2\times\ +6)}$

$= 2 \times ? + 6 = 34$

$= 2 \times ? = 28$

$\therefore ? = 14$

27(D). Given:

Initial profit % = 15%

Final profit % = 19.2%

Reduction in SP and CP = Rs. 140 each

We know that:

$\text{Profit \%} = \dfrac{(\text{Profit}\times 100)}{\text{CP}}$

Profit = SP − CP

Let the $CP = 100a$

$\therefore$ Profit on CP = 15% of 100a

$= 15a$

$\therefore$ SP = 115a

New CP = 100a − 140

New SP = 115a − 140

$\therefore$ New profit = SP − CP

$= 115a - 140 - (100a - 140)$

$= 115a - 140 - 100a + 140$

$= 15a$

$\therefore \text{Profit \%} = \dfrac{(\text{Profit}\times 100)}{\text{CP}}$

$\Rightarrow 19.2 = \dfrac{(15a \times 100)}{(100a - 140)}$

$\Rightarrow 19.2 \times (100a - 140) = 1500a$

$\Rightarrow 1920a - 2688 = 1500a$

$\Rightarrow 1920a - 1500a = 2688$

$\Rightarrow 420a = 2688$

$\Rightarrow a = \dfrac{2688}{420}$

$\Rightarrow a = 6.4$

$\therefore$ Original CP of the article = 100a

$= 100 \times 6.4$

$=$ Rs. 640

28(D). Given,

Ratio of A & B investments = 1500 : 2500

$= 15 : 25$

$= 3 : 5$

According to the question,

Half of the profit is shared equally the remaining is shared according to their investment.

So A's share of profit

$\Rightarrow \left(\dfrac{400}{2}\right) + \left(\dfrac{3}{8} \times 400\right) = 200 + 150$

$=$ Rs. 350

$\therefore$ B's share of profit

$\Rightarrow \left(\dfrac{400}{2}\right) + \left(\dfrac{5}{8} \times 400\right) = 200 + 250$

$=$ Rs. 450

29(B). According to the question,

$A\left(1 + \dfrac{12}{100}\right)^2 - A = (A + 1500) \times 8\% \times 3$

$A \times \dfrac{112}{100} \times \dfrac{112}{100} - A = A \times \dfrac{24}{100} + 360$

$A \times \dfrac{12544}{10000} - A - A \times \dfrac{24}{100} = 360$

$\dfrac{12544A - 10000A - 2400A}{10000} = 360$

$144A = 3600000$

$A = 25000$

Amount invested by Reet = Rs 25000

30(C). Given:

Simple interest on Rs. 4800 for $4\frac{1}{2}$ years = Rs. 1684.80

As we know,

Simple Interest $= \dfrac{(Principal \times Rate \times Time)}{100}$

Amount = Principal + Simple interest

Simple interest = 1684.80

$\Rightarrow 4800 \times 4\frac{1}{2} \times \dfrac{\text{Rate}}{100} = 1684.80$

$\Rightarrow \text{Rate} = \dfrac{1684.80}{(24 \times 9)}$

$\Rightarrow \text{Rate} = 7.8\%$

Amount for $6\frac{2}{3}$ years = Principal + Simple interest

$= 4800 + 4800 \times 6\frac{2}{3} \times 7.8\%$

$= 4800 + 4800 \times \dfrac{20}{3} \times \dfrac{78}{1000}$

$= 4800 + 2496$

$= 7296$

$\therefore$ The required amount = Rs. 7296

31(D). Given:

Length = 7 cm

Breadth = 4 cm

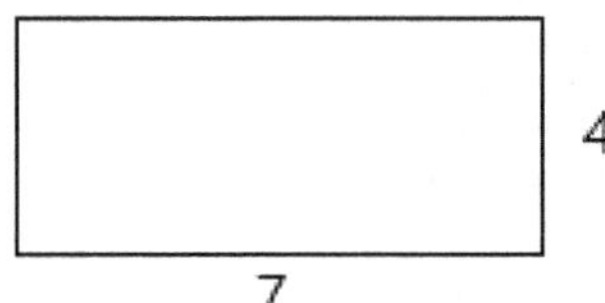

If we revolve sheet around length ,

Then

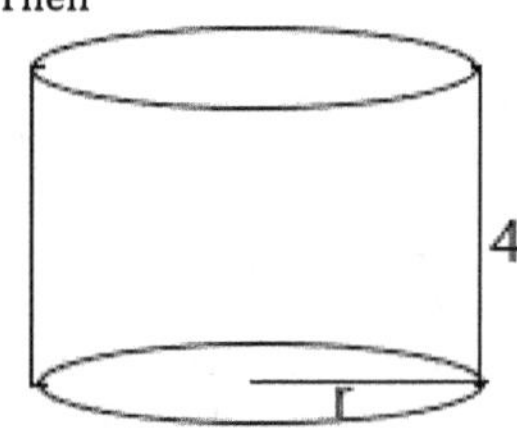

As we know,

Circumference of cylinder formed = length of rectangular sheet

$2\pi r = 7$

$2 \times \dfrac{22}{7} \times r = 7$

$r = \dfrac{7 \times 7}{2 \times 22}$

$r = \dfrac{49}{44}$ cm

Volume $= \pi r^2 h$

$= \dfrac{22}{7} \times \dfrac{49}{44} \times \dfrac{49}{44} \times 4$

$= \dfrac{7 \times 49}{22}$

$= 15.59$ cm^3

32(C). As we know,

Perimeter of a Square $= 4 \times$ Side of a square

$= 4 \times 12$

$= 48 cm$

Perimeter of a Equilateral Triangle $= 3 \times$ Side of a Equilateral Triangle

As given, same wire is bent to form Equilateral Triangle from which a square is made.

Perimeter of a Square = Perimeter of a Equilateral Triangle

$\Rightarrow 48 = 3 \times$ side of a Equilateral Triangle

$\Rightarrow$ Side of a Equilateral Triangle $= \dfrac{48}{3} = 16 cm$

Area of a Equilateral Triangle $= \dfrac{\sqrt{3}}{4} \times (\text{side})^2$

$= \dfrac{\sqrt{3}}{4} \times 16 \times 16$

$= 64\sqrt{3}$

$\therefore$ Area of a Equilateral triangle is $64\sqrt{3} cm^2$.

33(C). Given,
Digits are non-zero and multiple of 3 i.e., $3, 6, 9$.
Number doesn't have repetition of digits.
The numbers thus formed are
$369, 396, 639, 693, 936, 963$
Sum of these numbers $= 3996$ and it is divisible by both 74 as well as 9.

34(C). As we know,
$$\text{Average} = \frac{\text{Sum of all observations}}{\text{Total number of observations}}$$
Given,
The average age of a class of 40 students $= 12$ years
Total age of the class (only students) $= 40 \times 12 = 480$ years
If the teacher's age is also included, the average increases by one year.
So, the total age of the class (with teacher) $= 41 \times 13 = 533$ years
Age of the teacher $= 533 - 480 = 53$ years

35(D). Given,
Average of three number $= 28$
Let the number be x_1, x_2, x_3.
$x_1 = \frac{x_2}{2}$
$\therefore x_2 = 2x_1$ ..... (i)
$x_3 = 2x_2$ ..... (ii)
From equation (i), we get
$x_3 = 2(2x_1) = 4x_1$
$\frac{x_1 + x_2 + x_3}{3} = 28$
$x_1 + x_2 + x_3 = 28 \times 3$
From equation (i) and (ii), we get
$x_1 + 2x_1 + 4x_1 = 84$
$7x_1 = 84$
$x_1 = 12$
$\therefore x_3 = 4(12) = 48$

36(B). Let the actual number be x
According to the question
$\Rightarrow 20\%$ of $x + 36 = 200\%$ of x
$\Rightarrow \left(\frac{20}{100}\right) \times x + 36 = \left(\frac{200}{100}\right) \times x$
$\Rightarrow \frac{x}{5} + 36 = 2x$
$\Rightarrow 36 = 2x - \frac{x}{5}$
$\Rightarrow \frac{9x}{5} = 36$
$\Rightarrow x = 20$
40% of x
$\Rightarrow \left(\frac{40}{100}\right) \times 20 = 8$
$\therefore 40\%$ of actual number is 8.

37(D). Work done by $(A + B + C)$ in 1 minute $= \frac{1}{30}$
Work done by $(A + B)$ in 1 minute $= \frac{1}{50}$
Work done by C alone in 1 minute $= \frac{1}{30} - \frac{1}{50}$
$= \frac{5-3}{150}$
$= \frac{2}{150}$
$= \frac{1}{75}$
C alone can complete the work in 75 minutes.

38(C). A alone can finish the work in 48 days
A's one day work $= \frac{1}{48}$
A and B complete the whole work in $= 11\frac{1}{3}$ days
A and B work on alternate days, with B beginning so, we can say B will work only 6 days A will work only $11\frac{1}{3} - 6 = 5\frac{1}{3}$ days

If A's one day work $= \frac{1}{48}$ of work A complete in $= 1$ days
A's $5\frac{1}{3}$ days work $= \frac{1}{48} \times 5\frac{1}{3} = \frac{1}{48} \times \frac{16}{3} = \frac{1}{9}$
Remaining work $= 1 - \left[\frac{1}{9}\right] = \frac{8}{9}$
B complete $\frac{8}{9}$ work in $= 6$ days
$\Rightarrow$ B complete whole work in $= 6 \times \left[\frac{9}{8}\right] = \frac{27}{4}$ days
$\therefore$ B alone complete the work is $6\frac{3}{4}$ days.

39(A). Given,
A does 30% of a work in 30 days.
As we know,
$$\text{Efficiency} = \frac{Work}{Time}$$
Let total work be 100 units.
Then, efficiency of A $= \frac{30}{30} = 1$ unit / day
He then calls in B and they together finish the remaining work in 20 days.
So, remaining work $= 70$ units
Let the efficiency of B be x units/day, then
$\frac{70}{(1+x)} = 20$
$\Rightarrow 20 + 20x = 70$
$\Rightarrow 20x = 50$
$\Rightarrow x = 2.5$ units/day
$\therefore$ Working alone B would take $= \left(\frac{100}{2.5}\right) = 40$ days

40(D). Given:
Speed of train $= 72$ km/h
Length of train $= 220$ metre
Length of platform $= 330$ metre
Formula used: Speed $= \frac{Dis\tan ce}{Time}$
Speed (in m/s) $=$ Speed (in km/h) $\times \left(\frac{5}{18}\right)$
Speed $= 72 \times \left(\frac{5}{18}\right) = 4 \times 5 = 20$ m/s
Total distance to travel $= 220 + 330 = 550$ m
Time taken to cover the distance $= \frac{Dis\tan ce}{Speed}$
$\Rightarrow \frac{550}{20} = 27.5$ seconds
$\therefore$ The train takes 27.5 seconds to cross the 330 m long platform.

41(B). Due to stoppages, it covers 9 km less.
Time taken to cover
$9 km = \left(\frac{9}{54} \times 60\right)$ min $= 10$ min.

42(D). Given:
The HCF of two polynomials $= 3x + 1$
The LCM of two polynomials $= 30x^3 + 7x^2 - 10x - 3$
One polynomial $= 6x^2 + 5x + 1$
As we know,
The product of two polynomials $=$ Product of their HCF and LCM
Let the two polynomials be $f(x)$ and $g(x)$.
Here, $f(x) = 6x^2 + 5x + 1$
According to the question,
$f(x) \times g(x) = (3x + 1) \times (30x^3 + 7x^2 - 10x - 3)$
$\Rightarrow (6x^2 + 5x + 1) \times g(x) = (3x + 1) \times (30x^3 + 7x^2 - 10x - 3)$
$\Rightarrow (6x^2 + 2x + 3x + 1) \times g(x) = (3x + 1) \times (30x^3 + 15x^2 - 8x^2 - 4x - 6x - 3)$
$\Rightarrow [2x(3x + 1) + 1(3x + 1)] \times g(x) = (3x + 1) [15x^2(2x + 1) - 4x(2x + 1) - 3(2x + 1)]$
$\Rightarrow (3x + 1) \times (2x + 1) \times g(x) = (3x + 1) \times (2x + 1) \times (15x^2 - 4x - 3)$
$\Rightarrow g(x) = (15x^2 - 4x - 3)$

$\therefore$ The other polynomial is $15x^2 - 4x - 3$.

43(C). Given that,
The man was 32 years old when his first son was born.
So, the age of the man when his son was 7 years = 32 + 7 = 39 years.
The age of his wife is 35 years when his son is 7 years old.
So, the required age difference between man and his wife = 39 - 35 = 4 years.

44(A). It is given that,
We have to find the value of $1 - 2 + 3 - 4 + 5 - \underline{+} 101$.
The given series can be written as,
$\Rightarrow 1 - 2 + 3 - 4 + 5 - \ldots + 101 = (1 + 3 + \ldots\ldots + 101) - (2 + 4 + \ldots\ldots + 100)$
As, we can see that $(1, 3, \ldots\ldots, 101)$ is an AP with $a = 1$ and $d = 2$.
We know that general term of an AP is given by $a_n = a + (n - 1) \times d$
Therefore, according to the question,
$\Rightarrow a_n = 101 = 1 + (n - 1) \times 2$
$\Rightarrow n = 51$
We also know that the sum of terms of an AP
$S_n = \frac{\pi}{2} \times (2a + (n - 1)d)$
$\Rightarrow S_{51} = 1 + 3 + \ldots + 101 = \frac{51}{2} \times (2 + 50 \times 2) = 2601$
Similarly, $(2, 4, \ldots, 100)$ is an AP with $a = 2$ and $d = 2$
$\Rightarrow a_n = 100 = 2 + (n - 1) \times 2$
$\Rightarrow n = 50$
$\Rightarrow S_{50} = 2 + 4 + \ldots + 100 = \frac{50}{2} \times (4 + 49 \times 2) = 2550$
$\Rightarrow 1 - 2 + 3 - 4 + 5 - 101 = (1 + 3 + \ldots\ldots + 101) - (2 + 4 + \ldots\ldots + 100) = 2601 - 2550 = 51$

45(A). We know that,
Equation of ellipse: $\frac{x^2}{a^2} + \frac{y^2}{b^2} = 1$
Eccentricity (e) = $\sqrt{1 - \frac{b^2}{a^2}}$
Where, vertices = ($\pm$ a, 0) and focus = ($\pm$ ae, 0)
Now, according to the equation, vertices of the ellipse ($\pm$ 5, 0) and foci ($\pm$4, 0)
So, a = $\pm$5
$\Rightarrow a^2 = 25$
$\Rightarrow ae = 4$
$\Rightarrow e = \frac{4}{5}$
Now, $\frac{4}{5} = \sqrt{1 - \frac{b^2}{5^2}}$
$\Rightarrow \frac{16}{25} = \frac{25 - b^2}{25}$
$\Rightarrow 16 = 25 - b^2$
$\Rightarrow b^2 = 9$
$\therefore$ Equation of ellipse = $\frac{x^2}{25} + \frac{y^2}{9} = 1$

46(A). We know that,
$\sec^2\theta - \tan^2\theta = 1$
$\Rightarrow \sec^2\theta = 1 + \tan^2\theta$
$\Rightarrow \sec\theta = \sqrt{(1 + \tan^2\theta)}$
Given: $\cot 35° = m$
Find: The value of $\sec 55°$
$\Rightarrow \sec 55° = \sqrt{(1 + \tan^2 55°)}$

$\Rightarrow \sec 55° = \sqrt{(1 + \tan^2(90° - 35°))}$
$\Rightarrow \sec 55° = \sqrt{(1 + \cot^2 35°)}$
$\Rightarrow \sec 55° = \sqrt{(1 + m^2)}$

47(A). $\left(\frac{2}{x^2} - \sqrt{x}\right)^{10} = \sum {}^{10}C_r \left(\frac{2}{x^2}\right)^{10-r}\left(-x^{\frac{1}{2}}\right)^r$
$= \sum {}^{10}C_r \left(2x^{-2}\right)^{10-r}\left(-x^{\frac{1}{2}}\right)^r$
$= \sum {}^{10}C_r \left(2^{10-r}x^{-20+2r}\right)\left(-x^{\frac{r}{2}}\right)$
$= \sum {}^{10}C_r \left(2^{10-r}x^{-20+2r+\frac{r}{2}}\right)\left(-1^{\frac{r}{2}}\right)$
Now, for independent term, $\frac{-20 + 2r + r}{2} = 0$
$\Rightarrow \frac{(4r + r)}{2} = 20$
$\Rightarrow 5r = 40$
$\Rightarrow r = 8$
So, the independent term=
${}^{10}C_r \times 2^{10-r} \times (-1)^{\frac{r}{2}}$
$= {}^{10}C_8 \times 2^{10-8} \times (-1)^{\frac{8}{2}}$
$= \frac{10!}{8!2!} \times 2^2 \times 1$
$= \frac{10 \times 9}{2} \times 4$
$= 180$

48(B). Since there are 6 rings and 4 fingers
Then 1 st finger can have any 6 rings, hence 6 ways
2 nd finger can have the remaining 5 rings, hence 5 ways
3 rd finger can have the remaining 4 rings, hence 4 ways
4 th finger can have the remaining 3 rings, hence 3 ways
So, the total number of ways = 6 × 5 × 4 × 3
= 360

49(D). Average earning of the company = $\frac{27840}{8}$ = 3480
Earnings of the company in 1996-97 = 4320
$\Rightarrow$ Percentage = $\frac{4320}{3480} \times 100$ $\Rightarrow$ Percentage = 124.2% $\Rightarrow$ Percentage = 125% (approx)

50(C). Average earning of a company
$= \frac{(2640 + 3720 + 2520 + 3360 + 3120 + 4320 + 5040 + 3120)}{8}$
$= \frac{27840}{8} = 3480$
No. of company below the average earning = 5, No. of company above the average earning = 3, Ratio = 5 : 3

51(A). Victory is to Joy as Defeat is to Sorrow.
Victory always leads to joy, whereas defeat leads to Sorrow.
So, these are the human reactions shown by some actions.

52(C). A FISH is to GILLS then a MAN is to lungs.
A fish breathe through their gills, while a man breathes through their lungs.

53(B).

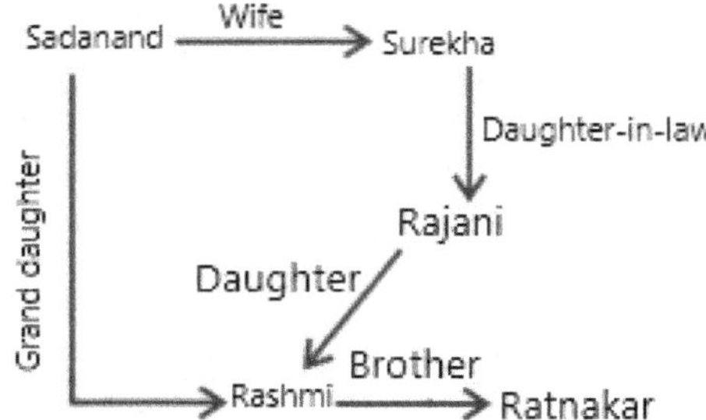

∵ Rashmi is the granddaughter of Sadanand.
Thus Sadanand became Rashmi's grandfather and Rashmi and Ratnakar have 'sister-brother' relation, so Sadanand and Ratnakar have 'grandfather-grandson' relation.

54(D). On checking option (D)-
Q&P#T%S@R
According to Question,

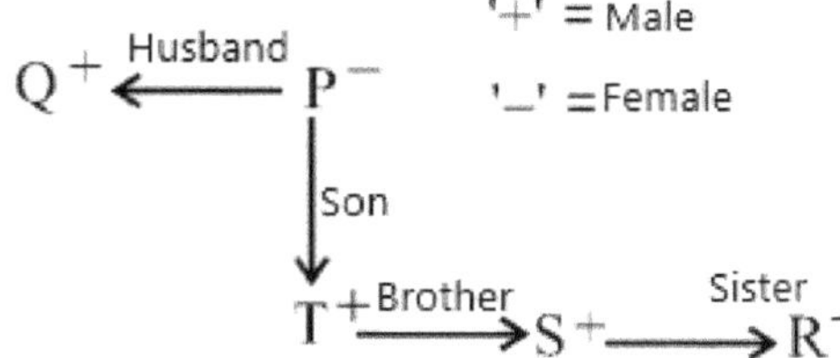

It is clear from the figure that S is definitely the brother of T.

55(D). The pattern followed here is: The arrows are placed as, In the first circle there is an arrow pointing upwards, then In the 2 nd circle, a new arrow comes which points downwards. In the 3rd circle there are 3 arrows in the order 1st upward, 2nd downward then 3rd upward, so, in the 4th circle there will be 4 arrows 1 st pointing upwards, 2 nd downwards, 3rd upwards, and 4 th downwards. So, figure D doesn't follow the pattern here.

56(A). The pattern followed is:
There are two '+' symbols which are diagonally opposite to each other and there are two square symbols diagonally opposite to each other, among which one is painted.
All follow the same pattern, except figure D.
Hence, the correct option is (D).

57(B). Figures A, C, and D are all rotations of the same shape but Figure B is a reflection. No matter how you turn the figure, it will not resemble the other three

58(A). Drawing the diagram,

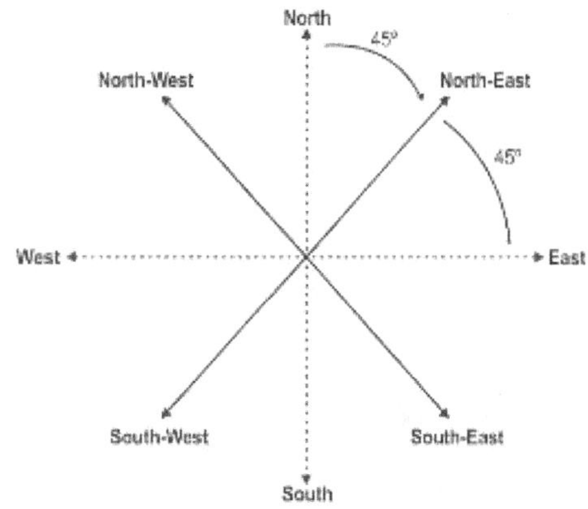

The direction is shifted 45° clockwise.
If the north becomes north-east, the north-east becomes east.

59(D).

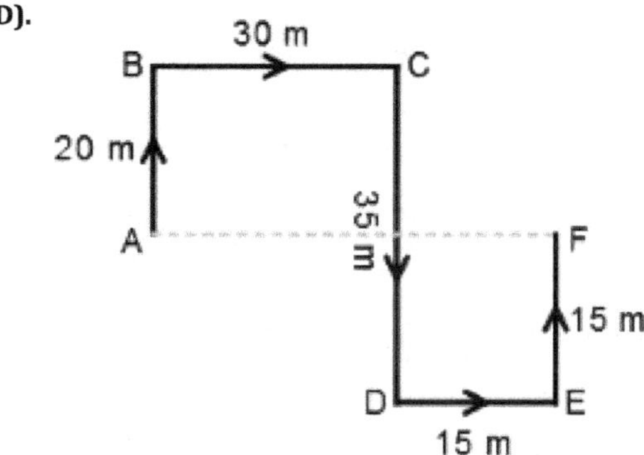

Required distance = AF
= 30 + 15
= 45 m
From the above diagram, AF is in the East direction from A.
So, the required answer is '45 m East'.

60(D). Given-
A is coded as 2 .
$2 = 2 \times 1$
M is coded as 26 .
$26 = 2 \times 13$
Z is coded as 52 .
$52 = 2 \times 26$
The numerical code is obtained on doubling the numerical position of the letter.
On applying the same logic in BET,
Code for B $= 2 \times 2 = 4$
Code for E $= 2 \times 5 = 10$
Code for T $= 2 \times 20 = 40$
Code for BET $= 4 + 10 + 40 = 54$

61(A). The pattern of code is as follows,
Here letters are coded as equivalent opposite letters.
Opposite of letter A = Z,
Opposite of letter P = K,
Opposite of letter T = G,
Opposite of letter I = R,
Opposite of letter T = G,
Opposite of letter U = F,
Opposite of letter D = W,
Opposite of letter E = V.

Similarly,

Therefore, the code for BEYOND is YVBLMW.

62(B). Answer figure 'B' will complete the given figure.

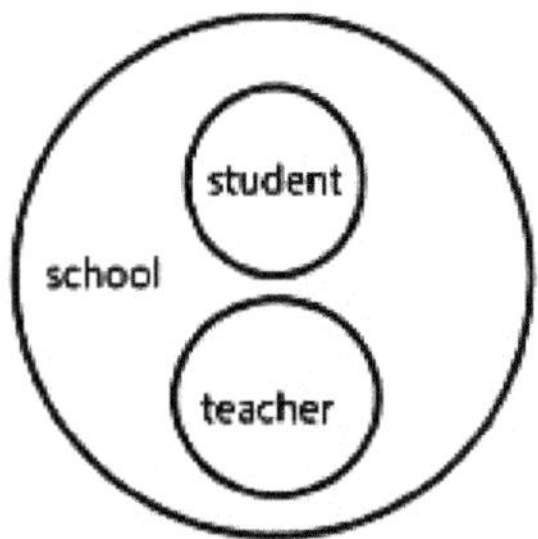

63(C). The figure made of lines is decreasing 1-1 in the next line and the point inside is also decreasing 1-1 so, the next figure will be 'C'.

64(D).

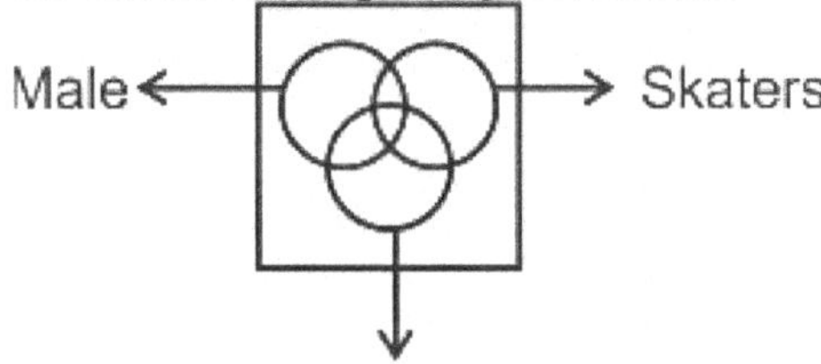

Both teachers and students are part of the school. Also, no student can be a teacher.

65(D). Some males are skaters, some males have brown-haired and some skaters have brown-haired
The correct Venn diagram representation is:

66(D). The pattern of the series is:
227 – 1× 6 = 221
221 – 2 × 5 = 211
211 – 3 × 4 = 199
199 – 4 × 3 = 187
187 – 5 × 2 = 177

67(C). The logic here is:
22 + (24) = 46
46 + (46 + 2) = 46 + 48 = 94
94 + (94 + 2) = 94 + 96 = 190
190 + (190 + 2) = 190 + 192 = 382
Thus, 382 is the next number in the series.

68(C). Anil ranks 7th from the top.
Rohit is 3 ranks behind Anil, which means Rohit's rank is 10th (7 + 3) from the top.
Rohit is 7 ranks ahead of Sumit, which means Sumit's rank is 17th (10 + 7) from the top.
Vijay is 32 ranks behind Sumit, which means Vijay's rank is 49th (17 + 32) from the top.

From Top		From Bottom
1		52
2		51
3		50
4		49
5		48
6		47
7	Anil	46
8		45
9		44
10	Rohit	43
16		37
17	Sumit	36
18		35
19		34
48		5
49	Vijay	4
50		3
51		2
52		1

Vijay's rank is 49th from the top and 4th from the bottom, which means the total number of students = 49 + 4 -1 = 52.

69(A). Given,
Height of five students A, K, L, M and T are compared. Height of K is more than only two students. Height of M is greater than T and Height of T is greater than K.
Five students -A, K, L, M and T are compared.
1. Height of K is more than only two students.
_ > _ > K > _ > _
2. Height of M is greater than T and Height of T is greater than K.
M > T > K
From condition 1 and 2, we get
M > T > K > _ > _
So, 3 students are smaller than T.

70(A). The least possible Venn diagram for the given statements is as follows,

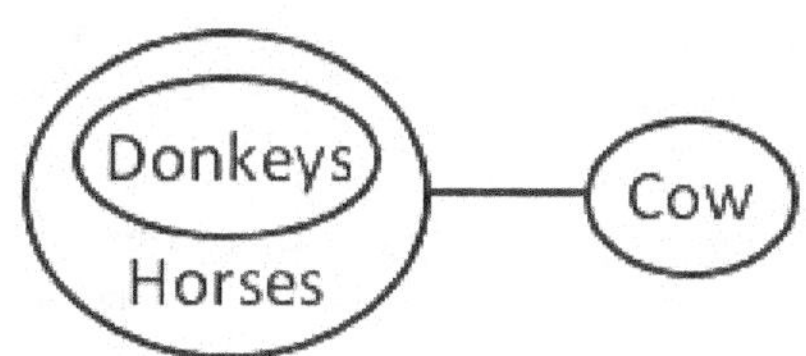

Conclusions:
I. Some cows are donkeys → False (All donkeys are horses and no cow is a horse, imply that no cows are donkeys)
II. Some horses are donkeys → True (All donkeys are horses imply that some horses are donkeys)
III. No donkeys is a cow → True (All donkeys are horses and no cow is a horse, imply that no donkeys are cow)
Therefore, the correct answer is 'Both conclusions II and III follows'.

71(A).   Statements:
1. All books are red.
2. No copy is red.
The least possible diagram for the given statements is as follows:

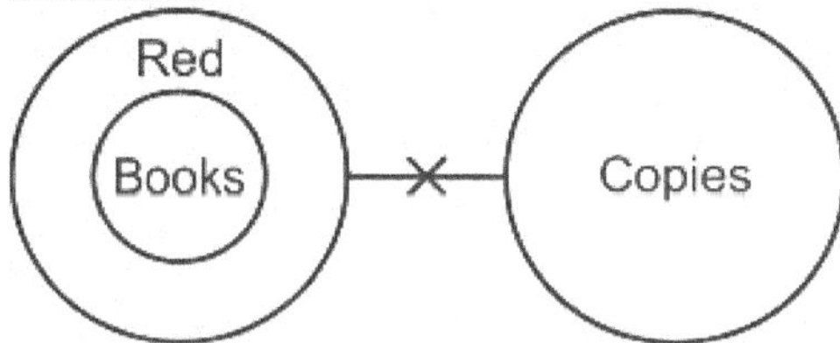

Conclusions:
I. Some books are copies → False (It is not possible because all books are red and no red is a copy so some books are copies it is not possible)
II. No book Is a copy → True (because all books are red and no red is a copy so no book is a copy)
III. All the copies are books → False (It is not possible because all books are red and no red is a copy so all copies are books it is not possible)
So, only conclusion II follows.

72(A).   The pattern followed here is:

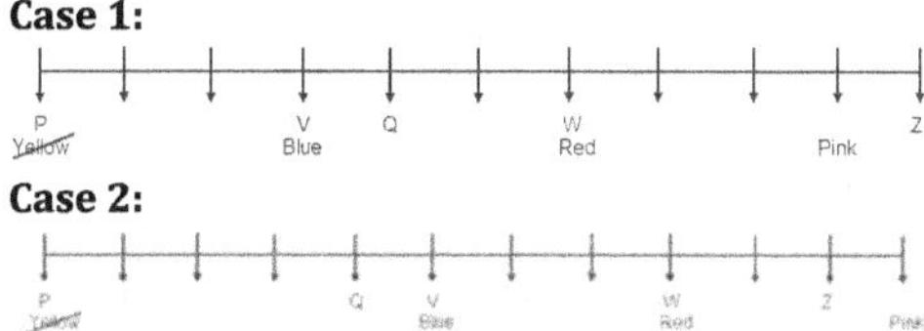

Therefore, "PNST" is odd among them.

73(A).

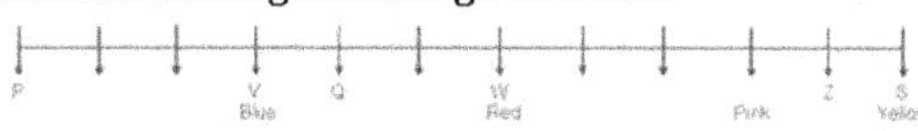

All follow the same pattern, except 'PV'.

Q.74 1) P sits fourth to the right of Q, who sits sixth to the right of Z.
2) No person sits to the right of P.
3) V, who is an immediate neighbor of Q, sits sixth to the right of the person who likes pink color.
4) P does not like the yellow color and V likes blue color.
5) The person who likes red color sits exactly between the person who likes pink color and the person who likes blue color.
6) W likes red color.
Case 1:

Case 2:

7) At least two people sit between W and Z.
8) S is an immediate neighbor of Z but does not like the color pink.
So, case 2 is eliminated.
9) The person who likes yellow color sits at one of the extreme ends.
10) Not more than four persons sit between the one who likes yellow and the one who likes Red.
The final arrangement is given below-

74(B).   So, 12 people are sitting in that row.

Q.75 1) A is sitting second to the left of the person who is 39 years old.
(Implies, both A and the person who is 39 years old are sitting in the second row. Also, there are only two possibilities i.e. A is sitting either on the 1st seat or the 2nd seat of the second row.)
2) The age of the person sitting right behind A is 1 year less than twice the age of A.
(Let us assume the age of A be X, implies, the age of the person sitting right behind him is 2X – 1.)
3) E is sitting two seats ahead of C whose age is numerically an even number.
4) K is sitting third to the right of E and the sum of their ages is 25 years.
(Implies, E is sitting in the first seat of the first row and K is sitting on the rightmost seat while C is sitting on the first seat of the 4th row. Also, as we know the age of the person sitting right behind A is 1year younger than twice the age of A (which will be numerically an odd number), implies, A is sitting on the 2nd seat in the 2nd row. Also, it means that D is sitting on the rightmost seat in the 2nd row.)

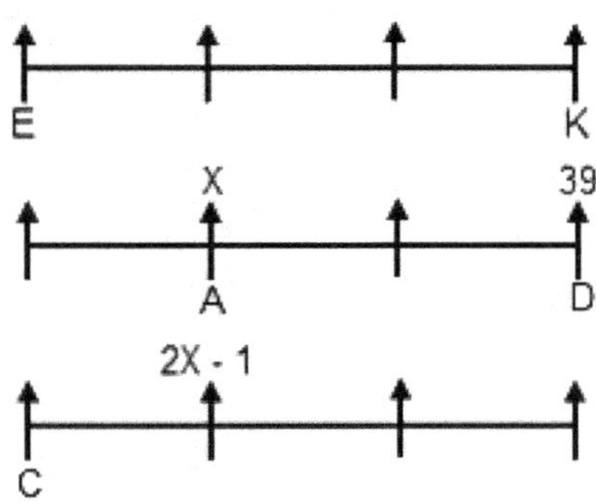

5) The age of K is 1 year less than thrice the age of the person who is sitting immediately behind him.

(Implies, K is 12 years old. Also, according to the 4th statement, the age of E is 13 years.)

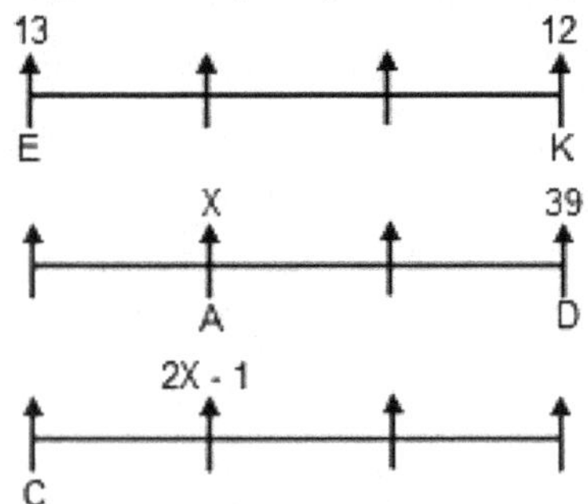

6) J is sitting immediately in front of F.

7) H is sitting second to the left of J and H is 21 years younger than J.

(It is only possible if F is sitting on the third seat from the left in the 3rd row and J is sitting immediately in front of him in the 2nd row.)

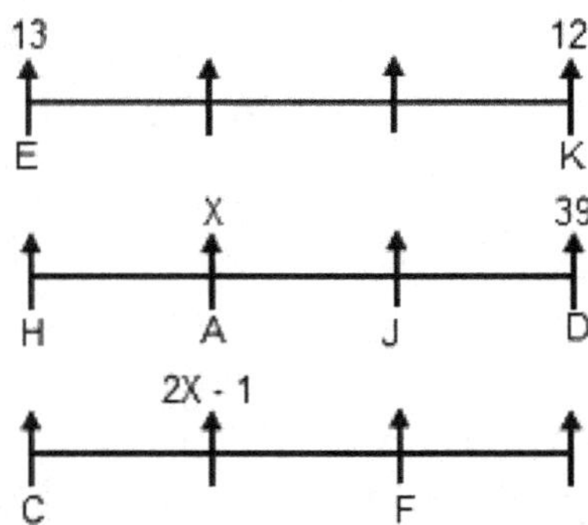

8) B is sitting to the immediate left of the person who is sitting right in front of D.

(Implies, B is sitting to the immediate left of K as it is the only possibility.)

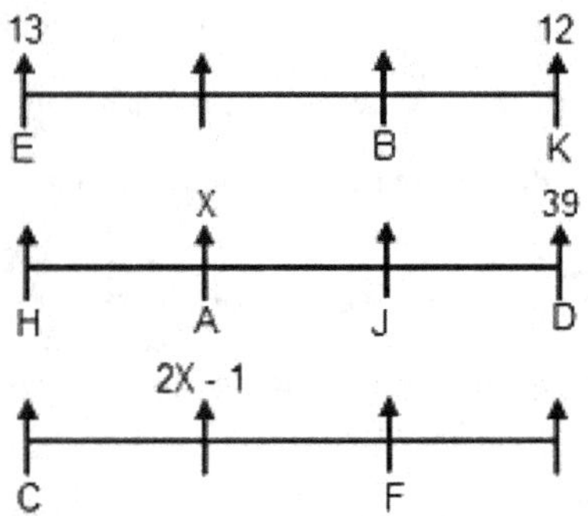

9) The difference between the ages of A and L is 47 years.

10) L is 15 years older than the person who is sitting second to his left.

(It is only possible if we place L on the rightmost seat in the 3rd row. Also, as the age of the person who is sitting second to the left of L is 2X – 1 years old, implies, the age of L is 2X + 14 years.

Now, 2X + 14 – X = 47 years

X = 33 years)

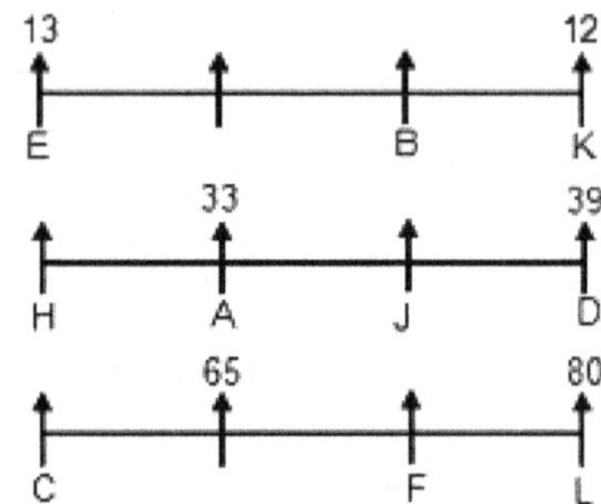

11) The difference between the ages of the two people who are sitting on the extreme ends in the third row is 8 years.

12) The age of H is 45 years less than the person sitting immediately behind him.

(Implies, the age of C is either 72 years or 88 years. Let us assume that C is 88 years old then that would mean H is 43 years old.)

13) The age of B is one third the age of the person who is sitting immediately behind E but half the age of the person who is sitting to his immediate left.

(Clearly, H is sitting immediately behind E. If the age of H is 43 years then the age of B would not be a natural number. Implies, the age of C is 72 years, the age of H is 27 years and the age of B is 9 years. Also, it means that the age of the person who is sitting to the immediate left of B is 18 years.)

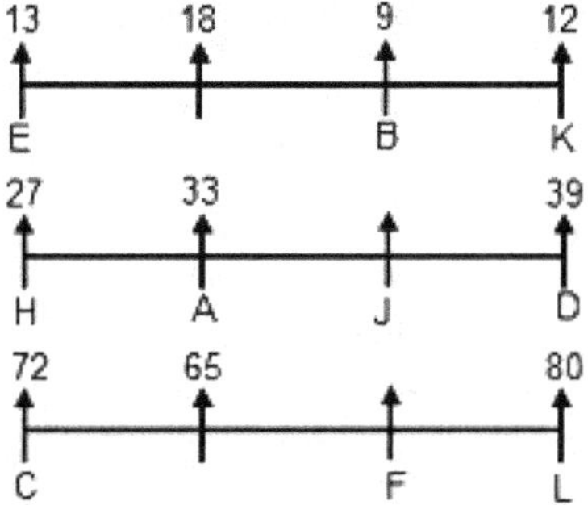

14) J is 6 years younger than F but 30 years younger than G.

(As J is 30 years younger than G, implies, G must be in the row that is ahead of J's row. Hence, G is sitting between E and B in the 1st row and he is 18 years old. Implies, J is 48 years old and F is 54 years old. Also, now that only I is left to be placed, we can safely say that I is sitting between C and F.)

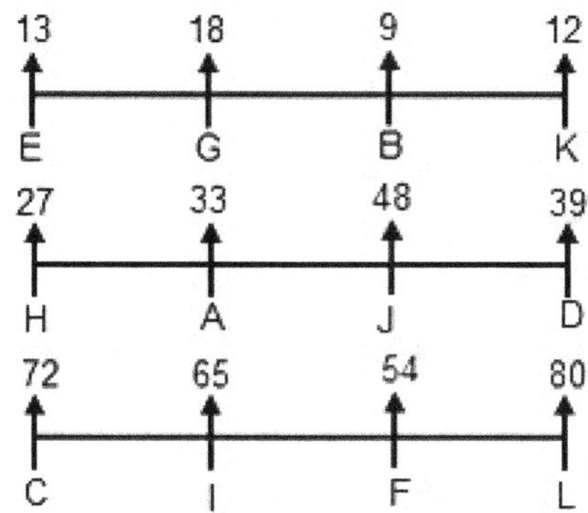

75(C). The age of E is 13 years and the age of L is 80 years. Thus, the difference between the ages of the person who is sitting on the leftmost seat of the 1st row and the person who is sitting on the rightmost seat of the 3rd row is 67 years.

76(C). 'निर्झरिणी' शब्द वर्तनी और उच्चारण की दृष्टि से शुद्ध और सार्थक है।
निर्झरिणी का अर्थ: नदी होता है।
नदी के पर्यायवाची शब्द: सरिता, तटिनी, सरि, सारंग, तरंगिणी, दरिया, निर्झरिणी होते है।

77(A). उर्वर शुद्ध शब्द है।
उर्वर. उपजाऊ
उर्वर के पर्याय: उपजाऊ, उर्वरा, ज़रखेज़, उपजवाला

78(A). 'छक्के छुड़ाना' इस मुहावरे का अर्थ है हराना है।
वाक्य प्रयोग - शिवाजी ने आक्रमण करके मुगलों के "छक्के छुड़ा दिए"।

79(C). 'पाटी पढ़ना' - मुहावरे का अर्थ 'सबक सीखना' है।
वाक्य प्रयोग- मैंने तो राम को स्कूल में उसके गलत कार्य के लिए "पाटी पढ़ा दिया"।

80(A). 'सिर उठाना' का तात्पर्य 'विरोध करना' है।
वाक्य प्रयोग- आज मैं देखता हूं कि कौन मेरे सामने "सिर उठाता है"।

81(B). शेर का स्त्रीलिंग शेरनी होता है।
वह संज्ञा शब्द जो हमें स्त्री जाति का बोध कराते हैं, वे शब्द स्त्रीलिंग संज्ञा शब्द कहलाते हैं।
जैसे:
- सजीव: माता, लड़की, भेद, गाय, भैंस आदि।
- निर्जीव: धोती, टोपी, सड़क, सजा, भीड़ आदि।

82(A). कुत्ता का स्त्रीलिंग कुतिया होता है।
वे संज्ञा या सर्वनाम शब्द जो स्त्री जाति का बोध कराते हैं, उसे स्त्रीलिंग कहते हैं।
जैसे- शिक्षिका, बालिका, अजा आदि।

83(C). 'संध्या और रात के बीच का समय' को एक शब्द में 'गोधूलि' कहेंगे।
अन्य शब्दों की वर्तनी अशुद्ध है।
- गोधूलि शब्द का अर्थ है - गो + धूल + ई = गोधूलि अर्थात गायों के पैरों से उठने वाली धूल।
- पुराने समय में जब गायें जंगल से चरकर वापस आती थीं तो पता चल जाता था कि शाम होने वाली है।
- इसलिए इस समय विशेष को गोधूलि बेला कहने लगे। अर्थात संध्या का समय।

84(B). दिए गए विकल्पों में अनुचित युग्म 'जहां कोई दूसरा न हो - एकाक्ष' है।
'जहां कोई दूसरा न हो' के लिए एक शब्द एकांत होगा।
'एकाक्ष' शब्द के लिए उचित वाक्यांश जिसके एक ही आँख हो होगा।

85(B). उपर्युक्त विकल्पों में से ' बाल्टी ' एक विदेशज शब्द हैं। बाल्टी (पुर्तगाली शब्द हैं) जिसका अर्थ होता है " पानी भरने का बर्तन, अन्य विकल्पों के शब्द देशज हैं। इसलिए सही विकल्प ' बाल्टी है।

86(B). उपरोक्त विकल्पों में फुनगी देशज शब्द है क्योंकि यह शब्द आम बोल-चाल की भाषा का शब्द है।
फुनगी का अर्थ है, वृक्ष की शाखा या घास का अगला भाग या सिरा या ऊपरी नोक, पर्वत की चोटी।
ऐसे शब्द जो किसी स्थान विशेष के लोगों द्वारा अपनी आवश्यकतानुसार बना लिए जाते है तथा सीमित क्षेत्र में ही प्रयुक्त किए जाते हैं, देशज शब्द कहलाते हैं। इसलिए, स्पष्ट है कि फुनगी ही सटीक विकल्प है।

87(C). दिए गए सभी विकल्पों में से 'गीत' शब्द पुल्लिंग है। अन्य शब्द रात, बात, मात ये सभी स्त्रीलिंग शब्द हैं।
विशेष:

लिंग	परिभाषा	उदाहरण
पुल्लिंग	जिन शब्दों के अंत में आ, आव, पा, न आ दि आते हैं वे शब्द अधिकतर पुल्लिंग होते हैं।	जैसे - बहाव, लोहा आदि।
स्त्रीलिंग	जिन शब्दों के अंत में ई, आवट, इया, ता, आई, आहट आदि प्रत्यय लगे हों, स्त्रीलिंग होते हैं।	जैसे - मित्र ता, थकावट आदि।

88(C). गुड़िया शब्द का बहुवचन गुड़ियाँ है।
जिन स्त्रीलिंग संज्ञाओं के अन्त में 'या' लगा होता है, उनमें 'या' के ऊपर चन्द्रबिन्दु लगाने से बहुवचन बनता है। जैसे:
बिंदिया - बिंदियाँ
चिड़िया - चिड़ियाँ
डिबिया - डिबियाँ
अन्य विकल्प असंगत एवं अनुचित उत्तर हैं।

89(C). दिए गए विकल्पों में से 'मंत्री' का उचित बहुवचन शब्द 'मंत्रीगण' होगा।
'मंत्री' पुल्लिंग शब्द है जिसका अर्थ होता है-
- राजा का प्रधान सलाहकार, अमात्य
- आदेश और सलाह देनेवाला राज्य का मुख्य व्यक्ति।

90(A). त्रुटि वाला वाक्यांश ' हमारी दुग्धशाला में शुद्ध गाय का घी बिकता है' है।
इस वाक्यांश का सही अनुरूप - 'हमारी दुग्धशाला में गाय का शुद्ध घी बिकता है' होगा।

91(C). त्रुटि वाला वाक्यांश ' शीघ्र भेजने की अनुकम्पन करें ' है।
इस वाक्यांश का सही रूप 'शीघ्र भेजने की अनुकम्पा करें' होगा।

92(A). दिए गए विकल्पों में से 'मूर्त' शब्द का विलोम शब्द 'अमूर्त' होगा।
मूर्त तत्सम शब्द है जिसका अर्थ 'आकार वाला' होता है। 'मूर्त' शब्द में 'अ' उपसर्ग के योग से 'अमूर्त' शब्द बना जिसका अर्थ 'अप्रत्यक्ष या निराकार' होगा।

93(C). 'वक्ता' का विलोम शब्द 'श्रोता' होता है। वक्ता के पर्यायवाची शब्द हैं - वाचक, व्याख्याता, भाषणकर्त्ता, तकरीर करने वाला।
श्रोता के पर्यायवाची शब्द हैं - सुनने वाला, श्रवणकर्ता।

94(B). 'अक्ष' शब्द 'कुशल' शब्द का पर्यायवाची नहीं है। अक्ष के पर्यायवाची शब्द हैं - किली, धुरा, धुरी, अक्षदंड।

95(C). 'पक्षी' शब्द का पर्यायवाची शब्द 'पंथी' नहीं है। पंथी के पर्यायवाची शब्द पथिक, बटोही, राही, यात्री, मुसाफिर, राहगीर, आदि हैं।

96(B). 'अनु + दित = अनुदित' में संधि का सही प्रयोग नहीं हुआ है। इसका संधि विच्छेद 'अनु + उदित' होता है। इसमें दीर्घ संधि है। शब्द + इतर = शब्देतर में गुण संधि का प्रयोग हुआ है। रजनी

+ ईश = रजनीश में दीर्घ स्वर संधि का प्रयोग हुआ है। अहम् + कार = अहंकार में व्यंजन संधि का प्रयोग हुआ है।

97(B). 'आ + औ = औ' वृद्धि संधि का नियम है। जब संधि करते समय जब अ, आ के साथ ए, ऐ हो तो 'ऐ' बनता है और जब अ, आ के साथ ओ, औ हो तो 'औ' बनता है। उसे वृधि संधि कहते हैं।
उदाहरण:
महा + औषध : महौषद (आ + औ = औ)

98(B). 'धनुः + टंकार' शब्द मिलकर 'धनुष्टंकार' शब्द बनाते है। तथा इसमें 'विसर्ग संधि' है। विसर्ग संधि विसर्ग के साथ स्वर या व्यंजन मेल से जो विकार होता है उसे विसर्ग संधि कहते हैं। उदाहरण - निः + चय = निश्चय, दुः + चरित्र = दुश्चरित्र, ज्योतिः + चक्र = ज्योतिश्चक्र, निः + छल = निश्छल।

99(D). "संत रैदास", यहाँ उचित विकल्प है, अन्य विकल्प असंगत है।

- रैदास यहाँ दासी, दास, चकोर किसी की भक्ति नहीं करना चाहते है।
- "प्रभु जी, तुम स्वामी हम दासा, ऐसी भक्ति करै रैदासा"
- रैदास सिर्फ राम को स्वामी मानकर और स्वयं को दास मानकर भक्ति करना चाहता है।

100(C). **"अनुराग बांसुरी"** ,"नूर मोहम्मद" की रचना है।
- अनुराग बांसुरी का रचना वर्ष1764 ईस्वी है।
- यह बरवै चौपाई छंद में है।
- चौपाइयों के बीच बीच में इन्होंने दोहे न लिखकर बरवै रखे हैं।
- इसकी भाषा है जो सूफी रचनाओं से बहुत अधिक संस्कृत गर्भित है।
- "इंद्रावती" भी नूर मोहम्मद की अन्य रचना है।

General Knowledge

1. Who is the author of the book titled "Crunch Time: Narendra Modi's National Security Crises"?
(a) Sreeram Chaulia (b) Tarun Das
(c) Kaushik Basu (d) V. R. Panchamukhi

2. Consider the following organizations:
1. Bangabhasha Prakasika Sabha
2. Landholders Society
3. Bengal British India Society
4. Indian League
Select the correct chronological order of founding of these organizations from the code given below:
(a) 1,2,3,4 (b) 1,3,2,4
(c) 2,1,3,4 (d) 2,3,4,1

3. An inscription by which of the following is found on the pillar containing Prayag Prasasti of Samudragupta?
(a) Jahangir (b) Shahjahan
(c) Aurangzeb (d) Dara Shikoh

4. Which amongst the following families was the first to have a matrimonial alliance with Akbar?
(a) Rathor (b) Sisodiya
(c) Kachwaha (d) Chauhan

5. Under whose leadership did the Revolt of 1857 proceed in Lucknow?
(a) Begum of Awadh (b) Tatya Tope
(c) Rani Lakshmi Bai (d) Nana Sahib

6. After the Revolt of 1857, the British government selected the sepoys from which provinces?
(a) Brahmins from Uttar Pradesh and Bihar
(b) East Bengali and Oriya
(c) Gorkhas, Sikhs and Punjabis from the Northern Province
(d) Maratha from Madras Presidency

7. While watching news, you hear about a place, of which you had never heard earlier. You want to know more about the place and you want to locate it on the map. Which of the following is/are required for you to be able to locate the place on the map?
(a) Only latitude of the place
(b) Only longitude of the place
(c) Both longitude and latitude of the place
(d) Latitude, longitude and altitude of the place

8. Inhabitants are unaware of the speed of rotation of the planet Earth because:
1. the angular velocity is constant for each place on the Earth's surface
2. the atmosphere rotates with the Earth
3. there are no nearby objects, either stationary or moving at a rate different from that of the Earth
Which of the above is/are the correct explanation(s)?
(a) 1 only (b) 1 and 2 only
(c) 2 and 3 only (d) 1, 2 and 3

9. While travelling to a hilly region, you notice a massive boulder, which was loosened by heavy rains and moved downhill. This has resulted due to which of the following processes?

1. Mass wasting
2. Erosion
3. Weathering
Select the correct answer using the code given below.
(a) 1 only (b) 1 and 2 only
(c) 2 and 3 only (d) 1, 2 and 3

10. Who co-chaired the 18th Annual General Meeting of the Indian Institute of Entrepreneurship (IIE), Guwahati on 19 January 2023?
(a) Hardeep Singh Puri and Piyush Goyal
(b) G Kishan Reddy and Dharmendra Pradhan
(c) G Kishan Reddy and Piyush Goyal
(d) Hardeep Singh Puri and Kiren Rijiju

11. Which of the following has signed a Memorandum of Understanding (MoU) with the government of Goa to jointly promote Goa as a high-potential tourism destination in the world?
(a) Vrbo (b) Expedia
(c) Skyscanner (d) Airbnb

12. What is the rank of India in World Happiness Index 2023?
(a) 139th (b) 142th
(c) 112th (d) 136th

13. What is the theme of World Wetlands Day 2023?
(a) Wetlands Action for People and Nature
(b) It's Time for Wetlands Restoration
(c) Wetlands and Water
(d) Wetlands and Biodiversity

14. Which one of the following statements about the process of photosynthesis is correct?
(a) Chemical energy is converted into light energy.
(b) Carbon dioxide is oxidized to form carbohydrate.
(c) Water molecule splits into hydrogen and oxygen.
(d) Light energy is directly used to split water.

15. How are evergreen plants with woody stems having naked seed classified?
(a) Angiosperms (b) Monocotyledons
(c) Pteridophytes (d) Gymnosperms

16. The term used for the conservation of ecosystems and natural habitats and the maintenance and recovery of viable populations of species in their natural surroundings is:
(a) Core conservation
(b) In situ conservation
(c) Ex situ conservation
(d) Peripheral conservation

17. The Election Commissioner can be removed by the:
(a) Chief Election Commissioner
(b) Prime Minister
(c) President on the recommendation of the Chief Election Commissioner
(d) Chief Justice of India

18. Which one of the following is not a constitutional body?

(a) Finance Commission
(b) Planning Commission
(c) Public Service Commission
(d) Election Commission

19. At least how many days of prior notice is required for the impeachment of the President of India?
(a) 7 days
(b) 14 days
(c) 21 days
(d) 30 days

20. Which of the following welfare schemes' achievements have been recongnised by the Guiness World Records?
(a) Pradhan Mantri Kaushal Vikas Yojana
(b) Pradhan Mantri Jan Dhan Yojana
(c) Pradhan Mantri Suraksha Bima Yojana
(d) Pradhan Mantri Krishi Sinchai Yojana

21. With reference to casual workers employed in India, consider the following statements:
1. All casual workers are entitled for Employees Provident Fund coverage.
2. All casual workers are entitled for regular working hours and overtime payment.
3. The government can by notification specify that an establishment or industry shall pay wages only through its bank account.
Which of the above statements are correct?
(a) 1 and 2 only
(b) 2 and 3 only
(c) 1 and 3 only
(d) 1, 2 and 3

22. Which among the following steps is most likely to be taken at the time of an economic recession?
(a) Cut in tax rates accompanied by increase in interest rate
(b) Increase in expenditure on public projects
(c) Increase in tax rates accompanied by reduction of interest rate
(d) Reduction of expenditure on public projects

23. ___________ won the gold medal in the men's 10m air rifle competition of the ISSF Shooting World Cup in Cairo, Egypt.
(a) Varun Tomar
(b) Bhavesh Shekhawat
(c) Anish Bhanwala
(d) Rudrankksh Patil

24. Select the statements regarding the Development Financial Institution (DFI) proposed in the budget 2021-22:
1. It will provide medium to long-term finance for infrastructure in the country.
2. Central government's share of expenditure in the National Infrastructure Pipeline (NIP) will be completely funded by this institution.
Select the correct answer using the code given below
(a) 1 only
(b) 2 only
(c) Both 1 and 2
(d) Neither 1 nor 2

25. The Indian Space Research Organization (ISRO) successfully conducted the Reusable Launch Vehicle Autonomous Landing Mission (RLV) from the Aeronautical Test Range (ATR) in ___________.
(a) Thiruvananthapuram
(b) Chitradurga
(c) Kulasekharapatnam
(d) Sriharikota

Mathematics

26. $3889 \div 12.952 - ? = 3854.002$
(a) – 3553.74
(b) 3553.74
(c) – 3453.74
(d) 3457.34

27. The loss percent incurred when an object is sold at Rs. 436 is equal to the profit percent which is gained when selling it at Rs. 464. Find the cost price of that object.
(a) Rs. 450
(b) Rs. 410
(c) Rs. 478
(d) Rs. 465

28. A tradesman allows a discount of 15% on the marked price. Find the ratio of the cost price to the Marked price in the particular case that the tradesman gets a profit of 19% on the cost price.
(a) 7 : 5
(b) 3 : 4
(c) 5 : 7
(d) 15 : 19

29. Rs. 6000 becomes Rs. 8340 in K years at simple interest. If the rate of interest is 13% per annum, what is the value of K ?
(a) 2 years
(b) 4 years
(c) 3 years
(d) 5 years

30. Find the rate of interest when a sum of Rs. 2600 amounts to Rs. 3146 in 3 years.
(a) 4%
(b) 3%
(c) 7%
(d) 9%

31. The inner diameter of a cylindrical wooden pipe is 24 cm and its outer diameter is 28 cm and its outer diameter is 28 cm . The length of the pipe is 35 cm . Find the mass of the pipe, if 1 cm^3 of wood has a mass of 0.6 g .
(a) 3.432 kg
(b) 4.253 kg
(c) 6.325 kg
(d) 6.236 kg

32. The diameter of the base of a cone-shaped tent is 24 meters and its height is 16 meters. What is the area of the canvas required to erect it?
(a) $\frac{5280}{7} m^2$
(b) $\frac{5180}{7} m^2$
(c) $\frac{4180}{7} m^2$
(d) $\frac{3480}{7} m^2$

33. Integers are listed from 700 to 1000 . In how many integers is the sum of the digits 10 ?
(a) 6
(b) 7
(c) 8
(d) 9

34. There are 35 mobile phones in a box, out of which the average weight of 12 mobile phones is 50 grams and the average weight of 11 mobile phones is 40 grams and the average weight of the remaining mobile phones is 45 grams, then find the average weight of all mobile phones. (approx.)
(a) 45 grams
(b) 48 grams
(c) 43 grams
(d) 40 grams

35. The average score of 84 students (boys and girls) in a test is 57 . The ratio of the number of boys to that of girls is 10 : 11 . The average score of boys is 20% less than that of girls. What is the average score of girls in the test?
(a) 68
(b) 60
(c) 65
(d) 63

36. If the price of the commodity is increased by 50% by what fraction must its consumption be reduced so as to keep the same expenditure on its consumption?

(a) $\frac{1}{4}$ (b) $\frac{1}{3}$

(c) $\frac{1}{2}$ (d) $\frac{2}{3}$

37. Rashmi and Pallavi can make a carpet in 3 days and 12 days more than the time taken if both of them worked together. Find the time in which Rashmi can make the carpet alone.

(a) 9 days   (b) 6 days

(c) 12 days   (d) 8 days

38. A, B, and C can do a piece of work in 22 days, 40 days, and 110 days respectively, working alone. Find the number of days in which the work will be done if A is assisted by B and C on alternate days.

(a) 14 days   (b) 16 days

(c) 18 days   (d) 20 days

39. Ravi and Kumar are working on an assignment. Ravi takes 6 hours to type 32 pages on a computer, while Kumar takes 5 hours to type 40 pages. How much time will they take, working together on two different computers to type an assignment of 110 pages?

(a) 7 hours 30 minutes   (b) 8 hours

(c) 8 hours 15 minutes   (d) 8 hours 25 minutes

40. Two trains with their speeds in the ratio of 3 : 4 are going in the opposite direction along parallel tracks. If each takes 3 seconds to cross a telegraph post, then the time taken by the trains, to cross each other completely, will be?

(a) 3 second   (b) 4 second

(c) 7 second   (d) 21 second

41. A man travels half of the distance with speed 'v' and one-fourth of the distance with '$2v$' and remaining distance with '$\frac{v}{4}$'. What is the average speed of the journey?

(a) $\frac{7v}{13}$ (b) $\frac{8v}{13}$

(c) $\frac{5v}{13}$ (d) $\frac{6v}{13}$

42. Find the smallest of all:
$3^{\frac{1}{4}}, 2^{\frac{1}{3}}, 5^{\frac{1}{6}}, 2^{\frac{1}{2}}$

(a) $3^{\frac{1}{4}}$ (b) $2^{\frac{1}{3}}$

(c) $5^{\frac{1}{6}}$ (d) $2^{\frac{1}{2}}$

43. At present, the sum of ages of Rahul and Karan is 63 years. The ratio of their ages after 7 years will be 7:4, what is the present age of Rahul?

(a) 40 years   (b) 42 years

(c) 29 years   (d) 34 years

44. If $x = \frac{\sqrt{5}+1}{\sqrt{5}-1}$ and $y = \frac{\sqrt{5}-1}{\sqrt{5}+1}$, then find the value of $x^2 + y^2 - 4$.

(a) 3   (b) 4

(c) 5   (d) 2

45. Find the points on the curve $4x^2 + 9y^2 = 1$, where the tangents are perpendicular to the line $2y + x = 0$?

(a) $\left(\frac{1}{2\sqrt{10}}, \frac{1}{3\sqrt{10}}\right)$ and $\left(\frac{-1}{2\sqrt{10}}, \frac{-1}{3\sqrt{10}}\right)$

(b) $\left(\frac{3}{2\sqrt{10}}, \frac{5}{3\sqrt{10}}\right)$ and $\left(\frac{-3}{2\sqrt{10}}, \frac{-5}{3\sqrt{10}}\right)$

(c) $\left(\frac{3}{2\sqrt{10}}, \frac{1}{3\sqrt{10}}\right)$ and $\left(\frac{-3}{2\sqrt{10}}, \frac{-1}{3\sqrt{10}}\right)$

(d) None of these

46. If sin A - cos A = 0, then the value of $\sin^4 A + \cos^4 A$ is:

(a) 0   (b) 1

(c) $\frac{1}{2}$ (d) $\frac{3}{4}$

47. Let $S = \{1, 2, 3, \ldots\}$, A relation R on $S \times S$ is defined by xRy if $\log_a x > \log_a y$ when $a = \frac{1}{2}$. Then the relation is

(a) reflexive only

(b) symmetric only

(c) transitive only

(d) both symmetric and transitive

48. What is $\sum_{r=0}^{n} 2^r C(n, r)$ equal to?

(a) 2^n (b) 3^n

(c) 2^{2n} (d) 3^{2n}

Ques (49-50): Direction : Study the following line graphs and answer the given questions.

The following line graph shows the total production (in Tonnes) of Onion and Potato in 6 different villages. The table below shows the total quantity of onions and potatoes imported from abroad as a percentage of their respective total production.

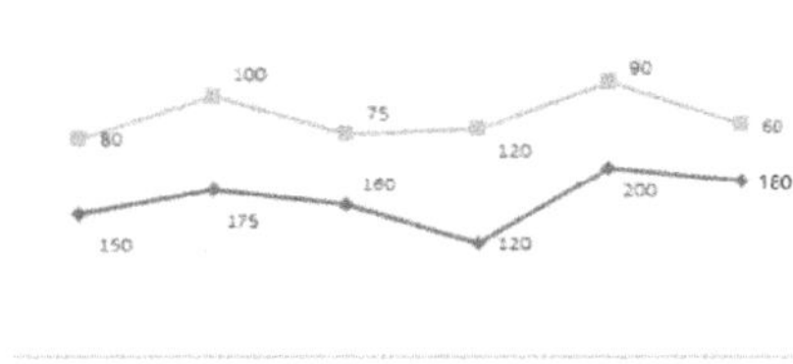

Village	Percentage of imported Onion	Percentage of imported Potato
A	20%	15%
B	12%	18%
C	15%	16%
D	25%	20%
E	8%	30%
F	10%	25%

Note : Total consumption of Onion or Potato = Production of Onion or Potato + Imported quantity of Onion or Potato

49. Total consumption of Onion and Potato together in village D is approximately what percent of total consumption of Onion in the villages B and C together?

(a) 73.33%   (b) 75.5%

(c) 72.66%   (d) 77.36%

50. If there are total 18 families in village E and 11 families in village F, then per family consumption of Onion in village F is how much more than the per family consumption of Onion in village E?

(a) 8 tonnes   (b) 4 tonnes

(c) 6 tonnes   (d) 10 tonnes

Reasoning

51. Direction : In the following question, select the related number from the given alternatives.

2 : 9 :: 3 :?

(a) 27
(b) 28
(c) 29
(d) 30

52. **Direction** : In the following question, select the related word from the given alternatives.

Television : Electricity :: Car : ?

(a) Tyre
(b) Fuel
(c) Brake
(d) Water

53. Introducing a man, Aman says, 'His wife is the only daughter of my maternal grandfather'. How is the man related to Aman?

(a) Grandfather
(b) Father
(c) Son
(d) Grandson

54. A is the son of C while C and Q are the sisters to one another. Z is the mother of Q. If P is the son of Z, which one of the following statements is correct?

(a) Q is the grandfather of A
(b) P is the maternal uncle of A
(c) P is the cousin of A
(d) Z is the brother of C

55. **Direction:** Choose the odd figure in the options.

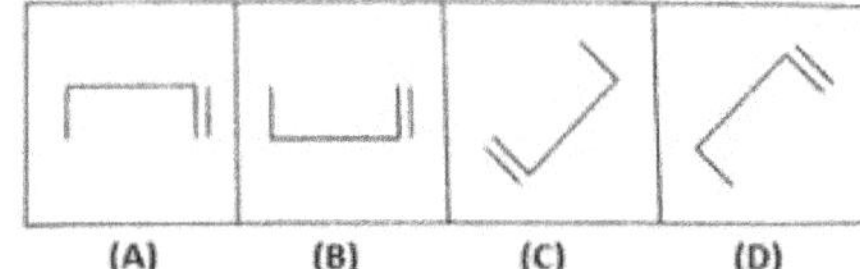

(A)　　(B)　　(C)　　(D)

(a) (A)
(b) (B)
(c) (C)
(d) (D)

56. **Direction** : Choose the odd figure in the options.

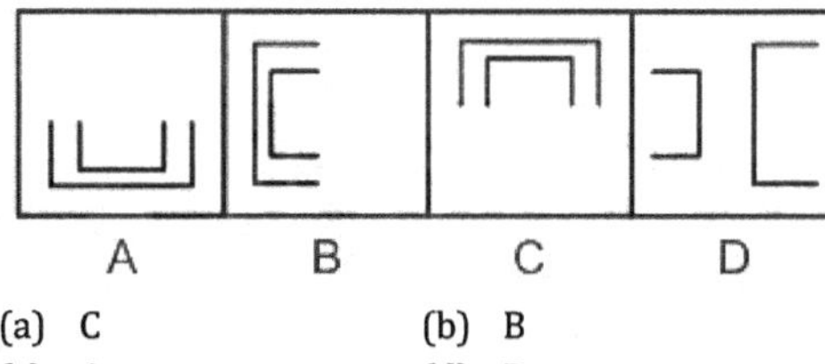

A　　B　　C　　D

(a) C
(b) B
(c) A
(d) D

57. **Direction:** Choose the odd figure in the options.

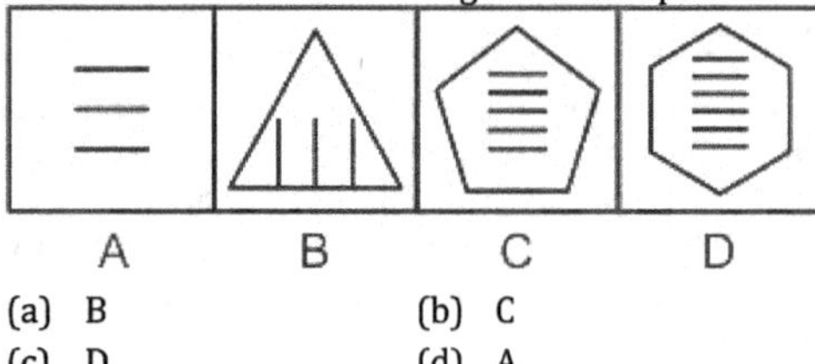

A　　B　　C　　D

(a) B
(b) C
(c) D
(d) A

58. Kunal walks 10 km towards the north. From there, he walks 6 km towards South. Then he walks 3 km towards east. How far and in which direction is he with reference to his starting point?

(a) 5 km, West
(b) 5 km, North-East
(c) 7 km, East
(d) 7 km, south-East

59. One morning at 7 O'clock. Rupesh started walking, while his back was towards the Sun. Then, he turned towards left, walked straight and then turned towards right and walked straight. Then, he again turned towards left. Now in which direction is he facing?

(a) North
(b) East
(c) West
(d) South

60. If 'ALPACA' means 'ACAPLA' in any language. So how to write 'ANIMAL' in this language?

(a) LAMNIA
(b) AAMLIN
(c) LAMINA
(d) ALAMIN

61. If HALE = NPGK then how will EAH be coded?

(a) TTR
(b) PLQ
(c) KPN
(d) NPK

62. **Direction** : Which of the answer figures will complete the figural series given in the problem figures?

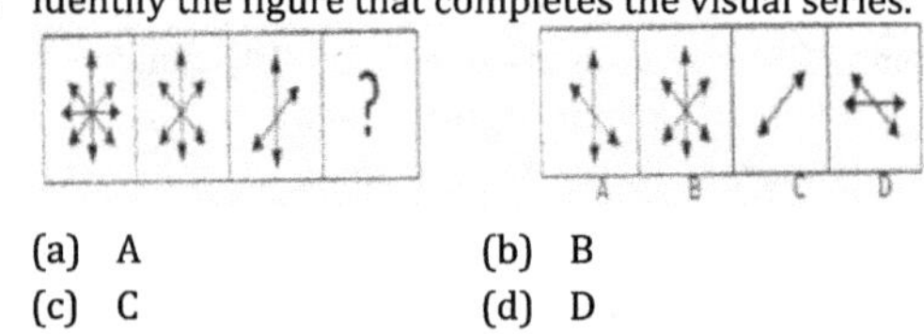

(a) A
(b) B
(c) C
(d) D

63. Identify the figure that completes the visual series.

(a) A
(b) B
(c) C
(d) D

Ques (64-65): Direction: Identify the diagram that best represents the relationship among classes given below:

64. Alphabets, Numbers, Vowels, Consonants

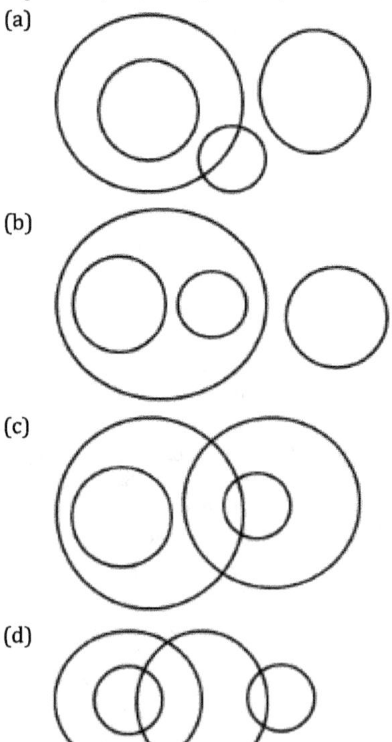

(a)

(b)

(c)

(d)

65. Triangles, hexagons and geometrical figures

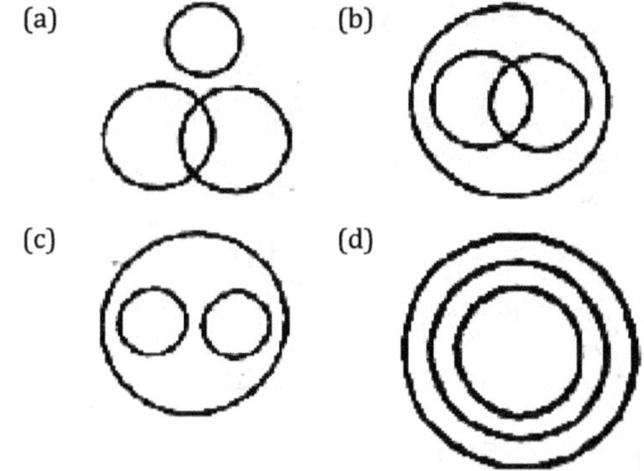

(a)   (b)   (c)   (d)

66. A series is given with one term wrong. Select that wrong term from the given alternatives.
8, 17, 36, 74, 154
(a) 74   (b) 17
(c) 154   (d) 8

67. Direction : In the following question, a series is given with one term missing. Choose the correct alternative from the given options.
23, 12, 13, 21 , _________, 112.5
(a) 63   (b) 44
(c) 45   (d) 54

68. There are five friends P, Q, R, S and T. S is shorter than T but taller than P. R is the tallest. Q is a little shorter than T but little taller than S. If they stand in the order of their heights who will be the shortest?
(a) S   (b) Q
(c) P   (d) T

69. A, B, C, D and E each having a different weight, D is heavier than A and E and B is lighter than C. Who is the heaviest among them?
(a) D   (b) B
(c) C   (d) Data insufficient

Ques (70-71): Direction: In the following question below some statements are given followed by some conclusions. Taking the given statements to be true even if they seem to be at variance from commonly known facts, read all the conclusions and then decide which of the given conclusions logically follows the given statements.

70. Statements:
Some cats are dogs.
All dogs are Deer.
Conclusions:
Some Deer are Cats.
All Deer are Cats.
No Deer is the dog.
(a) Only conclusion I follows
(b) Only conclusion III follows
(c) Only conclusion I and III follows
(d) Only conclusion II and II follows

71. Statements:
Some song are movie.
Some movie are video.
Conclusions:
I. Some song are video.
II. All video are movie.
(a) Neither conclusion I nor II follows.
(b) Only conclusion II follows.
(c) Both conclusions I and II follow.

(d) Only conclusion I follows.

Ques (72-73): Direction: Study the following information carefully and answer the given questions.
Eight friends - L, M, N, O, P, Q, R and S likes different colour - Pink, Yellow, Green, Red, White, Black, Orange and Purple but not necessarily in the same order. Each of them went for a picnic and spent in the multiples of Rs. 50 i.e. 50, 100, 150, 200, 250, 300, 350, 400 but not necessarily in the same order. Before coming back home, they all sat on a circular table facing the centre. The one who spent Rs. 350/- is three places to the right of O who likes Orange colour. The one who spends Rs. 250/- is three places to the left of P, who sits three places to the left of O. The difference of amounts spent by S who likes Black colour and P is maximum possible and they sat opposite to each other. There are only two persons sitting between Q and S. L sits sixth to the left of Q. Q likes green colour. L likes white colour spends Rs. 150/- and sits adjacent to the one who spends least. R sits 6th to the left of P who likes Red colour. There is only one person between N who likes Pink colour and the one who spends Rs. 50/-. R who likes Purple colour spends more amount at picnic than M. Difference in amounts spent by O and Q is Rs. 100/- and difference in amounts spent by O and S is Rs. 200/-.

72. Who among the following spent Rs. 100?
(a) R   (b) S
(c) Q   (d) O

73. Who is 6th to the left of one who likes Black colour?
(a) O   (b) N
(c) M   (d) R

74. Select the word which is different from the others.
(a) Football
(b) Volleyball
(c) Cricket
(d) Chess

75. Select the number which is different from the others.
(a) 7851   (b) 6432
(c) 5789   (d) 1325

General Hindi

76. प्रश्न में सही वर्तनी चुनिये:
(a) मत्रीमंडल   (b) मंत्रमंडल
(c) मंत्रयमंडल   (d) मंत्रिमंडल

77. प्रश्न में सही वर्तनी चुनिये:
(a) उत्पत्ती   (b) उत्पत्ति
(c) ऊत्पति   (d) उतपति

78. "अक्ल पर पत्थर पड़ना" मुहावरा का सही अर्थ है:
(a) ज्यादा बढ़ा-चढ़ाकर बोलना
(b) मुसीबत आना
(c) चोट लगना
(d) बुद्धि से काम न लेना

79. 'घर की मुर्गी दाल बराबर' मुहावरे का अर्थ है:
(a) घर की मुर्गी को बराबर दाल खिलाना।
(b) अपने आदमी को कम महत्व देना।
(c) घर की मुर्गी को दाल के बराबर मूल्वान समझना।
(d) मुर्गी और दाल खाना।

80. "गिरगिट की तरह रंग बदलना" मुहावरे का अर्थ है:

    (a) जगह न बदलना   (b) काम न करना
    (c) बातें बदलना   (d) काम समाप्त करना

81. हिन्दी के शब्दों का लिंग निर्धारण किसके आधार पर होता है?
    (a) प्रत्यय   (b) संज्ञा
    (c) क्रिया   (d) सर्वनाम

82. कवि का स्त्रीलिंग है:
    (a) कविइत्री   (b) कवित्री
    (c) कवयित्री   (d) कवियित्री

83. 'जो करने योग्य हो' उसके लिए उचित शब्द को पहचानिए।
    (a) करणीय   (b) कारणीय
    (c) कर्णीय   (d) कार्निय

84. 'धनुष की प्रत्यंचा से उत्पन्न ध्वनि' के लिए उचित एक शब्द का चयन कीजिए।
    (a) टांकर   (b) टनकर
    (c) टंकार   (d) तंकर

85. दिए गए विकल्पों में से कौन-सा शब्द स्त्रीलिंग है?
    (a) कुर्सी   (b) पेड़
    (c) शेर   (d) लड़का

86. निम्नलिखित में कौन सा शब्द पुल्लिंग है?
    (a) अँधेर   (b) नकेल
    (c) मुड़ेर   (d) बटेर

87. 'पा' लगाकर बनाये गए शब्द कहलाते हैं।
    (a) स्त्रीलिंग   (b) पुल्लिंग
    (c) हिंदी शब्द   (d) इनमे से कोई नही

88. 'आगरा' का बहुवचन होगा-
    (a) आगरे   (b) आगरों
    (c) आगरें   (d) बहुवचन नहीं होगा

89. हिन्दी में वचन होते हैं-
    (a) एक   (b) दो
    (c) तीन   (d) अनगिनत

90. निम्नलिखित प्रत्येक प्रश्न में तीन गद्यांश दिये गये हैं। त्रुटि वाले वाक्यांश को चुनें और उसके अनुरूप (A), (B), (C) पर चिन्ह लगाएँ। यदि वाक्य त्रुटिहीन हो, तो (D) पर चिन्ह लगाएँ:
    (a) अपने परिवार एवं प्रियजनों के विषय में
    (b) स्वास्थ्य संबंधी कुशल समाचार
    (c) शीघ्र भेजने की अनुकम्पन करें
    (d) कोई त्रुटि नहीं

91. निम्नलिखित प्रत्येक प्रश्न में तीन गद्यांश दिये गये हैं। त्रुटि वाले वाक्यांश को चुनें और उसके अनुरूप (A), (B), (C) पर चिन्ह लगाएँ। यदि वाक्य त्रुटिहीन हो, तो (D) पर चिन्ह लगाएँ:
    (a) भारतवर्ष के पर्वतीय क्षेत्र की
    (b) सुन्दरता, सारे विश्व में
    (c) सबसे सर्वोत्तम है
    (d) कोई त्रुटि नहीं

92. निम्नलिखित में से कौन-सा शब्द 'खर' का पर्यायवाची है?
    (a) गधा   (b) रावण
    (c) मूर्ख   (d) कुंठित

93. निम्न में से 'अभिमान' किसका विलोम है?
    (a) नम्रता   (b) विकर्षण
    (c) व्यय   (d) निरामिष

94. निम्न में से कौन सा विलोम - युग्म सही नहीं है?
    (a) अनुरक्ति - विरक्ति   (b) अनाथ - नाथ
    (c) अराग - सुराग   (d) अल्पायु-दीर्घायु

95. निम्नलिखित विकल्पों में 'अधीर' शब्द का पर्यायवाची नहीं है।
    (a) धैर्यहीन   (b) विलक्षण
    (c) व्यग्र   (d) आतुर

96. पो + इत्र की संधि क्या होगी?
    (a) पवित्र   (b) पावित्र
    (c) पोइत्र   (d) पाइत्र

97. 'शयन' का संधि-विच्छेद क्या होगा?
    (a) शे + यन   (b) शे + अन
    (c) शय + अन   (d) श + अन

98. 'देव्यागम' का संधि-विच्छेद क्या होगा?
    (a) देवी + आगम   (b) देव + आगम
    (c) देव्य + आगम   (d) देव्या + अगम

99. हिंदी की प्रसिद्ध रचना 'निर्मला' के रचनाकार कौन हैं?
    (a) जयशंकर प्रसाद   (b) मुंशी प्रेमचंद
    (c) रामधारी सिंह दिनकर   (d) वृन्दावन लाल वर्मा

100. निम्नलिखित में से कौन सी रचना जयशंकर प्रसाद द्वारा रचित है?
    (a) ध्रुवस्वामिनी   (b) प्रतिज्ञा
    (c) मृगनयनी   (d) उर्वशी

// Smart Answer Sheet //

Correct — Percentage of students who answered correctly.

Skipped — Percentage of students who skipped.

Q.	Ans.	Correct / Skipped	Q.	Ans.	Correct / Skipped	Q.	Ans.	Correct / Skipped
1	A	41.67% / 1.92%	2	A	17.15% / 4.8%	3	A	41.62% / 1.07%
4	C	47.94% / 1.09%	5	A	88.69% / 0.0%	6	C	60.69% / 1.72%
7	C	48.55% / 1.85%	8	D	65.67% / 1.48%	9	D	31.78% / 3.99%
10	B	53.03% / 1.75%	11	D	68.87% / 1.01%	12	D	49.85% / 1.2%
13	B	24.14% / 3.22%	14	D	81.92% / 0.0%	15	D	58.03% / 1.75%
16	B	47.42% / 1.9%	17	C	62.22% / 1.64%	18	B	85.72% / 0.0%
19	B	49.52% / 1.42%	20	B	78.93% / 0.0%	21	D	56.61% / 1.78%
22	B	55.71% / 1.51%	23	D	87.94% / 0.0%	24	A	11.08% / 4.55%
25	B	52.63% / 1.67%	26	A	42.83% / 1.62%	27	A	67.95% / 1.44%
28	C	50.23% / 1.86%	29	C	42.22% / 1.1%	30	C	46.41% / 1.59%
31	A	62.08% / 1.83%	32	A	41.7% / 1.81%	33	D	86.66% / 0.0%
34	A	85.05% / 0.0%	35	D	28.59% / 3.82%	36	B	66.27% / 1.3%
37	A	53.93% / 1.39%	38	B	32.33% / 3.5%	39	C	49.96% / 1.22%
40	A	13.74% / 4.26%	41	B	14.46% / 3.26%	42	B	62.06% / 1.29%
43	B	56.65% / 1.19%	44	A	44.14% / 1.35%	45	C	54.0% / 1.11%
46	C	81.19% / 0.0%	47	C	14.82% / 3.38%	48	B	83.25% / 0.0%
49	D	82.34%	50	C	49.55%	51	B	62.16%

		0.0%			1.82%			1.21%
52	B	82.97% 0.0%	53	B	61.79% 1.51%	54	B	40.5% 1.6%
55	B	60.58% 1.37%	56	D	65.64% 1.56%	57	D	68.16% 1.47%
58	B	16.72% 3.25%	59	D	80.81% 0.0%	60	C	40.04% 1.92%
61	C	85.54% 0.0%	62	C	27.65% 3.41%	63	C	84.49% 0.0%
64	B	79.65% 0.0%	65	C	68.18% 1.66%	66	A	88.29% 0.0%
67	B	76.09% 0.0%	68	C	16.75% 4.5%	69	D	50.3% 1.24%
70	A	83.02% 0.0%	71	A	84.89% 0.0%	72	C	13.05% 4.89%
73	B	17.29% 3.55%	74	D	77.95% 0.0%	75	B	57.39% 1.58%
76	D	89.34% 0.0%	77	B	89.96% 0.0%	78	D	50.6% 1.38%
79	B	83.08% 0.0%	80	C	44.52% 1.43%	81	B	63.69% 1.99%
82	D	25.11% 4.95%	83	A	65.81% 1.72%	84	C	51.33% 1.88%
85	A	43.54% 1.99%	86	A	26.75% 4.65%	87	B	86.21% 0.0%
88	D	88.72% 0.0%	89	B	88.03% 0.0%	90	C	67.14% 1.42%
91	C	60.66% 1.98%	92	A	80.52% 0.0%	93	A	69.21% 1.84%
94	B	62.93% 1.12%	95	B	49.88% 1.56%	96	A	62.61% 1.66%
97	B	55.87% 1.2%	98	A	64.85% 1.23%	99	B	42.74% 1.5%
100	A	57.35% 1.0%						

// Hints and Solutions //

1(A). A new book authored by Dr Sreeram Chaulia titled "Crunch Time: Narendra Modi's National Security Crises" was released on March 31 by the Minister of State for External Affairs, Meenakshi Lekhi. He is the Dean of the Jindal School of International Affairs of OP Jindal Global University.

5(A). During the Revolt of 1857, the rebellion in Lucknow was led by Begum Hazrat Mahal of Awadh. She declared his younger son Birjis Kadar as the Nawab of Awadh.

6(C). In the Revolt of 1857, soldiers from Uttar Pradesh, Bengal, and Bihar participated in a big way.

7(C). The grid helps people to locate places on the map. On small-scale maps, the grid is often made up of latitude and longitude lines. Latitude lines run east-west around the globe, parallel to the Equator, an imaginary line that circles the middle of the Earth. Longitude lines run north-south, from pole to pole. Latitude and longitude provide an absolute location for a place on the globe.
Two types of imaginary reference lines are used to locate positions or points and to make accurate globes and maps. These lines are called parallels of latitude and meridians of longitude.

8(D). While traveling in a bus or car, we can tell that it is moving either if we look outside or if the speed of the car or bus increases or decreases, and the same is the case for a rotational motion. In space, the earth does not experience any external torque while rotating on its own axis, and hence its angular velocity is always constant.
Also, the atmosphere around the earth rotates with the earth because of gravity, friction, and viscosity. There is nothing out there in the space either stationary or moving which we can consider as a reference to notice the rotation of the earth.

9(D). While travelling to a hilly region, you notice a massive boulder, which was loosened by heavy rains and moved downhill. This has resulted due to Mass wasting, Erosion and Weathering processes.
Mass movements/Mass wasting:
- It is the down-slope movement of Regolith (loose uncemented mixture of soil and rock particles that covers the Earth's surface) by the force of gravity without the aid of a transporting medium such as water, ice, or wind. Still, as we shall see, water plays a key role.
- Mass movements are part of a continuum of erosional processes between weathering and stream transport.
- Mass movement causes regolith and rock to move down-slope where sooner or later the loose particles will be picked up by another transporting agent and eventually moved to a site of deposition such as an ocean basin or lake bed.
- Mass movement processes are occurring continuously on all slopes; some act very slowly, others occur very suddenly, often with disastrous results.
- Weathering and erosion impact the surface of the land in many ways.
- Much of this relates to the mechanical, chemical, and biological processes breaking down rocks while shaping the landscape, including the formation of soils.
- Gravity has a large role in moving material downhill by a variety of means called mass wasting.
- Mass wasting is associated with a variety of serious landslide hazards that are often associated with heavy precipitation.

10(B). Union Minister for Tourism and Culture, G Kishan Reddy and Union Minister for Education and Skill Development and Entrepreneurship, Dharmendra Pradhan co-chaired the 18th Annual General Meeting of the Indian Institute of Entrepreneurship (IIE), Guwahati on 19 January 2023.
During the meeting, a holistic approach of the government for skill development in the North Eastern region was suggested. The Institute must enter into an understanding with leading Centres of excellence like IITs and IIMs and provide degree courses for students in cutting-edge courses like data analytics etc.

11(D). Airbnb has signed a Memorandum of Understanding (MoU) with the government of Goa to jointly promote Goa as a high-potential tourism destination in the world.
Airbnb provides an online marketplace that connects people who want to rent out their homes to tourists who intend to visit that locality.
It will help the Goa Tourism Department in developing such homestay capacity across the state.

12(D). In terms of overall happiness, India is now placed in the 136th position in 2023. Finland was ranked the happiest country in the world five times in a row as of March 2023, according to the World

Happiness Report followed by Denmark.

13(B). World Wetlands Day is observed globally on 2 February every year. The theme for World Wetlands Day 2023 is "It's Time for Wetlands Restoration", highlighting the urgent need to prioritize wetland restoration.

14(D). During photosynthesis, water is split into 2H+, [O], and electrons. This creates oxygen, one of the net products of photosynthesis. At the end of the process, oxygen and carbohydrates are generated.

15(D). Gymnosperms seeds are called as naked seeds. Coniferous forests have cones instead of seeds and are called gymnosperms. Pines, spruces, firs, and ginkgos are some examples of gymnosperms.

16(B). In situ conservation refers to the conservation of plant and animal species in their natural habitats.

17(C). The Election Commissioner can be removed by the President on the recommendation of the Chief Election Commissioner.

18(B). Planning Commission is not a constitutional body. Planning Commission of India was an organization in the Government of India, which formulated India's Five-Year Plans.

19(B). At least 14 days days of prior notice is required for the impeachment of the President of India. President comes under Parliament.

20(B). Pradhan Mantri Jan Dhan Yojana welfare schemes' achievements have been recognised by the Guinness World Records.
- Pradhan Mantri Jan Dhan Yojana is a National Mission on Financial Inclusion encompassing an integrated approach to bring about comprehensive financial inclusion of all the households in the country.
- It was launched by the Prime Minister of India Narendra Modi on 28 August 2014.
- The scheme was implemented with the aim to open a bank account for all citizens in India.
- Pradhan Mantri Jan Dhan Yojana entered into the Guinness Book of World Records in 2015.
- Banks have opened 11.50 crore accounts under the Pradhan Mantri Jan-Dhan Yojana.
- The Guinness Book said: "Most bank accounts opened in one week as part of the Financial Inclusion Campaign is 18,096,130 and was achieved by the Government of India from August 23 to 29, 2014."

21(D). The provisions of the Provident Fund Act, 1952, covers all types of employees, who are drawing salary/wages at the time of joining up to Rs. 15,000/- per month. Also, the employees drawing salary/wages more than Rs. 15,000/- per month can also come under the purview of the EPF Act at the discretion of the management and by submitting a joint undertaking to the Provident Fund Commissioner.

22(B). An increase in expenditure on public projects steps is most likely to be taken at the time of an economic recession.

23(D). Rudrankksh Patil won the gold medal in the men's 10m air rifle competition of the ISSF Shooting World Cup in Cairo, Egypt on 21 February 2023. Rudrankksh Patil defeated Germany's Maximilian Ulbrich 16-8 in the gold medal match to clinch the top prize.

24(A). Development Financial Institutions are organizations that are involved in medium to long-term financing at a low cost for development. Profit is not their prime motive rather they are guided by the developmental needs of the economy. So, statement 1 is correct.
Expenditure of National Infrastructure Pipeline will be shared between the centre, states and private sector in the ratio of 39, 40 and 21 respectively. DFI proposed in the budget helps in raising finance for the centre, states, and the private sector in meeting the expenditure towards National Infrastructure Pipeline. It has no commitment to completely fund the central government's share of expenditure in the National Infrastructure Pipeline. So, statement 2 is not correct.

25(B). The Indian Space Research Organization (ISRO) successfully conducted the Reusable Launch Vehicle Autonomous Landing Mission (RLV) from the Aeronautical Test Range (ATR) in Karnataka's Chitradurga on 2 April 2023.

26(A). Given:
$3889 \div 12.952 - ? = 3854.002$
$\Rightarrow \frac{3889}{12.952} - ? = 3854.002$
$\Rightarrow 300.262 - ? = 3854.002$
$\Rightarrow ? = 3854.002 - 300.262$
$\Rightarrow ? = -3553.74$

27(A). Given:
The loss percent incurred when an object is sold at Rs. 436 is equal to the profit percent which is gained when selling it at Rs. 464.
Loss = CP - SP
Gain = SP - CP
The loss percent incurred when an object is sold at Rs. 436
Loss = CP - 436
profit percent which is gained when selling it at Rs. 464.
Gain = 464 - CP
As per the question,
$\Rightarrow$ CP - 436 = 464 - CP
$\Rightarrow$ 2CP = 900
$\Rightarrow$ CP = $\frac{900}{2}$
$\Rightarrow$ CP = Rs. 450

28(C). The ratio of the cost price to the marked price is given as (100− Discount %) : (100+ Profit %)
$\Rightarrow CP : MP = (100-15\%) : (100 + 19\%) = 85 : 119$
$\therefore CP : MP = 5 : 7$
Alternate Solution:
Let the cost price be Rs. 100 .
Given that the profit $= 19\%$
So, the selling price $=$ Rs. 119
Also, the selling price $= 85\%$ of the Marked price
$\frac{119}{85} \times 100 =$ Marked price
Marked price $=$ Rs. 140
Cost price: Marked price $= 100 : 140 = 5 : 7$

29(C). Given:
Principal $=$ Rs. 6000
Amount $=$ Rs. 8340
Rate $= 13\%$
Time $= T$
Formula:

$$SI = \frac{PRT}{100}$$

According to the question,

Simple interest $= 8340 - 6000 = 2340$

By using formula, we get

Simple interest $= (6000 \times 13 \times T)100$

$\Rightarrow 2340 = 780 \times T$

$\Rightarrow 3 = T$

$\therefore$ The value of T is 3 years.

30(C). Given:

Principal $=$ Rs. 2600

Amount $=$ Rs. 3146

Time $=$ 3 years

Formula:

$$SI = \frac{(PRT)}{100}$$

$$A = P + SI$$

According to the question, we have

Simple interest is

$\Rightarrow SI = 3146 - 2600$

$\Rightarrow SI =$ Rs. 546

Now, Rate of interest is

$\Rightarrow SI = \frac{(PRT)}{100}$

$\Rightarrow 546 = \frac{(2600 \times R \times 3)}{100}$

$\Rightarrow R = \frac{546}{78}$

$\Rightarrow R = 7\%$

$\therefore$ The Rate of interest per annum is 7%.

31(A). Here, inner radius $(r) = \frac{24}{2}$ cm $= 12$ cm

Outer radius $(R) = \frac{28}{2}$ cm $= 14$ cm, $h = 35$ cm

Voume of the wood used in the pipe

$= \pi \left(R^2 - r^2 \right) h$

$= \frac{22}{7} \left[(14)^4 - (12)^2 \right] \times 35 \text{ cm}^3$

$= \frac{22}{7} \times 26 \times 2 \times 35 \text{ cm}^3 = 5720 \text{ cm}^3$

Mass of 1 cm^3 of wood $= 0.6$ g

$\therefore$ Mass of 5720 cm^3 of wood

$= 0.6 \times 5720$ g

$= 3.432$ kg

32(A). Given,

Diameter $d = 24m$

Radius, $R = \frac{24}{2} = 12m$

Height $H = 16m$

Slant height $L = \sqrt{R^2 + H^2}$

$= \sqrt{12^2 + 16^2}$

$= 20m$

The area of the canvas required to erect a tent is equal to the lateral surface area of the cone. So,

Canvas required $=$ Curved surface area of cone

$= \pi r l$

$= \frac{22}{7} \times 12 \times 20$

$= \frac{5280}{7} m^2$

33(D). Possible combination of three digits whose sum is 10 and the numbers formed with these three digits greater than 700 and less than 1000 are:

$0, 1, 9 \rightarrow 901, 910$

$0, 2, 8 \Rightarrow 802, 820$

$0, 3, 7 \Rightarrow 703, 730$

$1, 1, 8 \Rightarrow 811$

$1, 2, 7 \Rightarrow 712, 721$

So, we have 9 such numbers.

34(A). Given,

Total mobile phones in the box are 35.

The average weight of 12 mobile phones $= 50$ grams

Then, the total weight of 12 mobile phones $12 \times 50 = 600$ grams

The average weight of the next 11 mobile phones is 40 grams.

Then, the total weight of 11 mobile phones $11 \times 40 = 440$ grams

Remaining number of mobile phones $= 35 - 12 - 11 = 12$

The average weight of the remaining mobile phones is 45 grams.

Then, the total weight of the remaining mobile phones $12 \times 45 = 540$ grams

Now the total weight of 35 mobile phones $600 + 440 + 540 = 1580$ grams

$$\text{Average} = \frac{Total\ weight}{Total\ numbers\ of\ an\ item}$$

$= \frac{1580}{35}$

$= 45.12$ grams

$\therefore$ The average weight of all mobile phones is 45 grams.

35(D). Given:

Average score of 84 students $= 57$

Ratio of boy and Girl $= 10 : 11$

Average score of boys $= \left(\frac{80}{100} \right) \times$ Average score of girls

We know that:

$$\text{Average on 'n' numbers} = \frac{\text{Sum of n numbers}}{n}$$

sum of 'n' numbers $=$ (Average on 'n' numbers $) \times n$

The Total marks scored by 84 students $= 84 \times 57$

$= 4788$

Let the Number of boys and girls $= 10x$ and $11x$

$\because$ The total number of students $= 84$

$\therefore 10x + 11x = 84$

$\Rightarrow 21x = 84$

$\Rightarrow x = \frac{84}{21}$

$\Rightarrow x = 4$

Number of Boys $= 10x = 10 \times 4 = 40$

Number of Girls $= 11x = 11 \times 4 = 44$

Average score of boys $= \left(\frac{80}{100} \right) \times$ Average score of girls

$\Rightarrow$ (Average score of boys) : (Average score of girls) $= 4 : 5$

Let the Average score of boys $= 4y$

Average score of girls $= 5y$

Total marks scored by 40 boys $= 40 \times (4y)$

$= 160y$

Total marks scored by 44 girls $= 44 \times (5y)$

$= 220y$

$\because$ Total marks scored by 40 boys + Total marks scored by 44 girls $=$ Total marks scored by 84 students

$\therefore 160y + 220y = 4788$

$\Rightarrow 380y = 4788$

$\Rightarrow y = \frac{4788}{380}$

$\Rightarrow y = 12.6$

Average score of 44 girls $= 5y$

$= 5 \times 12.6$

$= 63$

36(B). Let the initial price of the commodity be 100.

After 50% increase in price, It will become, $100 \ldots 50\%$ increase > 150.

Now, we have to reduce the consumption to keep

expenditure 100.
Increase in price $= 150 - 100 = 50$
We have to reduce the consumption,
$$= \frac{50}{150} \times 100$$
$$= \frac{1}{3} \text{ or } 33.33\%$$

37(A). Let the time both of them together will take to make the carpet be x days.
Time taken by Rashmi alone $= x + 3$ days
Time taken by Pallavi alone $= x + 12$ days
One day work when they both work together = Sum of their individual per day work
$$\Rightarrow \frac{1}{x} = \frac{1}{x+12} + \frac{1}{x+3}$$
$$\Rightarrow \frac{1}{x} = \frac{2x+15}{x^2+15x+36}$$
$$\Rightarrow x^2 + 15x + 36 = 2x^2 + 15x$$
$$\Rightarrow 36 = 2x^2 - x^2$$
$$\Rightarrow x^2 = 36$$
$$\Rightarrow x = 6$$
Time taken by Rashmi to make carpet alone $= 6 + 3 = 9$ days

38(B). Given:
Time taken by A to complete the work $= 22$ days
Time taken by B to complete the work $= 40$ days
Time taken by C to complete the work $= 110$ days
Concept used:
Time taken by someone to complete the work in X days.
Then, part of the work done by him/her in 1 day is $\frac{1}{x}$.
Calculations:
Time taken by A to complete the work $= 22$ days
So, part of work done by A in 1 day $= \frac{1}{22}$
Similarly we can say,
Part of work done by B in 1 day $= \frac{1}{40}$
Part of work done by C in 1 da $= \frac{1}{110}$
Now $(A + B)$'s 1 day of work
$$= \{(\tfrac{1}{22}) + (\tfrac{1}{40})\} = \frac{31}{440}$$
And $(A + C)$'s 1 day of work
$$= \{(\tfrac{1}{22}) + (\tfrac{1}{110})\} = \frac{6}{110}$$
Work done in 2 days
$$= \{(\tfrac{31}{440}) + (\tfrac{6}{110})\} = \frac{55}{440} = \frac{1}{8}$$
Now, $\frac{1}{8}$ work is done in 2 days
So, total time required to complete the work $= 8 \times 2 = 16$ days

39(C). Number of pages typed by Ravi in 1 hour $= \frac{32}{6} = \frac{16}{3}$.
Number of pages typed by Kumar in 1 hour $= \frac{40}{5} = 8$.
Number of pages typed by both in 1 hour $= (\frac{16}{3} + 8) = \frac{40}{3}$.
$\therefore$ Time taken by both to type 110 pages
$$= (110 \times \tfrac{3}{40}) \text{ hours}$$
$= 8\frac{1}{4}$ hours (or) 8 hours 15 minutes.

40(A). Let the speed of two trains be $3a$ and $4a$ respectively.
Length of train $= 3a \times 3 = 9a$ meter
Length of other train $= 4a \times 3 = 12a$ meter
Then,
Time taken to cross each other

$$= \frac{(9a+12a)}{(3a+4a)}$$
$$= \frac{21}{7}$$
$= 3$ second
$\therefore$ 3 second required to cross each other.

41(B). Let the total distance of the journey be x. We know that
$$\text{Time} = \left(\frac{\text{Distance}}{\text{Speed}}\right)$$
So, total time $= \left(\frac{x}{2v}\right) + \left(\frac{x}{(4 \times 2v)}\right) + \left(\frac{x}{(4 \times (\frac{v}{4}))}\right)$
$$= \frac{13x}{8v}$$
$$\text{Average speed} = \frac{\text{Total distance}}{\text{Total time}}$$
$$= \frac{x}{\left(\frac{13x}{8v}\right)}$$
$$= \frac{8v}{13}$$

42(B). Concept:
Bring the denominators of the powers of all the numbers to same.
Calculation:
LCM of the denominators $4, 3, 6, 2$ is 12
The numbers can be written as
$3^{\frac{3}{12}}, 2^{\frac{4}{12}}, 5^{\frac{2}{12}}, 2^{\frac{6}{12}}$
$\because$ All the powers have denominators same,
$3^3, 2^4, 5^2, 2^6$
2^4 is the least of them.
$\therefore 2^{\frac{1}{3}}$ is least of them.

43(B). Let, the present age of Rahul is x.
Present age of Karan is $63 - x$
7 years later
Rahul's age after 7 years $= x + 7$
Karan's age after 7 years $= 63 - x + 7 = 70 - x$
According to the question,
$$\Rightarrow \frac{(x+7)}{(70-x)} = \frac{7}{4}$$
$$\Rightarrow 4x + 28 = 490 - 7x$$
$$\Rightarrow 11x = 462$$
$$\Rightarrow x = 42 \text{ years}$$
$\therefore$ present age of Rahul $= 42$ years

44(A). Given:
$x = \frac{\sqrt{5}+1}{\sqrt{5}-1}$ and $y = \frac{\sqrt{5}-1}{\sqrt{5}+1}$
Concept used:
$(x + y)^2 = x^2 + y^2 + 2xy$
$\Rightarrow x^2 + y^2 = (x + y)^2 - 2xy$
Calculation:
$$xy = \frac{\sqrt{5}+1}{\sqrt{5}-1} \times \frac{\sqrt{5}-1}{\sqrt{5}+1} = 1$$
$$x + y = \frac{\sqrt{5}+1}{\sqrt{5}-1} + \frac{\sqrt{5}-1}{\sqrt{5}+1} = \frac{\sqrt{5}+1}{\sqrt{5}-1} + \frac{\sqrt{5}-1}{\sqrt{5}+1}$$
$$= [\frac{5+1+2\sqrt{5}+5+1-2\sqrt{5}}{5-1}]$$
$$= \frac{12}{4}$$
$x + y = 3$
Putting values in $x^2 + y^2 = (x + y)^2 - 2xy$, we get
$x^2 + y^2 = 3^2 - 2 \times 1 = 7$
$\therefore x^2 + y^2 - 4 = 7 - 4 = 3$

45(C). Given:
Equation of curve is $4x^2 + 9y^2 = 1$ and the tangents to the given curve are perpendicular to the line $2y + x = 0$.
Let (x_1, y_1) be the point of contact.
The given equation of line $2y + x = 0$ can be

written as: $y = (\frac{-1}{2})x$.

Now by comparing the equation $y = (\frac{-1}{2})x$ with $y = mx + c$ we get: $m = \frac{-1}{2}$ and $c = 0$

So, the slope of the given line $2y + x = 0$ is $m_1 = \frac{-1}{2}$

As we know that slope of the tangent at any point say (x_1, y_1) to a curve is given by: $m = \left[\frac{dy}{dx}\right]_{(x_1, y_1)}$

Now by differentiating the equation of curve $4x^2 + 9y^2 = 1$ with respect to x we get

$$\Rightarrow 8x + 18y \cdot \frac{dy}{dx} = 0$$

$$\Rightarrow \frac{dy}{dx} = -\frac{4x}{9y}$$

$$\Rightarrow \left[\frac{dy}{dx}\right]_{(x_1, y_1)} = -\frac{4x_1}{9y_1}$$

So, the slope of the tangent is $m_2 = \frac{-4x_1}{9y_1}$

It is given that the tangents to the given curve are perpendicular to the line $2y + x = 0$.

As we know that, if L_1 and L_2 are two lines with slope m_1 and m_2 respectively and if they are perpendicular to each other then $m_1 \times m_2 = -1$.

$$\Rightarrow m_1 \times m_2 = -\frac{1}{2} \cdot -\frac{4x_1}{9y_1} = -1$$

$$\Rightarrow y_1 = -\frac{2}{9}x_1$$

$\because$ The point (x_1, y_1) lies on the curve $4x^2 + 9y^2 = 1$

$$\Rightarrow 4x_1^2 + 9y_1^2 = 1$$

By substituting $y_1 = -\frac{2}{9}x_1$ in the above equation we get

$$\Rightarrow 4x_1^2 + 9 \times \frac{4}{81} \times x_1^2 = 1 \Rightarrow x_1^2 = \frac{9}{40}$$

$$\Rightarrow x_1 = \pm\frac{3}{2\sqrt{10}}$$

When $\qquad x_1 = \frac{3}{2\sqrt{10}} \qquad$ then

$$y_1 = -\frac{2}{9}x_1 = -\frac{2}{9}\frac{3}{2\sqrt{10}} = \frac{1}{3\sqrt{10}}$$

Similarly when $\qquad x_1 = \frac{-3}{2\sqrt{10}} \qquad$ then

$$y_1 = -\frac{2}{9}x_1 = -\frac{2}{9}\frac{-3}{2\sqrt{10}} = \frac{-1}{3\sqrt{10}}$$

So, the points of contact are: $\left(\frac{3}{2\sqrt{10}}, \frac{1}{3\sqrt{10}}\right)$ and $\left(\frac{-3}{2\sqrt{10}}, \frac{-1}{3\sqrt{10}}\right)$

46(C). Given,

$\sin A - \cos A = 0$

$\Rightarrow \sin A = \cos A$

$\Rightarrow A = 45°$

$\Rightarrow \sin A = \cos A = \frac{1}{\sqrt{2}}$

Now,

$$\sin^4 A + \cos^4 A = \left(\frac{1}{\sqrt{2}}\right)^4 + \left(\frac{1}{\sqrt{2}}\right)^4$$

$$= \frac{1}{4} + \frac{1}{4}$$

$$= \frac{1}{2}$$

47(C). Here, $x\mathrm{R}y \Rightarrow \log_a x > \log_a y$ and $a = \frac{1}{2}$

$$\Rightarrow \frac{\log x}{\log\left(\frac{1}{2}\right)} > \frac{\log y}{\log\left(\frac{1}{2}\right)}$$

$\Rightarrow \log x > \log y$

$\Rightarrow x > y$

For reflexive, $x > x$ which is not true so the relation is not reflexive.

For symmetric, if $x > y$ then $y > x$ which is also not true.

For transitive, if $x > y$ and $y > z$ then $x > z$ so, the relation is transitive only.

48(B). $\Rightarrow {}^nC_0 2^0 + {}^nC_1 2^1 + {}^nC_2 2^2 + \ldots + {}^nC_{n-1}2^{n-1} + {}^nC_n 2^n \Rightarrow {}^nC_0 1^n 2^0 + {}^nC_1 1^{n-1}2^1 + {}^nC_2 1^{n-2}2^2 + \ldots + {}^nC_{n-1}2^{n-1} + {}^nC_n 2^n$

Comparing with binomial expansion $x = 1$ and $y = 2 \Rightarrow \sum_{r=0}^n 2^r C(n, r) = (1 + 2)^n \Rightarrow 3^n$

Ques (49-50): Given,

Total consumption of Onion or Potato = Production of Onion or Potato + Imported quantity of Onion or Potato.

We can prepare the following table:

Village	Onion production (In tonnes)	Potato production (In tonnes)	Imported quantity of Onion	Imported quantity of Potato	Consumption of Onion	Consumption of Potato
A	150	80	$\frac{20}{100} \times 150$ =0.2 × 150 = 30	$\frac{15}{100} \times 80$ = 0.15 × 80 = 12	150 + 30 = 180	80 + 12 = 92
B	175	100	$\frac{12}{100} \times 175$ = 0.12 × 175 = 21	$\frac{18}{100} \times 100$ = 0.18 × 100 = 18	175 + 21 = 196	100 + 18 = 118
C	160	75	$\frac{15}{100} \times 160$ = 0.15 × 160 = 24	$\frac{16}{100} \times 75$ = 0.16 × 75 = 12	160 + 24 = 184	75 + 12 = 87
D	120	120	$\frac{25}{100} \times 120$ = 0.25 × 120 = 30	$\frac{20}{100} \times 120$ = 0.2 × 120 = 24	120 + 30 = 150	120 + 24 = 144
E	200	90	$\frac{8}{100} \times 200$ = 0.08 × 200 = 16	$\frac{30}{100} \times 90$ = 0.3 × 90 = 27	200 + 16 = 216	90 + 27 = 117
F	180	60	$\frac{10}{100} \times 180$ = 0.1 × 180 = 18	$\frac{25}{100} \times 60$ = 0.25 × 60 = 15	180 + 18 = 198	60 + 15 = 75

49(D). Thus,

Total consumption of Onion and Potato together in village D

= 150 + 144

= 294 tonnes

Total consumption of Onion in villages B and C together

= 196 + 184

= 380 tonnes

So, required percentage = $\left[\frac{294}{380}\right] \times 100$

= 77.36 %

50(C). Thus,

Per household consumption of onion in village

F = $\dfrac{\text{Onion consumption in village F}}{\text{Total households in village F}}$

= $\dfrac{198}{11}$

= 18 tonnes

Per household consumption of onion in village

E = $\dfrac{\text{Onion consumption in village E}}{\text{Total households in village E}}$

$= \dfrac{218}{18}$

$= 12$ tonnes So, required difference $= 18 - 12$

$= 6$ tonnes

51(B). The pattern followed here is:

$(2 \times 2 \times 2) + 1 = 8 + 1 = 9$

Similarly,

$(3 \times 3 \times 3) + 1 = 27 + 1 = 28$

52(B). Television works by electricity.

Similarly,

A car runs on fuel.

53(B). Preparing the family tree using the following symbols:

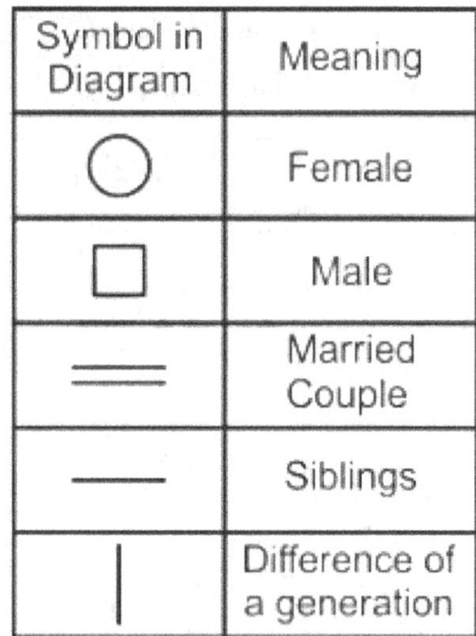

Symbol in Diagram	Meaning
◯	Female
▢	Male
═══	Married Couple
───	Siblings
│	Difference of a generation

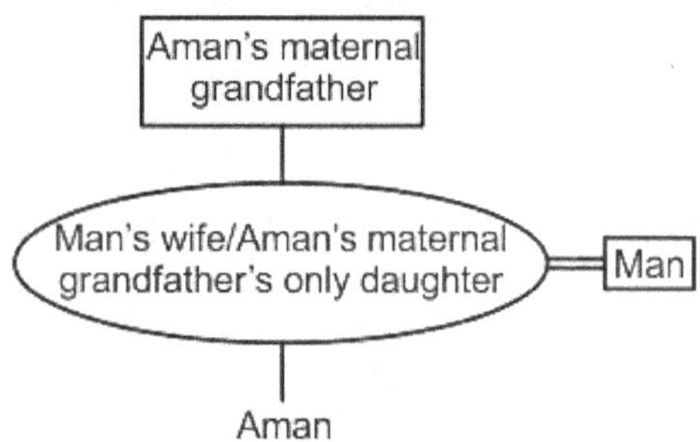

So, the man is the father of Aman.

54(B). With the above information we can draw the following family tree:

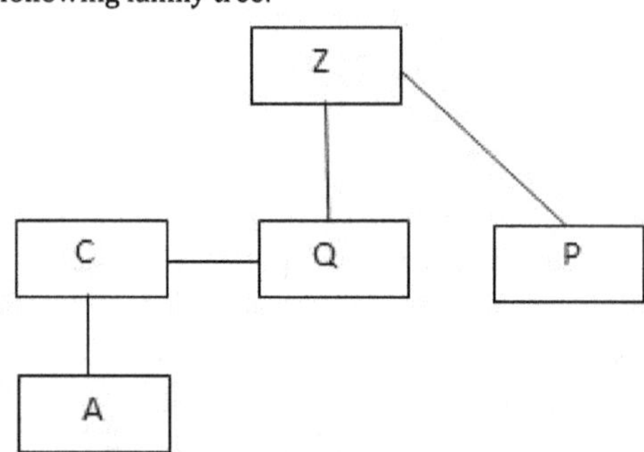

Since, C and Q are sisters to one another and A is the son of C. Hence, C is the mother of A, therefore, Z is maternal grandmother of A. As P is the son of Z. Hence, P is the maternal uncle of A.

55(B). In all the figures except (B), all the figures except are the rotated form of the same figure.

56(D). The logic followed is:

In all the options except (option D), all the faces open in the same direction, and the next figure can be obtained by 90º clockwise rotation.

Option (A):

Both the shapes are in the same direction.

90º clockwise rotation will give the next figure.

Option (B):

Both the shapes are in the same direction.

90º clockwise rotation will give the next figure.

Option (C):

Both the shapes are in the same direction.

90º clockwise rotation will not give the next figure.

Option (D):

Both the shapes are opposite to each other.

Thus figure D is not following the pattern.

57(D). The logic is:

A → Number of lines in the outside figure is 4 while the number of lines inside the figure is 3. So, the number of lines in the outside and inside figure is not equal.

B → Number of lines in the outside figure is 3 while the number of lines inside the figure is 3. So, the number of lines in the outside and inside figure is equal.

C → Number of lines in the outside figure is 5 while the number of lines inside the figure is 5. So, the number of lines in the outside and inside figure is equal.

D → Number of lines in the outside figure is 6 while the number of lines inside the figure is 6. So, the number of lines in the outside and inside figure is equal.

58(B).

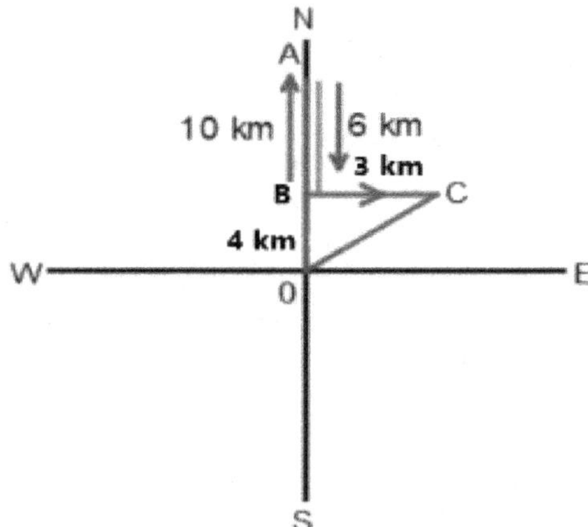

From the figure, we get OC which is the required distance,

$OC = \sqrt{(BO^2 + BC^2)}$

$OC = \sqrt{(4^2 + 3^2)}$

$OC = 5$ km (North-East)

59(D).

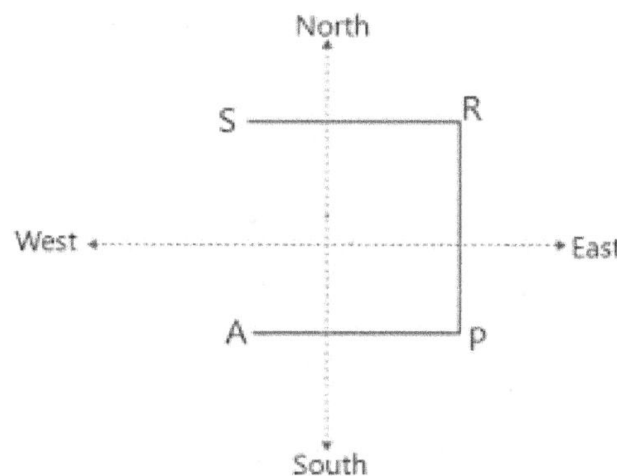

He is facing towards South.

60(C). 'ALPACA' is written backwards to obtain the coded word 'ACAPLA'.

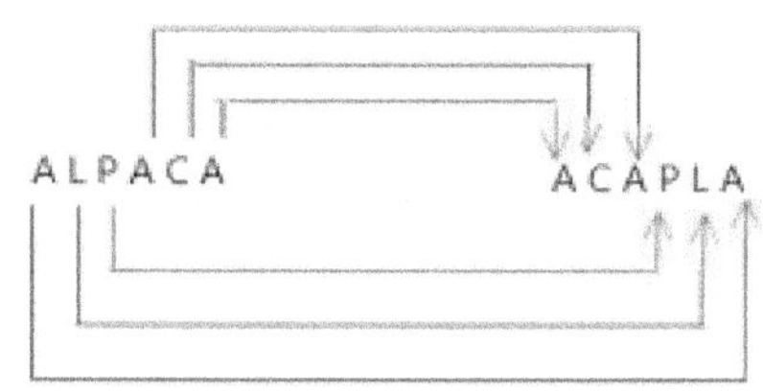

Similarly, ANIMAL is written as LAMINA.

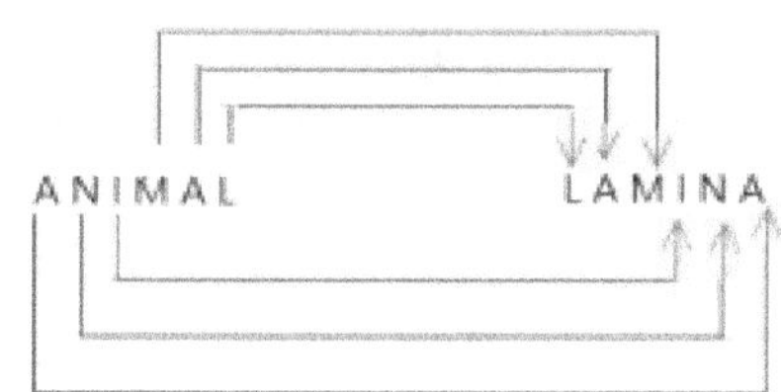

61(C). Given:
HALE = NPGK
We can say that:
H= N, A = P, L = G, E = K
So we can write:
EAH = KPN

62(C). The given problem figure will complete the answer figure series given in option (C).

63(C). The question figure will be completed by the figure given in option (C).

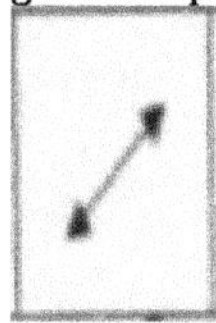

64(B). Vowels and consonants are parts of alphabets while numbers are not alphabets.

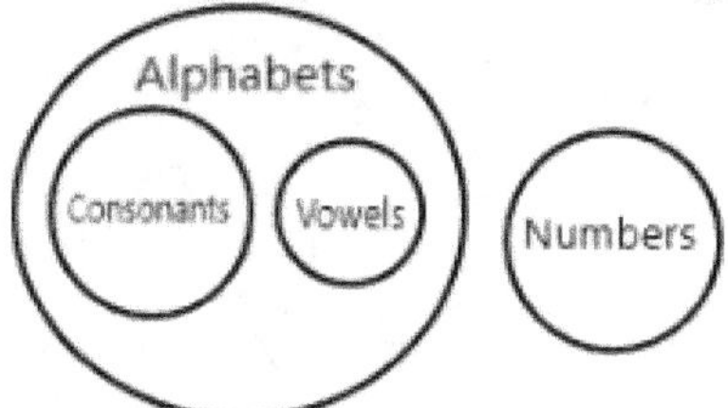

65(C). The Venn diagrams best represents the relationship between - triangles, hexagons and geometrical figures is shown below:

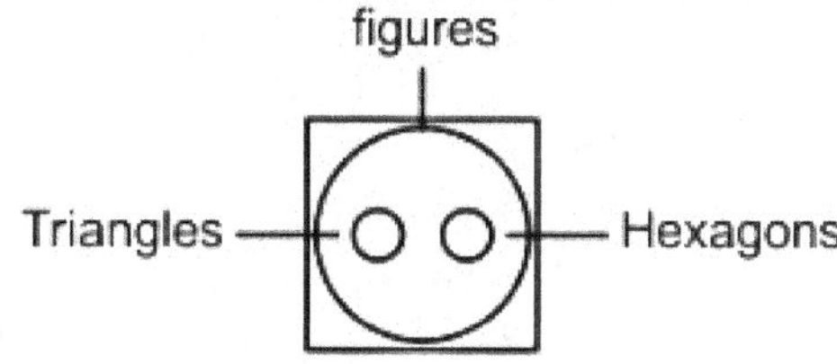

Both triangles and hexagons are geometrical figures.

66(A). The pattern followed here is:

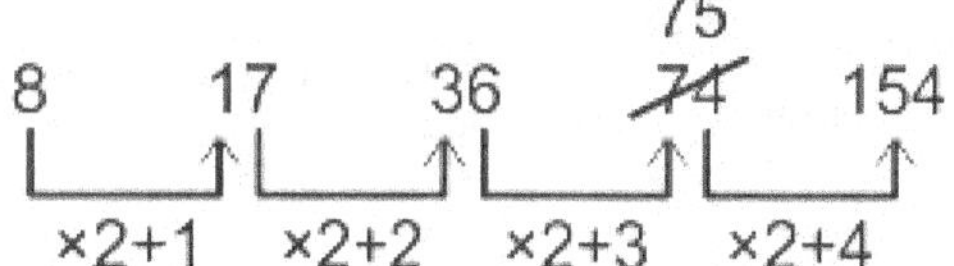

74 is the wrong term that doesn't follow the pattern here.
There should be 75 in place of 74.

67(B). The pattern followed here is as below:-

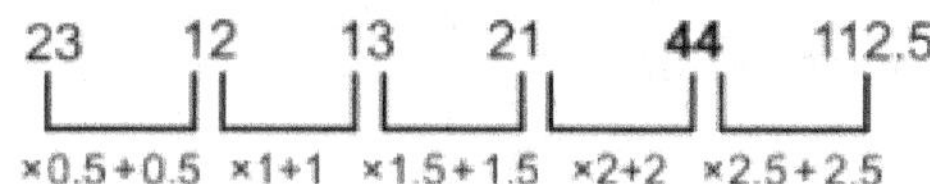

Therefore, 44 is the correct answer.

68(C). The logic follows here is:
There are five friends P, Q, R, S, and T.
1) S is shorter than T but taller than P
$\Rightarrow$ T > S > P
2) Q is a little shorter than T but a little taller than S
$\Rightarrow$ T > Q > S > P
3) R is the tallest
$\Rightarrow$ R > T > Q > S > P
Therefore, the correct order of five friends according to their height is
$\Rightarrow$ R > T > Q > S > P
From the above arrangement, it is clear that 'P' is the shortest among all.

69(D). Given,
A, B, C, D and E each having a different weight, D is heavier than A and E and B is lighter than C.
According to the given information,
D > A, E
and B < C
The heaviest of these cannot be known.

70(A). The least possible Venn diagram from the given statement is as follows:

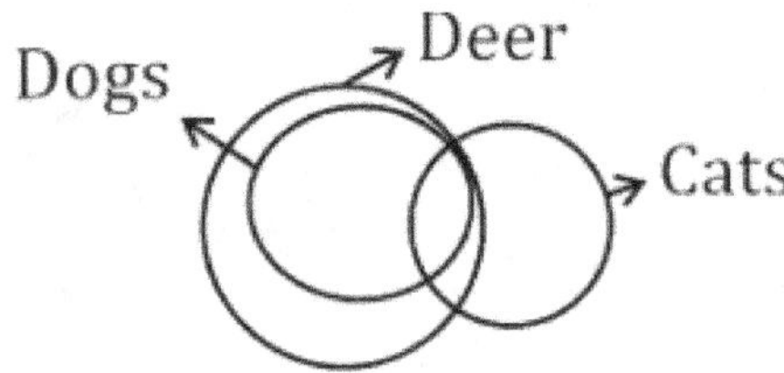

Conclusions:
Some Deer are Cats. (True) (It is possible because some deer are cats)
All Deer are Cats. (False) (It is not possible because all deers aren't cat)
No Deer is the dog. (False) (It is not possible because some deer are dogs)
So, the only conclusion I follows.

71(A). The least possible Venn diagram is as follows,

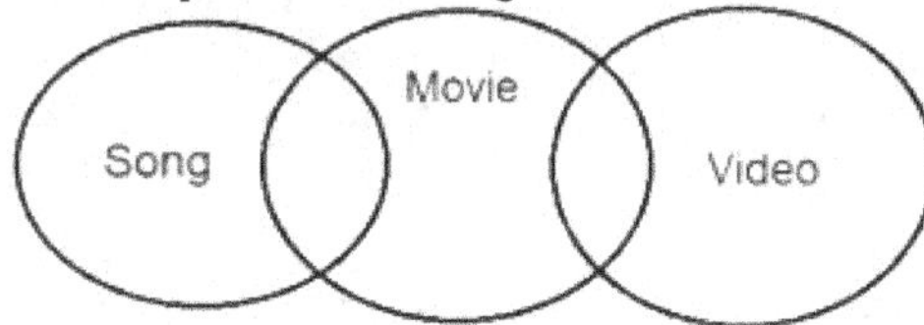

Conclusions:
I. Some song are video → It is possible but not definite, hence it is false.
II. All video are movie → It is possible but not definite, hence it is false.
Thus, neither conclusion I nor II follows.

Ques (72-73): Friends: L, M, N, O, P, Q, R and S
Colours: Pink, Yellow, Green, Red, White, Black, Orange and Purple
Spendings: 50, 100, 150, 200, 250, 300, 350, 400
1) The one who spent Rs. 350/- is three places to the right of O who likes Orange colour.

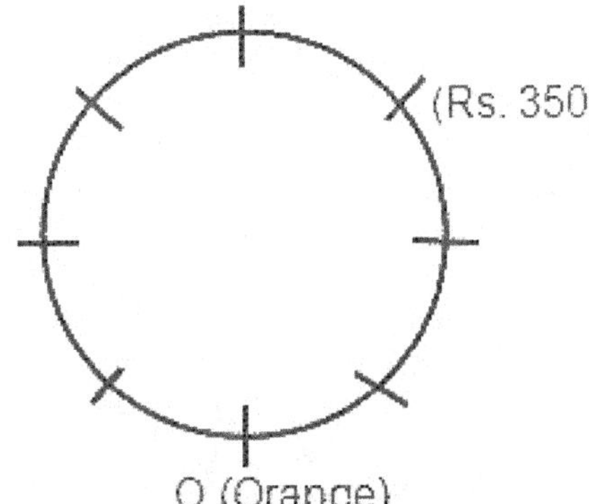

2) The one who spends Rs. 250/- is three places to the left of P, who sits three places to the left of O.

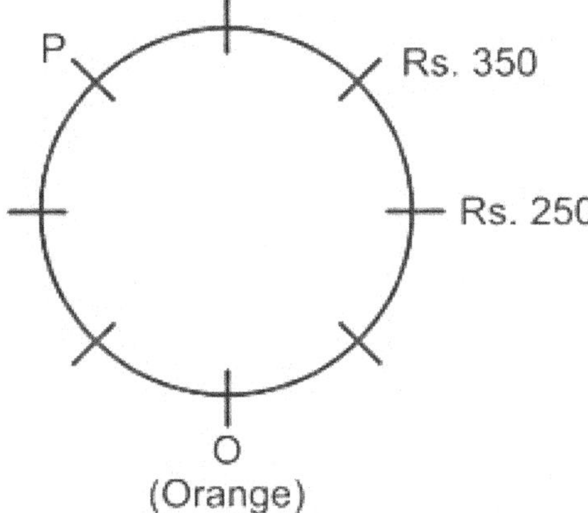

3) The difference of amounts spent by S who likes Black colour and P is maximum possible and they sat opposite to each other.

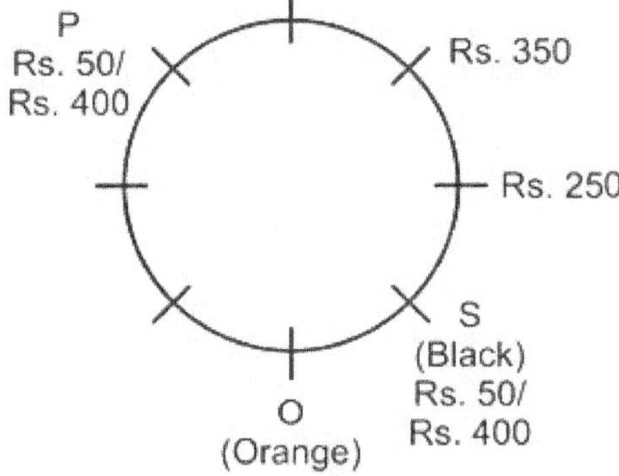

4) There are only two persons sitting between Q and S.

Case 1

Case 2

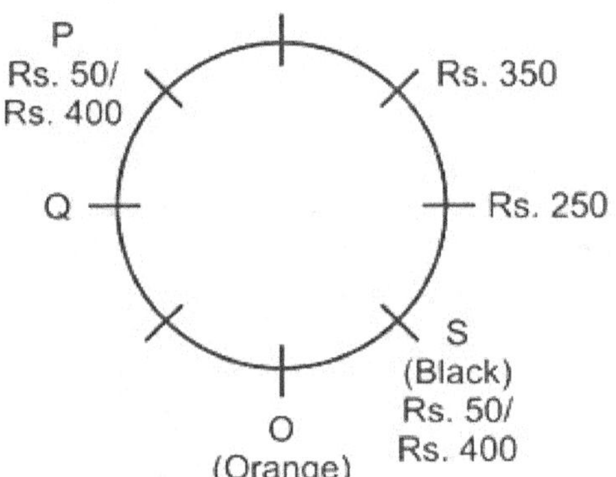

5) L sits sixth to the left of Q. Q likes green colour. (Case 2 will be eliminated here as it doesn't satisfy the condition)

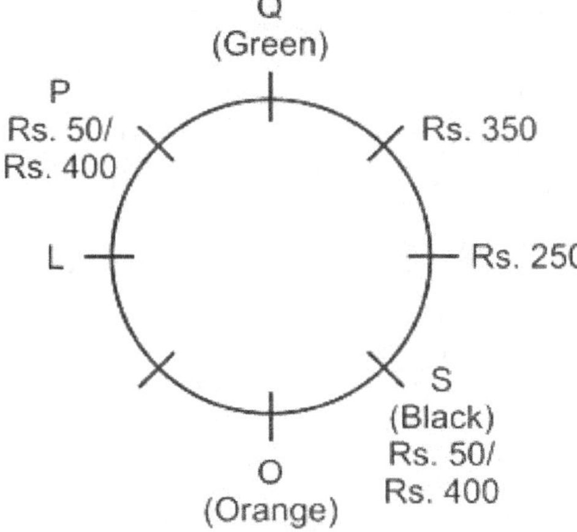

6) L likes white colour spends Rs. 150/- and sits adjacent to the one who spends least.

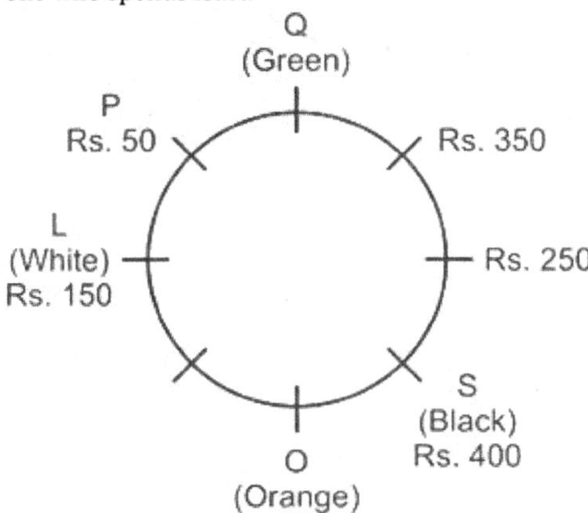

7) R sits 6th to the left of P who likes Red colour.

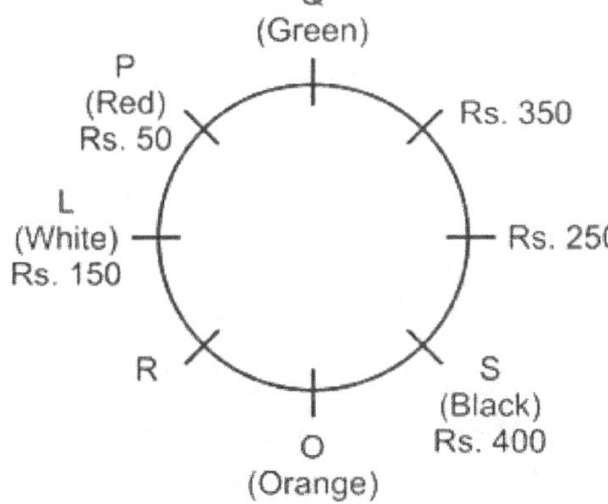

8) There is only one person between N who likes Pink colour and the one who spends Rs. 50/-.

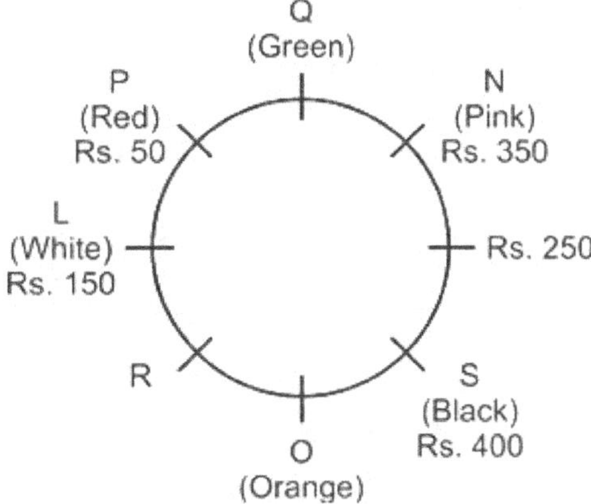

9) R who likes Purple colour spends more amount at picnic than M who likes Yellow.

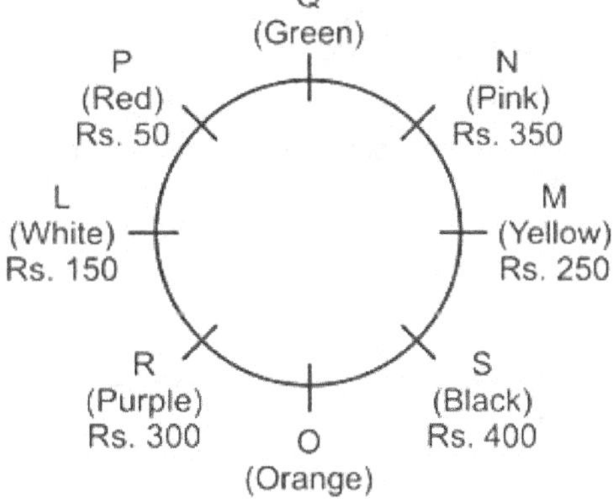

10) Difference in amounts spent by O and Q is Rs. 100/- and difference in amounts spent by O and S is Rs. 200/-. (So, Q spent Rs. 100 and O spent Rs. 200)

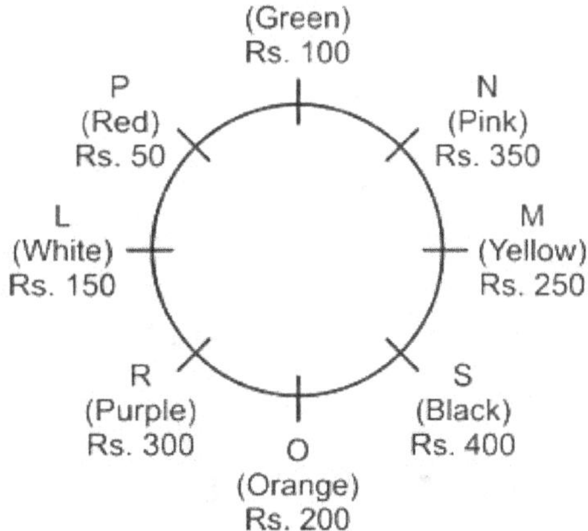

72(C). So, Q spent Rs. 100.

73(B). So, N sits 6th to the left of one who likes Black colour.

74(D). All except Chess are outdoor games. So, chess is the odd one here.

75(B). 7851, and 5789, 1325 are odd numbers.
6432, is an even number.
So, 6432 is different from the others.

76(D). मंत्रिमंडल सही वर्तनी है।
मंत्रिमंडल का अर्थ "राज्य के मंत्रियों का वर्ग" होता है।
उदाहरण : केंद्रीय मंत्रिमंडल नामक एक छोटी कार्यकारी निकाय है।

77(B). प्रश्न में सही वर्तनी उत्पत्ति है।
उत्पत्ति का अर्थ "जन्म होना या उत्पादन करना" होता है।
उदाहरण: कबीर की उत्पत्ति के संबंध में अनेक किंवदन्तियाँ हैं।

78(D). 'अक्ल पर पत्थर पड़ना' का अर्थ बुद्धि से काम न लेना है।
वाक्य प्रयोग: जब व्यक्ति का बुरा समय आता है तो उसकी अक्ल पर पत्थर पड़ जाते हैं।

79(B). घर की मुर्गी दाल बराबर: घर के व्यक्ति और वस्तु का कोई महत्व नहीं या अपने आदमी को कम महत्व देना।
वाक्य प्रयोग: अंतरा ने बहुत अच्छा खाना बनाया पर घर में उसे प्रशंसा नहीं मिली लेकिन जब पड़ोसियों ने खाना खाया तो वाह वाही मिली, इसे घर की मुर्गी दाल बराबर कहते हैं ।

80(C). मुहावरा: गिरगिट की तरह रंग बदलना
अर्थ: बातें बदलना
वाक्य प्रयोग : गिरगिट की तरह रंग बदलने से तुम्हारी कोई इज्जत नहीं करेगा।

81(B). हिन्दी में शब्दो का लिंग निर्धारण संज्ञा के आधार पर होता है , संज्ञा के द्वारा निर्जीव और सजीव दोनों का ज्ञान हो जाता है। जैसे पुल्लिंग में लड़का, घोड़ा, पेड़, बल्ब आदि और स्त्रीलिंग में बकरी, लड़की, घोड़ी, लाइट आदि।

82(D). 'कवि' का स्त्रीलिंग रूप ' कवयित्री ' है तथा अतिरिक्त विकल्प निरर्थक हैं।

83(A). 'जो करने योग्य हो' उसके लिए उचित शब्द 'करणीय' है।
- अन्य विकल्प वर्तनीगत अशुद्ध हैं।
- करणीय विशेषण शब्द है जिसके अर्थ हो सकते हैं - करने योग्य, करने के लायक, किया जाने योग्य, कर्तव्य।
- करण मूल शब्द है जिसका अर्थ करना होता है उसमें 'ईय' प्रत्यय का योग है।
- करण + ईय = करणीय।

84(C). 'धनुष की प्रत्यंचा से उत्पन्न ध्वनि' के लिए उचित एक शब्द 'टंकार' होगा।
धनुष के लिए अन्य शब्द - धातु आदि की टन-टन, टनाका है।
वह शब्द जो कसे हुए डोरे या तार आदि पर उँगली का आघात करने से होता है उसे टंकार कहते हैं।
दिए गए अन्य शब्द वर्तनीगत अशुद्ध हैं।

85(A). कुर्सी शब्द एक स्त्रीलिंग शब्द है।
विशेष:
संज्ञा के जिस रूप से व्यक्ति या वस्तु की नर या मादा जाति का बोध हो, उसे व्याकरण में 'लिंग' कहते है।
लिंग के तीन भेद किये गये हैं:
(1) पुल्लिंग
(2) स्त्रीलिंग और
(3) नपुंसकलिंग।

86(A). अँधेर' शब्द पुल्लिंग है।
'अँधेर' शब्द का वाक्य प्रयोग - इस नेता ने समाज में अंधेर मचा रखा है।
'अँधेर' से तात्पर्य यहाँ अनीति और अशांति से है।

वचन	परिभाषा	उदाहरण
लिंग - संज्ञा के जिस रूप से व्यक्ति या वस्तु की नर या मादा जाति का बोध हो, उसे व्याकरण में 'लिंग' कहते है। सरल शब्दों में- शब्द की जाति को 'लिंग' कहते है। हिन्दी में दो लिंग होते हैं—		
पुल्लिंग	जिन संज्ञा के शब्दों से पुरुष जाति का पता चलता है, उसे पुल्लिंग कहते हैं।	जैसे – पिता, राजा, कुत्ता, आदमी आदि।
स्त्री	जिन संज्ञा के शब्दों से स्त्री जाति का पता चलता है, उसे स्त्रीलिंग कहते	जैसे - माता, रानी, कुतिया, औरत आ

लिंग		
	हैं।	दि।

87(B). जिन संज्ञा शब्द के अंत में 'पा' लगाया जाता है उन्हें पुल्लिंग कहते हैं जैसे - बुढ़ापा, मोटापा, पुजापा आदि।
लिंग - संज्ञा के जिस रूप से व्यक्ति, वस्तु, की नर या मादा रूप में पहचान हो वह लिंग कहलाता है। जैसे- लड़का, लड़की आदि।
लिंग दो प्रकार के होते हैं - स्त्रीलिंग और पुल्लिंग।

लिंग के भेद	परिभाषा	उदाहरण
स्त्रीलिंग	जिन शब्दों से स्त्री जाति का बोध हो उ से स्त्रीलिंग कहते हैं।	नदी, माता, लड़की
पुल्लिंग	जिन शब्दों से पुरुष जाति का बोध हो उसे पुल्लिंग कहते हैं।	पिता, राजा घोड़ा,

88(D). 'आगरा' का बहुवचन नहीं होगा ।
किसी स्थान या जगह का कोई बहुवचन नहीं होता है|
अतः सही विकल्प (D) है।

89(B). हिन्दी में दो वचन होते हैं-एकवचन और बहुवचन
एकवचन - शब्द के जिस रूप से उसके एक होने का बोध हो, वह एकवचन कहलाते हैं । जैसे- स्त्री, घोड़ा, नदी, रुपया आदि।
बहुवचन - शब्द के जिस रूप से उसके एक से अधिक होने का बोध हो, वह बहुवचन कहलाते हैं । जैसे- स्त्रियाँ, घोड़े, नदियाँ, रूपये आदि।
अतः सही विकल्प (B) है।

90(C). त्रुटि वाला वाक्यांश ' शीघ्र भेजने की अनुकम्पन करें ' है। इस वाक्यांश का सही रूप 'शीघ्र भेजने की अनुकम्पा करें' होगा।

91(C). त्रुटि वाला वाक्यांश ' सबसे सर्वोत्तम है ' है। इस वाक्यांश का सही रूप 'सर्वोत्तम है' होगा क्योंकि सर्वोत्तम शब्द सबसे और उत्तम शब्द से मिलकर बना है।

92(A). 'गधा' शब्द 'खर' का पर्यायवाची है।
इसके अन्य पर्यायवाची धूसर, रासभ, गर्दभ, शीतलावाहन, चक्रीवान, शंखकर्ण, वैशाखनंदन आदि है।

93(A). नम्रता का विलोम अभिमान है।
नम्रता का अर्थ - नम्र होने का भाव।
अभिमान का अर्थ - अपनी प्रतिष्ठा या मर्यादा एवं सत्ता की अनुचित धारणा।

94(B). दिए गए विकल्पों से अनाथ - नाथ उचित विलोम शब्द का युग्म नहीं है।
अनाथ - नाथ का सही युग्म है अनाथ - सनाथ।
अनाथ का अर्थ है - असहाय।
सनाथ का अर्थ है - स्वामी रहित।

95(B). दिए गए विकल्पों में में 'विलक्षण' अधीर शब्द का पर्यायवाची नहीं है।
'विलक्षण' के पर्यायवाची - अदभुत, अनोखा, विचित्र, अजीब।
'अधीर' के पर्यायवाची- आतुर, धैर्यहीन, व्यग्र, बेकरार, उतावला।

96(A). 'पो + इत्र' की संधि 'पवित्र' होगी। शेष विकल्प त्रुटिपूर्ण हैं।
'पवित्र' में अयादि स्वर संधि है। पो + इत्र = पवित्र (ओ + इ = अवि, ए, ऐ तथा ओ, औ का मेल किसी अन्य स्वर के साथ होने पर क्रमशः अय्, आय्, अव् और आव् हो जाता है। इसे अयादि स्वर संधि कहते हैं।

97(B). 'शयन' का संधि-विच्छेद 'शे + अन' होगा।
'शयन' में अयादि संधि है। ए, ऐ तथा ओ, औ का मेल किसी अन्य स्वर के साथ होने पर क्रमशः अय्, आय्, अव् और आव् हो जाता है। इसे अयादि स्वर संधि कहते हैं।

98(A). 'देव्यागम' का संधि विच्छेद 'देवी + आगम' होगा।
'देव्यागम' में यण संधि है। जब इ, ई, उ, ऊ या ऋ का मेल यदि असमान स्वर से हो तो इ, ई का 'य', उ, ऊ का 'व' और ऋ का 'र' हो जाता है, तो इसे 'यण संधि' कहते हैं।

99(B). 'निर्मला' उपन्यास हिंदी के उपन्यास सम्राट मुंशी प्रेमचंद की रचना है। इनके अन्य उपन्यास – प्रेमा, प्रतिज्ञा, गोदान, प्रेमाश्रम, रंगभूमि, कर्मभूमि आदि हैं।

मुंशी प्रेमचंद भारत के उपन्यास सम्राट माने जाते हैं जिनके युग का विस्तार सन् 1880 से 1936 तक है। प्रेमचंद का वास्तविक नाम धनपत राय श्रीवास्तव था। वे एक सफल लेखक, देशभक्त नागरिक, कुशल वक्ता, जिम्मेदार संपादक और संवेदनशील रचनाकार थे।

100(A). ध्रुवस्वामिनी जयशंकर प्रसाद द्वारा रचित प्रसिद्ध हिन्दी नाटक है। यह प्रसाद की अंतिम और श्रेष्ठ नाट्य-कृति है। इसका कथानक गुप्तकाल से सम्बद्ध और शोध द्वारा इतिहाससम्मत है। यह नाटक इतिहास की प्राचीनता में वर्तमान काल की समस्या को प्रस्तुत करता है।

General Knowledge

1. "Lessons Life Taught Me Unknowingly" is an autobiography of which actor?
(a) Anupam Kher
(b) Boney Kapoor
(c) Rakesh Roshan
(d) Rishi Kapoor

2. Match the following:

	Provinces		Capital
A.	Central Province	1.	Patliputra
B.	Uttarapatha	2.	Toshali
C.	Prachya	3.	Taxila
D.	Dakshinapatha	4.	Suvarnagiri
E.	Avanti Rastra	5.	Ujjain

(a) A(3), B(5), C(1), D(4), E(2)
(b) A(1), B(4), C(3), D(5), E(2)
(c) A(1), B(3), C(2), D(4), E(5)
(d) A(4), B(3), C(4), D(2), E(5)

3. Period of geopolitical tension between the Soviet Union and the United States said to be Cold War Era, in which duration?
(a) 1914-1919
(b) 1939-1945
(c) 1947-1991
(d) 1991-2001

4. Which of the following statements is/are correct in context to Kushan rulers:
1. They repaired the Sudarshana lake in Kathiawar region.
2. They supported the development of Mahayana sect of Buddhism.
3. They were the first rulers to issue gold coins.
Select the correct answer using the codes given below:
(a) 1,2 and 3
(b) 2 and 3 only
(c) 1 and 3 only
(d) 2 only

5. Who organized the Kuka movement?
(a) Guru Ram Das
(b) Guru Nanak
(c) Guru Ram Singh
(d) Guru Gobind Singh

6. Kunwar Singh led the revolt of 1857 AD from which province?
(a) Punjab
(b) Bengal
(c) Bihar
(d) Maharashtra

7. Which one of the following factors does not affect the distribution of groundwater ?
(a) Amount of precipitation
(b) Rate of evaporation
(c) Ability of the ground surface to allow water to infiltrate into the groundwater system
(d) Distance from the sea

8. Which one of the following is a non-justiciable right ?
(a) Right to adequate livelihood
(b) Right against exploitation
(c) Right of accused
(d) Right to life and personal liberty

9. Which one of the following countries has the maximum time difference from Greenwich Mean Time (GMT)?
(a) India
(b) Nepal
(c) Sri Lanka
(d) Bhutan

10. SEWA founder and women's activist Ela Bhatt, who passed away in November 2022 belongs to which of the following city?
(a) Mumbai
(b) Ahmedabad
(c) Bangalore
(d) Kolkata

11. On 17 December 2022, which bank announced ZERO Fee Banking on savings accounts and waived fees on 25 commonly used banking services?
(a) ICICI Bank
(b) Axis Bank
(c) Yes Bank
(d) IDFC FIRST Bank

12. Alibaba Group recently sold its entire stake to which Indian company?
(a) PayTm
(b) Google
(c) Facebook
(d) Reliance

13. Consider the following statements.
1. The Indian Space Research Organisation (ISRO) and Japan Aerospace Exploration Agency (JAXA) have joined hands to launch a joint lunar polar exploration (LUPEX) mission.
2. The mission aims to send a lander and rover to the Moon's north pole around 2024.
3. While ISRO will provide the under-development H3 launch vehicle and the rover JAXA would be responsible for the lander.
Which of the above-given statements are correct?
(a) 1 only
(b) 1 and 3 only
(c) 1 and 2 only
(d) 1, 2 and 3

14. 'Kandhamal Haldi', which received GI tag recently, is a variety of turmeric indigenous to-
(a) North Bengal
(b) Southern Odisha
(c) Sangli, Maharashtra
(d) Alleppey, Kerala

15. Where does the photochemical reaction take place?
(a) Grana
(b) Cytoplasm
(c) Stroma
(d) Endoplasmic reticulum

16. Oceans cover most of the earth's surface, which is approximately?
(a) $\frac{3}{4}$
(b) $\frac{1}{2}$
(c) $\frac{1}{4}$
(d) $\frac{2}{3}$

17. Consider the following statements about Pradhan-Mantri Formalization of Micro food processing Enterprises scheme (PM-FME Scheme):
A. This scheme was launched by the Ministry of Agriculture.
B. It aims to enhance the competitiveness of existing individual micro-enterprises in the unorganized segment of the food processing industry.
C. Capacity building is an important component of this scheme.
Choose the correct statement/s.
(a) A and B
(b) B and C
(c) A and C
(d) A, B, C

18. Which of the following statements is/are correct about the new FDI policy?
1. An entity of a country, which shares a land border with India or where the beneficial owner of investment into India is situated in or is a citizen of any such

country, can invest only under the Government route.
2. This revised FDI policy aims to curb opportunistic takeovers/acquisitions of Indian companies due to the current Covid-19 pandemic.

(a) Only 1   (b) Only 2
(c) Both 1 and 2   (d) Neither 1 nor 2

19. Which of the following is/are incorrect?
1. Karve Committee is related to the MSME sector.
2. The Micro, Small, and Medium Enterprises (MSME) are classified into two enterprises as per the Micro, Small & Medium Enterprises Development (MSMED) Act, 2006.
3. Small scale enterprise is one in which investment in Plant and Machinery is more than twenty-five lakh rupees but does not exceed ten crore rupees.

(a) 1 and 2 only   (b) 2 and 3 only
(c) 1 and 3 only   (d) 1, 2 and 3

20. The 'SATH-E' project is associated with which of the following fields?

(a) Education   (b) Agriculture
(c) Transportation   (d) Communication

21. Which is the tax that is imposed by the Central Government, but the income received from it is divided between the Center and the States?

(a) Central duty   (b) Central excise duty
(c) Corporation tax   (d) None of these

22. Which is the highest bank in the banking system of India?

(a) State Bank of India
(b) Reserve Bank of India
(c) Central Bank of India
(d) Industrial Development Bank of India

23. Who has become the first Indian athlete to qualify for two different events of the Winter Olympics 2022?

(a) Manpreet Singh
(b) Mohammad Arif Khan
(c) Vishnu Saravanan
(d) Mairaj Ahmad Khan

24. With reference to the recent changes in the classification of MSMEs, consider the following statements:
1. Units in manufacturing with an investment in plant and machinery less than one crore are classified as micro-scale units.
2. Units in services with an annual turnover between ten lakhs and two crores are classified as medium-scale units.
Which of the statements given above is/are correct?

(a) 1 only   (b) 2 only
(c) Both 1 and 2   (d) Neither 1 nor 2

25. Which technology company has launched a platform that displays flood forecasts named 'FloodHub'?

(a) Microsoft   (b) Apple
(c) Google   (d) Meta

Mathematics

26. $0.002 \times 0.5 =$?

(a) 0.0001   (b) 0.001
(c) 0.01   (d) 0.1

27. Some fruits are bought at 15 for Rs. 140 and an equal number of fruits at 10 for Rs. 120 . If all the fruits are sold at Rs. 132 per dozen, then what is the profit percent in the entire transaction?

(a) $4\frac{1}{2}$ (b) $2\frac{1}{4}$
(c) $3\frac{1}{8}$ (d) 3

28. An article is marked 25% above its cost price. If $x\%$ discount is allowed on the marked price and still there is a profit of 5.5% , then the find value of x .

(a) 13.6   (b) 15.4
(c) 15.6   (d) 16.4

29. Find the difference in Simple interest and Compound interest on an amount of Rs. 32,000 at 20% per annum at the end of 3 years.

(a) 4096   (b) 5490
(c) 7650   (d) 7685

30. If a certain amount doubles itself in 5 years at simple interest then find the rate of interest per annum at which the sum was invested?

(a) 12.50%   (b) 15%
(c) 16.66%   (d) 20%

31. Perimeter of a square is $24\sqrt{2}$ cm. Its diagonal is:

(a) $6\sqrt{2}$ cm   (b) $8\sqrt{2}$ cm
(c) 8 cm   (d) 12 cm

32. The ratio of the sides of a rectangle is $3:4$. If the perimeter of the rectangle is 56 cm. Then find its sides.

(a) 12 cm and 16 cm   (b) 10 cm and 11 cm
(c) 22 cm and 6 cm   (d) 20 cm and 9 cm

33. Sum of three numbers a, b and c is $10 (a+b+c=10)$. If a , b and c are three positive integers, then what is their maximum product $(a \times b \times c)$?

(a) 50   (b) 48
(c) 36   (d) 42

34. A bike travels from R to S at the speed of 30 km/hr and from S to R at speed of 20 km/hr. What is the average speed of the bike?

(a) 30 km/hr   (b) 28 km/hr
(c) 32 km/hr   (d) 24 km/hr

35. The average marks obtained by Class A students is 79, while the average marks obtained by Class B students is 89. If there are 38 students in class A and 42 students in class B, find the average marks of all 80 students.

(a) 84.25   (b) 84.45
(c) 84.15   (d) 83.95

36. If 35% of a number is 805 . What is 62% of this number?

(a) 1426   (b) 281.75
(c) 523.25   (d) 1526

37. A certain number of men complete a work in 60 days. If there are 8 more men, the work can be finished in 10 days less. The number of men originally is?

(a) 30   (b) 32
(c) 36   (d) 40

38. P can finish a work in 15 days. In how many days can

P and Q together complete the job if Q is twice as fast as P ?

(a)   3 days
(b)   5 days
(c)   2 days
(d)   6 days

39. A can complete a work in 18 days, B can complete the same work 12.5% more efficiently than A. In what time, A and B can complete the same work working together?

(a)   8 days
(b) $8\frac{8}{17}$ days
(c)   9 days
(d) $4\frac{9}{17}$ days

40. Two buses start from a house at an interval of 5 minutes and move with a speed of 10 km/hr in the same direction. With how much speed (km/hr) should a woman coming from the opposite direction towards the house travel, to meet the buses at an interval of 3 minutes?

(a)   6.5
(b)   6
(c) $6\frac{1}{3}$
(d) $6\frac{2}{3}$

41. A train of 1000 m crosses a bridge in 2 min with a speed of 45 km/hrs while a person crosses the same bridge in 1 minute 40 seconds. Speed of person in km/hr is:

(a)   8 km/h
(b)   5 km/h
(c)   18 km/h
(d)   10 km/h

42. The L.C.M. of two prime numbers, x and $y(x > y)$ is 161. Then the value of $(x - y)$ is:

(a)   9
(b)   13
(c)   15
(d)   16

43. The present ages of three colleague's are in proportions 3 : 5 : 7. Four years ago, the sum of thier ages was 48. find thier present ages (in years)?

(a)   12 , 20 and 28 years
(b)   13 , 15 and 23 years
(c)   11 , 16 and 19 years
(d)   20, 24 and 27 years

44. If $f : R \to R$ and $g : R \to R$ are two fuctions defined as $f(x) = 2x$ and $g(x) = x^2 + 2$ then the value of (fog) 2 is:

(a)   4
(b)   6
(c)   12
(d)   10

45. Under which of the following conditions does a general second-degree equation ax^2 + 2hxy + by^2 + 2gx + 2fy + c = 0 (a ≠ 0) represent a circle?

(a)   h = g, a = b
(b)   h = g = f, a = b
(c)   h = 0, a = b
(d)   h = 0, g^2 + f^2 - c = a + b

46. If $4\sin^2 x - 2\cos^2 x = 2$, then find the value of $\tan x$.

(a) $\sqrt{3}$
(b) $\sqrt{2}$
(c)   1
(d)   None of these

47. In an entrance test, there are multiple-choice questions, with four possible answers to each question of which one is correct, The probability that a student knows the answer to a question is 90% , If the student gets the correct answer to a question, then the probability that he was guessing is:

(a) $\frac{37}{40}$
(b) $\frac{1}{37}$
(c) $\frac{36}{37}$
(d) $\frac{1}{9}$

48. In how many ways can the letters of the word SOFTWARE be arranged so that all the vowels be together?

(a)   102
(b)   360
(c)   4320
(d)   None of the above

Ques (49-50): Direction : Study the chart carefully and answer the question that follows.

Four trainers A, B, C, and D take classes in a month. The pie chart shows the total hours of classes taken by all four trainers.

Total Time = 60 hours

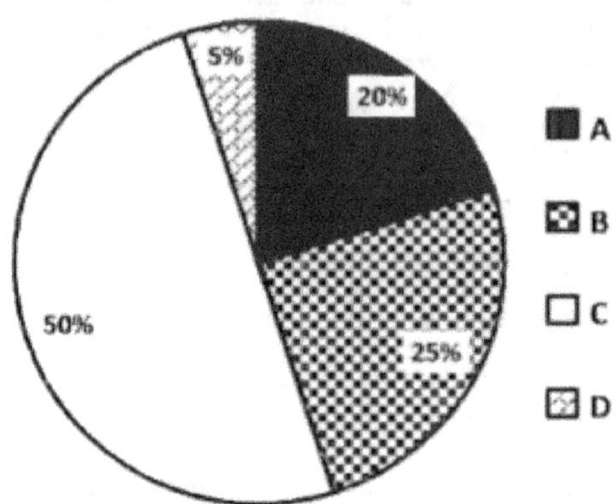

Note : (1) They can take classes for 1 hour (Basic class). 2 hours (Regular class) and 3 hours (Advance class). No trainer can leave class before time and cant take class before time and cant take class for any extra time.

(2) D doesn't take any regular class. He will take either Basic or Advance class.

49. Next month D takes 10 hours of classes. If the number of basic classes taken by D next month is twice the advance classes then find the difference between basic and advance classes taken by him.

(a)   1
(b)   2
(c)   3
(d)   4

50. The number of basic classes taken by A is 3 times the number of advance classes taken by A, with no regular classes. Find the total number of classes taken by A.

(a)   5
(b)   7
(c)   8
(d)   9

Reasoning

Ques (51-52): Direction : In the following question, select the related letters from the given alternatives.

51. YEAR: UHDN:: TIME : ?

(a)   PALP
(b)   PLPA
(c)   PLAA
(d)   PPAL

52. BRISTLE : BRUSH

(a)   Arm : Leg
(b)   Stage : Curtain
(c)   Recline : Chair
(d)   Key : Piano

53. Pointing to a photograph of a lady, a man said "She is the wife of father of mother of my only child". How is the lady in the photograph related to man?

(a)   Mother-in-law
(b)   Mother
(c)   Daughter
(d)   Aunt

54. P, Q, R, S, T and U are women. R is the only maternal aunt of S. P is sister in law of Q. Q is niece of R. T and R are the only children of U. How is T related to S?

(a) Sister
(b) Niece
(c) Aunt
(d) Mother

55. **Direction** : Choose the figure which is different from the rest.

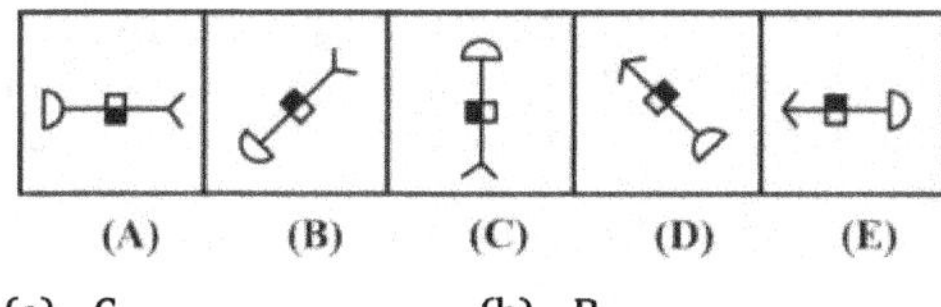

(a) C
(b) B
(c) A
(d) E

56. **Direction** : Choose the figure which is the different from the rest.

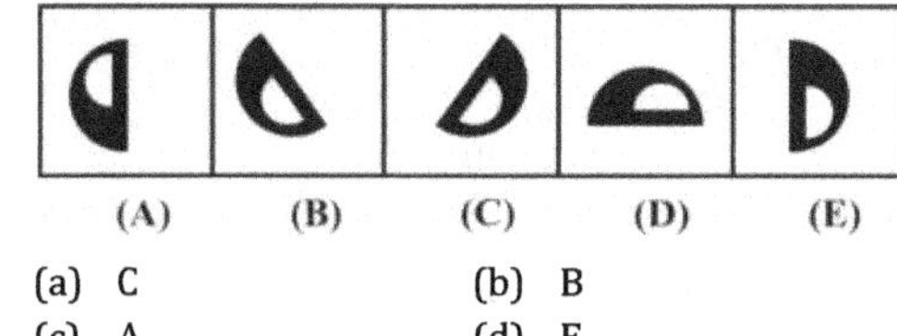

(a) C
(b) B
(c) A
(d) E

57. Find the odd figure out.

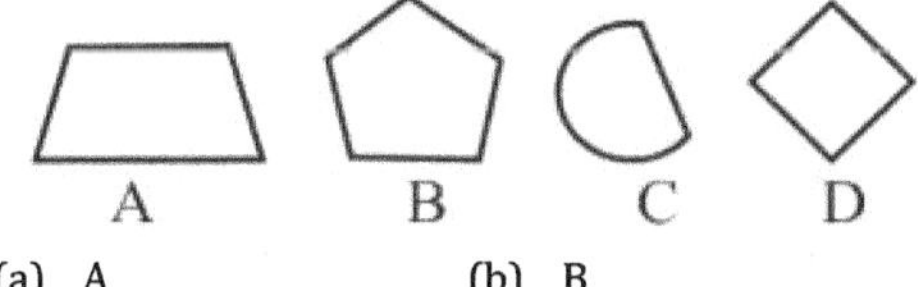

(a) A
(b) B
(c) C
(d) D

58. John went straight from a hotel and turned left after covering 3 km and travelled 5 km in that direction to reach point X. From here, he took a right turn and travelled 4 km, and again took a right turn and travelled 4 km, From here, he took a turn to reach point X straight. If John is now moving towards the North-West direction, in which direction did he start moving from the hotel ?

(a) North
(b) West
(c) South-East
(d) East

59. Two persons A and B, stand at the same point. A walks 6 km East, takes a right turn and walks 4 km and turns left and walks 2 km. B walks 3 km towards West; turns right and walks 2 km; turns right again and walks 11 km. How far is A from B ?

(a) 6 km
(b) 12 km
(c) 10 km
(d) 8 km

60. If 'air' is called 'green', 'green' is called 'red', 'red' is called 'sea', 'sea' is called 'blue', 'blue' is called 'water' and 'water' is called 'pink', then what is the color of grass?

(a) Green
(b) Air
(c) Red
(d) Pink

61. If in a language, 'one' is called 'two', 'two' is called 'three', 'three' is called 'four', 'four' is called 'five' and 'five' is called 'six'. Then what is the square of number 2?

(a) Three
(b) Four
(c) Five
(d) Six

Ques (62-63): Direction: Select the Answer figure that will complete the series of question figures.

62. **Problem Figures:**

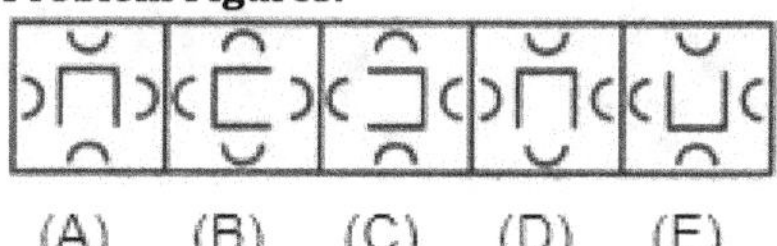

(A)   (B)   (C)   (D)   (E)

Answer Figures:

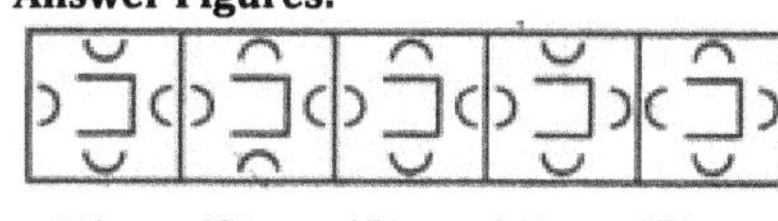

(1)   (2)   (3)   (4)   (5)

(a) (1)
(b) (2)
(c) (3)
(d) (5)

63.

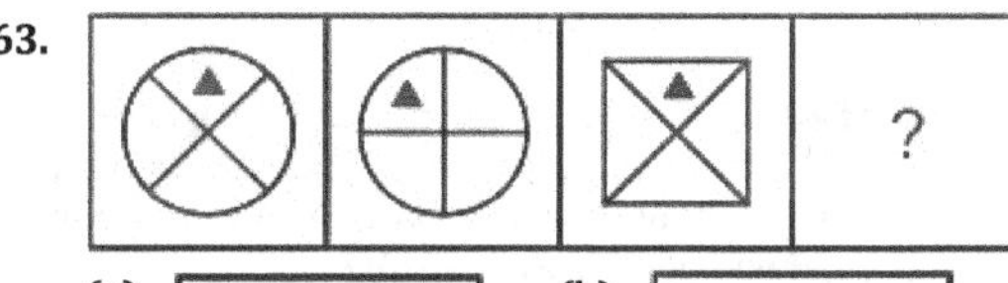

(a)

(b)

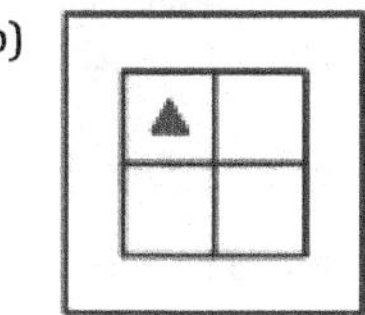

(c)

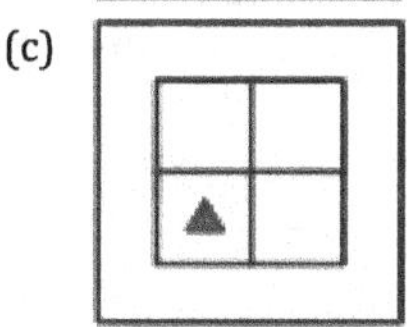

(d)

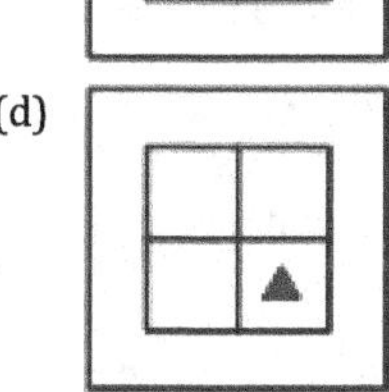

Ques (64-65): Direction: Identify the diagram that best represents the relationship among classes given below:

64. Elephants, Wolves, Animals

(a)

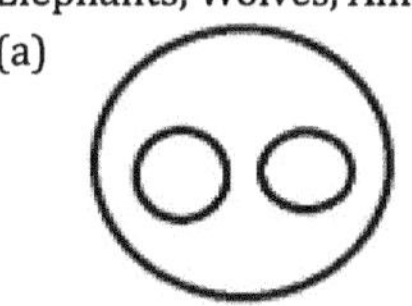

(b)

(c)

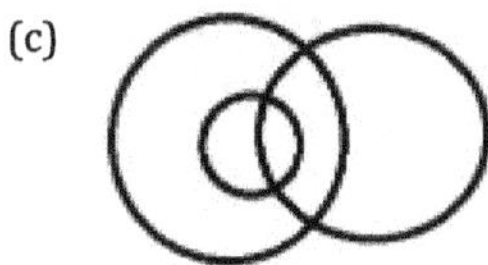

(d)

65. Badminton, Tennis, and Racket

(a)

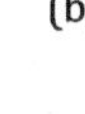

(b)

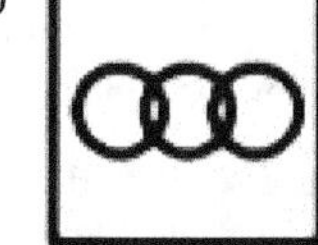

(c)    (d) 

66. The missing term in the series 21, 41, 66, 96, ___, 171, 216, 266 is:
(a) 142
(b) 131
(c) 125
(d) 117

67. What approximate value should come in place of the question mark (?) in the following number series?
26, 65, 145, ? , 577
(a) 323
(b) 224
(c) 255
(d) 325

68. In a row of 40 girls, when Komal moves four places to the left from her position, her position becomes 10th from the left end of the row. What was Swati's position from the right end of the row, if Swati was three places to the right of Komal's original position
(a) 7
(b) 21
(c) 22
(d) 24

69. Dinesh is taller than Chinku and Elina. Akash is not as tall as Elina. Chinku is taller than Akash. Dinesh is not as tall as Bikash. Who among them is next to the tallest one?
(a) Bikash
(b) Chinku
(c) Akash
(d) Dinesh

Ques (70-71): Direction: In the following question below some statements are given followed by some conclusions. Taking the given statements to be true even if they seem to be at variance from commonly known facts, read all the conclusions and then decide which of the given conclusions logically follows the given statements.

70. Statements:
I. Some white are red.
II. Some white are green.
Conclusions:
I. Some green are red.
II. Some red are not green.
(a) Only conclusion I follows
(b) Only conclusion II follows
(c) Both conclusion follows
(d) Neither conclusion I nor conclusion II follows

71. Statements:
Some inks are staplers.
No stapler is a marker.
All markers are dusters.
Conclusions:
I. Some dusters are not staplers.
II. All inks being markers is a possibility.
(a) If only conclusion I follows
(b) If only conclusion II follows
(c) If only conclusion II follows
(d) If neither conclusion I nor II follows

72. Select the set in which the numbers are related in the same way as are the numbers of the following set.
(3, 9, 27)
(a) (5, 25, 125)
(b) (6, 36, 215)
(c) (8, 16, 512)
(d) (11, 121, 110)

73. Select the word which is different from the others.
(a) Violin
(b) Sitar
(c) Flute
(d) Guitar

Ques (74-75): Direction: Read the information carefully and answer the following question:
A certain number of persons are sitting in a row. All of them are facing north. R is sitting 3rd from the left end. One person is sitting between R and T who is not sitting at any end. Three persons are sitting between T and O who is not the immediate neighbour of P. L is sitting immediate right of O. Three persons are sitting between L and N. One person is sitting between N and P who is sixth to the right of L. E is sitting 4th from the right end. Two persons are sitting between E and K who is sitting at one of the end. Four people are sitting between K and B. One person is sitting between B and H. Two persons are sitting between S and P. Number of persons sitting between R and O are equal to the number of persons sitting between S and H. P sits at the left of S. O is sitting at one of the extreme ends.

74. How many persons are sitting in the row?
(a) 21
(b) 23
(c) 20
(d) 22

75. What is the position of L with respect to H?
(a) 11th to the left
(b) 10th to the right
(c) 8th to the right
(d) 5th to the right

76. निर्देश: वर्तनी के अनुसार शुद्ध शब्द का चयन कीजिए
(a) स्वास्तीक
(b) स्वस्तिक
(c) स्वाशितक
(d) स्वष्तिक

77. किस शब्द की वर्तनी शुद्ध है?
(a) आधीन
(b) व्यवहारिक
(c) मिष्टान्न
(d) अत्यधिक

78. किस मुहावरे का अर्थ 'लज्जित होना' नहीं है?
(a) पानी पानी हो जाना
(b) घड़ों पानी पड़ना
(c) गांठ बांधना
(d) इनमें से कोई नहीं

79. 'थाली का बैंगन होना' इस मुहावरे का सही अर्थ क्या है?
(a) बहुत रुचिकर होना
(b) सर्वत्र सुलभ होना
(c) अस्थिर विचार का होना
(d) मनपसन्द का होना

80. 'गये थे रोजा छुड़ाने, नमाज गले पड़ी' लोकोक्ति का क्या अर्थ है?
(a) मुश्किल में पड़ जाना
(b) कष्ट पहुँचाना
(c) गरीब हो जाना
(d) उपकार करने के बदले स्वयं को दुख भोगना पड़ा

81. निम्न में से कौन सा विकल्प पुल्लिंग है?
(a) खोज
(b) घूस
(c) आइना
(d) चील

82. निम्नलिखित में से पुल्लिंग शब्द छाँटिए:
(a) गाजर
(b) आहट
(c) अनार
(d) अरहर

Ques (83-84): निर्देश : वाक्यांश के लिए दिए गए विकल्पों में से प्रयुक्त शब्द का चयन कीजिए।

83. जिसकी आशा न की गई हो:
(a) प्रतिआशा
(b) अप्रत्याशित

(c) आशातीत   (d) अप्रतिआशा

84. पृथ्वी के तीन ओर पानी वाला स्थान

(a) द्वीप   (b) प्रायद्वीप
(c) महाद्वीप   (d) उपरोक्त कोई नहीं

85. निम्नलिखित प्रश्न में, चार विकल्पों में से, उस विकल्प का चयन करें, जो दिए गए शब्द का सही स्त्रीलिंग वाला विकल्प है।
अभिमानी

(a) अभिमानीन   (b) अभिमानिनी
(c) अभिमानीय   (d) अभिमानीज

86. किस कारक में 'से' विभक्ति का प्रयोग साधन के अर्थ में होता है?

(a) अपादान   (b) कर्ता
(c) करण   (d) सम्प्रदान

87. पेड़ से पत्ता गिरता है में कौन सा कारक है?

(a) अधिकरण   (b) कर्म
(c) करण   (d) अपादान

88. 'गम्' धातु लृट् लकार मध्यमपुरुष बहुवचन का रूप है:

(a) गमिष्यतः   (b) गमिष्यथः
(c) गमिष्यथ   (d) गमिष्यावः

89. 'गाः' पद में विभक्ति वचन है:

(a) प्रथमा बहुवचन   (b) द्वितीया बहुवचन
(c) पंचमी एकवचन   (d) सप्तमी एकवचन

Ques (90-91): निर्देश: वाक्य के अशुद्ध भाग (त्रुटिपूर्ण भाग) का चयन कीजिए।

90. राम राज्य में (a)/शेर और बकरी एक घाट (b)/पर पानी पीती थी। (c)/कोई त्रुटि नहीं (d)

(a) (a)   (b) (b)
(c) (c)   (d) (d)

91. चन्द्रमा की स्वच्छ चाँदनी (a)/ जगती तल, पृथ्वी तल में, (b)/ और आकाश में फैली हुई हैं (c)/कोई त्रुटि नहीं (d)

(a) (a)   (b) (b)
(c) (c)   (d) (d)

92. निर्देश: दिए गए निम्नलिखित शब्दों में से विलोम शब्द का चयन करे।
जटिल

(a) कठिन   (b) कृतज्ञ
(c) सरल   (d) मुश्किल

93. रोशनी <u>नदी</u> किनारे बैठी है। दिए गए विकल्पों में रेखांकित शब्द का पर्यायवाची शब्द बताइये।

(a) पारावार   (b) झरना
(c) निर्झरिणी   (d) पानी

94. निम्नलिखित विकल्पों में से 'अश्व' किसका पर्यायवाची शब्द है?

(a) तुरंग   (b) शार्दूल
(c) शिखी   (d) पखेरू

95. विषाद शब्द का विलोम शब्द है:

(a) मृद   (b) वरदान
(c) आह्लाद   (d) स्तुति

96. दिए गये विकल्पों में से "उच्चारण" का सही संधि-विच्छेद चुनें।

(a) उच्च + चारण   (b) उत् + चारण
(c) अत + चारण   (d) अतः + चारण

97. पित्रदेश का सही संधि-विच्छेद है:

(a) पित्रा + देश   (b) पितृ + आदेश
(c) पित्र + आदेश   (d) पितृ + देश

98. प्रत्यूष का सही संधि-विच्छेद है:

(a) प्रती + ऊष   (b) प्रति + ऊष
(c) प्रति + उष   (d) प्रती + उष

99. निम्न में से किस पत्रिका से सम्बन्धित साहित्यकार नहीं हैं?

(a) नया ज्ञानोदय - रवीन्द्र कालिया
(b) पहल - ज्ञानरंजन
(c) तद्रव - अखिलेश
(d) दस्तावेज - रामचन्द्र तिवारी

100. 'साकेत' किसकी कृति है ?

(a) मैथिलीशरण गुप्त   (b) रामधारी सिंह दिनकर
(c) जयशंकर प्रसाद   (d) धर्मवीर भारती

// Smart Answer Sheet //

Correct — Percentage of students who answered correctly.

Skipped — Percentage of students who skipped.

Q.	Ans.	Correct / Skipped	Q.	Ans.	Correct / Skipped	Q.	Ans.	Correct / Skipped
1	A	84.81% / 0.0%	2	C	68.4% / 1.47%	3	C	41.62% / 1.34%
4	D	11.1% / 3.06%	5	C	62.91% / 1.2%	6	C	76.69% / 0.0%
7	D	67.24% / 1.71%	8	A	86.14% / 0.0%	9	D	52.78% / 1.84%
10	B	54.19% / 1.42%	11	D	76.71% / 0.0%	12	A	82.07% / 0.0%
13	C	40.59% / 1.52%	14	B	64.0% / 1.84%	15	A	50.93% / 1.03%
16	A	12.22% / 4.94%	17	B	79.4% / 0.0%	18	C	27.57% / 3.63%
19	C	53.82% / 1.56%	20	A	69.94% / 1.04%	21	B	54.65% / 1.63%
22	B	63.11% / 1.81%	23	B	54.37% / 1.81%	24	A	60.91% / 1.65%
25	C	60.39% / 1.79%	26	B	82.74% / 0.0%	27	C	32.76% / 4.12%
28	C	63.01% / 1.02%	29	A	69.88% / 1.16%	30	D	64.98% / 1.05%
31	D	78.28% / 0.0%	32	A	80.86% / 0.0%	33	C	63.39% / 1.01%
34	D	83.55% / 0.0%	35	A	55.04% / 1.8%	36	A	51.36% / 1.69%
37	D	84.64% / 0.0%	38	B	83.71% / 0.0%	39	B	12.85% / 4.59%
40	D	31.92% / 3.27%	41	C	26.83% / 3.14%	42	D	79.9% / 0.0%
43	A	65.05% / 1.84%	44	C	63.36% / 1.14%	45	C	68.54% / 1.08%
46	B	85.92% / 0.0%	47	B	54.32% / 1.45%	48	C	54.41% / 1.96%
49	B	63.83% / 1.21%	50	C	52.2% / 1.66%	51	B	42.72% / 1.3%
52	D	59.32% / 1.5%	53	A	81.21% / 0.0%	54	D	89.3% / 0.0%
55	B	41.51% / 1.45%	56	B	46.77% / 1.91%	57	C	59.94% / 1.38%
58	D	31.82% / 4.58%	59	A	47.43% / 1.71%	60	C	80.71% / 0.0%
61	C	48.3% / 1.2%	62	D	31.39% / 3.92%	63	B	27.12% / 4.82%
64	A	84.08% / 0.0%	65	B	87.28% / 0.0%	66	B	55.27% / 1.59%
67	D	64.18%	68	D	24.21%	69	D	31.75%

		1.12%			4.05%			4.79%
70	D	67.59% 1.6%	71	A	66.06% 1.4%	72	A	62.32% 1.47%
73	C	47.83% 1.0%	74	C	47.65% 1.59%	75	A	45.57% 1.64%
76	B	47.24% 1.62%	77	D	62.43% 1.8%	78	C	57.24% 1.38%
79	C	56.43% 1.9%	80	D	44.18% 1.91%	81	C	69.04% 1.43%
82	C	23.1% 3.57%	83	B	46.05% 1.05%	84	B	56.95% 1.98%
85	B	12.09% 3.04%	86	C	44.46% 1.3%	87	D	48.02% 2.0%
88	C	43.94% 1.63%	89	B	78.26% 0.0%	90	B	68.62% 1.65%
91	B	54.44% 1.32%	92	C	78.49% 0.0%	93	C	41.47% 1.65%
94	A	69.91% 1.51%	95	C	46.34% 1.8%	96	B	40.55% 1.15%
97	B	58.12% 1.45%	98	B	59.11% 1.26%	99	D	85.76% 0.0%
100	A	49.68% 1.77%						

// Hints and Solutions //

1(A). 'Lessons Life Taught Me Unknowingly' is an autobiography of Anupam Kher.

About 'Lessons Life Taught Me, Unknowingly':
- The autobiography of Padma Bhushan awardee gives a detailed account of his failures, rejections, and lessons learned in his life and in a career spanning 500 films.
- The autobiography shares the events in Kher's life that shaped his career and is an exciting account as it does not talk about his successes.
- The book was released in India on 5 August and will be released in the US on 15 October 2019.

2(C). The Mauryan empire was one of the greatest empires which ruled on India.

It has great historical significance. The rule of Mauryas ruled from 322-185 B.C. & under them, the majority of India remained united as a single state by the great founder emperor Chandragupta Maurya. With the help of Chanakya, Chandragupta Maurya laid the foundation of this great Mauryan empire.

3(C). Period of geopolitical tension between the Soviet Union and the United States said to be Cold War Era, in 1947-1991.

The Cold War was a period of geopolitical tension between the Soviet Union and the United States and their respective allies, the Eastern Bloc and the Western Bloc, after World War II.

The period is generally considered to span 1947 to the 1991 dissolution of the Soviet Union.

The term "cold" is used because there was no large-scale fighting directly between the two superpowers, but they each supported major regional conflicts known as proxy wars.

The West was led by the United States as well as the other First World nations of the Western Bloc that were generally liberal democratic but tied to a network of authoritarian states, most of which were their former colonies.

4(D). Kushanas are one of the branches of the Yue Chi tribes living at the Chinese frontier or in Central Asia. Kujula Kadphises laid the foundation of the Kushana Empire in India. Kadphises II (Viema Kadphises) issued a large number of gold coins and

spread his kingdom up to the East of Indus river. The first gold coins were not issued by the Kushanas. These were identical in weight with those issued by the Romans & the Parthians and have been found at various sites in north India & Central Asia. So, statement 3 is incorrect.

Kanishka was the greatest Kushana ruler. He started a new era known as the Shaka Era (78 AD). Kushans were the great patron of the Mahayana form of Buddhism. Kanishka convened the fourth Buddhist Council at Kundalvana in Kashmir where the doctrines of Mahayana Buddhism were finalised. It was held in Sanskrit. So, statement 2 is correct.

The famous Shaka ruler, Rudradaman I undertook the repairing of Sudarshana lake in Kathiawar region which had been in the use of irrigation for a long time dated back to the Mauryas. So, statement 1 is incorrect.

5(C). Guru Ram Singh organized the Kuka movement. The Kuka Rebellion was an armed rebellion in 1871–72 by the Kukas (named Namdhari Sikhs) of Punjab.

6(C). Kunwar Singh led the 'Revolt of 1857' in Bihar. He also led the revolt of 1857 at Jagdishpur. He was one of the main organisers of the fight against the British in Bihar in the revolt of 1857. He specialized in guerrilla warfare.

7(D). Plants need this shallow groundwater to grow, and, by the process of evapotranspiration, water is moved back into the atmosphere. Distance from the sea is not a direct factor affecting the distribution of groundwater.

8(A). The right to adequate livelihood comes under article 39 of DPSP. Therefore, It is Non Justiciable right.

9(D). Greenwich Mean Time of Bhutan is 6 hours and 0 minutes ahead.

10(B). SEWA founder and women's activist Ela Bhatt, who passed away in November 2022 belongs to Ahmedabad.

11(D). IDFC FIRST Bank on 17 December 2022 announced ZERO Fee Banking on savings accounts and waived fees on 25 commonly used banking services.

12(A). Chinese tech firm Alibaba has reportedly sold its entire stake in Paytm's parent company, One97 Communications Ltd. This block deal marked the transfer of 3.4 per cent equity, or 2.1 crore shares, of One97 Communications Ltd and resulted in Alibaba no longer being a shareholder in Paytm.

13(C). India's ISRO and Japan's JAXA are working on a joint lunar polar exploration (LUPEX) mission and the two space agencies have been working on the mission that aims to send a lander and rover to the Moon's south pole around 2024. So, statements 1 and 2 are correct.
- JAXA is likely to provide the under-development H3 launch vehicle and the rover ISRO would be responsible for the lander. So, statement 3 is incorrect.
- The Lunar Polar Exploration mission would demonstrate new surface exploration technologies related to vehicular transport and lunar night survival for sustainable lunar exploration in Polar Regions.Explore lunar polar region suitability for establishing a lunar base for sustainable activities
- Other targets of the mission include

demonstration of lunar and planetary surface exploration technologies e.g. vehicular transport and overnight survival.

So, statement 1 and 2 only is correct.

14(B). Odisha's Kandhamal Haldi (turmeric), famous for its healing properties, received GI tag as the Geographical Indications under sub-section (1) of Section 13 of the Geographical Indications of Goods (Registration and Protection) Act, 1999. The GI tag is awarded by the India Patent Office,

This GI tag gives an assurance of quality, allows a state or a geographical region to lay an exclusive claim over a product, and is often used as a reason to increase production rates.

For tribal people in Kandhamal, turmeric is the main cash crop. It is used for domestic and for cosmetic and medicinal purposes.

15(A). This reaction is completed in the grana part of the chlorophyll. It occurs in the stacks of Thylakoid. This reaction is also known as the Hill reaction. In this process break down of water takes place and hydrogen ion and electron is formed. In the photolysis of water, energy is received from the light. In the end, ATP is formed from ADP.

Cytoplasm- It assists the metabolic activities, and also provides shape to the cell. It fills up the cells where the organelles remain in their position.

Stroma Dark reaction takes place in it of the chlorophyll. Dark reaction is also known as the Calvin Benson cycle.

Endoplasmic reticulum- its function is to produce proteins for the cell to function.

16(A). Oceans cover approximately 71% of the Earth's surface, which is equivalent to $\frac{3}{4}$ of the total surface area. They are the largest of the Earth's habitats and contain the vast majority of the Earth's water.

17(B). Launched under the Aatmanirbhar Bharat Abhiyan, the PM-FME Scheme is a centrally sponsored scheme. It aims to enhance the competitiveness of existing individual micro-enterprises in the unorganized segment of the food processing industry and promote formalization of the sector. This scheme was launched by the Ministry of Food and Processing. Therefore statement A is Incorrect.

It seeks to provide support to Farmer Producer Organizations, Self Help Groups, and Producers Cooperatives along their entire value chain.

Under the PM-FME scheme, capacity building is an important component. The scheme envisages imparting training to food processing entrepreneurs, various groups, viz., SHGs / FPOs / Co-operatives, workers, and other stakeholders associated with the implementation of the scheme. Therefore statement B and C are correct. The Scheme adopts One District One Product (ODODP) approach to reap the benefit of scale in terms of procurement of inputs, availing common services and marketing of products. The States would identify food product for a district keeping in view the existing clusters and availability of raw material. The ODOP product could be a perishable produce based product or cereal-based products or a food product widely produced in a district and their allied sectors.

18(C). FDI is allowed in India under two modes: the automatic route or through the government route.

Companies don't need government approval in Automatic Route.

Companies need Government approval in Government mode.

Provisions of the New FDI policy:
- An entity of a country, which shares a land border with India or where the beneficial owner of investment into India is situated in or is a citizen of any such country, can invest only under the Government route. Therefore, statement 1 is correct.
- A transfer of ownership in an FDI deal that benefits any country that shares a border with India will also need government approval.
- Investors from countries not covered by the new policy only have to inform the RBI after a transaction rather than asking for prior permission from the relevant government department.

India shares land borders with Pakistan, Afghanistan, China, Nepal, Bhutan, Bangladesh, and Myanmar.

This revised FDI policy aims to curb opportunistic takeovers/acquisitions of Indian companies due to the current Covid-19 pandemic. Therefore, statement 2 is correct.
- China's investment in the Indian business space has been expanding rapidly.

19(C). In 1955, the Village and Small-scale Industries Committee, also called the Karve Committee, noted the possibility of using small-scale industries for promoting rural development.

A 'small-scale industry' is defined as the maximum investment allowed on the assets of a unit. This limit has changed over a period of time. In 1950 a small-scale industrial unit was one which invested a maximum of rupees five lakh.

It was believed that small-scale industries are more 'labour-intensive' i.e. they use more labour than the large-scale industries, therefore, generate more employment. But these industries cannot compete with the big industrial firms, it is obvious that the development of small-scale industry requires them to be shielded from the large firms. For this purpose, the production of several products was reserved for the small-scale industry; the criterion of the reservation being the ability of these units to manufacture the goods. They were also given concessions such as lower excise duty and bank loans at lower interest rates.

20(A). The 'SATH-E' project is associated with education fields.
- Project SATH-E is the acronym of 'Sustainable Action for Transforming Human Capital-Education'.
- Project SATH-E is associated with education.
- It was launched in 2017 to identify and build three 'role model' States for the school education sector.
- The project was implemented by NITI Aayog.
- In May 2017, the NITI Aayog wrote to all States offering assistance for improving their health and education sectors.
- The SATH-E initiative is based on formal agreements with the States and will be funded through a cost-sharing mechanism between NITI Aayog and the participating states.
- Jharkhand, Odisha and Madhya Pradesh were chosen as 'role model' States.

- The first phase of SATH-E was completed in March 2020.
- The second phase of the project SATH-E 2.0 was commenced by NITI Aayog for a 2-year term from October 2020.

21(B). Central excise duty is a tax that is levied by the central government, but the income received from it is divided between the center and the states.

22(B). Reserve Bank of India is the highest bank in India's banking system. The Reserve Bank of India (RBI) was established on 1 April 1935 and was nationalized in 1949.

23(B). Jammu and Kashmir-based alpine skier Mohammad Arif Khan has become the first Indian athlete to qualify for two different events of the Winter Olympics 2022.
He secured an Olympics quota spot in the men's giant slalom event, after booking his first Winter Olympics ticket in the alpine skiing slalom category in November 2021. The Beijing 2022 Winter Olympics are set to take place from February 4 to 20.

24(A). According to the revised classification for MSMEs composite criteria for classification have been devised. A micro-unit is defined as those in which Investment is less than 1 crore and turnover is less than 5 crore. So, statement 1 is correct.
A medium-scale unit is defined as those in which investment is greater than 10 crores and less than 20 crores, while turnover is greater than 50 crores and less than 100 crores. So, statement 2 is not correct.

25(C). American technology major Google has launched a platform that displays flood forecasts, namely 'FloodHub'.
This platform shows the area and time where floods could occur, in order to inform people about the natural calamity. Google has used an AI technique called transfer learning to make it work in areas where there is less data available.

26(B). Given:
$0.002 \times 0.5 = ?$
Now,
$0.002 \times 0.5 = ?$
$\Rightarrow \frac{(2 \times 5)}{(1000 \times 10)} = ?$
$\Rightarrow \frac{10}{10000} = ?$
$\Rightarrow ? = 0.001$

27(C). Given:
Fruits at 15 for Rs. 140 = Fruits at 10 for Rs. 120
Fruits sold at Rs. 132 per dozen
Profit > Loss
Profit = SP - CP
Profit percent $= \frac{\text{Profit}}{\text{C P}} \times 100$
Let total fruit brought be LCM of 10 and 15 = 30
So, Let 30 fruits are bought at 15 for Rs. 140 , then cost of 30 fruits $= \frac{140}{15} \times 30 = $ Rs. 280
30 fruits are also brought at 10 for Rs. 120 , then cost of 30 fruits $= \frac{120}{10} \times 30 = $ Rs. 360
Total cost of 60 fruits = Rs. 280 + Rs. 360 = Rs. 640
SP of 12 fruits = Rs. 132
SP of 1 fruit = Rs. 11
SP of 60 fruits = Rs. 11 $\times$ 60 = Rs. 660
Profit = SP − CP

= Rs. 660 - Rs. 640
= Rs. 20
Profit percent $= \frac{20}{640} \times 100 = 3\frac{1}{8}$
$\therefore$ The required profit percent $= 3\frac{1}{8}\%$

28(C). Given,
An article is Marked 25% above the cost price.
After giving $x\%$ discount still makes a profit of 5.5%
.
As we know,
Let the cost price of the article be 100 unit.
According to the question,
Selling price $= \left[\frac{(100 + \text{gain}\%)}{100}\right] \times$ cost price
The selling price of the article is
$= \left[\frac{(100 + 5.5)}{100}\right] \times 100$
$= 105.5$ units
The Marked price of the article is:
$= [100 + (100 \times 25\%)]$
$= 100 + 25$
$= 125$ units
Also,
The selling price of the article is:
Selling price = [Marked price - (Marked price $\times$ Discount %)]
$= [125 - (125 \times x\%)] = 105.5$
$\Rightarrow 125 - \frac{5x}{4} = 105.5$
$\Rightarrow \frac{5x}{4} = 19.5$
$\Rightarrow x = 19.5 \times \frac{4}{5}$
$\Rightarrow x = 15.6$
$\therefore$ The required value of x is 15.6 .

29(A). Given:
Sum, $(P) = $ Rs. $32,000$
Rate, $(R) = 20\%$
Time, $(T) = 3$ years
Simple interest $= \frac{(P \times R \times T)}{100}$
For compound Interest,
Amount, $(A) = P(1 + \frac{R}{100})^T$
Amount $= P + $ Compound interest
For the first year, Simple interest and Compound interest will be equal
For Simple interest,
Simple interest $= \frac{(P \times R \times T)}{100}$
$= \frac{(32,000 \times 20 \times 3)}{100}$
$= 19,200$
For Compound interest,
Amount, $(A) = P(1 + \frac{R}{100})^T$
$= 32,000 \times (1 + \frac{20}{100})^3$
$= 55,296$
Compound interest = Amount − Principle
$= 55,296 - 32,000$
$= 23,296$
Now, $23,296 - 19,200 = 4096$

30(D). Given:
Time = 5 years
SI $= \frac{\text{PRT}}{100}$
Where P is principal, R is rate of interest and T is time.
Sum doubles itself:
So, SI = 2P − P = P

$\Rightarrow P = \frac{P \times R \times 5}{100}$

$\Rightarrow R = 20\%$

So, rate of interest = 20%

31(D). Given,

Perimeter of a square is $24\sqrt{2}$ cm.

As we know,

Diagonal of square $= \sqrt{2} \times$ Side

The perimeter of square $= 4 \times$ Side

$\Rightarrow 24\sqrt{2}$ cm $= 4 \times$ Side

$\Rightarrow$ Side $= 6\sqrt{2}$ cm

Diagonal of square $= \sqrt{2} \times$ Side

$\Rightarrow$ Diagonal of square $= \sqrt{2} \times 6\sqrt{2}$ cm

$\Rightarrow$ Diagonal of square $= 12$ cm

$\therefore$ Diagonal of a square is 12 cm.

32(A). Given,

The ratio of the sides of a rectangle $= 3 : 4$

Perimeter $= 56$ cm

As we know,

Perimeter of rectangle $= 2(l + b)$

Where, $l =$ length

$b =$ breadth

Let the length of rectangle be $3x$.

And the breadth of rectangle be $4x$.

According to the question:

Perimeter of rectangle $= 2(l + b)$

$\Rightarrow 56 = 2(3x + 4x)$

$\Rightarrow 56 = 2 \times 7x$

$\Rightarrow x = 4cm$

Now,

The length of rectangle $= 3x = 3 \times 4 = 12$ cm

The breadth of rectangle $= 4x = 4 \times 4 = 16$ cm

$\therefore$ Its sides are 12 cm and 16 cm.

33(C). The possible combinations are $(5, 3, 2)(2, 4, 4), (3, 3, 4), (2, 2, 6), (7, 2, 1)$, $(8, 1, 1)$

Product of the combinations

$\Rightarrow 5 \times 3 \times 2 = 30$

$\Rightarrow 2 \times 4 \times 4 = 32$

$\Rightarrow 4 \times 3 \times 3 = 36$

$\Rightarrow 2 \times 2 \times 6 = 24$

$\Rightarrow 7 \times 2 \times 1 = 14$

$\Rightarrow 8 \times 1 \times 1 = 8$

36 is the maximum product among the combinations.

$\therefore$ 36 is the maximum product of $(a \times b \times c)$.

34(D). Given,

A bike speed from R to S is 30 km/hr.

and from S to R at speed of 20 km/hr

As we know,

Average Speed $= \frac{2 \times S_1 \times S_2}{(S_1 + S_2)}$

Average Speed $= 2 \times 30 \times \frac{20}{50} = 24$ km/hr

$\therefore$ The average speed is 24 km/hr.

35(A). Given:

Total number of student in class A = 38

Total number of student in class B = 42

Average marks of students in class A = 79

Average marks of students in class B = 89

According to the formula,

Average $= \frac{\text{Sum of all the terms}}{\text{Total number of terms}}$

So,

Total marks of students in class A = 79 × 38 = 38(80 – 1) = 38 × 80 – 38 = 3040 – 38 = 3002

Total marks of students in class B = 89 × 42 = 42(90 – 1) = 42 × 90 – 42 = 3780 – 42 = 3738

Total marks of students of class A and class B = 6740

Total students of class A and class B = 38 + 42 = 80

Average $= \frac{6740}{80} = 84.25$

$\therefore$ The average mark of all 80 students is 84.25.

36(A). Given:

35% of a number = 805

Calculation:

Let the number be X.

$\Rightarrow X \times 35\% = 805$

$\Rightarrow X \times \frac{35}{100} = 805$

$\Rightarrow X = 2300$

Now, 62% of number 2300

$= 62\%$ of 2300

$= 2300 \times \frac{62}{100}$

$= 1426$

$\therefore$ The 62% of the number is 1426 .

37(D). Let there be x men originally.

x men finish the work in 60 days and $(x + 8)$ finish it in 50 days.

x men finish the job in 60 days.

1 man can finish it in $60x$ days.

$(x + 8)$ men can finish the job in 50 days.

1 man can finish it in $50(x + 8)$ days.

according to the question,

$60x = 50(x + 8)$

$\Rightarrow 10x = 400$

$\Rightarrow x = 40$

So, there were 40 men originally.

38(B). P can complete job in 15 days so in 1 day P completes $\frac{1}{15}$ amount work.

Q is twice as fast as P . So Q takes half the time as P that means $\frac{15}{2}$ days.

In one day, Q does $\frac{1}{\frac{15}{2}} = \frac{2}{15}$ amount of work.

Then both work together,

In one day work done together = P 's one day work $+$ Q 's one day work.

$\therefore$ Work done $= \frac{1}{15} + \frac{2}{15} = \frac{3}{15} = \frac{1}{5}$

If in one day they finish $\frac{1}{5}$ work then entire work is done in 5 days.

39(B). Given:

Days taken by A to complete the work $= 18$ days

B is 12.5% more efficient than A

Concept used:

Efficiency is inversely proportional to the time.

Calculation:

$12.5\% = \frac{1}{8}$

Let efficiency of A be 8 units

And efficiency of B be 9 units.

$A : B$ (Efficiency) $= 8 : 9$

$A : B$ (Time)$= 9 : 8$

From this,

Time taken by $A = 9$ units

$\Rightarrow 9$ units $= 18$ days

$\Rightarrow 1$ unit $= 2$ days

$\Rightarrow 8$ units $= 2 \times 8 = 16$ days

Take L.C.M. of 16,18 and make it as total work i.e. 144 units Total work $= 144$ units

Total efficiency $A + B = 8 + 9 = 17$ units

Time taken $= \frac{144}{17} = 8\frac{8}{17}$

$\therefore$ The time taken by A and B to complete the work together is $8\frac{8}{17}$ days.

40(D). Let speed of the woman is x km/hr .
Distance covered in 5 minutes at 10 km/hr $=$
Distance covered in 3 minutes at $(10 + x)$ km/hr
$\therefore 10 \times \frac{5}{60} = \frac{3}{60} \times (10 + x)$
$\Rightarrow 50 = 3 \times (10 + x)$
$\Rightarrow 50 = 30 + 3x$
$\Rightarrow 50 - 30 = 3x$
$\Rightarrow 20 = 3x$
$\Rightarrow \frac{20}{3} = x$
$\therefore x = 6\frac{2}{3}$
So, the speed of woman is $6\frac{2}{3}$ km/hr .

41(C). Given:
Length of train $= 1000\ m$
Speed of train $= 45\ km/hr$
We know that:
Speed $= \dfrac{\text{Distance}}{\text{time}}$
$1\ km/hr = \frac{5}{18}\ m/sec$
$2\min = 120$ seconds
$1\min 40$ seconds $= 100$ seconds
Let length of bridge be $x\ m$.
According to the question:
$45 \times [\frac{5}{18}] = \frac{(x+1000)}{120}$
$\Rightarrow \frac{25}{2} \times 120 = x + 1000$
$\Rightarrow 1500 = x + 1000$
$\Rightarrow x = 1500 - 1000$
$\Rightarrow x = 500$
$\therefore$ Length of bridge is $500\ m$.
Let speed of person be km/sec .
$\Rightarrow k = \frac{500}{100}$
$\Rightarrow k = 5\ m/sec = 5 \times \frac{18}{5} = 18\ km/h$

42(D). As we know,
A prime number is a whole number greater than 1 whose only factors are 1 and itself.
According to question,
$161 = 23 \times 7$
$\Rightarrow x = 23 \quad \cdots (\because x > y)$
$\Rightarrow y = 7$
$\therefore x - y = 23 - 7 = 16$

43(A). Let the present age of three colleague's are : $3x, 5x$ and $7x$
Four years ago, their ages were $(3x - 4)$, $(5x - 4)$ and $(7x - 4)$.
According to the question,
$(3x-4) + (5x-4) + (7x-4) = 48$
$\Rightarrow 15x-12 = 48$
$\Rightarrow 15x = 60$
$\Rightarrow x = 4$
Their present ages are 12 years, 20 years and 28 years respectively.

44(C). $(fog)2 = f\{g(x)\}$
$\because f(x) = 2x$
and $g(x) = x^2 + 2$
$\therefore f\{g(x)\} = f\left(x^2 + 2\right)$
$= 2(x^2 + 2$
$= f\left(x^2 + 2\right)$
$= 2\left(x^2 + 2\right)$
$= 2x^2 + 4$
Therefore, $(fog)2 = 2 \times (2)^2 + 4$

$= 2 \times 4 + 4 = 12$

45(C). Given,
A general second-degree equation $ax^2 + 2hxy + by^2 + 2gx + 2fy + c = 0$ $(a \neq 0)$ represent a circle.
The general equation of any type of circle is represented by: $x^2 + y^2 + 2gx + 2fy + c = 0$, for all values of g, f and c.
$\Rightarrow x^2 + 2hxy + y^2 + 2gx + 2fy + c = 0$,
Comparing both equations, we get
$\Rightarrow a = 1, b = 1, 2h = 0$
$\Rightarrow a = b$ and $h = 0$

46(B). Given:
$4\sin^2 x - 2\cos^2 x = 2$
$\Rightarrow 2\sin^2 x - \cos^2 x = 1$
$\Rightarrow 2\sin^2 x - \cos^2 x = \sin^2 x + \cos^2 x$
$\Rightarrow \sin^2 x = 2\cos^2 x$
$\Rightarrow \tan^2 x = 2$
$\Rightarrow \tan x = \sqrt{2}$
Hence, the correct option is (B)

47(B). Let,
E_1 : He knows the answer.
E_2 : He does not know the answer.
X : He gets the correct answer.
Therefore, $P(E_1) = 90\% = \frac{9}{10}$
$P(E_2) = 1 - \frac{9}{10} = \frac{1}{10}$
$P(X \mid E_1) = 1$
$P(X \mid E_2) = \frac{1}{4}$
As we know that according to Bayes theorem:
$P(E_i \mid A) = \dfrac{P(E_i) \times P(A|E_i)}{\sum_{i=1}^{n} P(E_i) \times P(A|E_i)}, i = 1, 2, \ldots, n$
$\therefore P(E_2 \mid X) = \dfrac{\frac{1}{10} \cdot \frac{1}{4}}{\left[\frac{9}{10} \cdot 1 + \frac{1}{10} \cdot \frac{1}{4}\right]} = \frac{1}{37}$

48(C). Given,
Word = SOFTWARE
Arrangement of n letter of a word
Case 1: If there were no repeating letters $= n!$
Case 2: If there were "r" letter of one kind $= \frac{n!}{r!}$
Keeping all the vowel at one place and consider it as one vowel = SFTWR(OAE)
Here, n = 6 and number of vowel = 3
All letter can be arranged in 6! ways and vowel can be arranged in 3! ways
Total number of ways to arrange the word $= 6! \times 3! = 6 \times 5 \times 4 \times 3 \times 2 \times 1 \times 3 \times 2 \times 1 = 4320$
$\therefore$ Total number of ways to arrange the word = 4320

49(B). Let the number of basic classes be ' $2x$ '.
Let the number of advance classes be ' x '.
Total duration of basic classes $= 2x \times 1 = 2x$ hours
Total duration of advance classes $= x \times 3 = 3x$ hours
Total duration of his classes $= 2x + 3x = 5x$
$\Rightarrow 5x = 10$
$\Rightarrow x = 2$
Now,
Number of basic classes $= 2x = 2 \times 2$
$= 4$ classes
Number of advance classes $= x = 2$ classes
Difference between the number of advance classes and basic classes $= 4 - 2$
$= 2$

50(C). Let the basic classes taken by A be ' $3x$ '.
Let the the advance classes by A be ' x '.

Time duration for all basic classes $= 3x \times 1 = 3x$ hours

Time duration for all advance classes $= x \times 3 = 3x$ hours

Total time duration of $A's$ classes $= 3x + 3x = 6x$ hours

According to the question,

$6x = 12$

$\Rightarrow x = 2$

Now total classes = Total basic classes + Total advance classes

$\Rightarrow 3x + x = 4x$

$\Rightarrow 8$ classes

$\therefore$ A will take total of 8 classes.

51(B).

Alphabets	A	B	C	D	E	F	G	H	I	J	K	L	M
Positional value	1	2	3	4	5	6	7	8	9	10	11	12	13
Positional value	26	25	24	23	22	21	20	19	18	17	16	15	14
Alphabets	Z	Y	X	W	V	U	T	S	R	Q	P	O	N

The pattern followed here is:

Y   E   A   R

$\downarrow$-4 $\downarrow$+3 $\downarrow$+3 $\downarrow$-4

U   H   D   N

Similarly,

T   I   M   E

$\downarrow$-4 $\downarrow$+3 $\downarrow$+3 $\downarrow$-4

P   L   P   A

52(D). As a bristle is a part of a brush so, a key is a part of a piano.

53(A). According to Question,
On making relationship diagram-

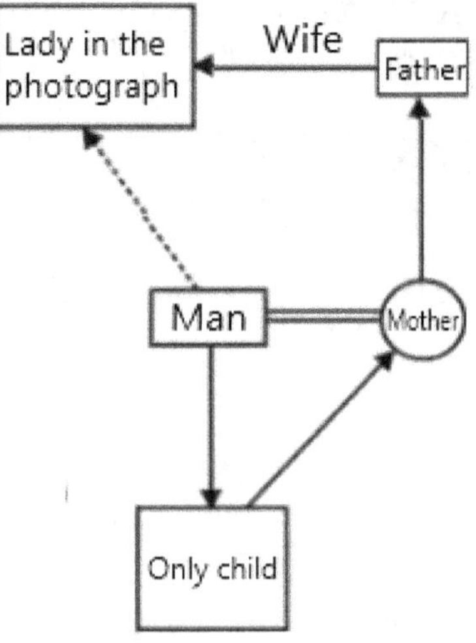

So, it is clear from the relation diagram that the woman in the picture is the mother-in-law of the man.

54(D). Preparing the family tree using the following symbols

Symbol in Diagram	Meaning
◯	Female
▢	Male
═	Married couple
—	Siblings
		Difference of a generation

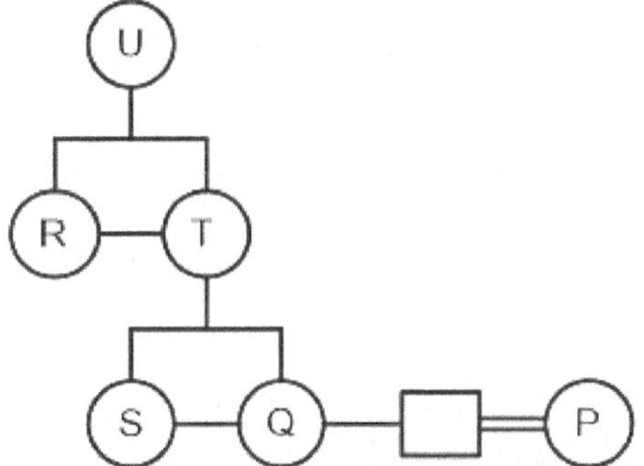

From the above figure it is clear that T is mother of S.

55(B). Figure (B) is different from the other figures in the given set of figures.

56(B). Figure (B) is different from the other figures in the given set of figures.

57(C). In figure A, B and D only straight lines are used whereas in figure C straight line as well as curved line is also used so figure C is different from all others.

58(D). Drawing the map according to given conditions assuming John started in North direction,

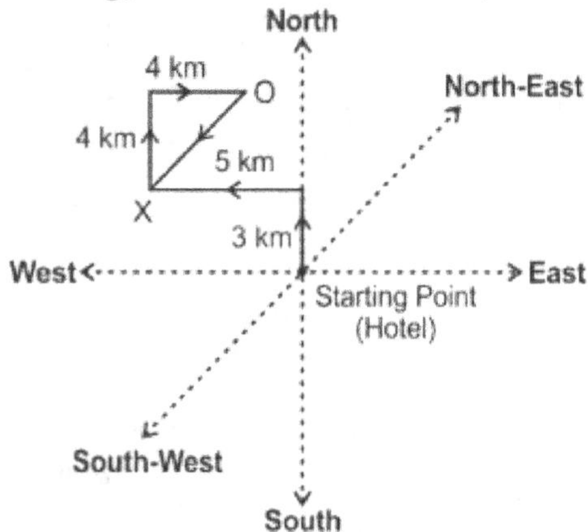

Given that OX is in North - West direction but in the diagram above, OX is in South - West.
Rotating the map clockwise 90°

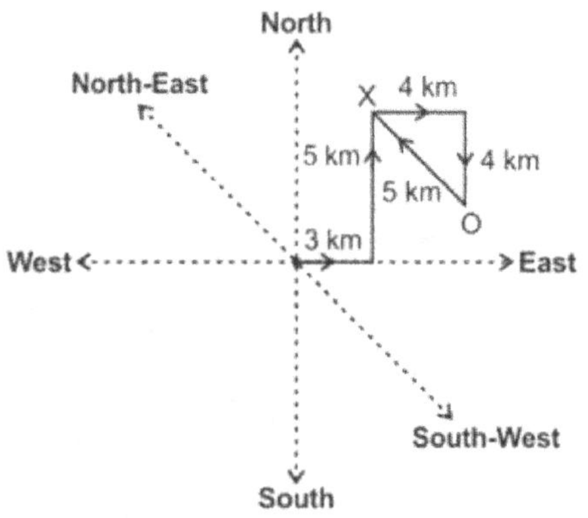

It is clear from the above map that OX is moving in North - West direction.
So, John started moving from the hotel in East direction.

59(A). According to the question,

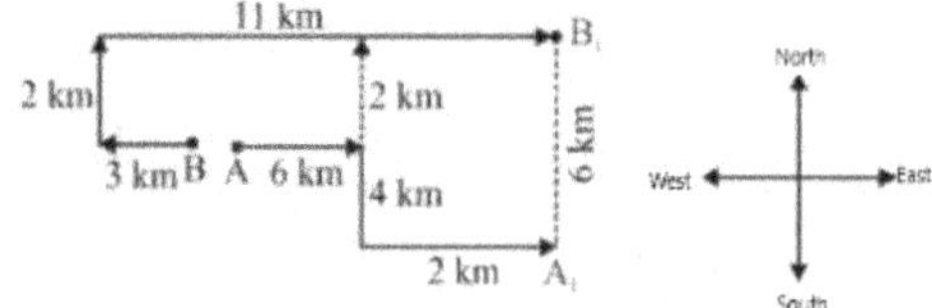

So, the distance between A and B will be 6 km.

60(C). According to the given information:

Word	Code
Air	Green
Green	Red
Red	Sea
Sea	Blue
Blue	Water
Water	Pink

We know that the color of the grass is green.
But in the statement, 'Green' is called 'Red'.
So, the color of the grass will be 'Red'.

61(C). According to the given information:

Word	Code
One	Two
Two	Three
Three	Four
Four	Five
Five	Six

So, the square of the number 2 is 4.
But in the statement, 'four' is called 'five'.

62(D). Three and two arcs are inverted alternately. The central element rotates 90 ° ACW and 180 ° alternately. Therefore the correct answer figure will be:

63(B). Logic: The circle of the first figure is rotated 45° to the left and the direction of the triangle inside is the same as before.
Following the same logic, if we rotate the 3rd image to the left by 45° and keep the direction of the inner triangle as same, we'll get:

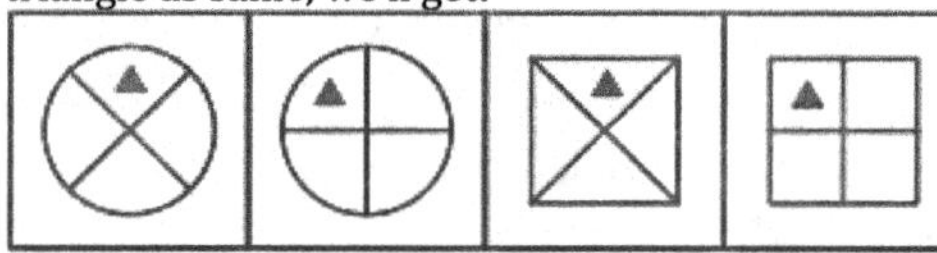

64(A). Elephants and Wolves bear no relationship to each other. But, both of them are animals.

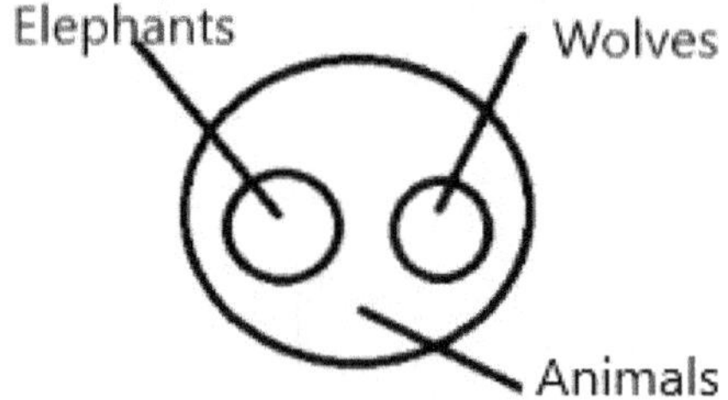

65(B). The racket is used in both Badminton and in Tennis. But racket is also used in other games as well.

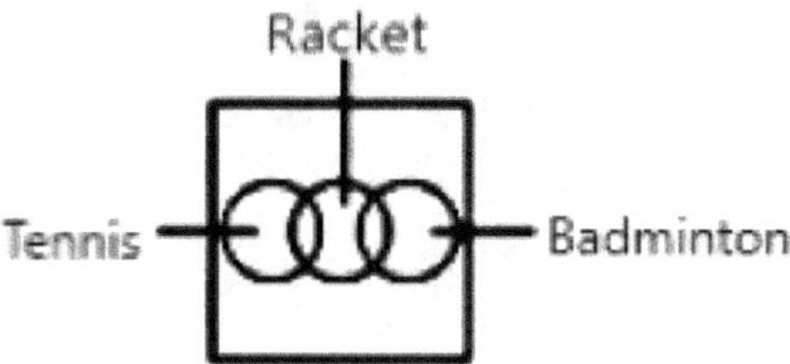

66(B). Given:
21, 41, 66, 96, ___, 171, 216, 266
21   41   66   96   **131**   171 216 266

+20 +25 +30 +35   +40 +45 +50

+5   +5   +5   +5   +5   +5

∴ The missing term is 131.

67(D). The series follows the following pattern:

$(2 + 3)^2 + 1 = 25 + 1 = 26$

$(3 + 5)^2 + 1 = 64 + 1 = 65$

$(5 + 7)^2 + 1 = 144 + 1 = 145$

$(7 + 11)^2 + 1 = 324 + 1 = 325$

$(11 + 13)^2 + 1 = 576 + 1 = 577$

∴ The required number in the series is 325.

68(D). Given,

In a row of 40 girls, when Komal moves four places to the left from her position, her position becomes 10th from the left end of the row.

Komal is 10th from the left end of the row by shifting 4.

Thus Komal's original position was 14th from the left end. Swati is 3rd to the right of Komal's original place.

Clearly, Swati is $14 + 3 = 17$ th from the left end.

Number of girls $= (40 - 17) = 23$ to the right of Swati

Thus, Swati is 24th from the right end of the row.

69(D). The logic follows here is:

1) Dinesh is taller than Chinku and Elina

⇒ Dinesh > Chinku/Elina

2) Akash is not as tall as Elina

⇒ Elina > Akash

3) Chinku is taller than Akash

⇒ Chinku > Akash

4) Dinesh is not as tall as Bikash

⇒ Bikash > Dinesh

Therefore, the correct order is:

Bikash > Dinesh > Chinku/Elina > Akash

As we can see Bikash is the tallest one.

Therefore, Dinesh is next to the tallest one.

70(D). According to the given information:

Statements:

I. Some white are red.

II. Some white are green.

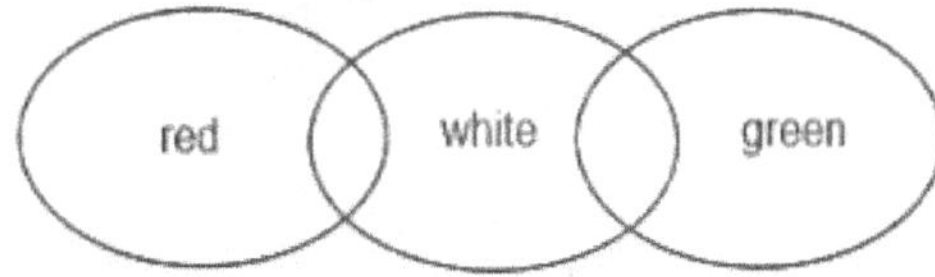

Conclusions:

I. Some green are red → It is possible but not definite, so false.

II. Some red are not green → It is possible but not definite, so false.

So, neither conclusion I nor conclusion II follows.

71(A).

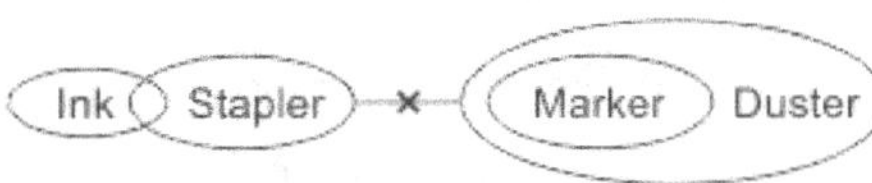

72(A). The pattern followed here is:

$(3, 9, 27) \rightarrow (3, 3^2, 3^3)$

Similarly,

$(5, 25, 125) \rightarrow (5, 5^2, 5^3)$

73(C). Flute is played by blowing across a hole at one end and covering other holes with the fingers.

Violin , Guitar and Sitar are string musical instruments.

So, Flute is the odd word.

Ques (74-75): Given:

A certain number of persons are sitting in a row. All of them are facing north.

1. R is sitting 3rd from the left end. One person is sitting between R and T who is not sitting at any end.

2. Three persons are sitting between T and O who is not the immediate neighbour of P.

3. L is sitting immediate right of O. O is sitting at one of the extreme ends.

4. Three persons are sitting between L and N.

5. One person is sitting between N and P, who is sixth to the right of L.

6. Two persons are sitting between S and P. P sits at the left of S.

O L R _ T N _ P _ _ S

7. E is sitting 4th from the right end. Two persons are sitting between E and K who is sitting at one of the end.

8. Four people are sitting between K and B.

9. One person is sitting between B and H.

H _ B _ E _ _ K

10. Number of persons sitting between R and O are equal to the number of persons sitting between S and H.

Now after combining the cases from the left end and the right end.

The final arrangement is as follows:

O L R _ T N P _ S H B E _ K

74(C). So, total of 20 persons are sitting in the row.

75(A). So L is sitting 11th to the left of H.

76(B). वर्तनी का अर्थ: भाषा की वर्तनी का अर्थ उस भाषा में शब्दों को वर्णों से अभिव्यक्त करने की क्रिया को कहते हैं। लिखने की रीति को वर्तनी कहते हैं।

उपरोक्त शब्दों में 'स्वस्तिक' वर्तनी के अनुसार शुद्ध रूप है बाकी सभी शब्द वर्तनी के अनुसार गलत शब्द है। स्वस्तिक का अर्थ चारणों का एक प्रकार, शरीर या पदार्थ पर लगाया जानेवाला एक मंगल चिह्न होता है।

77(D). दिए गए विकल्पो में 'अत्यधिक' की वर्तनी शुद्ध है।

अन्य की शुद्ध वर्तनी है-

आधीन - अधीन

व्यवहारिक - व्यावहारिक

मिष्ठान्न - मिष्टान्न

78(C). 'गांठ बांधना' मुहावरे का अर्थ - याद रखना होता है। अन्य सभी मुहावरों का अर्थ लज्जित हो जाना है। अतः सही विकल्प (C) 'गाँठ बांधना' है।

मुहावरे: गाँठ बांधना

अर्थ: याद रखना

वाक्य प्रयोग: जीवन मे हर एक अनुभव से मिले सबक को गाँठ बांधकर रखना चाहिए।

79(C). जब कोई शब्द समूह या पद या वाक्यांश निरंतर अभ्यास के कारण सामान्य अर्थ न देकर विशेष अर्थ व्यक्त करने लगे तो उसे मुहावरा कहते हैं।

'थाली का बैंगन होना' मुहावरे का अर्थ "अस्थिर विचार का होना अथवा ऐसा इंसान जिसके पास कोई सिद्धांत न हो" है।

वाक्य प्रयोग: वह तो थाली का बैंगन है, उसकी बात पर भरोसा मत करो।

80(D). उपरोक्त सभी विकल्पों में से 'गये थे रोजा छुड़ाने, नमाज गले पड़ीटे' लोकोक्ति का सही अर्थ 'उपकार करने के बदले स्वयं को दुख भोगना पड़ा' है।

लोकोक्ति: गये थे रोजा छुड़ाने, नमाज गले पड़ी, अर्थ- उपकार करने के बदले स्वयं को दुख भोगना पड़ा।

वाक्य: गली में लड़ाई हो रही थी मामले को सुलझाने गया था तो पुलिस मुझे ही पकड़ कर ले गई यह तो गये थे रोजा छुड़ाने,

नमाज पढ़ी गले वाली बात होगी।

दिए गए विकल्पों में सही उत्तर विकल्प (D) उपकार करने के बदले स्वयं को दुख भोगना पड़ा है। अन्य विकल्प इसके अनुचित उत्तर होंगे।

81(C). दिए गए विकल्पों में 'आइना' शब्द पुल्लिंग है।

किसी वाक्य में 'आइना आज साफ़ नज़र आ रही है' का प्रयोग करना उचित नहीं हैं। यहाँ 'रही' के स्थान पर 'रहा' होगा। इस प्रकार स्पष्ट है कि 'आइना' एक पुल्लिंग शब्द है।

जैसे - आइना आज साफ़ नज़र आ रहा है।

82(C). 'अनार' पुल्लिंग शब्द है।

अन्य विकल्पों का विश्लेषण:

गाजर, अरहर, आहट ये तीनो स्त्रीलिंग शब्द है।

हिन्दी भाषा में लिंग के दो भेद माने जाते हैं – पुल्लिंग तथा स्त्रीलिंग।

लिंग	परिभाषा	उदाहरण
पुल्लिंग	जिन शब्दों से पुरुष जाति का बोध होता है उन्हें पुल्लिंग शब्द कहते हैं ।	जैसे - पिता, भाई, लड़का, पेड़, सिंह शिव, हनुमान, बैल आदि ।
स्त्रीलिंग	जिन शब्दों से स्त्री जाति का बोध होता है उन्हें स्त्रीलिंग शब्द कहते हैं।	जैसे - माता, बहन, यमुना, गंगा, कुरसी, छड़ी, नारी बुआ, लड़की, लक्ष्मी, गाय आदि।

अतः विकल्प (C) सही है

83(B). "जिसकी आशा न की गई हो" वाक्यांश के लिए प्रयुक्त शब्द अप्रत्याशित होगा।

वाक्यांश: शब्द समूह का वह सार्थक रूप जिससे एक विचार की स्पष्ट एवं पूर्ण अभिव्यक्ति होती हो, उसे वाक्यांश कहते हैं। वाक्यांश का अर्थ वाक्य का अंश होता है।

84(B). पृथ्वी के तीन ओर पानी वाला स्थान वाक्यांश के लिए प्रयुक्त शब्द प्रायद्वीप होता है।

प्रायद्वीप: प्रायद्वीप भूमि के वो भाग होते हैं जिनके तीन तरफ जल तथा एक ओर स्थल होती है।

85(B). 'अभिमानी' शब्द का स्त्रीलिंग शब्द 'अभिमानिनी' होगा।

अभिमानी विशेषण शब्द है, जिसका अर्थ है-
- जिसे अभिमान हो, अपने मान-अभिमान का विशेष ध्यान रखने वाला, स्वाभिमानी अहंकारी, घमंडी, मगरूर।

अभिमानिनी - अभिमानी स्त्री, वह महिला जिसे घमंड हो।

86(C). करण कारक में 'से' विभक्ति का प्रयोग साधन के अर्थ में होता है। कारक ऐसे शब्दों को कहते हैं जो क्रिया के करने से होते हैं। उदाहरण के तौर पर वाक्य "राम को वनवास जाना था" को देखा जा सकता है। इस वाक्य में यह देखा जा सकता है कि राम कर्ता हैं और जाना क्रिया, लेकिन क्रिया एवं करता को मिलाने वाला "को" है। इस वाक्य में "को" कारक है।

करण कारक- जिसकी सहायता से कोई कार्य किया जाए, उसे करण कारक कहते हैं। इसके विभक्ति-चिह्न 'से' के द्वारा है। अथवा - वह साधन जिससे क्रिया होती है, वह करण कहलाता है। अर्थात, जिसकी सहायता से किसी काम को अंजाम दिया जाता है वह करण कारक कहलाता है।

87(D). "पेड़ से पत्ता गिरता है" में अपादान कारक है।

"वाक्य में जिस स्थान या वस्तु से किसी व्यक्ति या वस्तु की पृथकता अथवा तुलना का बोध होता है, वहाँ अपादान कारक होता है।" यानी अपादान कारक से विलगाव का बोध होता है। प्रेम, घृणा, लज्जा, ईर्ष्या, भय और सीखना आदि भावों की अभिव्यक्ति के लिए अपादान कारक का ही प्रयोग किया जाता है।

88(C). 'गमिष्यथ' यह पद मूलधातु 'गम' का 'लृट् लकार' मध्यम पुरुष बहुवचन है।

'गम-गच्छ' धातु से 'लृट् लकार' के विविध वचनों और पुरूषों में प्राप्त रूप इस प्रकार है:

'गम्' (परस्मैपद) धातु लृट् लकारः			
पुरुष	एकवचनम्	द्विवचनम्	बहुवचनम्
प्रथमपुरुषः	गमिष्यति	गमिष्यतः	गमिष्यन्ति
मध्यमपुरुषः	गमिष्यसि	गमिष्यथः	गमिष्यथ
उत्तमपुरुषः	गमिष्यामि	गमिष्यावः	गमिष्यामः

89(B). 'गाः' का अर्थ होता है गायों को, ओकारान्त 'गो' शब्द का यह द्विवचन रूप है।

90(B). वाक्य के (b) भाग में त्रुटि है, "पर पानी पीती थी।" के स्थान पर "पर पानी पीते थे।" होगा।

शुद्ध वाक्य:
"राम राज्य में शेर और बकरी एक घाट पर पानी पीते थे।"

91(B). वाक्य के (b) भाग में त्रुटि है, क्योंकि जगती तल और पृथ्वी तल अर्थ एक ही होता है।

शुद्ध वाक्य:
"चन्द्रमा की स्वच्छ चाँदनी पृथ्वी तल में और आकाश में फैली हुई हैं।"

92(C). दिए गए शब्दों में जटिल शब्द का विलोम शब्द सरल है जटिल शब्द के पर्यायवाची शब्द निम्न है, कठिन, मुश्किल तथा कृपण शब्द का अर्थ कंजूस होता है।

93(C). 'निर्झरिणी' शब्द 'नदी' का पर्यायवाची है।

'नदी' शब्द के अन्य पर्यायवाची - शैलजा, जलमाला, शैवालिनी, प्रवाहिनी, सरिता

अन्य विकल्प:

शब्द	पर्यायवाची
पारावार	समुद्र, अब्धि, सागर, वारीश, नीरनिधि, उदधि, अर्णव
झरना	प्रताप, उत्स, निर्झर, सोता, श्रोत
पानी	तोय, जीवन, वारि, पय, अमृत,

94(A). दिए गयें विकल्पों में से 'तुरंग' शब्द 'अश्व' का पर्यायवाची शब्द है।

'तुरंग' शब्द का पर्यायवाची 'अश्व' है।

'अश्व' के पर्यायवाची - रविपुत्र, हय, घोड़ा, सैंधव

अन्य विकल्प:

शब्द	पर्यायवाची
शार्दूल	वनराज, शेर, केसरी, केहरी
शिखी	नर्तकप्रिय, मोर, मेहप्रिय, सितापांग
पखेरू	गगनचर, चिड़िया, विहंग, नभचर

95(C). विषाद शब्द का विलोम शब्द 'आह्लाद' है।

विषाद का अर्थ - दुःख, अवसाद, उदासी, ग़म। (पुल्लिंग)

आह्लाद का अर्थ - प्रसन्न, हर्षित। (विशेषण)

अन्य विकल्प:

मृदः कटु, वरदानः अभिषाप, स्तुतिः निन्दा

96(B). 'उच्चारण' का सही सन्धि विच्छेद होगा - उत् + चारण।
- 'उच्चारण - उत् + चारण' में व्यंजन संधि है।
- 'उच्चारण - उत् + चारण' (त्/द् + च = च्च)।
- व्यंजन संधि करते समय त्/द् के साथ च् हो तो 'त्' का 'च' बन जाता है।

97(B). 'पित्रादेश' का संधि विच्छेद 'पितृ + आदेश' होगा। अतः 'पितृ + आदेश' है।

नियम- 'ऋ + आ = रा' होगा।

यण स्वर संधि - इ, ई, उ, ऊ या ऋ का मेल यदि असमान स्वर से हो तो इ, ई का 'य्'; उ, ऊ का 'व्' और ऋ का 'र्' हो जाता है।
- जैसे - यदि + अपि (इ + अ) = यद्यपि, अनु + एषण = अन्वेषण।

98(B). प्रत्यूष शब्द का सही संधि विच्छेद 'प्रति + ऊष' होगा।
इसमें 'इ +उ ' वर्णों की संधि हुई है और ' य ' वर्ण की उत्पत्ति हुई है।
इसलिए यहाँ पर यण संधि होगी।
क्योंकि जब इ, ई, उ, ऊ, ऋ के बाद कोई अन्य स्वर आता है तो ये क्रमश: य, व, र, ल् में परिवर्तन हो जाता है, यह परिवर्तन यण सन्धि का होता है।

99(D). "दस्तावेज - रामचन्द्र तिवारी" यह सही विकल्प है, क्योंकि दस्तावेज पत्रिका रामचन्द्र तिवारी द्वारा सम्पादित नही है।
दस्तावेज के सम्पादक:-डॉ॰ विश्वनाथ प्रसाद तिवारी
हिंदी की साहित्यिक पत्रिकाएँ, हिंदी साहित्य की विभिन्न विधाओं के विकास और संवर्द्धन में उल्लेखनीय भूमिका निभाती रहीं हैं।

कविता, कहानी, उपन्यास, निबंध, नाटक, आलोचना, यात्रावृत्तांत, जीवनी, आत्मकथा तथा शोध से संबंधित आलेखों का नियमित तौर पर प्रकाशन इनका मूल उद्देश्य है।
अधिकांश पत्रिकाओं का संपादन कार्य अवैतनिक होता है।

100(A). 'साकेत' मैथिलीशरण गुप्त की कृति है।
'साकेत महाकवि' मैथिलीशरण गुप्त का लिखा महाकाव्य है जो 12 सर्गों में लिखा गया है। शुरुआती सर्गों में श्रीराम को वनवास का आदेश, अयोध्यावासियों का करुण-रुदन और वनगमन की झांकियां हैं। अंत के सर्गों में लक्ष्मण की पत्नी व राजवधू उर्मिला के वियोग का वर्णन है। साकेत मुख्यत: उर्मिला को केन्द्र में रख कर ही लिखी गयी है।

General Knowledge

1. ' Chandimangala ' was composed in which one of the following languages during the 16 th century CE?
   (a) Sanskrit
   (b) Tamil
   (c) Bengali
   (d) Oriya

2. Chandragupta's advisor, Kautilya became very famous for his great text ______.
   (a) Kamasutra
   (b) Abhigyan Shakuntalam
   (c) Arthashastra
   (d) Manusmriti

3. Who among the following was responsible for the destruction of the famous Somnath temple on the Gujarat coast?
   (a) Muhammad Ghori
   (b) Mahmud of Ghazni
   (c) Bakhtiyar Khilji
   (d) Qutb-ud-din Aibak

4. As per the power rule established in late 1700s in Bengal, which of the following is not true?
   (a) Zamindars were responsible for paying revenue to the Company.
   (b) Village ryot paid rent to the zamindar.
   (c) Jotedars gave out loans to other ryots and sold their produce.
   (d) Ryots distributed the revenue demand (jama) over villages.

5. The real name of 'Frontier Gandhi' is:
   (a) Purushottam Das Tandon
   (b) Subhash Chandra Bose
   (c) Khan Abdul Ghaffar Khan
   (d) Abul Kalam Azad

6. Presided over the session of Banaras Hindu Mahasabha in August, 1923:
   (a) Swami Sahajanand
   (b) Rajendra Prasad
   (c) Lala Lajpat Rai
   (d) Pandit Madan Mohan Malaviya

7. With reference to the longitude of which of the following places is the India Standard Time determined?
   (a) Indore
   (b) Kanpur
   (c) Mirzapur
   (d) Varanasi

8. __________ layer in the earth's atmosphere which reflects radio waves from the earth thus helping radio communication.
   (a) Stratosphere
   (b) Mesosphere
   (c) Troposphere
   (d) Ionosphere

9. With reference to the global distribution of rainfall, consider the following statements.
   1. The latitudes of $35°$ and $40°$ in the north and south of the equator decrease towards the west.
   2. However, rainfall occurs between north and south of the equator and between latitudes in the western part of the first continents, which progressively decrease as they move east.
   Which of the above statements is correct?
   (a) Only 1
   (b) Only 2
   (c) Both 1 and 2
   (d) Neither 1 nor 2

10. Who has been appointed as the Director General of the News Services Division of All India Radio in August 2022?
    (a) Dr. Vasudha Gupta
    (b) Satish Reddy
    (c) Ravindra Kohli
    (d) Bipasha Jaiswal

11. Which of the following countries has designed the drone 'Haeil'?
    (a) Iran
    (b) North Korea
    (c) Ukraine
    (d) Turkey

12. Which country has declared national emergency due to Cyclone Gabrielle?
    (a) Malaysia
    (b) New Zealand
    (c) Australia
    (d) Indonesia

13. In February 2023 , which country lifted its temporary ban on the import of frozen seafood from India?
    (a) Iran
    (b) Oman
    (c) Saudi Arabia
    (d) Qatar

14. Which of the following options is correctly depicting the formula of power?
    (a) $P = VI$
    (b) $P = \dfrac{V^2}{R}$
    (c) $P = I^2 R$
    (d) All of the above

15. Phreatophytes are the plants adapted to grow in-
    (a) Moist shaded places
    (b) Rocky environments
    (c) Arid environments
    (d) Active volcanic lava

16. Sea turtles are called living fossils for they have been on the earth in their present form for over 150 million years. Of the five species of sea turtles found in the waters of the Indian subcontinent, which is the most populous species?
    (a) Keneps Ridley
    (b) Loggerhead
    (c) Olive Ridley
    (d) Flatback

17. Consider the following statements regarding Ek Bharat Shreshtha Bharat (EBSB) programme.
    1. It aims to promote engagement and thereby understanding amongst the people of different states/UTs to ensure a stronger united India.
    2. The NITI Aayog has been designated Nodal Ministry for coordination of the programme.
    Which of the statements given above is/are correct:
    (a) 1 only
    (b) 2 only
    (c) Both 1 and 2
    (d) Neither 1 nor 2

18. Select the correct answer by matching List 1 with List 2.

List 1	List 2
A. 93rd Amendment	1. Parliament's power to amend Fundamental Rights
B. 97th Amendment	2. Abolition of special privileges of Princely states, titles and pensions
C. 24th Amendment	3. Reservation for OBCs in unaided educational institutions
D. 26th Amendment	4. New cooperative Act

(a)   A - 1, B - 3, C - 2, D - 4
(b)   A - 3, B - 4, C - 1, D - 2
(c)   A - 4, B - 2, C - 3, D - 1
(d)   A - 3, B - 1, C - 2, D - 4

19. The electoral college for the election of the President consists of:
1. Elected members of both the Houses of Parliament
2. Elected members of the legislative assemblies of the states
3. Nominated members of both Houses of Parliament.
Select the correct answer using the code given below.
(a)   1 and 2 only   (b)   2 and 3 only
(c)   1 and 3 only   (d)   1, 2 and 3

20. In which of the following states, Central government has decided to install 4,000 telecom towers in 2022?
(a)   Odisha   (b)   Karnataka
(c)   Uttar Pradesh   (d)   Assam

21. Match the following plans and programmes:

Plans	Programmes
A. 1st Plan	1. Rapid Industrialisation
B. 2nd Plan	2. Community Development
C. 3rd Plan	3. Expansion of basic industries
D. 4th Plan	4. Minimum Needs Programme
E. 5th Plan	5. Achievement of self-reliance and growth with stability

Select the correct answer form the code below:
(a)   A-1, B-2, C-3, D-4, E-5
(b)   A-2, B-1, C-4, D-5, E-3
(c)   A-2, B-1, C-3, D-4, E-5
(d)   A-2, B-1, C-3, D-5, E-4

22. The strategy adopted under I.R.D.P. in the Seventh Plan was:
(a)   Adoption of total household approach
(b)   Adoption of village approach
(c)   Adoption of block approach
(d)   Adoption of district approach

23. Who won the National Hockey Championship 2023 ?
(a)   ITBP   (b)   BSF
(c)   Bhopal   (d)   Haryana

24. Consider the following statements with reference to SWAMITVA Scheme:
1. The Ministry of Rural Development (MoRD) is the Nodal Ministry for THE implementation of the scheme.
2. The scheme will help in streamlining planning and revenue collection in rural areas and ensuring clarity on property rights.
3. The scheme will enable the creation of better-quality Gram Panchayat Development Plans (GPDPs).
Which of the statements given above is/are correct?
(a)   1 only   (b)   2 and 3
(c)   2 only   (d)   1 and 3

25. In April 2023, the Indian Space Research Organisation has successfully completed two significant tests- Vikas Engine Test Campaign for the L110 Stage & System Demonstration Model tests for the Crew Module

Propulsion System for which of the following mission?
(a)   Mangalyaan 2   (b)   Chandrayaan 3
(c)   Gaganyaan   (d)   Pragyan

Mathematics

26. Subtract 3 kg 178 g from 8 kg 350 g.
(a)   5 kg 172 g   (b)   4 kg 272 g
(c)   4 kg172 g   (d)   4 kg 472 g

27. Suman sold an article for Rs. 882 after allowing 16% discount on its marked price. Had she not allowed any discount, she would have gained 20% on the cost price. What is the cost price of the article?
(a)   725   (b)   750
(c)   850   (d)   875

28. Akhil started a business by investing a certain amount of money in a business for 10 months.After Two months, Amit invested Rs. 4000 more than Akhil in the same business. If Akhil and Amit received Rs. 38500 and Rs. 42000 respectively as their profit after 10 months of starting Business, find Amit's investment?
(a)   Rs. 11000   (b)   Rs. 13000
(c)   Rs. 15000   (d)   Rs. 17000

29. If the difference between C.I. and S.I. on a certain sum at 10% interest rate is Rs. 50 for 2 years, then find Half of the sum.
(a)   2500   (b)   5000
(c)   250   (d)   7500

30. A sum amounts to Rs. 1210 in 2 years when invested at compound interest. If principal is Rs. 1000, then what is the rate of interest (in %)?
(a)   10   (b)   20
(c)   15   (d)   12

31. The area of a rectangle is 460 square metres. If the length is 15% more than the breadth, then what is the breadth of the rectangular field?
(a)   23 meters   (b)   20 meters
(c)   18 meters   (d)   21 meters

32. By melting a solid cone a sphere is made having a volume of $1047.816 m^3$ if the radius of the cone and sphere are equal then the height of the cone in m is:
(a) $25.2 m$ (b) $32.5 m$
(c) $35.2 m$ (d) $22.5 m$

33. Find the sum of a unit and tenth digit of 7^{181} .
(a)   3   (b)   9
(c)   7   (d)   1

34. The average age of 6 students is 11 years. If two more students of ages 14 and 16 years join. What will their now average age?
(a)   11   (b)   12
(c)   13   (d)   14

35. The marks of 5 students are 25, 35, 45, 50, 15 . Calculate the average marks.
(a)   30   (b)   34
(c)   35   (d)   32

36. If 30% of $C = 25\%$ of A and $2d\%$ of $C = A$, find the value of d ?

(a) 60   (b) 45
(c) 40   (d) 20

37. P, Q and R together can complete a work in 20 days. P alone can complete the work in 40 days; Q alone in 60 days then in how many days R alone can complete the work?

(a) 60   (b) 80
(c) 40   (d) 120

38. T alone can complete the work in 12 days. T and U together worked on a piece of work and completed one-third work in 3 days. In how many days can U alone complete the same piece of work?

(a) 36 days   (b) 40 days
(c) 25 days   (d) 30 days

39. 100 workers can make a bridge in 150 days. When 20% bridge was completed 25% workers left the job, find the number of days in which remaining work will be completed by remaining workers. (All workers have the same efficiency)

(a) 100 days   (b) 130 days
(c) 160 days   (d) 250 days

40. A man goes to a place at a speed of 70 km/hr and comes back with a different speed. If the average speed is 17.5 km/hr, then what is the return speed (in km/hr)?

(a) 12   (b) 52.5
(c) 10   (d) 20

41. From two places, 60 km apart, A and B start towards each other at the same time and meet each other after 6 hour. If A traveled with $\frac{2}{3}$ of his speed and B traveled with double of his speed, they would have met after 5 hours. The speed of A is:

(a) 4 km/h   (b) 6 km/h
(c) 10 km/h   (d) 12 km/h

42. Find HCF of 726 and 462 .

(a) 66   (b) 67
(c) 68   (d) 69

43. The ages of Vijender and Rishi are in the ratio 11 : 13. After 7 years, the respective ratio of their ages will be 20 : 23. What is the difference between their ages?

(a) 10 years   (b) 8 years
(c) 6 years   (d) 4 years

44. If both p and q belong to the set {1, 2, 3, 4}, then how many equations of the form $px^2 + qx + 1 = 0$ will have real roots?

(a) 12   (b) 10
(c) 7   (d) 6

45. If the centroid of a triangle formed by (4,x), (y,-5) and (7, 8) is (3, 5), then the values of x and y are respectively.

(a) 2, 12   (b) -12, 13
(c) 12, -2   (d) 13, -2

46. Find the value of $\sin(45° + x) + \sin(45° - x)$.

(a) $\sqrt{3}\cos x$ (b) $\sqrt{3}\sin x$
(c) $\sqrt{2}\cos x$ (d) $\sqrt{3}\cot x$

47. In what number of ways can the letters of the word 'ABLE' be arranged so that the vowels occupy even places?

(a) 2   (b) 4
(c) 6   (d) 8

48. There are 10 people seated in two rows (5 in 1 row) and there are two types of food items. Each row can be served any of the two food items but it must be different from the other row. In how many ways the food can be served?

(a) 6453300   (b) 2441200
(c) 7257600   (d) 6265800

Ques (49-50): Direction: Read the given information carefully and answer the following questions.

The given Tabulation represents the total number of visitors to the Exhibition on weekdays is 12500.

Days	Percentage of visitors
Monday	25%
Tuesday	24%
Wednesday	15%
Thursday	17%
Friday	19%

The table represents the ratio of the number of male to female visitors.

Days	Male : Female
Monday	13 : 12
Tuesday	7 : 5
Wednesday	2 : 1
Thursday	11 : 6
Friday	11 : 8

49. Find the average number of female visitors.

(a) 5500   (b) 1050
(c) 5250   (d) 1025

50. Find the ratio of male visitors on Friday to the female visitors on Monday.

(a) 13 : 12   (b) 12 : 11
(c) 13 : 11   (d) 11 : 12

Reasoning

51. **Direction:** In the following question, select the related number from the given alternatives.

13 : 184 :: 17 : ?

(a) 306   (b) 304
(c) 289   (d) 316

52. In the following question, select the related letter pair from the given alternatives.

DIRECTOR : IDERTCRO :: ? : ?

(a) FAMOUS : OUSFAM

(b) LEMON : ELNOM

(c) CAPACITY : ACAPICYT

(d) HEROIC : EHROCI

Ques (53-54): Direction : Read the following information carefully and answer the question that follows.

There are seven family members – P, Q, R, S, T, U, and V. R is the maternal grandmother of V. Q is the husband of R. S is the brother-in-law of Q. P is the nephew of S. T is the mother of V. U is the son-in-law of Q. There are four males in the family.

53. How is P related to Q?

(a) Daughter   (b) Son
(c) Nephew   (d) Son-in-law

54. Which of the following T's father?
(a) S   (b) R
(c) Q   (d) P

55. **Direction** : Choose the figure which is different.

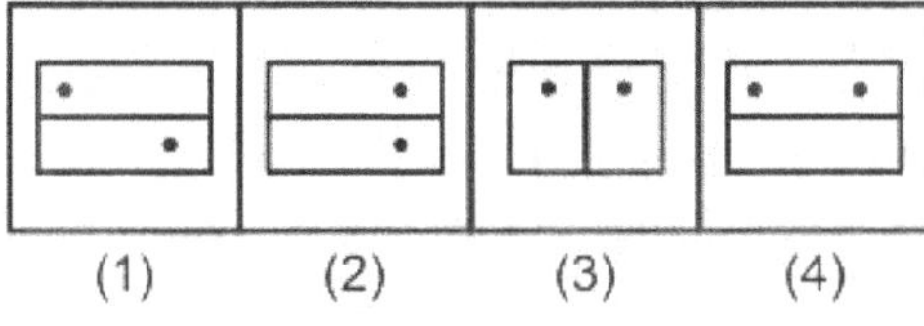

(1)   (2)   (3)   (4)

(a) 1   (b) 2
(c) 3   (d) 4

56. **Direction** : In the question, out of four figures marked 1, 2, 3, and 4, three are similar in a certain manner. However, one figure is not like the other three. Choose the figure that is different from the rest.

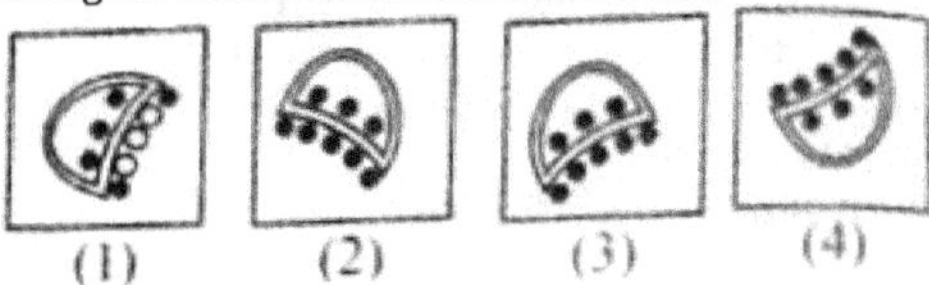

(1)   (2)   (3)   (4)

(a) 3   (b) 4
(c) 1   (d) 2

57. **Direction** : In the question, out of four figures marked, 1, 2, 3, and 4, three are similar in a certain manner. However, one figure is not like the other three. Choose the figure that is different from the rest.

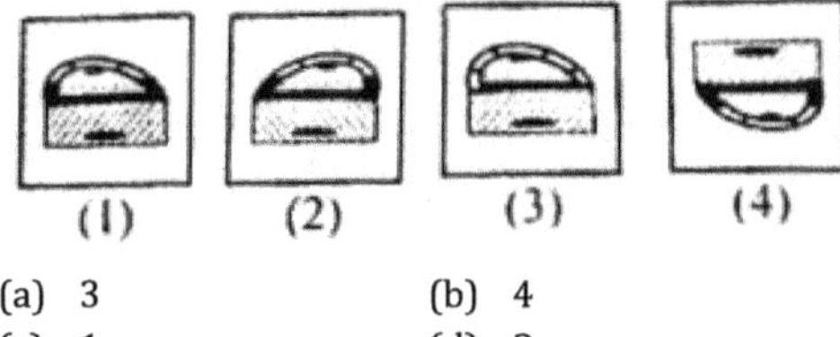

(1)   (2)   (3)   (4)

(a) 3   (b) 4
(c) 1   (d) 2

58. Kamini walks 30 m toward south from her home. Then she turns left and walks 40 m. She again turns left and walks 60 m to reach a book store. What is the shortest distance between her home and the book store?
(a) 50 m   (b) 60 m
(c) 40 m   (d) 80 m

59. Sameer walks 50 meters facing north and then turns anticlockwise by 270° and walks further for 50 meters. Then he turns clockwise by 45° and walks another 50 meters. Which direction is he facing now?
(a) North-East   (b) North-West
(c) South-East   (d) South-West

60. In a certain code language if BLOCK is written as 43, what will be code of HOUSE in same language?
(a) 68   (b) 61
(c) 67   (d) 63

61. In a certain code language if ELEPHANT is written as LEPEAHTN, what will be code of QUESTION in same language?
(a) UQSEITNO   (b) SEUQNOTI
(c) UQESTINO   (d) EUQITSON

62. The five unknown figures in the picture form a chain. Which of the options will be sixth in the series?

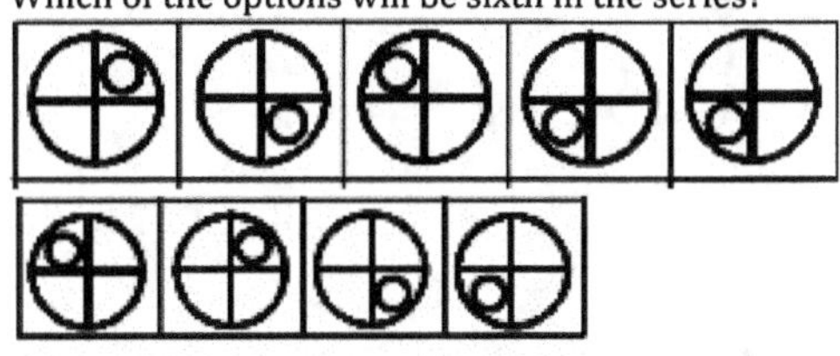

A   B   C   D
(a) A   (b) B
(c) C   (d) D

63. **Direction:** Fill in the blank box.

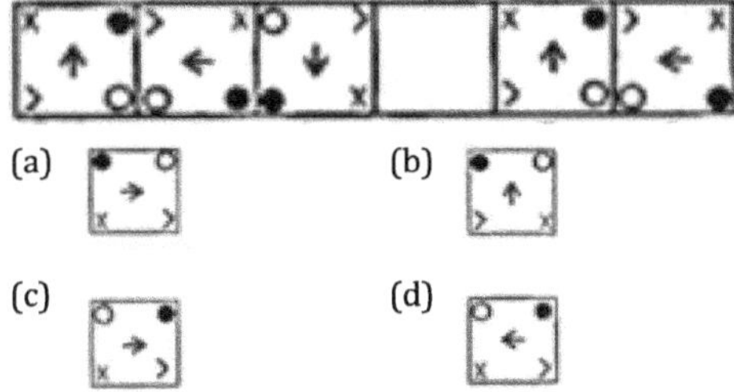

(a)   (b)

(c)   (d)

Ques (64-65): Direction: Identify the diagram that best represents the relationship among classes given below:

64. Sentence, Word, Number

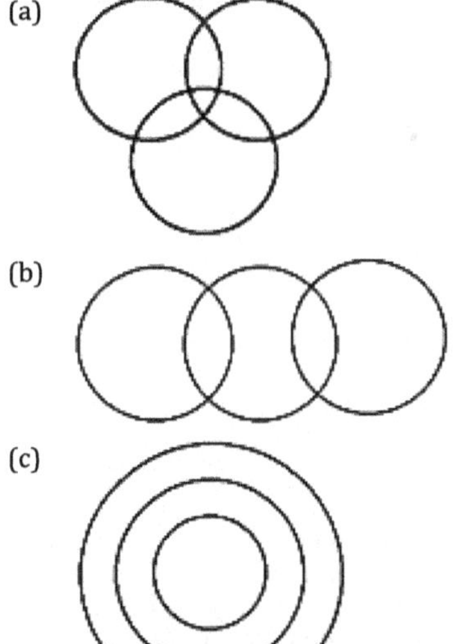

(a)

(b)

(c)

(d)

65. Water, Atmosphere and Hydrogen

(a)

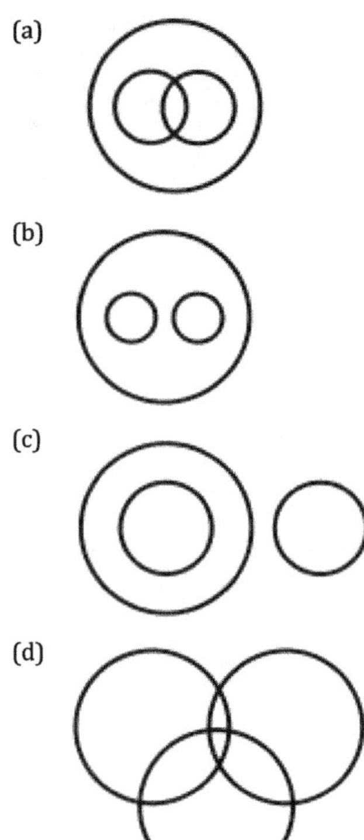

(b)

(c)

(d)

Ques (66-67): What number will come in place of the question mark (?) in the given series?

66. 0, 6, 24, 60, 120, 210, ?
    - (a) 336
    - (b) 633
    - (c) 300
    - (d) 436

67. 1, 24, 58, 125, 247, 446, ?
    - (a) 77
    - (b) 747
    - (c) 744
    - (d) 777

68. N and L are 22nd from the right and left respectively. M sits 13th from the right of N. If M and L have 4 seats in between them, how many seats are there in total?
    - (a) 20
    - (b) 24
    - (c) 25
    - (d) 27

69. 40 girl students are in a row and they are facing north. Kailash is sixth to the left of Sonam. If Sonam is 30th from the left end of the row, then what is the position of Kailash from the right end of the row?
    - (a) 17th
    - (b) 16th
    - (c) 15th
    - (d) 27th

Ques (70-71): Direction: In the following question below some statements are given followed by some conclusions. Taking the given statements to be true even if they seem to be at variance from commonly known facts, read all the conclusions and then decide which of the given conclusions logically follows the given statements.

70. **Statements:**
    I. Some tables are large.
    II. No large is blue.
    Conclusions:
    I. All large are tables.
    II. Some blue are large.
    - (a) Only conclusion I follows.
    - (b) Only conclusion II follows.
    - (c) Both conclusion follows.
    - (d) Neither conclusion I nor conclusion II follows.

71. **Statements:**
    Some tigers are rats.
    All rats are elephants.
    All tigers are cats.
    Conclusions:
    I. Some cats are elephants.
    II. Some elephants are tigers.
    III. Some cats are rats.
    - (a) Only conclusions II and III follows.
    - (b) All conclusions I, II and III follows.
    - (c) Only conclusions I and II follows.
    - (d) Only conclusions I and III follows.

Ques (72-73): Direction: This question is based on the information given below:
Four ladies A, B, C, D and four gentlemen E, F, G, H are sitting in a circle round a table facing each other under the following arrangement:
(i) No two ladies or two gentlemen are sitting side by side.
(ii) C, who is sitting between G and E, is facing D.
(iii) F is between D and A and is facing G.
(iv) H is to the right of B.

72. Who is sitting to the left of A?
    - (a) E
    - (b) F
    - (c) G
    - (d) H

73. E is facing whom?
    - (a) F
    - (b) B
    - (c) G
    - (d) H

74. Select the letter which is different from the others.
    - (a) FIL
    - (b) RUX
    - (c) ILO
    - (d) LOQ

75. Select the set in which the numbers are related in the same way, as the numbers of the following set.
    (9, 6, 27)
    - (a) (7, 5, 13)
    - (b) (3, 2, 21)
    - (c) (8, 6, 18)
    - (d) (6, 4, 16)

General Hindi

76. वर्तनी की दृष्टि से सही शब्द का चयन कीजिए:
    - (a) आक्रषण
    - (b) आकर्षण
    - (c) आर्कषण
    - (d) आर्कशण

77. वर्तनी की दृष्टि से सही शब्द का चयन कीजिए:
    - (a) विशेस
    - (b) विसेश
    - (c) विषेश
    - (d) विशेष

78. निम्नलिखित मुहावरे के सही अर्थ का चयन करें।
    'आये थे हरि भजन को ओटन लगे कपास'
    - (a) हरि भक्ति का मार्ग कठिन होता है
    - (b) उद्देश्य की प्राप्ति में असफल होना
    - (c) किसी कार्य विशेष की उपेक्षा कर किसी अन्य कार्य में लग जाना
    - (d) ईश्वर भक्ति करना

79. "दाल में काला होना" मुहावरे का अर्थ है:
    - (a) गड़बड़ होना
    - (b) काली दाल
    - (c) कल की दाल
    - (d) दाल में कंकड़

80. दिए गए वाक्य में सही मुहावरा भरें-

शत्रुओं से लड़ने के लिए भारतीयों को ______ तैयार हो जाना चाहिए।

(a) कपड़े पहनकर (b) नाक मारकर

(c) कमर कसकर (d) सुबह - सुबह

81. 'महोदय' शब्द का स्त्रीलिंग दिये गए विकल्पों में से कौन सा है?

(a) महोदयी (b) महोदया

(c) महोदाया (d) महोदय

82. इनमें से पुल्लिंग शब्द कौन-सा है?

(a) दया (b) निर्धनता

(c) बुढ़ापा (d) दुर्घटना

83. जो मुश्किल से प्राप्त हो, उसे कहते हैं:

(a) अलभ्य (b) सुलभ

(c) दुर्लभ (d) अलंघ्य

84. अवसर के अनुरूप बदल जाने वाले को कहते हैं:

(a) यथास्थितिवादी (b) आदर्शवादी

(c) भाववादी (d) अवसरवादी

85. संबंध कारक के लिए प्रयुक्त होने वाला चिन्ह है?

(a) में (b) के लिए

(c) रा (d) पर

86. पुरूषवाचक सर्वनाम से संबंधित नहीं है:

(a) मैं (b) हम

(c) कोई (d) तू

87. संज्ञा या सर्वनाम के जिस रुप से किसी अन्य शब्द के साथ संबंध या लगाव प्रतीत हो उसे कहते हैं:

(a) अपादान कारक (b) कर्म कारक

(c) करण कारक (d) संबंध कारक

88. उर्दू शब्द 'सौदा' का बहुवचन में क्या रूप होता है?

(a) उसका रूप परिवर्तित हो जाता है।

(b) उसके रूप में कोई परिवर्तन नहीं होता है।

(c) बहुवचन में उसके विकल्प का प्रयोग किया जाता है।

(d) उसके अन्त में 'गर' लगा देते हैं।

89. हिन्दी में 'मैं' का बहुवचन है-

(a) हम (b) हम दोनों

(c) हम सब (d) हम लोग

90. निम्नलिखित प्रश्न में, चार विकल्पों में से, उस सही विकल्प का चयन करें जो शुद्ध वाक्य का सबसे अच्छा विकल्प है।

(a) दो लड़के इधर आ रहे हैं।

(b) दो लड़का उधर आ रहे हैं।

(c) दो लड़के इधर आ रहे है।

(d) दो लड़का इधर आ रहा है।

91. निम्नलिखित प्रश्न में, चार विकल्पों में से, उस सही विकल्प का चयन करें जो शुद्ध वाक्य का सबसे अच्छा विकल्प है।

(a) हम आप से कहा था। (b) हमने आपसे कहो था।

(c) हमने आपसे कहा था। (d) हम आप से कहे थे।

92. 'चिरंतन' का विलोम शब्द है:

(a) अंत (b) आदि

(c) निरंतन (d) नश्वर

93. 'ठोस' का विलोम शब्द है:

(a) सघन (b) तरल

(c) घन (d) निर्धन

94. 'तलवार' का पर्यायवाची है:

(a) तूणीर (b) तीर

(c) चंद्रहास (d) वाण

95. इनमें से 'कोदण्ड' का पर्यायवाची कौन-सा है?

(a) भाला (b) तलवार

(c) फावड़ा (d) धनुष

96. 'अंतर्धान' शब्द का सही संधि - विच्छेद होगा:

(a) अंतर्ध + यान (b) अंतः + यान

(c) अंतः + ध्यान (d) अंतर + ध्यान

97. 'निरीह' का संधि विच्छेद इनमें से क्या है?

(a) निर + ईह (b) निः + रीह

(c) निः + ईह (d) निरि + ईह

98. कौन-सा विग्रह यण संधि' का नहीं है?

(a) राका + ईश (b) अति + उत्तम

(c) अनु + ईक्षण (d) यदि + अपि

99. इनमे से कौन सी कविता हरिवंश राय बच्चन की है?

(a) उर्मिला (b) कवासी

(c) मधुशाला (d) महाप्राण

100. 'भक्तमाल' कृति के रचनाकार है:

(a) अग्रदास (b) नाभादास

(c) नन्ददास (d) रसखान

// Smart Answer Sheet //

Correct — Percentage of students who answered correctly.

Skipped — Percentage of students who skipped.

Q.	Ans.	Correct / Skipped	Q.	Ans.	Correct / Skipped	Q.	Ans.	Correct / Skipped
1	C	51.55% / 1.13%	2	C	19.67% / 4.17%	3	B	68.15% / 1.19%
4	C	46.97% / 1.28%	5	C	55.54% / 1.93%	6	D	54.78% / 1.26%
7	C	40.13% / 1.06%	8	D	14.8% / 3.26%	9	C	28.82% / 4.24%
10	A	42.8% / 1.49%	11	B	53.91% / 1.68%	12	B	61.96% / 1.31%
13	D	48.31% / 1.97%	14	D	51.77% / 1.85%	15	C	40.32% / 1.21%
16	C	47.45% / 1.33%	17	A	45.88% / 1.33%	18	B	66.41% / 1.09%
19	A	85.91% / 0.0%	20	A	56.9% / 1.43%	21	D	58.22% / 1.85%
22	A	64.01% / 1.52%	23	A	51.58% / 1.97%	24	B	59.34% / 1.82%
25	C	25.36% / 3.75%	26	A	88.33% / 0.0%	27	D	53.5% / 1.32%
28	C	58.46% / 1.5%	29	A	82.36% / 0.0%	30	A	12.24% / 4.21%
31	B	41.66% / 1.95%	32	A	10.29% / 3.8%	33	C	80.62% / 0.0%
34	B	11.22% / 3.34%	35	B	88.75% / 0.0%	36	A	23.08% / 3.05%
37	D	49.65% / 1.04%	38	A	42.72% / 1.12%	39	C	51.56% / 1.72%
40	C	26.11% / 3.66%	41	B	28.23% / 4.5%	42	A	42.94% / 1.29%
43	C	40.52% / 1.02%	44	C	31.87% / 4.1%	45	C	87.17% / 0.0%
46	C	82.69% / 0.0%	47	B	47.47% / 1.93%	48	C	28.93% / 4.08%
49	D	45.53% / 1.7%	50	D	53.06% / 1.77%	51	B	76.77% / 0.0%

Q	Ans	%	Q	Ans	%	Q	Ans	%
52	C	42.31% / 1.64%	53	B	52.91% / 1.07%	54	C	19.68% / 3.99%
55	D	65.81% / 1.69%	56	C	50.5% / 1.21%	57	A	20.56% / 3.27%
58	A	17.16% / 3.98%	59	C	50.8% / 1.99%	60	A	69.72% / 1.05%
61	A	58.11% / 1.0%	62	A	82.86% / 0.0%	63	A	42.91% / 1.44%
64	D	67.29% / 1.13%	65	D	47.89% / 1.94%	66	A	61.32% / 1.82%
67	C	22.56% / 3.95%	68	C	82.98% / 0.0%	69	A	88.51% / 0.0%
70	D	60.57% / 1.12%	71	B	58.86% / 1.54%	72	B	89.15% / 0.0%
73	D	67.25% / 1.54%	74	D	53.3% / 1.25%	75	C	47.46% / 1.94%
76	B	85.25% / 0.0%	77	D	84.04% / 0.0%	78	C	54.83% / 1.58%
79	A	76.44% / 0.0%	80	C	85.68% / 0.0%	81	B	89.96% / 0.0%
82	C	79.65% / 0.0%	83	C	84.14% / 0.0%	84	D	88.96% / 0.0%
85	C	86.61% / 0.0%	86	C	56.19% / 1.08%	87	D	48.72% / 1.83%
88	B	47.14% / 1.97%	89	A	78.95% / 0.0%	90	A	50.45% / 1.09%
91	C	45.06% / 1.63%	92	D	76.0% / 0.0%	93	B	88.77% / 0.0%
94	C	83.31% / 0.0%	95	D	17.82% / 3.61%	96	C	58.99% / 1.07%
97	C	56.68% / 1.12%	98	A	65.28% / 1.3%	99	C	51.36% / 1.13%
100	B	56.01% / 1.48%						

// Hints and Solutions //

1(C). Chandimangala is a type of Mangalkavaya which was written in the 16-century and is an important asset of Bengali Literature .

- Chandimangal of Kavikankan Mukundaram Chakravarti is an epic work recounting the stories of Goddess Chandi.
- The book describes her constant battle to establish herself as a cult among human beings.
- The three books of Kavya try to establish the various manifestations of Goddess Chandi .
- The literary tradition is folk and is practiced even today among the rural women through pre-Aryan rituals .
- These include Panchalis - a long drawn narrative celebrating the glory of the deity, and Vratha Katha - includes chanting of rhymes on the performance of a vow.

2(C). The correct answer is Arthashastra.

The Arthashastra is an old Indian discourse on statecraft, economic policy, and military strategy, written in Sanskrit. It is one of the sources to learn about the history of the Mauryan Period.

- It had a wide influence on Sanskrit literature.
- Kautilya, also recognized as Vishnugupta and Chanakya, is traditionally credited as the author of the text.
- Arthashastra entails the science (sastra) of wealth/earth/polity (artha). 'Artha' however is a bit wider and an all-embracing term with different meanings.
  - In a simple way, 'Arthashastra' can be explained as ' science and art of politics and diplomacy .
- This treatise is divided into sixteen books dealing with virtually every topic concerned with the running of a state, taxation, law, diplomacy, military strategy, economics, bureaucracy, etc.
- The book is a masterwork that includes an array of topics like statecraft, politics, strategy, selection, and training of employees, leadership skills, legal systems, accounting systems, taxation, fiscal policies, civil rules, internal and foreign trade, etc .
- Arthashastra backs rational ethics to the conduct of the affairs of the state.
- The emphasis is on the systematization of law and uniformity of law throughout the empire.

Thus, it is clear that Chandragupta's advisor, Kautilya became very famous for his great text Arthashastra.

3(B). The correct answer is Mahmud of Ghazni.

Mahmud of Ghazni

- The first invasion of India by Mahmud of Ghazni took place in 1001 AD .
- Mahmud of Ghazni also known as Yamin ad-Dawlah Mahmud was the ruler of the Ghaznavid Empire from 997 C.E. until his death.
- Mahmud turned the former provincial city of Ghazni into the wealthy capital of an extensive empire which included modern-day Afghanistan, Pakistan, most of Iran and parts of northwest India.
- He was also the first ruler to carry the title Sultan.
- He is remembered as a hero of Islam by some, as a defiler of Hindu, Jain and Buddhist shrines by others.
- By establishing Muslim rule over a substantial part of the Indian Sub-continent, he permanently changed the nature of sub-continental politics, religion, and culture.

4(C). The correct answer is Jotedars gave out loans to other ryots and sold their produce.

Power rule in the late 1700s in Bengal .

- During the 1700s, the Zamindars were facing a major crisis, a class of rich peasants called the jotedars consolidated their power and position in the villages.
- They were most active in the regions of the NOrthern Bengal. They were also called gantidars or mandals.
- By the early 19th century, the jotedars had acquired vast areas of land. When the estates of the zamindars were auctioned because of their failure to pay taxes, jotedars were mostly the purchasers. Thus they emerged as the commanding figures in Northern Bengal.
- They controlled local trade and moneylending, thus exercising huge power and authority over the poorer cultivators. They mostly practised sharecropping.
- Their land was leased to sharecroppers who brought their own equipment, worked in the field, and handed over half the produce to the jotedars after the harvest. Thus they are able to control the peasants.
- The jotedars were housed in the villages themselves and had direct control over the villagers. They resisted the efforts of zamindars to increase the JAMA of the village, prevented zamindari officials from performing their duties.

5(C). During the civil disobedience movement, there was a non-violent movement of Pathans under the leadership of Abdul Ghaffar Khan of Utmanzai, a village near Peshawar. Ghaffar Khan was called as Frontier Gandhi because of his popularity.

6(D). The convention was presided over by Pandit Madan Mahan Malaviya. The Hindu Mahasabha was founded in Haridwar in 1915 by Malaviyaji and some Punjabi leaders.

7(C). With reference to the longitude of Mirzapur India Standard Time is determined.
The longitude passing through Royal Observatory Greenwich meridian is used as the standard time all over the world. Greenwich Mean Time in London is used as the standard time for all over the world as it has the standard meridian passing over it at 0°.
The 82°30' East longitude is taken as the Standard Time Meridian of India, as it passes through the middle of India (Mirzapur in Uttar Pradesh).

8(D). The layer in the earth's atmosphere which reflects radio waves from the earth thus, helping radio communication is Ionosphere.
It is a region where the air is electrically charged as the radiations from the sun knock off electrons from it. It plays an important role in the electricity of the atmosphere and forms the magnetosphere's inner edge.

9(C). In general, as we move from the equator to the poles, the rainfall continues to decrease. The world's coastal regions receive a greater amount of rainfall than the interior parts of the continents. Being great sources of water, the oceans receive more rainfall than the continents. Between the latitudes of 35° and 40° in the north and south of the Mediterranean Risa, there is a greater amount of rainfall on the eastern coasts, which is less when moving west. She goes. But, due to the west winds, between the latitudes of 45° and 65° north and south of the equator, rainfall first occurs in the western part of the continents, which is east. When going towards, it keeps decreasing at least.

10(A). Senior Indian Information Service officer Dr. Vasudha Gupta has been appointed as the Director General of the News Services Division of All India Radio. She has succeeded N Venudhar Reddy, who superannuated on 31 August 2022. Before her appointment, she was serving as Director General, Press Information Bureau (PIB). She is credited for establishing of Fact-Check system for the Government.

11(B). North Korea has designed the drone 'Haeil'. It can create massive radioactive waves through submarine explosions.

12(B). The New Zealand government on 14 Feb 2023, declared a national state of emergency after Cyclone Gabrielle lashed the North Island.

13(D). Qatar lifted its temporary ban on the import of frozen seafood from India. The ban was imposed in November 2022, just ahead of the FIFA World Cup following alleged detection of Vibrio cholera from a few consignments from India.

14(D). Electric Power: The rate at which electrical energy is dissipated into other forms of energy is called electrical power i.e.,

$$P = \frac{W}{t} = VI = I^2R = \frac{V^2}{R}$$

Where V = Potential difference, R = Resistance and I = current

From above equation it is clear that all options are correct.
Hence, the correct option is (D)

15(C). Phreatophytes are the deep-rooted plants to obtain water from deep inside the ground.
They are named so because they are derived water from the phreatic zone below the water table.
Extension of roots is an adaptation through which the desert plants are able to obtain water even in dry climatic conditions.
Masquet, Saltmarsh and Greasewood are examples of sub-soil plants.
Another type of adaptation in desert plants is the transformation of leaves into thorns.
The surface area of thorns is less than that of leaves, so the evaporation is less and they are able to retain more.

16(C). The Olive Ridley sea turtle is found in warm and tropical waters all over the world, including the Indian Ocean and the Bay of Bengal.

17(A). Union Ministry of HRD has decided to take forward the Ek Bharat Shreshtha Bharat (EBSB) programme by using innovative ways in view of the prevailing conditions of COVID 19.
Objectives to promote engagement and thereby understanding amongst the people of different states/UTs to ensure a stronger united India. Therefore statement 1 is correct.
The Ministry of Human Resource Development has been designated Nodal Ministry for coordination of the programme. Therefore statement 2 is not correct.

18(B).

List 1	List 2
A. 93rd A mendment	3. Reservation for OBCs in unaided e ducational institutions
B. 97th A mendment	4. New cooperative Act
C. 24th A mendment	1. Parliament's power to amend Fun damental Rights
D. 26th A mendment	2. Abolition of special privileges of Pr incely states, titles, and pensions

19(A). The President is elected not directly by the people but by members of the electoral college consisting of:
The elected members of both the Houses of Parliament; Therefore statement 1 is correct.
The elected members of the legislative assemblies of the states; and Therefore statement 2 is correct.
The elected members of the legislative assemblies of the Union Territories of Delhi and Puducherry. Thus, the nominated members of both Houses of Parliament, the nominated members of the state legislative assemblies, the members (both elected and nominated) of the state legislative councils (in case of the bicameral legislature) and the nominated members of the Legislative Assemblies of Delhi and Puducherry do not participate in the election of the President. Therefore statement 3 is incorrect.

20(A). In Odisha, c entral government has decided to install 4,000 telecom towers in 2022 to ensure that villages get access to internet connectivity. An allocation of ₹9,734 crores has been made for Odisha for the 2022-23 fiscal. 6,000 villages in the State remain out of mobile network Therefore, it has been decided to install 3,933 mobile towers.

21(D). Five-Year Plans are centralized and integrated national economic programs.

The First Five-year Plan(1951–1956) was launched in 1951. It was mainly focused on community development, which include development of the primary sector such as agriculture, fishing, forestry, mining, etc.

The second five year plan(1956–1961) was mainly focused on rapid industrialisation. It had long-term economic growth and hence patronised the development of basic and heavy industries.

The third five year plan(1961–1966) was mainly focused on expansion of basic industries. The basic strategy was the development of public sector and heavy industries so as to attain a self sustaining growth.

Achievement of self-reliance and growth with stability and a focus on agriculture's growth rate were the objectives of the fourth five-year plan (1969–1974).

The Minimum Needs Programme was introduced in the first year of the Fifth Five Year Plan(1974–78), to provide certain basic minimum needs and improve the living standards of people.

22(A). The strategy adopted under I.R.D.P. in the Seventh Plan was adoption of total household approach.

In view of the deficiencies noticed in the implementation of the Integrated Rural Development Programme (IRDP), it has been suggested that greater priority should be assigned to rural employment programmes by shifting resources away from IRDP. However, the experience of the working of poverty alleviation programmes is by no means uniform in the country. In general, the performance of IRDP has been better in the relatively developed regions which are well provided with infrastructure and where level of awareness among the beneficiaries is high.

23(A). The central ice hockey team of the Indo-Tibetan Border Police (ITBP) won the 12th edition of the National Ice Hockey Championship for men 2023 organized in Leh, Ladakh for the third time in a row. ITBP team defeated Ladakh Scouts 1-0 in the final match.

24(B). SWAMITVA Scheme:
- Union Budget 2021: SWAMITVA Scheme to be extended to all States/UTs, 1.80 lakh property-owners in 1,241 villages have already been provided cards
- SVAMITVA Scheme is a Central Sector scheme launched by Hon'ble Prime Minister of India on National Panchayat Day i.e 24th April 2020.
- The Ministry of Panchayati Raj (MoPR) is the Nodal Ministry for the implementation of the scheme. So, statement 1 is incorrect.
- In the States, the Revenue Department / Land Records Department will be the Nodal Department and shall carry out the scheme with the support of the State Panchayati Raj Department. Survey of India shall work as the technology partner for implementation.
- The scheme will help in streamlining planning and revenue collection in rural areas and ensuring clarity on property rights. Hence, statement 2 is correct.
- It is a scheme for mapping the land parcels in rural inhabited areas using drone technology and a Continuously Operating Reference Station (CORS).
- The scheme will enable the creation of better-quality Gram Panchayat Development Plans (GPDPs), using the maps created under this program. So, statement 3 is correct.

25(C). In April 2023, the Indian Space Research Organisation successfully completed two significant tests- Vikas Engine Test Campaign for the L110 Stage & System Demonstration Model tests for the Crew Module Propulsion System for the Gaganyaan mission in Mahendragiri, Tirunelveli District, Tamil Nadu.

26(A). On substracting 3 kg 178 g from 8 kg 350 g= 8 kg 350 g - 3 kg 178 g = 5 kg 172 g

27(D). Given:

Selling Price = Rs. 882

Discount $= 16\%$

Gain $= 20\%$

Formula Used:

$$\text{Marked price} = \frac{\text{Selling Price}}{\frac{(100-\text{Discount}\%)}{100}}$$

Cost price : Marked price $= (100-$ Discount $\%) : (100+ \text{profit} \%)$

$$\text{Marked price} = \frac{882}{\left[\frac{(100-16)}{100}\right]}$$

$= $ Rs. 1050

According to question,

New Discount $= 0\%$

Cost price : $1050 = (100 - 0) : (100 + 20)$

$$\text{Cost Price} = 1050 \times \frac{100}{120}$$

Cost Price $= 875$

28(C). Let Akhil's investment be Rs. ' x '

Amit's investment = Rs. $(x + 4000)$

Now, ratio of their investments = ratio of their share of profit

$(x \times 10) : [(x + 4000) \times 8] = 38500 : 42000$

$\Rightarrow \dfrac{10x}{(32000+8x)} = \dfrac{11}{12}$

$\Rightarrow 120x = 352000 + 88x$

$\Rightarrow 32x = 352000$

$\Rightarrow x = $ Rs. 11000

$\therefore$ Amit's investment $= 4000 + 11000 = Rs.\,15000$

29(A). Given:

The difference between S.I. and C.I. at 10% interest rate is Rs. 50

According to the question,

We know that,

$$\text{C.I.} - \text{S.I.} = P \times \left(\frac{R}{100}\right)^2$$

$\Rightarrow P \times \left(\frac{10}{100}\right)^2 = $ Rs. 50

$\Rightarrow P \times \left(\frac{1}{10}\right)^2 = $ Rs. 50

$\Rightarrow P \times \left(\frac{1}{100}\right) = $ Rs. 50

$\Rightarrow P = $ Rs. 5000

Now, half of the sum,

$\Rightarrow \dfrac{5000}{2} = 2500$

$\therefore$ Half of the sum is Rs. 2500 .

30(A). We know that,

$$C = P\left[\left(\frac{1+r}{100}\right)^n - 1\right]$$

$S = P + C$
Where
C = compound interest
P = Principal
r = rate
n = number of period
S = sum after n periods
In 2 years,
$P = 1000$
$S = 1210$
$\Rightarrow P + C = 1210$
$\Rightarrow 1000 + C = 1210$
$\Rightarrow P\left[(\frac{1+r}{100})^n - 1\right] = 210$
$\Rightarrow 1000 \times \left[(\frac{1+r}{100})^2 - 1\right] = 210$
$\Rightarrow (\frac{1+r}{100})^2 - 1 = 0.21$
$\Rightarrow (\frac{1+r}{100})^2 = 1.21$
$\Rightarrow \frac{r}{100} = (1.21)^{\frac{1}{2}} - 1 = 1.1 - 1 = 0.1$
$\Rightarrow r = 10\%$

31(B). Have given,
The area of a rectangle is 460 square metres.
Let the width = x meter
Then the length = $\frac{115x}{100}$ m
$= x \times \frac{115x}{100} = 460$
$\Rightarrow x^2 = \frac{(460 \times 100)}{115}$
$\Rightarrow x^2 = 400$
$\Rightarrow x = 20$ m

32(A). Formula used:
The volume of the cone = $\frac{1}{3}\pi r^2 h$
The volume of a sphere = $\frac{4}{3}\pi r^3$
Concept:
When melted,
The volume of a cone = The volume of a sphere
$\Rightarrow 1047.816 = (\frac{4}{3})\pi r^3$
$\Rightarrow 1047.816 = (\frac{88}{21})r^3$
$\Rightarrow r^3 = 1047.816 \times \frac{21}{88}$
$\Rightarrow r^3 = 11.907 \times 21$
$\Rightarrow r^3 = 250.047$
$\Rightarrow r = 6.3m$
The volume of a cone = The volume of a sphere
$\Rightarrow \frac{1}{3}\pi r^2 h = \frac{4}{3}\pi r^3$
$\Rightarrow h = 4r$
$\Rightarrow h = 4 \times 6.3$
$\therefore$ The height of the cone in m is $25.2m$

33(C). Last two digit of 7^n
$7^1 = 07$
$7^2 = 49$
$7^3 = 43$
$7^4 = 01$
$\Rightarrow$ Cyclicity of 7^n is 4
$\Rightarrow 7^{181} = 7^{4 \times 45 + 1} = 7^1 = 07$
$\Rightarrow$ Last two digits of 7^{181} is 07
$\therefore$ Required sum = $0 + 7 = 7$

34(B). Given,
Aerage age of 6 students = 11 years
Average of n numbers = $\frac{\text{sum of total numbers}}{n}$
Total age before new students were added
$= 11 \times 6 = 66$
Total age after new students were added
$= 66 + 14 + 16 = 96$
Let their current average age be x.

Then, according to the question,
$x = \frac{96}{8}$
$\Rightarrow x = 12$
$\therefore$ Their new average age = 12 years

35(B). Given:
Marks of 5 students are $25, 35, 45, 50, 15$.
Average = $\frac{\text{Sum of values}}{\text{Number of values}}$
Average = $\frac{(25+35+45+50+15)}{5}$
Average = $\frac{170}{5}$
Average = 34
$\therefore$ The average marks are 34.

36(A). Given:
30% of C = 25% of A
2 d% of C = A
According to the questions,
$\Rightarrow (\frac{30}{100}) \times C = (\frac{25}{100}) \times A$
$\Rightarrow (\frac{30}{25}) = \frac{A}{C}$
$\Rightarrow \frac{6}{5} = \frac{A}{C}$
According to the questions,
$\Rightarrow$ 2 d% of C = A
$\Rightarrow \frac{2\,d}{100} = \frac{A}{C}$
$\Rightarrow \frac{2\,d}{100} = \frac{6}{5}$
$\Rightarrow 2\,d = (\frac{6}{5}) \times 100$
$\Rightarrow d = 60$
$\therefore$ The value of d is 60.

37(D). Given,
(P+Q+R) can do 1 unit of work in $\frac{1}{20}$ days
P alone can do 1 unit of work in $\frac{1}{40}$ days
Q alone can do 1 unit of work in $\frac{1}{60}$ days
So, R alone can do 1 unit of work in =
$\frac{1}{20} - (\frac{1}{40} + \frac{1}{60})$
$= 120 - \frac{3+2}{120}$
$= \frac{1}{20} - \frac{1}{24}$
$= \frac{6-5}{120}$
$= \frac{1}{120}$
Therefore, R can complete the whole work in 120 days.

38(A). Given,
1 day work of T = $\frac{1}{12}$
Let U alone can complete the work in x days.
1 day work of U = $\frac{1}{x}$
Time taken by T and U to complete one-third work
= 3 days
Time taken by T and U in completing 1 full piece of work = $3 \div (\frac{1}{3})$ days = 9 days
1 day work of T and U working together = $\frac{1}{9}$
$\Rightarrow (\frac{1}{12}) + (\frac{1}{x}) - \frac{1}{9}$
$\Rightarrow \frac{1}{x} = (\frac{1}{9}) - (\frac{1}{12})$
$\Rightarrow x = 36$ days

39(C). Let the work efficiency of each worker be 'x' unit per day
Total work done by 100 workers per day = 100 × x
= 100x units
Total work = 100x × 150 = 15000x units

25% workers left the job after 20% bridge completion

Remaining work = 100% - 20%

$\Rightarrow$ 80% of 15000x = 12000x units

Remaining workers = 75% of 100 = 75

Time taken by 75 workers to complete the remaining work = $\frac{12000x}{75x}$ = 160 days

40(C). If distance of whole journey is same then average speed of journey is $= \frac{2ab}{a+b}$

$a =$ speed $_1$ and $b =$ speed $_2$

Given:

Average speed = 17.5 km/hr

Travelling speed $(a) = 70$ km/hr

Let the return speed be 'b' km/hr.

$\Rightarrow 17.5 = \left[\frac{2 \times 70 \times b}{70+b}\right]$

$\Rightarrow 17.5 \times (70 + b) = 140b$

$\Rightarrow 1225 + 17.5b = 140b$

$\Rightarrow 1225 = 122.5b$

$\Rightarrow b = 10$

$\therefore$ The Return speed is 10 km/hr

41(B). Let the distance between A and B is 60 km and the speed of $A = x$ kmph and that of $B = y$ kmph

According to the question, $x \times 6 + y \times 6 = 60$

or, $x + y = 10$ ......(i)

And, $\left(\frac{2x}{3} \times 5\right) + (2y \times 5) = 60$

or, $10x + 30y = 180$

or, $x + 3y = 18 \ldots$ (ii)

From equation (i) $\times 3$ - (ii)

$3x + 3y - x - 3y = 30 - 18$

or, $2x = 12$

So, $x = 6$ kmph

42(A). Factor of $726 = 2 \times 3 \times 11 \times 11$

Factor of $426 = 2 \times 3 \times 7 \times 11$

So, HCF $(726, 426) = 2 \times 3 \times 11 = 66$

43(C). Let the present ages of Vijender and Rishi be 11x and 13x, respectively.

According to the question:

$\frac{(11x+7)}{(13x+7)} = \frac{20}{23}$

260x + 140 = 253x + 161

260x - 253x = 161 – 140

7x = 21, x = 3

Difference between their ages

= 13x – 11x

= 2x

= 2 × 3 = 6 years

44(C). It is given that,

Both p and q belong to the set {1, 2, 3, 4} and the quadratic equation of the form, px^2 + qx + 1 = 0 has real roots.

By comparing the quadratic equation of the form, px^2 + qx + 1 = 0 with the standard quadratic equation ax^2 + bx + c = 0. We get, a = p, b = q and c = 1.

Now, we know that.

Discriminant (D) = b^2 - 4ac

Therefore, according to the question,

D = q^2 - 4p

$\because$ The roots are real.

$\Rightarrow$ D $\geq$ 0 $\Rightarrow$ q^2 - 4p $\geq$ 0

$\Rightarrow$ q$^2 \geq$ 4p

$\because$ p and q belong to the set {1, 2, 3, 4}

Case -1:

If p = 1 then q$^2 \geq$ 4 $\Rightarrow$ q $\in$ {2, 3, 4}

Hence, for p = 1, q can take 3 values.

So, three quadratic equation of the form, px^2 + qx + 1 = 0 can be formed for p = 1.

Case -2:

If p = 2 then q$^2 \geq$ 8 $\Rightarrow$ q $\in$ {3, 4}

Hence, for p = 2, q can take 2 values

So, two quadratic equation of the form, px^2 + qx + 1 = 0 can be formed for p = 2.

Case -3:

If p = 3 then q$^2 \geq$ 12 $\Rightarrow$ q $\in$ {4}

Hence, for p =1, q can take 1 value

So, only one quadratic equation of the form, px^2 + qx + 1 = 0 can be formed for p = 3.

Case -4:

If p = 4 then q$^2 \geq$ 16 $\Rightarrow$ q $\in$ {4}

Hence, for p =4 , q can take 1 value

So, only one quadratic equation of the form, px^2 + qx + 1 = 0 can be formed for p = 4.

So, in total we get, 3 + 2 + 1 + 1 = 7 possible quadratic equations of the form px^2 + qx + 1 = 0 that can be formed such that both p and q belong to the set {1, 2, 3, 4} and have real roots.

45(C). Here, vertices of triangle (4,x), (y,-5) and (7, 8) and Centroid = (3, 5)

So, $3 = \frac{4+y+7}{3}$

$\Rightarrow$ 11 + y = 9

$\Rightarrow$ y = -2

And, $5 = \frac{x+5+8}{3}$

$\Rightarrow$ x + 3 = 15

$\Rightarrow$ x = 12

$\therefore$ x = 12, and y = -2

46(C). As we know,

$\sin(X + Y) = \sin X \cos Y + \cos X \sin Y$

$\sin(X - Y) = \sin X \cos Y - \cos X \sin Y$

$\sin 45° = \frac{1}{\sqrt{2}}$

Now,

$\sin(45° + x) + \sin(45° - x) = \sin 45° \cos x + \cos 45° \sin x + \sin 45° \cos x - \cos 45° \sin x$

$= 2 \sin 45° \cos x$

$= \sqrt{2} \cos x$

47(B). In word ABLE, there are 2 vowels and 2 consonants.

Total number of letters = 4

Total number of even place = 2

There are 2 vowels to be filled in 2 places.

Hence, the number of ways = $^2C_2$ = 1

The vowels can arrange among themselves in 2! = 2 ways.

Now, the 2 consonants can fill the remaining 2 places in 2! = 2 ways.

Therefore, total number of ways = 1 × 2 × 2 = 4 ways.

48(C). Number of ways 10 people can be seated in a row = $^{10}C_5$ = 252

Number of ways 5 people can be seated in one row = 5!

Number of ways 5 people can be seated in the second row = 5!

Number of ways the people of the rows can be

arranged = 5! × 5!
Number of ways 2 food items can be arranged among 2 rows = 2!
= 2
Total number of ways the food can be served to these people = 252 × 5! × 5! × 2
= 7257600
∴ The people can be served in 7257600 ways.

Ques (49-50):

Days	Percentage of visitors	Number of visitors	Male : Female	Male visitors	Female visitors
Monday	25%	3125	13 : 12	1625	1500
Tuesday	24%	3000	7 : 5	1750	1250
Wednesday	15%	1875	2 : 1	1250	625
Thursday	17%	2125	11 : 6	1375	750
Friday	19%	2375	11 : 8	1375	1000

49(D). The number of visitors on Monday = 25% of 12500
Number of female visitors on Monday = $\frac{12}{25} \times 25\%$ of 12500
$\Rightarrow \frac{12}{25} \times \frac{25}{100} \times 12500 = 1500$
The number of visitors on Tuesday = 24% of 12500
Number of female visitors on Monday = $\frac{5}{12} \times 24\%$ of 12500
$\Rightarrow \frac{6}{13} \times \frac{26}{100} \times 12500 = 1250$
The Number of visitors on Wednesday = 15% of 12500
Number of female visitors on Wednesday = $\frac{1}{3} \times$ 15% of 12500
$\Rightarrow \frac{1}{3} \times \frac{15}{100} \times 12500 = 625$
The number of visitors of on Thursday = 17% of 12500
Number of female visitors on Thursday = $\frac{6}{17} \times$ 17% of 12500
$\Rightarrow \frac{6}{17} \times \frac{17}{100} \times 12500 = 750$
The number of visitors on Friday = 19% of 12500
Number of female visitors on Friday = $\frac{8}{19} \times$ 19% of 12500
$\Rightarrow \frac{8}{19} \times \frac{19}{100} \times 12500 = 1000$
So, the total number of female visitors = 1500 + 1250 + 625 + 750 + 1000
= 5125
Average of female visitors
$= \frac{\text{Total number of visitors}}{\text{Number of days}}$
= 1025
∴ Average of female visitors = 1025

50(D). The number of visitors on Friday = 17% of 12500
The number of male visitors on Friday = $\frac{11}{17} \times$ 17% of 12500
$\Rightarrow \frac{11}{17} \times \frac{17}{100} \times 12500 = 1375$
The number of visitors on Monday = 25% of 12500
The number of female visitors on Monday
$= \frac{12}{25} \times 25\% \times 12500$
$\Rightarrow \frac{12}{25} \times \frac{25}{100} \times 12500 = 1500$

The ratio of male visitors Friday to the female visitors Monday = 1375 : 1500
= 11 : 12
∴ The ratio of male visitors Friday to the female visitors Monday = 11 : 12

51(B). The pattern followed here is as follows,
13 : 184 → (13 × 13) + 15 = 184
Similarly,
17 → (17 × 17) + 15 = 304
Thus 17 is related to 304.

52(C). The logic follows here is:

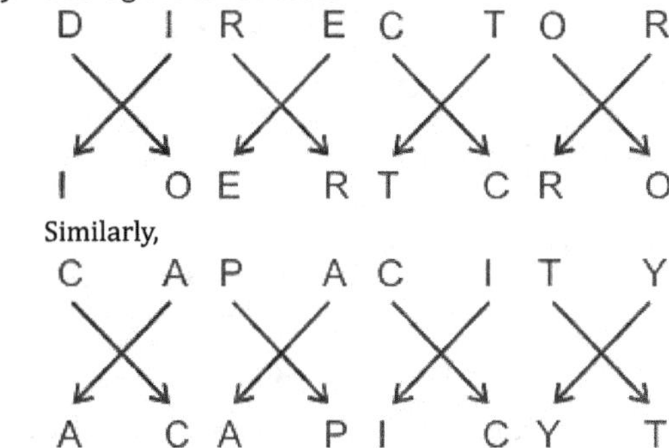

Ques (53-54): From the given information,
(i) T is the mother of V. R is the grandmother of V.

(ii) Q is the husband of R. S is the brother-in-law of Q.

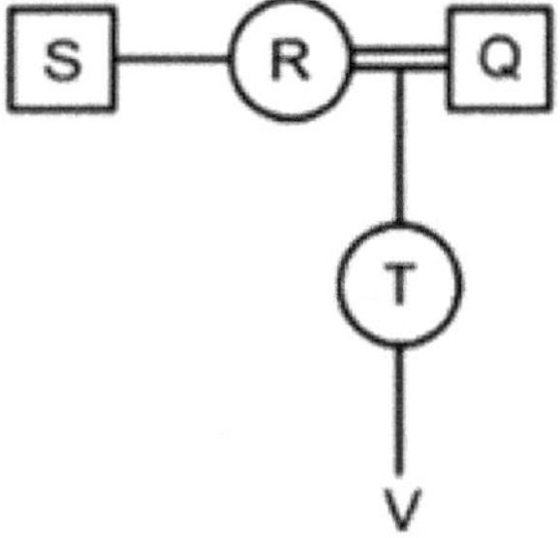

(iii) U is the son-in-law of Q. P is the nephew of S.

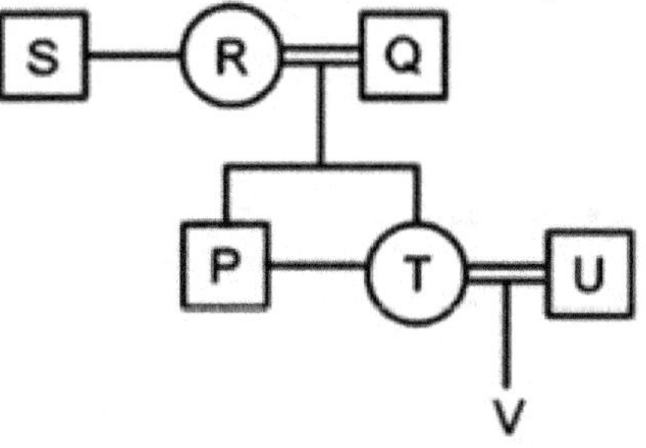

(iv) There are 4 males in the family. It means V is female.

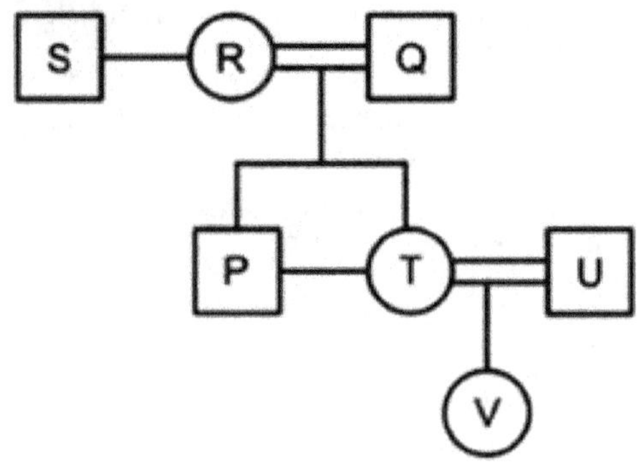

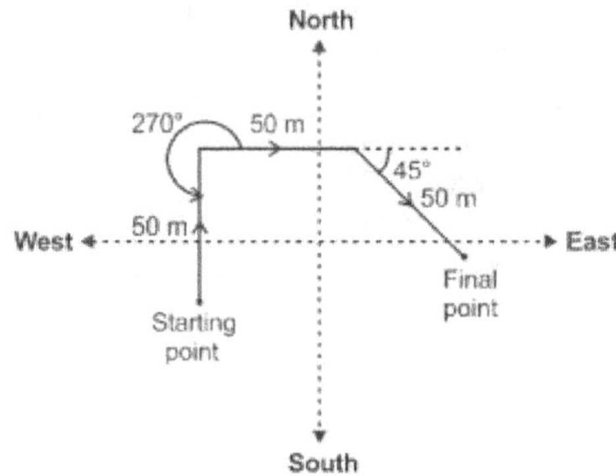

53(B). So, P is the son of Q.

54(C). So, Q is the father of T.

55(D). The logic follows here is:
Dots are in different rectangles.
Figure (1), (2) and (3) follow the same pattern.
In Figure (4), dots are in the same rectangle.
Thus, Figure (4) is different from others.
So, the correct answer is "4".

56(C). In the given question four figures are given. Figure 1 is different from the other figures because the circles given in all the 3 figures are completely black, while in figure 1 the circles are partly black and partly plain.

57(A). In the given question figure, figures 1, 2, 4 are similar while figure 3 is different from the others because the black line in figure (3) is shorter than the others.

58(A). We have drawn the figure according to the information given in the question,

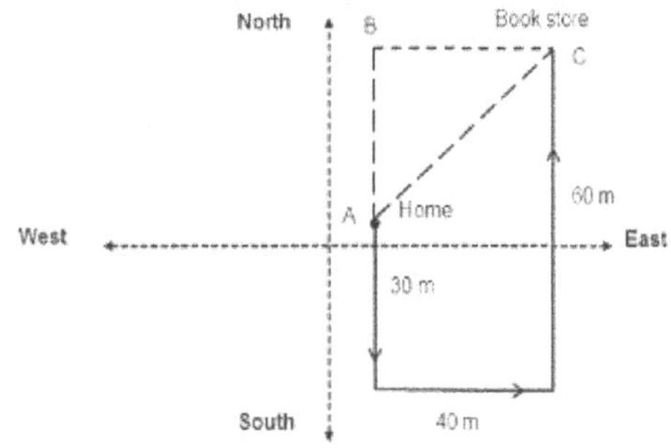

Here point A is her home and C is book store.
The shortest distance between her home and the book store

$AC^2 = 40^2 + (60 - 30)^2$

$AC^2 = 1600 + 900$

$AC^2 = 2500$

$AC = 50$ m

59(C). Sameer walked 50 m towards the north and then turned 270° in the anticlockwise direction i.e. towards the east and then walked from another 50 m.
From there he took a 45° turn in the clockwise direction i.e. towards the south-east and goes for 50 m.
The map of the path followed by Sameer is shown below:

So, Sameer is facing the "south-east" direction.

60(A). The table is alphabets place value:

Alphabets	A	B	C	D	E	F	G	H	I	J	K	L	M
Positional value	1	2	3	4	5	6	7	8	9	10	11	12	13
Positional value	26	25	24	23	22	21	20	19	18	17	16	15	14
Alphabets	Z	Y	X	W	V	U	T	S	R	Q	P	O	N

The pattern followed here is:
BLOCK → 2 +12 +15 + 3 +11= 43
HOUSE → 8 +15 + 21+19 + 5 = 68
So, 68 will be code of HOUSE in same language.

61(A). The pattern followed here is:
ELEPHANT is written as LEPEAHTN.

$$E L E P H A N T$$
$$\times \quad \times \quad \times \quad \times$$
$$L E P E A H T N$$

Similarly,
QUESTION=?

$$Q U E S T I O N$$
$$\times \quad \times \quad \times \quad \times$$
$$U Q S E I T N O$$

So, UQSEITNO will be code of QUESTION in same language.

62(A). The logic followed here is:
In the given series firstly it have 1 section gap then 2 section gap then 3 section gap and so on.

(1) (2) (3) (4) (5) (6)

63(A). Here the central element (arrow) moves one step anticlockwise in every next figure while the other four elements move one step clockwise.

64(D). The venn diagram that best represents the relationship between Sentence, Word, Number is shown below:

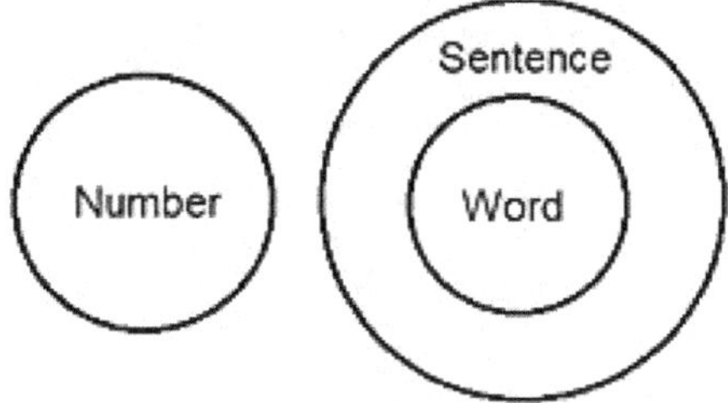

As in, sentences are made of words and numbers do not belong to any of them.

65(D). Hydrogen is a constituent of both Water and the Atmosphere. Water is present in the Atmosphere.

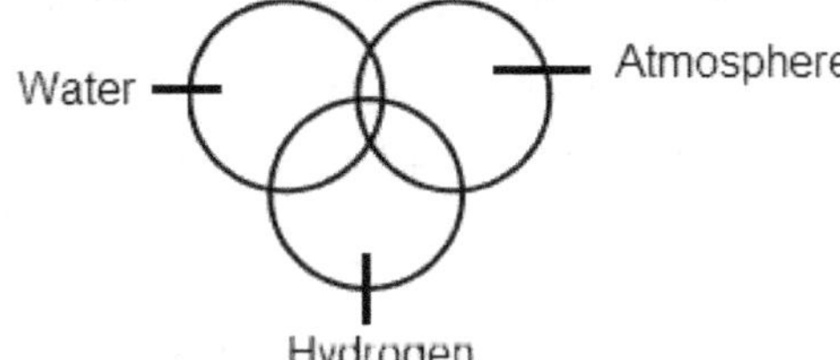

66(A). The pattern followed is:

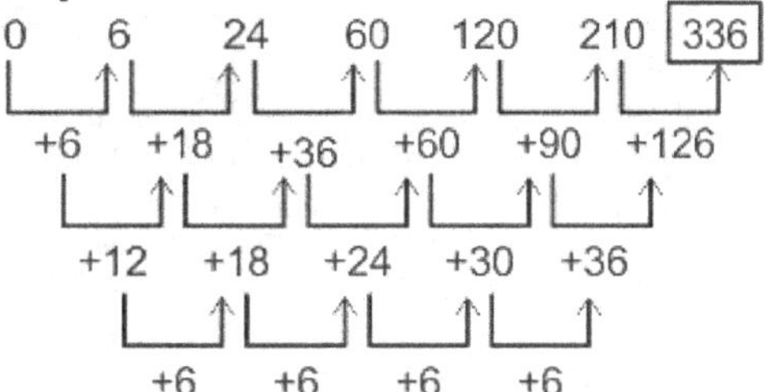

So, the correct answer is "336".

67(C). Here, the following logic is used:

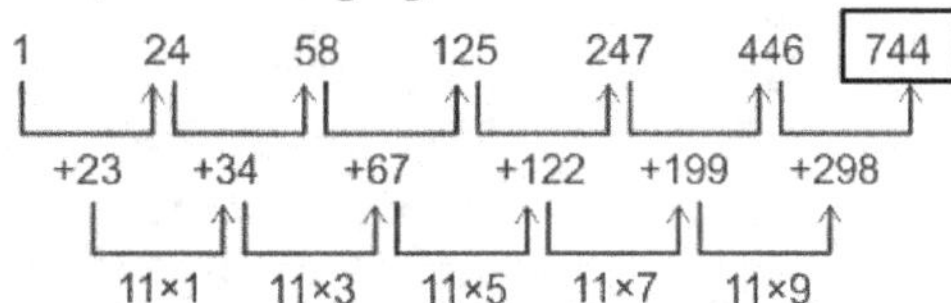

Therefore, '?' will be replaced by '744'.

68(C). N and L are 22nd from the right and left respectively. M sits 13th from the right of N. If M and L have 4 seats in between them.

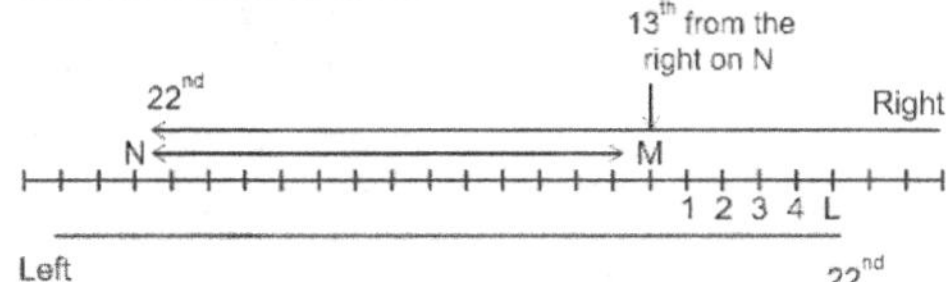

There are 25 seats.

69(A). Given,
40 girl students are in a row and they are facing north. Kailash is sixth to the left of Sonam.
According to the given information,

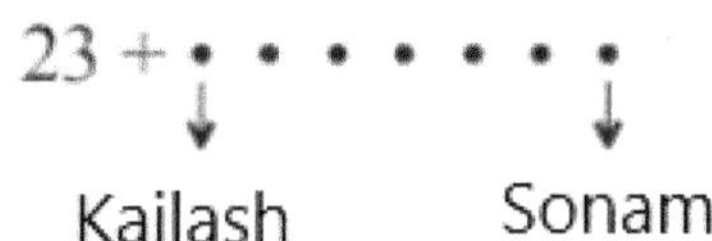

The position of Kailash from the right end = 40 - 23 = 17th

70(D). The least possible Venn diagram is:

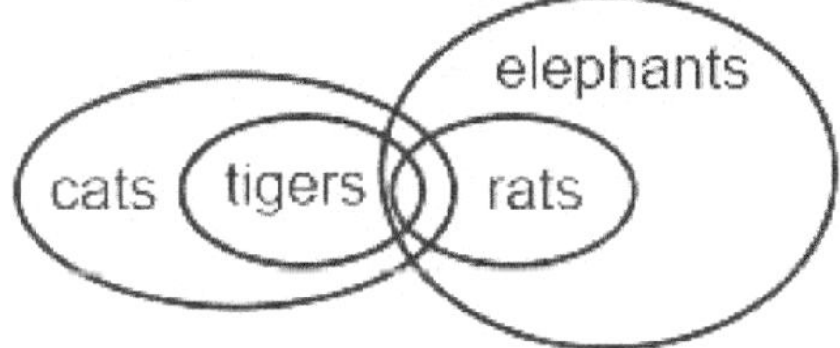

I. All large are tables. → False (As, Some tables are large → So, some large are tables)
II. Some blue are large → False (As, No large is blue. → So, Some blue are not large)
So, neither conclusion I nor conclusion II follows.

71(B). The least possible Venn diagram is:

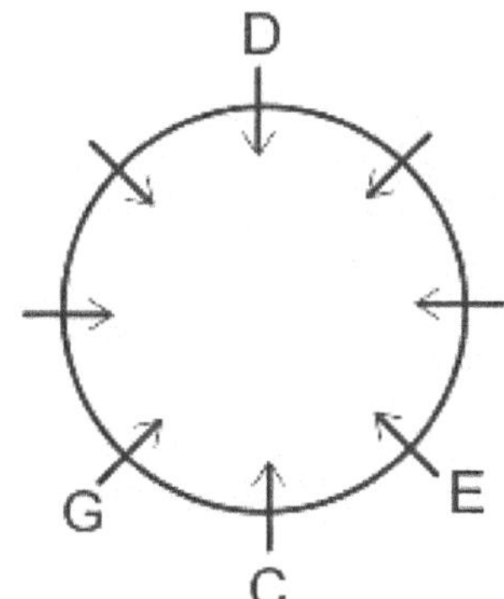

Conclusions:
I. Some cats are elephants → True (as some part of tiger and rats are common for cats and elephants as shown in the diagram above)
II. Some elephants are tigers → True (as some tigers are cats and all rats are elephants, implies some part of rats that are tigers are elephants too)
III. Some cats are rats → True (as some tigers are cats and all tigers are cats, implies some part of rats that are tigers are cats too)
So, all conclusions I, II and III follows.

Ques (72-73): Four ladies A, B, C, D and four gentlemen E, F, G, H are sitting in a circle around a table facing each other.
(ii) C, who is sitting between G and E, is facing D.

CASE 1:

CASE 2:

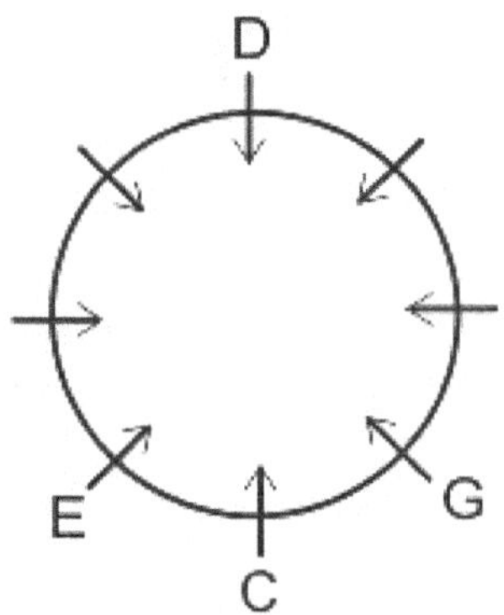

(iii) F is between D and A and is facing G.
(iv) H is to the right of B.

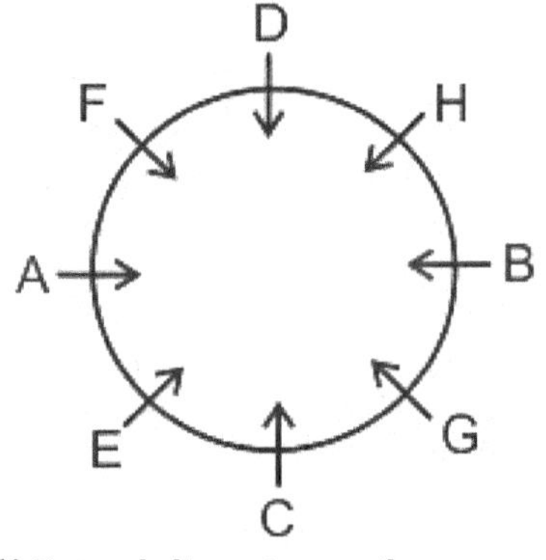

CASE 1:   CASE 2:

(i) No two ladies or two gentlemen are sitting side by side.
Case 1 is eliminated because B and D or H and G are sitting together and it is clearly mentioned that no two ladies or two gentlemen are sitting side by side.

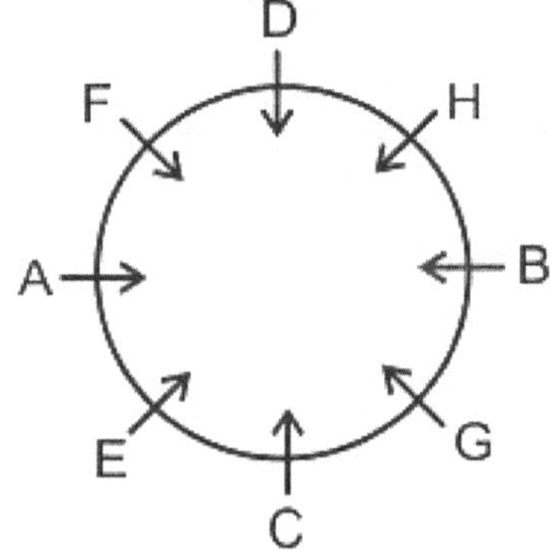

72(B). F is left to the A.

73(D). E is facing towards H.

74(D). Here, there is a gap of 3 letters between the first, second and third letters but in option (D) there is a gap of 3 between the first and the second letter and the difference between the second and the third letter by 2.
Logic:
(A) F(6) → I(9) → L(12)
(B) R(18) → U(21) → X(24)
(C) I(9) → L(12) → O(15)
(D) L(12) → O(15) → Q(17)

75(C). The pattern followed here is:
Subtract the second number from the first number then multiply the result with 9.
$9 - 6 = 3$ and $3 \times 9 = 27$
Only option (C) follows the rule,
$8 - 6 = 2$ and $2 \times 9 = 18$
Other options are not following the rule.
So, $(8, 6, 18)$ will be the correct answer.

76(B). वर्तनी की दृष्टि से आकर्षण सही शब्द है।
आकर्षण का अर्थ "किसी व्यक्ति या वस्तु की ओर सम्मोहित होना" होता है।
उदाहरण: लोग ज्यादातर छोटे बच्चे की ओर आकर्षित होते है।

77(D). वर्तनी की दृष्टि से विशेष सही शब्द है।
विशेष का अर्थ "असाधारण" होता है।
उदाहरण: घूमने के लिए श्याम ने विशेष व्यवस्था की थी।

78(C). 'आये थे हरि भजन को ओटन लगे कपास' का अर्थ किसी कार्य विशेष की उपेक्षा कर किसी अन्य कार्य में लग जाना, प्रमुख कार्य के उद्देश्य को छोड़कर अन्य कार्य में लग जाना,उच्च लक्ष्य लेकर चलना पर कोई घटिया सा काम करने लगना, वांछित कार्य छोडकर अन्य कार्य करने लग जाना है।
वाक्य प्रयोग: सोहन विदेश में नौकरी करता था और वह उस नौकरी को छोड़ कर अपने गांव लौटा इस उद्देश्य से कि वह अपने गांव के लोगों को अपने लिए विज्ञान के द्वारा प्रगतिशील बनाएगा और अपने गांव को विकसित करेगा, लेकिन जब सोहन अपने गांव आया तो यहां छोटे-मोटे कामों में लग गया और उसी में अपना सारा समय देने लगा ऐसी परिस्थिति में कहा जाता था कहा जाता है कि आए थे हरि भजन को ओटन लगे कपास।

79(A). "दाल में काला होना" मुहावरे का अर्थ गड़बड़ होना है।
वाक्य प्रयोग: जिस तरह से सेठ को पुलिस ने अकेले में बुलाया तो लगता है की दाल में काला है।
मुहावरा: ऐसे वाक्यांश, जो सामान्य अर्थ का बोध न कराकर किसी विलक्षण अर्थ की प्रतीति कराये, मुहावरा कहलाता है।

80(C). उपरोक्त रिक्त स्थान के लिए उचित मुहावरा है - कमर कसकर।
शत्रुओं से लड़ने के लिए भारतीयों को कमर कसकर तैयार हो जाना चाहिए।
'कमर कसकर' मुहावरे का अर्थ - तैयार होना।
वाक्य प्रयोग - तुम्हारे इम्तिहान नजदीक आ गए हैं अब तुम्हें पढ़ाई के लिए कमर कस लेनी चाहिए।

81(B). 'महोदय' शब्द का स्त्रीलिंग 'महोदया' होगा।
शब्द के जिस रूप से किसी प्राणी या वस्तु के स्त्री जाति के होने का बोध होता है, उसे स्त्रीलिंग कहते हैं। जैसे–औरत, शेरनी, धोबिन, नौकरानी, घोड़ी, मालिन आदि।

82(C). बुढ़ापा शब्द पुल्लिंग है।
अ, आ, आव, पा, पन, क, त्व, आवा तथा औड़ा से अंत होने वाली संज्ञाएँ पुल्लिंग होती हैं।
अः खेल, रेल, बाग, हार, यंत्र आदि।
आः लोटा, मोटा, गोटा, घोड़ा, हीरा आदि।

83(C). 'जो मुश्किल से प्राप्त हो' उसे 'दुर्लभ' कहते हैं।
दुर्लभ विशेषण शब्द है। जो शब्द संज्ञा या सर्वनाम की विशेषता बताते हैं, विशेषण कहलाते हैं।

84(D). अवसर के अनुरूप बदल जाने वाले को ' अवसरवादी' कहते हैं ।

अवसर का अर्थ 'मौका या सुयोग' है। अन्य विकल्प इसके अनुचित उत्तर हैं।

85(C). संज्ञा या सर्वनाम का वह रूप जो हमें किन्हीं दो वस्तुओं के बीच संबंध का बोध कराता है, वह संबंध कारक कहलाता है।

सम्बन्ध कारक के विभक्ति चिन्ह का, के, की, ना, ने, नो, **रा**, रे, री आदि हैं।

86(C). 'कोई' शब्द पुरूषवाचक सर्वनाम से संबंधित नहीं है।

जिन सर्वनाम शब्दों से वस्तु, व्यक्ति, स्थान आदि की निश्चितता का बोध नहीं होता वे अनिश्चयवाचक सर्वनाम कहलाते हैं जैसे- कोई, कुछ आदि।

पुरुषवाचक सर्वनाम: जिस सर्वनाम शब्द का प्रयोग बोलने वाला अपने लिए, सुनने वाले अर्थात जिससे बातें कर रहा है उसके लिए तथा उस व्यक्ति के लिए जिसके बारे में वह बात कर रहा है, प्रयुक्त करता है, वे सभी 'पुरुषवाचक सर्वनाम' कहलाते हैं; जैसे- मैं, मेरा, मुझे, हम, हमारा, हमें, तू, मेरा, तुझे, तुम, तुम्हारा, तुम्हें, वह आदि।

87(D). संज्ञा या सर्वनाम के जिस रुप से किसी अन्य शब्द के साथ संबंध या लगाव प्रतीत हो उसे संबंध कारक कहते हैं

जैसे- गंगा हिमालय से निकलती है।

88(B). उर्दू शब्द 'सौदा' का बहुवचन में उसके रूप में कोई परिवर्तन नहीं होता।

यदि 'सौदा' के अन्त में 'गर' लगा दें तो नया शब्द 'सौदागर' हो जायेगा जिसका अर्थ व्यापारी है।

89(A). हिन्दी में 'मैं' का बहुवचन 'हम' है।

" मैं " मे कहने वाले के साथ कोई नहीं होता ,पर "हम" से लगता है कि जो व्यक्ति बात कर रहा है उसके साथ कुछ और भी लोग हैं, जैसे " मैं कल मुंबई जा रहा हूँ" मतलब कहने वाला ही केवल जा रहा है।

90(A). दिए गए विकल्पों में शुद्ध वाक्य का सबसे अच्छा विकल्प है - दो लड़के इधर आ रहे हैं।

91(C). दिए गए विकल्पों में शुद्ध वाक्य का सबसे अच्छा विकल्प है 'हमने आपसे कहा था।'

92(D). 'चिरंतन' का विलोम शब्द नश्वर है।

चिरन्तन का अर्थ- हमेशा रहने वाला

नश्वर का अर्थ - मर्त्य

विपरीत (उल्टा) अर्थ बताने वाले शब्दों को विलोम शब्द कहते हैं।

उदाहरण: रात-दिन, धरती-आकाश

93(B). 'ठोस' का विलोम शब्द तरल है।

तरल का अर्थ – बहने वाला/ अस्थिर

ठोस का अर्थ – ठस/पक्का

विपरीत (उल्टा) अर्थ बताने वाले शब्दों को विलोम शब्द कहते हैं।

उदाहरण: रात-दिन, धरती-आकाश

94(C). चंद्रहास शब्द तलवार का पर्यायवाची है।

तलवार के अन्य पर्यायवाची- असि, करवाल, कृपाण, खडग, शाम्शीर, शायक, चंद्रहास, खंज

95(D). 'धनुष' शब्द 'कोदण्ड' का पर्यायवाची शब्द है। '

धनुष के अन्य पर्यायवाची इस प्रकार हैं- धनु, कमान, मेहराब, शरासन, धनुक आदि।

ऐसे शब्द जिनके अर्थ समान हों, पर्यायवाची शब्द कहलाते हैं।

पानी के पर्यायवाची शब्द हैं जल, नीर, अंबु, तोय आदि।

96(C). अंतर्ध्यान शब्द के सही संधि विच्छेद का विकल्प अंतः + ध्यान होगा।

अंतर्ध्यान मे विसर्ग संधि है।

विसर्ग के बाद स्वर या व्यंजन आने पर विसर्ग में जो विकार होता है, उसे विसर्ग सन्धि कहते हैं।

97(C). निरीह का सही संधि विच्छेद निः + ईह है।

यदि विसर्ग से पहले अ, आ को छोड़कर कोई अन्य स्वर आए और बाद में कोई भी स्वर आए तो भी विसर्ग 'र्' में बदल जाता है।

ई / इ : + अ / आ / इ / ई / उ / ऊ = र्

98(A). राका + ईश विग्रह यण संधि' का नहीं है। यह गुण संधि का विग्रह है।

- यण संधि - जब संधि करते समय इ, ई के साथ कोई अन्य स्वर हो तो ' य ' बन जाता है, जब उ, ऊ के साथ कोई अन्य स्वर हो तो ' व् ' बन जाता है , जब ऋ के साथ कोई अन्य स्वर हो तो ' र ' बन जाता है।
- गुण संधि - गुण संधि स्वर संधि का एक भेद अथवा प्रकार है। जब संधि करते समय (अ, आ) के साथ (इ, ई) हो तो 'ए' बनता है, जब (अ, आ) के साथ (उ, ऊ) हो तो 'ओ' बनता है, जब (अ, आ) के साथ (ऋ) हो तो 'अर' बनता है तो यह गुण संधि कहलाती है।

99(C). मधुशाला कविता हरिवंश राय बच्चन की है।

हिन्दी काव्य प्रेमियों में हरिवंश राय बच्चन सबसे अधिक प्रिय कवि रहे हैं और सर्वप्रथम 1935 में प्रकाशित उनकी 'मधुशाला' आज भी लोकप्रियता के सर्वोच्च शिखर पर है। हरिवंश राय बच्चन ने मधु, मदिरा, हाला (शराब), प्याला (कप या ग्लास), मधुशाला और मदिरालय की मदद से जीवन की जटिलताओं के विश्लेषण का प्रयास किया है।

100(B). "भक्तमाल" के रचनाकार "नाभादास" है।

भक्तमाल का रचना वर्ष 1585 ईस्वी है। 'भक्तमाल' की रचना व्रजभाषा में हुई है। इसकी भाषा शैली प्रौढ़ एवं परिमार्जित है । ' भक्तमाल' में नाभादास ने छप्पय छंद में अपने पूर्ववर्ती अथवा समसामयिक लगभग दो सौ भक्तों का चरित्रगान किया है।

1. Who wrote Discovery of India?
   (a) Mahatma Gandhi
   (b) Sardar Vallabhbhai Patel
   (c) Indira Gandhi
   (d) Jawaharlal Nehru

2. Who amongst the following was the last person converted by the Buddha?
   (a) Anand
   (b) Vasumitra
   (c) Goshal
   (d) Subhadda

3. Which one of the following is NOT correctly matched? Dynasties - Metals of coin
   (a) Kushanas - Gold and copper
   (b) Guptas - Gold and silver
   (c) Satavahanas - Gold
   (d) Kalachuris - Gold, silver and copper

4. Which one of the following was the capital of the Sultanate during the reign of Iltutmish?
   (a) Agra
   (b) Lahore
   (c) Badaun
   (d) Delhi

5. In which year did Lord Curzon cancelled the partition of Bengal?
   (a) 1911
   (b) 1904
   (c) 1906
   (d) 1907

6. When did the British government appoint the Sadler University Commission to improve education?
   (a) In 1919
   (b) In 1917
   (c) In 1921
   (d) In 1986

7. Consider the statements A, B, C about Autumn season in India and choose the correct answer:
   A. This season is also known as the south-west monsoon season.
   B. Winds blow from the Bay of Bengal and Arabian sea towards the land in this season.
   C. This season is marked by the onset and advance of monsoon.
   (a) B and C are true, A is false.
   (b) A, B, C all are false.
   (c) A and B are true, C is false.
   (d) A and C are true, B is false.

8. By which name the river Yarlung Tsangpo is known in India?
   (a) Subhansiri
   (b) Brahmaputra
   (c) Manas
   (d) Yangtze

9. Identify the type of soil on the basis of the given characteristics:
   1. The soil is porous because of its loamy nature.
   2. They occur all along the Indo-Gangetic-Brahmaputra plains.
   3. Porosity and texture provide good drainage and other conditions favourable for agriculture.
   Select the correct answer from the given alternatives:
   (a) Laterite soil
   (b) Alluvial Soil
   (c) Saline soil
   (d) Red and yellow soil

10. Which university was sought to be converted into Gati Shakti Vishwavidyalaya, as per a recent bill passed in Lok Sabha?
    (a) National Rail and Transportation Institute (NRTI)
    (b) BITS Pilani
    (c) Indira Gandhi Institute of Development Research
    (d) IIIT Hyderabad

11. Consider the following statements:
    1. Climate and Clean Air Coalition (CCAC) to reduce short lived climate pollutants is a unique initiative of the G20 group of countries.
    2. Short-lived climate pollutants have an overall warming influence on climate.
    Which of the statements given above is/are correct?
    (a) 1 only
    (b) 2 only
    (c) Both 1 and 2
    (d) Neither 1 nor 2

12. In which state did Defence minister Rajnath Singh inaugurate Siyom bridge in January 2023?
    (a) West Bengal
    (b) Goa
    (c) Arunachal Pradesh
    (d) Kerala

13. Which state government launched the portal for the creation of "One Family One Identity"?
    (a) Madhya Pradesh
    (b) Rajasthan
    (c) Uttar Pradesh
    (d) Himachal Pradesh

14. Which of the following is an example of binary fertilizer?
    (a) MOP
    (b) Ammonia
    (c) Urea
    (d) DAP

15. A Barometer kept in an elevator reads 760 mm when the elevator is at rest. When the elevator moves in the upward direction with increasing speed, the reading of the Barometer will be:
    (a) 760 mm
    (b) < 760 mm
    (c) > 760 mm
    (d) Zero

16. Stalactites and stalagmites consist of deposits of:
    (a) silica
    (b) magnesium carbonate
    (c) calcium carbonate
    (d) sodium carbonate

17. Which among the following view is supported by Evolutionary theory of origin of the state?
    (a) State is an artificial creation
    (b) State emerged at a particular period of time
    (c) State is a result of wars
    (d) State is a continuous development of human society

18. For the first time a joint sitting of both the houses took place in 1961 to resolve a deadlock on:
    (a) Dowry Prohibition Bill
    (b) Jammu and Kashmir Reorganisation Bill
    (c) Epidemic Disease Bill
    (d) Disaster Management Bill

19. After-following the recommendation of State Reorganization Commission, 1956, the number of elected MLAs in Bihar Legislative Assembly was:

(a) 318   (b) 330
(c) 320   (d) 321

20. Uttar Pradesh 'Start-up Fund' was launched on _______.
(a) 10th March, 2020   (b) 20th March, 2020
(c) 10th May, 2020   (d) 20th May, 2020

21. Which among the following States was the largest producer of wheat in India in the year 2015-16?
(a) Haryana   (b) Uttar Pradesh
(c) Punjab   (d) Bihar

22. A consumer co-operative store is set up by:
(a) Members
(b) Registrar of Co-operative Societies
(c) Central Government
(d) State Government

23. Which among the following cup/trophy is awarded for women in the sport of Badminton?
(a) Webb Ellis Cup   (b) Wisden Trophy
(c) Uber Cup   (d) Derby Cup

24. Which of the following sectors has been identified as Strategic Sectors for Public Sector Enterprises?
1. Space
2. Petroleum
3. Telecom
4. Banking
Select the correct answer using the code given below.
(a) 1, 2 and 4 only   (b) 2 and 3 only
(c) 1 and 4 only   (d) 1, 2, 3 and 4

25. What is the name of the new solar-powered electric vehicle recently developed by Lightyear?
(a) Model S   (b) Aptera
(c) Lucid Air   (d) One

Mathematics

26. Evaluate : $37.188 \div 3.6$
(a) 9.8   (b) 9.66
(c) 10.33   (d) 11.6

27. A shopkeeper marks his goods 30% higher than the cost price and allows a discount of 10% on the marked price. In order to earn 6.5% more profit, what discount percent should he allow on the marked price?
(a) 5   (b) 4
(c) 6   (d) 5.5

28. The cost price of 50 Coca-Cola Bottles is equal to the selling price of 40 Coca-Cola Bottles. Find the Profit/Loss percentage.
(a) 15%   (b) 25%
(c) 20%   (d) 30%

29. A principal amounts to $Rs.$ 6690 after 3 years and to $Rs.$ 10035 after 6 years on compound interest. Find the principal invested.
(a) $Rs.$ 4460   (b) $Rs.$ 4590
(c) $Rs.$ 4910   (d) $Rs.$ 5000

30. If the compound interest accrued on an amount of Rs. 17500 in two years is 6660.9375, what is the rate of interest?

(a) 16.5   (b) 17
(c) 17.5   (d) 16

31. If each side of a rectangle is increased by 12%, then by what percentage will its area increase?
(a) 12.65%   (b) 27.5%
(c) 25.44%   (d) 18.54%

32. A field is in the shape of the figure given below. Flowers are to be sown on the semi-circular ends. What will be the cost of sowing of flowers at the rate of 2 paisa/m^2, if the length of the field is 42 m?

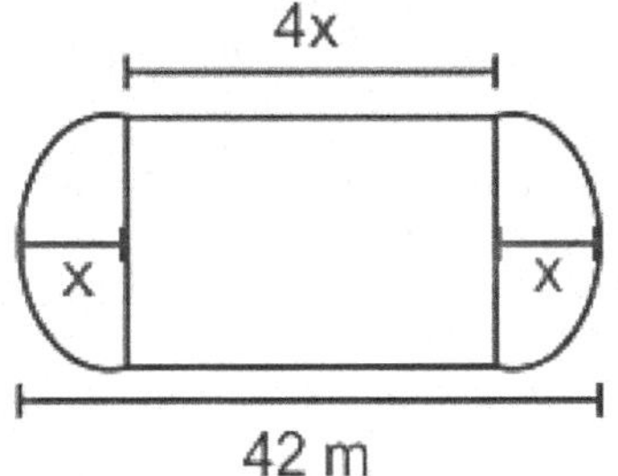

(a) Rs. 3.08   (b) Rs. 2.08
(c) Rs. 4.08   (d) Rs. 5.08

33. If the sum of two consecutive even numbers is 66, then the smaller one is:
(a) 34   (b) 32
(c) 42   (d) 24

34. The average of 5 consecutive even numbers P, Q, R, S, and T is 106. What is the product of Q and S?
(a) 11440   (b) 11024
(c) 10608   (d) 11232

35. Average weight of 25 Students of a class is 50 kg. If the weight of the class teacher is included, the average is increased by 1 kg. The weight of the teacher is:
(a) 76 kg   (b) 77 kg
(c) 74 kg   (d) 75 kg

36. In a survey, it was found that in a constituency, 55% of voters are male and the rest are female. 40% of the male voters are literate and $33\frac{1}{3}\%$ of the female voters are illiterate. What percentage of the voters are literate?
(a) 55%
(b) 34%
(c) 52%
(d) Can not be determined

37. Three persons A , B, and C complete a piece of work in 6 days for which they are paid a sum of Rs. 480.If the efficiency of A, B and C are in ratio 4 : 5 :7, then find the daily income of B?
(a) Rs. 25   (b) Rs. 30
(c) Rs. 150   (d) Rs. 20

38. The efficiency of A, B and C in the ratio as $A : B = 2 : 1$, and $B : C = 3 : 4$. They start working together and complete the work in 7 days. How much time taken by B and C work together to complete the same work?
(a) 13 days   (b) 10 days
(c) 12 days   (d) 15 days

39. P can complete a job in 30 days. Q alone can complete the same job in 20 days. P works for 18 days and then the remaining job is completed by Q. How many days will it take Q to complete the remaining job alone?

(a) 6 days   (b) 8 days

(c) 16 days   (d) 7 days

40. A train leaves from a station and moves at 40 km/hr. After 2 hours, another train leaves from the same station and moves in the same direction at a certain speed. If the second train catches up with the first train in 4 hours, what is the speed of the second train?

(a) 55 km/hr   (b) 50 km/hr

(c) 60 km/hr   (d) 65 km/hr

41. Mr. Prasad travelled equal distances at speeds of 2 km/hr, 4 km/hr , and 6 km/hr , and took a total of 55 minutes to complete. Find the total distance he travelled, in km .

(a) 2   (b) 1

(c) 4   (d) 3

42. The HCF and LCM of two numbers are 14 and 3920 respectively. If one of the numbers is 490 . Find the second number.

(a) 56   (b) 84

(c) 98   (d) 112

43. Rahul is 6 years younger than his elder brother Shyam. Rahul also has a sister who is 4 years younger to him. What is the difference between the age of Rahul and the average age of the three siblings?

(a) 7 months   (b) 7 months

(c) 2 months   (d) 8 months

44. Find the value of $(\cos 2p\pi + i \sin 2p\pi)(\cos 2q\pi + i \sin 2q\pi)$?

(a) 1   (b) i

(c) $\frac{1}{2}$ (d) -1

45. Which one of the following points lies inside a circle of radius 6 and centre at $(3, 5)$?

(a) (-2, -1)   (b) (0, 1)

(c) (-1, -2)   (d) (2, -1)

46. If $\tan\theta + \sin\theta = m$ and $\tan\theta - \sin\theta = n$. Then the value of $m^2 - n^2$ is:

(a) 4mn   (b) $\sqrt{mn}$

(c) $2\sqrt{mn}$ (d) $4\sqrt{mn}$

47. A box contains 5 green pencils and 7 yellow pencils. Two pencils are chosen at random from the box without replacement. What is the probability they are both yellow?

(a) $\frac{42}{234}$ (b) $\frac{6}{11}$

(c) $\frac{7}{12}$ (d) $\frac{7}{22}$

48. In a class of seven boys and three girls, four children are to be selected. In total how many ways can they be selected such a minimum of one boy should be there?

(a) 159   (b) 194

(c) 205   (d) 210

Ques (49-50): Direction: Study the following graph carefully and answer the question based on the information given below.

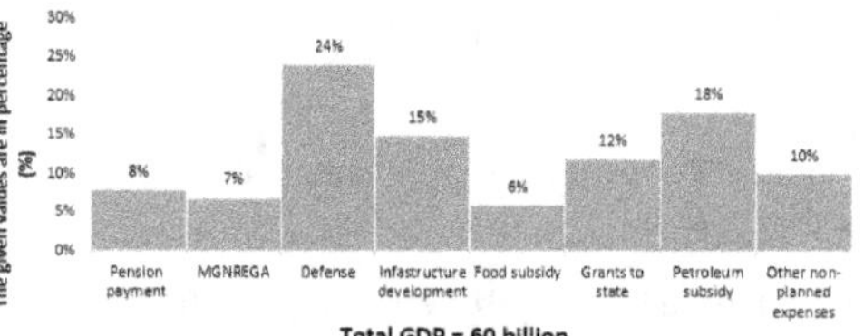

49. What is the ratio of the expenditure on Pension payment to that on Food subsidy?

(a) 4 : 5   (b) 8 : 3

(c) 4 : 3   (d) 5 : 4

50. What is the total sum of expenditure on Pension payment, Defence and Food subsidy together?

(a) 22.6 billion   (b) 22.8 billion

(c) 23.4 billion   (d) 20.8 billion

Reasoning

51. Select the option that is related to the third term in the same way as the second term is related to the first term.

Innocent : Guilty :: Moisten : ?

(a) Drench   (b) Dried

(c) Desire   (d) Wet

52. In the following question, select the related number from the given alternatives.

SAO : 35 :: NPC : ?

(a) 40   (b) 25

(c) 33   (d) 41

53. Pointing to a boy, a lady said, " He is the son of my grandmother's only child's husband's only daughter's husband." How is the lady related to the boy?

(a) Mother   (b) Grandmother

(c) Aunt   (d) Sister

54. Direction : Read the information carefully and answer the following question.

A+B means A is the father of B

A-B means A is the mother of B

A*B means A is the sister of B

A/B means A is the brother of B

In the given expression M+N*O/P , how is N related to P's brother?

(a) Brother   (b) Father

(c) Sister   (d) Mother

55. In the given question, there are four figures given out of which three are similar in some manner and one is not like the others. Select the figure which is odd one out.

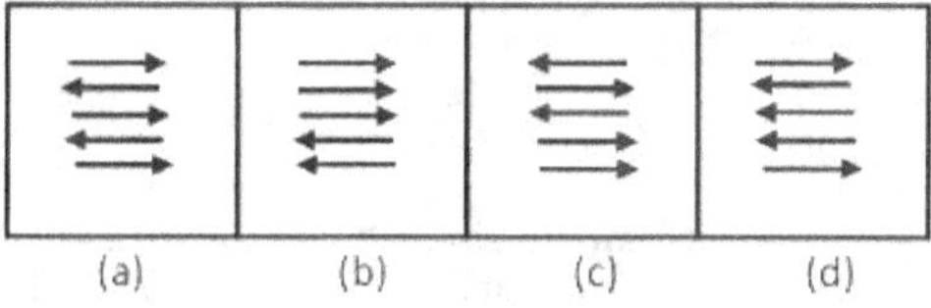

(a) d   (b) a

(c) b   (d) c

56. Select the figure that does not belong to the following group.

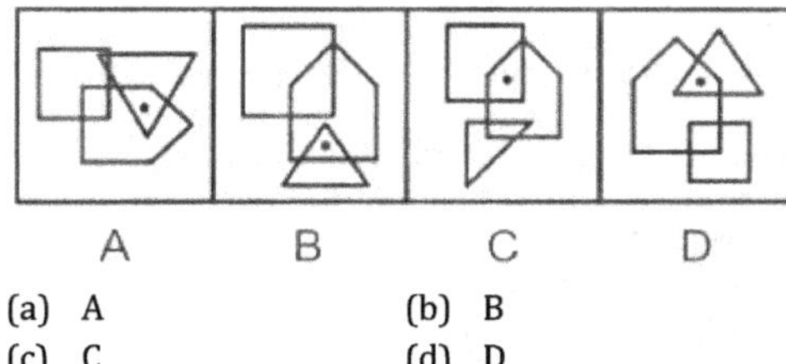

(a) A   (b) B
(c) C   (d) D

57. Four figures have been given, out of which three are alike in some manner and one is different. Select the one that is different.

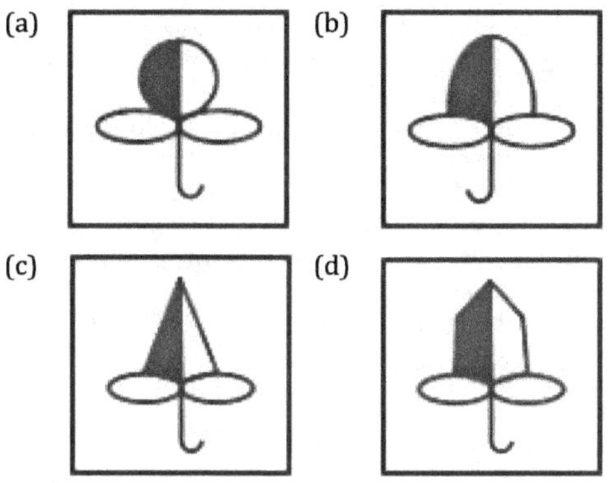

(a)   (b)

(c)   (d)

58. Sudhir leaves his home to go to the library and walks 20 m towards east. He then walks 35 m towards west and a further 5 m towards north. He then turns towards east and walks 15 m. Find the straight distance in meters between his initial and final positions.

(a) 2 m   (b) 5 m
(c) 10 m   (d) 15 m

59. A few telecommunication towers S, J, Z, E, N and B are plotted on a map. Z is 6 km to the north of S, which is 9 km to the west of J, which is 12 km to the north of B, which is 9 km to the east of N, which is 15 km to the north of E. Where is Z with respect to E?

(a) 33 km northwards   (b) 33 km southwards
(c) 9 km northwards   (d) 9 km southwards

60. If white is called 'blue', blue is called 'red', red is called 'yellow', yellow is called 'green', green is called 'black', black is called 'violet' and violet is called 'orange', then what would be the colour of human blood?

(a) Red   (b) Green
(c) Yellow   (d) Violet

61. In a certain code language, BAT is written YZG. How will SICK be wirtten in that same code?

(a) HRYV   (b) HRZP
(c) HRXP   (d) RHPX

62. Which of the option figure will replace the question mark (?) to continue the figure series given below?

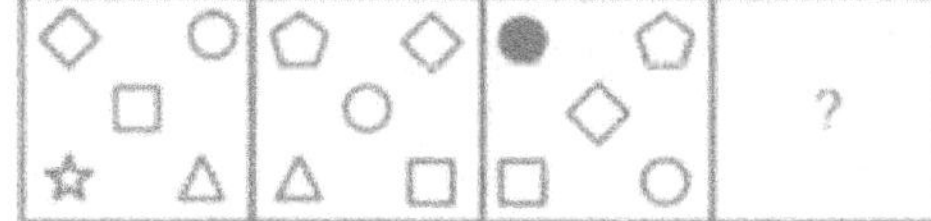

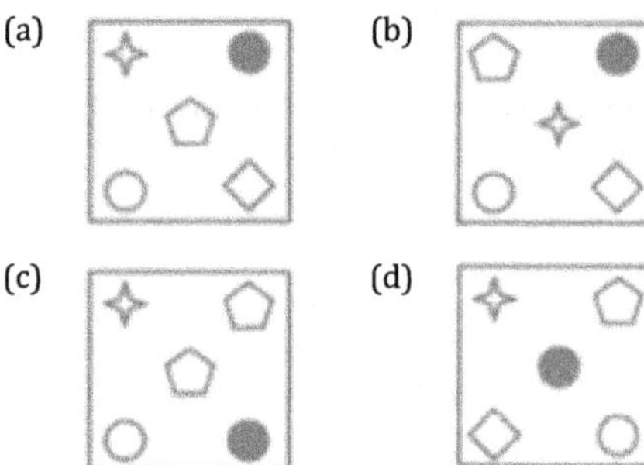

(a)   (b)

(c)   (d)

63. Direction: Select a figure from amongst the Answer Figures which will continue the same series as established by the five Problem Figures.

Problem Figures:

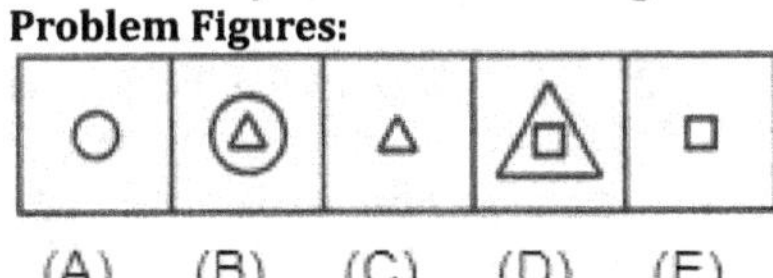

(A)   (B)   (C)   (D)   (E)

Answer Figures:

(1)   (2)   (3)   (4)

(a) (1)   (b) (2)
(c) (3)   (d) (4)

Ques (64-65): Direction: Identify the diagram that best represents the relationship among classes given below:

64. Singer, Musician, Businessman

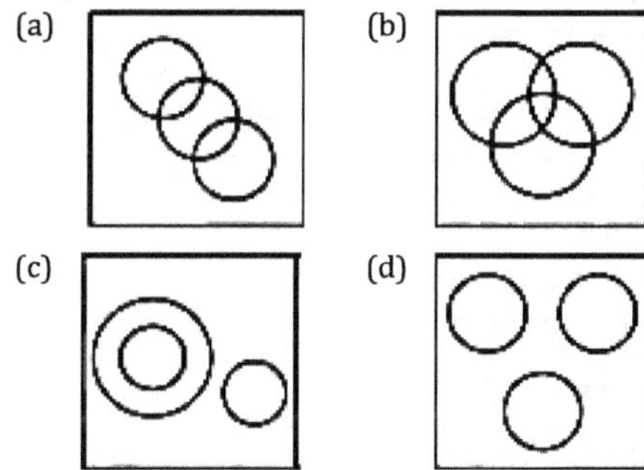

(a)   (b)

(c)   (d)

65. Fathers, women and doctors

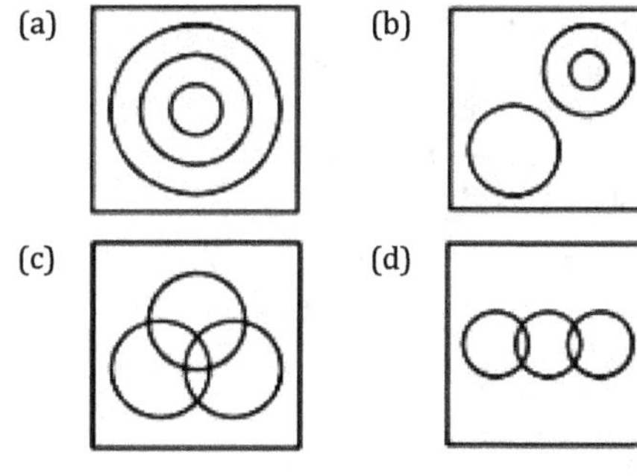

(a)   (b)

(c)   (d)

66. Direction : Select the number from among the given options that can replace the question mark (?) in the following series.

1, 9, 25, 49, 81, ?

(a) 91   (b) 111

(c) 121   (d) 94

67. **Direction** : Select the option that will correctly replace the question mark (?) in the series.

100, 96, 80, 44, ?

(a) -24   (b) 20

(c) -20   (d) 16

68. Suresh, Kamalesh, Mukesh, Amit, and Rakesh are friends. Suresh is shorter than Kamalesh but taller than Rakesh, Mukesh is the tallest. Amit is a little shorter than Kamalesh and a little taller than Suresh. Who has two persons taller and two persons shorter than him?

(a) Amit   (b) Kamalesh

(c) Rakesh   (d) Suresh

69. In a row of boys, Rahul's position from the right end is 39th and Pankaj's position from the left end is 53rd. After interchanging their position, Rahul's position becomes 64th from the right end. How many boys are there in the row?

(a) 118   (b) 117

(c) 116   (d) 120

Ques (70-71): Direction: In the following question below some statements are given followed by some conclusions. Taking the given statements to be true even if they seem to be at variance from commonly known facts, read all the conclusions and then decide which of the given conclusions logically follows the given statements.

70. **Statements:**

Some books are novels.

No novel is a diary.

Conclusions:

I. No book is a diary.

II. All diaries are books.

III. No diary is a novel.

(a) Either conclusion I or II and only conclusion III follows

(b) Only conclusion II follows

(c) Only conclusion I follows

(d) Only conclusion III follows

71. **Statements:**

Some cows are crows.

Some crows are elephants.

Conclusions:

I. Some cows are elephants.

II. All crows are elephants.

(a) If only conclusion I follows

(b) If only conclusion II follows

(c) If both conclusion I and II follows

(d) Neither I nor II follows

72. Select the letter which is different from the others.

(a) MLN   (b) ONP

(c) PRQ   (d) UTV

73. Select the letter which is different from the others.

(a) ZM   (b) RH

(c) XL   (d) NG

Ques (74-75): Direction: Study the following information carefully and answer the question that follow:

Fifteen persons from A to O are sitting in three rows namely Row-1, Row-2 and Row-3 facing north. Five persons are sitting in each row and seats of all rows are such that each seat is exactly behind or in front of another seat of a neighbouring row. Row-1 is to the north of Row-2 and Row-2 is to the north of Row-3.

It is given that Engineers are sitting in row-1, Doctors are sitting in row-2 and Teachers are sitting in row-3.

Further, it is given that:

1. The number of persons sitting between N and O is the same as the number of persons sitting between E and H.

2. Two persons are sitting between A and F but neither of them is doctorand F is sitting third to the left of A.

3. N and A are sitting in the same row but N is sitting at one of the ends and J is sitting exactly behind or in front of him.

4. E is a teacher and two persons are sitting between him and L but neither E nor L is sitting exactly behind J.

5. G is sitting exactly behind A but not exactly in front of L.

6. I is sitting exactly behind O.

7. K is neither an engineer nor sitting in the same row as I but he is sitting at one of the ends.

8. C is sitting immediate to the right of H.

9. D is not an engineer and not sitting at any of the ends.

10. M is sitting in the same row as G is sitting but they are not neighbours of each other.

11. G is sitting at one of the ends but not in front of L.

74. Select the odd one out.

(a) F-I-K   (b) D-O-C

(c) K-N-D   (d) B-L-F

75. How many persons are sitting between N and B?

(a) Two   (b) One

(c) Four   (d) Three

General Hindi

76. व्यंजन सम्बन्धी अशुद्ध वर्तनी है:

(a) श्राप   (b) खीझना

(c) गण्यमान्य   (d) सोडा

77. अशुद्ध वर्तनी है:

(a) पुनरवलोकन   (b) सौन्दर्य

(c) पुनरागमन   (d) अभयारण्य

78. 'अधजल गगरी छलकत जाय' इस कहावत का अर्थ है:

(a) गगरी भरी न होने के कारण छलकना

(b) अल्प ज्ञान पर इतराना

(c) ज्ञान प्रदर्शन करना

(d) अज्ञान प्रकट करना

79. 'कंगाली में आटा गीला करना' मुहावरे का अर्थ है:

(a) अकारण नुकसान होना

(b) काम-काज बन्द होना

(c) मुसीबत में ही मुसीबत आना

(d) व्यर्थ का काम करना

80. 'बालू से तेल निकालना' मुहावरे का अर्थ है:

(a) शीघ्र नष्ट होने वाली वस्तु   (b) असम्भव काम करना

(c) पूर्णतः स्वस्थ होना   (d) बहुत साधन सम्पन्न होना

81. "कहार" शब्द का स्त्रीलिंग है।

(a) कुम्हार   (b) कहारिन

(c) कुंआर   (d) कहारी

82. 'विदुषी का पुलिंग शब्द क्या है?

(a) आयुष्मान   (b) बलवान

(c) विधुर   (d) विद्वान

Ques (83-84): निर्देश : प्रत्येक प्रश्न के आगे दिए गए विकल्पों में से उचित

विकल्प चुनें।

83. आयोजन करने वाला व्यक्ति:
(a) आयोजक
(b) कार्यकर्ता
(c) अधिकारी
(d) आलोचक

84. जो पहले कभी नहीं हुआ:
(a) अजर
(b) भूतपूर्व
(c) अकथनीय
(d) अभूतपूर्व

85. 'माँ ने बच्चे को सुलाया' इस वाक्य में 'को' किस कारक की विभक्ति है?
(a) सम्प्रदान
(b) कर्म
(c) करण
(d) अपादान

86. किस वाक्यांश में अपादान कारक है?
(a) चोरी करने के कारण
(b) उसने
(c) नौकर को
(d) घर से निकाल दिया

87. किस शब्द में उपसर्ग का प्रयोग हुआ है?
(a) उपकार
(b) लाभदायक
(c) पढ़ाई
(d) अपनापन

88. 'श्रीमती' शब्द का बहुवचन होगा:
(a) श्रीमतिनी
(b) श्रीमतीएँ
(c) श्रीमतीय
(d) श्रीमतियाँ

89. 'मेला' का बहुवचन शब्द है:
(a) मेली
(b) मेलों
(c) मेले
(d) मेलियाँ

Ques (90-91): निर्देश: वाक्य के अशुद्ध भाग (त्रुटिपूर्ण भाग) का चयन कीजिए।

90. छायावाद के युग में (a)/ राष्ट्रवादी विचारधारा के (b)/ उन्नत स्वर (c)/ सुनने को मिलता है। (d)
(a) (a)
(b) (b)
(c) (c)
(d) (d)

91. दीपावली पर कुछ लोग (a)/ चमचमाती चाँदी के बर्तन (b)/ खरीदने का लोभ संवरण न कर सके। (c)/ कोई त्रुटि नहीं (d)
(a) (a)
(b) (b)
(c) (c)
(d) (d)

92. 'राजा' का विलोम शब्द कौन-सा होगा?
(a) रानी
(b) प्रजा
(c) रंक
(d) सेनापति

93. दिए गए विकल्पों में से 'गोष्ठी' का पर्यायवाची शब्द कौन-सा है?
(a) काया
(b) सभा
(c) कोष
(d) कलेवर

94. दिए गए विकल्पों में से 'स्तुति' शब्द का विपरीतार्थक शब्द कौन-सा है?
(a) प्रशंसा
(b) अशुभ
(c) शुभ
(d) निंदा

95. 'सामान्य' शब्द का विलोम है:
(a) श्रेष्ठ
(b) सर्वज्ञ
(c) साधारण
(d) विशिष्ट

96. 'सत्याग्रह' का संधि-विच्छेद है:
(a) सत्या + ग्रह
(b) सत + आग्रह
(c) सत्य + ग्रह
(d) सत्य + आग्रह

97. 'यशोदा' का सन्धि विच्छेद है:
(a) यशो + दा
(b) यश + दा
(c) यश: + दा
(d) य + शोदा

98. 'खंड' का संधि-विच्छेद है:
(a) खन + ड
(b) खण + ड
(c) खम् + ड
(d) इनमें से कोई नहीं

99. कौन-सी कृति महादेवी वर्मा की है?
(a) नीहार
(b) साकेत
(c) कामायनी
(d) प्रिय-प्रवास

100. कहानी 'बूढ़ी काकी तथा अन्य नाटक' की रचनाकार कौन हैं?
(a) सुधा अरोड़ा
(b) चित्रा मुद्गल
(c) राजी सेठ
(d) कृष्णा सोबती

// Smart Answer Sheet //

Correct — Percentage of students who answered correctly.

Skipped — Percentage of students who skipped.

Q.	Ans.	Correct / Skipped	Q.	Ans.	Correct / Skipped	Q.	Ans.	Correct / Skipped
1	D	66.92% / 1.54%	2	D	51.68% / 1.04%	3	C	32.34% / 4.82%
4	D	43.28% / 1.85%	5	A	45.07% / 1.66%	6	B	55.12% / 1.93%
7	B	63.54% / 1.4%	8	B	79.69% / 0.0%	9	B	59.69% / 1.05%
10	A	17.33% / 4.82%	11	B	59.5% / 1.37%	12	C	18.44% / 4.05%
13	C	87.72% / 0.0%	14	D	14.77% / 3.76%	15	B	61.74% / 1.18%
16	C	56.36% / 1.2%	17	D	47.72% / 1.65%	18	A	44.82% / 1.25%
19	B	28.73% / 3.34%	20	D	82.63% / 0.0%	21	B	84.29% / 0.0%
22	B	88.69% / 0.0%	23	C	66.27% / 1.9%	24	D	67.65% / 1.98%
25	D	41.27% / 1.28%	26	C	85.87% / 0.0%	27	A	44.84% / 1.34%
28	B	69.04% / 1.92%	29	A	15.2% / 3.13%	30	C	61.05% / 1.63%
31	C	42.81% / 1.6%	32	A	14.39% / 3.16%	33	B	43.7% / 1.78%
34	D	83.24% / 0.0%	35	A	41.57% / 1.67%	36	C	18.86% / 4.51%
37	A	44.08% / 1.86%	38	A	57.96% / 1.06%	39	B	79.67% / 0.0%
40	C	80.67% / 0.0%	41	D	77.92% / 0.0%	42	D	64.77% / 1.35%
43	D	47.17% / 1.81%	44	A	63.49% / 1.73%	45	B	11.66% / 4.34%
46	D	40.83% / 1.24%	47	D	61.05% / 1.95%	48	D	51.77% / 1.83%
49	C	82.65% / 0.0%	50	B	54.98% / 1.97%	51	B	51.29% / 1.27%
52	C	60.09% / 1.4%	53	A	49.28% / 1.46%	54	C	60.93% / 1.52%
55	A	48.86% / 1.87%	56	C	46.8% / 1.61%	57	B	53.89% / 1.47%
58	B	60.24% / 1.85%	59	A	53.19% / 1.8%	60	C	69.8% / 1.86%
61	C	46.0% / 1.83%	62	A	25.07% / 3.23%	63	D	46.19% / 1.1%
64	B	67.62% / 1.09%	65	D	53.46% / 1.13%	66	C	83.76% / 0.0%
67	C	79.35% / 0.0%	68	A	26.88% / 3.98%	69	C	45.16% / 1.43%
70	D	69.27%	71	D	67.45%	72	C	58.48%

Q.	Ans	%	Q.	Ans	%	Q.	Ans	%
		1.14%			1.27%			1.29%
73	B	66.09%	74	D	10.66%	75	A	26.5%
		1.72%			3.25%			3.13%
76	A	89.33%	77	A	66.5%	78	B	86.72%
		0.0%			1.13%			0.0%
79	C	82.61%	80	B	59.02%	81	B	58.04%
		0.0%			1.44%			1.81%
82	D	40.87%	83	A	42.76%	84	D	88.1%
		1.92%			1.24%			0.0%
85	B	51.58%	86	D	51.77%	87	A	85.84%
		1.22%			1.68%			0.0%
88	D	43.81%	89	C	41.08%	90	D	47.64%
		1.27%			1.23%			1.72%
91	B	51.22%	92	C	83.69%	93	B	46.14%
		1.09%			0.0%			1.57%
94	D	64.6%	95	D	76.82%	96	D	68.88%
		1.79%			0.0%			1.88%
97	C	45.57%	98	C	64.95%	99	A	67.66%
		1.22%			1.04%			1.11%
100	B	55.61%						
		1.72%						

// Hints and Solutions //

1(D). The "Discovery of India" was authored by Jawaharlal Nehru.

Books	Authors
My Experiments with Truth, Hind Swaraj, Key to Health	Mahatma Gandhi
Discovery of India, Glimpses of World History	Jawaharlal Nehru
Golden Threshold, The Broken Wing, Songs of Life, Death & the Spring, The Birds of Time, Songs of Life, The Sceptred Flute: Songs of India, The Feather of the Dawn	Sarojini Naidu
Poverty and Un-British Rule in India	Dadabhai Naoroji
Geeta Rahashya, The Arctic Home in the Vedas	Bal Gangadhar Tilak
The Indian War of Independence of 1857	V.D. Savarkar
Unhappy India	Lala Lajpat Rai

5(A). Lord Curzon partitioned Bengal on October 16, 1905, as a result of which the anti-secession movement broke out. The partition of Bengal was canceled in 1911 during the time of Lord Hardinge.

6(B). In 1917, the Calcutta University Commission was appointed by the Government of India under the Chairmanship of Mr. Michel Sadler, the Vice-Chancellor of the University of Leeds.

7(B). The statements A, B and C all are false.
- Th e period that starts in June and ends in September is referred to as the Southwest Monsoon' period.
- The Southwest Monsoon is the significant rainy season for India.
- This is the summer monsoon where the southwest monsoon holds away over the country.
- Southwest monsoon season that is marked by the onset and advance of monsoon is caused by the Arabian Sea and Bay of Bengal winds.

8(B). Brahmaputra the river Yarlung Tsangpo is known in India.
The source of the Yarlung Tsangpo river is the Chemayungdung glacier (Kailas range). The river flows through Tibet & China and enters India at Namcha Barwa (Arunanchal Pradesh) known as Dihang. When it enters Assam, it is joined by the river Lohit and known as the river Brahmaputra and drains into the Bay of Bengal.

9(B). Alluvial soils are formed mainly due to silt deposited by Indo-Gangetic-Brahmaputra rivers.
In coastal regions, some alluvial deposits are formed due to wave action. Most of the soil is Sandy and clayey soils are not uncommon. Porosity and texture provide good drainage and other conditions favorable for agriculture. They yield splendid crops of rice, wheat, sugarcane, tobacco, cotton, jute, maize, oilseeds, vegetables and fruits.

10(A). Lok Sabha passed Central Universities (Amendment), Bill 2022 for conversion of the National Rail and Transportation Institute (NRTI), a Deemed to be University into Gati Shakti Vishwavidyalaya (GSV), a Central University. As per the Education Ministry, the Gati Shakti University will be a world-class, multi-disciplinary, and futuristic institution for the transport sectors.

11(B). The Climate and Clean Air Coalition to Reduce Short-Lived Climate Pollutants (CCAC) was launched by the United Nations Environment Programme (UNEP) and six countries—Bangladesh, Canada, Ghana, Mexico, Sweden, and the United States—in 2012. So, the statement 1 is incorrect.
Short-lived climate pollutants (SLCPs) are agents that have a relatively short lifetime in the atmosphere – a few days to a few decades – and a warming influence on climate. The main short-lived climate pollutants are black carbon, methane and tropospheric ozone, which are the most important contributors to the human enhancement of the global greenhouse effect after CO_2. So, statement 2 is correct.

12(C). Defence minister Rajnath Singh inaugurated Siyom bridge in Arunachal Pradesh in January 2023.
The Siyom bridge on the Along-Yinkiong Road, a 100-meter 'Class-70' steel arch superstructure will facilitate faster induction of troops and heavy equipment to forward areas of the Upper Siang district, Tuting and Yinkiong regions along the Line of Actual Control (LAC). It was built by Border Roads Organisation.

13(C). Uttar Pradesh government launches portal for One Family, One ID. The Uttar Pradesh govt launched the portal for the creation of "One Family One Identity" in Feb 2023. It was launched to identify families as a unit for implementing the 'one job per family' proposal.

14(D). DAP is an example of binary fertilizer.

DAP i.e. Diammonium phosphate is a very famous fertilizer.

Fertilizers are substances which when added to the soil, help in supplying nutrients that are essential for the growth of plants and also help in aeration and water retention of soil.

They may be natural or synthetic.

Natural fertilizers include manure, compost, etc.

Synthetic or artificial fertilizers are the man-made ones that provide specific nutrients that the soil lacks.

Nitrogen (N), Phosphorous (P), and Potassium(K) are the macronutrients essential for the growth of plants.

15(B). A barometer is an instrument that measures atmospheric pressure. It is used in forecasting the weather and determining altitude. Please note that the elevator is going upwards with acceleration a. The net acceleration is the sum of a and g(acceleration due to gravity)

Pressure= Height of mercury column x

Density of mercury x gravity

As there is no compression of air in the elevator its density remains the same. Atmospheric pressure is also the same when the elevator is at rest or moving. The height of the mercury column will have a different reading when the elevator is at rest or moving.

$P = hdg = h'd(a+g) \quad - \cdots > h' = hg/(a+g)$

Effective g increases and the value of h decreases. Therefore, the reading of the barometer would be <760 mm.

16(C). Stalactites and stalagmites consist of deposits of calcium carbonate. The mineral deposits build up over time, forming the characteristic cone or cylinder shapes of stalactites and stalagmites.

17(D). The theory that explains the convincing origin of the state describes the state is the product of growth, a calm and composed evolution stretching over a long period of time and ultimately shaping itself into the complex structure of a modern state. Thus, we can say state is a continuous development of human society.

18(A). The first joint sitting took place in May 1961 when there were disagreements between the Lok Sabha and Rajya Sabha over a few amendments to the Dowry Prohibition Bill. The provision regarding the joint sitting of the two Houses has been invoked only thrice since 1950.

19(B). After following the recommendations of the State Reorganization Commission in 1956, the number of elected MLAs in the Bihar Legislative Assembly was 330. The number of seats in the House of people was 55 in Bihar. The State Reorganization Commission was set up in India in 1956, to recommend the reorganization of state boundaries along linguistic lines.

20(D). Uttar Pradesh 'Start-up Fund' was launched on 20th May, 2020 .

- On March 20, 2020, Uttar Pradesh Chief Minister Yogi Adityanath unveiled the 'UP Start-up Fund,' which would be maintained by the Small Industries Development Bank of India (SIDBI).

- The fund was established as part of the 2017 U.P. Information Technology and Start-up Policy

.

- The fund will be organised as a Fund of Funds.
- The fund would not engage directly in start-ups under this model; instead, it will invest in Alternative Investment Funds certified by the Securities and Exchange Board of India (SEBI).
- SIDBI will operate as the fund manager, and it will be properly managed.
- The state now has 18 incubators and over 1,800 start-ups in operation.
- In the start-up rankings of several states, the Centre named Uttar Pradesh as an "Inspiring Leader" in 2018.
- The key agency for the development of the start-up ecosystem is UP Electronics Corporation.

23(C). Uber Cup is awarded for women in the sport of Badminton.

The Uber Cup, sometimes referred to as the Women's World Team Championship, is a major international badminton competition contested by national women's badminton teams from various countries. It was first organized in 1956–1957 at an interval of three years. Then from 1984 it started happening at an interval of every two years.

24(D). The government in the Budget unveiled the Disinvestment/Strategic Disinvestment Policy and identified the following four sectors as strategic sectors, where bare minimum CPSEs would be retained.

- Atomic energy, Space and Defence
- Transport and Telecommunications
- Power, Petroleum, Coal and other minerals
- Banking, Insurance and financial services. So, statements 1, 2, 3 and 4 are correct.

25(D). In June 2022, Lightyear unveiled a new solar-powered electric vehicle, called the One, which can travel up to 450 miles on a single charge and uses solar panels to recharge the battery.

26(C). On Evaluating $37.188 \div 3.6 = \dfrac{37.188}{3.6} = 10.33$

27(A). Given:

Marked percentage on goods = 30%

Discount Percentage = 10%

Selling Price = Cost Price + Profit

Profit percent = $\dfrac{\text{Profit}}{\text{Cost Price}} \times 100$

Discount = Marked Price − Selling Price

Discount percent = $\dfrac{\text{Discount}}{\text{Marked Price}} \times 100$

Let the cost price be = 100a

Marked price = $100a + 100a \times \dfrac{30}{100} = 130a$

Selling price after discount

$= 130a - (130a \times \dfrac{10}{100})$

$= 117a$

Selling price for 6.5% more profit

$= 117a + 100a \times \dfrac{6.5}{100} \Rightarrow 117a + 6.5a = 123.5a$

$\therefore$ New Discount percent

$= \dfrac{(130a - 123.5a)}{130a} \times 100$

$= 5\%$

28(B). Given:

Cost Price of 50 Coca-Cola Bottles = Selling Price of

40 Coca-Cola Bottles
$\Rightarrow$ CP $\times$ 50 = SP $\times$ 40
$\Rightarrow \dfrac{\text{SP}}{\text{CP}} = \dfrac{50}{40}$
$\Rightarrow \dfrac{\text{SP}}{\text{CP}} = \dfrac{5}{4}$
Here, $\dfrac{\text{SP}}{\text{CP}} > 1$
This means SP > CP and there is a profit in the transaction.
Let the SP be 5x and CP be 4x.
So, Profit% = $\left(\dfrac{\text{SP} - \text{CP}}{\text{CP}}\right) \times 100\%$
$= \dfrac{5x - 4x}{4x} \times 100\%$
$= \left(\dfrac{1x}{4x}\right) \times 100\%$
$\Rightarrow \left(\dfrac{1}{4}\right) \times 100\%$
$= 25\%$
$\therefore$ The Profit percentage is 25%.

29(A). Given-
A principal amounts to $Rs.\,6690$ after 3 years and to $Rs.\,10035$ after 6 years.
Let the principal invested be P.
Amount after 3 years $A_1 = Rs.\,6690$
$\Rightarrow 6690 = P\left(1 + \dfrac{R}{100}\right)^3$ --- (1)
where R is rate of interest
Amount after 6 years $A_2 = Rs.\,10035$
$\Rightarrow 10035 = P\left(1 + \dfrac{R}{100}\right)^6$ --- (2)
On dividing equation (2) by equation (1) we get,
$\Rightarrow \dfrac{10035}{6690} = \left(1 + \dfrac{R}{100}\right)^3$
$\Rightarrow \left(1 + \dfrac{R}{100}\right)^3 = \dfrac{3}{2}$
On keeping $\left(1 + \dfrac{R}{100}\right)^3 = \dfrac{3}{2}$ in equation (1) we get,
$\Rightarrow 6690 = P \times \dfrac{3}{2}$
$\Rightarrow P = Rs.\,4460$

30(C). We know the formula for compound interest:
$\Rightarrow \text{CI} = \left[P\left\{\left(1 + \dfrac{R}{100}\right)^t - 1\right\}\right]$
Where,
CI = Compound interest, P = Principal, R = Rate of interest, t = Time period
Now,
$\text{CI} = \left[P\left\{\left(1 + \dfrac{R}{100}\right)^t - 1\right\}\right]$
$\Rightarrow 6660.9375 = \left[17500\left\{\left(1 + \dfrac{R}{100}\right)^2 - 1\right\}\right]$
$\Rightarrow \dfrac{6660.9375}{17500} = \left[\left\{\left(1 + \dfrac{R}{100}\right)^2 - 1\right\}\right]$
$\Rightarrow 0.380625 + 1 = \left(1 + \dfrac{R}{100}\right)^2$
$\Rightarrow \sqrt{1.380625} = \left(1 + \dfrac{R}{100}\right)$
$\Rightarrow 1.175 - 1 = \dfrac{R}{100}$
$\Rightarrow 0.175 \times 100 = R$
$\Rightarrow R = 17.5\%$
$\therefore$ Rate of interest = 17.5%

31(C). Given:
Side of rectangle increased by 12%,
As we know,
Area of rectangle = Length $\times$ Breadth
Let the length of rectangle = x units
And breadth of rectangle = y units
So, Area of rectangle = xy
New area of rectangle = $(x + 12\% \text{ of } x) \times (y + 12\% \text{ of } y)$
$= \left(\dfrac{112x}{100}\right) \times \left(\dfrac{112y}{100}\right)$

$= \dfrac{12544xy}{10000}$
Increase in area $= \left[\dfrac{(12544xy)}{10000}\right] - xy$
$= \dfrac{(12544xy - 10000xy)}{10000}$
$= \dfrac{2544xy}{10000}$
Required percentage $= \left[\dfrac{\left(\frac{2544xy}{10000}\right)}{(xy)}\right] \times 100$
$= \dfrac{(2544xy \times 100)}{(10000 \times xy)}$
$= 25.44\%$
$\therefore$ The area of rectangle is increased by 25.44%.

32(A). Given:
Length of the park = 42 m, rate of planting flowers
= 2 paisa/m^2
Concept:
Area of semi circle = $\dfrac{\pi r^2}{2}$
Calculations:
From the figure, length of the field = length of rectangle + length(radius) of two semicircles
$\Rightarrow 4x + x + x = 42$ meter
$6x = 42$ meter
$\Rightarrow x = 7$ m = radius
Area of two semi circle = $2 \times \dfrac{\pi r^2}{2}$
$= \dfrac{22}{7} \times 7 \times 7$
$\therefore$ Area of semi circular parts = 22×7 m^2
$= 154$ m^2
Rate of planting = 2 paisa/m^2
$\because$ 2 paisa = Rs. 0.02
Cost of sowing of flowers = 154×0.02 = Rs. 3.08

33(B). Let the smaller numbers be x
The other numbers are $(x + 2)$.
According to the question,
$x + (x + 2) = 66$
$\Rightarrow 2x = 64$
$\Rightarrow x = 32$
$\therefore$ The smaller one is 32.

34(D). Let consecutive even numbers P, Q, R, S and T are $n, n+2, n+4, n+6$ and $n+8$.
$\therefore \dfrac{n + (n+2) + (n+4) + (n+6) + (n+8)}{5} = 106$
$5n = 530 - 20$
$\Rightarrow n = \dfrac{510}{5}$
$\Rightarrow n = 102$
Consecutive even numbers are $102, 104, 106, 108$ and 110.
$Q \times S = 104 \times 108 = 11232$

35(A). Given,
Average weight of 25 Students of a class is 50 kg.
If the weight of the class teacher is included, the average is increased by 1 kg.
Average weight of 25 students of a class is 50 kg.
Sum = $25 \times 50 = 1250$
If the weight of the teacher is added then the average increases by 1 kg.
$\Rightarrow 26 \times 51 = 1326$
Weight of the teacher = 1326 - 1250
= 76 kg

36(C). Given,
Male voters = 55%
Literate male voters percentage = 40%

liliterate female voters percentage $= 33\frac{1}{3}\%$

Let the total voters are $= 100\%$

Female voters $= 100\% - 55\% = 45\%$

Literate male voters $= 55\% \times \frac{40}{100} = 22\%$

Literate female voters $= 45\% \times 66\frac{2}{3}\% = 30\%$

$\therefore$ Total literate voters $= 22\% + 30\% = 52\%$

37(A). Given that,

Total amount earned by A, B, and C in 6 days = Rs 480

The amount earned by them in 1 day $= \frac{480}{6} =$ Rs 80

Amount of money earned is proportional to the amount of work done

Let work done by A, B and C be $4x, 5x$ and $7x$.

$\therefore$ Total work done by A, B and C together $= 16x$

Work done by B $= 5x$

Daily income of B $= \frac{5x}{16x} \times 80 =$ Rs. 25

38(A). Given:

Ratio of efficiency $A : B = 2 : 1$

Ratio of efficiency $B : C = 3 : 4$

Total time taken by A, B and C to complete the work $= 7$ days

Calculation:

Ratio of Efficiency of A and $B = 2 : 1$

Ratio of Efficiency of B and $C - 3 : 4$

By equaling the value of B, we can find the ratio of efficiency of A, B and $C = 6 : 3 : 4$

Total work $= (6 + 3 + 4) \times 7$

$\Rightarrow$ Total work $= 13 \times 7 = 91$ units

Combined efficiency of B and $C = 3 + 4 = 7$ units/day

Time taken by B and c to complete the work $= \frac{91}{7} = 13$ days

$\therefore$ The time taken by B and C to complete the given work is 13 days.

39(B). Given,

P's 1 day work $= \frac{1}{30}$

Q's 1 day work $= \frac{1}{20}$

As we know,

Work = Efficiency $\times$ Time

P's 18 day work $= \frac{18}{30} = \frac{3}{5}$

Remaining work $= 1 - \frac{3}{5} = \frac{2}{5}$

Q's $\frac{2}{5}$ day work $= \frac{1}{20} \times \frac{5}{2} = \frac{1}{8}$

Q will complete the remaining job alone in 8 days.

40(C). Distance covered by the first train in 2 hrs = 40 × 2 = 80 km

Let the speed of the second train be x km/hr

According to the question

Speed $= \frac{Dis\tan ce}{Time}$

$\Rightarrow (x - 40) = \frac{80}{4}$

$\Rightarrow x - 40 = 20$

$\Rightarrow x = 20 + 40$

$\therefore x = 60$ km/hr.

41(D). Given,

Mr. Prasad travelled equal distances at speeds of 2 km/hr, 4 km/hr and 6 km/hr.

Let the distance be d km.

As we know,

Time $= \frac{Distance}{Speed}$

Total time $= 55$ minutes

$\therefore \frac{d}{2} + \frac{d}{4} + \frac{d}{6} = \frac{55}{60}$

$\Rightarrow \frac{6d+3d+2d}{12} = \frac{55}{60}$

$\Rightarrow \frac{11d}{12} = \frac{55}{60}$

$\Rightarrow d = \frac{55 \times 12}{60 \times 11}$

$\Rightarrow d = 1$ km

Total distance $= 3\,d = 3 \times 1 = 3$ km

42(D). Given:

HCF $= 14$

LCM $= 3920$

First number $= 490$

Product of the two numbers $=$ HCF $\times$ LCM

Let the second number be N.

$\Rightarrow 490 \times N = 14 \times 3920$

$\Rightarrow N = \frac{3920}{35}$

$\Rightarrow N = 112$

$\therefore$ The second number is 112.

43(D). Let, Rahul's age = x

$\therefore$ Rahul's brothers age = x + 6

$\therefore$ Rahul's sister's age = x - 4

$\therefore$ Their total age = (x + x + 6 + x - 4) = 3x + 2

$\therefore$ Their average age $= \frac{(3x+2)}{3} = x + \frac{2}{3}$

Required difference $= \left(x + \frac{2}{3}\right) - x$

$= \frac{2}{3}$ year = 8 months

44(A). The given equation is,

$= (\cos 2p\pi + i \sin 2p\pi)(\cos 2q\pi + i \sin 2q\pi)$

$= \cos 2(p + q)\pi + i \sin 2(p + q)\pi$

$= (\cos \pi + i \sin \pi)^{2(p+q)}$

$= (-1 + 0)^{2(p+q)}$

$= (-1)^{2(p+q)} = 1$

45(B). Here, radius = 6 and centre at $(3, 5)$

$\therefore$ Equation of circle

$= (x - 3)^2 + (y - 5)^2 = 6^2$

$\Rightarrow (x - 3)^2 + (y - 5)^2 = 36$

Now check the points,

(A) (-2, -1):

$\Rightarrow (-2-3)^2 + (-1-5)^2$

$= 25 + 36 > 36$

So, this point lies outside of circle.

(B) (0, 1):

$\Rightarrow (0 - 3)^2 + (1 - 5)^2$

$= 9 + 16 < 36$

So, point (0,1) lies inside the circle

46(D). Given:

$\tan \theta + \sin \theta = m$ and $\tan \theta - \sin \theta = n$

$\because mn = (\tan \theta + \sin \theta)(\tan \theta - \sin \theta)$

$= \tan^2 \theta - \sin^2 \theta$

$= \sin^2 \theta \left(\frac{1 - \cos^2 \theta}{\cos^2 \theta}\right)$

$= \frac{\sin^2 \theta}{\cos^2 \theta} \cdot \sin^2 \theta$

$mn = \tan^2 \theta \cdot \sin^2 \theta$

$\sqrt{mn} = \tan \theta \cdot \sin \theta$ ......(i)

Then, $m^2 - n^2 = (\tan \theta + \sin \theta)^2 - (\tan \theta - \sin \theta)^2$

$= 4 \tan \theta \cdot \sin \theta$

$= 4\sqrt{mn}$

47(D). Event A is choosing a yellow pencil first, and Event B is choosing a yellow pencil second.

Initially, there are 12 pencils, 7 of which are yellow.

Probability the first pencil is yellow $= P(A) = \frac{7}{12}$

If a yellow pencil is chosen, there will be 11 pencils left, 6 of which are yellow.

Probability the second pencil is yellow $= P(B) = \frac{6}{11}$

Two pencils are chosen at random from the box without replacement.

So events are independent of each other.

Probability they are both yellow:

$= P(A \cap B) = P(A) \times P(B)$

$= \frac{7}{12} \times \frac{6}{11} = \frac{7}{22}$

48(D). Given:

Number of boys in class $= 7$

Number of girls in class $= 3$

The total number of possible cases:

Case 1 :

When 1 boy and 3 girls are selected.

Total combination $= {}^{7}C_1 \times {}^{3}C_3$

$= \frac{7!}{1!(7-1)!} \times \frac{3!}{3!(3-3)!}$

$= \frac{7 \times 6!}{6!} \times \frac{3!}{3!}$

$= 7 \times 1$

$= 7$

Case 2 :

When 2 boys and 2 girls are selected.

Total combination $= {}^{7}C_2 \times {}^{3}C_2$

$= \frac{7!}{2!(7-2)!} \times \frac{3!}{2!(3-2)!}$

$= \frac{7 \times 6 \times 5!}{2 \times 5!} \times \frac{3 \times 2!}{2!}$

$= 21 \times 3$

$= 63$

Case 3 :

When 3 boys and 1 girl are selected.

Total combination $= {}^{7}C_3 \times {}^{3}C_1$

$= \frac{7!}{3!(7-3)!} \times \frac{3!}{1!(3-1)!}$

$= \frac{7 \times 6 \times 5 \times 4!}{3 \times 2 \times 1 \times 4!} \times \frac{3 \times 2!}{2!}$

$= 35 \times 3$

$= 105$

Case 4 :

When all 4 boys are selected $= {}^{7}C_4$

$= \frac{7!}{4!(7-4)!}$

$= \frac{7 \times 6 \times 5 \times 4!}{4! \times 3 \times 2 \times 1}$

$= 35$

$\therefore$ Total combination $= 7 + 63 + 105 + 35 = 210$

Hence, the correct option is (D).

49(C). Given,

Total GDP $= 60$ billion

Pension payment $= 8\%$

Food subsidy $= 6\%$

Now,

Pension payment $= \frac{8}{100} \times 60$

$= \frac{48}{10}$

$= \frac{24}{5}$

Food subsidy $= \frac{6}{100} \times 60$

$= \frac{36}{10}$

$= \frac{18}{5}$

Now required ratio $= \dfrac{\text{Pension payment}}{\text{Food subsidy}}$

$= \dfrac{\frac{24}{5}}{\frac{18}{5}}$

$= \frac{24}{5} \times \frac{5}{18}$

$= \frac{4}{3}$

So, Required ratio $= 4 : 3$

50(B). Given,

Pension payment $= 8\%$

Defence $= 24\%$

Food subsidy $= 6\%$

Now,

Required expenditure,

$(8 + 24 + 6)\%$ of 60 billion

$= 38\%$ of 60 billion

$= \frac{38}{100} \times 60$ billion

$= \frac{228}{10}$ billion

$= 22.8$ billion

51(B). Innocent and guilty are antonyms.

Similarly,

The antonym of moisten is Dried.

'Dried' is related to the third term in the same way as the second term is related to the first term.

Hence, "dried" is the correct answer.

52(C). In SAO : 35

$\Rightarrow$ Values of S, A, and O are 19, 1, and 15 respectively in the English alphabet and the next term is obtained by;

$\Rightarrow 19 + 1 + 15 = 35$

Similarly,

In NPC : ?

$\Rightarrow$ Values of N, P, and C are 14, 16, and 3 respectively in the English alphabet and the next term is obtained by;

$\Rightarrow 14 + 16 + 3 = 33$

53(A). By using the following symbols in the table given below, we can draw the following family tree:

Symbol in Diagram	Meaning
◯	Female
☐	Male
═══	Married Couple
──	Siblings
│	Difference of A Generation

According to the given information:

Statement: "He is the son of my grandmother's only child's husband's only daughter's husband."

Here, the boy is the son of lady's grandmother's only child's (i.e. lady's mother) husband's (i.e. lady's father) only daughter's (i.e. the lady) husband (i.e. lady's husband).

Thus the following family tree can be drawn:

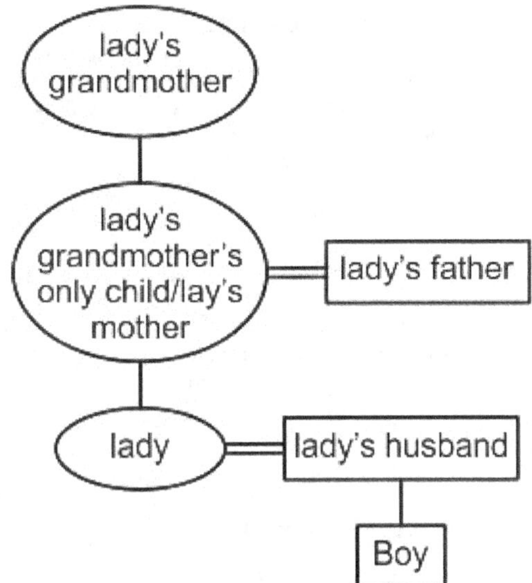

Therefore, the lady is ' Mothe r' of the boy.

54(C). Preparing the family tree using the following symbols:

Symbol in Diagram	Meaning
○	Female
□	Male
══	Married Couple
──	Siblings
│	Difference of A Generation

Given:
A+B means A is the father of B
A-B means A is the mother of B
A*B means A is the sister of B
A/B means A is the brother of B
Let us first decode the given symbols and then draw a family tree

A is				
Symbol	+	-	*	/
Meaning of B	Father	Mother	Sister	Brother

On checking: M+N*O/P
1) M+N
Here, M is the father of N.
2) N*O
Here, N is the sister of O.
3) O/P
Here, O is the brother of P.
• Thus, the following family tree can be drawn.

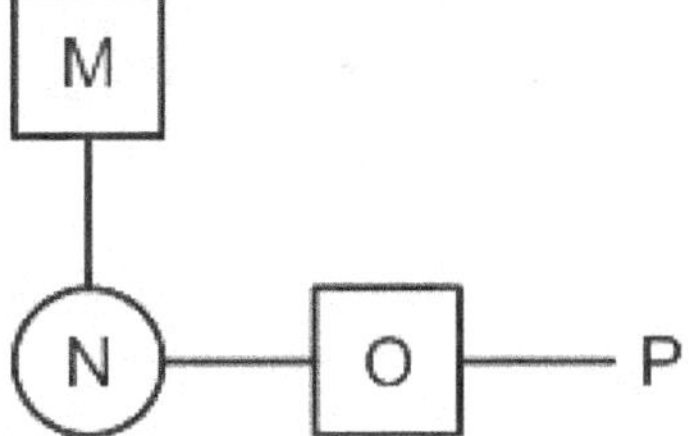

Clearly, N is 'Sister' of 'O' who is the brother of 'P'.

55(A). In each figure, three arrows are in east direction and two are in west direction except for figure (d). In figure (d), two arrows are in east direction and three are in west direction.

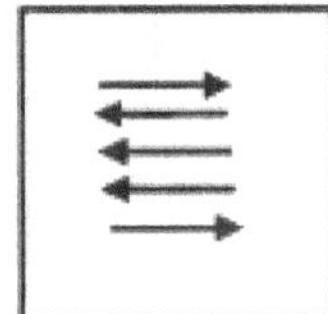

Hence, figure (d) is odd one out.

56(C).

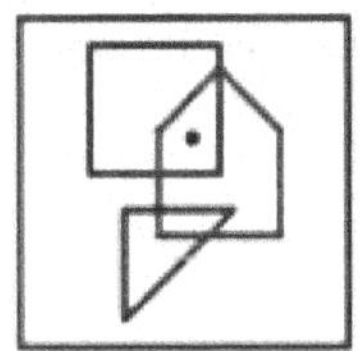

In all the given images except image C, the dot appears in the region common to pentagon and triangle.
Hence, figure C is the odd one among the given options.

57(B). The logic followed here is:
All the figures contain a left semi-shaded portion on the top.
All figure's bottom lines extend and bend to the right, except for figure (B).

Thus option (B) figure is different.

58(B). 1) Sudhir went 20 m in the East.
2) Then he took a U-turn and went 35 m in the west.
3) Then he went 5 m in the North.
4) Then he went 15 m in the East.
The path followed by Sudhir is shown in the map below:

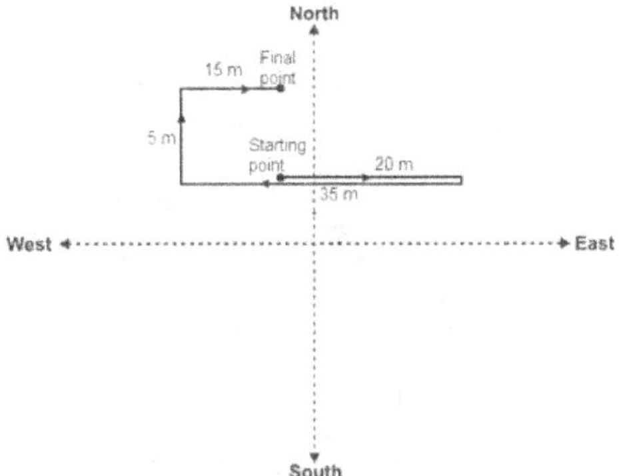

So, the distance between the starting and the final point of Sudhir is "5 m".

59(A). Given:
Telecommunication towers S, J, Z, E, N, and B are plotted on a map.
The direction chart according to the given statements is,

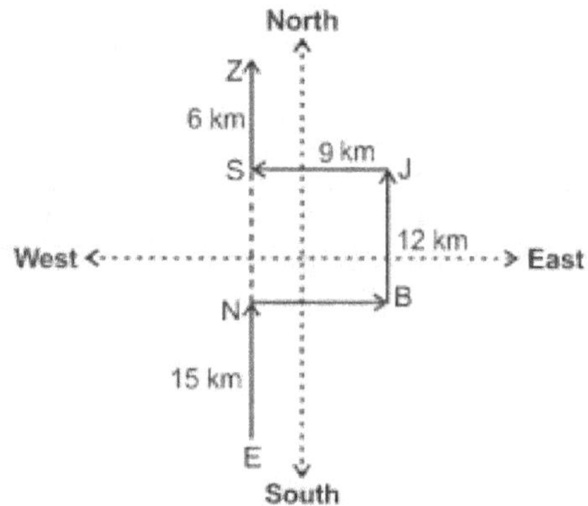

Therefore, Z is to the North of E.
The distance between Z and E is ⇒ 6 + 12 + 15 = 33.
So, the correct answer is "33 km northwards".

60(C). The logic follows here is:
White is called as blue.
Blue is called as red.
Red is called as yellow.
Yellow is called as green.
Green is called as black.
Black is called as violet.
Violet is called as orange.
The color of the human blood is red.
The red in question is called "yellow".

61(C). The pattern followed is:

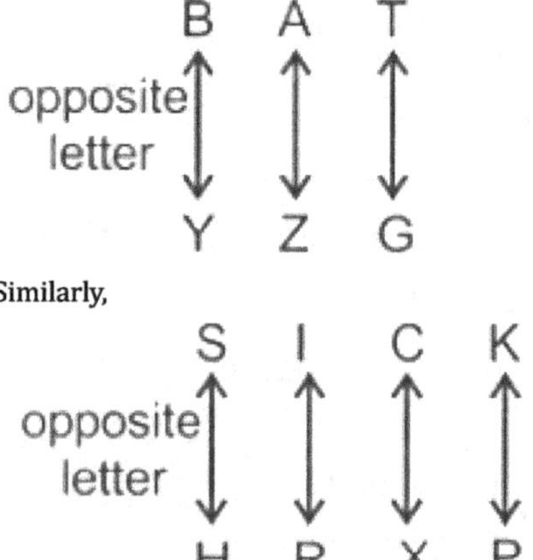

Similarly,

62(A). The option figure that will replace the question mark (?) to continue the figure series given below is option (A).
In 1 st and 2 nd figure, the triangle's appear as mirror image, same in 2 nd and 3 rd figure, square appear as mirror image, so in 4 th figure, the image of circle will appear as mirror image.
This is possible in all options except (D), so it is eliminated.
Again, the circle in the 1 st image is shifted to centre in the 2 nd image, again, the kite in the 2 nd image is shifted to centre in the 3 rd image, so the pentagon in 3 rd image will be shifted to centre in the 4 th image, i.e, the image that will follow the series.
Only option (A) and (C) has pentagon at its centre.

So, we eliminate option (B) here.
Now, we can see that the image of pentagon appears two times in option (C), but in the series this kind of pattern is not followed. So, clearly option (C) is eliminated.

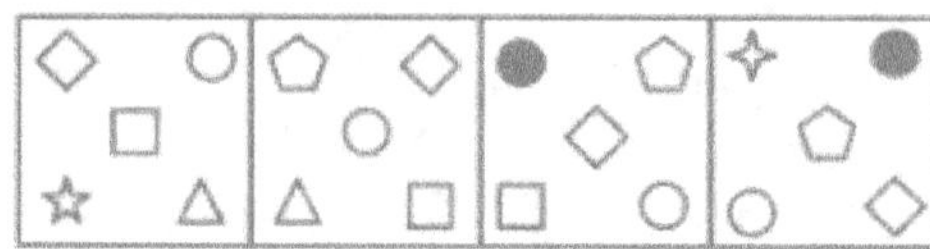

63(D). In one step, the existing element enlarges and a new element appears inside this element. In the next step, the outer element is lost.

64(B).

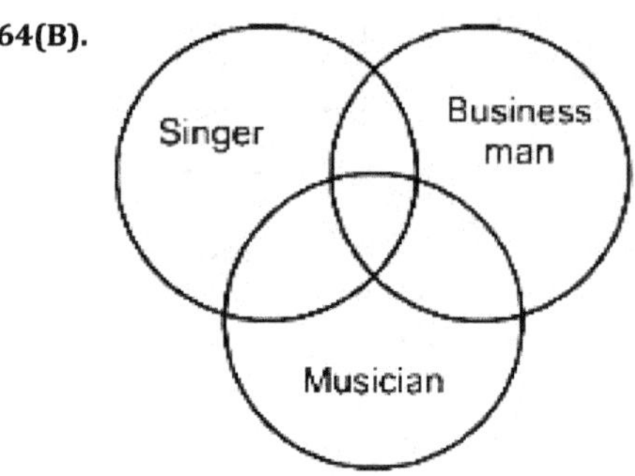

65(D). Fathers can never be women and also women can never be fathers.
Some fathers can be doctors and also some doctors can be fathers.
Some women can be doctors and also some doctors can be women.
This implies-
1) Doctor is common to women as well as to fathers.
2) There is no relation or connection between fathers and women.
Now,

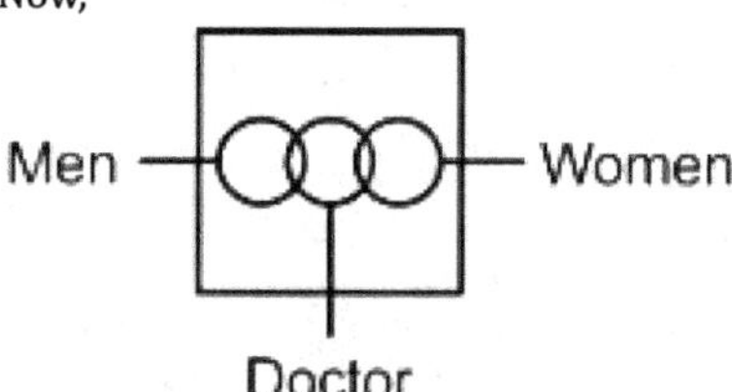

Thus, the Venn Diagram in option 4 of the given options is the correct representation.

66(C). The logic followed here is:
$1^2 = 1$
$3^2 = 9$
$5^2 = 25$
$7^2 = 49$
$9^2 = 81$
$11^2 = 121$
Therefore, 121 is the correct answer.

67(C). The pattern followed is,

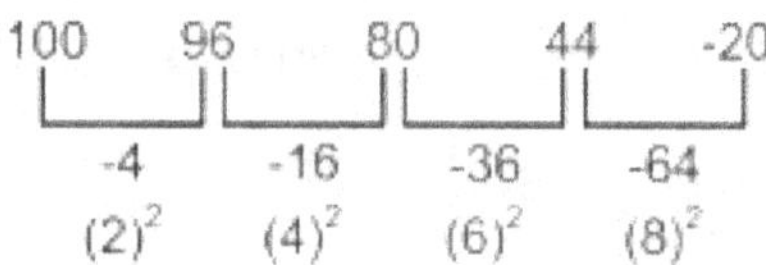

68(A). There are five friends we need to find a person who has two-person taller and shorter than him.
Suresh is shorter than Kamalesh and taller than

Rakesh. While Amit is shorter than Kamalesh and taller than Suresh.

i) Kamalesh > Amit > Suresh > Rakesh.

Also, Mukesh is the tallest among all.

ii) Mukesh > Kamalesh > Amit > Suresh > Rakesh.

As it can be seen that Amit is that person who has two-person shorter and taller than him.

69(C). The current positions of Rahul is the same as the previous positions of Pankaj.

Thus, the number of boys is = (53 rd from the left end + 64 th from the right end - 1) = 116

So, the right answer is 116.

70(D). The least possible Venn diagram for the given statements is as follows,

Books ◯ Novels —— Diary

Conclusions:

I. No book is a diary → False (It is possible but not definite, as there is no direct relation between book and diary Therefore it is possible but not definite).

II. All diaries are books → False (It is possible but not definite, as there is no direct relation between book and diary Therefore it is possible but not definite)

III. No diary is a novel → True (No novel is a diary, imply that no diary is a novel)

Therefore, the correct answer is only conclusion III follows.

71(D). The least possible Venn diagram is:

Cows ◯ Crows ◯ Elephant

I. Some cows are elephants. → False

II. All crows are elephants. → False

So, neither I nor II follows.

72(C). Here, the pattern is:

1st alphabet -1 = 2nd alphabet

And 1st alphabet +1 = 3rd alphabet

(A) M(13) L(12) N(14)

(B) O(15) N(14) P(16)

(D) U(21) T(20) V(22)

(C) P(16) R(18) Q(17)

73(B). The position value of the 1 st alphabet is twice that of the position value of the 2 nd alphabet.

(A) Z(26) M(13),

(C) X(24) L(12),

(D) N(14) G(7),

(B) R(18) H(8)

Ques (74-75): 1) Two persons are sitting between A and F but neither of them is doctor and F is sitting third to the left of A.

Case 1a:

| F | — | — | A | — | Engineers |

| — | — | — | — | — | Doctors |

| — | — | — | — | — | Teachers |

Case 1b:

| — | F | — | — | A | Engineers |

| — | — | — | — | — | Doctors |

| — | — | — | — | — | Teachers |

Case 2a:

| — | — | — | — | — | Engineers |

| — | — | — | — | — | Doctors |

| F | — | — | A | — | Teachers |

Case 2b:

| — | — | — | — | — | Engineers |

| — | — | — | — | — | Doctors |

| — | F | — | — | A | Teachers |

2) N and A are sitting in the same row but N is sitting at one of the ends and J is sitting exactly behind or in front of him.

Case 1a:

| F | — | — | A | N | Engineers |

| — | — | — | — | J | Doctors |

| — | — | — | — | — | Teachers |

Case 1b:

| N | F | — | — | A | Engineers |

| J | — | — | — | — | Doctors |

| — | — | — | — | — | Teachers |

Case 2a:

| — | — | — | — | — | Engineers |

| — | — | — | — | J | Doctors |

| F | — | — | A | N | Teachers |

Case 2b:

| — | — | — | — | — | Engineers |

| J | — | — | — | — | Doctors |

| N | F | — | — | A | Teachers |

3) E is a teacher and two persons are sitting between him and

L but neither E nor L is sitting exactly behind J.
So, cases 2a and 2b are rejected. We have the following cases now:

Case 1a:

F	—	—	A	N	Engineers
—	—	—	—	J	Doctors
E	—	—	L	—	Teachers

Case 1b:

F	—	—	A	N	Engineers
—	—	—	—	J	Doctors
L	—	—	E	—	Teachers

Case 2a:

N	F	—	—	A	Engineers
J	—	—	—	—	Doctors
—	E	—	—	L	Teachers

Case 2b:

N	F	—	—	A	Engineers
J	—	—	—	—	Doctors
—	L	—	—	E	Teachers

4) The number of persons sitting between N and O is the same as the number of persons sitting between E and H.
5) I is sitting exactly behind O.
6) K is neither an engineer nor sitting in the same row as I but he is sitting at one of the ends.

Case 1a:

F	—	O	A	N	Engineers
—	—	I	—	J	Doctors
E	—	H	L	K	Teachers

Case 1b:

F	—	O	A	N	Engineers
—	—	I	—	J	Doctors
L	H	—	E	K	Teachers

Case 2a:

N	F	O	—	A	Engineers
J	—	I	—	—	Doctors
K	E	—	H	L	Teachers

Case 2b:

N	F	O	—	A	Engineers
J	—	I	—	—	Doctors
K	L	H	—	E	Teachers

7) G is sitting exactly behind A but not exactly in front of L.
So, cases 1a and 2a are rejected.
8) C is sitting immediate to the right of H.

Case 1b:

F	—	O	A	N	Engineers
—	—	I	G	J	Doctors
L	H	C	E	K	Teachers

Case 2b:

N	F	O	—	A	Engineers
J	—	I	—	G	Doctors
K	L	H	C	E	Teachers

9) D is not an engineer and not sitting at any of the ends.
10) M is sitting in the same row as G is sitting but they are not neighbours of each other.
11) G is sitting at one of the ends but not in front of L.
So, case 1b is rejected.

N	F	O	B	A	Engineers
J	M	I	D	G	Doctors
K	L	H	C	E	Teachers

74(D). Unlike in other options, in B-L-F, both B and F are from the same row.
So, the correct answer is B-L-F.

75(A). F and O are sitting between N and B.
So, the correct answer is Two.

76(A). व्यंजन सम्बन्धी अशुद्ध वर्तनी "श्राप" है। श्राप शब्द में वर्णपरिवर्तन की अशुद्धि (शब्द की वर्तनी में किसी वर्ण के स्थान पर दूसरा वर्ण लिख देने के कारण) हुई है।
"श्राप" शब्द का शुद्ध रूप है - "शाप"

77(A). अशुद्ध वर्तनी "पुनरवलोकन" है।
पुनरवलोकन शब्द का शुद्ध रूप है – पुनर्वलोकन

78(B). 'अधजल गगरी छलकत जाय' इस कहावत का अर्थ "अल्प ज्ञान पर इतराना" है।
वाक्य प्रयोग - वह दसवी में दो बार फेल हो चुका है और बाते ऐसी करता है जैसे कितना होशियार हो सही कहा गया है अधजल गगरी छलकत जाए।

79(C). 'कंगाली में आटा गीला करना' मुहावरे का अर्थ "मुसीबत में ही मुसीबत आना" है।
वाक्य प्रयोग - वह तो पहले ही गरीबी से जूझ रहा था और अब उसकी नौकरी भी छूट गई।

80(B). 'बालू से तेल निकालना' मुहावरे का अर्थ "असम्भव काम करना" है।
वाक्य प्रयोग- यदि सरकार के पास पैसे नही है तो वह क्या "बालू से तेल निकालकर" पैसे लाएगी।

81(B). 'कहार' पुल्लिंग शब्द है जिसका स्त्रीलिंग "कहारिन" होता है।
अन्य विकल्प -
पुल्लिंग - स्त्रीलिंग
कुम्हार - कुम्हारिन
कहार - कहारिन
अन्य तथ्य -
लिंग - संज्ञा के जिस रूप से व्यक्ति या वस्तु की नर या मादा जाति का बोध हो, उसे व्याकरण में 'लिंग' कहते है।
पुल्लिंग - जिन संज्ञा शब्दों से पुरूष जाति का बोध होता है, उसे पुल्लिंग कहते है। (कुत्ता, बालक, खटमल, पिता, राजा, घोड़ा, बन्दर, हंस, बकरा, लड़का)
स्त्रीलिंग - जिस संज्ञा शब्द से स्त्री जाति का बोध होता है, उसे स्त्रीलिंग कहते है। (माता, रानी, घोड़ी, कुतिया, बंदरिया, हंसिनी, लड़की, बकरी, जूँ)

82(D). 'विदुषी' शब्द का पुलिंग 'विद्वान' है। 'विदुषी' का अर्थ है 'विद्वान महिला'।
अन्य विकल्प:
आयुष्मान: आयुष्मती
बलवान: बलवती
विधुर: विधवा

83(A). आयोजन करने वाला व्यक्ति: आयोजक
जब अनेक शब्दों के लिए एक शब्द का प्रयोग किया जाता है और उसका अर्थ वही रहता है तो उस शब्द को अनेक शब्दों के लिए एक शब्द या वाक्यांशों के लिए एक शब्द कहते हैं। भाषा में सरसता लाने के लिए हम इन शब्दों का उपयोग करते है।

84(D). जो पहले कभी नहीं हुआ: अभूतपूर्व
अभूतपूर्व एक विशेषण है और यह उन क्रियाओं के आगे या किसी घटना के आगे लगाया जाता है जो पहले कभी हुई नहीं हो जैसे सचिन तेंदुलकर द्वारा लगाए गए शतक या चांद पर मनुष्य का पहुंचना आदि। यह ऐसी घटनाएं हैं जो पहले नहीं हुई उन्हें अभूतपूर्व कहा जाता है।

85(B). 'माँ ने बच्चे को सुलाया' दिए गए वाक्य में कर्म कारक की विभक्ति है।
वह वस्तु या व्यक्ति जिस पर वाक्य में की गयी क्रिया का प्रभाव पड़ता है वह कर्म कहलाता है। कर्म कारक का विभक्ति चिन्ह 'को' होता है।

86(D). 'घर से निकाल दिया' में अपादान कारक है।
वाक्य में जिस स्थान या वस्तु से किसी व्यक्ति या वस्तु की पृथकता अथवा तुलना का बोध होता है, वहाँ अपादान कारक

87(A). उप + कार = उपकार
उपकार: संज्ञा पुलिंग [संस्कृत] [विशेषण उपकारक, उपकारी, उपकार्य, उपकृत]
लाभदायक संस्कृत [विशेषण] जो लाभ देने वाला हो; फ़ायदेमंद।
अपनापन [संज्ञा पुल्लिंग] आत्मीयता; घनिष्ठता
उपकार, शब्द में उपसर्ग का प्रयोग हुआ है। अन्य विकल्प में उपसर्ग का प्रयोग नही हुआ है।

88(D). श्रीमती शब्द का बहुवचन श्रीमतियाँ होगा।
संज्ञा के जिस रुप से किसी व्यक्ति, वस्तु, प्राणी, पदार्थ आदि के एक से अधिक होने का बोध होता है या पता चलता है उसे बहुवचन कहते हैं। जैसे-लड़के, बच्चे कपड़े पुस्तकें स्त्रियां टोपिया, गाड़ियां, ठेले, नदियां आदि।

89(C). दिए गए विकल्पों में से 'मेला' शब्द का उचित बहुवचन रूप 'मेले' है।
अन्य विकल्प व्याकरणिक दृष्टि से अनुचित हैं।
मेला पुल्लिंग शब्द है जिसका अर्थ है - उत्सव, देव दर्शन आदि शुभ अवसर पर एकत्र भीड़

90(D). वाक्य के (d) भाग में त्रुटि है, "सुनने को मिलता है।" के स्थान पर "सुनने को मिलते हैं।" होगा।
शुद्ध वाक्य:
छायावाद के युग में राष्ट्रवादी विचारधारा के उन्नत स्वर सुनने को मिलते हैं।

91(B). वाक्य के (b) भाग में त्रुटि है, "चमचमाती चाँदी के बर्तन " के स्थान पर "चाँदी के चमचमाते बतन" होगा।
शुद्ध वाक्य:
"दीपावली पर कुछ लोग चाँदी के चमचमाते बर्तन खरीदने का लोभ संवरण न कर सके।"

92(C). 'राजा' का विलोम शब्द रंक होगा।
एक ऐसा शब्द जिसका अर्थ दूसरे शब्द के अर्थ के विपरीत हो।
उदाहरण: "गर्म" और "ठंडा" विलोम हैं।

93(B). दिए गए विकल्पों में से 'गोष्ठी' का पर्यायवाची शब्द सभा होगा।
गोष्ठी के अन्य पर्यायवाची- सभा, महफिल, मीटिंग।

94(D). 'स्तुति' शब्द का विपरीतार्थक शब्द निंदा होता है।
स्तुति का अर्थ- प्रशंसा
निन्दा का अर्थ- बुराई करना

95(D). 'सामान्य' शब्द का विलोम ' विशिष्ट' है ।
शब्दो के अर्थ:
- सामान्य - मामूली, साधारण
- श्रेष्ठ - अति उत्तम, उत्कृष्ट
- सर्वज्ञ - सबकुछ जाननेवाला
- साधारण - सब जगह पाया जानेवाला, आम, साधारण दृश्य, साधारण पहनावा, सामान्य, मामूली
- विशिष्ट - विशेषता युक्त, असाधारण

96(D). 'सत्याग्रह' का संधि-विच्छेद है - सत्य + आग्रह।
'सत्याग्रह' में दीर्घ संधि है।
जब दो शब्दों की संधि करते समय (अ, आ) के साथ (अ, आ) हो तो 'आ' बनता है, जब (इ, ई) के साथ (इ, ई) हो तो 'ई' बनता है, जब (उ, ऊ) के साथ (उ, ऊ) हो तो 'ऊ' बनता है। उसे दीर्घ संधि कहते है। जैसे- विद्या + अभ्यास = विद्याभ्यास (आ + अ = आ) आदि।

97(C). 'यशोदा' का सन्धि विच्छेद है - यश: + दा।
'यशोदा' में विसर्ग संधि है।
विसर्ग के साथ स्वर अथवा व्यंजन के मिलने से जो विकार उत्पन्न होता है, उसे विसर्ग संधि कहते हैं। जैसे- नम: + कार = नमस्कार आदि।

98(C). 'खंड' का संधि-विच्छेद है - खम् + ड।
खंड में व्यंजन संधि है।
जब संधि करते समय व्यंजन के साथ स्वर या कोई व्यंजन के

मिलने से जो रूप में परिवर्तन होता है, उसे ही व्यंजन संधि कहते हैं। यानी जब दो वर्णों में संधि होती है तो उनमे से पहला यदि व्यंजन होता है और दूसरा स्वर या व्यंजन होता है तो उसे हम व्यंजन संधि कहते हैं। जैसे- अहम् + कार = अहंकार, उत् + लास = उल्लास आदि।

99(A). 'नीहार' नामक कविता संग्रह महादेवी वर्मा की कृति है, यह वर्ष 1930 में प्रकाशित हुई थी। नीहार महादेवी वर्मा की पहली कविता-संग्रह है।

महादेवी वर्मा 'पीड़ा की गायिका ' अथवा 'आधुनिक युग की मीरा ' के नाम से विख्यात हैं। ये श्रीकृष्ण में अटूट श्रद्धा रखती थीं । हिन्दी साहित्य जगत में श्रीमती महादेवी वर्मा जी का उच्चतम स्थान है।

सरस कल्पना, भावुकता एवं वेदनापुर्ण भावों के अभिव्यक्त करने की दृष्टि से इन्हें अपूर्व सफलता प्राप्त हुई है।

अन्य विकल्प -
- साकेत, मैथिलीशरण गुप्त की रचना है।
- कामायनी' जयशंकर प्रसाद तथा प्रिय-प्रवास अयोध्या सिंह उपाध्याय 'हरिऔध' की कृति है।

100(B). कहानी 'बूढ़ी काकी तथा अन्य नाटक' की रचनाकार चित्रा मुद्गल है। इस रचना के लिए में चित्रा मुद्गल को साहित्य अकादमी सम्मान से सम्मानित किया गया था। चित्रा मुद्गल नारी चेतना की प्रमुख लेखिकाओं में से एक है, उनकी प्रमुख रचना 'पोस्ट बॉक्स नम्बर-203 नाला सोपारा' है।

Mock Test 10

1. Who wrote the book 'Hind Swaraj'?
   (a) Mohandas Karamchand Gandhi
   (b) Gopal Krishna Gokhale
   (c) Bal Gangadhar Tilak
   (d) Maulana Azad

2. After the Santhal Uprising subsided, what was/were the measure/measures taken by the colonial government?
   1. The territories called 'Santhal Pargana' were created.
   2. It became illegal for a Santhal to transfer land to a non-Santhal.
   Select the correct answer using the code given below:
   (a) 1 only
   (b) 2 only
   (c) Both 1 and 2
   (d) Neither 1 nor 2

3. Who among the following were the founders of the "Hind Mazdoor Sabha" established in 1948?
   (a) B. Krishan Pillai, E.M.S. Namobodiripad and K.C. George
   (b) Jayaprakash Narayan, Deen Dayal Upadhyay
   (c) C.P Ramaswamy Iyer, K. Kamaraj and Veeressalingam Pantulu
   (d) Ashok Mehta, T.S. Ramanjuam and G.G. Mehta

4. With reference to the religious practices in India, the "Sathanakavasi" sect belongs to:
   (a) Budddhism
   (b) Jainism
   (c) Vaishnavism
   (d) Shaivism

5. The 'Moplah Rebellion' of 1921 was offshoot of:
   (a) Khilafat movement
   (b) The freedom struggle of 1857
   (c) Swadeshi movement
   (d) Non-cooperation movement

6. The Indian National Congress was founded in the year:
   (a) In 1865
   (b) In 1867
   (c) In 1885
   (d) In 1887

7. Examine the following statements and select the appropriate option.
   1. Most of the coalfields in India are found east of 78° East longitude.
   2. The states of Orissa, Chhattisgarh and Jharkhand constitute more than 50% of the total coal production of India.
   (a) 1 and 2 both true
   (b) 1 true, 2 false
   (c) 1 false, 2 true
   (d) 1 and 2 both false

8. The sea level is divided into the following major parts. Select the correct options.
   1. Continental Shelf
   2. Continental gradient
   3. Continental Ridges and Hills
   4. Shallow-deep sea plateau
   5. Deep Sea Plain
   6. Ocean depths
   (a) 1, 2, 3 and 5 only
   (b) 1, 2, 5 and 6 only
   (c) 1, 2, 4 and 6 only
   (d) 2, 3, 4, 5 and 6 only

9. In soil, water that is readily available to plant roots is known as which of the following?
   (a) Bound water
   (b) Hygroscopic water
   (c) Capillary water
   (d) Gravitational water

10. What is the rank of India in the 2022 Global Innovation Index, released in September 2022?
    (a) 30th
    (b) 10th
    (c) 20th
    (d) 40th

11. Which state has inaugurated a new vehicle location control centre and mobile app to boost security for women in January 2023?
    (a) Maharashtra
    (b) Andhra Pradesh
    (c) Assam
    (d) West Bengal

12. When was the 5th World Braille Day observed across the globe by the United Nations (UN)?
    (a) 4th January 2023
    (b) 3rd January 2023
    (c) 2nd January 2023
    (d) 1st January 2023

13. Which of the following company has been penalized by the Competition Commission of India (CCI) for abusing its dominant position in multiple markets?
    (a) Google
    (b) Microsoft
    (c) Meta
    (d) Apple

14. Which one of the following is NOT an electromagnetic wave?
    (a) Light wave
    (b) Radio wave
    (c) Sound wave
    (d) Microwave

15. With reference to 'Polycrack', the world's first patented heterogeneous catalytic process, which of the following statements is/are correct?
    1. It converts multiple feedstocks into hydrocarbon liquid fuels, gas, carbon, and water.
    2. It does not emit any hazardous pollutants into the atmosphere.
    3. It can be fed with un-segregated municipal solid waste with moisture up to 50%.
    Select the correct answer using the code given below.
    (a) 1 only
    (b) 1 and 3 only
    (c) 1, 2 and 3
    (d) 3 only

16. Which of the following is an example of air pollution?
    (a) Smoke and fog
    (b) Exhaust gas from cars
    (c) Gases from burning wood or charcoal
    (d) All of these

17. The important feature of democracy is to give prominence to which of the following?
    (a) Executive
    (b) Judiciary
    (c) Citizen
    (d) Civil society

18. Which of the following is a writ which can be enforced only against a public official?
    (a) habeas corpus
    (b) mandamus
    (c) Prohibition
    (d) Certiorari

19. When was the 'Shimla Agreement' signed between India and Pakistan?
    (a) 1972
    (b) 1978
    (c) 1976
    (d) 1974

20. The New Industrial Policy (2016) of Government of Jharkhand has given top priority to rural electrification

with an objective of?
(a) 70% Electrification by 2017
(b) 80% Electrification by 2017
(c) 90% Electrification by 2017
(d) 100% Electrification by 2017

21. In general, the main objective of monetary policy is:
(a) control money supply
(b) controlling private banks
(c) control the stock market
(d) deregulation of the precious metals market

22. The current rate of cash reserve ratio declared by the Reserve Bank of India is:
(a) 11%   (b) 10%
(c) 9%   (d) 8%

23. Which Indian cricketer has surpassed Kapil Dev's 434 wickets in Test Cricket in March 2022?
(a) Ravichandran Ashwin
(b) Harbhajan Singh
(c) Jayant Yadav
(d) Mohammed Shami

24. With reference to the newly announced strategic disinvestment policy in the budget 2021, consider the following statements:
1. Under this policy disinvestment proceeds will be credited into the National Investment and Infrastructure Fund.
2. Strategic disinvestment in India includes the transfer of management control from the government to the private sector.
Which of the statements given above is/are correct?
(a) 1 only   (b) 2 only
(c) Both 1 and 2   (d) Neither 1 nor 2

25. Consider the following statements regarding International Space Station (ISS):
1. The International Space Station (ISS) is a modular space station (habitable artificial satellite) in low Earth orbit.
2. The ISS programme is a multi-national collaborative project between four participating space agencies.
Which of the statements given above is/are correct?
(a) 1 only   (b) 2 only
(c) Both 1 and 2   (d) Neither 1 nor 2

Mathematics

26. Direction: What should come in place of the question mark (?) in the following question?
14.28% of 630 + 32% of ? = 202
(a) 310   (b) 320
(c) 330   (d) 350

27. If an item is sold at a 10% discount to Rohit and a 30% discount to Abhishek and difference between their selling price is Rs. 240. Find the marked price of the article.
(a) Rs. 1200   (b) Rs. 1100
(c) Rs. 1000   (d) Rs. 1500

28. Rakesh marked the price of an article 30% above the cost price and sells that article after giving a 10% discount and makes a profit of Rs. 340. Find the cost price of the article.

(a) Rs. 2000   (b) Rs. 3000
(c) Rs. 4000   (d) Rs. 2500

29. A sum of money at simple interest amounts to Rs. 4,480 in 2 years and Rs. 5,200 in 5 years. What is the original sum?
(a) Rs. 4,000   (b) Rs. 3,500
(c) Rs. 3,000   (d) Rs. 2, 500

30. A person deposited $Rs.\,400$ for 2 years, $Rs.\,550$ for 4 years and $Rs.\,1200$ for 6 years. He received a total of $Rs.\,1020$ as simple interest. Find the rate percent per annum.
(a) 10%   (b) 15%
(c) 25%   (d) 30%

31. A conical figure is reformed where the radius is increased by 20 percent and the height is reduced by 20 percent. What is the change in the volume of the figure?
(a) 15.2 percent increase
(b) 20 percent increase
(c) 20 percent decrease
(d) 15.2 percent decrease

32. The curved surface area of a cylinder is $594 cm^2$ and its vol is $1336.5 cm^3$. What is the height (in cm) of the cylinder?
(a) 114 cm   (b) 21 cm
(c) 24.5 cm   (d) 10.5 cm

33. If the number 2632A4878 is completely divisible by 9. Find the possible value of 'A'.
(a) 5   (b) 4
(c) 2   (d) 3

34. Without considering the salary of the boss, the average salary reduces by Rs. 1000. What will be salary of boss if average salary of 11 employees and the boss is Rs. 18000 ?
(a) Rs. 30000   (b) Rs. 27000
(c) Rs. 36000   (d) Rs. 29000

35. The average price of 20 books is Rs. 14, while the average price of 18 of these books is Rs. 13. Out of the remaining two books, if the value of one book is 21.05% of the other, what will be the value of each of these two books?
(a) Rs. 36, Rs. 10   (b) Rs. 38, Rs. 8
(c) Rs. 40, Rs. 6   (d) Rs. 25, Rs. 21

36. If the number when subtracted from 37.5% of itself gives the result as 35, find the original number.
(a) 90   (b) 49
(c) 56   (d) 72

37. Sakshi can do a piece of work in 20 days. Tanya is 25% more efficient than Sakshi. The number of days taken by Tanya to do the same piece of work is:
(a) 15   (b) 16
(c) 18   (d) 25

38. A can do a piece of work in 12 hours, while B can do it in 8 hours. If A and B both work together, so in how many hours the work will be completed?
(a) 10 hours   (b) 4 hours
(c) 5 hours 15 minutes   (d) 4 hours 48 minutes

39. A can do 20% of a work in 4 days. B can do 33.33% work in 10 days. They worked together for 9 days. C complete the remaining work in 6 days. B and C together will complete 75% of the same work in:

(a) 15 days   (b) 12 days

(c) 10 days   (d) 9 days

40. Two trains running in opposite directions cross a man standing on the platform in 25 seconds and 32 seconds respectively and they cross each other in 30 seconds. The ratio of their speed is:

(a) 4 : 3   (b) 2 : 5

(c) 5 : 6   (d) 1 : 3

41. Ramdev covers a distance of 30 km at a speed of 60 km/hr and another 50 km at a speed of 100 km/hr, what is his average speed for the whole journey?

(a) 100 km/hr   (b) 82 km/hr

(c) 80 km/hr   (d) 85 km/hr

42. If the product of two numbers is 3360 and their LCM is 96, find their HCF.

(a) 35   (b) 33

(c) 34   (d) 29

43. A is two years older than B who is twice as old as C. If the total of the ages of A, B and C be 27, the how old is B?

(a) 7   (b) 8

(c) 9   (d) 10

44. If $4x + 5y = 14$ and $x - 5y = 16$ then the value of x and y are:

(a) 10 and $\frac{-6}{5}$ (b) 6 and 2

(c) 10 and $\frac{6}{5}$ (d) 6 and -2

45. What is the focus of the parabola $4x^2 + y = 0$?

(a) $\left(0, \frac{-1}{18}\right)$ (b) $\left(0, \frac{1}{2}\right)$

(c) $\left(0, \frac{1}{4}\right)$ (d) $\left(0, \frac{-1}{16}\right)$

46. Find the value of $\cot A \cot 2A - \cot 2A \cot 3A - \cot 3A \cot A$

(a) 1   (b) 0

(c) $\frac{1}{2}$ (d) $\frac{\sqrt{3}}{2}$

47. If A and B are two events such that $P(A) = 0.5, P(B) = 0.6$ and $P(A \cap B) = 0.4$, then what is $P(\overline{A \cup B})$ equal to?

(a) 0.9   (b) 0.7

(c) 0.5   (d) 0.3

48. There are 20 points in a plane, how many triangles can be formed by these points if 5 are colinear?

(a) 1130   (b) 550

(c) 1129   (d) 1140

Ques (49-50): Direction: The line chart given below shows the sales (in crores) of campany A and D from July to Decermber.

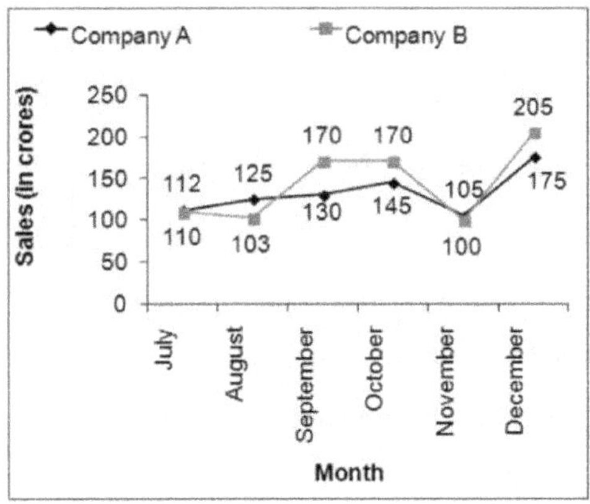

49. The sales of company A in November is how much percent more than the sales of company B in November?

(a) 5   (b) 10

(c) 8   (d) 15

50. The sales of company B is same in which two months?

(a) October and November

(b) August and November

(c) August and November

(d) July and August

Reasoning

51. If FLOW is related to RIVER then STAGNANT is related to:

(a) Pool   (b) Rain

(c) Stream   (d) Canal

52. If DOG is to RABIES then MOSQUITO is to:

(a) Plague   (b) Death

(c) Malaria   (d) Sting

Ques (53-54): DIRECTIONS : Study the following information and answer the questions given below it:

All the six members of a family A, B, C, D, E and F are travelling together. B is the daughter of C but C is not the father of B. A and C are a married couple. E is the sister of C. D is the son of A. F is the sister of B.

53. How many male members are there in the family?

(a) 1   (b) 2

(c) 3   (d) 4

54. Who is the father of B?

(a) D   (b) F

(c) E   (d) A

55. **Direction :** Choose the figure which is different from the rest.

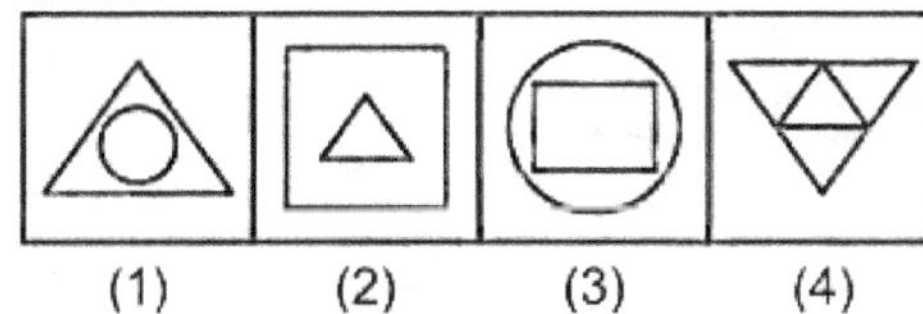

(a) 1   (b) 2

(c) 3   (d) 4

56. **Direction:** Out of given figure, three figures are similar in a certain way, one figure is not like the others. Find out the figure which does not belongs the group.

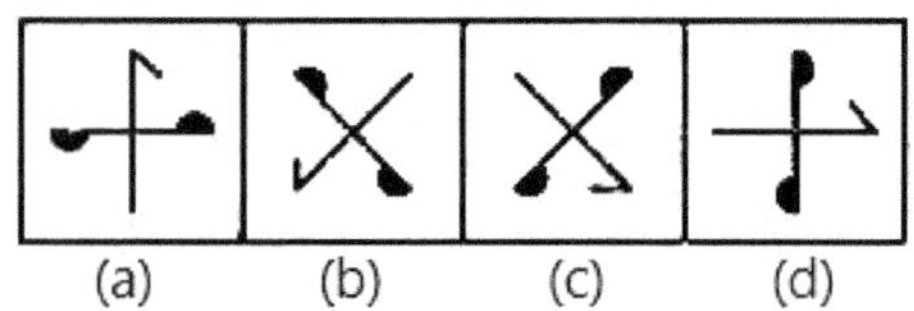

(a)   (b)   (c)   (d)

(a) c   (b) d
(c) b   (d) a

57. Direction : Find the odd one out.

A	B	C	D
☆	☆	☆	☆

(a) C   (b) A
(c) D   (d) B

58. A girl starts from her house and walks 4 km towards East and walks 5km after taking a right turn. She then turns right and walks 4 km and takes another right and walks 3km. Which direction should she walk to reach her house?

(a) South   (b) West
(c) East   (d) North

59. Point B is 3 metres north of point A. Point C is 3 metres west of point B. Point D is 5 metres south of point C. Point E is 7 metres east of point D. In which of the following directions is point E, with reference to point B?

(a) South-East   (b) North-East
(c) South   (d) None of these

60. In a certain code language, "REPORT" is written as "PERTRO". How is "SECOND" written in that code language?

(a) CSENOD   (b) CESDNO
(c) ESDNOC   (d) EDNOCS

61. If in a certain code EDITION is written as 3891965 , then how TIDE will be written in that code?

(a) 3819   (b) 1983
(c) 1839   (d) 1586

62. Direction: Select a figure from amongst the Answer Figures which will continue the same series as established by the five Problem Figures.
Problem Figures:

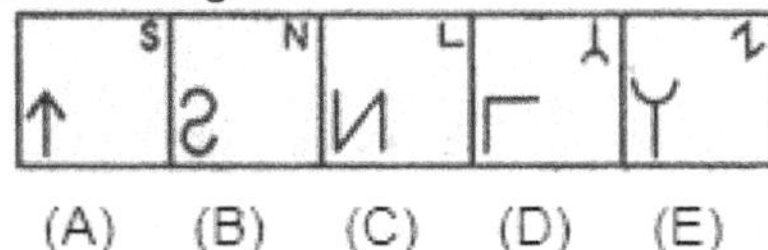

(A)   (B)   (C)   (D)   (E)

Answer Figures:

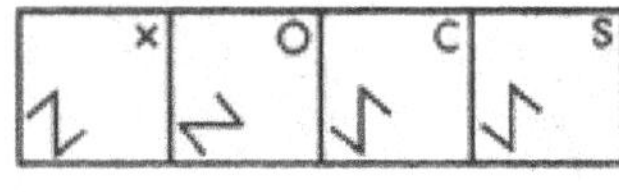

(1)   (2)   (3)   (4)

(a) 1   (b) 2
(c) 3   (d) 4

63. Direction: Select a figure from amongst the Answer Figures which will continue the same series as established by the five Problem Figures.
Problem Figures:

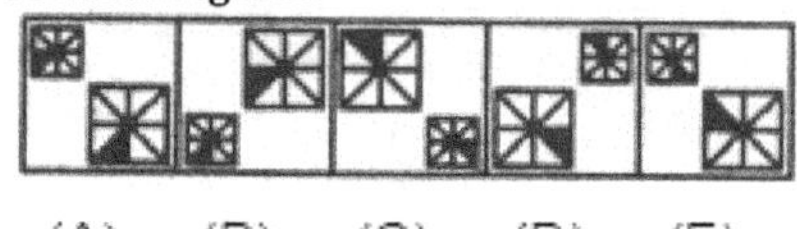

(A)   (B)   (C)   (D)   (E)

Answer Figures:

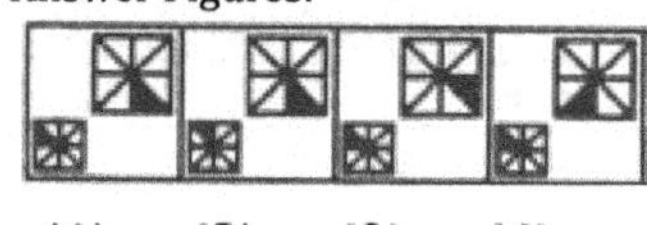

(1)   (2)   (3)   (4)

(a) (1)   (b) (2)
(c) (3)   (d) (4)

Ques (64-65): Direction: Identify the diagram that best represents the relationship among classes given below:

64. Furniture, Chair, Table

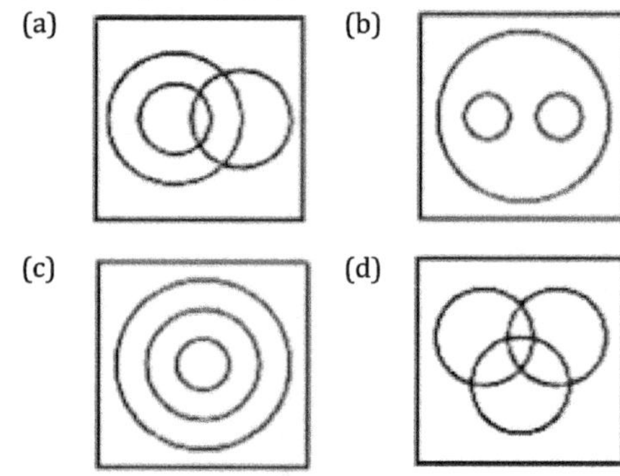

(a)   (b)

(c)   (d)

65. Jharkhand, Goa, Panaji

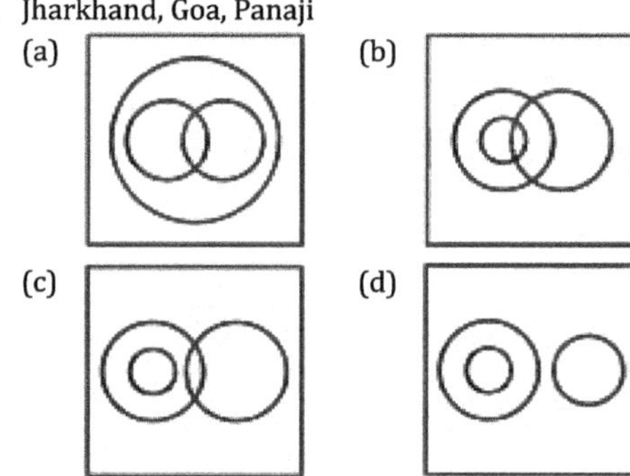

(a)   (b)

(c)   (d)

66. Find the two missing terms in the series:
8, 4, 12, 6, ?, 9, ? and select the answer from the following:

(a) (12, 18)   (b) (18, 27)
(c) (12, 27)   (d) (15, 36)

67. Which number does not belong to the class of others?
11, 21, 51, 81, 91, 111

(a) 11   (b) 81
(c) 91   (d) 111

68. Aarti is older than Saumya. Muskan is elder to Aarti but younger than Kashish. Kashish is older than Saumya. Saumya is younger than Muskan. Gargi is the eldest. Who is the youngest?

(a) Saumya   (b) Kashish
(c) Aarti   (d) Muskan

69. B, F, J, K and W each of different weights, F is heavier than just J . Heavier than B, F and W but not as much as K , who is the third heaviest?

(a) B
(b) F
(c) K
(d) W

Ques (70-71): Direction: In the following question below some statements are given followed by some conclusions. Taking the given statements to be true even if they seem to be at variance from commonly known facts, read all the conclusions and then decide which of the given conclusions logically follows the given statements.

70. Statement:
Some schools are houses.
Some colleges are schools.
Conclusion :
I. Some colleges are houses.
II. Some colleges are not houses.

(a) Only I follows
(b) Only II follows
(c) Either I or II follows
(d) Neither I nor II follows

71. Statements:
All wallets are bags.
Some bags are envelopes.
Conclusions:
I. Some wallets are envelopes.
II. No wallet is an envelope.
III. No bag is an envelope.

(a) Both Conclusions I and II follows
(b) Both Conclusion II and III follows
(c) Either Conclusion I or II follows
(d) Both Conclusion I and III follows

Ques (72-73): Direction: Study the following information carefully and answer the question given below.
Certain representatives of the countries sitting on a circular conference table. They all are facing inside. There are some seats vacant between them. Not more than three representatives sitting together. The total number of seats around the table is a prime number.
Two seats between A and the one who belongs to Brazil. There is only one seat between the one who belong to Israel and the one who belong to Thailand. The one who belongs to Brazil sits three places away from I who belong to Syria. The one who belongs to Japan sits second to the right of the one who belongs to India. The one who belongs to Argentina is the immediate neighbour of the one who belongs to Japan and the one who belongs to Israel. There are three seats between the one who belongs to Thailand and the one who belongs to Egypt. A belongs to India and C belongs to Argentina. The one who belongs to Indonesia sits exactly between the one who belongs to Thailand and the one who belongs to Egypt. The one who belongs to Syria and K are immediate neighbours of each other. There are exactly five seats between K and the one who belongs to Canada. L who belongs to Iran and B who belongs to Brazil are immediate neighbours of each other. There are two seats between the one who belongs to Canada and the one who belongs to Japan. There is only one seat between E and H, who belongs to Israel. There are three seats between K who belongs to Germany and F who belongs to Indonesia. D who belongs to Canada sits immediate left of A. J is an immediate neighbour of C. There is one more person sitting on the table who is G who belongs to Egypt. No one sits to the immediate right of B.

72. Who among the following sits 10th to right of the one who belongs to India?
(a) H

(b) K
(c) The one who belongs to Syria
(d) The one who belongs to Egypt

73. What is the position of the one who belongs to Indonesia with respect to I?
(a) Third to left
(b) Fifth to the right
(c) Fifth to the left
(d) Sixth to the left

74. Find the odd number pair from the given alternatives.
(a) 6 - 93
(b) 7 - 81
(c) 6 - 56
(d) 8 - 91

75. Select the word which is different from the others.
(a) Hindi
(b) Urdu
(c) Hindu
(d) Maithili

76. निम्नलिखित में से शुद्ध वर्तनी का चयन कीजिए।
(a) स्वयम्वर
(b) चन्चल
(c) सन्यासी
(d) मण्डल

77. निम्न में शुद्ध वर्तनी पहचानिए-
(a) अद्वितीय
(b) सूचिपत्र
(c) महिना
(d) परिक्षा

Ques (78-80): निर्देश : उस विकल्प का चयन करें जो दिए गए मुहावरे का सही अर्थ है।

78. कमर टूटना
(a) थक जाना
(b) जीत जाना
(c) कमर टूट जाना
(d) चोट लगना

79. माथे पर बल पड़ना
(a) सिर दर्द होना
(b) पसंद करना
(c) गुस्सा करना
(d) असंतोष प्रकट करना

80. आठ-आठ आँसू रोना
(a) पछताना
(b) बहुत अधिक विलाप करना
(c) आश्चर्यचकित होना
(d) गिन चुनकर रोना

81. 'मंत्री' शब्द का लिंग क्या है?
(a) पुल्लिंग
(b) स्त्रीलिंग
(c) नपुंसकलिंग
(d) उभयलिंग

82. अपवाद को छोड़कर वर्णमाला के अक्षरों के नाम किस लिंग में होते हैं?
(a) पुल्लिंग
(b) स्त्रीलिंग
(c) नपुंसकलिंग
(d) उभयलिंग

83. 'वह बात जो जन साधारण में चलती आ रही है' इस वाक्यांश के लिए एक सार्थक शब्द दीजिए।
(a) कूपमंडूक
(b) किवदंती
(c) किंकर्तव्य
(d) कपोल-कल्पित

84. "सामान्य नियम के विरुद्ध बात": वाक्यांश के लिए एक शब्द होगा ।
(a) विवाद
(b) संवाद
(c) वाद
(d) अपवाद

85. संज्ञा अथवा सर्वनाम के अंत में लगने वाले प्रत्यय हैं:
(a) कृत प्रत्यय
(b) तद्धित प्रत्यय

(c) स्त्री प्रत्यय   (d) इनमें से सभी

86. किस शब्द में उपसर्ग नहीं है:
(a) अपवाद   (b) पराजय
(c) प्रभाव   (d) ओढ़ना

87. निम्न में से किस विकल्प के सभी शब्दों में उपसर्ग तथा प्रत्यय (दोनों) का प्रयोग हुआ है ?
(a) अनुकरणीय, निश्चल   (b) आबालवृद्ध, अपकीर्ति
(c) झगड़ालू, ससुराल   (d) अलौकिकता, प्रशासनिक

88. बहुवचन शब्द की पहचान कीजिए:
(a) टोपी   (b) जटाएँ
(c) बहन   (d) मुनि

89. 'सहेली' के उचित बहुवचन शब्द का चयन कीजिए।
(a) सखा   (b) सहेलीएँ
(c) सहेलियों   (d) सहेलियाँ

90. निम्नलिखित में से शुद्ध वाक्य का चयन कीजिए-
(a) गन्दा पानी उबालकर पियें।
(b) पड़ोसी ने मुझे स्वतंत्रता दिवस की बधाई दिया।
(c) यमुना का पानी गन्दा और प्रदूषित है।
(d) बच्चा लोग क्रिकेट खेलता है।

91. निम्नलिखित में से शुद्ध वाक्य का चयन कीजिए-
(a) सीधी लकीर खींचना बहुत कठिन है।
(b) जंक फूड से मोटापा बढ़ती है।
(c) हरा पेड़ ऑक्सीजन देते हैं।
(d) मेरे घर में तुम्हारी स्वागत है।

92. 'ज्योतिर्मय' का विलोम शब्द है:
(a) प्रकाशित   (b) सकारात्मक
(c) जागृति   (d) तिमिरमय

93. 'हर्ष' का विलोम शब्द है:
(a) विषाद   (b) प्रहर्ष
(c) खुशी   (d) नीरव

94. ' उन्नयन ' का विलोम शब्द है:
(a) आगमन   (b) गतिमान
(c) अचेतन   (d) अवनयन

95. 'अतिवृष्टि' का विलोम शब्द है:
(a) अनायास   (b) अनावृष्टि
(c) अप्रतिम   (d) अनावृत्ति

96. 'सद्भावना' का संधि विच्छेद बताइये।
(a) सत + भावना   (b) सत् + भावना
(c) सद्धा + भावना   (d) स + भावना

97. 'प्रत्युपकार' में कौन सी संधि है?
(a) व्यंजन संधि   (b) विसर्ग संधि
(c) यण् संधि   (d) गुण संधि

98. 'तदनन्तर' का संधि विच्छेद होगा:
(a) तत् + अन्तर   (b) तत् + अनत्र
(c) तत् + अन्तर   (d) त + अन्नतर

99. निम्न में से किस लेखक की आत्मकथा का नाम 'क्या भूलूं क्या याद करूँ' है?
(a) हरिवंश राय बच्चन   (b) अब्दुल कलाम
(c) भारतेंदु हरिशचंद्र   (d) जयशंकर प्रसाद

100. 'हिंदी साहित्य की भूमिका' के लेखक कौन हैं?
(a) रामचंद्र शुक्ल   (b) डॉ. रामकुमार वर्मा
(c) हजारीप्रसाद द्विवेदी   (d) रामविलास शर्मा

// Smart Answer Sheet //

Correct — Percentage of students who answered correctly.

Skipped — Percentage of students who skipped.

Q.	Ans.	Correct / Skipped	Q.	Ans.	Correct / Skipped	Q.	Ans.	Correct / Skipped
1	A	77.74% / 0.0%	2	C	41.13% / 1.44%	3	D	42.24% / 1.55%
4	B	45.73% / 1.48%	5	A	56.47% / 1.39%	6	C	40.04% / 1.5%
7	A	51.38% / 1.2%	8	B	64.9% / 1.69%	9	C	57.92% / 1.92%
10	D	55.7% / 1.93%	11	D	87.12% / 0.0%	12	A	50.71% / 1.31%
13	A	64.21% / 1.47%	14	C	52.52% / 1.11%	15	C	62.43% / 1.7%
16	D	78.71% / 0.0%	17	C	13.68% / 4.95%	18	B	40.3% / 1.03%
19	A	55.57% / 1.09%	20	D	56.01% / 1.13%	21	A	52.76% / 1.39%
22	B	43.77% / 1.66%	23	A	59.43% / 1.06%	24	B	45.62% / 1.38%
25	A	54.51% / 1.85%	26	D	48.9% / 1.03%	27	A	25.37% / 4.92%
28	A	49.92% / 1.64%	29	A	46.99% / 1.2%	30	A	16.3% / 3.92%
31	A	62.42% / 1.94%	32	B	56.14% / 1.11%	33	A	58.84% / 1.21%
34	D	63.73% / 1.2%	35	B	13.28% / 4.94%	36	C	43.09% / 1.89%
37	B	86.74% / 0.0%	38	D	11.16% / 3.93%	39	C	18.74% / 3.43%
40	C	65.88% / 1.93%	41	C	12.01% / 3.75%	42	A	79.21% / 0.0%
43	D	62.61% / 1.25%	44	D	57.62% / 1.51%	45	D	52.71% / 1.32%
46	A	43.49% / 2.0%	47	D	50.17% / 1.78%	48	A	63.23% / 1.78%
49	A	65.36% / 1.61%	50	A	88.35% / 0.0%	51	A	46.9% / 1.16%
52	C	85.91% / 0.0%	53	B	48.95% / 1.65%	54	D	78.66% / 0.0%
55	D	43.91% / 1.21%	56	C	54.97% / 1.31%	57	A	43.75% / 1.87%
58	D	54.2% / 1.26%	59	A	49.67% / 1.29%	60	B	66.22% / 1.79%
61	B	85.04% / 0.0%	62	C	63.61% / 1.62%	63	A	63.37% / 1.38%
64	B	50.99% / 1.03%	65	D	58.37% / 1.22%	66	B	46.69% / 1.17%
67	B	60.11% / 1.96%	68	A	47.06% / 1.47%	69	D	54.74% / 1.2%
70	D	83.45% / 0.0%	71	C	57.32% / 1.32%	72	D	27.44% / 4.65%
73	C	18.82% / 3.99%	74	C	85.7% / 0.0%	75	C	78.4% / 0.0%
76	D	61.7% / 1.47%	77	A	78.68% / 0.0%	78	A	79.42% / 0.0%
79	A	87.13% / 0.0%	80	B	52.39% / 1.85%	81	D	81.52% / 0.0%
82	A	82.34% / 0.0%	83	B	40.95% / 1.74%	84	D	64.69% / 1.29%
85	B	59.39% / 1.54%	86	D	81.7% / 0.0%	87	D	63.99% / 1.42%
88	B	85.06%	89	D	42.37%	90	A	47.13%

		0.0%			1.28%			1.11%
91	A	82.46%	92	D	55.63%	93	A	61.77%
		0.0%			1.09%			1.81%
94	D	42.92%	95	B	41.85%	96	B	68.54%
		1.22%			1.77%			1.15%
97	C	76.29%	98	A	42.45%	99	A	53.47%
		0.0%			1.16%			1.16%
100	C	67.09%						
		1.02%						

// Hints and Solutions //

1(A). Mohandas Karamchand Gandhi wrote the book 'Hind Swaraj', expressing his views on Swaraj and Modern civilisation in 1909.

It is written in a dialogic form i.e., as a discussion between the Reader and the Editor of a journal/newspaper. Hind Swaraj or Indian Home-Rule comprises of 20 short chapters. Primarily Hind Swaraj deals with two issues:
- a critique of modern civilization,
- the nature and structure of Indian Swaraj and the means and methods to achieve it.

2(C). After the Santhal Rebellion (1855–56) the Santhal Pargana was created, covering 5,500 square miles from the districts of Bhagalpur and Birbhum. The colonial state hoped that the Santhals could be reconciled by creating a new territory for the Santhals and imposing certain special laws within it. It became illegal for a Santhal to transfer land to a non-Santhal. The British government made laws so that the tribals' land could not be taken by outsiders (dicus).

3(D). The Hind Mazdoor Sabha (HMS) is a National Trade Union Centre in India. It was founded in West Bengal in 1948. Its founders included Basawan Singh (Sinha), Ashok Mehta, R.S. Ruikar, Mani Benkara, Shibnath Benerajee, R.K. Khedgikar, T.S. Ramanujam, VS. Mathur, G.G. Mehta.

4(B). With reference to the religious practices in India, the "Sathanakavasi" sect belongs to Jainism.

5(A). The 'Moplah Rebellion' of 1921 was offshoot of Khilafat movement. The Moplah Rebellion, also known as the Moplah Riots of 1921 was the culmination of a series of riots by Mappila Muslims of Kerala in the 19th and early 20th.

6(C). A retired English I.C.S. 72 political workers with the help of officer A.O. Hume laid the foundation of the Indian National Congress in Bombay in December, 1885.

7(A). 78° East longitude passes through Ladakh > Himachal Pradesh > Uttarakhand > Uttar Pradesh > Madhya Pradesh > Maharashtra > Telangana > Andhra Pradesh > Karnataka > Tamil Nadu.
States with major coalfields:
- Jharkhand ranks first in coal reserves and its production. Most of the coalfields are located in a narrow belt running in an east-west direction along 24 degrees north latitude. The major coal mining centers of the state are Auranga, Bokaro, Dhanbad, Jharia, Giridih, Karanpur, Ramgarh.
- Odisha has the second largest coal reserves in the country. It carries more than 24 percent of the total coal reserves. It produces about 15 percent of the total coal production of India. Most of the state's coal reserves are found in the districts of Sambalpur, Dhenkanal and Sundergarh.

- Chhattisgarh has the third largest coal reserves in India. It carries about 17 percent of the total coal reserves. However, the state ranks first in the production of coal.

As it is understood that Odisha, Chhattisgarh, Jharkhand are located at 78° East latitude and they constitute more than 50% of the total coal production of India.

8(B). Sea Level Division: Can be divided into various parts such as Continental Shelf, Continental Slope, Continental Rise or Foot, Deep Ocean Basin, Abyssal Plain and Abyssal Hills, Oceanic Trench, Seamount and Gayotes.
- Continental Shelf: It is the submerged edge of a continent which is a gently sloping plain. It is located close to the continental margin. The Siberian Shelf in the Arctic Ocean is the largest continental shelf in the world. It is made of granite rock.
- Continental Slope: It is the slope between the outer edge of the continental shelf and the deep ocean floor. The steep-sided continental slope separates the continental shelf from the deep ocean floor. It is considered to be the end zone of the continent.
- Deep Sea Plain: It is also known as abyssal plain. Abyssal plain is an underwater plain on the deep sea floor, usually found at depths between 3,000 meters (9,800 ft) and 6,000 meters (20,000 ft).
- Oceanic Depths: Ocean depths or trenches are vertical depressions in the deepest parts of the ocean. Trenches are long, narrow depressions on the ocean floor that form at the boundary of tectonic plates where one plate is pushed, or subducted, under another.

9(C). Capillary water is retained on the soil particles by the nature of surface tensions. The gravity cannot remove the strong force from the soil particles. The molecules of capillary water are present in a liquid state. Plant roots are able to absorb it.

10(D). India climbed six notches to 40th position in the Global Innovation Index 2022, according to a report by the Geneva-based World Intellectual Property Organization. Turkiye and India entered the top 40 for the first time, placing at 37th and 40th, respectively. Switzerland has topped the ranking for the 12th consecutive year. The Index was started in 2007 was created by Soumitra Dutta.

11(D). West Bengal (WB) Chief Minister (CM) Mamata Banerjee inaugurated a new vehicle location control centre and mobile app, as a part of efforts to enhance security for women in West Bengal.

12(A). The 5th World Braille Day was observed across the globe on 4th January 2023 by the United Nations (UN) to highlight and raise awareness about the importance of Braille as a means of communication for the partially sighted and blind.

13(A). The Competition Commission of India (CCI) has imposed a penalty of Rs 1337.76 crore on Google for abusing its dominant position in multiple markets. In its order, the CCI said, Google has perpetuated its dominant position in the online search market resulting in the denial of market access for competing search apps.

14(C). Sound wave is not an electromagnetic wave. It is a mechanical wave. When sound wave propagates, particles of the medium oscillates along the direction of propagation of the wave.

E.M waves don't require any medium for propagation. Examples: Light waves are also known as Photon is a best and only example of electromagnetic waves.

15(C). Indian Railways has commissioned the country's first governmental Waste to Energy Plant at Bhubaneswar in East Coast Railway.

This Waste to Energy Plant works on a patented technology called POLYCRACK, is the first-of-its-kind in Indian Railways and fourth in India.

It is the world's first patented heterogeneous catalytic process that converts multiple feedstocks into hydrocarbon liquid fuels, gas, carbon and water.

Polycrack Plant can be fed with all types of Plastic, Petroleum sludge, Un-segregated MSW (Municipal Solid Waste) with moisture up to 50%, E-Waste, Automobile fluff, Organic waste including bamboo, garden waste, etc., and Jatropha fruit and palm bunch.

16(D). Smoke and fog, Exhaust gas from cars and Gases from burning wood or charcoal are examples of air pollution. Air pollution refers to the presence of harmful substances in the air.

17(C). The essential feature of democracy is giving prominence to the citizen. One of the key features of democracy is that by the people, from the people and to the people. People occupy the centre stage here.

18(B). The writ of Mandamus is such that it can be enforced only against a public official.

Mandamus writ is used by the court to order the public official who has failed to perform his duty or refused to do his duty, to resume his work. Besides public officials, Mandamus can be issued against any public body, a corporation, an inferior court, a tribunal, or government for the same purpose.

19(A). The 'Shimla Agreement' between India and Pakistan was done in 1972.

The Simla Agreement was a peace treaty signed between India and Pakistan on 2 July 1972 in Shimla, the capital city of the Indian state of Himachal Pradesh. It followed the Indo-Pakistani War of 1971, which began after India intervened in East Pakistan as an ally of Bengali rebels who were fighting against Pakistani state forces in the Bangladesh Liberation War.

20(D). Industrial policy 2016 aimed at higher capital formation, increasing the wages of the people and provide employment opportunities to the people.

- The Government of Jharkhand gave priority to industrial growth in order to reduce poverty and employment.
- It aimed to create an industry-friendly environment to maximize investment in mineral and natural resource-based industries.
- Under this policy, the state government collaborated with GAIL for the infrastructure development of the power.
- Rural Electrification has been accorded top priority with an objective of 100% electrification by 2017.

21(A). Monetary policy implemented by the Reserve Bank of India (RBI) aims to reduce inflationary pressures. For this money supply is controlled and for this bank rate, SLR, CRR etc. are used.

22(B). The rate of cash reserve ratio declared by the Reserve Bank of India at the time of asking the question was 10%. Presently the CRR rate is 4.50% in february 2023.

23(A). India spinner Ravichandran Ashwin on 6 March 2022 surpassed Kapil Dev's 434 wickets in the second Test against Sri Lanka.

- He became India's second-highest wicket-taker behind Anil Kumble, who finished his career with 619 Test scalps.
- He achieved the feat on day 3 of the ongoing first Test match between India and Sri Lanka at Mohali.

24(B). Disinvestment means the sale or liquidation of assets by the government, usually Central and state public sector enterprises, projects, or other fixed assets.

To address various problems associated with central public enterprises, the government has brought out this policy to completely overhaul the government's presence in various sectors and minimize the number of PSUs to an absolute minimum. This Policy covers existing CPSEs, Public Sector Banks, and Public Sector Insurance Companies.

25(A). The International Space Station (ISS) serves as a microgravity and space environment research laboratory in which scientific experiments are conducted in astrobiology, astronomy, meteorology, physics, and other fields.

The International Space Station (ISS) is a modular space station (habitable artificial satellite) in low Earth orbit.

The ISS program is a multi-national collaborative project between five participating space agencies:
- NASA (United States),
- Roscosmos (Russia),
- JAXA (Japan),
- ESA (Europe),
- CSA (Canada)

26(D). Given:

14.28% of 630 + 32% of ? = 202

$$\Rightarrow \frac{1}{7} \times 630 + \frac{32}{100} \times ? = 202$$

$$\Rightarrow 90 + \frac{8}{25} \times ? = 202$$

$$\Rightarrow \frac{8}{25} \times ? = 112$$

$$\Rightarrow ? = 112 \times \frac{25}{8}$$

$$\Rightarrow ? = 350$$

∴ 350 should come in place of the question mark (?).

27(A). Given:

Difference between selling price when the discount rate is 10% and 30% = Rs. 240

Formula used:

$$\text{Selling price} = \frac{(100 - Discount\%)}{100} \times \text{Marked price}$$

Let the marked price be 'x'.

Rohit buy the article at $= \frac{90}{100} \times x$

Abhishek buy the article $= \frac{70}{100} \times x$

Difference between selling price = 240

$$\Rightarrow \frac{20}{100} \times x = 240$$

$$\Rightarrow x = 1200$$

∴ Marked price = Rs. 1200

28(A). Given:

Marked price = 30% above the cost price

Discount = 10%

Profit = Rs. 340

Formula used:

Marked price = (cost price) $\times \dfrac{(100+\%above)}{100}$

Selling price = Marked price $\times \dfrac{(100-discount)}{100}$

Profit = Selling price - Cost price

Let the cost price be Rs. x.

Marked price = x $\times \dfrac{(100+30)}{100}$

$\Rightarrow$ Marked price $= \dfrac{130x}{100}$

$\Rightarrow$ Marked price $= 1.3x$

Selling price $= 1.3x \times \dfrac{(100-10)}{100}$

$\Rightarrow$ Selling price $= 1.3x \times \dfrac{90}{100}$

$\Rightarrow$ Selling price $= 1.3x \times 0.9$

$\Rightarrow$ Selling price $= 1.17x$

Selling price – cost price = Profit

$\Rightarrow 1.17x{-}x = 340$

$\Rightarrow 0.17x = 340$

$\Rightarrow x = \dfrac{340}{0.17}$

$\Rightarrow x = Rs.\,2000$

∴ The cost price of an article is Rs. 2000.

29(A). Difference between the amount we get after 5 years and 2 years = 5200 – 4480 = Rs. 720

This difference equal to the simple interest we earn in 3 years.

∴ Simple interest for 1 year $= \dfrac{720}{3}$ = Rs. 240

$\Rightarrow$ Simple interest for 2 year = Rs. 480

$\Rightarrow$ Original sum = 4480 – 480 = Rs. 4000

30(A). Given-

A person deposited $Rs.\,400$ for 2 years, $Rs.\,550$ for 4 years and $Rs.\,1200$ for 6 years.

Let the rate percent per annum be R.

First principal $P_1 = Rs.\,400$

First time period $T_1 = 2$ years

First simple interest $SI_1 = \dfrac{P_1 \times R_1 \times T_1}{100}$

$\Rightarrow SI_1 = \dfrac{400 \times R \times 2}{100}$

$\Rightarrow SI_1 = Rs.\,8R$

Second principal $P_2 = Rs.\,550$

Second time period $T_2 = 4$ years

Second simple interest $SI_2 = \dfrac{P_2 \times R_2 \times T_2}{100}$

$\Rightarrow SI_2 = \dfrac{550 \times R \times 4}{100}$

$\Rightarrow SI_2 = Rs.\,22R$

Third principal $P_3 = Rs.\,1200$

Third time period $T_3 = 6$ years

Third simple interest $SI_3 = \dfrac{P_3 \times R_3 \times T_3}{100}$

$\Rightarrow SI_3 = \dfrac{1200 \times R \times 6}{100}$

$\Rightarrow SI_3 = Rs.\,72R$

According to the question,

A total of $Rs.\,1020$ is received as simple interest.

$\Rightarrow 8R + 22R + 72R = 1020$

$\Rightarrow 102R = 1020$

$\Rightarrow R = 10\%$

31(A). Given:

A conical figure is reformed where the radius is increased by 20 percent and the height is reduced by 20 percent.

Let original radius of the cone $= r$ unit

Original height of the cone $= h$ unit

Original volume of the cone $= \dfrac{1}{3}\pi r^2 h$

New radius of the cone $= r + \dfrac{20}{100}r = \dfrac{6}{5}r$ unit

New height of the cone $= h - \dfrac{20}{100}h = \dfrac{4}{5}h$ unit

New volume of the cone $= \dfrac{1}{3}\pi \left(\dfrac{6}{5}r\right)^2 \left(\dfrac{4}{5}h\right)$

Change in the volume of the figure

$= \dfrac{\left[\dfrac{1}{3}\pi\left(\dfrac{6}{5}r\right)^2\left(\dfrac{4}{5}h\right)\right] - \left[\dfrac{1}{3}\pi r^2 h\right]}{\dfrac{1}{3}\pi r^2 h} \times 100$

$= \dfrac{\dfrac{19}{125} \times \left[\dfrac{1}{3}\pi r^2 h\right]}{\dfrac{1}{3}\pi r^2 h} \times 100$

$= 15.2\%$

32(B). Curved surface area of cylinder $= 2\pi rh = 594$

$\Rightarrow rh = 594 \times \dfrac{7}{44}$

$\Rightarrow rh = 94.5$

Volume of cylinder $= \pi r^2 h = 1336.5$

$\Rightarrow r^2 h = 425.25$

$\Rightarrow \dfrac{r^2 h}{rh} = \dfrac{425.25}{94.5}$

$\Rightarrow r = 4.5$

$\Rightarrow h = \dfrac{94.5}{4.5}$

$\Rightarrow h = 21cm$

∴ Height of cylinder $= 21cm$

33(A). Given:

Number 2632A4878 is divisible by 9.

As we know,

The Sum of all digits should be divisible by 9.

The number is 2632A4878.

$\Rightarrow 2+6+3+2+A+4+8+7+8$

$\Rightarrow 40 + A$

Put $A = 5$

$\Rightarrow 40 + 5 = 45$

$\Rightarrow 45$ is divisible by 9

The value of 'A' is 5.

34(D). Given,

Without boss, there are 11 employees.

Average $= 18000 - 1000 = 17000$

Total salary of 11 members $= 11 \times 17000 = $ Rs. 187000

With boss, total salary 12 people $= 12 \times 18000 = $ Rs. 216000

Salary of boss $= 216000 - 187000 = $ Rs. 29000

35(B). Given:

The average price of 20 books = Rs. 14

The average price of 18 books = Rs. 13

Formula Used:

Average $= \dfrac{Sum\,of\,terms}{Number\,of\,terms}$

Let the price of remaining 2 books be x and y.

x = 21.05%y

$\Rightarrow$ x = 0.2105y

The average price of 20 books = Rs. 14

$\Rightarrow$ Total price of 20 books = Rs. 14 × 20 = Rs. 280

The average price of 18 books = Rs. 13

$\Rightarrow$ Total price of 18 books = Rs. 13 × 18 = Rs. 234

Total price = Price of 18 books + Price of 2 books

$\Rightarrow$ 280 = 234 + x + y

$\Rightarrow$ 46 = (1 + 0.2105)y

$\Rightarrow$ y = 38

$\Rightarrow$ x = 0.2105y = 0.2105 × 38

$\Rightarrow$ x = 8

∴ The value of each of these two books is Rs. 38 and Rs. 8 respectively.

36(C). Given:
Let the original number be 100x.
The number when subtracted from 37.5%
So, New number $= 100x \times \left(\frac{100-37.5}{100}\right) = 62.5x$
Resulting number = 35 = 62.5x
$\Rightarrow$ x = 0.56
$\Rightarrow$ 100x = 0.56 × 100 = 56
$\therefore$ Original value of number is 56.

37(B). Ratio of times taken by Sakshi and Tanya
$= 125 : 100 = 5 : 4$
Suppose Tanya takes x days to do the work.
$5 : 4 :: 20 : x$
$\Rightarrow x = \left(\frac{4 \times 20}{5}\right)$
$\Rightarrow x = 16$ days
Hence, Tanya takes 16 days to complete the work.

38(D). Given:
A can complete the work in 12 hours
A's one - hour work $= \frac{1}{12}$
B can complete the work in 8 hours
B's one - hour work $= \frac{1}{8}$
Let the total time taken by A and B to complete the work be x hours
A and B's one - hour work $= \frac{1}{12} + \frac{1}{8}$
$\frac{1}{12} + \frac{1}{8} = \frac{1}{x}$
$\Rightarrow x = 4.8$ hr = 4 hr and (0.8×60) min = 4 hours 48 minutes
The total time is taken by A and B to complete the work is 4 hours and 48 minutes

39(C). Given:
Time taken by A to complete 20% work = 4 days
Time taken by B to complete 33.33% of work = 10 days
They worked together for 9 days
C completed the remaining work in 6 days
As we know,
Work = Time × Efficiency
Time taken by A to complete 100% work = 4 × 5
= 20 days
Time taken by B to complete 100% work = 10 × 3
= 30 days
L.C.M of 20 and 30 = 60 = Total work
Efficiency of $A = \frac{60}{20}$
= 3 units/day
Efficiency of $B = \frac{60}{30}$
= 2 units/day
Worked done by A and B together in 9 days
$= (3 + 2) \times 9$
= 45 units
Remaining work $= (60 - 45)$ units
= 15 units
C can complete the remaining work in 6 days
Efficiency of $C = \frac{15}{6} = 2.5$ units/day
Total efficiency of B and $C = (2 + 2.5)$ units/day
= 4.5 units / day
Now, 75% of total work = 75% of 60 units
= 45 units
Required time $= \frac{45}{4.5}$ days
= 10 days
$\therefore B$ and C can complete 75% work in 10 days.

40(C). Given:
Two train crosses the man in 25 seconds and 32 seconds respectively.

Two trains running in opposite direction and they crosses each other in 30 second
When two running object moving in opposite direction their relative speed = Sum of their speed
Let, the speed of the 1st train be x m/sec and that of the 2nd train is y m/sec
When a train crosses a standing man it cross its won length
1st train cross the man in 25 second
$\Rightarrow$ Length of 1st train is 25x meter
2nd train cross the man in 32 seconds
$\Rightarrow$ Length of the 2nd train is 32y meter
Relative speed of two trains is (x + y) m/sec
In 30 seconds they cross each other
$\Rightarrow$ In 30 seconds the cross 30(x + y) meter
Accordingly,
30(x + y) = 25x + 32y
$\Rightarrow$ 30x + 30y = 25x + 32y
$\Rightarrow$ 30x - 25x = 32y - 30y
$\Rightarrow$ 5x = 2y
$\Rightarrow \frac{x}{y} = \frac{2}{5}$
$\Rightarrow$ x : y = 2 : 5
$\therefore$ The ratio of the speed of two trains is 2 : 5.

41(C). Given:
In first case:
Speed $(S_1) = 60$ km/hr
Distance $(D_1) = 30$ km
In second case:
Speed $(S_2) = 100$ km/hr
Distance $(D_2) = 50$ km
Formula:
Average Speed $= \frac{\text{Total Distance}}{\text{Total Time}}$
Time $= \frac{\text{Distance}}{\text{Speed}}$
Total Distance $= 30 + 50 = 80$ km
According to the question:
In first case:
Time $= \frac{30}{60} = \frac{1}{2}$ hrs
In second case,
Time $= \frac{50}{100} = \frac{1}{2}$ hrs
Total Time $= \frac{1}{2} + \frac{1}{2} = \frac{2}{2} = 1$ hrs
Average Speed $= \frac{\text{Total Distance}}{\text{Total Time}}$
Average Speed $= \frac{80}{1} = 80$ km/hr
$\therefore$ The average speed of whole journey is 80 km/hr.

42(A). Given,
Product of two numbers = 3360
LCM = 96
Let the HCF be x.
As we know,
Product of two numbers = LCM × HCF
$3360 = 96 \times x$
$\Rightarrow x = \frac{3360}{96}$
$\Rightarrow x = 35$
$\therefore$ Their HCF is 35.

43(D). Let C ' age be x years.
Then,
B ' age $= 2x$ years
A 's age $= (2x + 2)$ years
$\therefore (2x + 2) + 2x + x = 27$
$\Rightarrow 5x = 25$
$\Rightarrow x = 5$
So, B 's age $= 2x = 10$ years

44(D). Given,
$$4x + 5y = 14 \text{ ....(1)}$$
$$x - 5y = 16 \text{ .....(2)}$$
Adding equation (1) and (2), we get
$$4x + 5y + x - 5y = 14 + 6$$
$$\Rightarrow 5x = 30$$
$$\Rightarrow x = 6$$
Putting the value of x in eqaution (1), we get
$$\Rightarrow 4 \times 6 + 5y = 14$$
$$\Rightarrow 5y = -10$$
$$\Rightarrow y = -2$$

45(D). Given:
$$4x^2 + y = 0$$
$$\Rightarrow \frac{-y}{4} = x^2$$
On comparing the given equation with $x^2 = -4ay$
$$4a = \frac{1}{4} \Rightarrow a = \frac{1}{16}$$
Focus $= (0, -a) = \left(0, \frac{-1}{16}\right)$

46(A). To find the value of the given equation,
$$3A = A + 2A$$
Taking cot on both sides,
$$\Rightarrow \cot 3A = \cot(A + 2A)$$
$$\Rightarrow \cot 3A = \frac{\cot A \cot 2A - 1}{\cot 2A + \cot A}$$
$$\Rightarrow \cot 3A \cot 2A + \cot 3A \cot A = \cot A \cot 2A - 1$$
$$\Rightarrow \cot A \cot 2A - \cot 2A \cot 3A - \cot 3A \cot A = 1$$

47(D). P(A) = 0.5, P(B) = 0.6, P(A ∩ B) = 0.4
$$\Rightarrow P(A \cup B) = P(A) + P(B) - P(A \cap B)$$
$$\Rightarrow P(A \cup B) = 0.5 + 0.6 - 0.4$$
$$\Rightarrow P(A \cup B) = 0.7$$
$$\Rightarrow P(\overline{A \cup B}) = 1 - P(A \cup B)$$
$$\Rightarrow 1 - P(A \cup B) = 1 - 0.7$$
$$\Rightarrow P(\overline{A \cup B}) = 0.3$$

48(A). Given:
Number of points in plane n = 20.
Number of colinear points m = 5.
Number of triangles from by joining n points of which m are colinear $= {}^nC_3 - {}^mC_3$
Therefore the number of triangles $= {}^{20}C_3 - {}^5C_3$
$$= \frac{20!}{(20-3)!.3!} - \frac{5!}{(5-3)!.3!}$$
$$= 1140\text{-}10$$
$$= 1130$$

49(A). Given,
Sales of company A in November = 105 crores
Sales of company B in November = 100 crores
Let sales of company A in November be m% more than sales of company B in November.
Sales of company A = sales of company B + sales of company B $\times \left(\frac{m}{100}\right)$
$$\Rightarrow 105 = 100 + 100 \times \left(\frac{m}{100}\right)$$
$$\Rightarrow 105 = 100 + m$$
$$\Rightarrow m = 105 - 100$$
$$\Rightarrow m = 5$$
∴ The sales of company A in November be 5% more than sales of company B in November.

50(A). The sales of company B is same in September and October = 170 crores.
From above sales of company B is same for September and October.

51(A). If FLOW is related to RIVER then STAGNANT is related to Pool.
The pool water remains stagnant.

52(C). As Rabies is caused by Dog, Similarly, Malaria is caused by Mosquito.
Rabies is caused by viruses and is transmitted by bites of canines most commonly dogs. Malaria is caused by protozoa-plasmodium transmitted by bites of mosquitoes from female anopheles.

53(B).

Symbol	Character/Relationship
☐	Male
○	Female
⬡	Unknown Gender
——	Married Couple
←→	Siblings
≈	Cousins
☐↓	Is father of
○↓	Is mother of
↓☐	Is the son of
↓○	Is the daughter of

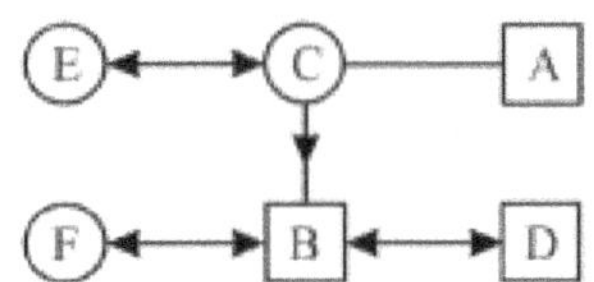

After the analysis of the Family tree, it is clear that A and D are the only male members in the family.

54(D).

Symbol	Character/Relationship
☐	Male
○	Female
⬡	Unknown Gender
——	Married Couple
←→	Siblings
≈	Cousins
☐↓	Is father of
○↓	Is mother of
↓☐	Is the son of
↓○	Is the daughter of

After the analysis of the Family tree, it is clear that A is the father of B.

55(D). The logic follows here is:
In figure 1, 2, and 3 outer figure and the enclosed figure are different.
But,
In figure 4 both the outer and the enclosed figure are the same.

56(C). Except in Figure (b) in all the other figures, one shaded semicircle attached to the line and the small line segment attached to the other line, face each other.

57(A). In all figures except figure C, 2 stars are connected with one line
Whereas in figure C, no line is connected between the edge of the side of the star.

58(D). The girl's path of travel is as follows:

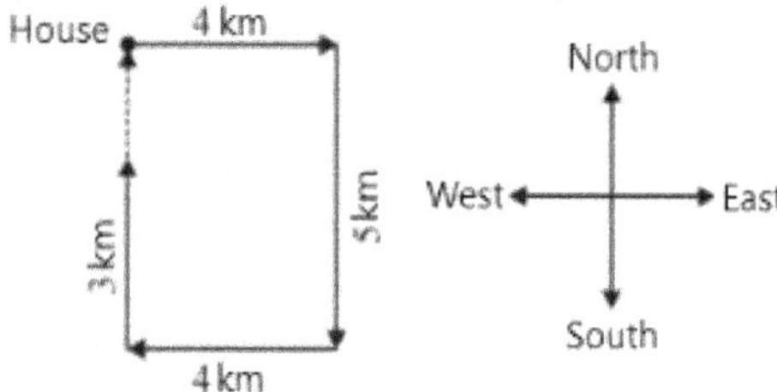

59(A). From the given information, we can draw the following diagram:

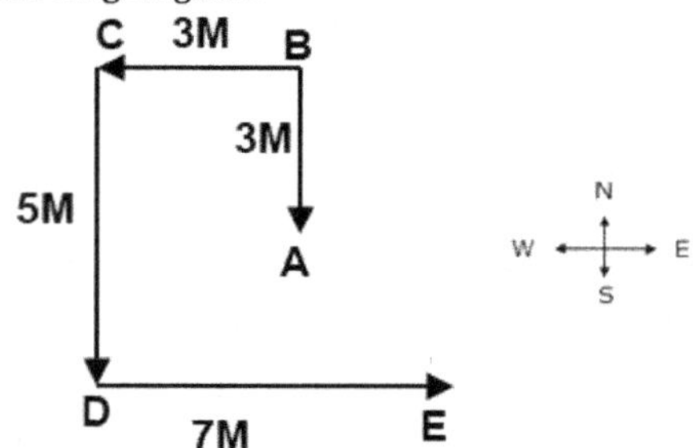

Therefore, Point E is south-east of point B.

60(B). The pattern used here is,

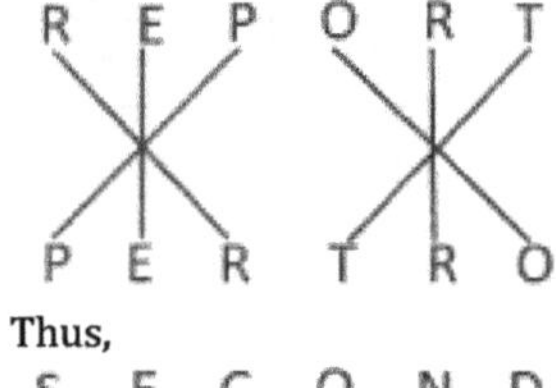

Thus,

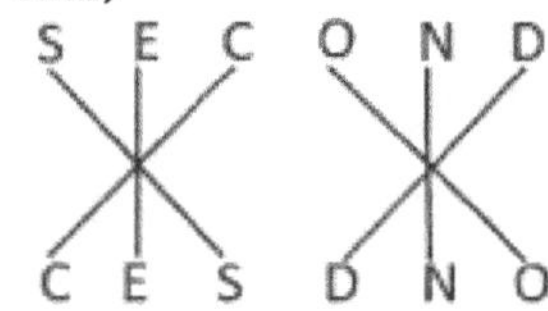

So, 'CESDNO' is the correct answer.

61(B). The pattern followed here is,

E	D	I	T	I	O	N

3	8	9	1	9	6	5

Similarly,

T	I	D	E
1	9	8	3

62(C). Figure (3) of answer figure i.e.,

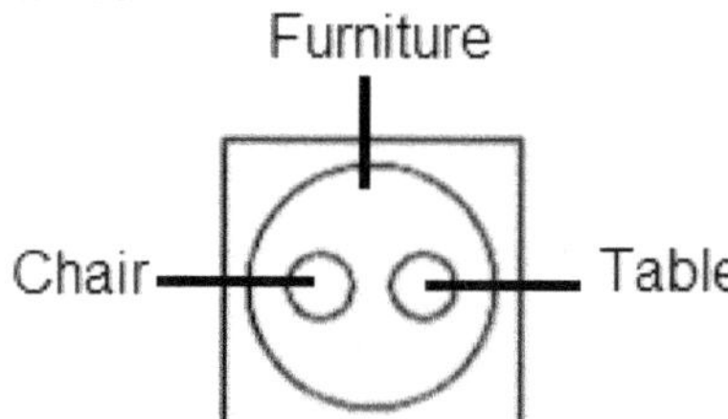

will continue the same series as established by the five Problem Figures.
In each step, element at the upper-right position gets enlarged, inverts vertically and reaches the lower-left corner; the existing element at the lower-left position, is lost and a new small element appears at the upper-right position.

63(A). Figure (1) from the answer figure i.e.,

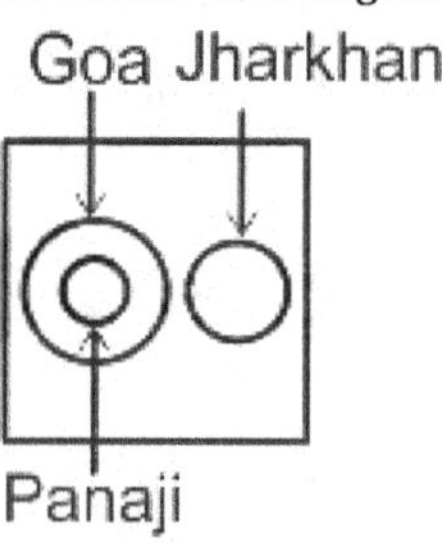

will continue the same series as established by the five problem figures.
Both the larger and the smaller squares move to the adjacent corner ACW in each turn. Also, the shading in the smaller square moves 1, 2, 3, 4, 5, ... steps ACW sequentially and the shading in the larger square moves 1, 2, 3, 4, 5,.... steps CW sequentially.

64(B). As, Chair and Table both are Furniture so, they both will come under furniture only.
So, the correct Venn diagram that represents them will be:

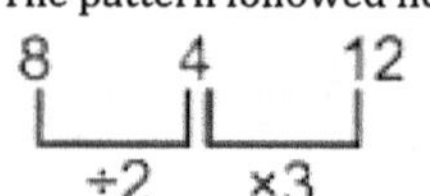

65(D). Panaji is the capital of Goa. So, Panaji is in the inner circle of Goa.
The correct Venn diagram representation is:

66(B). The pattern followed here is,

8   4   12
÷2   ×3

Taking last digit as first digit for next pattern

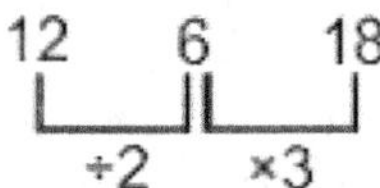

Similarly,

67(B). The pattern followed here is:
11 + 10 = 21
21 + 30 = 51
51 + 30 = 81
81 + 10 = 91
91 + 30 = 121 ≠ 111

68(A). Person: Aarti, Saumya, Muskan, Kashish, and Gargi
i) Aarti is older than Saumya.
Aarti > Saumya
ii) Muskan is elder to Aarti but younger than Kashish.
Kashish > Muskan > Aarti
iii) Kashish is older than Saumya.
iv) Saumya is younger than Muskan.
Kashish > Muskan > Aarti > Saumya
v) Gargi is the eldest.
Gargi > Kashish > Muskan > Aarti > Saumya
Therefore , Saumya is the youngest.

69(D). Given,
B, F, J, K and W each of different weights, F is heavier than just J . Heavier than B, F and W but not as much as K .
As per the given information, ascending order of weights:
$J > F > W > B > K$
Thus, W is the third heaviest.

70(D). The least possible Venn Diagram for the given statements will be as follows:

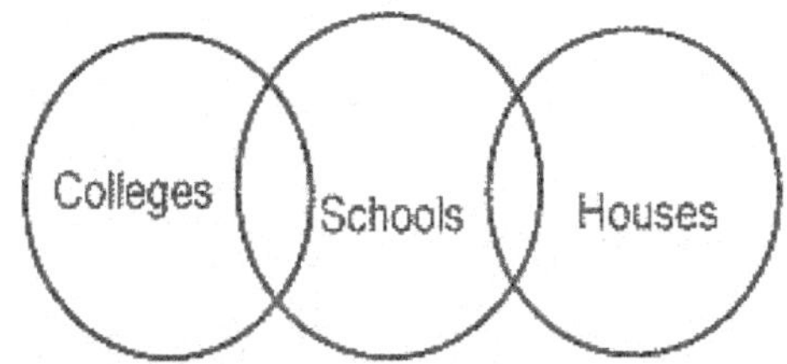

I. Some colleges are houses → False (There is no direct relation given between colleges and houses so it can be possible but not definite, hence, false)
II. Some colleges are not houses → False (There is no direct relation given between colleges and houses so it can be possible but not definite, hence, false)
So, Neither I nor II follows.

71(C). The least possible Venn Diagram for the given data is:

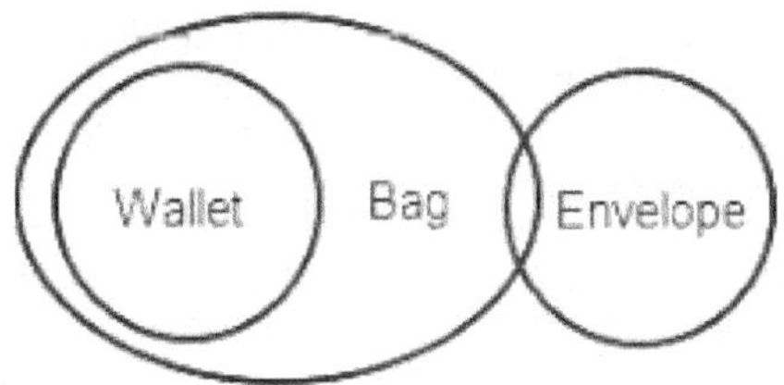

Conclusions:
I. Some wallets are envelopes → False (It is possible but not definite, therefore it is false)
II. No wallet is an envelope → False (It is possible but not definite, therefore it is false)
III. No bag is an envelope → False (As some bags are envelope therefore it is false.)
None of the conclusions are true but conclusions I and II form a complementary pair.
Thus, either conclusion I or II follows.

Ques (72-73): 1) A belongs to India and C belongs to Argentina.
2) Two seats between A and the one who belongs to Brazil.
3) The one who belongs to Japan sits second to the right of the one who belongs to India.
4) The one who belongs to Argentina is the immediate neighbour of the one who belongs to Japan and the one who belongs to Israel.

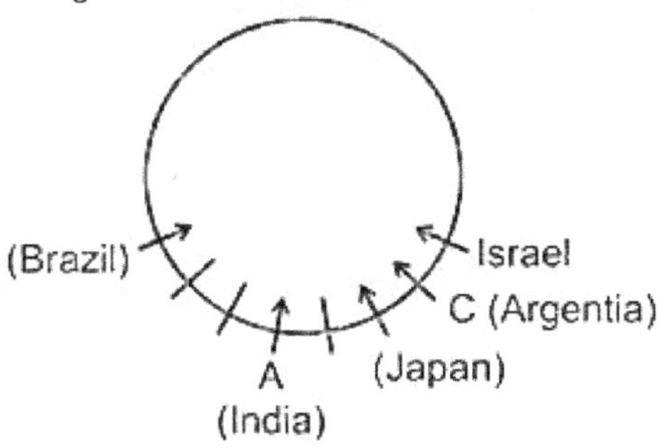

5) The one who belongs to Brazil sits three places away from I who belong to Syria.
6) There is only one seat between the one who belong to Israel and the one who belong to Thailand.
7) The one who belongs to Canada sits immediate left of the one who belongs to India.
8) There is only one seat between E and H, who belongs to Israel.
9) D who belongs to Canada sits immediate left of A.

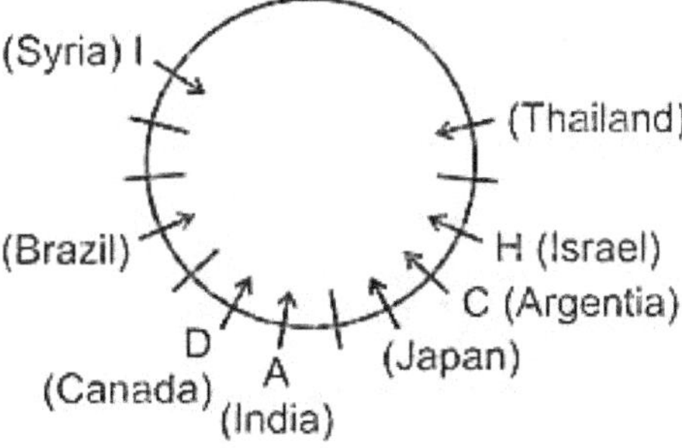

10) There are three seats between the one who belongs to Thailand and the one who belongs to Egypt.
11) No one sits to the immediate right of B.
12) L who belongs to Iran and B who belongs to Brazil are immediate neighbours of each other.
13) J is an immediate neighbour of C.

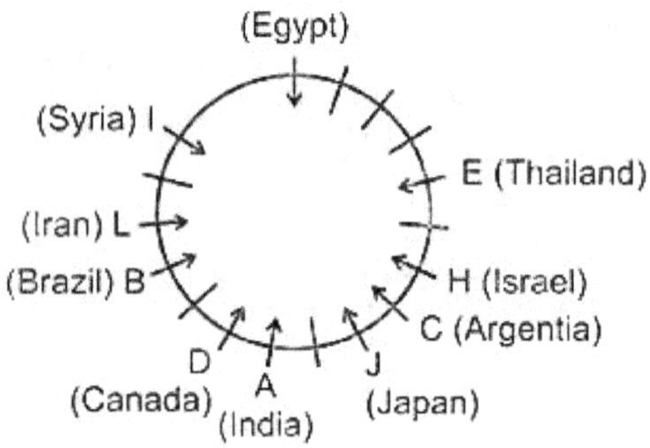

14) The one who belongs to Syria and K are immediate neighbours of each other.

15) There are three seats between K who belongs to Germany and F who belongs to Indonesia.

16) The one who belongs to Indonesia sits exactly between the one who belongs to Thailand and the one who belongs to Egypt.

17) There is one more person sitting on the table who is G who belongs to Egypt.

Therefore, the final arrangement is,

72(D). Thus, "the one who belongs to Egypt" sits 10th to right of the one who belongs to India.

73(C). Thus, the one who belongs to Indonesia sits "Fifth to the left" with respect to I.

74(C). Here the logic is:
By subtracting the digit of the second number in the pair will give the first number in the pair.
(A) 6 – 93 → 9 – 3 = 6
(B) 7 – 81 → 8 – 1 = 7
(C) 6 – 56 → 5 – 6 = -1
(D) 8 – 91 → 9 – 1 = 8
All follows the same logic except "6 - 56"

75(C). All options except 'Hindu' are names of different languages, while 'Hindu' is a person who follows the religion Hinduism.
Therefore, ' Hindu ' is the odd one here.

76(D). दिए गए विकल्पों में से मण्डल शब्द की वर्तनी शुद्ध है।
- 'मण्डल' का अर्थ गोलाई, वृत्त है।
- मण्डल पुल्लिंग शब्द है।

अन्य विकल्प -

शुद्ध वर्तनी	अशुद्ध वर्तनी	अर्थ
स्वयंवर	स्वयम्वर	पति चयन संबंधी उत्सव
चंचल	चन्चल	अस्थिर
संन्यासी	सन्यासी	स्वयं को ईश्वर को समर्पित करना

77(A). दिए गए सभी विकल्पों में शुद्ध वर्तनी वाला शब्द- अद्वितीय।
अद्वितीय विशेषण शब्द है जिसका अर्थ बेजोड़ या अनोखा होता है।

वर्तनी- लिखने की रीति को वर्तनी या अक्षरी कहते हैं। यह हिज्जे भी कहलाती है। किसी भी भाषा की समस्त ध्वनियों को सही ढंग से उच्चरित करने के लिए ही वर्तनी की एकरूपता स्थिर की जाती है। जिस भाषा की वर्तनी में अपनी भाषा के साथ अन्य भाषाओं की ध्वनियों को ग्रहण करने की जितनी अधिक शक्ति होगी, उस भाषा की वर्तनी उतनी ही समर्थ समझी जायेगी। अतः वर्तनी का सीधा सम्बन्ध भाषागत ध्वनियों के उच्चारण से है।

78(A). मुहावरा- 'कमर टूटना' अर्थ – थक जाना।
वाक्य- भारतीय सैनिकों की बहादुरी से पाकिस्तानी फौज की कमर टूट गई।

79(A). मुहावरा- 'माथे पर बल पड़ना' अर्थ – असंतोष प्रकट करना
वाक्य- मनोहर का रिपोर्टकार्ड पढ़ते ही पिताजी के माथे पर बल पड़ गया।

80(B). मुहावरा- 'आठ-आठ आँसू रोना' अर्थ– बहुत अधिक विलाप करना।
वाक्य- जिस समय पढ़ना था तब तो तुम आवारागर्दी करते रहे, अब फेल हो जाने पर आठ-आठ आँसू रोने से क्या फायदा।

81(D). 'मंत्री' शब्द उभयलिंग है।
जिन शब्दों का प्रयोग पुल्लिंग तथा स्त्रीलिंग दोनों में किया जाता है, उसे उभयलिंग कहा जाता है।
जैसे- प्रधानमन्त्री, मुख्यमन्त्री, इंजीनियर, डॉक्टर, राज्यपाल आदि उभयलिंगी शब्द हैं।

82(A). अपवाद को छोड़कर वर्णमाला के अक्षरों के नाम 'पुल्लिंग' में होते हैं।
जिन संज्ञा शब्दों से पुरुष जाति का पता चलता है, पुल्लिंग होते हैं।

83(B). "वह बात जो जनसाधारण में चलती आ रही है" उसे 'किवदंती ' कहते हैं।
- लोक जीवन में किवदंती का बहुत महत्व है।
- जो परंपराएं या कहानियां, कथाएं पीढ़ियों-दर-पीढ़ियों एक से दूसरी को सुनाई जाती रही हो, वह किवदंती कहलाती हैं।
- इसलिए यह शब्द दिए गए वाक्य में सार्थक शब्द है।

84(D). "सामान्य नियम के विरुद्ध बात": वाक्यांश के लिए एक शब्द होगा।- अपवाद
- सामान्य नियमों का उल्लंघन अपवाद कहलाता है। यह समाज में चले आ रहे हैं "सामान्य नियमों के विरुद्ध" की गई बात को दर्शाता है।
- असामान्यता या छूट इसके पर्यायवाची हो सकते हैं।
- अपवाद का विलोम- अनुसमर्थन हो सकता है।

85(B). संज्ञा, सर्वनाम और विशेषण के अंत में लगाने वाले प्रत्यय 'तद्धित प्रत्यय' कहलाते हैं।
प्रत्यय वे शब्द हैं जो दूसरे शब्दों के अन्त में जुड़कर, अपनी प्रकृति के अनुसार, शब्द के अर्थ में परिवर्तन कर देते हैं।

86(D). दिए गए विकल्पों में से 'ओढ़ना' शब्द में उपसर्ग नहीं है।
ओढ़ना शब्द 'ना' प्रत्यय लगा कर बना है।
जो शब्दांश शब्दों के प्रारम्भ में जुड़ कर उनके अर्थ में कुछ विशेषता लाते हैं, वे उपसर्ग कहलाते हैं।

87(D). दिए गए विकल्पों में से 'अलौकिकता, प्रशासनिक' शब्दों मे उपसर्ग और प्रत्यय दोनों का उपयोग हुआ है।
अ+लौकिक + ता = अलौकिकता
प्र + शासन + इक = प्रशासनिक

88(B). दिए गए विकल्पों में से 'जटाएँ' शब्द बहुवचन है जिसका एकवचन रूप 'जटा' है।
जटा स्त्रीलिंग शब्द है जिसका अर्थ है - गुथे एवं लिपटे हुए बालों की लट (जैसे—साधु-संतों की जटा)।

89(D). दिए गए विकल्पों में से 'सहेली' शब्द का उचित बहुवचन शब्द 'सहेलियाँ' है।
सहेली के पर्यायवाची शब्द हैं -अलि, भट्टू, संगिनी, सहचारिणी, आली, सखी, सहचरी, सजनी, सैरन्ध्री।

90(A). 'गन्दा पानी उबालकर पियें।' शुद्ध वाक्य है क्योंकि वाक्य में लिंग, वचन, पुरुष, काल, कारक, आदि का क्रिया के साथ ठीक-ठीक प्रयोग किया गया है।

91(A). 'सीधी लकीर खींचना बहुत कठिन है।'- शुद्ध वाक्य है क्योंकि वाक्य में लिंग, वचन, पुरुष, काल, कारक, आदि का क्रिया के साथ ठीक-ठीक प्रयोग किया गया है।

92(D). 'ज्योतिर्मय' का विलोम शब्द तिमिरमय है।
- ज्योतिर्मय का अर्थ: जगमगाता हुआ
- तिमिरमय का अर्थ: अंधकारयुक्त

93(A). 'हर्ष' शब्द का विलोम शब्द विषाद है,
- 'हर्ष' शब्द का अर्थ- खुशी, उत्साह
- 'विषाद' शब्द का अर्थ- दुःख, निराशा

94(D). 'उन्नयन' का विलोम शब्द अवनयन है।
- उन्नयन का अर्थ: जिसकी आँखें ऊपर उठी हो
- अवनयन का अर्थ: जिसकी आँखें नीचे झुकी हो

95(B). 'अतिवृष्टि' का विलोम शब्द अनावृष्टि है।
- अतिवृष्टि का अर्थ- अत्यधिक वर्षा
- अनावृष्टि का अर्थ- सूखा, अनावर्षण

96(B). 'सद्भावना' का संधि विच्छेद 'सत् + भावना' होता है। इसमें व्यंजन संधि है। व्यंजन से स्वर अथवा व्यंजन के मेल से उत्पन्न विकार को व्यंजन संधि कहते हैं। एक व्यंजन के दूसरे व्यंजन या स्वर से मेल को व्यंजन-संधि कहते हैं। व्यंजन से स्वर अथवा व्यंजन के मेल से उत्पन्न संधि को व्यंजन संधि कहते हैं।

97(C). 'प्रत्युपकार' में यण् संधि है। प्रत्युपकार का संधि विच्छेद 'प्रति + उपकार' होता है। यण संधि स्वर संधि का एक भेद अथवा प्रकार है। जब संधि करते समय इ, ई के साथ कोई अन्य स्वर हो तो ' य ' बन जाता है, जब उ, ऊ के साथ कोई अन्य स्वर हो तो ' व् ' बन जाता है, जब ऋ के साथ कोई अन्य स्वर हो तो ' र ' बन जाता है। जैसे:
अनु + अय = अन्वय
सु + अस्ति = स्वस्ति
सु + आगत = स्वागत
धातु + इक = धात्विक
अनु + ईक्षा = अन्वीक्षा
वधू + आगमन = वध्वागमन

98(A). 'तदनन्तर' का संधि विच्छेद 'तत् + अन्तर' होता है। इसमें व्यंजन संधि है। जब संधि करते समय व्यंजन के साथ स्वर या कोई व्यंजन के मिलने से जो रूप में परिवर्तन होता है, उसे ही व्यंजन संधि कहते हैं। जब किसी वर्ग के पहले वर्ण (क्, च्, ट्, त्, प्) का मिलन किसी वर्ग के तीसरे या चौथे वर्ण से या (य्, र्, ल्, व्, ह) से या किसी स्वर से हो जाये तो क् को ग् , च् को ज् , ट् को ड् ,

त् को द् , और प् को ब् में बदल दिया जाता है।
उदाहरण :
सत् + आशय : सदाशय
तत् + अन्तर : तदनन्तर
उत् + घाटन : उद्घाटन

99(A). क्या भूलूं क्या याद करूँ हरिवंश राय बच्चन की बहुप्रशंसित आत्मकथा तथा हिन्दी साहित्य की एक कालजयी कृति है। यह चार खण्डों में है: 'क्या भूलूँ क्या याद करूँ', 'नीड़ का निर्माण फिर', 'बसेरे से दूर' और 'दशद्वार से सोपान तक'।
इसके लिए बच्चनजी को भारतीय साहित्य के सर्वोच्च पुरस्कार 'सरस्वती सम्मान' से सम्मनित भी किया जा चुका है। हिन्दी प्रकाशनों में इस आत्मकथा का अत्यंत ऊचा स्थान है।
उनकी सबसे प्रसिद्ध कृति मधुशाला है। भारतीय फिल्म उद्योग के प्रख्यात अभिनेता अमिताभ बच्चन उनके सुपुत्र हैं। उनकी मृत्यु 18 जनवरी 2003 में सांस की बीमारी के वजह से मुंबई में हुई थी।

100(C). हजारीप्रसाद द्विवेदी द्वारा रचित रचना:
- रचना: हिंदी साहित्य की भूमिका
- प्रकाशन वर्ष: 1940

अन्य विकल्प:

रचनाकार	रचनाएँ
राम चंद्र शुक्ल	'चिन्तामणि' भाग 1 और 2 तथा 'विचार वीथी, 'हिन्दी साहित्य का इतिहास', 'सूरदास', 'रसमीमांसा', 'त्रिवेणी' आदि।
डॉ. राम कुमार वर्मा	'हिंदी साहित्य का आलोचनात्मक इतिहास', मौन करुणा, आत्म समर्पण आदि।
राम विलास शर्मा	प्रेमचंद और उनका युग (1941), भाषा और साहित्य में पाकिस्तान (1941), भारतेंदु हरिश्चन्द्र, गोस्वामी तुलसीदास और मध्यकालीन भारत (1944), निराला (1946) आदि।

'हिंदी साहित्य की भूमिका' के लेखक हजारीप्रसाद द्विवेदी हैं। अतः इसका सही उत्तर विकल्प (C) 'हजारीप्रसाद द्विवेदी' होगा। अन्य विकल्प सही उत्तर नहीं हैं।

www.ingramcontent.com/pod-product-compliance
Lightning Source LLC
LaVergne TN
LVHW080552200726

843510LV00008B/1082